About the Author

Joycelyn M. Pollock received her Ph.D. in Criminal Justice at the State University of New York at Albany. She also obtained a J.D. at the University of Houston, and passed the Texas Bar in 1991. She is a University Distinguished Professor at Texas State University.

The first edition of *Ethics in Crime and Justice: Dilemmas and Decisions* was published in 1986 and continues to be one of the leading texts in the field. Dr. Pollock has also published *Women's Crimes, Criminology and Corrections* (2015); *Criminal Law*, 11th Ed. (2016); *Prisons and Prison Life: Costs and Consequences* (2014); *Crime and Justice in America: An Introduction* (2012); *Morality Stories, 2nd Ed.* (with Michael Braswell and Scott Braswell, 2007); *Women, Prison and Crime, 2nd Ed.* (2002); *Sex and Supervision: Guarding Male and Female Inmates* (1986); *Counseling Women Prisoners* (1999); *Criminal Women* (2000); and *Prison: An American Institution, 2nd Ed.* (Editor, 2006). In addition to publishing these and other texts, she maintains an active research agenda, primarily in the areas of police ethics and women's prisons.

In addition to teaching at Texas State University, Dr. Pollock has delivered training to police officers, probation officers, parole officers, constables, and other groups in the areas of sexual harassment, ethics, criminology, and other subjects. She has taught at the Houston Police Academy and the Bill Blackwood Law Enforcement Management Institute, and has been a guest speaker for the International Association of Policewomen, the Texas Juvenile Justice Association, and the Southwest Legal Institute, among other groups. In 1998, she was awarded a Fulbright Teaching Fellowship to Turku School of Law in Turku, Finland. She was also a recipient of a Senior Scholar Justice award from the Open Society Institute. The Academy of Criminal Justice Sciences has honored her with the Bruce Smith Award for outstanding contributions to the field of criminology and the ACJS Fellows Award for contributions to criminal justice research. In 2008, she was awarded the Distinguished Alumni award from the State University at Albany, School of Criminal Justice.

NINTH EDITION

Ethical Dilemmas and Decisions in

CRIMINAL JUSTICE

JOYCELYN M. POLLOCK
Texas State University

CENGAGE
Learning®

Australia • Brazil • Mexico • Singapore • United Kingdom • United States

Ethical Dilemmas and Decisions in Criminal Justice, Ninth Edition

Joycelyn M. Pollock

Product Director: Marta Lee-Perriard

Sr. Product Manager: Carolyn Henderson-Meier

Associate Content Developer: Jessica Alderman

Product Assistant: Valerie Kraus

Sr. Marketing Manager: Kara Kindstrom

Art and Cover Direction, Production Management, and Composition: Lumina Datamatics, Inc.

Manufacturing Planner: Judy Inouye

Cover Image: Image Source/ Getty Images

> For product information and technology assistance, contact us at
> **Cengage Learning Customer & Sales Support, 1-800-354-9706.**
>
> For permission to use material from this text or product,
> submit all requests online at www.cengage.com/permissions
> Further permissions questions can be e-mailed to
> **permissionrequest@cengage.com.**

Library of Congress Control Number: 2015951153

Student Edition:
ISBN: 978-1-305-57737-4

Loose-leaf Edition:
ISBN: 978-1-305-66105-9

Cengage Learning
20 Channel Center Street
Boston, MA 02210
USA

Cengage Learning is a leading provider of customized learning solutions with employees residing in nearly 40 different countries and sales in more than 125 countries around the world. Find your local representative at **www.cengage.com.**

Cengage Learning products are represented in Canada by Nelson Education, Ltd.

To learn more about Cengage Learning Solutions, visit **www.cengage.com.**

Purchase any of our products at your local college store or at our preferred online store **www.cengagebrain.com.**

Printed in the United States of America
Print Number: 02   Print Year: 2017

To Greg and Eric, as always

Brief Contents

Preface | xv

PART I   **ETHICS AND THE CRIMINAL JUSTICE SYSTEM ▪ 1**

CHAPTER 1   MORALITY, ETHICS, AND HUMAN BEHAVIOR ▪ 1

CHAPTER 2   DETERMINING MORAL BEHAVIOR ▪ 24

CHAPTER 3   JUSTICE AND LAW ▪ 54

CHAPTER 4   BECOMING AN ETHICAL PROFESSIONAL ▪ 85

PART II   **POLICE ▪ 113**

CHAPTER 5   THE POLICE ROLE IN SOCIETY ▪ 113

CHAPTER 6   POLICE DISCRETION AND DILEMMAS ▪ 146

CHAPTER 7   POLICE CORRUPTION AND RESPONSES ▪ 183

PART III   **LAW ▪ 223**

CHAPTER 8   LAW AND LEGAL PROFESSIONALS ▪ 223

CHAPTER 9   DISCRETION AND DILEMMAS IN THE LEGAL PROFESSION ▪ 252

CHAPTER 10   ETHICAL MISCONDUCT IN THE COURTS AND RESPONSES ▪ 293

PART IV   **CORRECTIONS ▪ 327**

CHAPTER 11   THE ETHICS OF PUNISHMENT AND CORRECTIONS ▪ 327

CHAPTER 12   DISCRETION AND DILEMMAS IN CORRECTIONS ▪ 367

CHAPTER 13   CORRECTIONAL PROFESSIONALS: MISCONDUCT AND RESPONSES ▪ 402

CHAPTER 14   MAKING ETHICAL CHOICES ▪ 434

Bibliography ▪ 469

Name Index ▪ 503

Subject Index ▪ 511

Case Index ▪ 519

Contents

Preface   xv

| PART I | ETHICS AND THE CRIMINAL JUSTICE SYSTEM | 1 |

Chapter 1   Morality, Ethics, and Human Behavior   1

Why Study Ethics?   4

Defining Terms   8
   Morals and Ethics   8
   Duties   11
   Values   11

Making Moral Judgments   13

Analyzing Ethical Issues and Policies   16

Analyzing Ethical Dilemmas   17

Conclusion   20

Chapter Review   20

Study Questions   21

Writing/Discussion Exercises   21

Key Terms   22

Ethical Dilemmas   22

Chapter 2   Determining Moral Behavior   24

Ethical Systems   26
   The Ethics of Virtue   28
   Natural Law   30
   Religion   32
   Ethical Formalism   35
   Utilitarianism   38
   The Ethics of Care   39

Egoism: Ethical System or Not?   42

Other Methods of Ethical Decision
   Making   44
   Using Ethical Systems to Resolve
     Dilemmas   44

Relativism, Absolutism, and
   Universalism   46
   Toward a Resolution: Situational Ethics   48

Conclusion   49

Chapter Review   50

Study Questions   51

Writing/Discussion Exercises   52

Key Terms   52

Ethical Dilemmas   52

Chapter 3   Justice and Law   54

Origins of the Concept of Justice   56

Distributive Justice   57

Corrective Justice   63
   Substantive Justice   64
   Procedural Justice   67

Wrongful Convictions   70

Race, Ethnicity, and Justice   73

Restorative Justice   75

Immoral Laws and the Moral Person   77

Conclusion   81

Chapter Review   81

Key Terms   82

Study Questions   82

Writing/Discussion Exercises   83

Ethical Dilemmas   83

Chapter 4   Becoming an Ethical Professional   85

Individual Influences   86
  Biological Factors   87
  Learning Theory   90
  Kohlberg's Moral Stage Theory   91
Workgroup and Organizational Influences   96
  Ethical Climate and Organizational Justice   100
  Ethics Training   103
  Leadership   104

Societal and Cultural Influences   107
Conclusion   108
Chapter Review   109
Study Questions   110
Writing/Discussion Exercises   111
Key Terms   111
Ethical Dilemmas   111

PART II   POLICE   113

Chapter 5   The Police Role in Society   113

Crime Fighter or Public Servant?   116
  Crime Fighter   116
  Public Servant   116
  History of Policing: From Public Servant to Crime Fighter   119
  Future of Policing   122
Power and Discretion   123
  Discretion and Duty   124
Formal Ethics for Police Officers   128
  The Law Enforcement Code of Ethics   128
The Police Subculture   129
  Themes and Value Systems   129
  The Cop Code   130

  Police Culture and "Noble Cause"   131
  Police Culture, Loyalty, and the Blue Curtain of Secrecy   133
  Police Culture Today   137
Conclusion   142
Chapter Review   143
Study Questions   144
Writing/Discussion Exercises   144
Key Terms   144
Ethical Dilemmas   144

Chapter 6   Police Discretion and Dilemmas   146

Discretion and Discrimination   148
  A Racial Divide   149
  Racial Profiling   152
  Police Shootings of Blacks   156
Discretion and the Use of Force   157
  What We Know and Don't Know   158
  Factors in the Use of Force   160
  Use of Tasers (CEDs)   161
  Responses to Uses of Force   163
Discretion and Criminal Investigations   165
  Proactive Investigations   166
  Reactive Investigations   173

Conclusion   178
Chapter Review   179
Study Questions   180
Writing/Discussion Exercises   180
Key Terms   180
Ethical Dilemmas   180

Chapter 7   **Police Corruption and Responses**   **183**

Economic Corruption   186
   Gratuities   187
   Graft   190
Abuse of Authority   191
   Professional Courtesy and Ticket
     Fixing   191
   On-Duty Use of Drugs and Alcohol   192
   Sexual Misconduct   193
Criminal Cops   196
Costs of Corruption   197
   Consent Decrees   198
Explanations of Deviance   200
   Individual Explanations   201
   Organizational Explanations   204
   Societal Explanations   207

Reducing Police Corruption   208
   "Rotten Apple" Responses   208
   "Rotten Barrel" Responses   213
   Societal Responses   218
Conclusion   220
Chapter Review   220
Study Questions   220
Writing/Discussion Exercises   221
Key Terms   221
Ethical Dilemmas   221

PART III   **LAW**   **223**

Chapter 8   **Law and Legal Professionals**   **223**

The Role of Law   225
Justifications for Law   226
   Preventing Harm to Others   227
   Preventing Offensive Behavior   227
   Preventing Harm to Self
     (Legal Paternalism)   227
   Preventing Harm to Societal Morals
     (Legal Moralism)   228
Paradigms of Law   230
   Consensus Paradigm   230
   Conflict Paradigm   231
   Pluralist Paradigm   232
First, Let's Kill All the Lawyers   233

Law and the Legal Professional   234
Legal Agent or Moral Agent?   237
Ethics for Legal Professionals   239
   Ethical Guidelines for Judges   243
Culture and Ethics   246
Conclusion   248
Chapter Review   248
Study Questions   249
Writing/Discussion Exercises   249
Key Terms   250
Ethical Dilemmas   250

Chapter 9   **Discretion and Dilemmas in the Legal Profession**   **252**

Ethical Issues for Defense Attorneys   254
   Responsibility to the Client   255
   Conflicts of Interest   258
   Zealous Defense   259
   Confidentiality   261
   Duty Regarding Perjury   264
Ethical Issues for Prosecutors   265
   Use of Discretion   266
   Duty to Disclose   269
   Conflicts of Interest   270
   Plea Bargaining   272
   Media Relations   274

   Expert Witnesses   275
   Zealous Prosecution   282
Ethical Issues for Judges   284
   Conflict of Interest   284
   Use of Discretion   285
Conclusion   289
Chapter Review   289
Study Questions   290
Writing/Discussion Exercises   290
Key Terms   291
Ethical Dilemmas   291

Chapter 10   **Ethical Misconduct in the Courts and Responses**   **293**

Ethical Misconduct   294
   Defense Attorney Misconduct   295
   Prosecutorial Misconduct   296
   Judicial Misconduct   302
Factors in Wrongful Conviction   306
Explanations for Misconduct   309
   *Explanations of Prosecutor
      Misconduct   309*
   Explanations for Misconduct of Judges   312
Responding to Misconduct   312
   Professional and Judicial Sanctions   313
   Rethinking Prosecutorial Immunity   314
   Better Training, Better Supervision   314
   Conviction Integrity Units   315

   Mandatory DNA Testing   315
   *Private Crime Labs and Enhanced
      Due-Process Procedures   316*
**Judicial Independence and the
  Constitution   318**
   Judicial Activism   320
Conclusion   323
Chapter Review   323
Study Questions   324
Writing/Discussion Exercises   324
Key Terms   325
Ethical Dilemmas   325

PART IV   **CORRECTIONS**   **327**

Chapter 11   **The Ethics of Punishment and Corrections**   **327**

**Rationales for Punishment and
  Corrections   329**
   Retribution   332
   Prevention Rationale   335
Ethical Frameworks for Corrections   340
   Utilitarianism   341
   Ethical Formalism   341
   Ethics of Care   342
   Rawlsian Ethics   342
Punishments   343
   Supermax Prisons   345
   Private Prisons   348
   Capital Punishment   352
**Formal Ethics for Correctional
  Professionals   356**

**Occupational Subcultures in
  Corrections   358**
   The Correctional Officer Subculture   358
   Treatment Professionals   362
   *The Probation/Parole Officer
      Subculture   362*
Conclusion   363
Chapter Review   363
Study Questions   365
Writing/Discussion Exercises   365
Key Terms   365
Ethical Dilemmas   365

Chapter 12   **Discretion and Dilemmas in Corrections**   **367**

Correctional Officers   369
   A New Era of Corrections?   372
   Relationships with Inmates   373
   *Sexual Relationships and Sexual Abuse in
      Prison   375*
   Use of Force   380
   Maintaining Morality in Prison   382
   Jail Officers   382
Treatment Staff   385
Community Corrections   390
   Caseload Supervision   392
   Parole Officers   394
   Halfway Houses   395

Conclusion   398
Chapter Review   398
Study Questions   399
Writing/Discussion Exercises   400
Key Terms   400
Ethical Dilemmas   400

Chapter 13   **Correctional Professionals: Misconduct and Responses**   **402**

Misconduct and Corruption   403
  California   405
  Mississippi   409
  Texas   410
  Florida   410
  Treatment Professionals   415
  Community Corrections   415
Explanations for Misconduct   418
  Individual Explanations   419
  Organizational Explanations   421
  Societal Explanations   424

Responses to Corruption   424
  *A New Era? Procedural Justice/Restorative
    Justice   427*
Conclusion   431
Chapter Review   431
Study Questions   432
Writing/Discussion Exercises   432
Key Terms   432
Ethical Dilemmas   432

Chapter 14   **Making Ethical Choices**   **434**

Just Wars and Just Means   435
  The Response to 9/11   438
Utilitarianism versus Human
  Rights–Based Policing   458
Ethical Dilemmas and Decisions   461
Conclusion   466

Chapter Review   466
Study Questions   467
Writing/Discussion Exercises   467
Key Terms   467
Ethical Dilemmas   468

Bibliography   469
Name Index   503
Subject Index   511
Case Index   519

Preface

The first edition of this book was published in 1986, thus this 9th edition marks the 30th year of its existence! When I first wrote the book, there were very few textbooks for a course covering criminal justice ethics. Now there are probably a dozen, so I appreciate that readers continue to find value in this one. Over the years, the book has been shaped by current events, reviewers' comments, and the many individuals who have provided feedback. I want to thank each and every person who has contacted me through e-mail, letters, or personally at conferences. I welcome and appreciate all feedback. Please continue to let me know what you think and help me make the book better and more accurate.

Since the first edition, this text has provided the basic philosophical principles necessary to analyze ethical dilemmas, and it has also included current news events to show that these are not simply "ivory tower" discussions. Each edition has incorporated recent news, sometimes requiring updates even as the book goes to press. The book also identifies themes that run through the entire system, such as discretion and due process. In each edition, I have tried to improve the coverage and structure of the book without changing the elements that work for instructors.

This edition has been the most challenging I have faced in quite some time because there has been a veritable explosion of interest and news in the area of criminal justice ethics: law enforcement use of force, prosecutorial misconduct identified in exonerations, and mandatory minimums are only a few topics that have garnered a great deal of national attention recently. As with prior years, it is difficult not to devote more space to law enforcement than courts or corrections, since the troubles there seem to receive greater coverage by both the academic and popular press. However, in the last several years, examples of prosecutorial misconduct have been in the news much more often, as well as other factors involved in wrongful convictions. These topics began to be covered in this book several editions ago, but now it seems a tipping point has been reached in public consciousness so that concern is resulting in legislative activity. Similarly, the scandals in the Florida prison system and Rikers Island Jail in New York City have led to investigations. Systemic issues such as mandatory minimums, the lack of indigent defense, and mass imprisonment have even entered the presidential campaign, with candidates making criminal justice reform part of their platforms. These are interesting times for those in criminal justice, and it is important to note that the discussion cannot be just about law but, also, must involve a discussion about professional ethics and how to ensure that the great discretion that comes with being a criminal justice professional is used ethically.

This edition keeps the basic structure of devoting three chapters each to police, courts, and corrections with four introductory chapters. For this edition, I have not changed the organization of the chapters too much, or the chapter objectives or study questions, so instructors should experience an easy transition in terms of course material. All of the Walking the Walk boxes remain the same as well. The focus of revisions has been, instead, on covering relevant academic work and news. The changes are described in more detail below.

New to This Edition

- **Chapter 1: Morality, Ethics, and Human Behavior** – The beginning of the chapter was rewritten. It now discusses current events, including Ferguson, Missouri, and the aftermath; wrongful convictions; and national scandals in prisons to set the stage as to why it is important to conduct ethical analysis. The format of the chapter remains roughly the same, but certain discussions have been deleted (e.g., Messner and Rosenfeld's cultural strain explanation) to make room for an expanded discussion of the analysis of ethical *issues* compared to the existing discussion of *dilemmas*. The definitions of ethical issues and ethical dilemmas has been moved up to the first section and then a section on analyzing an ethical issue has been added using the preexisting paragraphs of Fast and Furious and the critical thinking checklist. The section on morality and behavior has been deleted as it is repetitive of the discussion in Chapter 4. The In the News box on public corruption has been updated with more recent data. The Michael Vick dogfighting box has been removed. There has been a Quote & Query box added since there was not one before.

- **Chapter 2: Determining Moral Behavior** – The story of Detective Poole has been removed from the chapter opening and used for an integrated "ethical dilemma" analysis near the end of the chapter. The chapter now opens with a new story of a Florida officer who was dubbed "the dirtiest cop" to trigger the question, why is something defined as right or wrong? Another added section in the front of the chapter is an ethical issue analysis on whether officers' names should be released to the public after officer-involved shootings. Many chapters will now have an ethical issue analysis and an ethical dilemma analysis. The news item on the Wall Street broker who said Lehman Brothers was a corrupt culture was deleted as was the old "In the News" corrupt politicians box, and a new news story was used that discusses the 30 most corrupt politicians in New York along with the governor's commission to investigate corruption.

- **Chapter 3: Justice and Law** – The beginning of the chapter has been rewritten to begin by asking the question, "What is justice?" and immediately moves to definitions and the relationship between justice and ethics. The two biggest changes to the chapter are a new section on race and ethnicity and justice implications, and a new section on procedural justice and the work of Tom Tyler. The section on CEO's salaries has been updated. Also added are: a news box on a CEO deciding to give all employees a minimum salary of $70,000, a news box on a family's decision to forgive their daughter's killer, and a news box about wrongful convictions.

- **Chapter 4: Becoming an Ethical Professional** – The beginning of the chapter has been rewritten and the chapter has been reorganized to reflect individual, work-group, organizational, and cultural/societal influences on ethical decision making. The existing material on biological, learning and moral development research has been put under individual influences on behavior as well as a new section on Rokeach's value survey. The workgroup section has utilized the existing information on Bandura's techniques of moral neutralization and also the concepts of bounded ethicality and ethical fading. Added is a section on ethical climate studies. The organizational influence section utilizes the existing leadership and ethics training material and adds a section referencing organizational justice. The cultural/societal section briefly discusses legal and cultural influences on organizational behavior. New news boxes have been added on a major ethical scandal in Hidalgo County, Texas, and the interrogation tactics that led to wrongful convictions by Burge and Guevarra in the Chicago Police Department. A new policy box has been added on whether to institute pension forfeiture policies.

- **Chapter 5: The Police Role in Society** – The beginning of the chapter has been changed to introduce the national discussion of policing issues that has emerged since Ferguson. The discussion of crime control versus being a public servant in the last edition has been expanded with current discussions of the warrior versus guardian model (which is very similar) and Radley Balko's book and articles on the "rise of the warrior cop." The recent events concerning the 1032 military equipment sharing program is discussed. The history of policing section has remained substantially the same. An expanded discussion is offered of the police role in a free, democratic society. News boxes were added on police nonfeasance, updated news on the San Francisco "testilying" scandal, and a box on police officers who violated the blue curtain of secrecy. The information on the Gallup poll results on trust in police has been updated.

- **Chapter 6: Police Discretion and Dilemmas** – The beginning of the chapter has been changed to an introduction that highlights the scope of power and discretion officers have and how law and policy don't resolve decisions that involve race relations, the use of force, and other decision making. The order of the topics has been rearranged to bring force up to the second topic area in view of its current importance. Updated national poll numbers on public trust in police have been added. New boxes on Maricopa County (racial profiling) and Albuquerque (use of force) have been added. There is updated information on the numbers of police shootings and a discussion of the scarcity of good data. The organization of the use-of-force section has been revised to include subheadings of "what we know," "factors," and "responses." Updated news on undercover operations has been added as well as new information on interrogation practices.

- **Chapter 7: Police Corruption and Responses** – All news boxes have been updated. Added sections include the costs of civil lawsuits and an expanded discussion of consent decrees. The corruption section has been rearranged to two categories: economic corruption and abuse of authority, with new examples for different types. A few types of misconduct have been added (ticket fixing, theft). The sexual misconduct section has been expanded with more recent studies. A discussion of PTSD was added as an individual explanation for corruption. Organizational factors have been subdivided into small work-group (exemplified by narcotics task forces) and larger organizational issues to reflect the same organization as Chapter 4. "Perverse incentives" (e.g., pressure from Compstat) has been added as an organizational factor. Within the suggestions to reduce misconduct discussion, a section on body cameras has been added, along with a section on public databases of misconduct. Added or expanded discussions include police decertification, secrecy of discipline or personnel records of officers, Christopher Dorner's "manifesto" alleging unfairness and bias in LAPD's disciplinary process, the arbitration process, and societal responses to misconduct. An ethical issue box on whether police disciplinary proceedings should remain exempt from public disclosure laws was added.

- **Chapter 8: Law and Legal Professionals** – A new box on the suicide of Kalief Browder has been added to illustrate the potential failure of due process. The Michael Morton case, which opened the chapter, has been updated to reflect more current events, as has the news box on same-sex marriage. The section on paradigms has been substantially shortened in line with reviewers' comments that it was less relevant to the discussion of ethics than other topics. The white-collar crime box has been removed. The section "Let's kill all the lawyers" that was in Chapter 10 has been moved here to consolidate the idea of the role of lawyers and public perceptions of them and to make room in Chapter 10 for more examples of misconduct. The box on Tenaha, Texas (asset forfeiture) has been updated. A discussion on underfunding of indigent defense has been added. The legal agent/moral agent discussion has been shortened. The number of states who have adopted subsections g and h of Rule 3 has been updated. A discussion about campaign financing and judicial elections has been added, moving the section that had been in Chapter 10 up to this chapter. Throughout the chapter minor revisions have updated and streamlined the information.

- **Chapter 9: Discretion and Dilemmas in the Legal Profession** – Chapter 9 has been slightly reorganized with subheadings added. The Criminal Justice Standards have been updated to reflect the 4th edition. The discussion on indigent defense has been expanded and updated. News stories have been added, including the DOJ investigation into Missoula, Montana's lack of prosecution of alleged sexual assault, and the misconduct charges against John Jackson, the prosecutor in the Willingham case. The discussion on asset forfeiture has been expanded and updated to reflect current events. The Daubert standard for scientific evidence has been clarified. Updated news on the FBI's review of hair analysis cases has been added as well as more current examples of crime lab scandals.

- **Chapter 10: Ethical Misconduct in the Courts and Responses** – The opening story has remained the same but this chapter has been reorganized by providing subheadings to better assist the student in identifying the types of misconduct, the reasons for misconduct, and the responses. Numerous subheadings have been added and discussions have been consolidated and streamlined. New news boxes have been added on attorney misconduct (legal services for sex) and prosecutor misconduct (the Scarcella scandal in New York City and the jailhouse informant scandal in Orange County, California). The Ted Stevens prosecution scandal news box has been enlarged to add two other cases of federal prosecutor misconduct. Also, studies of the prevalence of prosecutor misconduct have been added and the discussion on jailhouse informants has been expanded. New news stories of federal judge misconduct have been added. The wrongful conviction section has been retitled, reorganized, and updated with current numbers and research. The section on judicial activism has been slightly rewritten.

- **Chapter 11: The Ethics of Punishment and Corrections** – The beginning of this chapter has been rewritten to introduce the reader to current events occurring in corrections and to emphasize how Chapters 11–13 are similar in organization to the set of three chapters each for police and law. Current correctional legislation and/or issues were discussed ("ban the box," reentry initiatives, etc.) indicating a shift in the penal harm era. New news boxes have been provided for a lawsuit against the

BOP (Bureau of Prisons) for their placement of the mentally ill in supermax ADX, Nebraska's law abolishing the death penalty, and *Hall v. Florida*, 2014. The box on Rikers Island was updated along with a longer in-text discussion. The discussion on private prisons has been updated and expanded with new information.

- **Chapter 12: Discretion and Dilemmas in Corrections** – The opening of the chapter remains the same. The discussion of *Brown v. Plata* has been updated. The discussion of PREA that was in Chapter 13 has been moved to Chapter 12 to consolidate (and enlarge) the sexual abuse in prison discussion, and there is a new subheading created to more easily find this discussion. Now there is a use of force section and sexual abuse section set up in somewhat similar ways to the discretion sections in the parallel police chapter (Chapter 6).

- **Chapter 13: Correctional Professionals: Misconduct and Responses** – The opening has remained the same, but Chapter 13 has been substantially reorganized to provide subheadings and case studies of prison corruption and abuse, which are enlarged discussions of current events in Florida, California, Colorado, and Texas. A new discussion of PTSD as an individual explanation of correctional officer misconduct has been added. Several new stories regarding probation and parole officer misconduct have been added. An ethical issue box has been added. The procedural justice discussion has been utilized as a response to corruption. An expanded discussion of societal explanations of misconduct has been added.

- **Chapter 14: Making Ethical Choices** – The last chapter of the book has been updated with current news, largely news concerning Edward Snowden and other revelations concerning the use of surveillance by the NSA and local law enforcement. Other news concerned the release of the "torture" report by the Select Committee on Intelligence, the decision not to prosecute anyone for the CIA enhanced interrogation activities, and new information on whistleblowers. A discussion of human rights-based policing has been added with new material.

Features

There are several boxed features found in *Ethical Dilemmas and Decisions in Criminal Justice*, 9th Edition, which highlight and provide real-world examples of key concepts and issues.

IN THE NEWS This feature has been present since the earliest editions of this book. Each chapter presents news items that relate to the discussion. In every edition, some of the news stories are kept, but most are cycled out to make room for current events. Examples include:

Ferguson, Missouri police-citizen conflict

Walter Scott case

Kalief Browder case

QUOTE AND QUERY Another long-time feature of the book, the Quote and Query boxes offer some classic and current quotes meant to illustrate a point or issue from the chapter's discussion. There is a query following the quote that spurs the reader to think about the quote in the context of the discussion.

WALKING THE WALK Introduced in the 6th edition, these boxes describe individuals who display ethical courage. This feature proved to be so popular that every chapter now has one.

CHAPTER DILEMMAS Each chapter has a featured dilemma followed by an extended analysis under law, policy and ethics. The feature makes explicit the focus of the book, illustrated by its title, *Dilemmas and Decisions*.

CHAPTER ISSUES A new feature to the 9th edition are featured "issues" boxes similar to dilemma boxes. These present a current issue or policy in policing, courts, or corrections followed by an extended analysis under law, policy and ethics. The addition of the issues boxes show how issues can be analyzed in a similar way to personal dilemmas.

Pedogogical Aids

In addition to the boxed features, *Ethical Dilemmas and Decisions in Criminal Justice*, 9th Edition, has several pedagogical aids designed to enhance student learning and comprehension.

KEY TERMS As in previous editions, key terms are highlighted and defined in the chapters.

STUDY QUESTIONS These questions identify important points and concepts in the chapter and can be used for test reviews or test questions.

WRITING/DISCUSSION QUESTIONS These questions cover more abstract concepts and are designed to provide an opportunity to employ critical thinking skills in a writing or discussion exercise.

ETHICAL DILEMMAS Since the first edition of this book, dilemmas have been provided at the back of each chapter that are designed to be representative of what criminal justice professionals might face in the field. Many of the dilemmas describe true incidents and have been provided by police officers, probation officers, lawyers, and other criminal justice professionals. Others have been gleaned from news events or the media.

CHAPTER OBJECTIVES Chapter-opening learning objectives preview the key content in each chapter for the reader.

CHAPTER REVIEW At the end of each chapter, the chapter objectives are presented again, but there is also a short summary of content. These reviews summarize the key content of the chapter for the reader.

Ancillaries

A number of supplements are provided by Cengage Learning to help instructors use *Ethical Dilemmas and Decisions in Criminal Justice* in their courses and to aid students in preparing for exams. Supplements are available to qualified adopters. Please consult your local sales representative for details.

For the Instructor

ONLINE INSTRUCTOR'S MANUAL The manual includes learning objectives, a detailed chapter outline (correlated to PowerPoint slides), lecture notes, assignments, media tools, ethical dilemmas, and classroom discussions/activities. The manual is available for download on the password-protected website and can also be obtained by e-mailing your local Cengage Learning representative.

ONLINE TEST BANK Each chapter of the test bank contains questions in multiple-choice, true/false, completion, and essay formats, with a full answer key. The test bank is coded to the learning objectives that appear in the main text, references to the section in the main text where the answers can be found, and Bloom's taxonomy. Finally, each question in the test bank has been carefully reviewed by experienced criminal justice instructors for quality, accuracy, and content coverage. The test bank is available for download on the password-protected website and can also be obtained by e-mailing your local Cengage Learning representative.

CENGAGE LEARNING TESTING, POWERED BY COGNERO This assessment software is a flexible online system that allows you to import, edit, and manipulate test bank content from the *Ethical Dilemmas and Decisions in Criminal Justice* test bank or elsewhere, including your own favorite test questions; create multiple test versions in an instant; and deliver tests from your LMS, your classroom, or wherever you want.

ONLINE POWERPOINT LECTURES Helping you make your lectures more engaging while effectively reaching your visually oriented students, these handy Microsoft PowerPoint® slides outline the chapters of the main text in a classroom-ready presentation. The PowerPoint slides are updated to reflect the content and organization of the new edition of the text and feature some additional examples and real-world cases for application and discussion. Available for download on the password-protected instructor companion website, the presentations can also be obtained by e-mailing your local Cengage Learning representative.

For the Student

Mindtap Criminal Justice

With MindTap™ Criminal Justice for *Ethical Dilemmas and Decisions in Criminal Justice*, you have the tools you need to better manage your limited time, with the ability to complete assignments whenever and wherever you are ready to learn. Course material that is specially customized for you by your instructor in a proven, easy-to-use interface keeps you engaged and active in the course. MindTap helps you achieve better grades today by cultivating a true understanding of course concepts and with a mobile app to keep you on track. With a wide array of course-specific tools and apps—from note taking to flashcards—you can feel confident that MindTap is a worthwhile and valuable investment in your education.

You will stay engaged with MindTap's video cases and You Decide career scenarios and remain motivated by information that shows where you stand at all times—both individually and compared to the highest performers in class. MindTap eliminates the guesswork, focusing on what's most important with a learning path designed specifically by your instructor and for your Ethics course. Master the most important information with built-in study tools such as visual chapter summaries and integrated learning objectives that will help you stay organized and use your time efficiently.

Acknowledgments

I thank the reviewers for this new edition. They are:

David D. Legere, J.D., New England College

Patrick McGrain, Gwynedd Mercy University

Amy Pinero, Baton Rouge Community College

Deborah Woodward Rhyne, University of Central Florida, Cocoa

Jerry L. Stinson II, Southwest Virginia Community College

The staff members at Cengage have been integral to the development of this edition as well. They are: Carolyn Henderson Meier, Senior Product Manager; Jessica Alderman, Associate Content Developer; and Kara Kindstrom, Senior Marketing Manager. Thanks also to Kailash Rawat, Associate Program Manager at Lumina Datamatics, and Jeri Freedman, copyeditor.

As always, I thank my colleagues and chairperson, Christine Sellers, at Texas State University for support through the years. I also wish to thank those individuals in the field who have emailed me with questions and suggestions for the book and hope that they continue to do so. Most importantly, I thank my husband, Eric Lund, for all that he does.

—**Joycelyn Pollock**
jpl2@txstate.edu

Morality, Ethics, and Human Behavior

Scott Waddle (the subject of the Walking the Walk box on p. 19).

Steve Liss/The LIFE Images Collection/Getty Images

In 2015, it would be hard not to be aware of the events that took place in Ferguson, Missouri (Michael Brown), Staten Island, New York (Eric Garner), North Charleston, South Carolina (Walter Scott), Baltimore, Maryland (Freddie Gray), and Cleveland, Ohio (Tamir Rice). Five black males lost their lives in these cities at the hands of police officers. There is debate and divisiveness about whether these events represent a "police problem" or a problem with citizens who, through their actions, compel police to use force in self-defense. But we have been here before. In 1991, Rodney King was beaten by LAPD and sheriff's deputies on the side of a California freeway. What followed included the now famous videotape, the officers involved being acquitted in a state court, the Los Angeles riot where 53 died, and, the eventual federal conviction of two of the officers. Rodney King became a nationally known figure representing the problem of police use of force, especially

Chapter Objectives

1. Explain the difference between ethical issues and ethical dilemmas.

2. Give examples of how discretion permeates every phase of the criminal justice system and creates ethical dilemmas for criminal justice professionals.

3. Explain why the study of ethics is important for criminal justice professionals.

4. Learn the definitions of the terms *morals*, *ethics*, *duties*, *supererogatories*, and *values*.

5. Describe what behaviors might be subject to moral/ethical judgments.

against minorities. In the next decade, much was written about this problem and sincere attempts, such as community policing initiatives, were made by law enforcement agencies around the country to address the enmity between law enforcement and minority communities.

Today, it seems as if the intervening 20 years had never happened. Michael Brown's death by a Ferguson, Missouri, police officer became a flashpoint similar to King's beating, triggering protests and mob violence. Once again, we, as a nation, are focused on law enforcement and whether there is abuse of the awesome power invested in those who wear police uniforms. It is with this backdrop that we open the ninth edition of this ethics text. Make no mistake, even though the discussions that have been generated pose legal questions (e.g., the legal test for use of force) and bring in academic researchers to present national statistics and correlates in the use of force, ethics is a part of this debate as well. It seems that at no other time in history, except perhaps during the civil unrest of the 1960s, has so much attention been focused on law enforcement and the criminal justice system. Laws, police, courts, and corrections have increasingly captured national attention. As crime rates have continued to drop across the country, there is growing concern that our criminal justice system is bloated, and, worse, unfair, especially against certain groups of citizens. Each of the paragraphs below briefly reviews current national attention and activity in the major subsystems of the criminal justice system: law, police, courts, and corrections.

We are seeing a growing chorus of discontent against the federal government's expansion of criminal laws, especially when such laws eliminate the requirement of criminal intent. "Overcriminalization" is said to be an issue that liberals and conservatives can agree upon, even if for different reasons. Recently, there has been enough political will to begin a discussion to roll back mandatory minimum sentencing, argue for moderation in drug sentencing and allow judges the discretion to consider mitigating factors, at least on the federal level.

As previously mentioned, the events in Ferguson, Missouri, and other places have spurred national attention to law enforcement, especially law enforcement's use of force against minorities. For instance, the 21st Century Panel on Policing was quickly formed by President Obama and, in early March 2015, the panel issued a comprehensive report with recommendations for major changes in training, accountability, and the culture of policing. Recently revealed is the fact that there are no good national figures for how many people are killed and/or injured by law enforcement officers. This lack of knowledge has spurred lawmakers in states and Congress to propose legislation requiring such data to be recorded and submitted to a state and/or national database. Responses to the perceived problem of misuse of force have been suggested, including body cameras, civilian review boards, the use of independent prosecutors after a police shooting, and implicit bias training that shows officers how their subconscious can identify black citizens as more dangerous, spurring them to be quicker to use deadly force.

A more concerted effort to document police misconduct is growing as well. A libertarian think tank (the Cato Institute) created and maintains a website that collects and displays news stories of police misconduct (**www.policemisconduct.net**), and the ACLU has initiated a drive to submit open records requests in several large cities for disciplinary records to develop a database of officers who have been the target of numerous brutality lawsuits. The Justice Department has initiated and completed investigations in many major cities across the United States that result in "consent decrees," agreements whereby the city agrees to a certain set of changes in policies and procedures to address issues of inappropriate use of force and violations of rights of citizens to prevent being sued by the Civil Rights Division of the Department of Justice.

Police are not the only target of scrutiny. The continuing news stories of the wrongfully convicted have led to the development of Innocence Projects around the country, where volunteer lawyers and students investigate cases and, in a growing number of cases, are successful in exonerating their clients. The National Registry of Exonerations (**www.law.umich.edu/special/exoneration/Pages/about.aspx**) notes that 1,570 people have been released from prison because their conviction has been found to be the result of inaccurate eyewitness testimony, false confession, and/or misconduct on the part of system actors. Conviction integrity units have also emerged in prosecutors' offices around the country. These prosecutors either work with Innocence Projects or identify cases on their own to investigate as potential wrongful convictions. Prosecutors have come under scrutiny themselves for unethical and illegal actions with a few being criminally charged for their actions that contributed to sending innocent people to prison.

Prisons and correctional professionals have come into the spotlight as well. Major reports from science and policy groups have criticized our "mass imprisonment," which makes our country stand apart from all its peers in the number of citizens incarcerated. The Colson Commission was formed by Congress to evaluate the problem of over-imprisonment at the federal level. Efforts are under way across the nation to find better solutions to the problem of recidivism. Spurring these efforts in certain states are prison scandals, such as those in Florida, where prisoners' deaths have been the target of external investigations, and Rikers Island jail in New York, where systemic abuses have been revealed.

The thread that ties all these national trends together is abuse of power and/or a lack of adherence to the principles of justice, equity, and compassion. The purpose of this book is to take a careful look at ethical decision making by criminal justice professionals. The criminal justice system can be examined using political, legal, organizational, or sociological approaches; however, in this book we shift the lens somewhat and look at the system from an ethics perspective. Asking whether something is legal, for instance, is not necessarily the same as asking whether something is right.

Ethical discussions in criminal justice focus on *issues* or *dilemmas*. **Ethical issues** are broad social questions, often concerning the government's social control mechanisms and the impact on those governed—for example, what laws to pass, what sentences to attach to certain crimes, whether to abolish the death penalty, and whether to build more prisons. The typical individual does not have much control over these issues. Other issues may be more discrete and can be said to be policy choices—for example, mandatory DNA collection for all misdemeanant arrestees, disclosing police officers' names to the public when they have been involved in shooting, or utilizing an "open file" policy in a prosecutor's office. Individuals may have control over these decisions, but they are often developed over the course of time through committees or other group decision-making processes.

While ethical issues are broad social questions or policy decisions, **ethical dilemmas** are situations in which one person must make a decision about what to do. Either the choice is unclear or the right choice will be difficult because of the costs involved.

At times, one's belief regarding an ethical issue gives rise to a personal dilemma. In 2000, George Ryan, then governor of Illinois, declared a moratorium on use of the death penalty in his state when at least five individuals on death row were exonerated through the use of DNA evidence. One of his last acts as he left office in 2003 was to commute

ethical issues
Difficult social or policy questions that include controversy over the "right" thing to do.

ethical dilemmas
Situations in which it is difficult for an individual to make a decision, either because the right course of action is not clear or because the right course of action carries some negative consequences.

the sentences of all 160 prisoners on death row to life without parole. Governor Ryan faced a difficult personal dilemma because he was in a position to do something about his belief that the death penalty was implemented in a way that could never be just. There was strong support and strong opposition to his action, indicating the depth of his dilemma and the seriousness of the issue. In a sad and ironic footnote to this story, Ryan ended up in prison himself after being convicted of federal racketeering charges and sentenced to a six-and-a-half-year sentence in a federal prison. Evidence proved that he had been involved in a system of "sweetheart deals" and backroom bribes selling government contracts since he had been secretary of state (Schaper, 2007).

In this book, ethical *issues* and ethical *dilemmas* will be analyzed. As you will see, the approach taken in both types of analysis is similar. Throughout the book we approach decision making using the framework of applying, *law*, *policy*, and then *ethics*. In each chapter, there will be at least one ethical issue or ethical dilemma that will be presented and analyzed. You will see that tools of ethical reasoning are necessary for a good analysis. It is for this reason that we must first explore the foundations of ethics.

Why Study Ethics?

Although the decisions faced by professionals associated with the criminal justice system—ranging from legislators who write the laws to correctional professionals who supervise prisoners—may be different, they also have similarities, especially in that these professionals all experience varying degrees of **discretion**, authority, and power. If decisions were totally bounded by legal rules or policy regulations, then, perhaps, there would be less reason for ethical analysis; however, the greater role discretion plays in a profession, the more important is a strong grounding in ethics.

discretion The authority to make a decision between two or more choices.

Legislators have the power to define certain acts as illegal and, therefore, punishable. They also have the power to set the amount of punishment. Public safety is usually the reason given for criminalizing certain forms of behavior. In other cases, legislators employ moral definitions for deciding which behaviors should be illegal. "Protection of public morality" is the rationale for a number of laws, including those involving drugs, gambling, and prostitution. On June 26, 2015, in *Obergefell v. Hodges*, the Supreme Court held that all states must license and recognize same-sex marriages. Before the Supreme Court issued its decision, legislators in some states passed laws allowing same-sex marriages, while in other states, legislators passed laws defining such marriages as illegal. The arguments for and against such laws are based in morality, not public safety. How do legislators use their great discretion to balance the rights of *all* people? We explore these questions in more detail in Chapter 3, which covers the concept of justice, and in Chapter 8, which begins our discussion of the law and legal professionals.

Part of the reason that legislators are not held to very high esteem in this country is that we perceive that their discretion is unethically influenced by lobbyists and personal interests rather than the public good. A clear example of this was the case of Jack Abramoff, a lobbyist who eventually ended up in prison. At the height of his Washington influence, however, he provided lawmakers with private seats in athletic skyboxes, expensive dinners, hunting trips, and cash. His most notorious dealings involved lobbying activities for Indian tribes. Lawmakers were lobbied to either approve or block the building of casinos. Amazingly, Abramoff's firm at one point was obtaining money from one client to advance their interest in building a casino while, at the same time, taking money from another client to block it. Much of the money charged to clients ended up in the pockets of legislators. The 2010 movie *Casino Jack and the U.S. of Money* is based on Jack Abramoff. The case illustrates that sometimes lawmakers' positions are not taken from moral or ethical stances at all, but rather according to which lobbyist has managed to persuade them.

Police officers, who enforce the laws created by legislators, also have a great deal of discretionary power. Most of us, in fact, have benefited from this discretion when we receive a warning instead of a traffic ticket. Police officers have the power to deprive people of their liberty (through arrest) and the power to decide which individuals to investigate and perhaps target for undercover operations. They also have the power to decide that lethal force is warranted, hence the great current debate in this country that focuses on police shootings, especially of minorities. In the United States, we enjoy constitutional protections against untrammeled police power, and police act as the guardians of the law, not merely enforcers for those in power. In Chapters 5, 6, and 7, the ethical use of police discretion is discussed in more detail.

Prosecutors probably face the least public scrutiny of all criminal justice professionals—which is ironic because they possess a great deal of discretion in deciding whom and how to prosecute. They decide which charges to pursue and which to drop, which cases to take to a grand jury, how to prosecute a case, and whether to pursue the death penalty in homicide cases. Although prosecutors have an ethical duty to pursue justice rather than conviction, some critics argue that at times their decision making seems to be influenced by politics or factors other than the goal of justice.

Defense attorneys have ethical duties similar to prosecutors in some ways; however, they also have unique duties to their client. After deciding whether to take a case or not, they decide whether to encourage a client to agree to a plea deal, what evidence to utilize and how to try the case, and whether to encourage a client to appeal.

Judges also possess incredible power, typically employed through decisions to deny or accept plea bargains, decisions regarding rules of evidence, and decisions about sentencing. Chapters 8, 9, and 10 explore the ethical issues of legal professionals in the criminal justice system.

Finally, correctional officials have immense powers over the lives of some citizens. Probation officers make recommendations in presentence reports and violation reports that affect whether an individual goes to prison. Prison officials decide to award or take away "good time," and they may punish an inmate with segregation; both types of decisions affect the individual's liberty. Correctional officers make daily decisions that affect the life and health of the prisoners they supervise. Parole officials decide when to file a violation report, and make other decisions that affect a parolee as well as his or her family members. In short, all correctional professionals have a great deal of discretion over the lives of those they control. The ethical issues and dilemmas of correctional professionals are discussed in Chapters 11, 12, and 13.

Although the professionals discussed face different dilemmas, they also share the following common elements:

- *They each have discretion—that is, the power to make a decision.* Although the specific decisions are different, they all involve power over others and the potential deprivation of life, liberty, or property.
- *They each have the duty of enforcing the law.* Although this concept is obvious with police, it is also clear that each of the professionals mentioned has a basic duty to

uphold and enforce all laws; they serve the law in their professional lives. You may have heard the phrase "we are a nation of laws, not men." What this means is that no one is supposed to be above the law, no matter how powerful, and no one is supposed to take the law into their own hands, no matter how clear the guilt.

- *They must accept that their duty is to protect the constitutional safeguards that are the cornerstone of our legal system—specifically, due process and equal protection.* Due process protects each of us from error in any governmental deprivation of life, liberty, or property. We recognize the right of government to control and even to punish, but we have certain protections against arbitrary or unlawful use of that power. Due process protects us against such abuses. We also expect that the power of our government will be used fairly and in an unbiased manner. Equal protection should ensure that what happens to us is not determined by the color of our skin, our gender, our nationality, or the religion we practice. Laws are for everyone, and the protection of the law extends to all of us. Although a fair amount of evidence indicates that different treatment does exist, the ideal of equal protection is an essential element of our legal system and should be an operating principle for everyone working in this system.

- *They are public servants.* Their salaries come from the public purse. Public servants possess more than a job; they have taken on special duties involving the public trust. Individuals such as legislators, public officials, police officers, judges, and prosecutors are either elected or appointed guardians of the public's interests. Arguably, they must be held to *higher standards* than those they guard or govern. Temptations are many, and, unfortunately, we find examples of *double standards*, in which public servants take advantage of their positions for special favors, rather than higher standards of exemplary behavior.

The Josephson Institute (2005), which is heavily involved in ethics training for corporations and public agencies, identifies the ethical principles that should govern public servants: public service (treating the office as a public trust), objective judgment (striving to be free from conflicts of interest), accountability (upholding open decision making), democratic leadership (observing the letter and spirit of the law), and respectability (avoiding the appearance of impropriety).

It would be ideal if all public servants possessed the characteristics identified by Delattre as shown in the Quote and Query box; however, even public servants of good character are sometimes perplexed as to the right course of action in situations they encounter in their professional duties. It is also true that there are all too many cases of public servants who have forgotten their mission of public service and substituted private enrichment. The In the News box provides depressing evidence that not all public servants have the public's interest in mind.

Ethical issues for professionals in the justice system include relationships with citizens and others over whom they have power (e.g., whether to use one's authority to coerce a citizen to provide sex, money, or other benefits), their relationship with their agency (e.g., whether to hide misconduct or rule breaking or whether to be lax about keeping up with professional training

---

QUOTE & QUERY

Part of what is needed [for public servants] is a public sense of what Madison meant by wisdom and good character: balanced perception and integrity. Integrity means wholeness in public and private life consisting of habits of justice, temperance, courage, compassion, honesty, fortitude, and disdain for self-pity.

(Delattre, 1989b: 79)

 Do you believe that this is asking too much of our public servants?

((•)) IN THE NEWS | *Public Corruption*

Citizens for Responsibility and Ethics in Washington (CREW), a citizen watchdog group, releases an annual report titled "CREW's Most Corrupt," which highlights corrupt members of Congress. The latest report is for 2013 and identifies 17 sitting members of Congress who have violated laws or engaged in serious breaches of ethics. The report was compiled by analyzing media reports, Federal Election Commission reports, court documents, and travel disclosure reports. The list includes legislators who received financial benefits from those who arguably may have benefited from the legislators' voting decisions. "Unjust enrichment" is a perennial problem of legislators, and in the report is a 2012 Rasmussen poll finding that 60 percent of the American public believe that members of Congress are willing to sell their vote.

Of course it isn't only federal politicians who use their position for self-gain. A *Report to Congress* from the Department of Justice reflects that investigations and prosecutions of public corruption at the state and local level have remained relatively consistent through the years with about 133 state and 272 local officials convicted in 1993 and 100 state and 319 local officials convicted in 2012. On the other hand, there seems to be a decline of federal officials convicted with 595 in 1993 but only 369 in 2012. While it may be wished that federal officials have become more honest over the years, there is no extraneous evidence to support that conclusion.

Powerful Assemblyman Sheldon Silver is only the latest well-known politician to be arrested for corruption in New York. An article graphic in the *New York Times* illustrates 30 previous individuals who had been accused of using their public office for personal gain (*www.nytimes.com/interactive/2014/07/23/nyregion/23moreland-commission-and-new-york-political-scandals.html?_r=0*).

Sources: Citizens for Responsibility and Ethics in Washington, 2013; Department of Justice, 2012; Rashbaum and Kaplan, 2015.

obligations), or their relationships with one another (e.g., whether to informally sanction a colleague when they speak out about misconduct). Professionals in the criminal justice system have unique powers and, therefore, unique ethical issues that they must be sensitive to in order to understand their ethical obligations and duties.

Felkenes (1987: 26) explained why the study of ethics is important for criminal justice professionals:

1. Professionals are recognized as such in part because [a] "profession" normally includes a set of ethical requirements as part of its meaning. . . . Professionalism among all actors at all levels of the criminal justice system depends upon their ability to administer policy effectively in a morally and ethically responsible manner.

2. Training in ethics helps develop critical thinking and analytical skills and reasoning abilities needed to understand the pragmatic and theoretical aspects of the criminal justice system.

3. Criminal justice professionals should be able to recognize quickly the ethical consequences of various actions and the moral principles involved.

4. Ethical considerations are central to decisions involving discretion, force, and due process which require people to make enlightened moral judgments.

5. Ethics is germane to most management and policy decisions concerning such penal issues as rehabilitation, deterrence, and just deserts.

6. Ethical considerations are essential aspects of criminal justice research.

In answer to a similar question, Braswell (1996/2002: 8) explained the following five goals of a study of ethics:

- Become aware of and open to ethical issues.
- Begin developing critical thinking skills.
- Become more personally responsible.
- Understand how the criminal justice system is engaged in a process of coercion.
- Develop **wholesight** (which roughly means exploring with one's heart as well as one's mind).

wholesight
Exploring issues with one's heart as well as one's mind.

The comprehensive nature of these two lists requires few additions; however, we also could note that individuals who ignore ethics do so at their peril. They may find themselves sliding down a slippery slope of behaviors that threaten their career and personal well-being. Even if their actions are not discovered, many people suffer from personal crises when their actions are in conflict with their conscience. Three basic points are reiterated below:

- We study ethics because criminal justice is uniquely involved in coercion, which means there are many and varied opportunities to abuse such power.
- Almost all criminal justice professionals are public servants and, thus, owe special duties to the public they serve.
- We study ethics to sensitize students to ethical issues and provide tools to help identify and resolve the ethical dilemmas they may face in their professional lives.

Defining Terms

morals   Principles of right and wrong.

ethics   The discipline of determining good and evil and defining moral duties.

The words **morals** and **ethics** are often used in daily conversation. For example, when public officials use their offices for personal profit or when politicians accept bribes from special interest groups, they are described as unethical. When an individual does a good deed, engages in charitable activities or personal sacrifice, or takes a stand against wrongdoing, we might describe that individual as a moral person. Often, the terms *morals* and *ethics* are used interchangeably. This makes sense because they both come from similar root meanings. The Greek word *ethos* pertains to custom (behavioral practices) or character, and *morals* is a Latin-based word with a similar meaning. As Box 1.1 shows, the inquiry into how to determine right and wrong behavior has perplexed humans for thousands of years. Philosophers through the ages owe much to the great Greek philosophers who discussed what the "good life" meant.

Morals and Ethics

Morals and morality refer to what is judged as good conduct. Immorality refers to bad conduct. We would judge someone who intentionally harms a child for their own enjoyment, or someone who steals from the church collection plate as immoral. Some of us disagree on whether other behaviors, such as abortion, capital punishment, or euthanasia, are immoral. How to resolve such questions will be the subject of the next chapter.

BOX 1.1 \ Socrates, Plato, Aristotle, and the Stoics

Socrates (469–399 BCE)

Socrates associated knowledge with virtue. He believed that bad acts are performed through ignorance. The wisest man was also the most virtuous. He believed that all people acted in a way to serve their own interests, but some people, because they were ignorant, pursued short-term happiness that would, in the long run, not make them happy. True happiness could come only from being virtuous, and virtue comes from knowledge. Thus, Socrates believed his role was to strip away self-deception and incorrect assumptions; hence, the so-called Socratic method of questioning a person's beliefs. The concept of *eudaimonia* is translated as happiness, but it is much more than that and is sometimes translated as flourishing. Self-actualization, to borrow Abraham Maslow's term, might be similar to the Greek concept of *eudaimonia*, the idea that one's happiness involved the pursuit of excellence and virtue.

Plato (423–347 BCE)

Plato was a student of Socrates. In fact, it is his writings that are the source for what we know about Socrates's ideas. Because his writings were largely in the form of dialogues, with Socrates as the main character in many of them, it is hard to distinguish Socrates's ideas from Plato's. Another difficulty in summarizing Plato's ideas about ethics is that he undertook a wide-ranging exploration of many topics. His writings included discussions of ethical and political concepts, as well as metaphysical and epistemological questions. In *The Republic*, he, like Socrates, associates virtues with wisdom. The four virtues he specifically mentions are wisdom, courage, moderation, and justice. Three of the virtues are associated with the three classes of people he describes as making up society: the rulers (wisdom), the soldiers (courage), and the merchants (moderation since they pursue lowly pleasures). Justice is the idea that each person is in the place they should be and performs to their best ability. Plato discussed the concept of *eudaimonia*, mentioned above, which can be considered self-completion or self-actualization. A good life would be one that fit the nature of the person—that is, moderation for the merchant class, courage for the solder, and wisdom for leaders. There is, of course, the need for all virtues in every life to some degree.

Aristotle (384–322 BCE)

Aristotle was a student of Plato. Aristotle did not believe, as did Socrates, that bad behavior came from ignorance. He believed some people had weak wills and did bad things knowing they were bad. The idea of *eudaimonia* is part of Aristotle's discussions of what it means to live a good life. Again, this concept, although translated as happiness, has more to do with flourishing or self-actualization. The good life is one devoted to virtue and moderation. The so-called Golden Mean was choosing actions that were moderate and between two extremes. For instance, courage was the virtue whereas the deficiency was cowardice and the excess was foolhardiness. Generosity is the mean between stinginess and wastefulness, and so on. Aristotle's virtue theory is discussed more fully in the next chapter.

Stoics (Third Century BCE, Includes Zeno, Seneca, and Epictetus)

The Stoic philosophical school is associated with the idea that man is a part of nature and the essential characteristic of man is reason. Reason leads to virtue. Virtue and morality are simply rational action. While Plato divided people into the three classes of leaders, soldiers, and everyone else, the Stoics simply saw two groups: those who were rational/virtuous and those who were irrational/evil. They perceived life as a battle against the passions. They argued that people should not seek pleasure, but should seek virtue, because that is the only true happiness. Moreover, they should seek virtue out of duty, not because it will give them pleasure.

For further information, go to:

Stanford Encyclopedia of Philosophy: http://plato.stanford.edu; and the Internet Encyclopedia of Philosophy: www.iep.utm.edu

The term *ethics* refers to the study and analysis of what constitutes good or bad conduct (Barry, 1985: 5; Sherman, 1981: 8). There are several branches, or schools, of ethics:

- **Meta-ethics** is the discipline that investigates the meaning of ethical systems and whether they are relative or are universal, and are self-constructed or are independent of human creation.
- **Normative ethics** determines what people ought to do and defines moral duties based on ethical systems or other means of analysis.
- **Applied ethics** is the application of ethical principles to specific issues.
- **Professional ethics** is an even more specific type of applied ethics relating to the behavior of certain professions or groups.

While these definitions of ethics refer to the *study* of right and wrong behavior, more often, in common usage, *ethics* is used as an adjective (ethical or unethical) to refer to behaviors relating to a profession, while *moral* is used as an adjective to describe a person's actions in other spheres of life. Most professions have codes of conduct that describe what is ethical behavior in that profession. For instance, the medical profession follows the Hippocratic Oath, a declaration of rules and principles of conduct for doctors to follow in their daily practices; it dictates appropriate behavior and goals.

Even though professional ethics restricts attention to areas of behavior relevant to the profession, these can be fairly inclusive and enter into what we might consider the private life of the individual. For instance, psychiatrists are judged harshly if they engage in romantic relationships with their patients. These rules usually are included in codes of ethics for these professions. When private behavior affects professional decision making, it becomes an ethical issue, such as when school bus drivers abuse drugs or alcohol, or when scientists are paid to do studies by groups who have a vested interest in seeing a particular outcome.

Public servants are especially scrutinized. We are very much aware of how politicians' private behavior can affect their career in politics. President Clinton's affair with intern Monica Lewinsky was a serious blow to his political career, and not just because he prevaricated in the congressional investigation. More recently Anthony Weiner's political career as a U.S. congressman was over after it was revealed he "sexted" (sent a sexually suggestive picture) to a woman, who reported it to the press. When he attempted a political comeback in a run for mayor of New York City in 2013, more sexting by Weiner was revealed under the pseudonym of "Carlos Danger." Such behavior, while a boon to late night comics, is tragically inexplicable behavior for a serious public servant. In professions involving the public trust, such as politics, education, and the clergy, there is a thin line between one's private life and one's public life. Citizens assume that if one is a liar and cheat in one's private life, then that also says something about how they would make decisions as a public servant. If one displays extremely poor judgment and disrespect for his family in his private life, he is not a good fit for public office. What about police officers, prosecutors, judges, or others in the criminal justice professions? They are also public servants. Should private decisions, such as whom they have sex with or whether they divorce their spouse, concern us?

For our purposes, it does not make a great deal of difference whether we use the formal or colloquial definitions of *morals* and *ethics*. This text is an applied ethics text, in that we will be concerned with what is defined as right and wrong behavior in the professions relevant to the criminal justice system and how people in these professions make decisions in the course of their careers. It also is a professional ethics text, because we are concerned primarily with professional ethics in criminal justice.

Duties

The term **duties** refers to those actions that an individual must perform to be considered moral. For instance, everyone might agree that one has a duty to support one's parents if able to do so, one has a duty to obey the law (unless it is an immoral law), and a police officer has a moral and ethical duty to tell the truth on a police report. Duties are what you must do in order to be good.

duties   Required behaviors or actions, that is, the responsibilities that are attached to a specific role.

Other actions, considered **supererogatories**, are commendable but not required. A good Samaritan who jumps into a river to save a drowning person, risking his or her own life to do so, has performed a supererogatory action. Those who stood on the bank receive no moral condemnation, because risking one's life is above and beyond anyone's moral duty. Of course, if one can help save a life with no great risk to oneself, a moral duty does exist in that situation.

supererogatories   Actions that are commendable but not required in order for a person to be considered moral.

Police officers have an ethical duty to get involved when others do not. Consider the 2001 attack on the World Trade Center. One of the most moving images of that tragedy was of police officers and firefighters running toward danger while others ran away. This professional duty to put oneself in harm's way is why we revere and pay homage to these public servants. Many civilians also put themselves in harm's way in this disaster, and because they had no professional duty to do so, they could be said to be performing supererogatory actions.

There are also **imperfect duties**, general duties that one should uphold but do not have a specific application as to when or how. For instance, most ethical systems support a general duty of generosity but have no specific duty demanding a certain type or manner of generosity. Another imperfect duty might be to be honest. Generally, one should be honest, but, as we will see in Chapter 2, some ethical systems allow for exceptions to the general rule.

imperfect duties   Moral duties that are not fully explicated or detailed.

Values

Values are defined as elements of desirability, worth, or importance. You may say that you value honesty; another way of saying that is that one of your values is honesty. Others may value physical health, friendships, material success, or family. Individual values form value systems. All people prioritize certain things that they consider important in life. Values only become clear when there is a choice to be made; for instance, when you must choose between friendship and honesty, or material success and family. Behavior is generally consistent with values. For instance, some individuals believe that financial success is more important than family or health. In this case, we may assume that their behavior will reflect the importance of that value and that these persons will be workaholics, spending more time at work than with family and

values   Judgments of desirability, worth, or importance.

BOX 1.2 \ Values Exercise			
Achievement	Altruism	Autonomy	Creativity
Emotional well-being	Family	Health	Honesty
Knowledge	Justice	Love	Loyalty
Physical appearance	Pleasure	Power	Recognition
Religious faith	Skill	Wealth	Wisdom

Arrange these values in order of priority in your life. What life decisions have you made that have been affected by the ordering of these values? Did you think of them directly when making your decision?

endangering their health with long hours, stress, and lack of exercise. Others place a higher priority on religious faith, wisdom, honesty, and/or independence than financial success or status. Consider the values in Box 1.2. Which, if any, do you believe are more important than others? Do you ever think about the values by which you live your life? Do you think that those professionals who are caught violating laws and/or ethical codes of conduct have a clear sense of their value system?

Values as judgments of worth are often equated with moral judgments of goodness. We see that both can be distinguished from factual judgments, which can be empirically verified. Note the difference between these factual judgments:

"He is lying."
"It is raining."

and these value judgments:

"She is a good woman."
"That was a wonderful day."

The last two judgments are more similar to moral judgments, such as "Lying is wrong" or "Giving to charities is good." Facts are capable of scientific proof, but values and moral judgments are not.

Some writers think that value judgments and moral judgments are indistinguishable because neither can be verified. Some also think that values and morals are relativistic and individual. In this view, there are no universal values; values are all subjective and merely opinions. Because they are only opinions, no value is more important than any other value (Mackie, 1977: 22–24).

In contrast, others believe that not all values are equal, and that some values, such as honesty, are always more important than other values, such as pleasure. In this view, values such as charity, altruism, integrity, knowledge, and responsibility are more important or better than the values of pleasure or wealth. You may value personal pleasure over charity or honesty, but to someone who believes in universal values, you would be wrong in this view. This question is related to a later discussion in Chapter 2 concerning whether ethics are relative or absolute.

As stated earlier, values imply a choice or a judgment. If, for instance, you were confronted with an opportunity to cheat on an exam, your values of success and honesty would be directly at odds. Values and morals are similar, although values indicate the *relative* importance of these constructs, whereas morals prescribe or pro-scribe behavior. The value of honesty is conceptually distinct from the moral rule against lying.

In the United States, success is defined almost exclusively by the accumulation of material goods, not by doing good deeds. The financial meltdown this country experienced in 2008 seems to be a good example of this. The widespread issuance of bad loans and the creation of the derivative markets were arguably due to the way the incentive systems were set up and the value placed on making money. The fact that such financial instruments were "toxic" and that the housing bubble was bound to col-lapse, along with the fortunes of many people who had invested or had obtained loans they couldn't afford, didn't seem to matter. The value system that precipitated the eco-nomic disaster seems to be fairly clear.

An explicit value system is part of every ethical system, as we will see in Chapter 2. The values of life, respect for the person, and survival can be found in all ethical systems. Certain values hold special relevance to the criminal justice system and those profes-sionals who work within it; privacy, freedom, public order, justice, duty, and loyalty are all values that will come up frequently in later discussions.

Making Moral Judgments

We make moral or ethical judgments all the time: "Abortion is wrong." "Capital pun-ishment is just." "It's good to give to charity." "It's wrong to hit your spouse." "You should put in a day's work for a day's pay." "You shouldn't take credit for someone else's work." These are all judgments of good and bad behavior. We also make choices, knowing that they can be judged as right or wrong. Should you fake a sickness to your boss to get a day in the sun? Should you give back extra change that a clerk gave you by mistake? Should you tell a friend that her husband is having an affair even though he asked you not to tell? Should you cut and paste sections of Wikipedia into your term paper? These are all ethical decisions in that they can be judged as right or wrong.

Not all behaviors involve questions of ethics. Acts that can be judged as ethical or unethical, moral or immoral, involve four elements: (1) acts (rather than beliefs) that are (2) human and (3) of free will (4) that affect others.

ACT First of all, some act must have been performed. For instance, we are concerned with the *act* of stealing or the *act* of contributing to charity, rather than an idle thought that stealing a lot of money would enable us to buy a sailboat or a vague intention to be more generous. We are not necessarily concerned with how people feel or what they think about a particular action unless it has some bearing on what they do. The inten-tion or motive behind a behavior is an important component of that behavior in some ethical systems; for instance, in ethical formalism (which we will discuss in Chapter 2), one must know the intent of an action to be able to judge it as moral or immoral. How-ever, one also must have some action to examine before making a moral judgment.

ONLY HUMAN ACTS Second, judgments of moral or ethical behavior are directed specifically to human behavior. A dog that bites is not considered immoral or evil, although we may criticize pet owners who allow their dogs the opportunity to bite. Nor do we consider drought, famine, floods, or other natural disasters immoral even though they result in death, destruction, and misery. The devastating earthquakes that hit Haiti in 2010 and Nepal in 2015 are not considered immoral, although individuals who could have helped victims and did not might be. Philosophers widely believe that only humans can be moral (or immoral) because of our capacity to reason. Because only humans have the capacity to be good—which involves a voluntary, rational decision and subsequent action—only humans, of all members of the animal kingdom, have the capacity to be bad.

There is much more to this argument, of course, and there are those who argue that some mammals show moral traits, if not moral sensibilities. Shermer (2004: 27–28), for instance, recognizes a pre-moral sense in animals, including shame or guilt in dogs, food sharing in bats, comforting and cooperative behaviors in chimpanzees, lifesaving behaviors in dolphins and elephants, and defending behaviors in whales. He argues that mammals, especially apes, monkeys, dolphins, and whales, exhibit attachment and bonding, cooperation and mutual aid, sympathy and empathy, direct and indirect reciprocity, altruism and reciprocal altruism, conflict resolution and peace-making, deception and deception detection, community concern and caring about what others think, and awareness of and response to the social rules of the group.

Does this mean, then, that these mammals can be considered moral or immoral? Although perhaps they may be placed on the continuum of moral awareness closer to humans than other species, one could also argue that they do not possess the rationality of humans. They do not, as far as we know, freely choose to be good or bad, nor do they judge their fellow animals as right or wrong. It may explain, however, why there is such moral condemnation toward those who abuse or injure certain animals, especially mammals such as cats, dogs, and monkeys.

FREE WILL In addition to limiting discussions of morality to human behavior, we usually further restrict our discussion to behavior that stems from free will and free action. Moral culpability is not assigned to persons who are not sufficiently aware of the world around them to be able to decide rationally what is good or bad. The two groups traditionally exempt from responsibility in this sense are the young and the insane, similarly to what occurs when ascribing legal culpability.

Arguably, we do not judge the morality of their behavior because we do not believe that they have the capacity to reason and, therefore, have not freely chosen to be moral or immoral. Although we may chastise a two-year-old for hitting a baby, we do so to educate or socialize, not to punish, as we would an older child or adult. We incapacitate the violent mentally ill to protect ourselves, but we consider them sick, not evil. This is true even if their actual behavior is indistinguishable from that of other individuals we do punish. For example, a murder may result in a death sentence or a hospital commitment, depending on whether the person is judged to be sane or insane, responsible or not responsible.

AFFECTS OTHERS Finally, we usually discuss moral or immoral behavior only in cases in which the behavior significantly affects others. For instance, throwing a rock off a bridge would be neither good nor bad unless you could possibly hit or were aiming at a person below. If no one is there, your behavior is neutral. If someone is below, however, you might endanger that person's life, so your behavior is judged as bad.

All the ethical issues and dilemmas we will discuss in this book involve at least two parties, and the decision to be made affects at least one other individual in every case. In reality, it is difficult to think of an action that does not affect others, however indirectly. Even self-destructive behavior is said to harm the people who love us and who would be hurt by such actions.

Indeed, even a hermit living alone on a desert island may engage in immoral or unethical actions. Whether he wants to be or not, the hermit is part of human society; therefore, some people would say that even he might engage in actions that could be judged immoral if they degrade or threaten the future of humankind, such as committing suicide or polluting the ocean. We sense that these elements are important in judging morality when we hear the common rationale of those who, when judged as doing something wrong, protest, "But nobody was hurt!" or "I didn't mean to."

One's actions toward nature also might be defined as immoral, so relevant actions include not only actions done to people but also those done to animals and to the environment. To abuse or exploit animals is defined by some people as immoral. Judgments are made against cockfighting, dog racing, laboratory experimentation on animals, and hunting. The growing area of environmental ethics reflects increasing concern for the future of the planet. The rationale for environmental ethics may be that any actions that harm the environment affect all humans. It also might be justified by the belief that humankind is a part of nature—not superior to it—and part of natural law should be to protect, not exploit, our world.

Thus far, we know that morality and ethics concern the judgment of behavior as right or wrong. Furthermore, such judgments are directed only at voluntary human behavior that affects other people, the earth, and living things. We can further restrict our inquiries regarding ethics to those behavioral decisions that are relevant to one's profession in the criminal justice system. Discussions regarding the ethics of police officers, for instance, would concern issues such as the following:

- Whether to take gratuities
- Whether to cover up the wrongdoing of a fellow officer
- Whether to sleep on duty

Discussions regarding the ethics of defense attorneys might include the following:

- Whether to devote more effort to private cases than appointed cases
- Whether to allow perjury
- Whether to attack the character of a victim in order to defend a client

Of course, all of these actions affect other people, as do most actions taken as a professional. Most behaviors that might be judged as ethical or not for criminal justice professionals fall into four major categories:

- Acts involving citizens/clients (i.e., misuses of authority, harassment, malfeasance, or misfeasance)
- Acts involving other employees (i.e., harassment, gossip, lying)
- Acts involving one's organization (i.e., theft, work ethic, filing false reports)
- Acts involving those one supervises (i.e., arbitrary discipline, unrealistic demands, discouraging honest criticism)

In this text, we will present some of the unique issues and dilemmas related to each area of the criminal justice system. It is important, first, however, to explore the means available for analyzing and evaluating the "right" course of action.

Analyzing Ethical Issues and Policies

"Critical thinking skills" has become an overused and abused term in education, but the core idea of critical thinking is to be more cognizant of facts as opposed to concepts, assumptions, or biases, and the use of objective reasoning to most effectively reach a decision or understand a problem. Paul and Elder (2003) explain that all reasoning is based on assumptions, points of view, and data or evidence, but reasoning is shaped by concepts and ideas that affect our interpretations of the data, which then lead us to conclusions that give meaning to the data. In order to be a critical thinker, one must ask these types of questions:

- What information am I using in coming to a conclusion?
- What information do I need to settle the question?
- Is there another way to interpret the information?
- What assumption has led me to my conclusion?
- Is there another point of view I should consider?
- What implication or consequence might be the result of this conclusion?

In each of the discussions throughout the book that subject issues or policies to an ethical analysis, critical thinking will be required. One of the most important elements of critical thinking is to separate facts from concepts and identify underlying assumptions.

The ethical systems will not be covered until Chapter 2; thus, the ethical analysis below will use general concepts concerning right and wrong. In all analyses, we will begin by determining if there is any relevant law, then if there are relevant policies, and, finally, ethical principles will be applied.

ETHICAL ISSUE

Was the "Fast and Furious" Operation Wrong?

The gun trafficking operation called "Fast and Furious" by the ATF and federal prosecutors became a major scandal when it was discovered that one of the guns was implicated in the death of a U.S. federal agent in Mexico. The operation involved allowing illegal gun sales and following the guns to track down major players in gun trafficking rings. Unfortunately, it was reported that federal agents lost track of nearly 1,400 guns of the 2,000 they tried to follow. One of those guns was found at the scene of a murder of a federal agent by drug cartel members in Mexico. Interestingly, the operation had been undertaken before during the Bush administration in 2006. Called Operation Wide Receiver, the same plan to allow illegal guns to "walk" in order to track them was carried out. E-mails from several ATF agents and assistant attorneys general indicated their discomfort with the plan and their concern about the consequences of allowing hundreds of guns to go to Mexico, arguably straight into the hands of drug dealers (Yost, 2012a). The exposure of the failings of the operation led to calls for the impeachment of Attorney General Eric Holder, but a congressional report, issued in September of 2012, did not uncover any evidence that Holder was aware of the operation. Rather, it was reported that an assistant deputy attorney general (Jason Weinstein) had learned about Operation Wide Receiver and the Fast and Furious operation and signed off on several wiretap applications for it. He, and other high-ranking Justice officials, did not understand or did not care that the firearms were ending up in the hands of criminals. The agents and prosecutors most directly involved evidently decided that the goal of leaving the guns in order to catch bigger criminals was more important than the risk to public safety.

Since 1993, at least a dozen complaints against this officer were sustained for various counts of battery, perjury, theft of city resources, conduct unbecoming, official misconduct, breach of duty, and excessive force. Police departments are required to forward serious sustained cases of misconduct to a state agency called the Criminal Justice Standards and Training Commission who decide whether the officer should lose his or her license. In this particular officer's case, seven cases were on file. In each case, he kept his state peace officer certification. In no case did they look at his record as a whole, only the most immediate case reported. The cases included disobeying a direct order and continuing to chase a suspect and then covering up his role in the subsequent accident by lying on a police report, striking a teenager in the face three times, striking a handcuffed man in the face and punching him in the stomach, head-butting a handcuffed man, spitting in the face of a handcuffed man, and working a second job while under suspension and then lying about it. In another case, he was fired after having an empty vodka bottle, cocaine, crack pipes, and false identifications in his police vehicle, but he won his job back after his union helped him file a grievance.

More recently, he was arrested again after he allegedly forcefully moved a man from the police lobby area, handcuffed him, placed him into a holding area, and held him against his will because the man wanted to file a formal complaint against the officer for excessive force. The officer was charged with first-degree felony kidnapping, tampering with a witness, and misdemeanor battery. He was finally terminated from employment in 2012 after the newspaper's investigative report that called him the "dirtiest cop." Evidently at least one person thinks that judgment is wrong: He has been reported as saying: "I'm conceited about only one thing in life, and that is that I'm an excellent police officer" (Cormier, 2011; German Bosque Arrested. . ., 2013). It is possible to examine each of the actions that make up this officer's record, evaluating each act as right or wrong, or we can examine the decisions of those in his police department who allowed him to continue to be a police officer or the system rules that allowed him to keep his license. In any of these analyses, we must utilize some type of method for determining good or bad. Ethical systems help us do that.

In this chapter, we will deal with the "why" of ethical judgments. Whether an act is right or wrong is an age-old question and there are classic answers to the question: "What is good?" Ethical systems help us analyze actions as good or bad, ethical or unethical, moral or immoral. Before we discuss ethical systems, we will analyze an ethical issue without the benefit of them. After the ethical systems have been discussed go back and reanalyze this ethical issue using one or more of the ethical systems that we will cover in this chapter.

ETHICAL ISSUE

"Does the Public Have the Right to Know the Identity of a Police Officer After a Shooting?"

One of the criticisms leveled against the Ferguson, Missouri, police department in the aftermath of the Michael Brown shooting was that there was a six-day lag between the shooting and when the police department identified the officer involved as Darren Wilson. When Eric Garner died in Staten Island, the officer involved, Daniel Pantaleo, was identified quickly after the video of the event circulated in the news media, even though New York has extremely protective legislation protecting officers' identities in discipline investigations. The other officers involved were not identified (Goodman and Baker, 2015). In South Carolina, when Walter Scott was shot by Officer Michael Slager on April 4, 2015, the police chief released the officer's name, again after the video of the event began circulating in the news media. It is unclear what might have happened if the video had not been recorded on a cellphone camera by a bystander.

(continued)

When there is a shooting by a police officer, should the police department release the name of the officer(s) involved? This is a hotly contested issue since when officers' names are released after shootings, they are reportedly the subject of death threats. Especially recently, relations between police departments and some communities have sunk to dangerous levels of enmity, and officer-involved shootings may serve as a flashpoint for retaliatory violence. Certainly, police have a right to be concerned after the 2014 assassinations of Officers Wenjian Liu and Rafael Ramos in New York City by a man supposedly "avenging" the death of Michael Brown. In Arizona, a bill was quickly written and passed by the state legislature that would mandate officers' names be kept private for 60 days after a shooting as a "cooling off" period (SB 1445). Governor Doug Ducey vetoed the bill on March 30, 2015 ("Ducey vetoes bill. . .", 2015), but proponents argue such protection is necessary.

In one case in Fairfield County, Virginia, the complexity of the issue was frustratingly clear to members of the Board of Supervisors, who were conflicted about whether they owed the public transparency in revealing the names and details of a shooting or should keep the information private while the disciplinary and legal procedures ensued; however, after 17 months, the investigation had not been completed and the public had lost trust that the response to the shooting was fair and unbiased. Due process for the victim and the officer(s) involved must be balanced against the public's right to know. Release of investigatory information during an active investigation or before any legal proceedings may bias the case; however, there is widespread belief among citizens that police officer shootings are not investigated thoroughly and that the victims of such shootings do not receive a fair investigation unless there is public pressure on the criminal justice system. The result is that some jurisdictions release very little information, sometimes not even the officer's name, and other jurisdictions release thousands of pages of investigatory reports (Olivo, 2015).

Law

The law is different across jurisdictions regarding how much may be revealed about ongoing investigations. If legislation like Arizona's is more successful in other locales, it may soon be illegal to disclose an officer's name. Generally, it is left to the discretion of the police department and city administrators as to whether and when to release an officer's name after a shooting. Eventually his or her name must be revealed, but the issue revolves around how soon and how many details of the shooting should be released. There is no law that mandates the disclosure of this type of information, but there are laws that exempt police investigatory reports from open records requests. At least 26 states completely shield discipline records from public disclosure (Goodman and Baker, 2015).

Policy

Police and city administrators owe a duty to the public they serve but they also owe a duty of care to the officers who are their employees. They have a responsibility to ensure that their actions do not needlessly put officers in harm's way. In recent cases, officers who become the target of public scrutiny have had their personal information revealed to the public by hackers and been the target of threats. The public has a right to a fair and impartial investigation and it is more difficult to believe this is occurring when secrecy shields even the officer's name. Ultimately, it is an issue of rights with the officer and his/her family members' rights balanced against the rights of the public and shooting victim's family.

Ethics

Even before the benefit of a discussion of ethical systems that will follow, individuals may argue that the public's right to know must outweigh the right of the officer to have his identity remain private. Civilians involved in shootings and accused of other criminal acts are routinely identified in the news media before due process might exonerate them. Only juveniles and rape victims are protected from public identification. It is important to note that the issue of safety can be divorced from the issue of public identification. Only unreasonable or evil people would agree that officers or their families deserve extra-judicial punishment; therefore, one can agree with the "rightness" of public identification without also supporting the potential aftermath. The ethical solution would be to serve the public's need/right to know and the officer's right to safety.

Ethical Systems

Our principles of right and wrong form a framework for the way we live our lives. But where do these principles come from? Before you read on, answer the following question: If you believe that stealing is wrong, why do you believe this to be so? You probably said it is because your parents taught you or because your religion forbids it—or maybe because society cannot tolerate people harming one another. Your answer is an indication of your **ethical system**.

ethical system
A structured set of principles that defines what is moral.

Ethical systems have a number of characteristics. First, they are the source of moral beliefs. Second, they are the underlying premises from which you make judgments. Third, they are beyond argument. That is, although ethical decisions may become the basis of debate, the decisions are based on fundamental truths or propositions that are taken as a given by the individual employing the ethical system.

C. E. Harris (1986: 33) referred to such ethical systems as *moral theories or moral philosophies* and defined them as a systematic ordering of moral principles. To be accepted as an ethical system, the system of principles must be internally consistent, must be consistent with generally held beliefs, and must possess a type of "moral common sense." Baelz (1977: 19) further described ethical systems as having the following characteristics:

- *They are prescriptive.* Certain behavior is demanded or proscribed. They are not just abstract principles of good and bad but have substantial impact on what we do.
- *They are authoritative.* They are not ordinarily subject to debate. Once an ethical framework has been developed, it is usually beyond question.
- *They are logically impartial or universal.* Moral considerations arising from ethical systems are not relative. The same rule applies in all cases and for everyone.
- *They are not self-serving.* They are directed toward others; what is good is good for everyone, not just the individual.

We don't consciously think of ethical systems, but we use them to make judgments. For instance, we might say that a woman who leaves her children alone to go out drinking has committed an immoral act. That would be a *moral judgment*. Consider that the moral judgment in any discussion is only the tip of a pyramid. If forced to defend our judgment, we would probably come up with some rules of behavior that underlie the judgment. Moral rules in this case might be:

> "Children should be looked after."
> "One shouldn't drink to excess."
> "Mothers should be good role models for their children."

But these moral rules are not the final argument; they can be considered the body of the pyramid. How would you answer if someone forced you to defend the rules by asking "why?" For instance, "Why should children be looked after?" In answering the "why" question, one eventually comes to some form of ethical system. For instance, we might answer, "Because it benefits society if all parents watched out for their children." This would be a utilitarian ethical system. We might have answered the question, "Because every parent's duty is to take care of their children." This is ethical formalism or any duty-based ethical system. Ethical systems form the base of the pyramid. They are the foundation for the moral rules that we live by.

The ethical pyramid is a visual representation of this discussion. In Figure 2.1, the moral judgment discussed above is the tip of the pyramid, supported by moral rules on which the judgment is based. The moral rules, in turn, rest upon a base, which is one's ethical system. Probably the most commonly utilized ethical systems by individuals when making personal decisions about their own behavior or judgments about others are religion and utilitarianism. The most commonly utilized ethical systems in

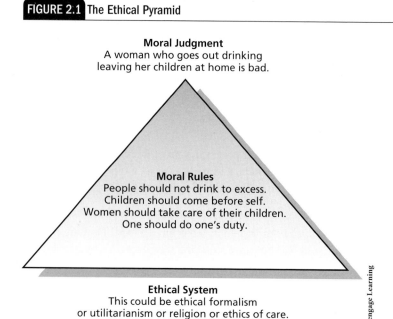

FIGURE 2.1 The Ethical Pyramid

Moral Judgment
A woman who goes out drinking
leaving her children at home is bad.

Moral Rules
People should not drink to excess.
Children should come before self.
Women should take care of their children.
One should do one's duty.

Ethical System
This could be ethical formalism
or utilitarianism or religion or ethics of care.
The rules are logically inconsistent with egoism.

© Cengage Learning

philosophical conversations are ethical formalism and utilitarianism because of the stark differences between them. We will discuss the ethical systems in somewhat of a chronological order, beginning with Aristotle and the Ethics of Virtue.

The Ethics of Virtue

The question of what it means to be a good person is an ancient one. Socrates, Plato, and Aristotle were not the first to explore virtue, but we will begin our discussion of ethical systems with Aristotle. As you read in the last chapter, Socrates associated virtue with knowledge. Ignorance led to bad behavior because if one was rational and wise, he or she would know what virtue was and behave accordingly. The four virtues identified by Socrates and Plato are justice, wisdom, fortitude, and temperance. Recall that Plato associated these virtues with the three classes of citizens: leaders (wisdom), soldiers (fortitude or courage), and all others (temperance). Aristotle disagreed with the idea that bad behavior occurred only through ignorance and argued that there were people who chose to behave in ways that were not virtuous. In *Nicomachian Ethics*, he answers the **ethics of virtue** question, "What is a good person?" One answer is that to be good, one must do good. Virtues that a good person possesses include thriftiness, temperance, humility, industriousness, and honesty. The goal of life, according to Aristotle, is *eudaimonia*, translated as "happiness," but another translation is "flourishing." The meaning of this word does not mean simply having pleasure, but also living a good life, reaching achievements, and attaining moral excellence.

Aristotle defined virtues as "excellences." These qualities are what enable an individual to move toward the achievement of what it takes to be human. Aristotle distinguished intellectual virtues (wisdom, understanding) from moral virtues (generosity,

ethics of virtue The ethical system that bases ethics largely upon character and possession of virtues.

eudaimonia The Greek term denoting perfect happiness or flourishing, related to the way to live a "good life."

self-control). The moral virtues are not sufficient for "the good life"; one must also have the intellectual virtues, primarily "practical reason." Aristotle believed that we are by nature neither good nor evil but become so through training and the acquisition of habits:

> [T]he virtues are implanted in us neither by nature nor contrary to nature: we are by nature equipped with the ability to receive them and habit brings this ability to completion and fulfillment. (Aristotle, quoted in Prior, 1991: 156–157)

Habits of moral virtue are obtained by following the example of a moral exemplar, that is, a parent or virtuous role model. These habits are also more easily instilled when "right" or just laws also exist. Moral virtue is a state of character in which choices are consistent with the **principle of the Golden Mean**. This principle states that virtue is always the median between two extremes of character. For instance, proper pride is the mean between empty vanity and undue humility, and so on. The Catalog of Virtues derived from the writings of Aristotle appears in Box 2.1. It should be noted that it is difficult to understand some of Aristotle's virtues because of the passage of time and the problems of translation. Generally, however, the idea is that the right way to behave is a balance between an excess and a deficiency of any element of character.

Moral virtue comes from habit, which is why this system emphasizes character. The idea is that one does not do good because of reason; rather, one does good because of the patterns of a lifetime. Those with good character will do the right thing, and those with bad character usually will choose the immoral path. Every day we are confronted with numerous opportunities to lie, cheat, and steal. When a cashier looks the other way, we could probably filch a $20 bill from the cash drawer, or when a clerk gives us a $10 bill instead of a $1 bill by mistake, we could keep it instead of handing it back. We don't because, generally, it does not even occur to us to steal. We do not have to go through any deep ethical analysis in most instances when we have the opportunity to do bad things, because our habits of a lifetime dictate our actions.

Somewhat related to the ethics of virtue ethical system are the Six Pillars of Character promulgated by the Josephson Institute of Ethics (2008). The Six Pillars of Character echo Aristotle's virtues. They include:

principle of the Golden Mean Aristotle's concept of moderation, in which one should not err toward excess or deficiency; this principle is associated with the ethics of virtue.

BOX 2.1 \ Catalog of Virtues

Courage (balance between cowardice and foolhardiness)
Temperance (balance between self-indulgence and asceticism)
Liberality (balance between meanness and too generous)
Munificence (similar to liberality; balance between stinginess and being profligate)
Magnanimity (balance between being vain and being petty)
Proper ambition (balance between being without ambition and having too much)
Good temper (balance between being quick to anger and not showing anger when warranted)
Truthfulness (balance between unnecessary truths and lying)
Wittiness (balance between being a bore and being a clown)
Friendliness (balance between obsequiousness and being unfriendly)
Modesty (balance between being too humble and too boastful)
Righteous indignation (balance between being envious and being spiteful)

Source: *Nicomachean Ethics*, Aristotle. Adapted from: www.cwu.edu/~warren/Unit1/aristotles_virtues_and_vices.htm.

1. *Trustworthiness.* This concept encompasses honesty and meeting one's obligations. Honesty means to be truthful, forthright, and sincere, and the pillar also involves loyalty, living up to one's beliefs, and having values.

2. *Respect.* This pillar is similar to the second portion of the categorical imperative of Ethical Formalism, which will be discussed subsequently. The concept admonishes us to treat each person with respect and not as a means to an end. The idea is also similar to the Golden Rule in Christianity.

3. *Responsibility.* This means standing up for one's choices and being accountable. Everyone has a moral duty to pursue excellence, but, if one fails, the duty is to take responsibility for the failure.

4. *Fairness.* This concept involves issues of equality, impartiality, and due process. To treat everyone fairly doesn't necessarily mean to treat everyone the same, but rather, to apply fairness in one's dealings with everyone.

5. *Caring.* This pillar encompasses the ideas of altruism and benevolence. It is similar to the ethics of care, which will be described later in the chapter.

6. *Citizenship.* This includes the duties of every citizen, including voting, obeying the law, being a good steward of the natural resources of one's country, and doing one's fair share.

One difficulty with the ethics of virtue is in judging the primacy of moral virtues. For instance, in professional ethics there are often conflicts that involve honesty and loyalty. If both are virtues, how does one resolve a dilemma in which one virtue must be sacrificed? Another difficulty is that it is not a system that provides an analysis of what to do in a given dilemma. If one is truly perplexed as to what the right course of action should be, this system does not help much in that it basically concludes that a virtuous person will act virtuously. The ethics of virtue probably explains more individual behavior than other ethical systems because most of the time, if we have developed habits of virtue, we do not even think about the possible bad acts we might do. However, when faced with a true dilemma—that is, a choice where the "right" decision is unclear—the ethics of virtue does not provide any equation or approach to find the right answer.

Aristotelian virtue ethics certainly influenced later thinkers, but as the timeline displayed in Box 2.2 shows, other ethical systems eclipsed this older system for centuries. More recently, Alasdair MacIntyre (1991), a contemporary philosopher, has done much to resurrect virtue ethics. He defines virtues as those dispositions that will sustain us in the relevant "quest for the good, by enabling us to overcome the harms, dangers, temptations and distractions which we encounter, and which will furnish us with increasing self-knowledge and increasing knowledge of the good." MacIntyre (1999) also seems to endorse an ethics-of-care approach because he discusses virtue as necessary to care for the next generation. He sees life as one of "reciprocal indebtedness" and emphasizes "networks of relationships" as the locale of giving and receiving the benefits of virtues. This language is similar to the ethics of care, which will be discussed in a later section of this chapter.

natural law The idea that principles of morals and rights are inherent in nature and not human-made; such laws are discovered by reason but exist apart from humankind.

Natural Law

The **natural law** ethical system holds that there is a universal set of rights and wrongs that is similar to many religious beliefs, but without reference to a specific supernatural figure. Originating most clearly with the Stoics, natural law is an ethical

BOX 2.2 \ Timeline of Ethics

Socrates (469–399 BCE)	
Plato (429–347 BCE)	
Aristotle (384–322 BCE)	VIRTUE THEORY
St. Augustine (354–430)	NATURAL LAW
	RELIGION
St. Thomas Aquinas (1225–1274)	RELIGION
John Locke (1632–1704)	SOCIAL CONTRACT
Adam Smith (1723–1790)	EGOISM
Immanuel Kant (1724–1804)	ETHICAL FORMALISM
Jeremy Bentham (1748–1832)	UTILITARIANISM
John Stuart Mill (1806–1873)	UTILITARIANISM
Ayn Rand (1905–1932)	EGOISM
John Rawls (1921–2002)	ETHICAL FORMALISM + UTILITARIANISM
Alisdair MacIntyre (1929–)	NEO-VIRTUE THEORY
Nel Noddings (1929–)	ETHICS OF CARE

system wherein no difference is recognized between physical laws—such as the law of gravity—and moral laws. Morality is part of the natural order of the universe. Further, this morality is the same across cultures and times. In this view, Christians simply added God as a source of law (as other religions added their own prophets and gods), but there is no intrinsic need to resort to a supernatural figure because these universal laws exist quite apart from any religion (Maestri, 1982; Buckle, 1993).

The natural law ethical system presupposes that what is good is what is natural, and what is natural is what is good. The essence of morality is what conforms to the natural world; thus, there are basic inclinations that form the core of moral principles. For instance, the preservation of one's own being is a natural inclination and thus is a basic principle of morality. Actions consistent with this natural inclination would be those that preserve one's own life, such as in self-defense, but also those that preserve or maintain the species, such as a prohibition against murder. Other inclinations are peculiar to one's species—for instance, humans are social animals; thus, sociability is a natural inclination that leads to altruism and generosity. These are natural and thus moral. The pursuit of knowledge or understanding of the universe might also be recognized as a natural inclination of humans; thus, actions that conform to this natural inclination are moral.

The Greek philosophers recognized natural law, but we also see it clearly in later writings, such as St. Augustine, who is attributed with a famous quote: "An unjust law is no law at all." This concept refers to the idea that if man's law contradicts the law of nature, then it is not only wrong, it may not even be considered law. St. Thomas Aquinas, in *Summa Theologiae*, distinguished natural law from God's law, and placed reason at the epicenter of the natural law system: "Whatever is contrary to the order of reason is contrary to the nature of human beings as such; and what is reasonable is in accordance with human nature as such" (Aquinas as cited in Buckle, 1993: 165).

Natural law theory defines good as that which is natural. The difficulty of this system is identifying what is consistent and congruent with the natural inclinations of humankind. How do we know which acts are in accordance with the natural order of things? Who determines the natural laws? Natural law has been employed to restrict the rights and liberties of groups of people; for instance, historically, the so-called "natural" superiority of whites was used to support and justify slavery, and the "natural" role of women as childbearers restricted their employment opportunities. Today, natural law is sometimes employed to oppose same-sex marriage. Opponents to same-sex marriage argue that the only natural marriage is between heterosexuals joined together for the purpose of procreation. Proponents argue that humans are naturally sociable and there is a natural human need for bonding, noting that many heterosexual marriages are for reasons other than procreation, but that does not make them unnatural. The fundamental problem with this ethical system is: how does one know whether a moral rule is based upon a true natural law or a mistaken human perception?

Religion

St. Augustine and St. Thomas Aquinas described natural laws, but they were also Christian theologians who placed morality and ethics into the discussion of sin. Religion, by definition, provides moral guidelines and directions on how to live one's life. For instance, Christians and Jews are taught the Ten Commandments, which prohibit certain behaviors defined as wrong. The authority of **religious ethics**, in particular Judeo-Christian ethics, stems from a willful and rational God. For believers, the authority of God's will is beyond question, and there is no need for further examination because of His perfection. The only possible controversy comes from human interpretation of God's commands. Indeed, these differences in interpretation are the source of most religious strife.

religious ethics The ethical system that is based on religious beliefs of good and evil; what is good is that which is God's will.

Religious ethics is, of course, much broader than simply Judeo-Christian ethics. Religions such as Buddhism, Confucianism, and Islam also provide a basis for ethics because they offer explanations of how to live a "good life" and address other philosophical issues, such as "What is reality?" Pantheistic religions—such as those of primitive hunter-gatherer societies—promote the belief that there is a living spirit in all things and tend not to be as judgmental as religions we are more familiar with, such as Christianity, Judaism, or Islam. A religion must have a willful and rational God or god figure before there can be a judgment of right and wrong, thus providing a basis for an ethical system. Those religions that do have a god figure consider that figure to be the source of principles of ethics and morality.

It is also true that of the religions we might discuss, many have similar basic moral principles. Many religions have their own version of the Ten Commandments. In this regard, Islam is not too different from Judaism, which is not too different from

Christianity. What Christians know as the Golden Rule actually predates Christianity, and the principle can be found in all the major religions, as well as offered by ancient philosophers:

- Christianity: "Do unto others as you would have them do unto you."
- Hinduism: "Do naught to others which, if done to thee, would cause thee pain: this is the sum of duty."
- Buddhism: "In five ways should a clansman minister to his friends and familiars . . . by treating them as he treats himself."
- Confucianism: "What you do not want done to yourself, do not do unto others."
- Judaism: "Whatsoever thou wouldst that men should not do unto thee, do not do that to them."
- Isocrates: "Do not do to others what would anger you if done to you by others."
- Diogenes Laertius, *Lives of the Philosophers*: "The question was once put to Aristotle how we ought to behave to our friends; and his answer was, 'As we should wish them to behave to us.'"
- The Mahabharata: "This is the sum of all true righteousness, deal with others as thou wouldst thyself be dealt by. Do nothing to thy neighbor which thou wouldst not have him do to thee hereafter." (Reiman, 1990/2004: 147; Shermer, 2004: 25)

A fundamental question discussed by philosophers and Christian religious scholars is whether God commands us not to commit an act because it is inherently wrong (e.g., "Thou shalt not kill"), or whether an act acquires its "badness" or "goodness" solely from God's definition of it. Another issue in Western religious ethics is how to determine God's will. Some believe that God is inviolable and that positions on moral questions are absolute. This is a legalist position. Others believe that God's will varies according to time and place—the situationalist position. According to this position, situational factors are important in determining the rightness of a particular action. Something may be right or wrong depending on the circumstances (Borchert and Stewart, 1986: 157). For instance, lying may be wrong unless it is to protect an innocent, or stealing may be wrong unless it is to protest injustice and to help unfortunates. Some would say that it is impossible to have an *a priori* knowledge of God's will because that would put us above God's law: We ourselves cannot be "all-knowing." Thus, for any situation, if we are prepared to receive God's divine commands, we can know them through faith and conscience. This discussion has focused on Christianity; therefore Box 2.3 briefly describes some of the other major world religions.

According to Barry (1985: 51–54), human beings can "know" God's will in three ways:

- *Individual conscience.* An individual's conscience is the best source for discovering what God wants one to do. If one feels uncomfortable about a certain action, it is probably wrong.
- *Religious authorities.* These authorities can interpret right and wrong for us and are our best source if we are confused about certain actions.
- *Holy scriptures.* The third way is to go directly to the Bible, Quran, or Torah as the source of God's law. Some believe that the written word of God holds the answers to all moral dilemmas.

BOX 2.3 \ Overview of Major World Religions

Judaism

Judaism is older than Christianity or Islam, with the Torah, rather than the Bible, as its foundational text. As with Christianity and Islam, there are various movements or divisions under Judaism, but, generally, Judaism incorporates a monotheistic belief in God with recognized prophets, including Abraham and Moses. Judaism teaches that Jesus was not the Messiah or son of God (similar to Islam) and not a prophet (dissimilar from Islam) because of disagreements with Jewish teachings. The definition of what is good in Judaism comes from the Torah, the Talmud, and religious authorities. Judaism's definitions of goodness lie in virtues and religious faith. Believers are exhorted to lead a righteous life that includes helping the needy. Virtues include benevolence, faith, and compassion. The Jewish version of the Golden Rule is: "What is hateful to you, do not do unto others." Falsehoods, unkind actions, stealing, revenge are wrong. Shalom (peace) is the path one should live one's life by which could equate to pleasantness and kindness in dealings with others.

Islam

One of the newest, yet largest, religions is Islam. Like Christianity, this religion recognizes one god, Allah. Jesus and other religious figures are recognized as prophets, as is Muhammad, who is considered to be the last and greatest prophet. Islam is based on the Quran, which is taken much more literally as the word of Allah than the Bible is taken by most Christians. There is a great deal of fatalism in Islam: *Inshallah*, meaning, "If God wills it," is a prevalent theme in Muslim societies, but there is recognition that if people choose evil, they do so freely. The five pillars of Islam are (1) repetition of the creed (*Shahada*), (2) daily prayer (*Salah*), (3) almsgiving (*Zakat*), (4) fasting (*Sawm*), and (5) pilgrimage (*Hajj*).

Another feature of Islam is the idea of the holy war. In this concept, the faithful who die defending Islam against infidels will be rewarded in the afterlife (Hopfe, 1983). This is not to say that Islam provides a legitimate justification for terroristic acts. Devout Muslims protest that terrorists have subverted the teachings of Islam and do not follow its precepts, one of which is never to harm innocents.

Buddhism

Siddhartha Gautama (Buddha) attained enlightenment and preached to others how to do the same and achieve release from suffering. He taught that good behavior is that which follows the "middle path" between asceticism and hedonistic pursuit of sensual pleasure. Essentials of Buddhist teachings are ethical conduct, mental discipline, and wisdom. Ethical conduct is based on universal love and compassion for all living beings. Compassion and wisdom are needed in equal measures. Ethical conduct can be broken into right speech (refraining from lies, slander, enmity, and rude speech), right action (abstaining from destroying life, stealing, and dishonest dealings, and helping others lead peaceful and honorable lives), and right livelihood (abstaining from occupations that bring harm to others, such as arms dealing and killing animals). To follow the "middle path," one must abide by these guidelines (Kessler, 1992).

Confucianism

Confucius taught a humanistic social philosophy that included central concepts such as *Ren*, which is human virtue and humanity at its best, as well as the source of moral principles; *Li*, which is traditional order, ritual, or custom; *Xiao*, which is familial love; and *Yi*, which is rightness, both a virtue and a principle of behavior—that is, one should do what is right because it is right. The *doctrine of the mean* exemplifies one aspect of Confucianism that emphasizes a cosmic or natural

(continued)

order. Humans are a part of nature and are included in the scheme of life. Practicing moderation in one's life is part of this natural order and reflects a "way to Heaven" (Kessler, 1992).

Hinduism

In Hinduism, the central concept of *karma* can be understood as consequence. Specifically, what one does in one's present life will determine what happens in a future life. The goal is to escape the eternal birth/rebirth cycle by living one's life in a moral manner so no bad karma will occur (Kessler, 1992). People start out life in the lowest caste, but if they live a good life, they will be reborn as members of a higher caste, until they reach the highest Brahman caste, and at that point the cycle can end. An early source for Hinduism was the Code of Manu. In this code are found the ethical ideals of Hinduism, which include pleasantness, patience, control of mind, refraining from stealing, purity, control of the senses, intelligence, knowledge, truthfulness, and non-irritability (Hopfe, 1983).

Strong doubts exist as to whether any of these methods are true indicators of divine command. Our consciences may be no more than the products of our psychological development, influenced by our environment. Religious authorities are, after all, only human, with human failings. Even the Bible seems to support contradictory principles. For instance, advocates of capital punishment can find passages in the Bible that support it (such as Genesis 9:6: "Whoever sheds the blood of man, by man shall his blood be shed. . ."), but opponents to capital punishment argue that the New Testament offers little direct support for execution and has many more passages that direct one to forgive, such as Matthew 5:38–40: ". . . Offer no resistance to injury. When a person strikes you on the right cheek, turn and offer him the other."

The question of whether people can ever know God's will has been explored through the ages. St. Thomas Aquinas (1225–1274) believed that human reason was sufficient not only to prove the existence of God but also to discover God's divine commands. Others believe that reason is not sufficient to know God and that it comes down to unquestioning belief, so reason and knowledge must always be separate from faith. These people believe that one can know whether an action is consistent with God's will only if it contributes to general happiness, because God intends for us to be happy, or when the action is done through the *holy spirit*—that is, when someone performs the action under the influence of true faith (Borchert and Stewart, 1986: 159–171).

To summarize, the religious ethics system is widely used and accepted. The authority of the god figure is the root of all morality; basic conceptions of good and evil or right and wrong come from interpretations of the god figure's will. Many people throughout history have wrestled with the problem of determining what is right according to God.

Ethical Formalism

Ethical formalism is a deontological system. A **deontological ethical system** is one that is concerned solely with the inherent nature of the act being judged. If an act or intent is inherently good (coming from a good will), it is still considered a good act even if it results in bad consequences. According to the philosopher Immanuel Kant (1724–1804), the only thing that is intrinsically good is a *good will*. On the one hand, if someone does an action from a good will, it can be considered a moral action

ethical formalism
The ethical system espoused by Kant that focuses on duty; holds that the only thing truly good is a good will, and that what is good is that which conforms to the categorical imperative.

deontological ethical system
The study of duty or moral obligation emphasizing the intent of the actor as the element of morality.

even if it results in bad consequences. On the other hand, if someone performs some activity that looks on the surface to be altruistic but does it with an ulterior motive—for instance, to curry favor or gain benefit—that act is not judged as "good" just because it results in good consequences. Gold, Braswell, and McCarthy (1991) offer the example of a motorist stranded by the side of the road; another driver who comes along has a decision to help or to pass by. If the driver makes a decision to stop and help, this would seem to be a good act. Not so, according to ethical formalism, unless it is done from a good will. If the helper stops because he or she expects payment, wants a return favor, or for any reason other than a good will, the act is only neutral—not moral. Only if the help springs from a good will can we say that it is truly good.

Kant believed that moral worth comes from doing one's duty. Just as there is the law of the family (father's rule), the law of the state and country, and the law of international relations, there is also a universal law of right and wrong. Morality, according to Kant, arises from the fact that humans, as rational beings, impose these laws and strictures of behavior upon themselves (Kant, trans. Beck, 1949). Kant was a Christian, but he also believed that what is good could be discovered through pure reason.

According to Kant, **hypothetical imperatives** are commands that designate certain actions to attain certain ends. An example is, "*If* I want to be a success, *then* I must do well in college," or "*If* I want people to like me, *then* I must be friendly." By contrast, a **categorical imperative** commands action that is necessary without any reference to intended purposes or consequences. The "imperative of morality" according to Kant needed no further justification (Kant, trans. Beck, 1949: 76). The following constitute the principles of Kant's categorical imperative of morality (Bowie, 1985: 157):

- *Act only on that maxim through which you can at the same time will that it should become a universal law.* In other words, for any decision of behavior to be made, examine whether that behavior would be acceptable if it were a universal law to be followed by everyone. For instance, a student might decide to cheat on a test, but for this action to be moral, the student would have to agree that everyone should be able to cheat on tests.

- *Act in such a way that you always treat humanity, whether in your own person or that of any other, never simply as a means but always at the same time as an end.* In other words, one should not use people for one's own purposes. For instance, being friendly to someone so that you can use her car is using her as a means to one's own ends. Even otherwise moral actions, such as giving to charity or doing charitable acts for others, would be considered immoral if done for ulterior motives such as self-aggrandizement.

- *Act as if you were, through your maxims, a lawmaking member of a kingdom of ends.* This principle directs that the individual's actions should contribute to and be consistent with universal law. However, the good act must be done freely. If one is compelled to do a good act, the compulsion removes the moral nature of the act. Only when we freely choose to abide by moral law and these laws are self-imposed rather than imposed from the outside are they a reflection of the higher nature of humans.

hypothetical imperatives
Statements of contingent demand known as if-then statements (if I want something, then I must work for it); usually contrasted with categorical imperatives (statements of "must" with no "ifs").

categorical imperative
The concept that some things just must be, with no need for further justification, explanation, or rationalization for why they exist (Kant's categorical imperative refers to the imperative that you should do your duty, act in a way you want everyone else to act, and don't use people).

A system such as ethical formalism is considered to be an *absolutist system*—if something is wrong, it is wrong all the time, such as murder or lying. To assassinate evil tyrants such as Adolf Hitler, Saddam Hussein, or Osama Bin Laden might be considered moral under a teleological system, more fully discussed below as concerned with consequences, because ridding the world of dangerous people is a good end. However, in the deontological view, if the act and intent of killing are wrong, then killing is always wrong; thus, assassination must be considered immoral in all cases, regardless of the good consequences that might result. This absolute judgment is criticized by those who argue that there are sometimes exceptions to any moral rule such as "one should not lie." In a well-known example, Kant argued that if someone asked to be hidden from an attacker in close pursuit and then the attacker asked where the potential victim was hiding, it would be immoral to lie about the victim's location. This seems wrong to many and serves to dissuade people from seeing the value of ethical formalism. However, according to Kant, an individual cannot control consequences, only actions; therefore, one must act in a moral fashion without regard to potential consequences. In the example, the attacker may not kill the potential victim, the victim may still be able to get away, or the attacker may be justified. The victim may have even left the place you saw them hide and move to the very place you offer to the attacker as a lie. Also, to not say anything is an option to lying. The point is that no one person can control anything in life, so the only thing that makes sense is to live by the categorical imperative.

Kant also defended his position with semantics—distinguishing untruths from lies with the explanation that a lie is a lie only when the recipient is led to believe or has a right to believe that he or she is being told the truth. The attacker in the previous scenario or an attacker who has one "by the throat" demanding one's money has no right to expect the truth; thus, it would not be immoral not to tell this person the truth. Only if one led the attacker to believe that one was going to tell the truth and then did not would one violate the categorical imperative. To not tell the truth when the attacker doesn't deserve the truth is not a lie, but if one intentionally and deliberately sets out to deceive, then that is a lie—even if it is being told to a person who doesn't deserve the truth (Kant, ed. Infield, 1981).

This ethical framework follows simply from the beliefs that an individual must follow a self-imposed moral law and that one is capable of using reason to determine right actions because any action can be evaluated by using the principles just listed. Criticisms of ethical formalism include the following (Maestri, 1982: 910):

- *Ethical formalism seems to be unresponsive to extreme circumstances.* If something is wrong in every circumstance regardless of the good that results or good reasons for the action, otherwise good people might be judged immoral or unethical.

- *Morality is limited to duty.* One might argue that duty is the baseline of morality, not the highest aspiration of it. Further, it is not always clear where one's duty lies. At times one might face a dilemma where two duties conflict with each other.

- *The priority of motive and intent over result is problematic in some instances.* It may be seriously questioned whether the intention to do good, regardless of result or perhaps with negative result, is always moral. Many would argue that the consequences of an action and the actual result must be evaluated to determine morality.

Other writers present variations of deontological ethics that do not depend so heavily on Kant (Braswell, McCarthy, and McCarthy, 2002/2007). The core elements of any deontological or duty-based ethical system are the importance placed on intention and the use of a predetermined set of principles to judge morality rather than looking at the consequences of an act.

Utilitarianism

utilitarianism
The ethical system that claims that the greatest good is that which results in the greatest happiness for the greatest number; major proponents are Bentham and Mill.

teleological ethical system
An ethical system that is concerned with the consequences or ends of an action to determine goodness.

Utilitarianism is a teleological ethical system. A **teleological ethical system** judges the consequences of an act. Even a bad act, if it results in good consequences, can be defined as good under a teleological system. The saying "the end justifies the means" is a teleological statement. Jeremy Bentham (1748–1832), a major proponent of utilitarianism, believed that the morality of an action should be determined by how much it contributes to the good of the majority. According to Bentham, human nature seeks to maximize pleasure and avoid pain, and a moral system must be consistent with this natural fact.

The "utilitarian doctrine asserts that we should always act so as to produce the greatest possible ratio of good to evil for everyone concerned" (Barry, 1985: 65). That is, if one can show that an action significantly contributes to the general good, then it is good. In situations where one must decide between a good for an individual and a good for society, then society should prevail, despite the wrong being done to an individual. This is because the utility or good derived from that action generally outweighs the small amount of harm done (because the harm is done only to one, whereas the good is multiplied by the many). For instance, if it could be shown that using someone as an example would be an effective deterrent to crime, whether or not the person was actually guilty, the wrong done to that person by this unjust punishment might be outweighed by the good resulting for society. This assumes that citizens would not find out about the injustice and lose respect for the authority of the legal system, which would be a negative effect for all concerned.

Although utilitarianism is quite prevalent in our thinking about ethical decision making, there are some serious criticisms of it:

- *All "pleasures" or benefits are not equal.* Bentham did not judge the relative weight of utility. He considered pleasure to be a good whether it derived from vice, such as avarice or greed, or from virtue, such as charity and kindness. Later utilitarians, primarily John Stuart Mill (1806–1873), believed that utilities (benefits) had different weights or values. In other words, some were better than others. For instance, art offers a different utility for society than alcohol, altruism carries more benefit than pleasure, and so on. But who is to determine which is better? Determining what is good by weighing utilities makes sense, but the actual exercise is sometimes very difficult.

- *The system presumes that one can predict the consequences of one's actions.* In the well-known "lifeboat" dilemma, five people are in a lifeboat with enough food and water only for four. It is certain that they will survive if there are only four; it is also certain that they will all perish if one does not go overboard. What should be done? Under ethical formalism, it would be unthinkable to sacrifice an innocent, even if it means that all will die. Under utilitarian ethics, it is conceivable that the murder of one might be justified to save the others. But this hypothetical situation points out the fallacy of the utilitarian argument. In reality, it is not known whether any will survive. The fifth might be murdered and five minutes later a rescue ship appears on the horizon. The fifth might be murdered but then the remaining four be eaten by sharks. Only in unrealistic hypothetical situations does one absolutely know the consequences of one's action. In real life, one never knows if an action will result in a greater good or ultimate harm.

- *There is little concern for individual rights in utilitarianism.* Ethical formalism demands that each individual must be treated with respect and not be used as a means to an end. However, under utilitarianism, the rights of one individual may be sacrificed for the good of many.

Utilitarianism has two forms: act utilitarianism and rule utilitarianism. The basic difference between the two can be summarized as follows: In **act utilitarianism**, only the basic utility derived from one action is examined. We look at the consequences of any action for all involved and weigh the units of utility accordingly. In **rule utilitarianism**, one judges that action in reference to the precedent it sets and the long-term utility of the rule set by that action.

On the one hand, act utilitarianism might support stealing food when one is hungry and has no other way to eat because the utility of survival would outweigh the loss to the store owner. On the other hand, rule utilitarianism would be concerned with the effect that the action would have if made into a rule for behavior: "Any time an individual cannot afford food, he or she can steal it" would contribute to a state of lawlessness and a general disrespect for the law. Such a rule would probably not result in the greatest utility for the greatest number. With rule utilitarianism, then, we are concerned not only with the immediate utility of the action but also with the long-term utility or harm if the action were to be a rule for all similar circumstances. Note the similarity between rule utilitarianism and the first principle of the categorical imperative. In both approaches, one must judge as good only those actions that can be universalized.

In summary, utilitarianism holds that morality must be determined by the consequences of an action. Society and the survival and benefit of all are more important than any individual. Something is right when it benefits the continuance and good health of society. Rule utilitarianism may be closer to the principles of ethical formalism because it weighs the utility of such actions after they have been made into general laws. The difference between ethical formalism and rule utilitarianism is that the actions themselves are judged right or wrong depending on the motives behind them under ethical formalism, whereas utilitarianism looks to the long-term consequences of the prescribed rules to determine their morality. Which of the ethical systems support Joseph Darby's decision described in the Walking the Walk box?

act utilitarianism The type of utilitarianism that determines the goodness of a particular act by measuring the utility (good) for all, but only for that specific act and without regard for future actions.

rule utilitarianism The type of utilitarianism that determines the goodness of an action by measuring the utility of that action when it is made into a rule for behavior.

The Ethics of Care

The **ethics of care** is based on human relationships and needs. The ethics of care has been described as a feminine morality because women in all societies are the childbearers and consequently seem to have a greater sensitivity to issues of care. Noddings (1986: 1) points out that the "mother's voice" has been silent in Western, masculine analysis: "One is tempted to say that ethics has so far been guided by

ethics of care The ethical system that defines good as meeting the needs of others and preserving and enriching relationships.

WALKING THE WALK

Joe Darby was a military reservist from a low-income family who grew up in Pennsylvania and settled in Maryland. The 372nd was a military police unit based in his town, and almost everyone had some ties to the military. Darby's unit was deployed to Iraq.

One fateful day in January 2004, Darby began his march into the history books by asking Specialist Charles Graner for some pictures of the surrounding countryside. Graner gave him a CD of pictures. Clicking through the pictures to decide which ones to send home, he stumbled on some that, at first, made him laugh; then, as others appeared on the computer screen, he grew more and more disgusted. "They just didn't sit right with me," he said later.

The pictures were the infamous torture photos taken in the Abu Ghraib prison by Graner and others. Whether Graner didn't remember that they were on the CD or didn't care will never be known; however, once Darby saw the pictures, he couldn't stop thinking about them. He had not been present and did not know that soldiers had been posing the prisoners nude, forcing them to simulate masturbation and homosexual acts, using dogs to intimidate and attack the naked prisoners, and placing them on stools and telling them if they fell off they would be electrocuted.

Darby had seen other things at the prison, though, which he related years later in news accounts—things like a helicopter flying into the prison grounds in the middle of the night with a prisoner being hustled into the interrogation room by men who not only were nameless but who never revealed whether they were military intelligence, CIA, or civilian contractors. When they left the next morning, the prisoner was dead and the soldiers were told to "clean it up."

The pictures of Charles Graner and Sabrina Harmon (another military police specialist) posing next to the body of this man are part of the group of photos that were plastered across newspapers, shown on televisions, and appeared on Internet sites around the world. The scandal tarnished the reputation of the United States, probably contributed to an increase in the Iraqi insurgency, ruined careers, and ended up with the soldiers in the pictures serving prison time.

So why did Darby do it? Why did he burn copies of the pictures onto a disk and give them to the Criminal Intelligence Division (CID) rather than to his commanding officer?

He said later that it was because things had been reported to his superiors before and nothing happened, and, besides, Ivan Frederick, one of those who appeared in the pictures, was the commanding officer of the night shift. Darby first turned in the envelope with the photos to CID investigators and said he didn't know where it came from, but then he admitted that he had gotten the pictures from Graner. He was promised that his name would be kept confidential.

Once investigators obtained the photos, they immediately began an investigation and questioned all those in the pictures who were then, inexplicably, allowed to remain in the compound. Tension and paranoia were intense, and Darby said he literally feared for his life, hoping that no one would discover that it was he who had turned them in. "I'm not the kind of guy to rat somebody out," he said later. "I've kept a lot of secrets for soldiers . . . but this crossed the line to me. I had the choice between what I knew was morally right and my loyalty to other soldiers. I couldn't have it both ways."

At some point, his name was leaked to the press, and then-secretary of defense Donald Rumsfeld announced in the congressional hearing about Abu Ghraib that Darby was the one who turned in the photos. Darby was sitting in a crowded mess hall in Iraq when the hearing was being aired on the television. The room became quiet. Although some soldiers shook Darby's hand, many regarded him as a traitor. So did most of his neighbors and even some of his family. His wife endured weeks of threats and vandalism before she was taken into protective custody by the military. Neighbors said he was a rat, a traitor, and should fear for his life. Darby, too, was removed from Iraq ahead of his unit and reunited with his wife in seclusion and under heavy guard. He was told that it wasn't safe to return to their hometown, and he didn't. They are not welcome there. His tour of duty was extended through the trials, which lasted through 2006. In 2005, Darby received the John F. Kennedy Profile in Courage Award.

Today, the media storm that Darby created has finally died down and he is a civilian trying to create a new life. He does not regret what he did. "I've always had a moral sense of right and wrong. And I knew that, you know, friends or not, it had to stop," Darby says.

Sources: Hylton, 2006; CBS.news.com, 2005; CBS.news.com, 2007; Gourevitch and Morris, 2008.

Logos, the masculine spirit, whereas the more natural and perhaps stronger approach would be through Eros, the feminine spirit."

The ethics of care is founded in the natural human response to care for a newborn child, the ill, and the hurt. There are similarities in the ethics of care's idea that morals derive from natural human impulses of compassion and Jean-Jacques Rousseau's (1712–1778) argument that it is humans' natural compassion that is the basis of human action and the idea that morality is based in emotion rather than rationality, that is, "What I feel is right is right, what I feel is wrong is wrong" (Rousseau, as cited by Ruggiero, 2001: 28).

Carol Gilligan's work on moral development in psychology identified a feminine approach to ethical decision making that focused on relationships and needs instead of rights and universal laws. The most interesting feature of this approach is that while a relatively small number of women emphasized needs over rights, no men did. She attributed this to Western society, in which men and women are both socialized to Western ethics, which are primarily concerned with issues of rights, laws, and universalism (Gilligan, 1982).

Applying the ethics of care does not necessarily lead to different solutions, but perhaps to different questions. In an ethical system based on care, we would be concerned with issues of needs rather than rights. Other writers point to some Eastern religions, such as Taoism, as illustrations of the ethics of care (Gold et al., 1991; Larrabee, 1993). In these religions, a rigid, formal, rule-based ethics is rejected in favor of gently leading the individual to follow a path of caring for others. In criminal justice, the ethics of care is represented to some extent by the rehabilitative ethic rather than the just-deserts model. Certainly the "restorative justice" movement is consistent with the ethics of care because of its emphasis on the motives and needs of all concerned, rather than simply retribution. In personal relationships, the ethics of care would promote empathy and treating others in a way that does not hurt them. In this view, meeting needs is more important than securing rights.

In their text, Braswell and Gold (2002) discuss a concept called **peacemaking justice**. They show that the concept is derived from ancient principles, and it concerns care as well as other concepts: "Peacemaking, as evolved from ancient spiritual and wisdom traditions, has included the possibility of mercy and compassion within the framework of justice" (2002: 25). They propose that the peacemaking process is composed of three parts: connectedness, caring, and mindfulness:

peacemaking justice   An ancient approach to justice that includes the concepts of compassion and care, connectedness, and mindfulness.

- *Connectedness* has to do with the interrelationships we have with one another and all of us have with the earth.
- *Caring* is similar to Noddings's concept that the "natural" inclination of humans is to care for one another.
- *Mindfulness* involves being aware of others and the world in all personal decision making (Braswell and Gold, 2002: 25–37).

To summarize, the ethics of care approach identifies the needs of all individuals in any ethical situation and attempts to maximize them. It is different from utilitarianism, however, in that one person cannot be sacrificed for others. Also, there is an attempt to resolve situations through human relationships and a sense that decisions should come from compassion rather than attention to rights or duties.

Egoism: Ethical System or Not?

egoism   The ethical system that defines the pursuit of self-interest as a moral good.

Very simply, **egoism** postulates that what is good for one's survival and personal happiness is moral. The extreme of this position is that all people should operate on the assumption that they can do whatever benefits themselves. Others become solely the means to ensure happiness; there is no recognition of the rights of others under this system. For this reason, some have rejected egoism as an ethical system entirely, arguing that it is fundamentally inconsistent with one of the elements ("they are not self-serving") (Baelz, 1977).

psychological egoism   The concept that humans naturally and inherently seek self-interest, and that we can do nothing else because it is our nature.

Psychological egoism refers to the belief that humans are naturally egoists and that it would be unnatural for them to be any other way. All species have instincts for survival, and self-preservation and self-interest are merely part of that instinct. Therefore, it is not only moral to be egoistic, but it is the only way we can be, and any other explanations of behavior are mere rationalizations. In behaviors that appear to be altruistic, such as giving to charity or volunteering, the argument goes that these acts provide psychic and emotional pleasure to the individual and that is why they do them, not for some other selfless reason. Even though acts such as running into a burning building or jumping into a river to save victims seem altruistic, psychological egoists believe that these acts occur because of the personality makeup of individuals who derive greater pleasure from being considered heroes, or enjoy the adrenalin rush of the dangerous act, more than the feeling of security derived from staying on the sidelines.

enlightened egoism   The concept that egoism may appear to be altruistic because it is in one's long-term best interest to help others in order to receive help in return.

Enlightened egoism is a slight revision of this basic principle, adding that each person's objective is long-term welfare. This may mean that we should treat others as we would want them to treat us to ensure cooperative relations. Even seemingly selfless and altruistic acts are consistent with egoism because these acts benefit the individual by ensuring reciprocal assistance. For instance, if you help your friend move when he asks you to, it is only because you expect that he will help you when you need some future favor. Under egoism, it would be not only impossible but also immoral for someone to perform a completely selfless act. Even those who give their lives to save others do so perhaps with the expectation of rewards in the afterlife. Egoism completely turns around the priorities of utilitarianism to put the individual first, before anyone else and before society as a whole; however, because long-term interests often dictate meeting obligations and helping others, enlightened egoists might look like altruists.

Adam Smith (1723–1790), the "father" of free enterprise, promoted a type of practical egoism, arguing that individuals pursuing their own personal good would lead to nations prospering as well. Capitalism is based on the premise that everyone pursuing self-interest will create a healthy economy: Workers will work harder to get more pay; owners will not exploit workers too badly because they might quit; merchants will try to get the highest price for items, whereas consumers will shop for the lowest price; and so on. Only when government or liberal do-gooders manipulate the market, some argue, does capitalism not work optimally. Ayn Rand (1905–1982) is perhaps the best-known modern writer/philosopher associated with egoism. She promoted both psychological egoism (that humans *are* naturally selfish) and ethical egoism (that humans *should be* self-interested). Libertarians utilize Rand's writings to support their view of limited government and fierce individualism.

Most philosophers reject egoism because it violates the basic tenets of an ethical system. Universalism is inconsistent with egoism, because to approve of all people acting in their own self-interest is not a logical or feasible position. It cannot be right for both me and you to maximize our own self-interests because it would inevitably lead to conflict. Egoism would support exploitative actions by the strong against the weak, which seems wrong under all other ethical systems. However, psychological egoism is a relevant concept in natural law (self-preservation is natural) and utilitarianism (hedonism is a natural inclination). But if it is true that humans are *naturally* selfish and self-serving, one can also point to examples that indicate that humans are also altruistic and self-sacrificing. One thing seems clear: When individuals are caught doing illegal acts, or acts that violate their professional codes of ethics, or acts that harm others, such as those described in the In the News box, it is usually only egoism that can justify their behavior.

(•) IN THE NEWS | *Corruption in High Places*

The *New York Times* reported that over 30 public officials in New York have been caught in corruption scandals in the last decade. Most recently, three state legislators were arrested on federal charges; one of them was accused of trying to bribe his way onto the mayoral ballot of New York City, another for bribery in relation to sponsoring legislation. A partial list includes: Assemblymen (and women) William Boyland (convicted of bribery), Nelson Castro (pleaded guilty to perjury and making false statements), Mike Cole (censored for spending the night at a female intern's home after drinking), Sam Hoyt (banned from having interns after having an affair with one), Diane Gordon (convicted of offering to help a developer get a parcel of city-owned land in return for building her a house), Micah Kellner (sanctioned for sexually harassing his staff members), Vito Lopez (fined for sexually harassing staff members), and Brian McLaughlin (pleaded guilty to racketeering charges in various criminal schemes to steal taxpayer money). In addition to Assemblymen/women, the list included Senators Pedro Espada (convicted of siphoning hundreds of thousands of dollars from his nonprofit health care network), Efrain Gonzalez (pleaded guilty to using hundreds of thousands of dollars from nonprofit agencies to pay for personal expenses), Shirley Huntley (pleaded guilty to stealing state grant money and falsifying evidence), Carl Kruger (pleaded guilty to bribery and conspiracy), Vincent Leibell (pleaded guilty to obstruction of justice and tax charges), Thomas Libous (charged with lying to FBI who were investigating whether he obtained a job for his son using his influence), and Kiram Monserrate (expelled because of assault and mail fraud). Former governor David Paterson was fined for soliciting and receiving free Yankee tickets and lying under oath about it and former governor Elliot Spitzer resigned after he was exposed as patronizing prostitutes. Others have been found guilty of a range of other criminal and/or corrupt actions, most often using their office to solicit and receive kickbacks, gifts, and other illegal and unethical benefits

Governor Andrew M. Cuomo set up a commission in July 2013 to investigate corruption, which included 25 commission members, including three co-chairs, with diverse backgrounds in law enforcement and government. Reports indicate that they almost immediately began receiving pressure from the Governor's Office to divert their attention away from some people; for instance, subpoenas to a media-buying firm that had placed millions of dollars' worth of advertisements for the New York State Democratic Party were withdrawn and the newspaper investigation discovered that the target had produced ads for the governor. In response to criticism, the governor explained that he had the right to monitor and direct the work of a commission he had created. Some believe that his purpose in creating the commission was only to force the legislature to pass a package of ethics reforms, although the result was deemed fairly weak. Finally, he abruptly disbanded the commission halfway through its proposed 18-month life. Federal prosecutors are investigating the roles of Mr. Cuomo and his aides in the panel's shutdown and have seized the investigation files that the commission staff had begun, so there may be further names to add to the list in the future.

Source: Rashbaum and Kaplan, 2015.

Other Methods of Ethical Decision Making

Some modern writers present approaches to applied ethics that do not directly include the ethical systems discussed thus far. For instance, Krogstand and Robertson (1979) described three principles of ethical decision making:

imperative principle
The concept that all decisions should be made according to absolute rules.

- The **imperative principle** directs a decision maker to act according to a specific, unbending rule.
- The **utilitarian principle** determines the ethics of conduct by the good or bad consequences of the action.
- The **generalization principle** is based on this question: "What would happen if all similar persons acted this way under similar circumstances?"

utilitarian principle
The principle that all decisions should be made according to what is best for the greatest number.

These should sound familiar because they are, respectively, religious or absolutist ethics, utilitarianism, and ethical formalism. Ruggiero (2001) proposes that ethical dilemmas be evaluated using three basic criteria. The first principle is to examine one's obligations and duties and what one has promised to do by contract or by taking on a role (this is similar to ethical formalism). The second principle is to examine moral ideals such as how one's decision squares with prudence, temperance, justice, honesty, compassion, and other ideals (this is similar to Aristotle's ethics of virtue). The third principle is to evaluate the act to determine if it would result in good consequences (this is utilitarianism).

generalization principle   The principle that all decisions should be made assuming that the decision would be applied to everyone else in similar circumstances.

Close and Meier (1995: 130) provide a set of questions more specific to criminal justice professionals and sensitive to the due process protections that are often discarded in a decision to commit an unethical act. They propose that the individual decision maker should ask the following questions:

1. Does the action violate another person's constitutional rights, including the right of due process?

2. Does the action involve treating another person only as a means to an end?

3. Is the action illegal?

4. Do you predict that your action will produce more bad than good for all persons affected?

5. Does the action violate department procedure or professional duty?

The most simple test is the so-called "front page" test. This ethical check asks us to evaluate our decision by whether or not we would be comfortable if it was on the front page of the newspaper. Public disclosure is often a good litmus test for whether something is ethical or not.

Using Ethical Systems to Resolve Dilemmas

As discussed in Chapter 1, if confronted with an ethical dilemma, one can follow a series of steps to come to an ethical resolution:

1. *Identify the facts.* Identifying all relevant facts is essential as a first step. Sometimes individuals facing a dilemma do not know all the facts, and sometimes the decision to find the facts is an ethical dilemma unto itself.

2. *Identify relevant values and concepts.* One's values of duty, friendship, loyalty, honesty, and self-preservation are usually at the heart of professional ethical dilemmas.

3. *Identify all possible moral dilemmas for each party involved.* Recall that this was to help us see that sometimes one's own moral or ethical dilemma is caused by others' actions. Usually one's ethical dilemma is prefaced upon others' ethical (or unethical) decisions.

4. *Decide what is the most immediate moral or ethical issue facing the individual.* This is always a behavior choice, not an opinion.

5. *Resolve the ethical or moral dilemma by using an ethical system or some other means of decision making.*

ETHICAL DILEMMA

Detective Russell Poole was a Robbery-Homicide Division investigator with the Los Angeles Police Department. In 1998, he was assigned an investigation regarding the alleged beating of Ismael Jimenez, a reputed gang member, by LAPD officers, and a suspected cover-up of the incident. In his investigation, he uncovered a pattern of complaints of violence by the anti-gang task force in the Ramparts Division. Gang members told Poole and his partners that a number of officers harassed them, assaulted them, and pressured them to provide untraceable guns. The beating occurred because Jimenez would not provide the officers with a gun. In a search of the house of Officer Rafael Perez, a member of the anti-gang task force, Poole found a box with a half-dozen realistic replica toy guns. He concluded that a number of the officers in the division were "vigilante cops" and requested that the investigation proceed further.

After Poole informed his superiors of what his investigation had uncovered, Bernard Parks, the LAPD chief at the time, ordered Poole to limit his investigation solely to the Jimenez beating. Poole prepared a 40-page report on the Jimenez case for the district attorney's office, detailing the pattern of complaints, alleged assaults, and other allegations of serious wrongdoing on the part of the Rampart officers. Poole's report never reached the district attorney's office because his lieutenant, enforcing the chief's orders, replaced his detailed report with a two-page report written by the lieutenant and another supervisor. Poole knew that in not providing the district attorney's office with all the information he uncovered, he could be charged with obstruction of justice, and the report provided so little information that the officer probably would not even be charged. Poole's lieutenant then asked him to put his name on the report (Golab, 2000).

Following the steps of analysis above, it is important for Poole to know all the facts that are relevant; for instance, if his superiors were telling him to avoid exposing the other wrongdoing because of an ongoing larger federal investigation, that would be an important fact to know to determine why he was being told to mislead the prosecutor. Concepts and values at issue include duty, loyalty, legality, and integrity. In regard to the third step, Poole's dilemma was created by the unethical/illegal acts of the police officers and the acts of his superiors. His immediate dilemma is whether to sign the misleading report.

Law

It is possible that obstruction of justice charges could be brought against intentionally misleading prosecutors as to the amount and quality of evidence against any particular offender.

Policy

It is important in a hierarchical organization for subordinates to follow the orders of superiors. However, it is also important that any organization reward and not punish those who live up to high ideals of honesty and mission. Obviously, Poole would be following formal policies to cooperate with the district attorney's office to pursue criminal convictions when warranted. Often in organizations there are formal and informal policies. Informal policies may act to obstruct the formal goals of the organization; in this case, there was a concerted effort to suppress the Rampart Division investigative findings.

Ethics

Poole reported that he never considered putting his name on a report he knew was wrong. His superiors, coworkers, and colleagues described him as "professional," "hard working," "loyal, productive, thorough, and reliable,"

(continued)

"diligent," "honest," and "extremely credible." He was known as a first-rate investigator and trusted by the D.A.'s office to provide thorough and credible testimony. In other words, his habits in his professional life were directly contrary to participating in a cover-up. From all accounts, Poole represented many of Aristotle's virtues (Golab, 2000).

Natural law and religious ethics do not give us clear answers to Poole's dilemma. However, ethical formalism does in that Kant's categorical imperative can be applied to his choice to sign or not sign the report. This dilemma illustrates that sometimes duties conflict: in this case, his duty to follow the law conflicted with his duty to obey his superiors. The first part of the categorical imperative is to act in such a way that you would agree should be universal. Not exposing or pursuing evidence of corruption would not be an action that we would want universalized, so signing the doctored report fails the first part of the categorical imperative. The second part of the imperative is to not treat others as a means to an end. It seems clear that Poole's superiors were attempting to use him to further their goals. Their behavior, then, violates this part of the imperative. If Poole does mislead the prosecutor by signing, then he is violating this imperative as well. The last portion of the imperative is that in order to be moral, behavior must be autonomous and freely chosen. If Poole were frightened or pressured into doing something, then the action would not be moral regardless of what it was. If, for instance, he believed that the district attorney would find out and come after him for falsifying a legal document, then he might not sign it, but it would not be because of a good will and, therefore, could not be considered a moral act.

Applying utilitarianism to Detective Russell Poole's dilemma, it seems clear that his superiors were engaged in damage control. They did not want a scandal, especially considering that it had not been that long since the Rodney King incident. By suppressing evidence of further wrongdoing, they probably assumed that they could keep the information from the public and deal with it internally. Applying the utilitarian ethical system to Poole's dilemma requires determining which choice (to sign or not to sign) results in the greatest benefit to all (society, the department, his peers, and Poole himself). Did the greatest benefit lie in exposing the corruption or trying to hide it?

Actually, the attempt to suppress the actions of the Ramparts Division officers was unsuccessful anyway. A year after Poole refused to sign the report that protected Officer Rafael Perez, Perez was prosecuted for stealing a large amount of cocaine from the evidence room. In a plea arrangement, he told investigators from the D.A.'s office the whole story of the Ramparts Division officers, leading to the biggest scandal in LAPD's history (Golab, 2000; Boyer, 2001). This illustrates one of the problems with utilitarianism: if people sacrifice their integrity for what they consider is a good cause, the result may be that they lose their integrity and still do not achieve their good cause.

Under the ethics of care, individual needs should be considered to determine the best course of action. Unfortunately, sometimes individuals' needs are not met even when they do the right thing. Detective Poole knew what the right course of action was. He also knew that he would pay a price for doing it. In fact, after he refused to sign the report he was transferred to a less prestigious position and denied a promotion. He was vilified and treated as a traitor by some officers when he went public with his evidence of a cover-up. Ultimately, he resigned from the Los Angeles Police Department (Golab, 2000). This illustrates the sad fact that doing the right thing sometimes comes at a price.

Relativism, Absolutism, and Universalism

Ethical relativism describes the position that what is good or bad changes depending on the individual or group, and that there are no moral absolutes. Relativists believe that what is right is determined by culture and/or individual belief and that there are no universal laws. Absolutism, as previously discussed under ethical formalism, is the position that, if something is wrong, it is always wrong. Universalism is a similar concept in that it is the position that what is considered wrong is wrong for all people for all time and if one wants to perform a certain act, one would have to agree that anyone else should be able to do it as well. Universalism is basically the Golden Rule: Do unto others as you would have them do unto you.

One may look to anthropology and the rise of social science to explain the popularity of moral relativism. Over the course of studying different societies—past and present, primitive and sophisticated—anthropologists have found that there are very few universals across cultures. Even those behaviors often believed to be universally condemned, such as incest, have been institutionalized and encouraged in some societies (Kottak, 1974: 307). Basically, **cultural relativism** defines good as that which contributes to the health and survival of society. Hunting and gathering societies that must contend with harsh environments may hold beliefs allowing for the euthanasia of burdensome elderly, whereas agricultural societies that depend on knowledge passed down through generations may revere their elderly and accord them an honored place in society.

Cultural relativists recognize that cultures have very different definitions of right and wrong, and moral relativists argue that there are no fundamental or absolute definitions of right and wrong. In opposition to this position, absolutists argue that just because there may be cultural norms endorsing such things as cannibalism, slavery, or having sex with six-year-olds, the norms do not make these acts moral and there are absolute rights and absolute wrongs whether we agree with them or not.

Although cultural relativism holds that different societies may have different moral standards, it also dictates that individuals within a culture conform to the standards of their culture. Therein lays a fundamental flaw in the relativist approach: If there are no universal norms, why should individuals be required to conform to societal or cultural norms? If their actions are not accepted today, it might be argued, they could be accepted tomorrow—if not by their society, perhaps by some other.

An additional inconsistency in cultural relativism as a support for moral relativism is the prohibition against interfering in another culture's norms. The argument goes as follows: Because every culture is correct in its definitions of morality, another culture should not step in to change those definitions. However, if what is right is determined by which culture one happens to belong to, why then, if that culture happens to be imperialistic, would it be wrong to force cultural norms on other cultures? Cultural relativism attempts to combine an absolute (no interference) with a relativistic "truth" (there are no absolutes). This is logically inconsistent (Foot, 1982).

Cultural relativism usually concerns behaviors that are always right in one society and always wrong in another. Of course, what is more common is behavior that is judged to be wrong most of the time, but acceptable in certain instances. As examples: killing is wrong except possibly in self-defense and war; lying is wrong except when one lies to protect another. Even absolutist systems may accept some exceptions. The **principle of forfeiture** associated with deontological ethical systems holds that people who treat others as means to an end or take away or inhibit their freedom and well-being forfeit the right to protection of their own freedom and well-being (Harris, 1986: 136). Therefore, people who aggress first forfeit their own right to be protected from harm. This could permit self-defense (despite the moral proscription against taking life) and possibly provide justification for lying to a person who threatens harm. Critics of an absolutist system see this exception as a rationalization and a fatal weakness

QUOTE & QUERY

The "Gestalt Prayer" of humanistic psychotherapist Fritz Perls:
I do my thing and you do your thing.
I am not in this world to live up to your expectations,
And you are not in this world to live up to mine.
You are you, and I am I, and if by chance we find each other, it's beautiful.
If not, it can't be helped.

(Source: Tolliver, 1981)

Is this a statement consistent with egoism? Do you believe that we should not judge each other? Are there absolute wrongs that cannot be ignored?

cultural relativism The idea that values and behaviors differ from culture to culture and are functional in the culture that holds them.

principle of forfeiture The idea that one gives up one's right to be treated under the principles of respect for persons to the extent that one has abrogated someone else's rights; for instance, self-defense is acceptable according to the principle of forfeiture.

to the approach; in effect, moral rules are absolute *except* for those exceptions allowed by some "back-door" argument.

Relativism allows for different rules and different judgments about what is good; proponents argue that it promotes tolerance. Universalists would argue that if moral absolutes are removed, subjective moral discretion leads to egoistic (and nationalistic) rationalizations. They would argue that things like the Holocaust, slavery, the slaughter of Native American Indians, the Armenian genocide, Japanese-American internment, the Bataan Death March, and torture in Abu Ghraib and Guantanamo happen because people promoting what they consider to be a good end (security or progress) do not apply absolute rules of morality and ethics and, instead, utilize relativism: It is okay for me to do this to you, at this time, because of what I consider to be a good reason, but you can't do it to me.

Toward a Resolution: Situational Ethics

Situational ethics is often used as a synonym for *relativism*; however, if we clarify the term to include certain fundamental absolute elements, it might serve as a resolution to the problems inherent in both an absolutist and a relativist approach to ethics. Recall that relativism, on the one hand, is criticized because it must allow any practice to be considered "good" if it is considered good by some people; therefore, even human sacrifice and cannibalism would have to be considered moral—a thoroughly unpalatable consequence of accepting the doctrine. Absolutism, on the other hand, is also less than satisfactory because we all can think of some examples when the "rule" must be broken. Even Kant declined to be purely absolutist in his argument that lying isn't really lying if told to a person who is trying to harm us. What is needed, then, is an approach that resolves both problems.

Hinman (1998) resolves this debate by defining the balance between absolutism and relativism as **moral pluralism**. In his elaboration of this approach, he stops short of an "anything goes" rationale but does recognize multicultural "truths" that affect moral perceptions. The solution that will be offered here, whether one calls it situational ethics or some other term, is as follows:

1. There are basic principles of right and wrong.
2. These principles can be applied to ethical dilemmas and issues.
3. These principles may call for different results in different situations, depending on the needs, concerns, relationships, resources, weaknesses, and strengths of the individual actors.

Situational ethics is different from relativism because absolute laws are recognized, whereas under relativism there are no absolute definitions of right and wrong. What are absolute laws that can be identified as transcendent? Natural law, the Golden Rule, and the ethics of care could help us fashion a set of moral absolutes that might be general enough to ensure universal agreement. For instance, we could start with the following propositions:

- Treat each person with the utmost respect and care.
- Do one's duty or duties in such a way that one does not violate the first principle.

situational ethics The philosophical position that although there are a few universal truths, different situations call for different responses; therefore, some action can be right or wrong depending on situational factors.

moral pluralism The concept that there are fundamental truths that may dictate different definitions of what is moral in different situations.

These principles would not have anything to say about dancing (as immoral or moral), but they would definitely condemn human sacrifice, child molestation, slavery, and a host of other practices that have been part of human society. Practices could be good in one society and bad in another. For instance, if polygamy was necessary to ensure the survival of society, it might be acceptable; if it was to serve the pleasure of some by using and treating others as mere objects, it would be immoral. Selling daughters into marriage to enrich the family would never be acceptable because that is not treating them with respect and care; however, arranged marriages might be acceptable if all parties agree and the motives are consistent with care.

This system is not too different from a flexible interpretation of Kant's categorical imperative, a strict interpretation of rule-based utilitarianism, or an inclusive application of the Golden Rule. All ethical systems struggle with objectivity and subjectivity, along with respect for the individual and concern for society. Note that egoism does not pursue these goals and that is why some believe it cannot be accepted as a legitimate ethical system. Interestingly, situational ethics seems to be entirely consistent with the ethics of care, especially when one contrasts this ethical system with a rule-based, absolutist system. In the ethics of care, you will recall, each individual is considered in the equation of what would be the "good."

Conclusion

Ethical systems provide the guidelines or principles to make moral decisions. Box 2.4 ("The Major Ethical Systems") summarizes the key principles of these ethical systems. It can happen that moral questions are decided in different ways under the same ethical system. For instance, if facts are in dispute, two people using utilitarianism may "weigh" the utilities of an act differently. Capital punishment is supported by some because of a belief that it is a deterrent to people who might commit murder; others argue it is wrong because it does not deter (this is an argument about facts between two utilitarians). Others believe that capital punishment is wrong regardless of its ability to deter (this would be an argument by those following a religious ethics system or ethics of care). Most arguments about capital punishment get confused during the factual argument about the effectiveness of deterrence. "Is capital punishment wrong or right?" is a different question than "Does capital punishment deter?"

Another thing to consider is that none of us is perfect; we all have committed immoral or unethical acts that we know were wrong. Ethical systems help us to understand or analyze morality, but knowing what is right is no guarantee that we will always do the right thing. Few people follow such strong moral codes that

BOX 2.4 \ The Major Ethical Systems

Ethics of virtue. What is good is that which conforms to the Golden Mean.
Natural law. What is good is that which is natural.
Religion. What is good is that which conforms to God's will.
Ethical formalism. What is good is that which conforms to the categorical imperative.
Utilitarianism. What is good is that which results in the greatest utility for the greatest number.
Ethics of care. What is good is that which meets the needs of those concerned.
Egoism. What is good is that which benefits me.

they *never* lie or *never* cause other people harm. One can condemn the act and not the person. The point is that just because some behaviors are understandable and perhaps even excusable does not make them moral or ethical. Another point is that few people consistently use just one ethical system in making moral decisions. Some of us are fundamentally utilitarian and some predominantly religious, but we may make decisions using other ethical frameworks as well.

Finally, it should be noted that while philosophical discussions typically emphasize the differences between these ethical systems, in many, if not most, cases where individuals face a dilemma about the right thing to do, the ethical systems agree. For instance, the first dilemma at the back of this chapter asks, should you report your friend for stealing from the store where you both work? Under ethics of virtue, the virtuous person would not condone or participate in theft. Even Aristotle said that a friend who is a scoundrel is more scoundrel than friend and deserves no loyalty. Under natural law, theft violates trust, which is one of the building blocks of society itself; therefore, it is unnatural to steal (except perhaps in life-threatening circumstances) and unnatural to condone stealing. Religion would obviously condemn the act and encourage stopping it since we are instructed that we are "our brother's keepers." Ethical formalism would look to your duty as a manager and apply universalism to determine that it was necessary to stop the stealing by reporting it. Utilitarianism would weigh the benefits and determine that it was not beneficial to anyone except your friend to allow her to get away with the theft. Finally, ethics of care would be concerned for your friend as well and would perhaps arrive at a solution where she might be persuaded to return the item and quit the job without undergoing any public retribution. Only egoism might support keeping quiet if it meant losing a friend; however, even enlightened egoism might support reporting the friend since she might turn around and use the incident against you at a later time.

Ethical systems are more complex to apply than they are to explain. For instance, utilitarianism is fairly easy to understand, but the measurement of utility for any given act is often quite difficult. Ethical formalism says to "do one's duty," but it does not help us when there are conflicting duties. The ethics of care emphasizes relationships but is vague in providing the steps necessary to resolve ethical dilemmas. More applied approaches utilize steps one can take to resolve ethical dilemmas, such as the "front page" test (exposing the decision to outside scrutiny). Whether morals are relative or absolute has been debated throughout time. The concept of situational ethics is offered as a way to reconcile the question as to whether ethics are universal or not, and it is also true that in many ethical dilemmas, these systems arrive at the same answer as to what is the right thing to do.

Chapter Review

1. **Define deontological and teleological ethical systems and explain ethical formalism and utilitarianism.**

   A deontological ethical system is one that is concerned solely with the inherent nature of the act being judged. If an act or intent is inherently good (coming from a good will), it is still considered a good act even if it results in bad consequences. A teleological ethical system judges the consequences of an act. The saying "the end justifies the means" is a teleological statement. Kant's ethical formalism defines good as that which conforms to the categorical imperative, which includes the universalism principles, the idea that we shouldn't use people, and the stricture that we must do our duty through a free will in order to be considered moral.

Utilitarianism, associated with Jeremy Bentham, defines good as that which contributes to the greatest utility for the greatest number.

2. **Describe how other ethical systems define what is moral—specifically, ethics of virtue, natural law, religion, and the ethics of care.**

Under the ethics of virtue, goodness is determined by the virtues. Aristotle and others have identified what are considered to be moral virtues. Those who possess such virtues will make the right decision when faced with a moral dilemma. Under natural law, good is determined by what is natural. Moral rules are considered similar to other natural laws, such as gravity. Even if humans have not discovered these moral rules, or disagree about what they are, they still exist. Under Judeo-Christian religion, what is good is determined by God's will. One can know God's will through one's religious leaders or the Bible. Other religions also have statements of good and evil and sources to use to determine what is good. The ethics of care is based on the emotions of relationships. Caring is the basis of this morality.

3. **Discuss the argument as to whether egoism is an ethical system.**

Most who write in the area of applied ethics reject egoism as an ethical system because it is self-serving and logically inconsistent. It doesn't make sense to have a universal rule that everyone should pursue self-interest, because our self-interests will inevitably conflict. Proponents of ethical egoism also believe in psychological egoism, the idea that we are, by nature, purely self-interested. Under this view, we are egoists and, therefore, to pursue our self-interest is good.

4. **Explain the controversy between relativism and absolutism (or universalism).**

Absolutist ethics allow no exceptions to moral rules for exceptional circumstances. Relativism seems to allow individuals to define anything as morally acceptable, even acts that would be considered wrong under universal moral rules. The compromise is situational ethics, which propose a very few absolute rules that will support different decisions in different circumstances.

5. **Identify what is good according to each of the ethical systems discussed in the chapter.**

Under *ethics of virtue*, what is good is that which conforms to the Golden Mean. Under *natural law*, what is good is that which is natural. Under *religion*, what is good is that which conforms to God's will. Under *ethical formalism*, what is good is that which conforms to the categorical imperative. Under *utilitarianism*, what is good is that which results in the greatest utility for the greatest number. Under *ethics of care*, what is good is that which meets the needs of those concerned. Under *egoism*, what is good is that which benefits me.

Study Questions

1. What are the elements of any ethical system, according to Baelz? What are the three parts of the ethical pyramid?

2. What are the three parts of the categorical imperative? What is the difference between act and rule utilitarianism?

3. What are the three ways to know God's will? What are the Six Pillars of Character?

4. What are Krogstand and Robertson's three principles of ethical decision making?

5. Explain the differences between situational ethics and relativism.

Writing/Discussion Exercises

1. Write an essay (or discuss) the ethical systems in regard to the following situations:

    a. In the movie *Sophie's Choice,* a woman is forced to choose which one of her children to send to the gas chamber. If she does not decide, both will be killed. How would ethical formalism resolve this dilemma? How would utilitarianism resolve it?

    b. There is a continuing debate over whether the United States had to bomb Hiroshima and Nagasaki at the end of World War II. Present the arguments on both sides. Now consider this: Are they utilitarian arguments, ethical formalist arguments, or some other?

2. Write an essay on (or discuss) the basic nature of humans. Are we basically altruistic? Basically egoistic? Include in this essay responses to the following and examples to support your answer: What are the "natural" inclinations of human beings? Do you think most people do the right thing out of habit or out of reason?

3. Write an essay (or discuss) whether ethics and morals are relative or absolute. Are there absolute moral truths, or is morality simply an individual's definition of right and wrong? Should everyone have the right to decide which behaviors are acceptable for them? Should all cultures have the right to decide what is right? If you believe there are absolute definitions of right and wrong, what are they?

Key Terms

act utilitarianism
categorical imperative
cultural relativism
deontological ethical system
egoism
enlightened egoism
ethical formalism
ethical system
ethics of care

ethics of virtue
eudaimonia
generalization principle
hypothetical imperatives
imperative principle
moral pluralism
natural law
peacemaking justice
principle of forfeiture

principle of the Golden Mean
psychological egoism
religious ethics
rule utilitarianism
situational ethics
teleological ethical system
utilitarianism
utilitarian principle

ETHICAL DILEMMAS

Situation 1

You are the manager of a retail store. The owner of the store gives you permission to hire a fellow classmate to help out. One day you see the classmate take some clothing from the store. When confronted by you, the peer laughs it off and says the owner is insured, no one is hurt, and it was under $100. "Besides," says your acquaintance, "friends stick together, right?" What would you do?

Situation 2

You are in a lifeboat along with four others. You have enough food and water to keep only four people alive for the several weeks you expect to be adrift until you float into a shipping lane and can be discovered and rescued. You will definitely all perish if the five of you consume all the food and water. There is the suggestion that one of you should die so the other four can live. Would you volunteer to commit suicide? Would you vote to have one go overboard if you choose by straws? Would you vote to throw overboard the weakest and least healthy of the five? If you were on a jury judging the behavior of four who did murder a fifth in order to stay alive, would you acquit them or convict them of murder? Would your answer be different if the murdered victim was your son or daughter?

Situation 3

You aspire to be a police officer and are about to graduate from a criminal justice department. Your best friend has just been hired by a local law enforcement agency, and you are applying as well. When you were freshmen, you were both caught with marijuana in your dorm room. Although you were arrested, the charges were dismissed because it turned out that the search was illegal. The application form includes a question that asks if you have ever been arrested. Your friend told you that he answered no because he knew this agency did not use polygraphs as part of the hiring process. You must now decide whether to also lie on the form. If you lie, you may be found out eventually, but there is a good chance that the long-ago arrest will never come to light. If you don't lie, you will be asked to explain the circumstances of the arrest, and your friend will be implicated as well. What should you do?

Situation 4

You have a best friend who has confessed a terrible secret to you. Today the man is married and has two children. He has a good family, a good life, and is a good citizen. However, 14 years earlier he killed a woman. A homeless person was accused of the crime but died before he could be tried and punished. Nothing good can come of this man's confession. His family will suffer, and no one is at risk of being mistaken as the murderer. What would you advise him to do? (Some may recognize this dilemma as coming from Dostoyevsky's *The Brothers Karamazov*.)

Situation 5

You are working in internal affairs, and in the course of another investigation, you discover disturbing evidence regarding the police chief's son, who is also an officer in the department. Several informants have confided in you that this individual has roughed them up and taken their drugs, yet you find no record of arrest or the drugs being logged in the evidence room. When you write your report, your sergeant tears it up and tells you that there is not enough evidence to justify an investigation and for you to stick to what you are told to do. What would you do? What would you do if the chief calls you into his office the next day and offers you a transfer to a high-status position that will definitely lead to a promotion?

3

Justice and Law

Occupy Wall Street protesters being arrested in April 2012.

It may seem strange that an ethics book has a chapter on justice, but the concept of justice is integrally related to ethics and, obviously, especially relevant in a discussion of ethical issues related to criminal justice professionals. Professionals in the criminal justice system serve and promote the interests of law and justice, so before we explore the ethical issues and dilemmas that confront them, this chapter begins with a discussion of justice itself.

Many of the major philosophers and ethicists frame their discussion of ethics around the concept of justice. We will discuss Aristotle's views of justice below. More recently, Michael Sandel (2009), a popular Harvard professor, has an ethics course, book, and website titled *Justice: What's the Right Thing to Do?* His approach places ethical questions within the context of justice. This juxtaposition of justice and ethics is consistent with ethical formalism to the extent that moral duties derive from

Chapter Objectives

1. Describe the three themes included in the definition of justice.

2. Define Aristotle's two forms of justice described in the chapter.

3. Under corrective justice, distinguish between substantive and procedural justice, including how procedural justice impacts wrongful convictions and perceptions of racial discrimination.

4. Explain the concept of restorative justice and the programs associated with it.

5. Describe civil disobedience and when it may be appropriate.

rights. For instance, a child has a right to be cared for, which creates a moral duty for parents. Other potential rights are more controversial; for instance, does one have a right to healthcare? Does one have a right to be told the truth in all situations? Injustice occurs when rights are denied, thus, discussions of justice and ethics overlap.

According to Lucas (1980: 3), justice "differs from benevolence, generosity, gratitude, friendship, and compassion." Justice is not something for which we should feel grateful, but rather, something upon which we have a right to insist. Justice should not be confused with "good." Some actions may be considered good but not demanded by justice. For instance, the recipients of charity, benevolence, and forgiveness do not have a right to these things; therefore, it is not an injustice to withhold them. Although the idea of need is important in some discussions of justice, it is not the only component or even the primary one; that is why ethical formalism (which focuses on duty) is more consistent with justice than the ethics of care (which focuses on need). It is important to understand that what is just and what is good are not necessarily the same.

People can be described as displaying unique combinations of generosity and selfishness, altruism and self-interest. Some writers insist that the need for justice arises from the nature of human beings and that we are not naturally generous, openhearted, or fair. On the one hand, if we were to behave all the time in accordance with those virtues, we would have no need for justice. On the other hand, if humans were to always act in selfish, grasping, and unfair ways, we would be unable to follow the rules and principles of justice. Therefore, we uphold and cherish the concept of justice in our society because it is the mediator between people's essential selfishness and generosity. In other words, justice is the result of a logical and rational acceptance of the concept of fairness in human relations.

Anthony Walsh (2000) presents the interesting idea that justice is a biologically adaptive trait. He uses evolutionary psychology to argue that the sense of justice is emotional rather than rational and is the result of natural selection. His argument, simplified, is that humans, similar to other animal species, have "cheaters" and "suckers." Cheaters are those who do not engage in "reciprocal altruism" (basically, cooperation). Suckers are those who are continually taken advantage of by cheaters. They are not optimally adapted for survival, and if they perish, cheaters would perish as well because they need victims to take advantage of. Thus, "grudgers" evolve as a response; they may be fooled once by cheaters, but they are outraged and demand punishment when they are victimized. This adaptation successfully ensures the continued existence of grudgers as well as cheaters. Our "moral outrage," in other words, is an evolutionary response, as is our emotional demand for justice.

Any discussion of justice includes at least three continuing themes: fairness, equality, and impartiality. **Fairness** is related to equal treatment. Parents ordinarily give each child the same allowance unless differences between the children, such as age or duties, warrant different amounts. Children are sensitive to issues of fairness long before they grasp more abstract ideas of justice. No doubt every parent has heard the plaintive cry, "It's not fair—Johnny got more than I did" or "It's not fair—she always gets to sit in the front seat!" What children are sensing is unequal and, therefore, unfair treatment. The concept of fairness is inextricably tied to equality and impartiality.

Equality refers to equal shares or equal treatment as well. There is a predisposition to demand equity or equal shares for all, or equal shares for similar people. The concept of equality is also present in retributive justice in the belief that similar crimes should be punished equally ("equal justice for all"). In contrast to the concept of equal

fairness the condition of being impartial, the allocation of equal shares or equal opportunities.

equality the same value, rights, or treatment between all in a specific group.

(•) IN THE NEWS | *"Too Big to Jail?"*

Recent reports indicate that the Justice Department has charged over 4,000 people with mortgage fraud alone based on the economic meltdown of 2008 due to mortgage-backed derivatives; however, hardly any top executives have been charged, despite the fact that their companies are paying billion-dollar fines for criminal behavior. Law professor Brandon L. Garrett, author of a recent book *Too Big to Jail*, analyzed 303 non-prosecution and deferred prosecution agreements with corporations from 2001 to 2014. Individuals were charged in only 34 percent of the cases that involved all types of white-collar and corporate crimes. Only 42 percent of those charged received any jail time. This is despite the fact that companies paid huge fines and admitted criminal culpability; for example, Siemens paid over $1.6 billion for bribery, Pfizer paid $2.3 billion for bribing doctors, and Tyson Foods paid a $4 million fine for bribery. Prosecutors explain that they would like to prosecute executives, but it is harder to prove cases of individual culpability. Critics argue that top executives are unlikely to be prosecuted because of other reasons.

Source: Stewart, 2015.

---

impartiality not favoring one party or interest more than another.

shares is the idea of needs or deserts; in other words, we should get what we need or, alternatively, what we deserve by status, merit, or other reasons.

Impartiality is also related to the concept of equal treatment. At the core of our system of criminal justice is the theme of impartiality. Our symbol of justice represents, with her blindfold, impartiality toward special groups and, with her scales, proportionally just punishments. Impartiality implies fair and equal treatment of all without discrimination and bias. It is hard to reconcile the ideal of "blind justice" with taking individual circumstances into consideration when determining culpability or punishment. Most would argue, individual differences and circumstances should be taken into consideration—if not during a finding of guilt or innocence, then at least when sentencing occurs. The blindfold may signify no special treatment for the rich or the powerful, but then it must also signify no special consideration for the young, for the misled, or for extraordinary circumstances. The In the News box above illustrates that those who believe the justice system is not impartial may be right.

Origins of the Concept of Justice

justice The quality of being impartial, fair, and just; from the Latin *justitia*, concerning rules or law.

Justice originated in the Greek word *dike*, which is associated with the concept of everything staying in its assigned place or natural role (Feinberg and Gross, 1977: i). This idea is closely associated with the definitions of justice given by Plato and Aristotle.

According to Plato, justice consists of maintaining the societal status quo. Justice is one of four civic virtues, the others being wisdom, temperance, and courage (Feibleman, 1985: 173). In an ordered state, everyone performs his or her role and does not interfere with others. Each person's role is the one for which the individual is best fitted by nature; thus, *natural law* is upheld. Moreover, it is in everyone's self-interest to have this ordered existence continue because it provides the means to a good life and appropriate human happiness.

In Aristotle's conception of justice, the lack of freedom and opportunity for some people—slaves and women, for instance—did not conflict with justice, as long as the individual was in the role for which, by nature, he or she was best suited. In other words, those with the highest intellect should be given schooling, those who were musical should be the musicians in society, and those with qualities that were suited to servitude should be slaves. Aristotle lived in a time where slavery was an accepted practice and slaves were considered to be different in aptitude and character from free men, but even Aristotle recognized that injustice may occur when someone placed into slavery, for instance, a vanquished enemy, might not be "naturally" suited to slavery. Aristotle associated justice with the law; if a person violated the law, he would be considered unjust. However, he didn't view justice solely as a function of law. A person's dealings with others in all areas of life determined whether he could be considered just or unjust.

Distributive Justice

Aristotle distinguished between two types of justice: distributive justice and corrective justice. **Distributive justice** concerns what measurement should be used to allocate society's resources, dealing with issues such as affirmative action, welfare, free schooling, and other goods and opportunities and how society distributes them among its members. **Corrective justice** concerns unfair advantage or undeserved harm between people. Justice demands remedies or compensations to the injured party.

> **distributive justice** Justice that concerns what measurement should be used to allocate society's resources.

The concept of the appropriate and just allocation of society's goods and interests is one of the central themes in all discussions of justice. According to one writer, justice always involves *rightful possession* (Galston, 1980: 117–119). The goods that one might possess include:

- Economic goods (income or property)
- Opportunities for development (education or citizenship)
- Recognition (honor or status)

> **corrective justice** Justice that concerns when unfair advantage or unjust enrichment occurs (either through contract disputes or criminal action) and what the appropriate remedy might be to right the wrong.

If there was enough of everything (goods, opportunity, status) for everyone, issues of distributive justice would not arise; it is only because there is usually a condition of scarcity that a problem arises with the allocation of goods. Two valid claims to possession are *need* and *desert*. The principles of justice involve the application of these claims to specific entitlements. Different writers have presented various proposals for deciding issues of entitlement.

Lucas (1980: 164–165) identified distributions based on need, merit, performance, ability, rank, station, worth, work, agreements, requirements of the common good, valuation of services, and legal entitlement. Despite differences, all schemes include some concept of need and merit (also see Raphael, 1980: 90). A major conflict in distributive justice is between need and merit. The difficulty in distributing society's goods lies in deciding the weight of each of the criteria discussed above. The various theories can be categorized as egalitarian, Marxist, libertarian, or utilitarian, depending on the factors that are emphasized (Beauchamp, 1982):

- *Egalitarian theories* start with the basic premise of equality or equal shares for all.
- *Marxist theories* place need above desert or entitlement.
- *Libertarian theories* promote freedom from interference by government in social and economic spheres; therefore, merit, entitlement, and productive contributions are given weight over need or equal shares.
- *Utilitarian theories* attempt to maximize benefits for individuals and society with a mixed emphasis on entitlements and needs.

BOX 3.1 \ Annual CEO Salaries – 2013/2014		
John Hammergren	McKesson Pharm	$151.2 million
Charif Souki	Cheniere Energy	$141.9 million
Mario J. Gabelli	Gamco Investors, Inc.	$85 million
Satya Nadella	Microsoft Corp	$84.3 million
Jay N. Levine	Springleaf Holdings, Inc.	$78.7 million
Tom L. Ward	Sandridge Energy Inc	$71.1 million
Anthony G. Petrello	Nabors Industries Ltd	$68.2 million
Lawrence J. Ellison	Oracle Corp	$67.2 million
Ralph Lauren	Polo Ralph Lauren	$66.7 million
Michael Fascitelli	Vornado Realty	$64.4 million
Richard Kinder	Kinder/Morgan	$60.9 million
David Cote	Honeywell	$55.8 million
George Paz	Express Scripts	$51.5 million
Jeffrey Boyd	Priceline	$50.2 million
Stephen Hemsley	United Health Group	$48.8 million

Note: Different sources have different lists of highest paid executives due to differences in computing stock options and other compensation sources.

Source: *Forbes*, 2015.

How do the theories apply to the wide disparities in salaries found in the United States? For instance, the CEO's salaries, as shown in Box 3.1, are dramatically higher than average salaries of American workers. Is that fair, or is that just compensation for reaching the pinnacle of one's career? Ironically, a recent study shows that the companies with the highest paid executives do not perform better, and, in fact, there is an inverse correlation between compensation and company performance. In other words, the study showed that companies with the highest paid executives perform correspondingly worse for their shareholders than the companies with lower average executive pay (Adams, 2014). Thus, evidence doesn't seem to support a merit-based argument for such compensation differences.

In 2011, the Occupy Wall Street movement began as disgust over the economic disparity between the 1 percent (who own most of the wealth of the country) and the other 99 percent. The movement tapped into the growing discontent in this country over the increasing disparity between the wealthiest and the rest of the population, especially since the recession of 2008. There is a growing recognition that the wide disparity between CEO compensation and average worker's compensation is unsustainable. In 2010, Congress included in the Dodd-Frank law a requirement that companies disclose the CEO–worker pay ratio each year. Evidently, this requirement is largely ignored by American businesses, but those who compute such statistics report that the gap is widening dramatically. According to one study done by the Economic Policy

Institute, CEO pay rose from 20 times that of average worker pay in 1965 to almost 296 times average worker pay in 2013. Compensation for executives includes base pay, bonuses, perquisites, and grant-date value of stock options. Equilar, a compensation computing company, reported that average CEO salary in 2014 was around $14.3 million, an increase of about 5 percent from 2013. Some executive salary–to–worker salary ratios are much higher than the average; for instance, Robert Iger, head of Walt Disney, makes 2,238 times more than the average worker; Satya Nadella, Microsoft's chief, earns 2,012 times the average employee's salary. Companies dispute the calculation of executive compensation and salary ratios, arguing that stock options are not really compensation until they are realized (Morgenson, 2015).

Egalitarian distribution systems would pay people equally, or at least equal people doing equal work would get paid equally. There is very little debate that men and women, for instance, should be paid equal salaries if they do the same work. Lilly Ledbetter had been paid less than her male colleagues for 40 years, but she lost her equal pay case because the Supreme Court agreed with her company that she should have brought the suit earlier (even though she was not aware of the pay discrepancy; *Ledbetter v. Goodyear*, 550 U.S. 618, 2007). Congress, in response, passed the Lilly Ledbetter Equal Pay Act (Pub.L.222-3. S. 181); this redefined the statute of limitations as when a person finds out about the disparity.

Even though gender disparate pay in equal jobs is clearly wrong, when jobs are not exactly the same, it is more difficult to determine fairness. Obviously, few would agree that workers in all jobs and all professions should be paid the same amount of money. First, not many people would be willing to put up with the long hours and many years of schooling needed in some professions if there were no incentives. Second, some types of jobs demand more responsibility and involve greater stress than others. Thus, even egalitarian systems, which would start with the premise of equal pay, would support calculating "worth" or effort and pay accordingly.

Marxist distribution systems propose that we pay people according to need. This sounds fair in one sense because people would get only what they need to survive at some predetermined level. In that case, a person with two children would earn more than a person with no children. Libertarian advocates, on the other hand, would have no trouble arguing that vast disparities in economic remuneration are acceptable and should be left to the free market. High salaries promote competition and competition promotes quality, therefore if a CEO or athlete earns a salary that is extremely

(•) IN THE NEWS | *Sharing the Wealth*

Dan Price, the founder of Gravity Payments, ignited a media firestorm in April 2015 when he made an announcement that he would raise all 120 employees' salaries to $70,000—even clerks, customer service representatives, and salespeople. The company processes credit card payments and to increase his employee's minimum pay, Price, who started the company at the age of 19, is cutting his own $1 million salary to $70,000 and using the anticipated profits of the very successful company to fund the pay increases. He said he was doing so because of an article he read describing a social science study that discovered people's emotional well-being was affected by salaries less than $75,000, but that salaries over that amount did not contribute proportionally to happiness.

Source: P. Cohen, 2015

disproportionate to anyone else, it must be because they have a skill or talent that the rest of us are willing to pay for.

Even if one subscribed to a libertarian approach, how should salary be calculated? Should workers be paid based on their production or as a salary? If so, how would one pay secretaries, teachers, or customer service workers, whose production is more difficult to measure? How would one pay police officers—by the number of arrests? Thus far, we have discussed only salaries, but in the workplace other goods are also distributed, such as promotions, merit increases, job postings, desirable offices, and parking places. How should these "perks" be awarded if production isn't easily measured?

Utilitarian systems of distribution would allow economic disparities if they contributed to the greater good. For instance, doctors should make more money than many other workers because it takes so long for someone to get the credentials to become a doctor. Since it is difficult to become a doctor, not many people would go through with it unless there were some rewards to look forward to. Also, doctors contribute to the greater good by curing the sick and injured and help the economic prosperity of the society by keeping people healthy, thus it benefits all of us that the compensation is sufficient to keep adequate numbers of people interested in medicine as a profession.

Minimum pay laws can be justified under a utilitarian system, but not a libertarian one. Federal minimum wage is $7.25 per hour but states can set their own wage laws and many have set minimum wages higher than the federal law. The following states have set minimum wages at $9.00 per hour or higher: California, Oregon, Washington, Connecticut, Massachusetts, Rhode Island, and Vermont (National Conference of State Legislators, 2015). The argument for such laws is that more money in workers' pockets improves the economy since low-income workers spend a greater percentage of their income on consumable goods than do those at the top of the socioeconomic ladder. The raise in pay goes straight back to the economy and the boost is good for everyone except business owners, who see a net profits decline.

Just distribution of other goods in society is also problematic. There are perennial arguments over how much people should receive in entitlement programs, such as food stamps and TANF (Temporary Assistance for Needy Families, formerly Aid to Families with Dependent Children [AFDC]). The principle of need is the rationale we use to take from the financially solvent, through taxes, and give to those who have little or nothing. There is always resentment over this redistribution because of the belief that some people choose not to work and take advantage of governmental "hand-outs" even though there is no evidence that the percent of cheaters is any different from that in other government programs.

The issue of universal healthcare has become a divisive controversy in this country. In March 2012, the Supreme Court heard arguments on the consolidated cases challenging the Patient Protection and Affordable Care Act (colloquially referred to as "Obamacare") of 2010. Twenty-six states and the National Association of Small Businesses joined to oppose the law. The legal issue was whether federal law could force individuals to purchase insurance. Opponents argued that it was beyond the scope of federal power. Proponents argued that without this provision, the other parts of the healthcare bill, such as requiring insurance companies to cover preexisting conditions and adult children, would be unfeasible. The Court's ruling in July of 2012 upheld the legislation, finding federal power to force people to buy health insurance or face fines existed under the government's taxing and regulation of commerce powers. In *King v. Burwell* (June 25, 2015), opponents challenged the use of subsidies, but the Supreme

Court ruled in favor of the healthcare law again. Interestingly, some argue that the national debate over this issue is very similar to what occurred during Franklin Delano Roosevelt's "New Deal" to get the country out of the Great Depression. The creation of the Civilian Conservation Corps, Social Security, Medicaid, and Medicare were all vigorously opposed and legally challenged at the time even though they have come to be integral parts of American's financial well-being today. Whether the federal government has the legal authority to mandate everyone buy insurance is a legal question; whether a government-run health system is more efficient or effective than the private market is an empirical argument; however, whether everyone deserves to have basic healthcare is a philosophical and moral discussion.

Another good to be distributed in society is opportunity. There is a compelling argument that although the *ideal* of education is that everyone is this country has equal access to educational opportunities; the *reality* is that, because of unequal tax bases, school districts are incredibly unequal and distribute the opportunity of education unequally. States struggle with how to fund poor school districts, and "Robin Hood" laws, which take from rich districts to subsidize poor districts, are bitterly opposed by parents, who move to a district specifically for the resources it provides students. There are also perennial arguments about charter schools and voucher systems with some arguing for choice and parental control, and others arguing that the basis of a democracy is a well-funded public school system.

Another issue in distributive justice is affirmative action, which is the subject of the Ethical Issue box in this chapter. John Rawls' theory of justice is perhaps the best-known modern conception of justice. He elegantly combines utilitarian and rights-based concepts in his theory. Basically, he proposes an equal distribution unless a different distribution would benefit the disadvantaged. Rawls believes that any inequalities of society should be to the benefit of those who are least advantaged (Rawls, 1971: 15):

- Each person is to have an equal right to the most extensive total system of basic liberties compatible with a similar system of liberty for all.
- Social and economic inequalities are to be arranged so that they are both reasonably expected to be to everyone's advantage and attached to positions and offices open to all (except when inequality is to the advantage of those least well-off).

So, for instance, Rawls may argue for a purely objective hiring scoring system except when one gives extra points for those who are least well-off, and tax rebates that are equally distributed, except if they are a bit more favorable for those in the lower income brackets. Rawls uses a heuristic device that he calls the **veil of ignorance** to explain the idea that people will develop fair principles of distribution only if they are ignorant of their position in society, for they just as easily may be "have-nots" as "haves" (Rawls, 1971: 12). Thus, justice and fairness are in everyone's rational self-interest because, under the veil of ignorance, one's own situation is unknown, and the best and most rational distribution is the one that is most equal to all.

Rawls' theory of justice has been criticized. First, some argue that the veil of ignorance is not sufficient to counteract humanity's basic selfishness: given the chance, people would still seek to maximize their own gain, even if doing so involves a risk (Kaplan, 1976: 199). Second, Rawls' preference toward those who are least well-off may be contrary to the good of society. Rawls states that "all social values—liberty and

veil of ignorance
Rawls' idea that people will develop fair principles of distribution only if they are ignorant of their position in society, so in order to get objective judgments, the decision maker must not know how the decision would affect him or her.

opportunity, income and wealth, and the bases of self-respect—are to be distributed equally unless an unequal distribution of any, or all, of these values is to the advantage of the least favored." This may be ultimately dysfunctional for society, for if those who are least well-off have the advantages of society preferentially, there will be no incentive for others to excel. Also, some argue that Rawls is wrong to ignore desert in his distribution of goods (Galston, 1980: 3).

ETHICAL ISSUE

Should Black Applicants to Police Departments That Serve Communities That Are Disproportionately Black Be Given Preferential Treatment?

This question is extremely controversial. One of the issues that came up after the Ferguson, Missouri, incident in the summer of 2014, involving the shooting of Michael Brown, was that the police department was 94 percent white, while the community was 67 percent black. One argument is that preferential hiring of minorities strengthens police departments by helping the department more closely reflect the neighborhoods it polices. The opposing argument is that quota systems and the pressure to hire minorities lower hiring standards. Further, even those who are qualified are stigmatized because of a perception that they were hired only because of their gender, race, or ethnicity. There is also little evidence that black officers are more effective in citizen interactions or less biased than white officers in stop-and-frisk and other discretionary actions. Should hiring decisions be made partially based on race when applicants are roughly similar in education, background, and civil service test scores?

Law

In *Ricci v. DeStefano* (129 S. Ct. 2658, 2009), the Supreme Court held, in a 5–4 decision, that the city of New Haven's decision to throw out firefighters' promotion test results because no blacks scored high enough to be promoted was discriminatory. City officials feared that the test itself would be ruled invalid because of the disparate impact, prompting them to ignore the test scores that placed only whites and two Hispanics in the eligible category for promotion. The Supreme Court held, in a suit brought by white firefighters who scored highly on the exam, that the city had failed to show a strong basis of evidence that there had been disparate treatment of minorities in the past that needed to be overcome. The case signals the continuing trend in the law to look disfavorably upon affirmative action programs if they impose disparate impact on any race (white included)

and/or that are not created to overcome clear evidence of historical discrimination toward minorities. In *Fisher v. University of Texas* (570 U.S. ____, 2013), the Supreme Court considered whether the university's admission process was a violation of the equal protection clause of the Fourteenth Amendment. The University of Texas accepted all students who graduated within the top 10 percent of their high school, but for other admissions, race was considered one factor among many, and was considered because of a lack of racial and ethnic representation in the student body as compared to the state population. The Court ruled in a 7 to 1 opinion (with Justice Kagen recusing herself) that the lower courts did not apply strict scrutiny in their analysis of whether using race was a necessary procedure to secure diversity and remanded the case back to the Fifth Circuit. In July of 2014, the Fifth Circuit, in a 2–1 decision, ruled that the university had proven under strict scrutiny that race was a necessary factor to apply to achieve the governmental objective of diversity. Fisher vowed to appeal the ruling. This case is relevant to police departments' hiring procedures because it appears, like universities, police departments must meet the strict scrutiny standard if they desire to award points or preferential consideration to the applicant's race, ethnicity, or gender.

Policy

Agencies differ on their policies regarding affirmative action. Some agencies continue to aggressively recruit minorities and may have policies that favor minority and female applicants, but it may be the case that affirmative action programs are simply policy choices today and not legally mandated. In fact, policy choices that attempt to promote the interests of minorities may be the subject of discrimination suits themselves, as was seen by the *Ricci* case above. Because of the *Fisher* case we know that any attempt to use affirmative action must meet a strict scrutiny test; that is, the use of race, ethnicity, or gender as a factor in hiring must meet an important governmental objective and must be the only way to meet such objective. Even departments that want to hire minorities find it difficult to do so. Kringen (2014) found that race/ethnicity interacted with other factors and that minority applicants were more likely to not make it through the hiring process due to issues related to employment history, criminal history, and financial issues. In addition to disqualification, black and female applicants were more likely to self-select out of the process during the initial stages.

Ethics

A utilitarian argument to be made for affirmative action is that it is better for the community to have a diversified police force. Recall that John Rawls would argue that equality should apply unless the different treatment benefits the least advantaged.

That is basically what affirmative action programs do since they are based on the idea that blacks and other minorities have been historically disadvantaged. Ethical formalism would not provide a rationale for affirmative action since one might argue that the decision to hire someone based on their race, ethnicity, or gender to achieve diversity is using these individuals, which violates the categorical imperative. An ethics of care perspective would go "outside the box" of deciding whether affirmative action was right or wrong, and perhaps provide remedial assistance to minorities and those who have trouble meeting hiring standards, but then use the same standards for everyone. As with all the issues that arise from distributive justice choices, these decisions are not easy to make.

How are these concepts of distributive justice relevant to criminal justice? First, the discussion illuminates the issues regarding the appropriateness of affirmative action in the hiring and promotion of police officers and other criminal justice professionals. Should your race give you an edge in hiring decisions? What if the profession is one, such as policing, that historically has been closed to minorities? Another issue that is related to distributive justice is how much to pay police officers or correctional officers compared to other professions. Most people believe that police are underpaid. If so, how much is a fair salary, and how does that salary compare to others, such as elementary school teachers? The criteria you use to determine these answers should have some basis in the distribution systems discussed earlier.

Finally, there is a connection between distributive justice and corrective justice, which will be discussed next. If it is true that socioeconomic status predicts criminal predisposition, should we care? Is it fair that poor people tend to end up in prison and those with more resources usually receive less punishment? Further, should we consider issues of distributive justice (i.e., what someone has by accident of birth) in any discussion of corrective justice (i.e., what people deserve when they commit a crime)? For example, is a rich person who embezzles from their employer equally culpable as a desperately poor individual who commits a theft? Reiman (2007) argues that economic power affects lawmaking, lawbreaking, enforcement, and punishment practices; literally, he argues that the rich get richer and the poor get prison under our system of justice. Clearly, distributive justice is an important concept in any discussion of the criminal justice system.

▋ Corrective Justice

Recall that in addition to distributive justice, Aristotle also described corrective justice, which is concerned with balancing unfair advantage. We will not discuss the types of issues relevant to civil law, such as contract disputes and other forms of business or consumer conflicts. We will concentrate, instead, on the concept of justice as it applies to determining guilt and dispensing punishment for criminal violations. As with distributive justice, the concepts of equality and desert, fairness and impartiality are

substantive justice   Concerns just deserts—in other words, the appropriate amount of punishment for a crime.

important. Two components of corrective justice should be differentiated. **Substantive justice** involves the concept of just deserts, or how one determines a fair punishment for a particular offense, and **procedural justice** concerns the steps we must take before administering punishment.

Substantive Justice

procedural justice   The component of justice that concerns the steps taken to reach a determination of guilt, punishment, or other conclusion of law.

Substantive justice refers to issues of inherent fairness in what we do to people in the name of justice. For instance, whether capital punishment is a fair punishment for the crime of murder is a substantive justice question. Many believe that the only just punishment is death because that is the only punishment of a degree equal to the harm caused by the offender. Others might say that life imprisonment is equitable and fair. Since the beginning of codified law, just punishment has been perceived as proportional to the degree of harm incurred. This was a natural outcome of the early, remedial forms of justice, which provided remedies for wrongs. For instance, the response to a theft of a slave or the killing of a horse involved compensation. The only just solution was the return or replacement of the slave or horse. This remedial or compensatory system of justice contrasts with a punishment system: the first system forces the offender to provide compensation to the victim or the victim's family, and the second apportions punishment based on the degree of harm suffered by the victim. They both involve a measurement of the harm, but in the first case, measurement is taken to adequately compensate the victim, and in the second it is to punish the offender. In a punishment-based system, the victim is a peripheral figure. The state, rather than the victim, becomes the central figure—serving both as victim and as punisher. Two *philosophies* of substantive justice (or how to calculate appropriate punishment) can be identified: retributive justice and utilitarian justice.

retributive justice   The component of justice that concerns the determination and methods of punishment.

lex talionis   A vengeance-oriented justice concerned with equal retaliation ("an eye for an eye; a tooth for a tooth").

lex salica   A form of justice that allows compensation; the harm can be repaired by payment or atonement.

RETRIBUTIVE JUSTICE   The concept of **retributive justice** is one of balance. The criminal must suffer pain or loss proportional to what the victim was forced to suffer. In an extreme form, this retribution takes the form of *lex talionis*, a vengeance-oriented justice concerned with equal retaliation ("an eye for an eye; a tooth for a tooth"). A milder form is *lex salica*, which allows compensation; the harm can be repaired by payment or atonement (Allen and Simonsen, 1986: 4). A life for a life might be easy to measure, but most cases involve other forms of harm. How does one determine the amount of physical or mental pain suffered by the victim, or financial loss such as lost income or future loss, in most crimes? And if the offender cannot pay back financial losses, how does one equate imprisonment with fines or restitution?

Historically, corporal and capital punishment were used for both property crime and violent crime. With the development of the penitentiary system in the early 1800s, punishment was more likely to be measured by the number of years of imprisonment rather than amounts of physical pain. The greater ease of measuring out prison sentences probably contributed to the rapid acceptance of those sentences. However, a term of imprisonment is much harder to equate to a particular crime. Although one can intuitively understand the natural balance of a life for a life, $10 for $10, or even a beating for an assault, it is much harder to argue that a burglary of $100 is equal to a year in prison or that an assault is equal to a term of two years. A year in prison is hard to define. Research on prison adjustment indicates that a year means different things to different people. For some, it might be no more than mildly inconvenient; for others, it might lead to suicide or mental illness (Toch, 1977).

In earlier systems of justice, the status of the victim was important in determining the level of harm and, thus, the punishment. Nobles were more important than free men, who were more important than slaves. Men were more important than women. Punishment for offenders was weighted according to these designations of the worth of the victim. Although we have no formal system for weighing punishment in this way and have rejected the worth of the victim as a rationale for punishment (except in a few cases, such as assaulting a police officer or president), many believe that our justice system still follows this practice informally. People argue that harsher sentences are given when the victim is white than when the victim is black and when the victim is rich as opposed to poor.

Our system of justice has rejected these discriminations, at least formally, but other distinctions in offenders' culpabilities are accepted. For instance, we don't hold juveniles fully responsible for their actions because they are considered less than rational. See the In the News box for the Supreme Court's treatment of juvenile culpability.

In Rawls' (1971) theory of justice, retributive punishment is limited in such a way as to benefit the least advantaged, similarly to the distributive justice scheme discussed earlier. In this philosophy of justice, the offender is punished until the advantage changes and the offender becomes the least advantaged. What is a just punishment for any offense should be considered using the veil of ignorance so one does not know whether one is the offender, the victim, or a disinterested bystander. Critics argue that Rawls' system would create a situation wherein an offender may victimize a large corporation or a well-off victim and still be more disadvantaged, dictating that no punishment is due him or her. Most of us would not countenance this definition of justice.

One other issue that must be addressed in any discussion of retributive justice is the concept of mercy. From the very beginnings of law, there has been the element of forgiveness or mercy, even though the offender deserves to be punished. Even tribal societies had special allowances and clemencies for offenders, usually granted by the king or chief. For instance, the concept of **sanctuary** allowed offenders respite from punishment as long as they were within the confines of church grounds. Benefit of clergy, dispensation, and even probation are examples of mercy by the court. However, it must be made clear that mercy is different from just deserts. If, on the one hand, because of

sanctuary Ancient right based on church power; allowed a person respite from punishment as long as he or she was within the confines of church grounds.

(( )) IN THE NEWS | *What Is the Just Punishment for Juvenile Murder?*

In *Roper v. Simmons*, 543 U.S. 551 (2005), the Supreme Court determined that execution for anyone who committed murder before the age of 18 was cruel and unusual and, thus, a violation of the Eighth Amendment. In 2010, the Supreme Court decided *Graham v. Florida*, 560 U.S. 48. The majority held that life without parole for a person who was under 18 when he committed a non-homicide crime was also a violation of the Eighth Amendment. It was cruel and unusual to punish a juvenile in this way because of differences in the brain's maturity between juveniles and adults, and because one could not come to the determination that the juvenile was a "worst of the worst" offender due to

their youth and probable capacity to change. In 2012, the Supreme Court consolidated two cases: juveniles Evan Miller and Kuntrell Jackson participated in murders when they were 14 and were sentenced to mandatory life without parole terms. In June of 2012, the Supreme Court ruled that a mandatory life without parole sentence was a violation of the Eighth Amendment in that the mandatory nature of the sentence did not allow for a consideration of the juvenile's youth and culpability. Obviously the justices decided this case on legal grounds, but it is also a moral question—are juveniles less culpable, even for murder, than adults and should they receive less punishment?

circumstances of the crime, of the criminal, or of the victim, the offender deserves little or no punishment, then that is what he or she deserves, and it is not mercy to give a suspended sentence or probation. On the other hand, if an offender truly deserves the punishment and is instead forgiven, then the individual has been granted mercy.

Murphy (1985/1995) proposes that retributive emotions derive from self-respect, that it is a healthy response to an injury to feel angry, resentful, and, yes, even vengeful. However, it is also acceptable to forgive and extend mercy to one's assailant if the forgiveness extends not from a lack of self-respect but rather from a moral system. For instance, he points out that many religions include the concept of "turning the other cheek" and extending mercy to enemies. Mercy is appropriate when the offender is divorced in some way from his or her offense. One way to this separation is true repentance.

Murphy (1988: 10) summarizes the points of mercy as follows:

1. It is an autonomous moral virtue (separate from justice).

2. It is a virtue that tempers or "seasons" justice—something that one adds to justice.

3. It is never owed to anyone as a right or a matter of desert or justice.

4. As a moral virtue, it derives its value at least in part because it flows from love or compassion while not losing sight of the importance of justice.

5. It requires a generally retributive outlook on punishment and responsibility.

Therefore, mercy is related to justice but is not necessarily a part of it. It is connected with a change in the offender because, typically, there must be repentance before mercy is extended. Also, it is connected with the compassion, charity, or benevolence of the victim. Other questions of mercy remain, however. Who has the right to extend mercy? In the accompanying news box, the parents of a murdered girl forgave their daughter's murderer.

(((•))) IN THE NEWS | *Forgiveness*

Nineteen-year-old Conor McBride shot his girlfriend Ann Grosmaire in the head as she kneeled in front of him begging him not to shoot. He then turned himself in to the police department. When filling out his booking paperwork he listed Ann's mother on his visiting list, an automatic response because she had become like a second mother to him since he had been spending so much time at Ann's house. What happened in the subsequent months may seem unbelievable to some, but is not completely without precedent either. The two families began a journey that ultimately led to both sides seeking and participating in a restorative justice process that allowed all parties to sit together and talk through what happened and what should happen to Conor. Restorative justice programs are usually limited to property crimes and, certainly, rarely appropriate in homicide cases. Families of victims understandably rarely want to sit across the table from their loved one's murderer. But in this case, the Grosmaires did. The prosecutor was skeptical and surprised when he was asked to organize and participate in the process. During the pre-plea conference, Conor described the events leading up to the shooting and the shooting itself. The story did not supply any understandable reason for why Conor shot Ann: The couple fought, he was tired, she told him she wished he was dead, he had picked up the shotgun thinking he would shoot himself, and he chose, instead, to kill her. He said he wasn't thinking. The Grosmaires, shaken from hearing for the first time that their daughter had been shot when she was on her knees in front of Conor, were asked what they felt was a fair punishment, as were Conor's parents. Their responses ranged from 5 to 20 years. The prosecutor was not obligated to concur, but reduced his preliminary 40-year sentence down to 20 years in deference to the parents' wishes. The Grosmaires explain that their willingness to forgive arose through their faith in their religion. When Kate found out she was on Conor's visiting list, she went to visit him in jail, Andy gave her a message: "Tell him I love him, and I forgive him." They visit him in prison about once a month.

Source: Tullis, 2013.

UTILITARIAN JUSTICE Retributive justice serves as a rationale for and as a means to determine the appropriate level of punishment: in this approach, an offender is punished simply be he or she deserves to be. However, **utilitarian justice** only supports punishment if it benefits society. Cesare Beccaria (1738–1794) and Jeremy Bentham (1748–1832) provided a utilitarian rationale for proportionality in punishment. Punishment should be based on the seriousness of the crime: The more serious the crime (or the greater the reward the crime offered the criminal), the more serious and severe the punishment should be to deter the individual from committing the crime. A utilitarian framework of justice would justify punishment on the basis of deterrence.

Bentham's **hedonistic calculus**, for instance, is concerned with measuring the potential rewards of the crime so the amount of threatened pain could be set to deter people from committing that crime. The use of proportionality in this scheme is deterrence, not balance. In a retributive system, we measure to determine the proportional amount of punishment to equalize the wrong; in a utilitarian system, we measure to determine the amount of punishment needed to deter. We see that under the utilitarian framework, there is no necessity for perfect balance. In fact, one must threaten a slightly higher degree of pain or punishment than the gain or pleasure that comes from the criminal act; otherwise, there would be no deterrent value in the punishment.

In some cases, retributive notions of justice and utilitarian notions of justice may conflict. If a criminal is sure to commit more crime, the utilitarian could justify holding him in prison as a means of incapacitation, but to hold him past the time "equal" to his crime would be seen as an injustice under a retributive system. We might punish an offender more seriously than he "deserves" under a utilitarian system if it could be shown to deter many others. Deterrence is the primary reason to punish at all under a utilitarian system, but desert is the only determinant of a retributive system of justice. Correctional rehabilitation is prevention, not deterrence per se, but it is also acceptable under a utilitarian justice system and irrelevant and unsupported by a retributive one.

We subscribe to both utilitarian and retributive rationales for punishment. Amid any discussion of the costs and benefits of prison programs, diversion programs, or the correct punishment for different groups, the concept of desert is ever present.

utilitarian justice
The type of justice that looks to the greatest good for all as the end.

hedonistic calculus Jeremy Bentham's rationale for calculating the potential rewards of a crime so the amount of threatened pain could be set to deter people from committing that crime.

Procedural Justice

We turn now to the procedure of administering punishment—our legal system. Law includes the procedures and rules used to determine guilt, decide punishment, or resolve disputes. It is important to keep in mind that justice and law are not the same thing. You might think of justice as the concept of fairness, while law is a system of rules.

The law is an imperfect system. Fuller (1969: 39) explored the weaknesses of law and described ways that the procedure of law may fail to achieve justice. Generally, there is a tension between having no rules and making ad hoc decisions for each individual case, and a system of rules that is too stringent with no exceptions made for extraordinary circumstances.

The tension between rules and a more abstract conception of justice is found in several Supreme Court cases. In 1993, the Supreme Court heard *Herrera v. Collins* (503 U.S. 902, 1993). Herrera was convicted of killing two police officers. Evidence was overwhelming and it included an officer's eyewitness testimony, Herrera's social security card left at scene of the first murder, and testimony it was his girlfriend's car that sped away. He also had a handwritten letter in his pocket when he was arrested in which he implicated himself in the killings. A jury convicted Herrera of capital murder in the killing of one of the officers, and he pleaded guilty to killing the second.

Nine years later, Herrera filed a habeas corpus petition to the Supreme Court to overturn both convictions. New evidence consisted of three sworn statements. One was written by a lawyer for Herrera's dead brother, Raul, claiming that Raul confessed to him that he had killed Rucker and Carrisalez. The second, signed by a former cell-mate of Raul's, claimed the same thing. The third, signed by Raul's son, claimed that he had witnessed his father shoot both officers. The evidence seemed ridiculously weak and suspiciously convenient, blaming the murders on a dead man, yet it was this case of probably many others, that the Supreme Court chose to decide a fundamentally important question: what effect should new evidence of innocence have on a conviction when appeals are exhausted? In other words, should innocence trump legal rules that dictate a finite number of appeals?

The Supreme Court majority issued a narrow holding that Herrera did not prove a constitutional violation by his actual innocence evidence. Some justices who concurred argued that there could be actual innocence evidence that would create a procedural right to rehear the case, but Justice Rehnquist wrote the opinion, and, in dictum argued there was no independent constitutional right for relief based on true innocence and the only recourse in a situation where evidence was discovered after appeals were exhausted was pardon or clemency. Justice Scalia, in his concurring opinion, wrote: "There is no basis, tradition, or even in contemporary practice for finding that in the Constitution the right to demand judicial consideration of newly discovered evidence of innocence brought forward after a conviction" (at 427).

In another case dealing with whether new evidence of innocence should trump legal rules, Justice Scalia wrote in a dissent that the Court had "never held that the Constitution forbids the execution of a convicted defendant who has had a full and fair trial but is later able to convince a habeas court that he is 'actually innocent'" (*In re Troy Anthony Davis*, 2009, p. 2). Especially in light of the increasing number of wrongful convictions brought to light, the position that innocence is not protected by the Constitution or procedural due process is quite amazing, yet the Supreme Court has never established clearly that innocence trumps legal rules (Bazelon, 2015).

In *Holland v. Florida* (530 U.S. 631, 2010), the majority of the Supreme Court did uphold fairness over rules in holding that the time for filing a federal habeas corpus petition could be extended by "equitable tolling" when the conduct of an attorney was sufficiently egregious to warrant the extension. Holland had lost two direct appeals and had one year to file a federal habeas corpus appeal. Despite his many pleas to his attorney to get an appeal in before the deadline, the attorney failed to do so. Because the deadline was missed, Holland was barred from filing a habeas petition appealing his death sentence. He filed his own *pro se* (without legal assistance) petition arguing that the deadline be waived because of the attorney's negligence. The Eleventh Circuit denied relief, but the Supreme Court held that courts must look at the totality of circumstances on a case-by-case basis to determine whether or not the deadline should be extended. Consistent with his opinion in prior cases, Justice Scalia dissented.

We are left to assume that although a system of law is necessary for the ordered existence of society, it sometimes does not result in justice. "Moral rights" may differ from "legal rights," and "legal interests" may not be moral. Shakespeare's *The Merchant of Venice* (excerpted in the Quote and Query box) addresses many of the issues discussed. Here, the plea for mercy emphasizes the relationship between justice and mercy. Shylock's demand for the court's enforcement of his legal right (his pound of flesh) and the unwillingness of the court to deny it, despite the clear implication that it would be a tragedy, illustrate how law sometimes has little to do with justice. Then Portia's surprise argument—that because Shylock's contract mentioned only flesh and not blood, so no blood could be spilled, and thus Shylock is denied his compensation—is a superb illustration of the law's slavish devotion to technical rules over substance. As a legal trick, this interpretation of a contract has not been improved upon yet, in fiction or in reality.

In our system of justice, **due process** exemplifies procedural justice. Our constitutional rights of due process (found in the Fifth, Sixth, and Fourteenth Amendments) require careful inquiry and investigation before punishment or forfeiture of any protected right can be carried out by the state. An individual has the right to due process whenever the government seeks to deprive that person of the protected rights of life, liberty, or property. Due process is the sequence of steps taken by the state that is designed to eliminate or at least minimize error. Procedural protections may include:

- Notice of charges
- Neutral hearing body
- Right of cross-examination
- Right to present evidence
- Representation by counsel
- Statement of findings
- Appeal

These protections do not eliminate deprivation or punishment, but they do result in more accurate and just decisions. Thus, if due process has been violated—by use of a coerced confession, tainted evidence, or improper police or court procedures—an injustice has occurred. The injustice does not arise because the offender does not deserve to be punished, but rather, because the state does not deserve to do the punishing, having relied on unfair procedures.

PROCEDURAL JUSTICE RESEARCH One of the most interesting and potentially policy-relevant avenues of social science research in recent years has been in the area of "procedural justice." This research is extremely relevant to our discussion here in that it illustrates the importance of procedural justice as it affects the legitimacy of the entire justice system. Thibaut and Walker (1975) conducted observations of courtroom settings and discovered some participants may not have been happy with the outcome, but they perceived the process as fair; in other words, the perception of the *process* (or procedures) of justice was as important, if not more important, than the *outcome*. From this research, two criteria for procedural justice were established: voice (which refers to an individual's ability to have a say during the proceedings), and control (which is the ability or power to have some influence over the outcome).

QUOTE & QUERY

The quality of mercy is not strained;
It droppeth as the gentle rain from heaven
Upon the place beneath. It is twice blest;
It blesseth him that gives and him that takes.
...
It is an attribute to God himself,
And earthly power doth then show likest God's
When mercy seasons justice. Therefore, Jew,
Though justice be thy plea, consider this,
That, in the course of justice, none of us
Should see salvation. We do pray for mercy,
And that same prayer doth teach us all to render
The deeds of mercy. I have spoke thus much
To mitigate the justice of thy plea,
Which if thou follow, this strict court of Venice
Must needs give sentence 'gainst the merchant there.

William Shakespeare, The Merchant of Venice, Act 4, Scene 1

 What is the magistrate in this passage asking Shylock to do? How do you believe mercy should "season" justice? What would be procedural justice in this case? What would be substantive justice?

due process
Constitutionally mandated procedural steps designed to eliminate error in any governmental deprivation of protected liberty, life, or property.

Tyler (1990) and his colleagues are best known for carefully developing the measurement of perceptions of procedural justice and establishing the association between perceptions of procedural justice and perceived "legitimacy" (of the police or other criminal justice agency) (Tyler, 1990; 2003; 2004; 2006a; Tyler and Fagan, 2008; Sunshine and Tyler, 2003a & b). The elements of procedural justice have been further developed as: *voice* (allowing the citizen the chance to speak), *neutrality* (fairness in decisions), *respect* (using respectful language and not demeaning the citizen), and *trustworthiness* (the idea that the actions of the officer are for the public good; Tyler and Huo, 2002; Tyler, 2006a). This growing body of research has established the relationship between one or a number of these elements and citizens' satisfaction with police, their view that police power is legitimate, and even their willingness to comply with the law (Mazerolle, Bennett, Davis, Sargeant and Manning, 2013). Research continues in this area to isolate, analyze, and validate the constructs of procedural justice and legitimacy (see, Gau, 2014; Rottman. 2007), but there seems to be no doubt that perceptions of procedural justice, that is, how the person is treated by justice officials, have a great deal to do with perceptions of legitimacy and willingness to comply with the law.

Concepts of procedural justice apply to professionals in criminal justice organizations as well. A growing body of research, using police officers and correctional officers for the most part, supports the idea that individuals in justice organizations who feel they are not treated fairly are less satisfied, more likely to quit, and more likely, perhaps, to treat others badly or engage in corrupt behaviors (Lambert, 2003; Lambert, Hogan, and Allen, 2006; Lambert, Hogan, and Griffen, 2007; De Angelis and Kupchik, 2007; Shane, 2012; Farmer, Beehr, and Love, 2003; Wolfe and Piquero, 2011; Harris and Worden, 2014; Reynolds, 2015). The importance of treating people fairly and providing due process protections is a theme that runs through not only law, but also ethics. In the following two sections, we take a closer look at procedural justice by examining the evidence related to wrongful convictions and the presence of racism in the criminal justice system.

Wrongful Convictions

There is no greater example of injustice than an innocent person being convicted of a crime and spending years in prison, or, worse, being executed. One of the reasons that many people distrust our justice system is that there seems to be a small—but steady—stream of exonerations. Radelet, Bedau, and Putnam (1992) and Christianson (2004) gathered together cases where innocent defendants were convicted of crimes they did not commit. More recently a national registry of false convictions has been created by the University of Michigan Law School and the Center on Wrongful Convictions at Northwestern University School of Law. The registry is the result of gathering together all the known cases of false convictions or cases where convictions have been overturned because of egregious errors or misconduct in procedural justice (www.law .umich.edu/special/exoneration/Pages/about.aspx). Currently 1,587 cases have been entered into the registry. About half of all cases involve black defendants. Nearly half were homicide cases, including 101 death sentences. About 43 percent of the cases involved mistaken eyewitness identification, and 24 percent involved false or misleading forensic evidence (Yost, 2012b).

The **Innocence Project** was created by Barry Scheck and Peter Neufeld in 1992 at Cardozo Law School. Now Innocence Project sites exist all across the country. The project is an affiliation of groups of lawyers, journalists, and, often, students in many states that identify cases where people may have been falsely convicted and there is DNA evidence still on file that could be used to prove or disprove their protestations of innocence. This organization has been pivotal in getting the wrongly accused off death row and freed from prison.

In a study conducted by the Columbia Law School, 328 cases in which the individuals were exonerated (usually by DNA) were examined. In 125 cases, a mistaken verdict depended upon false confessions, usually of the mentally ill, the mentally handicapped, and juveniles. The study also found that 68 percent of all death verdicts handed down between 1973 and 1995 were reversed because of serious errors. Between 1993 and 2002, 90 death row inmates had their convictions overturned because of errors in procedural justice. The errors involved defense lawyers' incompetence, and also police and prosecutors suppressing exculpatory evidence or engaging in other types of professional misconduct. Almost 10 percent of the cases sent back for retrial resulted in not-guilty verdicts. The study concluded that the high rate of errors occurred because of the indiscriminate use of the death penalty and factors such as race, politics, and poorly performing law enforcement systems (Columbia Law School, 2002). It should be noted that prosecutors have objected to the study's methodology, arguing that the study counted cases where the evidence was weak but the defendant might still be guilty. Further, they argue that the number of exonerations is quite small compared to the number of convictions (Liptak, 2004; Columbia Law School, 2002).

More recently, Acker and Redlich (2011) looked at 266 exonerees convicted of murder. They identified the following as reasons for the false convictions: false eyewitness identification, invalid forensic science, false confessions, informant/jailhouse informant testimony, government misconduct, and bad lawyering. The authors propose that evidence indicates 2.3 percent of all murder convictions may be error (2011:17), and that an important point to consider is that the true criminal goes on to commit more crimes. In their review, they found that 49 rapes and 19 murders occurred because police and prosecutors focused on the wrong suspect (2011: 18).

Others have also identified the reasons for false convictions, mentioning:

- Mistaken eyewitness testimony
- Perjury by informants
- Police and prosecutorial misconduct
- False confessions
- "Junk science"
- Ineffective assistance of counsel
- Racial bias
- **Confirmatory bias** (when a specific suspect has been fixated upon and other possibilities are ignored) (Schehr and Sears, 2005).

Brandon Garrett's (2011) study of 250 exonerees found that 70 percent were minorities. Racial bias in wrongful convictions has been attributed to individual factors and structural factors. Structural factors include systemic bias against minorities

Innocence Project
An organization (www.innocenceproject.org) staffed by lawyers and law students who reexamine cases and provide legal assistance to convicts when there is a probability that serious errors occurred in their prosecution.

confirmatory bias Fixating on a preconceived notion and ignoring other possibilities, such as in regard to a specific suspect during a police investigation.

QUOTE & QUERY

Is it better for 100,000 guilty men to walk free rather than have one innocent man convicted? The cost-benefit policy answer is no.

(prosecutor) Quoted in Liptak, 2004: 3.

No rate of preventable errors that destroy people's lives and destroy the lives of those close to them is acceptable.

(law professor) Quoted in Liptak, 2004: 3.

 Do either of these statements represent ethical formalism? Which statement represents utilitarian thinking? Why does it have to be a choice between letting guilty people go free and punishing innocents?

in all institutions of society (political, economic, and social) that leads to different opportunities and treatment. Individual factors include racism, a higher rate of error in cross-racial identification, stereotyping, and lack of resources among minority defendants.

Several studies have used different sources to estimate wrongful convictions. Asking justice professionals to estimate is typically the way such studies arrive at their figures and these estimates range from 0.5 percent to 15 percent, depending on which sources were used (inmate reports illustrated the higher figure). The average estimate is around 1 to 3 percent of all felony cases (Poveda, 2001; Ramsey, 2007; Zalman, Smith, and Kiger, 2008; Krajicek, 2015). The Quote and Query box presents two perceptions of the costs involved in wrongful convictions.

The state of Texas executes the most people and also has exonerated the most offenders, including Clarence Brandley, Delma Banks, James Curtis Giles, Joyce Ann Brown, Michael Morton, and Cameron Todd Willingham. Randall Dale Adams, another freed inmate, was the subject of the documentary *The Thin Blue Line*. He was convicted in 1976 of killing a Dallas police

(((•))) IN THE NEWS | *Who Is Guilty?*

One case illustrates the damage to truth and justice when the principles of procedural justice are compromised. In 1982 a teen couple were shot and killed on Chicago's South Side. The investigation targeted Anthony Porter, a known gang member and criminal of low intelligence who was seen near the location by multiple witnesses. Just 50 hours away from being executed, his case was one of the first to be taken up by Professor David Protess, his investigator, and students at the Medill Innocence Project at Northwestern University. Their investigation uncovered evidence of coerced witness testimony and improper interrogation of Porter and led them to Alstory Simon. They obtained a statement from Simon's ex-wife who said he admitted the killing. Simon even confessed to the killing in 1999 in a news broadcast. After the broadcast, the state attorney's office secured Porter's release and charged Simon with the murder. He pleaded guilty and received a 37-year sentence. However, after serving 15 years, Simon was also released in 2015 after the new state's attorney decided he was coerced into admitting guilt by Protess and his investigator.

Simon is now suing Northwestern University and Protess for $40 million in damages, alleging the university allowed a "culture of lawlessness" and unethical conduct among faculty and journalism students who worked in the Medill Innocence Project.

The suit alleges Protess and the investigator manufactured evidence, coaxed false statements from witnesses, intimidated Simon into confessing and set him up with a lawyer, Jack Rimland, who coached him to plead guilty to receive lucrative movie contracts. Protess had already left the university in 2011 as a result of an investigation about the methods he allowed his students to use (e.g., allegations included giving witnesses money for drugs, lying about their identities, and flirting with witnesses). In the Simon case, the allegations are that Paul Ciolino, the investigator, impersonated a police officer, confronted Simon while armed, showed him a video of an actor falsely claiming to have witnessed the killing and told Simon he would receive a short sentence if he confessed. Ciolino allegedly promised large sums of money from book and movie deals if he gave a statement.

Porter and Simon have both been released, arguably because of the ethical violations of, first, justice professionals, and, second, those who were successful at getting Porter's conviction overturned. Anita Alvarez, the current state attorney, has stated the office's Conviction Integrity Unit at this point cannot determine who killed the couple. The zeal to obtain justice by ignoring procedural justice has resulted evidently in no justice for anyone.

Sources: Hinkel and O'Connell, 2015; McLaughlin, 2014.

officer who stopped a car driven by David Harris. Harris said Adams was the gunman. Adams said he wasn't even in the car. Harris eventually confessed that he killed the officer alone. The prosecutor withheld the fact that he had made a deal with Harris to testify and hid his lengthy criminal record. Adams spent years in prison and on death row before finally being released (Hall, 2002; Kirchmeier et al., 2009).

Growing numbers of exonerated individuals each have their own story, but the factors that lead to their wrongful convictions often are similar and include unethical actions that thwart procedural justice, such as coercive interrogations, use of lying jailhouse informants, and suppressing exculpatory evidence. Due process is designed to minimize error, but procedural justice can be subverted by those who feel that they are above the law.

Race, Ethnicity, and Justice

The major constructs of procedural justice research include *neutrality* (fairness in decisions) and *respect* (using respectful language and not demeaning the citizen). There is strong evidence that the reason the relationship between police departments and minority communities is problematic is because the residents in these communities feel these two aspects of procedural justice are missing. Recently, this issue has become headline news, but the problem has been simmering for years.

In March 2012, 17-year-old Trayvon Martin was shot and killed by George Zimmerman, a neighborhood watch volunteer who was suspicious of the boy. Zimmerman was acquitted of any crime arguing self-defense, despite the fact that Martin was unarmed and Zimmerman ignored police orders not to approach him. Other killings or shootings of black men have been captured and received wide exposure through the news media and Youtube.com, such as Oscar Grant in California who was shot by a transit officer when he mistakenly pulled his gun instead of his Taser (similar to the more recent killing of Eric Harris by reserve deputy Robert Bates in Tulsa, Oklahoma).

The shooting of Michael Brown in Ferguson, Missouri, in the summer of 2014 seemed to be the lightning rod that sparked national outrage and spontaneous grassroots movements with slogans like "Black Lives Matter." Then in April 2015, the public saw an amateur video of Officer Michael Slager shooting at and killing Walter Scott, stopped for a traffic violation, who was running away at the time. Slager was fired and indicted for murder, but before this event had even left the news cycle, another black man's death occurred in Baltimore. Freddie Gray ran from police, was pursued, caught, and placed in a police van. At some point while in police custody, he incurred a crushed voice box and a nearly severed spinal cord. He died several days later. Baltimore erupted into violent protests and the governor called out the National Guard to restore order. Deaths of black men by the hands of police have now caught the attention of the media, and through the media, the entire country, sparking concern as to why there is no national database of police killings, much less any national numbers at all on police use-of-force incidents. Although the tragic deaths of individuals like Walter Scott, Freddie Gray, and Eric Harris are the most clear examples that explain the rancor between the police and minority communities, the problem is much broader.

There is a large difference in the perceptions of blacks and whites regarding the criminal justice system. For instance, in a Gallup Poll, 71 percent of whites said murder charges against O. J. Simpson were probably or definitely true, but only 28 percent of blacks agreed (reported in Mitchell and Banks, 1996: Bl). More current figures also show large differences. In a combined Gallup Poll of 2011–2014, 59 percent of whites, but only 36 percent of blacks, had a great deal or a lot of confidence in the police. About 59 percent of whites stated that the honesty and ethics of police officers was very high or high, compared with 45 percent of blacks. About one in four young black males reported being treated unfairly by a police officer in the preceding 30 days (Newport, 2014).

The issue of race permeates the criminal justice system, with discussions concerning the disproportional representation of blacks in certain crime categories, racial profiling by police, lack of access to competent attorneys, and disparate sentencing. Recent news stories illustrate that at each stage of the system there seems to be disparate treatment. A two-year study by the Vera Institute of 222,542 criminal cases found that black and white defendants received different treatment by the Manhattan District Attorney's office. Even after controlling for factors like the seriousness of the charges and a defendant's criminal history, blacks and Latinos were more likely than whites to be denied bail. They were also offered harsher plea deals; that is, when the charge was a misdemeanor drug offense, black defendants were 27 percent more likely than whites to get a plea offer that included incarceration (Editorial Board, 2014).

A recent study by Professor Baumgartner (UNC-Chapel Hill) of 1.3 million stops made over 12 years by the Charlotte-Mecklenburg Police Department found that though blacks make up less than a third of the city's driving-age residents, they are pulled over by police more frequently, receive more tickets, and are the subjects of roadside searches twice as often as whites. Only about 5 percent of the city's traffic stops lead to police searches, but the rate for young black males is almost three times that rate. Police officers reported encountering force three times as often when black drivers and passengers were involved. Baumgartner's study showed that whites were more likely to be pulled over for speeding, running red lights and stop signs, and driving while intoxicated while black drivers were more likely to be stopped for seat belts, vehicle registration, and equipment. Blacks were three times more likely to be searched during a seat-belt stop. The police chief disputed that the report supported racial profiling, arguing that most of the stops of blacks took place in primarily black communities with high crime rates (Gordon, 2015).

The argument that blacks are more heavily policed because they are disproportionately responsible for crime has been a long-standing defense to racial profiling, saturation patrols, and stop-and-frisks. A study of crime in communities, however, shows that it is income, not race or ethnicity, that seems to be the primary factor in crime. Peterson (2012) reviewed neighborhood crime studies to show that blacks and other minorities are much more likely than whites to live in structurally disadvantaged neighborhoods, and it is these neighborhoods that contribute disproportionally to crime statistics. What they found was that crime rates in the few white neighborhoods that had similar levels of structural disadvantage were similar to minority neighborhoods in their crime levels. In other words, it is not race that is the crux of the crime problem; it is structural disadvantage.

The Justice Department's report of Ferguson, Missouri, reported that a disproportionate number of arrests, citations and traffic stops of blacks, and onerous fines that included late charges, which quickly increased the original amount to thousands of dollars more, were among the factors in the public anger that led to the protests after Michael Brown's death in 2014.

Similarly, in California, a 2012 state analysis found that assessments tacked onto tickets by California lawmakers increased the price of traffic tickets exponentially (e.g., a $500 traffic ticket actually cost $1,953). A more recent study found that traffic fines impacted the poor and the working class disproportionately because they couldn't pay and had their licenses suspended, and the data showed that blacks were far more likely than others to be pulled over for a traffic stop (Williams, 2015).

The justification for the minor traffic stops and searches are that they are a law enforcement tool to fight crime. The argument against them is that the citizens who are pulled over and treated like criminals lose faith that the criminal justice system is fair. This is why procedural justice is so important—not only because it is a right of all citizens to be treated fairly but also because, in the long run, it leads to better police-community relations and compliance with the law.

Restorative Justice

What would a system of justice be like if the emphasis were on the victim's rights, needs, and compensation? In a system with a primary emphasis on the victim rather than the offender, money would be spent on victim services rather than prisons. It would be victims who would receive job skills training, not offenders. Some of the money that now goes to law enforcement and corrections would be channeled to compensation programs for victims of personal and property crimes. Victims would be helped even if their offenders were not caught. The major goal would not be punishment but service. Offenders would be peripheral figures; they would be required to pay restitution to victims, and punishment would occur only if they did not fulfill their obligation to their victims. Could such a system work? Would such a system provide better justice?

Although the restorative justice movement does not propose quite this level of radical restructuring, it does dramatically redesign the justice system and offers a new alternative to retributive justice. **Restorative justice** is a term used to describe a number of programs that seek to move compensation back to center stage in the justice system, instead of retribution. A similar, but not identical, philosophy has been called "peacemaking justice" by Braswell and Gold (2002). Programs that require the offender to confront the victim and provide compensation, and programs that place the victim in the middle of the process of deciding what to do about the offender, can be categorized under the restorative justice rubric. The propositions of the movement are as follows (Van Ness and Strong, 1997):

restorative justice
An approach to corrective justice that focuses on meeting the needs of all concerned.

1. Justice requires restoring victims, offenders, and communities who have been injured by crime.

2. Victims, offenders, and communities should have the opportunity to be a fully active part of the justice process.

3. Government should restore order, but the community should establish peace.

The roots of restorative justice can be found as far back as Roman and Grecian law. Both were based on repayment to victims. The response to offenses was compensatory, and only when the offender refused to provide compensation was physical punishment employed. Gradually, however, this compensation-to-the-victim approach was relegated to civil law, and criminal law became almost solely concerned with punishment.

In the 1970s, a trend toward "community justice" was part of the larger movement of community empowerment and development. Community justice boards or local justice committees were created as part of the justice system (Schweigert, 2002). This model actually comes from earlier examples of tribal justice, such as the Maori tribal council of New Zealand, which involves members of the families of both the victims and the offenders. The model uses reintegrative shaming, and responsibility for the crime is shared by the offender's family. Another example is the Skokomish Community Peacemaking Panel. Tribal peacemakers are selected from community members, and an adversarial system is specifically rejected in favor of one that seeks to solve the issue rather than simply to assess punishment.

Hallmarks of community justice models include the idea that justice should be informal, employ local leadership, and encourage community participation. The goal is to repair the harm and promote the health of the community, not simply punish the offender. Customs and traditions create the authority employed to resolve disputes (Schweigert, 2002: 25). In community or restorative justice models, crime is viewed as a natural human error that should be dealt with by the community. Offenders remain a part of the community.

In retributive justice, the question is "Who did it?" while in restorative justice, the question is "What is the harm?" In retributive justice, the question is "Which laws were broken?" while in restorative justice, the question is "What needs to be done to repair the harm?" In retributive justice, the question is "What should the punishment be?" while in restorative justice, the question is "Who is responsible for this repair?"

Types of restorative justice programs include victim–offender mediation (or victim–offender reconciliation programs), whereby victims and offenders get together so the victim can make it clear to the offender what harm has occurred and they can decide together how to make it right. Reparative boards have community members (rather than justice officials) decide what should happen after a crime has been committed and an offender identified. Family group conferencing and circle sentencing include family members and other interested parties in the decision on what should happen to an offender (Braithwaite, 2002). It has been found that victims are more satisfied in restorative justice programs than with traditional sentencing (79 percent compared to 57 percent). Offenders were also more likely to successfully satisfy their restitution orders in such programs (Braithwaite, 2002: 71).

Community reparative boards are more commonly used with youthful offenders. They are also called youth panels, neighborhood boards, or community diversion boards, and they have been in use since the 1920s. These boards reemerged in the mid-1990s. The goals are to involve the community, provide the opportunity for the offender to take responsibility for his or her actions, and facilitate the development of prevention (Braithwaite, 2002: 73).

Family group conferencing comes from the Maori tribal model and was made a part of national legislation in New Zealand in 1989. It includes conferences of offenders, victims, families, and interested or involved others to resolve the problem. Circle sentencing, a similar model, comes from the Navajos in North America. Everyone involved directly in a criminal offense sits in a circle and gets a turn to speak. The entire circle decides what should be done. The goal is not to respond only to the current offense but also to heal the community (Braithwaite, 2002: 76).

There are potential problems with, and some criticisms of, these types of programs (Braithwaite, 2002; Dzur and Wertheimer, 2002). For instance, victims may feel pressured to forgive before they are ready. Less due process may be given to offenders because the goal is not to punish; thus, issues of guilt or innocence may be unresolved. However, restorative justice seems to offer an alternative to our traditional retributive justice system that can be supported by ethics of care, utilitarianism, religion, and possibly other ethical systems. It is more akin to older systems of law that focused on compensation rather than punishment. While legal sanctions usually do not make the victim "whole" or change the offender, restorative justice attempts to do both.

Immoral Laws and the Moral Person

In this discussion, we have argued that procedural justice may not be equivalent to substantive justice. In other words, just because the legal rules have been followed does not necessarily mean that justice occurs. Nelson Mandela, for instance, was tried by a court of law before he was imprisoned, but that legal system was part of a brutal regime of oppression. In his trial, he argued that the process was illegitimate because it did not conform to principles of natural laws of justice. The Walking the Walk box below describes his life.

What is the moral duty of individuals when laws and governmental edicts are themselves immoral? Examples might include the laws of the Spanish Inquisition in the fifteenth century that resulted in large numbers of people being tortured and killed

WALKING THE WALK

Nelson Mandela was imprisoned in South Africa for 27 years. He began fighting apartheid in the 1940s. In 1964, he was convicted of sabotage and treason and sentenced to a life term of imprisonment for his activities in the African National Congress Party, which had been outlawed by the government. Throughout his decades in prison, he refused to compromise his position in order to gain his release, arguing that "only free men can negotiate." However, he did begin secret talks in the late 1980s when he was approached by the ruling white party leaders, who gradually came to the realization that apartheid could not continue as South Africa became in danger of being torn apart by race-based violence. Eventually, Mandela's reputation grew to worldwide proportions, and he was released in 1990. In 1991, he was elected president of the African National Congress when the ban against the political party was lifted. In 1994, black South Africans voted for the first time and Mandela was elected as president of a democratic South Africa, formally bringing to an end the era of apartheid. He was awarded the Nobel Peace Prize in 1993 along with Frederik de Klerk, the South African president who released him from captivity.

After apartheid ended, Mandela was instrumental in averting a civil war between blacks and whites. There was a strong possibility that it might happen; small numbers of blacks began a pattern of violence toward those who had co-operated with the separatist government. "Necklaces" made of burning rubber were used to burn victims alive in a pattern of retaliation. This violence was condemned by Mandela and others, and, instead, Truth and Reconciliation panels were created. These panels brought out into the open the horrors of apartheid and the brutal system that developed to protect it, but promised amnesty for those who admitted their wrongdoing. The Truth and Reconciliation panels, as well as earlier conciliatory gestures, such as Mandela congratulating the white rugby team during his only term (1994–1998) as president (memorialized in the movie *Invictus*), and his refusal to use his power to attack and punish the vanquished white ruling party, led to South Africa coming out of a brutal, repressive regime to a democracy with minimal civil strife.

Throughout his life, Mandela's principles served as the guiding light for his actions and, because of those actions, a whole country was changed.

Sources: Nelson Mandela Foundation website, www.nelsonmandela.org (accessed June 14, 2012); Bryson, 2010.

for having dissenting religious beliefs, and the Nuremberg laws of Nazi Germany stripping Jewish citizens of their citizenship, as well as later laws requiring Jews to give themselves up to be transported to concentration camps and often to their death. Examples in the United States might include the internment laws during World War II that forced U.S. citizens of Japanese descent to give up land and property and be confined in camps until the end of the war, and the Jim Crow laws that once forced blacks to use different doors and water fountains than whites.

These laws are now thought of as immoral, but they were not considered so by many people at the time. The most common examples of immoral laws are those that deprive certain groups of liberty or treat some groups differently, giving them either more or fewer rights and privileges than other groups. Boss (2001) has described unjust laws as having the following characteristics:

- They are degrading to humans.
- They are discriminatory against certain groups.
- They are enacted by unrepresentative authorities.
- They are unjustly applied.

Most ethical systems would condemn such laws, and an objective ethical analysis would probably prevent the passage of such laws in the first place. The example of Japanese American internment can be used to illustrate how one might use ethical systems to judge a specific law. The religious ethical framework would probably not provide moral support for the action because it runs contrary to some basic Christian principles, such as, "Do unto others as you would have them do unto you." Ethical formalism could not be used to support this law because it runs counter to the categorical imperative that each person must be treated as an end rather than as a means, and to the universalism principle. The principle of forfeiture could not justify the action because these were innocent individuals, many of whom were fiercely loyal to the United States. The only ethical framework that might be used to support the morality of this law is utilitarianism. Even under utilitarianism, however, we must be able to show that the total utility derived from the action outweighed the negative effect on those impacted. Did it save the country from a Japanese invasion? Did the benefits outweigh the harm to Japanese Americans?

Are there any laws today that might be considered immoral? Many argue that holding the detainees in Guantanamo for years without any due process, is in violation of the Geneva Convention and our own laws and has no ethical or moral justification. Defenders argue that our actions have been necessary and morally justified as self-defense. Unfortunately, actions that may seem reasonable when in the grip of fear, in retrospect, may not be legally or morally justifiable.

Martin Luther King, Jr., Mahatma Gandhi, and Henry David Thoreau agreed with St. Augustine that "an unjust law is no law at all." There is a well-known story about Thoreau, jailed for nonpayment of what he considered unfair taxes. When asked by his friend Ralph Waldo Emerson, "Henry, what are you doing in there?" Thoreau responded, "The question is, what are you doing out there?" The point of the story is that if a law is wrong, a moral person is honor-bound to disobey that law. Box 3.2 addresses civil disobedience. Another story concerns Socrates. About to be punished for the crime of teaching radical ideas to youth, he had the opportunity to escape and was begged by his friends to leave the country, yet he willingly accepted his death

---

BOX 3.2 \ Civil Disobedience

1. It must be nonviolent in form and actuality.
2. No other means of remedying the evil should be available.
3. Those who resort to civil disobedience must accept the legal sanctions and punishments imposed by law.
4. A major moral issue must be at stake.
5. When intelligent men [*sic*] of good will differ on complex moral issues, discussion is more appropriate than action.
6. There must be some reason for the time, place, and target selected.
7. One should adhere to "historical time."

Source: Hook, quoted in Fink (1977: 126–127).

---

by hemlock because, he argued, he had benefited from living in a society of laws all of his life and could not reject law simply because he didn't like the resolution of his trial. This position supports the notion that one should never place one's own moral code above the duly enacted laws of the land. One should change the laws, if they are believed to be wrong, through the process of legislation and appeal, not by committing unlawful acts, because the latter is dangerous to the stability of society.

Civil disobedience is the voluntary disobedience of established laws based on one's moral beliefs. Rawls (1971) defined it as a public, nonviolent, conscientious, yet political act contrary to law and usually done with the aim of bringing about a change in the law or policies of the government. Many great social thinkers and leaders have advocated breaking certain laws thought to be wrong. Philosophers believe that the moral person follows a higher law of behavior that usually, but not necessarily, conforms to human law. However, it is an exceptional person who willfully and publicly disobeys laws that he or she believes to be wrong. Psychological experiments show us that it is difficult for individuals to resist authority, even when they know that they are being asked to do something that is wrong.

> **civil disobedience**
> Voluntarily breaking established laws based on one's moral beliefs.

The Milgram experiments are often used to show how easily one can command blind obedience to authority. In these experiments, subjects were told to administer shocks to individuals hooked up to electrical equipment as part of a learning experiment (Milgram, 1963). Unbeknownst to the subjects, the "victims" were really associates of the experimenter and faked painful reactions only when the subjects thought they were administering shocks. In one instance, the subject and the "victim" were separated, and the subject heard only cries of pain and exclamations of distress, then silence, indicating that the "victim" was unconscious. Even when the subjects thought they were harming the "victims," they continued to administer shocks because the experimenter directed them to do so and reminded them of their duty (Milgram, 1963).

Although it is always with caution that one applies laboratory results to the real world, history shows that individual submission to authority, even immoral authority, is not uncommon. Those who turned in Jewish neighbors to Nazis and those who participated in massacres of Native Americans in this country were only following the law or instructions from a superior authority. The point is that it is a rare individual who stands up to legal authority, even when he or she believes the law to be wrong.

To determine what laws are unjust, Martin Luther King, Jr., used the following guidelines: "A just law is one that is consistent with morality. An unjust law is any that degrades human personality or compels a minority to obey something the majority does not adhere to or is a law that the minority had no part in making" (quoted in Barry, 1985: 3). Remember that civil disobedience occurs when the individual truly believes the law to be wrong and therefore believes that the enforcement of it or obedience to it would also be wrong. We are not referring to chronic lawbreaking because of immediate rewards. Indeed, most criminals have a fairly conventional sense of morality. They agree with the laws, even though they break them. Even those gray-area laws that involve disagreement over the "wrongness" of the behavior are not proper grounds for disobedience unless one believes that the government is immorally oppressing certain people.

There is a widespread belief that law is synonymous with morality and that as long as one remains inside the law, one can be considered a moral person. Callahan (1982: 64) points out the following:

> *We live in a society where the borderline between law and ethics often becomes blurred. For many, morality is simply doing that which the law requires; a fear of punishment is the only motivation for behavior in some minimally acceptable way.*

We should always remember that law is considered the basement of morality; even if you never break a law that does not automatically make you a moral person. There are immoral acts that are not illegal, and once in a great while some laws are immoral. Luckily, very few of us find that a higher standard of morality conflicts with existing law.

Before we conclude the chapter, one more dilemma will be presented along with a discussion of how consideration of law, policy, and ethics would help us in determining the right thing to do.

ETHICAL DILEMMA

You are a prosecutor involved in a case concerning a brutal murder. No DNA evidence was uncovered at the scene and there were no witnesses. The state lab examiners are unable to match a boot print left at the scene to the suspect's boot, but you find an expert who is willing to testify to a match. You also discover your expert has been sanctioned in another state for overstating her qualifications and her testimony has been excluded in other states because it does not meet legal tests for admission of expert testimony. Would you share such information with the defense? Would you use this expert's testimony at all?

Law

In *Brady v. Maryland* (373 U.S. 83,1963), the Supreme Court held that due process required that prosecutors divulge any exculpatory information to the defense. Not doing so could result in a reversal of a conviction. In order for scientific evidence to be admitted, it must meet the "*Daubert* standard" in most states. This guidance came from the Supreme Court in *Daubert v. Merrell Dow*

Pharmaceuticals Inc. (509 U.S. 579,1993). Before admitting scientific evidence, the *Daubert* standard requires the information to be proven relevant and reliable based on a number of criteria provided by the Court, including whether the findings were subject to peer review and whether the theory or method is accepted in the scientific community. The guidance still leaves a great deal of discretion to the judge in whether or not to admit expert testimony.

Policy

Since a National Academy of Science's 2009 report on forensic science, many in the criminal justice system are more skeptical of forensic testimony, especially in the areas where the examiner uses subjective judgment to determine whether a match exists between footprints, bite marks, or hair. That doesn't mean this type of evidence is not still being admitted, but it does mean that many district attorney offices are more careful now in the use of such testimony. Some offices may have policies that direct whether prosecutors can "shop" for experts or whether they must utilize only the state lab examiners. It is possible office policies exist that promote an "open file" approach where nothing in the case is hidden from defense. If that was the case, then the defense would know everything about the expert witness that the prosecutor knows. Most offices do not have open file policies, however.

Ethics

Recall that the steps in making an ethical decision are to identify the facts, the concepts, the ethical dilemmas, the main dilemma, and then resolve it by applying an ethical system. In this case, the facts known to the prosecutor are that the boot print match has been made by one expert but not by the state forensic examiner, and that there is information that calls into question the expert witness's credentials. The relevant concepts are justice, of course, but also professionalism, honor, and honesty. The two dilemmas are whether to use the expert witness testimony and whether to share the negative information with the defense counsel. The utilitarian ethical system would weigh up the costs and benefits of both sides. Since it is possible that any conviction that resulted might be overturned, it would serve the greater good to share the information if the testimony was used. It's possible that the greater good would also be served by not utilizing such problematic testimony, especially since the defense counsel would probably discredit the expert witness on the stand with the information provided. Ethical formalism would also probably not support utilizing such information since the system requires one to do one's duty and follow the categorical imperative. In this case, the prosecutor probably would not want to universalize the practice of using potentially discredited expert witnesses. The duty of a prosecutor is to seek justice, not a conviction; therefore, it is one's ethical duty to make sure that all the protections of due process occur in any prosecution.

Conclusion

In this chapter, we have explored the origins and components of justice. Typically, justice includes the concepts of fairness, equality, and impartiality. Justice was defined by Aristotle as being either distributive or corrective. Distributive justice concerns the allocations of goods and opportunities in society. Corrective justice is the central concern of the criminal justice system and can be further divided into substantive and procedural issues. Substantive justice is concerned with the fairness of what we do to offenders; procedural justice is concerned with the procedures that must be undertaken before punishment occurs. Research shows that people who perceive they are treated unfairly by justice professionals lose faith in the procedural justice of the system and are less likely to follow the law. The failings of procedural justice can be seen in wrongful convictions and the different perceptions of minorities and whites toward the criminal justice system. Restorative justice is a new approach that actually has ancient roots. It focuses attention on the victim rather than the offender. A special concern is when the legal system or a law can be considered to be unjust and immoral. Principles of civil disobedience allow us to provide guidance as to when a moral person might legitimately oppose a law.

Chapter Review

1. **Describe the three themes included in the definition of justice.**

    Most definitions of justice include the concepts of fairness (equal treatment), equality (equal shares), and impartiality (absence of bias). Justice acts to mediate our impulses of selfishness and fairness. Justice is distinguished from goodness.

2. **Define Aristotle's two forms of justice described in the chapter.**

    Aristotle described two forms of justice: distributive justice (which concerns the fair distribution of goods and opportunities in society) and corrective justice (which concerns the fair resolution in controversies when unjust enrichment or unfair advantage occurs, either through civil or criminal wrongs).

3. **Under corrective justice, distinguish between substantive and procedural justice, including how procedural justice impacts wrongful convictions and perceptions of racial discrimination.**

   Substantive justice concerns the inherent fairness of a law or punishment. Substantive justice can be supported by either retribution or utilitarian rationales. Procedural justice is concerned with legal administration or the steps taken before punishment is administered. For instance, a substantive justice question would be "Is capital punishment just?" while a procedural justice question would be "What due process should apply before a decision of capital punishment is just?" Procedural justice research shows that when people are treated in conformance to justice concepts (voice, neutrality, equity, dignity), they feel the entire justice system is more legitimate. When procedural justice is not followed, wrongful convictions are more likely to occur and groups of citizens (especially minorities) feel that justice professionals treat them unfairly.

4. **Explain the concept of restorative justice and the programs associated with it.**

   Restorative justice puts the emphasis on making the victim whole and maintaining bonds between the community, the victim, and the offender. Types of restorative justice programs include victim–offender mediation (or victim–offender reconciliation programs), reparative boards, family group conferencing, and circle sentencing.

5. **Describe civil disobedience and when it may be appropriate.**

   Laws that may be subject to civil disobedience must be immoral and unjust. For instance, they could be degrading, discriminatory, enacted by unrepresentative authorities, or unjustly applied. Civil disobedience must be nonviolent, there should be no other alternative, one must accept the legal consequences, and there should be a major moral issue at stake. If people of good will disagree on the matter, then civil disobedience is not appropriate.

Key Terms

civil disobedience	impartiality	retributive justice
corrective justice	Innocence Project	sanctuary
distributive justice	justice	substantive justice
due process	*lex salica*	utilitarian justice
equality	*lex talionis*	veil of ignorance
fairness	procedural justice	
hedonistic calculus	restorative justice	

Study Questions

1. Explain how Plato and Aristotle associated status with justice.
2. Describe distributive and corrective justice. Identify how different systems under distributive justice would allocate the resources of society.
3. Describe Rawls' system of distributive and corrective justice.
4. Describe retributive and utilitarian rationales for punishment, which is a substantive justice issue. Explain due process and how it fits with procedural justice. What are the elements of due process?
5. Describe some types of restorative justice programs. What ethical systems support restorative justice?

Writing/Discussion Exercises

1. Write an essay on (or discuss) how the government should distribute societal resources such as education and healthcare. How would you answer the argument of a couple who did not believe they should have to pay school taxes because they have no children? What about the argument that rich school districts should share their wealth with poor districts (keeping in mind that those who pay higher taxes in that district might have moved there because of the reputation of the school)? What are the arguments for and against universal healthcare?

2. Write an essay on (or discuss) the following issues under substantive and procedural justice:

    a. What is the proper punishment for a burglary, for a murder in an armed robbery, and for a million-dollar embezzlement? If you were being punished for a crime, would you rather receive a year in prison or 50 lashes? Why do we not use corporal punishment for criminal offenders? Do you think we should? Are there situations in our justice system where victims or offenders are treated differently than others because of who they are?

    b. An 87-year-old man living in Chicago is exposed as a soldier who took part in killing hundreds of Jewish concentration camp victims. U.S. extradition procedures are followed to the letter, and he is extradited to Israel to stand trial, as Israeli law determines that courts in Israel have jurisdiction over Nazi war crimes. Israeli legal procedure is followed without error, and he is convicted of war crimes and sentenced to death.

    c. Federal law enforcement agents determine that a citizen of another country participated in a drug cartel that sold drugs in the United States. A small group of agents goes to the foreign country, kidnaps the offender, drugs him, and brings him back to the United States to stand trial. Upon challenge, the government agents explain that, although these actions would have been unconstitutional and illegal against a citizen of the United States in this country, because they were conducted on foreign soil against a non-U.S. citizen, they were not illegal.

3. Write an essay on (or discuss) whether civil disobedience is ever justified. Discuss war protesters or anti-abortion activists who are arrested for trespassing and so on. If you believe that civil disobedience might be justified, when and in what circumstances would it be acceptable?

ETHICAL DILEMMAS

Situation 1

Two individuals are being sentenced for the exact same crime of burglary. You are the judge. One of the individuals is a 20-year-old who has not been in trouble before and participated only because the other individual was his friend. The second person has a history of juvenile delinquency and is now 25. Would you sentence them differently? How would you justify your decision?

Situation 2

In your apartment building there lives a young man who appears to be of Middle Eastern descent. You notice that other young men often visit him and that they come and go at odd hours of the day and night. You engage in a conversation with him one day, and during the course of the conversation, he states that "the United States deserved what happened on September 11 because of their imperialistic actions across the world and their support for the oppression of the Palestinian people." You think it is your duty to report him to the local police, and they appear to be interested in your report. One day, you observe him being taken away in handcuffs, and you never see him again. Several weeks later, his apartment is vacant, and you do not know what happened to his belongings. Would you attempt to find out what happened to him? Do you believe you should investigate further?

Situation 3

You are serving on a jury for a murder trial. The evidence presented at trial was largely circumstantial and, in your mind, equivocal. During closing, the prosecutor argues that you must find the defendant guilty because he confessed to the crime. The defense attorney immediately objects, and the judge sternly instructs the jury to disregard the prosecutor's statement. Although you do not know exactly what happened, you suspect that the confession was excluded because of some procedural error. Would you be able to ignore the prosecutor's statement in your deliberations? Should you? Would you tell the judge if the jury members discussed the statement and seemed to be influenced by it?

Situation 4

You are a probation officer who must prepare sentencing recommendation reports for the judge. The juvenile defendant to be sentenced in one case grew up in a desperately poor family, according to school records. He had a part-time job in a local grocery store, stocking the shelves and providing general cleanup. The store owner caught him stealing meat. Actually, this is the second time he has been caught stealing food. The first time he shoplifted at the store, the deferred adjudication included his commitment to work for the store owner. He explained that he was trying to help his mother, who could not provide enough food for his family. In general, failure to succeed at deferred adjudication results in a commitment to a juvenile facility. What would you recommend to the judge?

Situation 5

You are an ardent Tea Party activist who believes the government has encroached unlawfully upon the sovereign rights of the state and the privacy rights of individuals. You do not believe that your taxes should go to anything other than national security and a few restricted activities, such as the federal highway system. Any other governmental programs are theft as far as you're concerned. Your group has organized a sit-in, and you discover that they plan to block the entrance to a publicly funded health clinic to demonstrate their ire at the federalization of healthcare. You know that the planned activities will constitute trespass and you may get arrested. Would you participate? Why or why not?

4

Becoming an Ethical Professional

Dr. Lawrence Kohlberg (discussed on p. 92).

I n this chapter, we shift from the discussion of "What is ethical?" to "Why do some people act ethically and others act unethically?" Why people act the way they do has been the question for philosophers, religious scholars, psychologists, sociologists, psychiatrists, economists, and, more recently, criminologists. There is an obvious overlap between the question we ask in criminology—"Why do people commit crime?"—and the one we ask here: "Why do people commit unethical acts?" In some cases, when the unethical acts are also crimes, the question is exactly the same.

The sections that follow very briefly explore influences on ethical decision making. We will approach this question in a way that is visually represented in Figure 4.1. Individual characteristics may be the most important factor in whether or not someone acts unethically. Arguably, one's morals and value systems are fairly well established by the time one enters the workforce;

Chapter Objectives

1. Be able to describe biological influences on the ethical behavior of criminal justice professionals, including major research findings.

2. Describe psychological theories that attempt to explain individual differences in behavior.

3. Describe research that addresses work group influences on behavior.

4. Become familiar with organizational influences on behavior.

5. Become familiar with cultural and societal influences on ethical behavior.

FIGURE 4.1 Spheres of Influence on Ethical Decision making

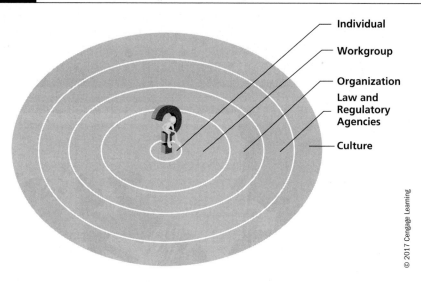

- Individual
- Workgroup
- Organization
- Law and Regulatory Agencies
- Culture

© 2017 Cengage Learning

thus, a dishonest, egoistic employee will be more likely to choose unethical behavior when the opportunity exists than another employee who values honesty and lives by a strong moral code. The section on individual influences on ethical behavior will be the first and longest discussion in the chapter because we assume that, generally, an adult's character is fairly well formed by the time they begin their professional life. There is also evidence to indicate, however, that our ethical decision making can be influenced by external factors, even into adulthood. An employee can be influenced by peers in a micro-climate of a workgroup distinct from the larger organization. In ethical scandals, it is often the case that the deviant behavior is limited to a small work group or division. For instance, in the chapters to follow, rogue narcotics taskforces in several cities are described that behave in ways quite different from the larger police department. Micro-climates can be created in even medium-sized organizations if they are isolated and unmonitored. Organizational influences (e.g., reward structures, training, and leadership) also play an important role in encouraging ethical behavior or facilitating unethical behavior. Finally, cultural and societal factors may influence the level of ethical behavior one finds in any given public service organization.

Individual Influences

Why do some people lie and others tell the truth in similar situations? Why would some people take advantage of others while others never would? How does one develop from an amoral infant to a virtuous adult? These are fascinating questions, and we can only skim the surface of the vast amount of literature that exists on the subject, briefly discussing biological and psychological research that helps us understand moral development and ethical decision making.

Biological Factors

Biological explanations have not been well received by many people despite a growing body of evidence that biology plays an important role in human behavior. Pinker (2002), for instance, discusses several false paradigms that have influenced sociology and psychology, including the "blank slate" or *tabula rasa* (the concept that humans are sponges, born with few or no instincts), "the noble savage" (the concept that humans are naturally peaceful and altruistic), and, the "ghost in the machine" (the concept that the body is separate from the mind, and that there is a consciousness apart from a physical entity). Contrary to these premises, which are popular in sociology, anthropology, and philosophy, the more we learn about the brain, the more we understand why we think the way we do, feel the way we do, and behave the way we do are fundamentally processes of the brain influenced by brain chemicals, neural pathways, and external factors that affect brain functioning.

Phineas Gage was a railroad worker in the early part of the twentieth century and became a textbook celebrity when an accident resulted in an iron spike impaling itself into his head. He miraculously recovered but changed from being a shy, soft-spoken, easygoing individual to one who was irascible, quick to anger, unpleasant, and quarrelsome (Pinker, 2002). The physical trauma to his brain changed his personality. This fact is not very controversial today, but other connections between the biological structures, chemical makeup, and processes of the brain and human behavior are less understood, and, therefore, more controversial. We will only briefly mention three implications for moral development that arise from research in this area: genetic influences on personality traits, sex differences, and frontal lobe development and injury.

Genetic influences continue to be denied despite accumulated findings that identical twins are more similar than fraternal twins in the presence of schizophrenia, autism, dyslexia, learning disabilities, gambling addictions, and criminality (Pinker, 2002; Fishbein, 2000). Genetics seems to influence personality traits that may impact ethical decision making, including such differences as whether someone is introverted/extroverted, neurotic/stable, incurious/open to new experiences, agreeable/antagonistic, and conscientious/undirected (Pinker, 2002). Some of these have clear implications for one's ability to develop moral decision making. Although his position was controversial, Wilson (1993) argued that values such as sympathy, fairness, self-control, and duty are moral "senses" that are inherent in humans and arise through a combination of genetics and socialization.

Shermer (2004) also argues that these traits are inherited, although he supports a group selection argument—specifically, eons ago human groups that held these traits were more likely to survive than groups that did not. In an interesting twist to the philosophical debate as to whether morals exist apart from humans (natural law explanations) or are created by them (relativism positions), Shermer argues that they are both: they transcend humans in the sense that our moral senses have been created by evolutionary factors that have taken place over the millennia; however, they are "of us" in the sense that they are human emotions, sentiments, and behaviors. Shermer (2004: 37) states that asking why humans should be moral is like asking why we should be hungry or jealous. The answer is because we are hardwired for these feelings and emotions through genetic selection.

Paul Zak (2012), a neuro-economist, focuses on the importance of oxytocin, going so far as to call it the "moral molecule." Neuro-economics only began in the 1990s when the so-called Chicago school of economics' rational models of economic decision making didn't work. Humans aren't necessarily rational in their decision making and so neuro-economists like Zak utilize the work of neuroscientists to reach new understandings of how brain chemicals like oxytocin may help explain behavior. He argues that this hormone promotes human bonding and trust. Oxytocin stimulates uterine contractions in pregnant women and is released during the act of nursing an infant, but it also is released when people pet their dogs, have sex, or hug someone. The brain releases oxytocin in settings where there are feelings of trust and safety and this leads to greater feelings of trust, which promotes altruistic reciprocity.

Zak's findings support the theory that oxytocin increases levels of trust and generosity. Evidently a small number of people have normal levels of oxytocin but few receptors in the brain so they cannot feel the effects of it. These individuals are, according to Zak, "at best selfish and at worst psychopaths" (quoted in Haederle, 2010: 47). Testosterone is found to counteract the effect of oxytocin, and those who are administered testosterone are less likely to be generous and trusting and more likely to punish opponents (Zak, 2012). This particular finding is interesting considering other research that indicates sex differences in ethical decision making exist.

Are women more "moral" than men? Studies show that women are less likely than men to cheat and more likely to recognize ethical issues (Emerson and McKinney, 2010; Lau and Haug, 2011; White, 1999; Hatamyar and Simmons, 2002). Over 70 studies examining sex differences in brain functioning found evidence that men are more antisocial, commit more serious types of offenses, and more often have serious childhood conduct disorders. There are also sex differences in delinquency, school performance, hyperactivity, impulsivity, and attention deficit disorders. These differences all seem to be related to brain development prenatally and during puberty and may influence the brain's ability to absorb "moral messages" or act upon them (Ellis and Pontius, 1989). As you probably know, the strongest correlate of criminality is sex, especially when considering only violent or victim-harming crimes. It is such a strong predictor that most people use the male pronoun when speaking of criminals unless there is specific reason to assume a female offender. Oddly, criminology textbooks devote very little attention to why women are so much less likely than men to commit victim-harming crimes but the answer may lie, at least partially, in biology (Pollock, 2014).

The frontal lobes of the brain seem to be implicated in feelings of empathy, shame, and moral reasoning. Individuals with frontal-lobe damage (like Phineas Gage) display characteristics that may be related to unethical behaviors, including increased impulsiveness, decreased attention span, tendency toward rude, unrestrained, tactless behavior, and a tendency to not be able to follow instructions, even after being able to verbalize what is required (Ellis and Pontius, 1989).

Several researchers have noted that moral decision making seems to take place in different regions of the brain, influenced by emotion centers (e.g., the amygdala) and areas responsible for rational thinking (e.g., the frontal lobes) (Moll et al., 2005; Shermer 2004). In a well-known hypothetical moral dilemma, a woman is hiding from enemy soldiers with others in a cellar when her baby starts crying. When test subjects are asked to imagine what they would do in this situation, two areas of the subjects' brains light up in MRIs—the inferior parietal lobe, which is related to rational but impersonal thinking, and the part of the brain connected with emotion, which evidently reacts with horror to the solution of smothering the baby to protect others (Vedantam, 2007). This indicates that moral decision making is both rational *and* emotional.

Researchers found that when subjects performed altruistic acts, their behavior triggered the pleasure center of the brain, connected with food and sex. This indicates that moral behaviors are hardwired into humans' basic impulses. Other research indicated that those with damage to the ventromedial prefrontal cortex, which is related to emotions, were unable to have any feelings regarding moral judgments (e.g., sympathy for others' pain and suffering or good feelings from altruism), although they were quite able to impersonally and coldly evaluate costs and benefits. The argument of some researchers is that morality lies in empathy, which derives from the emotional center of the brain. They say that only much later in evolution did the reasoning area of the brain develop and become involved in moral decision making (Vedantam, 2007).

This is an interesting scientific discussion that seems to parallel the distinction between ethical systems seated in emotion compared to those based in rationality. Emotion-based ethical systems such as ethics of care utilize the premises and approach of earlier philosophers such as David Hume (1711–1776) who believed that moral decisions were ultimately emotional. This is in contrast to rational, formulistic ethical systems such as utilitarianism and ethical formalism that presume that intellectual development is necessary for moral decision making and that ethical and moral decisions can be arrived at through reason.

There also seems to be a related discussion between theories of behavior that focus on rational choice versus normative/emotional factors. For instance, rational-choice theories of crime argue that criminals choose to commit crime based on rationally weighing the opportunities and risks (e.g., Cohen and Felson, 1979) and theories in business ethics presume that employees look at financial stakes and detection risk (e.g., Tabish and Jha, 2012). These theories view the individual as rationally weighing risk and reward. Other explanations of behavior point to emotional or relationship-based decision making (e.g., social bond theory, Hirschi, 1969). Some theorists mix the two approaches in that shame or guilt is used a perceived risk that is correlated with not committing the crime. Since, arguably, shame is an emotion based on relationships, this is an explanation that utilizes both rational and emotional motivations for behavior (see, Grasmick and Bursik, 1990). To complicate things further, other researchers have found that instrumental factors (risk of being caught, level of punishment) are only statistically significant in affecting decisions about committing crimes when moral norms are low (Kroneberg, Heintze, and Mehlkop, 2010).

Jonathan Haidt (2001) describes the relationship between emotions and rationality as a rider on an elephant, with the "elephant" representing the subjective, emotional component of humans' reactions to behavioral choices and the "rider" representing cognitive, rational, ethical decision making. The point of this discussion is that the rider can't control the elephant very

QUOTE & QUERY

Reason is, and ought only to be the slave of the passions, and can never pretend to any other office than to serve and obey them.

Source: David Hume, A Treatise of Human Nature (1739)

 What is David Hume saying in this quote? Does he believe that moral beliefs arise from one's heart or one's head?

well; in other words, emotional reactions and responses overwhelm rationality in many circumstances.

Others refer to the two as System 1 decision making (emotional, intuitive, immediate), and System 2 thinking (rational, deliberate, taking time to weigh various options) (Bazerman and Tenbrunsel, 2011). Whether one's initial "gut" reaction is the correct ethical decision in any dilemma is a philosophical question that takes us back to the previous chapter. It is interesting to note that research indicates that when workers are busy and stressed, they are more likely to make unethical choices because, possibly, the brain processes responsible for rationally deciding the correct action are already overloaded with other demands (Bazerman and Tenbrunsel, 2011). When individuals have time to reflect on their ethical choices after the fact, they often report that they wished they had done something different. Immediate decisions are influenced by biological instincts, emotional needs, and socialized values, and these influences are not necessarily operating at a conscious level. Thus, a worker may cheat on an expense voucher because of an emotional urge to get something they want and then create a post hoc rationalization for why it wasn't really dishonest (e.g., "everyone does it" or "the company doesn't pay me enough").

Learning Theory

Quite different from biological explanations of crime, learning theorists believe that children learn what they are taught, including morals and values as well as behavior. In other words, our beliefs about right or wrong and behavior are shaped by rewards and punishments, especially during our childhood. This learning can take place through modeling or by reinforcement. Note that criminology has also developed learning theory somewhat separately from what has occurred in psychology. Sutherland (1947) and Burgess and Akers (1966), and then Akers (1998) have utilized learning theory to explain criminality.

In **modeling**, values and moral beliefs come from those whom one admires and aspires to identify with. It is no surprise that, when asked who has been important in their moral development, most people say it is their parents, because primary caregivers are the most significant people in life during the important formative years. Although we may not hold exactly the same views and have exactly the same values as our parents, they are influential in our value formation. Note the similarity of this description of moral growth to that of Aristotle's who believed that one became virtuous by following the example of virtuous people.

Another way learning takes place is through **reinforcement**. Behaviors and beliefs that are reinforced (either through material rewards or through more subjective rewards, such as praise) are repeated and eventually become permanent. In one experiment, children were told a hypothetical story in which an adult punished a neutral act, such as a child practicing a musical instrument. The children later defined that act as bad, despite the intrinsic neutrality of the action. This indicates the power of adult definitions and punishment in the child's moral development (Boyce and Jensen, 1978: 133–170). Large gains in moral maturity (at least as measured by paper-and-pencil tests of expression of beliefs) can be achieved by direct manipulation of rewards for such beliefs (Boyce and Jensen, 1978: 143).

Albert Bandura (born 1925) described how the successful use of rewards is related to the child's age. As the child matures, concrete rewards and external sanctions

modeling Learning theory concept that people learn behaviors, values, and attitudes through relationships; they identify with another person and want to be like that person and pattern themselves after the "model."

reinforcement Rewards.

are replaced by symbolic and internal controls, such as one's conscience(Bandura, 1964). Eventually Bandura described the individual as not simply a passive recipient of rewards, but rather, as an active participant in the construction and meaning of rewards (Bandura, 1969, 1971). In this view, individuals are active, not passive; self-reflective, not merely acted upon; and self–regulating, not merely controlled by external forces. Bandura's later work revolved around his development of the concept of self-efficacy and moral identity. **Self-efficacy** can be defined as the individual's feelings of competence, and this sense is developed by comparing the self to others. The idea of a **moral identity** is composed of *moral agency*, which involves intent, anticipation of consequences, and self-regulation; and *moral efficacy*, which is the belief that one can successfully decide to act in moral ways.

Recall from Chapter 1 that values and ethics are related. Milton Rokeach (1918–1988) developed a value survey that is still in wide use today. He proposed that there are terminal values which would be the preferences for one's ideal life: True Friendship, Mature Love, Self-Respect, Happiness, Inner Harmony, Equality, Freedom, Pleasure, Social Recognition, Wisdom, Salvation, Family Security, National Security, A Sense of Accomplishment, A World of Beauty, A World at Peace, A Comfortable Life, and An Exciting Life. There are also instrumental values, which are one's preferences for *how to live* one's life: Cheerfulness, Ambition, Love, Cleanliness, Self-Control, Capability, Courage, Politeness, Honesty, Imagination, Independence, Intellect, Broad-Mindedness, Logic, Obedience, Helpfulness, Responsibility, and Forgiveness (Rokeach, 1973).

One's values are formed during childhood, perhaps through modeling and/or reinforcement. Much research exists that evaluates the correlation between values and behavior, although findings are mixed. Fritzsche (1995), for instance, found that value systems related to different types of wrongdoing in the workplace (e.g., bribery, conflict of interest, product misrepresentation). For instance, he found that the values of wisdom and honesty were negatively related to lying and independence was positively related to whistleblowing. The idea that different values affect different types of ethical behavior is an interesting finding and suggests the complexity of ethical decision making.

Kohlberg's Moral Stage Theory

Developmental theories propose that individuals mature physically, cognitively, and emotionally. Physical development—such as height and weight—can be charted by a pediatrician. Intellectual development is measured by a variety of intelligence tests and is charted against a normal curve of development. Emotional or social development also progresses at a predictable and normal pace, although it may be more difficult to measure. Social maturity is marked by the ability to empathize with others and a willingness to compromise one's desires with others' needs. An emotionally mature person balances individual needs with others' demands; however, that development might be stunted by negative environmental influences.

Jean Piaget (1896–1980) believed individuals went through stages of cognitive, or intellectual, growth that was related to their moral awareness. Piaget studied the rules that children develop in their play. These rules reflect the perceptions that children hold of themselves and others and move from egocentrism to

self-efficacy
Individuals' feelings of competence and confidence in their own abilities and power, developed by comparing self to others.

moral identity
Composed of *moral agency*, which involves intent, anticipation of consequences, and self-regulation; and *moral efficacy*, which is the belief that one can successfully decide to act in moral ways.

developmental theories
Approaches to behavior proposing that individuals have normal growth phases in areas such as morality and emotional maturity.

cooperativeness. Lawrence Kohlberg (1927–1987) carried on with Piaget's work and more fully described the stages that each individual passes through in moral development (Kohlberg, 1984).

Kohlberg's moral stages consist of three levels of moral reasoning, with two stages in each level. According to Kohlberg and his colleagues, each stage involves qualitative differences in the way the individual sees the world. Cognitive development and moral development are integrated—that is, one must grow intellectually in order to achieve a higher moral stage. One cannot skip stages, they are hierarchical; however, some people will not advance to the highest stages (Hersh, 1979: 52).

At the *pre-conventional level*, the person approaches a moral issue motivated purely by personal interests. The major concern is the consequence of the action for the individual. Young children first start sharing when they perceive benefit to themselves, such as giving someone their doll in exchange for a game or a ball, or they grudgingly share because they fear punishment from an adult if they do not.

At the *conventional level*, people perceive themselves as members of society, and living up to role responsibilities is paramount in believing oneself to be good. Children enter this level when they are capable of playing with other children according to rules. Games and play are training grounds for moral development because they teach the child that there are defined roles and rules of behavior. For instance, a game of softball becomes a microcosm of real life when a child realizes that he or she is not only acting as self but also as a first baseman, a role that includes certain specific tasks. Children learn to submerge individual interest to conform to rules and role expectations.

At the *post-conventional level*, a person moves beyond the norms and laws of a society to determine universal good—that is, what is good for all societies. Few people reach this level, and their actions are observably different from the majority. For instance, Mahatma Gandhi might be described as having a post-conventional morality. He acted in accordance with his belief in a higher order of morality. At this level of moral development, the individual assumes the responsibility of judging laws and conventions. In Figure 4.2, the six stages are illustrated.

Kohlberg advanced the possibility of a seventh stage, which has been described as a "soft" stage of ethical awareness with an orientation of cosmic or religious thinking. It is not a higher level of reasoning, but is qualitatively different. According to Kohlberg, in this highest stage individuals have come to terms with questions such as "Why be just in a universe that is largely unjust?" This is a different question than the definition of justice that forms the content of the other stages. In this stage, one sees oneself as part of a larger whole, and humanity as only part of a larger cosmic structure. This stage focuses on *agape*—a nonexclusive love and acceptance of the cosmos and one's place in it (Kohlberg, 1983; Power and Kohlberg, 1980).

Kohlberg has been criticized for focusing too much on the concept of justice, ignoring other aspects of morality. In fact, it is argued that the way he defines moral development is culturally biased, reflecting only Judeo-Christian concepts of morality. He has also been criticized for focusing too much on rational thinking as opposed to emotional aspects of morality (Levine, Kohlberg, and Hewer, 1985: 99). There has also been research that indicates the stages are not necessarily invariant or form a coherent explanation for people's moral beliefs (Boyce and Jensen, 1978; Bandura, 1991: 49).

Kohlberg's moral stages The view that moral development is hierarchical; each higher developmental stage is described as moving away from pure egoism toward altruism.

FIGURE 4.2 Kohlberg's Moral Stages	
Pre-conventional Level: Egoistic	*Stage 1* has a punishment and obedience orientation. What is right is that which is praised; what is wrong is that which is punished. The child submits to an authority figure's definition and is concerned only with the consequences attached to certain behaviors, not with the behavior itself.
	Stage 2 has an instrument-and-relativity orientation. The child becomes aware of and is concerned with others' needs. What is right is still determined by self-interest, but the concept of self-interest is broadened to include those who are within the child's sphere of relationships. Relationships are important to the child, and he or she is attached to parents, siblings, and best friends, who are included in the ring of self-interest. There is also the emerging concept of fairness and a recognition that others deserve to have their needs met.
Conventional Level: Fitting into Society	*Stage 3* has an interpersonal concordance orientation. The individual performs conventionally determined good behavior to be considered a good person. The views of "significant others" are important to self-concept. Thus, individuals will control their behavior so as to not hurt others' feelings or be thought of as bad.
	Stage 4 has a law-and-order orientation. The individual is concerned not just with interpersonal relationships but also with the rules set down by society. The law becomes all-important. Even if the laws themselves are wrong, one cannot disregard them, for that would invite social chaos.
Post-conventional Level: Transcending Society	*Stage 5* has a social contract orientation. The person recognizes interests larger than current laws. This individual is able to evaluate the morality of laws in a historical context and feels an obligation to the law because of its benefits to societal survival.
	Stage 6 centers on universal ethical principles. The person who has reached this stage bases moral judgments on the higher abstract laws of truth, justice, and morality.

Source: Kohlberg, 1984.

Another criticism is that Kohlberg's research can be described as sexually biased because he interviewed only boys in early research. Carol Gilligan (1982, 1987), one of Kohlberg's students, researched an apparent sex difference in moral reasoning and proposed that women may possess a morality *different* from men. Most men, it seems, analyze moral decisions with a rules or justice orientation (Stage 4), whereas many women see the same moral dilemma with an orientation toward needs and relationships (Stage 3). Gilligan labeled this a *care perspective*. A morality based on the care perspective (which is similar to the ethics of care system described in Chapter 2) would be more inclined to look at how a decision affects relationships and addresses needs, whereas the justice perspective is concerned with notions of equality, rights, and universality.

In Gilligan's study, although both men and women raised justice and care concerns in responses to moral dilemmas, among those who focused on one or the other, men focused exclusively on justice, whereas half of the women who exhibited a focus did so on justice concerns and the other half on care concerns (Gilligan, 1987). She also found that male and female respondents alike were able to switch from a justice perspective to a care perspective (or back again) when asked to do so; thus, their orientation was more a matter of perspective than an inability to see the other side. What Gilligan points out in her research is that the care perspective completely drops out when one uses only male subjects—which is what Kohlberg did in his early research for the moral stage theory.

In later studies, researchers have found small or no differences between men and women using stage scoring. The type of ethical dilemma seems to be important with dilemmas involving interpersonal relationships bringing out care concerns more than others (Jaffee and Hyde, 2000; Rothbart, Hanley, and Albert, 1986; Flanagan and Jackson, 1987; Walker, 1986; Thoma, 1986; Loo, 2003). Other research has found that moral orientations showed no stability over time or circumstance (Jaffee and Hyde, 2000).

There also seems to be mixed evidence of a correlation between moral stage scores and behavior (Lutwak and Hennessy, 1985). Almost all studies of moral development utilize measures of moral judgment derived from Kohlberg's research. The more involved method is to interview subjects and code their responses into Kohlberg's moral stages, however, this method is time-consuming and expensive, and therefore, paper-and-pencil tests have been developed. These so-called "**recognition tests**" require the subject merely to recognize and identify certain moral principles and agree with them. The most common is Rest's DIT (Defining Issues Test). Recognition tests may be less helpful in predicting behavior than "production" measures, which require the subject to actually reason through a dilemma and provide some rationale, but they have the advantage of cost effectiveness (Gavaghan, Arnold, and Gibbs, 1983; Aleixo and Norris, 2000).

recognition tests
Paper-and-pencil tests that measure an individual's ability to recognize and/or agree with moral terms.

Using these measures of morality, research has been accumulating as to what attributes are associated with higher scores on ethical reasoning. Although findings seem to be mixed, some correlates seem to be emerging. Strength of religious belief (but not necessarily church attendance) and being female have been observed as being correlated with higher scores and, to some extent, ethical behavior. Some research has also found older individuals have higher scores on measures of morality. In studies on college campuses, it has been found by some researchers that business students exhibit lower scores on measures of ethics than other majors. Also, some studies do find moral development and actions to be correlated (Greenberg, 2002; Seiler, Frischer, and Ooi, 2010; Ashkanasy, Windsor, and Trevino, 2006). Lau and Haug (2011), for instance, found that ethical beliefs were related to cheating in a college sample. In another study, "honesty scores" for people in three organizations were compiled from an attitudinal questionnaire about beliefs. It was found that the organization with the highest average honesty score had the least employee theft, and the organization with the lowest average honesty score had the most employee theft (Adams, 1981).

In contrast, other studies have found no correlation between ethical beliefs and behavior. In a study of clinical psychology students, only 37 percent indicated that they would actually do the ethically correct act that they identified as the correct response in an ethical dilemma (reported in Verges, 2010: 499). Thus, it appears that many people can identify the ethical choice, but they do not necessarily follow through and do the right thing when faced with a dilemma. It is possible that the reason the gap exists between belief and behavior is the disjunction between System 1 (emotional,

ETHICAL DILEMMA

You are a well-respected professional, successful in your field due to years of hard work. Your brother is a high-level mobster, responsible for perhaps dozens of murders and about to be indicted on felony counts of murder, extortion, and a range of other crimes. He also has been an informant for the FBI for over 10 years, providing them information that resulted in the arrests of his competitors. Right before he is arrested, he disappears. Now the FBI wants you to help them find him. You refuse. The fallout of your refusal threatens your reputation and livelihood. Would you cooperate to help catch him? Alternatively, change the scenario to a brother who is brilliant but seems to be increasingly disturbed. He then disappears. One day you see the newspaper has published a "manifesto" from the Unabomber, a mysterious figure who has sent 16 bombs through the U.S. mail, killing three people and injuring dozens. You recognize the letter as very probably written by your brother and have a strong suspicion that he is the Unabomber. Would you go to the FBI with your suspicions?

Law

There is no law that requires uninvolved relatives to help law enforcement catch their criminal siblings. As long as one has not aided, abetted, or encouraged crime, or assisted in a flight from justice, there is no legal duty to assist law enforcement's efforts to capture loved ones who are suspected of crimes.

Policy

Since these individuals are not making a decision as employees of an organization, there are no policy issues involved.

Ethics

In both of these dilemmas the values of loyalty and love are weighed against public safety and justice. The first scenario reflects the situation faced by William Bulger, who was president of the University of Massachusetts and forced to resign when he refused to help capture his infamous brother, James "Whitey" Bulger. The second is the dilemma of Ted Kaczynski's brother David, who did go to the FBI, an act that led directly to the capture of the Unabomber. These two brothers saw their ethical duties differently. Are there differences between the two situations that would lead to a different decision, or was it simply two different people resolving a similar dilemma in a different way? Our emotional reaction no doubt is "family first"; however, David Kaczynski's actions very probably saved lives. After rationally applying utilitarianism, it seems one would support sacrificing one's criminal brother for the safety and security of others. Ethical formalism would probably also support such actions. Ethics of care, on the other hand, would attempt to resolve the situation by trying to meet the needs of all, for instance, by brokering a deal for the brother to give up in return for something that was needed. This is what Kaczynski's brother attempted to do, possibly saving his brother from the death penalty.

impulse-based) and System II (rational, deliberate) decision making described earlier. In the featured dilemma, the right thing to do is not easily determined and may depend on whether one's focus is more in line with rational decision making or emotional relationship-based decision making.

To summarize: individual explanations of behavior include biological (e.g., oxytocin receptors) and psychological (e.g., modelling or moral development stage) explanations. There is strong evidence that both rational and emotional components to decision making exist when one is faced with an ethical dilemma. There is also mixed research as to whether individuals' beliefs and values predict their behavior. Research has found that people may believe the right thing to do is one thing and act in a different way entirely. Part of the reason for this may lie in external influences. Read the news story here and determine whether individual explanations of behavior or workgroup and organizational explanations, which we will discuss in the following section, better explain the actions described.

((·)) IN THE NEWS | Corruption in the County

Hidalgo County is a border county in Texas. Corruption is, if not endemic, certainly pervasive if one considers that former Hidalgo sheriff Brig Marmolejo served time in prison for his participation in drug-related crimes. The former sheriff of neighboring Cameron County, Conrado Cantu, was sentenced to 24 years in prison without parole for accepting bribes from drug traffickers and laundering drug money. More recently former sheriff Lupe Trevino was convicted of money laundering for taking money from a major drug trafficker and sentenced to five years in prison.

His son, Jonathan Trevino, was also convicted of a number of crimes and sentenced to 17 years in prison after a secret federal investigation proved that he was the recruiter and organizer of a band of law enforcement officers who took protection money from drug dealers to escort them through the county in marked police cars, and then robbed them of their drugs and money. The Panama Unit was a narcotics task force made up of deputies from the sheriff's department and officers from the Mission Police Department. The sheriff's son was appointed head of the unit when he was 23 and barely out of the academy. Young Trevino surrounded himself with close friends to fill out the unit. At one bust in 2010, unit members confiscated $50,000 and, realizing no one would find out, took the money home and split it up rather than submit it as evidence. From there, they begin to steal both money and drugs from those they busted, and, eventually, instead of investigating drug dealers to arrest them, the group identified dealers to rob.

A narcotics investigator was approached in 2012 by members of the Panama Unit because of his success in identifying and arresting drug dealers. He thought they wanted to work with him to achieve arrests, but they told him they weren't interested in arrests, they wanted the drugs. Instead of joining the rogue unit he went to the DEA who referred him to the FBI. He wore a wire for six months to obtain evidence. He had heard rumors of their activities before and Jonathan Trevino appeared to be invulnerable because of being the sheriff's son. Their activities became so brazen that there was a rumor that Hidalgo County deputies were going to be shot because too many drug dealers had been robbed by the crew and the cartel heads didn't know who they were, only that they were deputies. Before the investigation was over, the cooperating detective was under investigation by internal affairs himself after a source alleged he was the mastermind of some home invasions. He assumed he was being set up in case the Panama Unit members were exposed. Even after the indictments came down for Jonathan Trevino and the Panama Unit's members, due partially to the evidence obtained from him, internal affairs pursued him. He argued it was because the sheriff was retaliating for exposing his son to prosecution. He was also moved out of the detective position he had held back into patrol. Sheriff Trevino denied the charge that he was retaliating and declared he could move deputies anywhere he wanted. The investigator then brought a whistleblower lawsuit against the sheriff's department. Others in the department had filed another civil lawsuit alleging that Sheriff Trevino terminated them in retaliation for not working on his reelection campaign. Other claims alleged that he did not base promotions on test scores or seniority once he won the sheriff's position, but instead, promoted people who were well connected politically. At one point, there had been talk of Lupe Trevino running for Congress because he was so popular and powerful in Hidalgo County. Talking to a reporter after he was convicted of money laundering, he said he was in prison only because of the notoriety of his son.

Sources: Maril, 2014; Del Bosque, 2013a; Del Bosque, 2013b; Bells, 2015.

Workgroup and Organizational Influences

Any organization is made up of individuals who each have their own fairly well-established ethical and value systems. It is also the case, however, that individuals sometimes behave in ways that are contrary to their belief systems and/or their belief systems may change when exposed to external influences. Bandura (2002) sees social and moral maturity as constantly changing and reacting to outside influences, including family, peers, and social institutions. These external influences affect our ethical decision making even into adulthood. In this section, we will focus specifically on the work group and organization.

Bandura believed that individuals developed their moral identity through reinforcement, the development of empathy, and strengthening one's self-regulatory ability (self-control). He argues, however, that this self-regulation can be "turned off," leading to inhumane acts, through cognitive restructuring via several different mechanisms. Many of these mechanisms are most powerful in a small group setting, which is why workgroup influences on ethical decision making must be examined. Bandura's mechanisms are described as follows (1990, 1991, 2002):

- *Moral justification.* This is an appeal to a higher or more important end to justify the act (e.g., terrorists who are fighting for a cause). Similar to utilitarianism, the idea here is that the end justifies the means.

- *Euphemistic labeling.* By using words that downplay the seriousness of actions, the true moral nature of such actions is ignored (e.g., sanitizing language, such as "wasting" or "whacking" instead of killing, and the term "collateral damage" for killing civilians in times of war).

- *Advantageous comparison.* This is an argument that the action may be wrong, but it isn't as bad as some other actions (e.g., "What was done at Abu Ghraib wasn't as bad as the actions of insurgents who cut off the heads of civilian contractors").

- *Displacement of responsibility.* This argument basically removes the individual as a free-thinking agent of his or her own actions in order to deny culpability (e.g., "I was only following orders" or "I had to do it because the rules say so.").

- *Diffusion of responsibility.* In this situation, the individual can redefine his or her responsibility for an action by diffusing it among a number of people (e.g., mob action, or the observation that "everyone is doing it").

- *Disregard or distortion of the consequences.* By misidentifying the consequences of one's actions, one can deny one's responsibility for harm (e.g., when a criminal says "the insurance will take care of it," or a prosecutor excuses misconduct by a belief that all defendants are guilty).

- *Dehumanization.* Humans feel the most sympathy/empathy for those who are most like us and who are closest to us, and we feel the least for those who are most unlike us. Therefore, dehumanization is a process to strip the victim of any qualities of similarity that may create sympathy (e.g., the use of terms such as *gooks, slant-eyes, pigs, wetbacks*, and other dehumanizing references; in policing, there are a large number of terms used against citizens in high-crime neighborhoods whether or not they are actually offenders, for example, *mopes, thugs, low-lifes*).

These should sound familiar to criminology students because they hold much in common with Sykes and Matza's (1957) techniques of neutralization. These mechanisms were described as being used by juvenile delinquents to excuse or justify their delinquency, and included: the denial of responsibility (placing blame on the other party), the denial of injury (the action does not actually harm anyone), the denial of victim (the victim wasn't harmed or deserved it), the condemnation of the condemners (rejecting the judgers), and the appeal to higher authorities (end justifies the means thinking or loyalty to a deviant group).

Bandura argues that it takes a certain constellation of conditions to create human atrocities, not necessarily "monstrous" people (Bandura, 1991: 89). Also, he purports that the shift to immoral acts and attendant justifications is probably gradual, not immediate. The important point to note is that inhibitions are lessened when there is social support for inhuman acts; that is, an individual in a workgroup that generates some of these mechanisms (e.g., dehumanization or moral justification) has a much stronger probability of engaging in unethical behavior than someone who does not have that influence. Bandura also noted though that external conditions are not all-powerful; the individual adapts and reinterprets them within his or her own internal cognitive processes (Bandura, 2002). In the news box below, the actions of Jon Burge and his subordinates can arguably be explained by Bandura's moral disengagement theory.

(⬥) IN THE NEWS | *Jon Burge and the Midnight Crew of Area 2*

The actions of Jon Burge and his infamous midnight crew that operated out of Area 2 in Chicago in the 1980s is definitely out of the shadows. Mayor Rahm Emmanuel has authorized a $5.5 million "reparations" fund to compensate Burge's victims. This money will be paid by Chicago taxpayers in addition to the estimated $100 million that has been paid in settlements and lawsuit judgments related to Burge's use of torture to obtain false confessions. Eric Caine, for instance, spent 25 years in prison for a 1986 double murder. He was implicated by Aaron Patterson who confessed after being beaten by Burge. Caine also confessed after being hit so hard in the head that his eardrum was ruptured. Both men's confessions were eventually thrown out and prosecutors dropped the charges. They joined a growing number of exonerated who were tortured by Burge and his men until they confessed to crimes. Some of those tortured by Burge and his men did commit the crimes they were accused of; but others did not and confessed only to stop the torture. Patterson and Caine were released after spending decades in prison. Caine won a $10 million judgment in 2013.

For many years, no one in authority believed the stories that defendants were telling about why they confessed to crimes they did not commit. Even defense attorneys had a hard time believing that in a police precinct, police officers would beat individuals so badly that they damaged internal organs. Some were choked to the point of unconsciousness, others were handcuffed to a hot radiator so that their bodies would be burned. Still others were subjected to electric shocks and others were subjected to Russian Roulette.

There is an argument that city officials are anxious to describe the situation as entirely the fault of one deviant detective, but the sheer number of cases and the prevalence of the activity indicate it was a systemic problem, at least in Area 2. Other detectives have been named by the exonerated, including Kenneth Boudreau who has been implicated in a dozen cases where confessions have been thrown out, and Ray Guevara, who has been accused of beating suspects, falsely translating statements of Spanish-speaking suspects, and threatening witnesses with criminal charges if they did not say what he wanted them to say. In 2009, a federal jury awarded $21 million to Juan Johnson after finding Guevara intimidated and threatened witnesses to get them to testify against Johnson, who spent more than 11 years in prison until he was acquitted in a retrial. Guevara invoked his Fifth Amendment right in a retrial of Armando Serrano and Jose Montanez after a witness recanted and swore that Guevara intimidated him into falsely accusing the two.

Still, it seems to be Burge that is at the center of the most cases, including James Kluppelberg. Kluppelberg was freed after spending 24 years in prison on a wrongful conviction in an arson murder case that killed 28-year-old Elva Luperio and her five children. Four years after the fire, a suspect falsely tied Kluppelberg to the arson to avoid prison time and police arrested him even though they already had a potential suspect. A woman, who was convicted of setting another fire shortly before the arson-murder, admitted she "may have set" the blaze but couldn't remember because she was intoxicated. Detectives withheld this information from Kluppelberg and prosecutors. Kluppelberg claims in a lawsuit that police beat him until he falsely confessed to the crime.

Chicago taxpayers also paid $12.3 million to Ronald Kitchen and Marvin Reeves, who spent more than two decades in prison for the 1988 murders of five because of their false confessions and the testimony of a jailhouse informant who lied. In this case, as in others, the city settled before the plaintiffs could force former mayor Richard Daley to testify. He was the Cook County State Attorney and then mayor during the time period that Burge and his Area 2 subordinates used their tortuous methods to obtain confessions. Some argue that he is culpable because he failed to investigate police torture allegations against Burge and allegedly participated in a conspiracy to cover it up.

Finally, in 2006, a special prosecutor's report concluded that Burge and others in Area 2 had indeed tortured criminal suspects for two decades. The investigation uncovered dozens of cases—some where the individuals were still in prison. More recently, Daniel Yellon, dean of Loyola Law School, has been appointed by a federal judge to review cases for evidence of wrongful convictions that are connected to Burge if the defendants are still serving prison sentences. The review covers over 100 cases. Those that are potential wrongful convictions will be assigned to private attorneys.

Burge was convicted in 2010—but only of perjury and obstruction of justice for lying in a federal civil case. He testified that he knew nothing of the torture and did not participate in any actions described and, thus, was subsequently charged and convicted for his lie. Since the statute of limitations for more serious charges had long run out, he could not be charged for any of the abuse that took place. He was sentenced to four years in federal prison and was recently released. He still receives his $4,487 a month pension and won a court case when the city attorney tried to overturn the police pension board's decision to allow him to keep it despite the fact that, considering all the settlements and lawsuit judgments that have occurred thus far, he has cost the city in excess of $100 million and, considering the number of pending lawsuits as the wrongfully convicted win their release, that number will go much higher.

As stated above, Mayor Rahm Emmanuel and the city council have also approved a $5.5 million reparation fund for Burge's victims. Each will get up to $100,000 in addition to any civil judgment they receive, and they and their children will receive free tuition at city colleges. According to the city attorney who negotiated the plan: "We do this not because it's required legally. It is not. We do it because we think it's the right thing to do—for the victims, their families and the city."

Sources: Spielman, 2013; Meisner, 2013; Shelton, 2013; Spielman, 2013; Shaw, 2014; Korecki, 2014; Schmadeke, 2015; Mills, 2015.

Others besides Bandura have explained how individuals may engage in unethical behavior. Bazerman and Tenbrunsel (2011) present the concept of **bounded ethicality**. This refers to the cognitive structuring whereby decisions are interpreted using variables that do not include ethics; often in the context of a group decision-making process. For instance, in the infamous Ford Pinto case, where the automobile company's executives estimated that it would be less costly to pay a few wrongful death lawsuits than issue a recall, the decision making was purely economic without any consideration given to the morality of knowing some victims would die because of the faulty design. In some decision making, **ethical fading** occurs whereby the ethical ramifications of the decision choices may be addressed initially, but, over time, become removed from the decision-making process. These forces are incredibly powerful when operating as group influences and could account for the atrocities that were committed in the name of justice described in the In the News box about Jon Burge and his fellow detectives.

Another important concept Bazerman and Tenbrunsel (2011) discuss is "motivated blindness," which occurs when there are real and substantial pressures to ignore ethical issues. For instance, mortgage brokers who approved mortgages for people who could not afford them leading to the 2007–2008 recession, Arthur Anderson

bounded ethicality
This concept refers to the cognitive structuring whereby decisions are interpreted using variables that do not include ethics; for instance, companies evaluate decisions based only on economic factors rather than whether or not the action is moral.

ethical fading
This concept refers to the situation whereby decision makers, who might have initially questioned whether an action was ethical or not, over time drop that element of the discussion and concentrate on other factors so that the decision is eventually made without taking into consideration whether it is ethical or not.

auditors who did not report Enron's creation of phony subsidiaries to hide debt, and fund managers who sent their client's money to Bernard Madoff's impossibly lucrative investment fund, which turned out to be a Ponzi scheme, all profited from ignoring the ethical red flags of their behavior. More recently, in 2014, schedulers at Veterans Administration hospitals and medical centers were found to be entering false data regarding the time it took to see a doctor because of supervisor pressure and incentives to stay within timelines. Even though it was taking veterans six months to see doctors, records showed only weeks (by changing the date of the request) to bolster the ratings of the facility. Similarly, teachers and administrators in Atlanta were convicted of felony tampering charges in 2015 due to their cheating on student test results, arguably because they would face negative consequences if their schools were found to be low achieving.

Motivational forces can operate on a micro-level within small work groups or on the organization as a whole. Formal incentives (such as bonuses and quotas) typically occur at an organizational level. Organizations that desire to improve ethical decision making among workers need to review their reward systems. Do they reward unethical behavior unintentionally by focusing only on numbers and quotas? Are the messages about "how" to achieve goals ethically as powerful as the messages about what goals to achieve? Are there compliance systems in place to monitor worker's behavior, not just measures of productivity? While compliance systems have multiplied in response to ethical scandals, ironically there is some indication, at least in business settings, that they may increase rather than decrease unethical behavior. The reason seems to be that compliance systems create the perception that it is a mere rule-breaking issue as opposed to one's moral identity that is impacted by unethical behavior in the workplace (Bazerman and Tenbrunsel, 2011).

Ethical Climate and Organizational Justice

A growing body of research explores the ability to measure the "ethical climate" of an organization. The Ethical Climate Questionnaire (ECQ) includes questions regarding respondents' perceptions of how they (and other workers) behave and/or believe in regard to a range of ethical behaviors. Research shows that leadership, the reward structure, and organizational messages affect the ethical climate (Victor and Cullen, 1987; Mulgan and Wanna, 2011). Victor and Cullen (1988) discovered that there are significant differences in ethical climates even within one organization. These researchers identified theoretical scales indicating the primary vehicle of decision making as the following: self interest, company profit, efficiency, friendship, team interest, social responsibility, personal morality, company rules/procedures, and laws/professional codes. They also identified three basic ethical orientations: egoism, benevolence (utilitarianism), and principle (ethical formalism). In their research, these theoretical scales were tested and results showed the strongest, most robust scales could be described as: caring, law/code, rules, instrumental (egoism), and independence. They did find that strong differences emerged between companies in the ethical climate scores of employees. They also found that job level in organizations also showed significant differences in their ethical climate scores.

Other researchers have used the ECQ to find that ethical climate does affect work behavior; in stores where employees scores showed high levels of instrumentality (egoism), their scores of negative hypothesized behavior were also higher (they were given "what would you do?" scenarios). Correspondingly, stores where employees' aggregate scores were higher on caring, service, law/code, and independence showed lower negative behavior scores (Wimbush, Shepard, and Markham, 1997).

Other research shows that a strong ethics program results in less pressure to perform unethical acts, less misconduct, and less retaliation against whistleblowers. In the National Business Ethics Survey, it was found that among the businesses with the strongest ethics programs, 30 percent of respondents reported unethical behavior, but in the organizations with the weakest programs, fully 89 percent of employees reported misconduct (Hopkins, 2013). Gardner (2007), among many others, reports that organizations which express and enforce a strong ethical code (e.g., product quality or fairness for the customer) are also likely to have ethical workers. Others discuss how the organizational culture (i.e., rituals, myths, symbols, anecdotes, informal codes of conduct) reinforce ethics (or counteract a formal ethics code) (Jondle, Ardichvili, and Mitchell, 2014).

As mentioned in the last chapter, procedural justice involves the belief that one is being treated fairly by justice professionals. In management science, the same concept is called organizational justice, which refers to the idea that workers feel they are being treated fairly in the organization. Perceptions of a lack of organizational justice lead to negative behaviors, and perceptions of the presence of organizational justice lead to positive employee behaviors, including what has been called organizational citizenship behaviors (OCB). These refer to employee discretionary behaviors that are not required but contribute to the health of the organization (Katz, 1964; Bateman and Organ, 1983). According to Tyler (2011), these extra-role behaviors are normally not influenced through instrumental means, such as rewards and sanctions.

While the vast bulk of organizational justice research has occurred in the private/profit sector, there has been research conducted in criminal justice organizations. Lambert (2003), for instance, in various studies with colleagues, found that distributive (outcome) and procedural justice perceptions had significant positive effects on job satisfaction, but only perceptions of procedural justice was related to organizational commitment; both dimensions of organizational justice were related to job stress and organizational commitment, but only procedural justice influences job satisfaction (Lambert, Hogan, and Allen, 2006; Lambert, Hogan, and Griffen, 2007).

De Angelis and Kupchik (2007) found that when police officers perceived departmental investigations of citizen complaints were conducted in a fair and objective manner, they had a positive attitude toward the department, regardless of the outcome in the investigation. Shane (2012) found officers were more likely to perceive that the disciplinary process was fair when supervisory discretion was reduced by utilizing a disciplinary matrix for disciplinary outcomes. Reynolds and Hicks (2014), in a small, phenomenological study, found that unfair policies create perceptions of uncertainty among officers, making them question their status within the department; officers focused more on the fairness of procedures (procedural justice) rather than the actual outcome (distributive justice), and fair treatment was interpreted by the officers as the department could be trusted and that they were valued by the administration.

Farmer, Beehr, and Love (2003) found that both distributive (outcome) and procedural (interactional) perceptions of justice were positively related to officers' job performance, job satisfaction, and organizational commitment. Wolfe and Piquero (2011) found that officers who perceived that organizational procedures were fair were less likely to engage in police misconduct (measured by self-reports). In addition, favorable perceptions of organizational justice were related to a lower likelihood of adhering to the code of silence. Harris and Worden (2014) found that when officers perceived a disciplinary system as harsh or unfair, it led to negative police behaviors. This area of research is still developing and studies use a variety of measures for relevant constructs making synthesis of findings difficult.

The problem with much of this research is that it measures the organization as a whole. It seems clear that a worker's beliefs and feelings about the organization is related to but distinct from his or her supervisor, peers, or small workgroup (Lavelle, Rupp, and Brockner, 2007). For instance, Reynolds (2015), in his study of organizational justice in police departments, suggests that officers' perceptions of the fairness of supervisors are distinct from perceptions of the organization as a whole. As noted in the Jon Burge case described in the In the News box on p. 98, the activities of the "Midnight Crew" in Area 2 evidently did not extend to other divisions in the city. Recall that the city of Chicago attempted to rescind Burge's pension. Due process required that the pension board make the decision, and they refused to rescind the pension despite the fact that the taxpayers of Chicago will be paying Burge's pension and the civil judgments brought against him by the wrongfully convicted. In the issue analysis below, this topic is explored more fully.

ETHICAL ISSUE

Should Public Servants Have Their Pensions Rescinded If They Have Been Found to Engage in Unethical and/or Illegal Behavior While Employed?

Law

There is nothing to prevent states and localities from passing pension forfeiture laws. Generally, these laws are aimed at elected officials rather than those hired or appointed as public servants. It is unlikely that they could be applied retroactively because of contractual obligations. Limiting the discussion to public servants, this would constitute a governmental deprivation that would require due process, for example, a pension review board to evaluate the forfeiture for example. The few states that have such laws typically limit the offenses for which a pension can be forfeited. (For more information, see: www.governing .com/blogs/view/gov-scandals-spur-action-on-pension-forfeitures.html.)

Policy

As long as pension forfeiture policies are transparent and applied equally and fairly to wrongdoers, there is no reason why they should not be put in place. In some instances, such as former governor Rod Blagojevich (convicted of bribery) and former assistant coach Jerry Sandusky (convicted of child molestation), the situation of a former public servant being in prison and still drawing a public pension seems ironic and unfair. Whether such forfeitures have a deterrent effect is another question. Since they seem to be either nonexistent or rarely employed, the deterrent effect is probably minimal.

Ethics

Are pension forfeitures ethical? As noted above, the deterrent effect is probably minimal which would be the utilitarian rationale for such policies. It is important to note that pensions do not only support the public servant who committed the unethical and/or illegal act, but also, his or her family; therefore, ethics of care would be concerned with the loss of support for spouses, dependent children, and other family members. Under ethical formalism, recall that in order for the policy to satisfy the categorical imperative, it would have to be fair regardless of who received the forfeiture. The major ethical concern would be that only some violators would have their pensions taken away.

Ethics Training

The number of ethics courses and compliance officers in business grew in response to the Enron fraud and bankruptcy scandal which prompted the Sarbanes-Oxley Act of 2002 that held CEOs responsible for the actions of their employees. The question is whether ethics training is effective. Kohlberg (1976) described the following as necessary for moral growth:

- Being in a situation where seeing things from other points of view is encouraged
- Engaging in logical thinking, such as reasoned argument and consideration of alternatives
- Having the responsibility to make moral decisions and to influence one's moral world
- Being exposed to moral controversy and to conflict in moral reasoning that challenges the structure of one's present stage
- Being exposed to the reasoning of individuals whose thinking is one stage higher than one's own
- Participating in creating and maintaining a just community whose members pursue common goals and resolve conflict in accordance with the ideals of mutual respect and fairness

Most professional schools today (in law, medicine, and business) require at least one class in professional ethics. Typically, these classes present the opportunity to examine the ethical dilemmas that individuals may encounter as members of that profession and help students discover the best way to decide ethical issues. Part of the task is to provide what might be called indoctrination to the values and codes of behavior of that profession. More general criminal justice ethics courses exist in college and university curriculums (this text is written for such a class). In law enforcement and corrections academy classes, ethics is part of the curriculum as well. According to Sherman (1982: 17–18), criminal justice ethics courses should "stimulat[e] . . . the moral imagination" by posing difficult moral dilemmas and encourage analytical skills and the tools of ethical analysis. Sherman also believed that such courses should elicit a sense of moral obligation and personal responsibility, and an understanding of the morality of coercion.

There are differences in focus and scope between ethics classes in a university or college environment and an ethics training course in a professional organization or academy; however, whether they are effective or not is a question that could be addressed for either venue. Most of the research focuses on business ethics. It also typically has only measured whether or not training results in a different level of moral beliefs—for instance, a higher moral stage score as measured by Rest's DIT or other paper-and-pencil test of ethical beliefs, not whether changes in behavior have occurred as a result of ethics training. It is obviously very difficult to study whether ethics training might influence actual behavior. Research to date has obtained mixed results, but findings indicate that training is more effective if it is longer (rather than shorter), involves participatory learning methods, and is tailored to the specific organization. It also seems to be the case that training has more impact on reasoning ability (Type II thinking) than on intuitive judgments of right and wrong (Type I thinking)

(Jones, 2009; Seiler, Fischer, and Ooi, 2010). Sekerka (2009) found that ethics training can affect and shape organizational culture and affects a positive perception of organization by employees. Antes et al. (2009), after a meta-analysis of ethics training, report that the overall effectiveness of ethics instruction is modest. Success is related to course content and delivery method. They report that content should include ethical decision making, problem solving, and ethical sensitivity, and stand-alone courses are more successful than attempting to insert ethics in other courses.

As noted, all the research reviewed thus far has occurred in business applications. The only studies of ethics training in law enforcement have been reviews of prevalence and content. Wyatt-Nichol and Franks (2010), using a survey of police chiefs, found that training was more often pre-service, mostly lecture and discussion, and usually four hours or less. The chiefs surveyed thought ethics training was important and believed that the focus should shift from rules to shared values and problem solving. Ethics classes covered off-duty conduct, falsifying reports, excessive use of force, use of position for private gain, failure to report others' misconduct, providing false testimony, gifts and gratuities, and using police property for private use.

Interestingly, Skogan, Van Craen, and Hennessy (2014) noted that there was a paucity of strong academic research directed to evaluations of training in police academies in general, much less any attempt to measure the effect of ethics training in particular. There have been a few studies that have employed procedural justice concepts in a training venue and then measured the effects of such training. Skogan et al. (2014) developed, implemented, and analyzed the effects of an eight-hour training session that was administered to Chicago police officers. The training was based on procedural justice concepts and delivered by academy trainers. A survey was developed to measure adherence to procedural justice concepts (neutrality, voice, respect, trust). This study found that police officers who went through the training increased adherence to procedural justice concepts, except for trust. Researchers also found that those officers who went through the training showed an enduring difference in adherence to procedural justice concepts compared to those who had not gone through the training.

Rosenbaum and Lawrence (2012; also see Schuck and Rosenbaum, 2011) presented findings from an evaluation of a 20-hour training unit included in the traditional academy instruction. The researchers were able to utilize a randomized control design with a control group of cadets going through traditional training. They were evaluated on both attitudinal measures and through a video assessment of their interactions with citizens. Results were mixed as to how well the training affected the officers' interactions with citizens using procedural justice concepts.

These evaluations were not directed to ethics training per se; however, procedural justice training does seem to be related to the concepts, values, and principles reflected in an ethics training course. It is interesting to note that virtually no research has been conducted on the intersection between organizational justice (how the officers perceive they are treated by the organization) and procedural justice (how officers interact with the citizenry).

Leadership

In October of 2014, Julia Pierson, the first female head of the Secret Service, stepped down after several scandals regarding the behavior of Secret Service agents became front-page news. No one accused her of being involved in the unethical activities or

(°) IN THE NEWS | *Not So Secret Scandal*

Whistleblowers testifying to a Senate committee reported that Secret Service agents and managers engaged in sexual misconduct in 17 different countries. Several years ago, Secret Service agents in the advance team preparing for President Obama's visit to Cartagena, Columbia, allegedly engaged in a night of heavy drinking and prostitution and didn't pay a prostitute resulting in an altercation in their hotel. More recently, two Secret Service supervisors were removed from the president's detail for sending sexually explicit e-mails to a female agent. Most recently two agents returned to the White House after a night of drinking and drove into a traffic barrier in the midst of a bomb investigation. It was reported that supervisors averted the imminent arrest of the driver. Observers noted both driver and passenger seemed to be intoxicated. The whistleblowers testifying to a congressional committee described an organization that seemingly tolerated a range of unethical behaviors, including heavy drinking, hiring prostitutes, having extramarital affairs with other agents, and sexual relationships with foreign nationals that were not properly reported.

Source: Leonnig, C. and Nakamaura, D. 2014.

engaging in any kind of cover-up; however, her resignation reveals the expectation that we have of leaders. If there is a culture of impropriety or a pattern of transgressions in any organization, we look to the leader for fault. The scandal is described more fully in the In the News box.

Coincidentally, in April of 2015 Michele Leonhart, the first female head of the Drug Enforcement Administration (DEA), stepped down for much the same reason when it was revealed that DEA agents had engaged in sex parties in Columbia paid for by drug cartel leaders. It was also revealed that some agents had received gifts of cash and guns from cartel affiliates and, during the parties, laptops and Blackberries with sensitive governmental information were left accessible to cartel members and potentially compromised (Johnson, 2015).

In any organization, there are those who will almost always make ethical choices, those who will usually make unethical ones, and those who can be influenced one way or the other. The best course of action is to reward those in the first group and identify those in the second group and encourage them to find other employment or at least remove them from temptation. Then organizational leaders must create an atmosphere for the third group that encourages ethical decision making. This can be done by promoting ethical administrators, rewarding morally courageous behavior, and providing clear and powerful organizational policies that emphasize worthwhile goals and honest means.

Trautman (2008) describes a "Corruption Continuum," which details how organizations can become corrupt through the actions of its leaders; specifically, (1) administrative indifference toward integrity, (2) ignoring obvious ethical problems, and (3) creating a hypocrisy- and fear-dominated culture, all leading to (4) a survival-of-the-fittest approach by individual employees (who will commit unethical acts to protect themselves).

Administrators and managers do not necessarily ensure that an organization will be free from corruption merely by not engaging in corrupt practices themselves; they must take affirmative steps to encourage ethical actions. Issues that could be examined in a discussion of ethical leadership include the practice of recruitment, training, discipline and reward structures, and evaluation of performance. Souryal (1992: 307) offers advice to leaders who would like to advance ethical decision making and emphasizes the importance of organizational support for ethical actions. Ethical leaders should do the following:

1. Create an environment that is conducive to dignified treatment on the job.
2. Increase ethical awareness among the ranks through formal and informal socialization.
3. Avoid deception and manipulation in the way officers are assigned, rewarded, or promoted.
4. Allow for openness and the free flow of unclassified information.
5. Foster a sense of shared values and incorporate such values in the subculture of the agency.
6. Demonstrate an obligation to honesty, fairness, and decency by example.
7. Discuss the issue of corruption publicly, expose corrupt behavior, and reward ethical behavior.

Metz (1990) offers a similar set of advice. He proposes that ethical administrators follow these steps:

1. Establish realistic goals and objectives.
2. Provide ethical leadership (meaning, set a moral tone by actions).
3. Establish formal written codes of ethics.
4. Provide a whistleblowing mechanism.
5. Discipline violators of ethical standards.
6. Train all personnel in ethics.

When top leaders take responsibility for their subordinates' behavior, they will lead and administer with greater awareness, interaction, and responsibility. Because of this responsibility, a supervisor or administrator must be concerned with how the workplace treats the worker, how the worker views the mission, and how the public views the organization. A strong ethical leader would have a personal relationship with subordinates—without showing favoritism. This personal relationship is the foundation of modeling, identification, and persuasive authority. Strong leadership involves caring and commitment to the organization. A strong leader is someone who is connected with others but also has a larger vision, if you will, of goals and mission.

Schafer's (2010a, 2010b) research on police leadership supports these concepts. In a survey of police managers attending an FBI national academy career development course, survey respondents identified ineffective leaders as possessing five acts of commission: a focus on self, ego/arrogance, closed-mindedness, micromanagement, and capriciousness; and five acts of omission: poor work ethic, failure to act, ineffective communication, lack of interpersonal skills, and a lack of integrity (Schafer, 2010a). He also looked at what was considered effective leadership. The strongest factor emerged as honesty and integrity (37 percent identified that as the first element of good leadership; 2010b: 651). Integrity, along with a work ethic, communication skills, and caring for the needs of employees were the most commonly agreed elements of good leadership. Finally, leaders must never lose sight of the organizational mission; for public servants, the mission is public service.

Societal and Cultural Influences

It is important to note that the organizational culture is subject to external influences. External influences are both objective (e.g., laws and regulations that constrain the organization) and normative (public belief systems). We see these external influences operating in for-profit organizations as well as public service organizations such as those in criminal justice. Messages filter from the public to the organization in terms of what will be tolerated and what will not be; for instance, our popular media glorified the Wall Street values of money as the sole measure of success until the bankruptcy of Enron, at which time public pressure on Congress led to the Sarbanes-Oxley Act, which put more accountability on CEOs of companies. The crash of 2008 led to public pressure for banking regulations, and there was a new Consumer Protection Agency created (although Congress has stalled and delayed funding it).

The message can also be "we don't care." For instance, when Tom Brady, star quarterback of the Patriots, was suspended for four games in May 2015, public sentiment was decidedly mixed with many, if not most, people winking at the rule violations of "Deflategate," seemingly taking the position that deflating the game balls was only a rule violation, "not a felony." If rule breaking is not considered serious by the public, you can be sure it will not be by organizational actors.

Because of the events in Ferguson, Missouri, and Baltimore, Maryland, there is currently a strong public backlash against police use of force, especially against minority men. Whether justified or not, this public sentiment has resulted and will continue to result in strong external pressure on police organizations to improve training, tighten up use-of-force policies, and improve discipline systems. The public pressure has also spurred discussion of behavioral constraints such as the use of body cameras, citizen review panels, and special prosecutors that may be imposed from the outside. We will discuss these events in more detail in the chapters to follow, but suffice it to say here that outside regulations such as laws that constrain and restrict public servants' behavior and pressure from the public and policymakers do have an impact on organizational culture, and, in turn, on the individual behaviors of the professionals in the organization. In each subsystem of the criminal justice system (police, courts, and corrections), we will examine individual, organizational, and systemic (cultural or societal) responses to unethical behavior.

WALKING THE WALK

Thomas Tamm grew up with the FBI in his blood. Both his father and uncle were highly regarded ranking officials in the bureau. His brother became an FBI agent. It is said that, as a child, Tamm played in J. Edgar Hoover's office. Thus, you would not have expected that in the early morning hours of August 1, 2007, a squad of heavily armed FBI agents would roust his family from bed with a search warrant, seizing his and his child's computers and other personal items. His alleged crime? He leaked the fact that the federal government was engaged in spying on its own citizens, against the laws of the land.

Tamm, like his relatives, had pursued a career in public service, as a prosecuting attorney in the Department of Justice. In his job with the Department of Justice's Office of Intelligence Policy and Review, he had access to highly classified wiretap transcripts of suspected terrorists. In 2004, he discovered evidence that the National Security Agency was gathering domestic intelligence illegally without going through the Foreign Intelligence Surveillance Court for warrants. At first, Tamm tried to use accepted channels to address the problem, but when superiors and others in the government did not seem to be interested in investigating the acts of illegal spying, he met with Eric Lichtblau, a *New York Times* reporter. The explosive story of illegal domestic spying won Lichtblau a Pulitzer Prize, raised the important question of the extent of presidential power, spurred Congress to change the Foreign Intelligence Surveillance Act to retroactively make the wiretapping legal so that the acts of the president would not be attacked as illegal, and left Tamm with a federal indictment over his head for divulging national secrets.

Tamm had been subject to increasing depression and anxiety after leaking the story and eventually resigned from the Department of Justice under a cloud of suspicion in 2006. After the investigation narrowed to him, 18 federal agents raided his house with guns drawn, terrifying his wife and small child. When he became the target of the investigation, he was pressured to plead guilty to one felony count of revealing classified information, but he refused.

Since then he has lived under a potential indictment, even though those who were involved in the illegal spying have been promised immunity for their actions. When asked why he did it, he responded, "I had taken an oath to uphold the Constitution." In 2009, he received the Ridenhour Truth-Telling Prize from the Nation Institute and Fertel Foundation (the honor is named for Ron Ridenhour, the soldier who was instrumental in bringing the My Lai massacre to the public's attention). In 2011, the Justice Department quietly dropped all charges against Tamm. Still, the cost to Tamm was high: He has lost his career, and in an interview after the charges were dropped, he indicated he was still in "dire financial straits." When interviewed, he said he would do it again: "Well, the oath that I took was to preserve and protect the Constitution of the United States against enemies foreign and domestic. . . . And I honestly thought I had an ethical obligation to talk to somebody about what I thought was an illegal abuse of executive authority."

Sources: Isikoff, 2008; Memmott, 2011.

Conclusion

This chapter shifted the focus from "What is ethical or moral?" to "Why do people act in ethical or unethical ways?" More specifically, we are interested in any findings that shed light on how to ensure that criminal justice professionals act ethically. Philosophers, religious scholars, biologists, psychologists, sociologists, and criminologists have all tried to explain why people do bad things. Biology, learning theory, and Kohlberg's moral stages were used to explain why people's ethical belief systems develop the way they do, but it was also noted that research finds that people's beliefs sometimes do not match their behavior. Philosophy, biology, and psychology all seem to be consistent in the theme that ethical decision making is both emotional and rational.

Research also shows that even adults can be influenced to change their beliefs and behavior given external influences. Bandura discusses moral disengagement and Bazerman and Tenbrunsel explain that bounded ethicality and ethical fading explain why some unethical behavior occurs. It is probable that these forces are more powerful in small work groups as opposed to the organization itself; however, the organization can incentivize unethical behavior unwittingly by rewarding goals over methods. This leaves the question for organizations how to best ensure ethical behavior by professionals and other employees in the organization. It seems clear that training alone is not sufficient and must be combined with ethical leadership.

Ethical leadership is absolutely essential for the ethical organization. Ethical leaders owe a duty to their employees to take responsibility for their own behavior and to create an environment conducive to employees acting ethically, which includes open communication and the use of fair and appropriate discipline. How criminal justice professionals perform their job determines whether justice is a reality or an illusion. The greatest protection against corruption of power is a belief in and commitment to the democratic process and all it entails. If one desires a career in criminal justice, one must ask these questions:

Do I believe in the Constitution?

Do I believe in the Bill of Rights?

Do I truly believe in the sanctity and natural right of due process?

If a person views these protections as impediments, nuisances, or irrelevant, that person should not be a public servant. In the Walking the Walk box presented on page 107, an individual's attempt to act on those beliefs is described.

In the next nine chapters, we examine the criminal justice system by allocating three chapters each to three areas of study: police, courts, and corrections. In Chapters 5, 6, and 7, we will discuss ethics as they relate to policing in the United States. Chapters 8, 9, and 10 are devoted to professionals in the court system. Chapters 11, 12, and 13 explore the ethics of correctional professionals. In each set of three chapters, we begin in the first chapter (Chapters 5, 8, and 11) with some overarching issues that relate to the profession itself, the formal ethics and mission of the professions described in those chapters, and any occupational subcultures that exist. In the second chapter in each set (Chapters 6, 9, and 12), the focus is on the discretion inherent in the roles related to that set and the dilemmas related to such roles. Finally, in the third chapter in each set (Chapters 7, 10, and 13), the parameters and prevalence of corruption and misconduct are described, along with measures that have been suggested to reduce them.

Chapter Review

1. **Be able to describe biological influences on the ethical behavior of criminal justice professionals, including major research findings.**

   Individual explanations include *biological theories*, which propose that we commit good or bad acts because of biological predispositions, which may be inherited or not. Attention has focused on brain chemicals, such as oxytocin, that influence behavior. Genetic traits may also be a factor. Biological sex differences may be an influence on men's and women's predisposition to crime and, also, unethical behavior. Research indicates that both the rational and emotion centers of the brain are implicated in ethical choices.

2. **Describe psychological theories that attempt to explain individual differences in behavior.**

   Learning theory argues that our behavior is based on the rewards we have received in our past. Albert Bandura's more sophisticated social learning theory presents the individual as an active participant in adapting and interpreting the rewards of his or her environment. Lawrence Kohlberg's *moral stage theory* explains that people's behavior is influenced by the intellectual and emotional stage of development and that one reaches or does not reach higher stages of development based on environmental factors. Kohlberg's theory proposes a hierarchy of moral stages, with the highest stage holding the most perfect moral principles, which are universal. Carol Gilligan found that women were more likely to have a Stage 3 relationship orientation to ethical judgments, while men were more likely to have a Stage 4 "law and order" orientation.

3. **Describe research that addresses work group influences on behavior.**

   Research indicates that adults can be influenced by peers and, especially, small groups in ethical decision making. Bandura's moral disengagement theory explained that individuals behaved ethically through self-regulatory mechanisms (conscience) but that these mechanisms could be "turned off" through cognitive restructuring using the following: moral justification (appealing to higher principles), euphemistic labeling (downplaying the seriousness of the act), making comparisons (arguing it isn't as bad as something else), displacing responsibility (arguing someone else is at fault), diffusion of responsibility (by acting in a mob), disregarding the consequences (acting in such a way to ignore the effect of one's action), and dehumanization (pretending one's victims are less than human).

4. **Become familiar with organizational influences on behavior.**

   In addition to small work groups, the organization itself can also affect ethical decision making of individuals. Reward structures, leadership, and training all can either incentivize or discourage unethical behavior. Research on organizational justice indicates that employees who perceive they are being treated fairly are more likely to engage in organizational citizenship behavior. Research on training and ethics programs indicate that they can be successful in affecting the level of unethical behavior in the workplace. According to Sam Souryal and other authors, leaders should create an environment that treats employees with dignity and respect, set realistic goals, increase ethical awareness through training and having a formal written code, avoid deception, allow for openness and transparency, foster a sense of shared values, present an example of honesty and fairness, expose corrupt behavior (and provide a whistle blowing mechanism) and reward ethical behavior.

5. **Become familiar with cultural and societal influences on ethical behavior.**

   The public can affect the ethical climate of an organization in what messages organizational leaders and members receive as to what will be tolerated and what will not be. When the public places more value on winning than sportsmanship in sports, organizations are more likely to break rules; when the public reelects politicians convicted of criminal transgressions, the message is received that the rules don't matter; and, when juries acquit officers in clear cases of illegal uses of force, it seems obvious that no change will occur in that city's pattern of police behavior. The public exerts power in pressuring legislators to enact laws and regulations, but also in the normative pressure displayed in public opinion.

Study Questions

1. Briefly explain how biological approaches might explain antisocial behavior. What are some differences between males and females noted by biological researchers? Explain modeling and reinforcement.

2. Explain Kohlberg's moral development theory. What problems do critics have with his theory? How does Carol Gilligan disagree with Kohlberg's stage theory?

3. Explain why behavior does not always conform with beliefs. Mention specifically bounded ethicality and ethical fading.

4. What necessary elements did Kohlberg identify for reaching higher moral stages?

5. What are some standards that can be applied to good leadership? What advice do Souryal and Metz offer to those who desire to be good leaders?

Writing/Discussion Exercises

1. Develop an essay on (or discuss) the development of morality. Who has been the greatest influence on your moral development? Why? How? Why do you think people behave in ways that hurt other people? Have you ever done something you knew to be wrong? Why did you do it?

2. Develop an essay on (or discuss) the relationships between morality, moral/ethical teaching, and criminality. Do thieves have the same moral beliefs as others? Do they know that stealing is wrong? Can we successfully predict which individuals will perform unethical or immoral actions?

3. Develop an essay on (or discuss) what an ideal ethical organization would be. What would be the characteristics of leadership? Training? Employees? How does one create such an organization as a change agent if the existing organization is rife with corruption?

Key Terms

bounded ethicality	Kohlberg's moral stages	recognition tests
developmental theories	modeling	reinforcement
ethical fading	moral identity	self-efficacy

ETHICAL DILEMMAS

Situation 1

You are a prosecutor trying your first case. You are thrilled with how well it is going. Every objection you make is upheld, and every objection the defense makes is overruled. The judge shakes her head affirmatively every time you make a point and scowls and makes disparaging comments about and to the defense attorney. As the trial proceeds, you begin to see that it is going so well not because of your legal expertise, but rather, because the judge is obviously and seriously biased against the defense. You do not know if she simply does not like the defense attorney or if she does this in all the trials, but you do know that she is making it extremely difficult for the jury to ignore her and, thus, is violating the due process rights of the accused. Should you be grateful for your good luck and accept an easy conviction or make a stand against the judge's actions?

Situation 2

You are a police officer assigned to the juvenile division. For the most part, you enjoy your job and believe that you have sometimes even made a difference when the juvenile has listened to you and stayed out of trouble (at least as far as you knew). One day you are told repeatedly by your captain to pick up a juvenile, even though you don't think there is any probable cause to do so. This is the third time you have been ordered to pick him up and bring him into the station. You discover that the detectives are trying to get the juvenile to become an informant because he is related to a suspected drug dealer. Should you participate in the attempt to intimidate him or refuse to do so?

Situation 3

Your partner has been on the force 25 years, and you value her opinion greatly. However, you have noticed that she has become progressively more lethargic and unenthusiastic about the job. When dispatch asks for available cars, she won't let you respond. When you see accidents on the highway, she instructs you to go around the block so that you won't have to stop. Even when you receive calls, she tells you to advise dispatch that you are otherwise occupied. You believe that she has become burned out and isn't performing up to the standard that you know she is capable of. What, if anything, would you do about it?

Situation 4

You are a rookie police officer and are riding with a field training officer (FTO). During your shift, the FTO stops at a convenience store and quickly drinks four beers in the back room of the store. He is visibly affected by the beers, and the smell of alcohol is noticeable. What should you do? What if the FTO had just written a favorable evaluation of you even though you should have received a reprimand for an improper disposition of a traffic accident?

Situation 5

You are a senior getting close to graduation and are taking too many classes during your last semester. You find yourself getting behind in class and not doing well on tests. One of the classes requires a 30-page term paper, and you simply do not have the time to complete the paper by the due date. While you are on the Internet one day, you see that term papers can be purchased on any topic. You ordinarily would do your own work, but the time pressure of this last semester is such that you see no other way. Do you purchase the paper and turn it in as your own?

5

The Police Role in Society

© Desiree Mueller / SuperStock

Police, 1928.

Oscar Grant, Levar Jones, John Crawford III, Tamir Rice, Michael Brown, Eric Garner, Walter Scott, Freddie Gray . . . some of these names are more familiar than others; all were black men (or boys) killed by police officers. It is not clear why the Michael Brown shooting in the summer of 2014 in particular triggered a national scrutiny of police officers' actions, but that shooting, followed by the Walter Scott and Freddie Gray killings have indeed sparked a national debate about the mission and actions of police across the country. Even though the impetus of the attention was an accusation that black men were the target of discriminatory policing and illegal uses of force, the conversation has become much wider with questions about police militarization, misconduct, and oversight mechanisms.

Perhaps one of the triggers for the broader focus on policing was the image of heavily armed police officers in armored vehicles responding to the protestors in Ferguson, Missouri, in

Chapter Objectives

1. Describe the two different missions of law enforcement in a democracy.

2. Explain the types of control that police have at their disposal.

3. Provide the justification for police power and the basic ethical standards that derive from this justification.

4. Identify the differences between the formal ethics of law enforcement and the values of the police subculture.

5. Describe recent research findings on the police subculture.

August 2014. This view of camouflage-clad police with guns pointed at the citizenry, using rubber bullets and stun grenades against the very people they are sworn to protect, resulted in an almost visceral negative reaction of Americans to the governmental show of force, sparking a second look at the issue of the "militarization" of American policing. National support for police deteriorated when a video emerged of an officer pointing an assault rifle at protestors. The attention led to his firing, perhaps wrongfully so, since he reported seeing firearms in the crowd and was pelted with water and urine immediately before he aimed his weapon yelling at the crowd "I will f—ing kill you. Get back" and telling journalists who asked for his name: "Officer Go F—Yourself." Other officers reportedly shot rubber bullets into nonviolent protestors and charged people with "failing to disperse" who were nowhere near the protests (Golgowski, Wagner, and Siem, 2014).

Since August 2014 there has been a steady stream of news stories, opinion pieces, and other media attention to the issue of use of force. Officer Darren Wilson was no-billed by a St. Louis grand jury for the shooting of Michael Brown, but this event only energized the debate as journalists educated the public regarding the number of people shot by police last year (about 460), the likely undercounting of those killings, the legal test of reasonableness for when an officer is allowed to use force, and the very unlikely event that an officer who shoots in error will face legal consequences (Mador, 2014).

The events in Ferguson spurred more concern than just over use of force. When it was revealed that the town's revenue was largely based on funds from petty arrests and fines, the ensuing discussion became how the criminal justice system has, in essence, "criminalized poverty" in that poor people who can't afford fines incur even heavier financial penalties for nonpayment, which then lead to jail sentences where, in some locales, they are charged for medical care and basic necessities that leave them with even more debt. These fines are usually for nonviolent petty offenses leading to a related discussion of "over-policing" (Mador, 2014). The Department of Justice report of Ferguson that came afterward showed not only a pattern of racism, but also of "classism" where friends of those in power had tickets fixed, while those without connections were slapped with ever-growing late fees. These larger issues go well beyond policing; however, it is police officers who have been the targets of media attention.

Police officers today no doubt feel attacked misunderstood, wrongfully blamed, and unappreciated. Harsh scrutiny is directed at police actions, and officers no doubt feel unfairly excoriated by the public and the media. However, there is an important reason for such scrutiny. The police represent the "thin blue line" between disorder and order. They are also the personification of the power of the state. No other criminal justice professional comes under as much constant and public scrutiny—but no other criminal justice professional wields as much power and authority over the citizenry.

Police have the choice to arrest or not to arrest, to mediate or to charge, and in decisions to use deadly force, they even hold the power of life and death. If such power is used fairly, legally, and ethically, they are our protectors. If such power is used abusively, arbitrarily, and/or in corrupt ways, they become our oppressors. In non-democratic countries, police are feared because they act with impunity to maintain those in power; in some areas of Mexico and South America, police are viewed as corrupted by the drug cartels. Abusive power and economic corruption exist in the United States as well, although, not in pervasive patterns as in some other countries. No doubt the scrutiny police officers endure helps to keep it that way.

In this chapter, we deconstruct the nature of policing and uncover some of the structural and historical precedents for current events. We first explore the dual mission of crime fighter and public servant and explain how the roles affect perceptions of duty and the way discretion is employed. The philosophical justification for police power is discussed, as well as the limits of such power. Codes of ethics followed by the informal, subcultural codes of behavior that also influence officer behavior complete the chapter.

In January of 2013, there were more than 12,000 police departments in the United States, employing an estimated 477,000 sworn officers and 128,000 non-sworn personnel. The number of law enforcement personnel has increased by about a third between 1987 and 2013. Even though there are a few extremely large police departments (New York City Police Department has over 34,000 officers), most police departments are very small with about 48 percent employing fewer than 10 officers. About 27 percent of all officers were members of a racial or ethnic minority, which is about double the percentage in 1987 (Reeves, 2015: 1-3). Because of the large differences between departments, it is extremely difficult to have a conversation about "policing" in this country. Most of the news stories concern corruption in large cities, but that does not mean that small towns do not have problems as well. There are also major differences in informal culture, policies, and discipline systems in departments even in cities of the same size.

As we discuss issues of law enforcement ethics in these chapters, it is important to remember that the vast majority of officers are honest and ethical. We focus on the few officers who abuse their position or forget their mission; however, this in no way should be taken as a criticism of the thousands upon thousands of officers who perform their job well, every day, in every city in the country. Nor should we forget the thousands of officers who go above and beyond the call of duty. Officers risk their lives to save victims, sacrifice their health and take time away from family to address the needs and problems of the citizenry. We must focus on the actions of the deviant few to discover the elements of the profession that open the door to such behavior, but we should always remember that the vast majority of officers are more typical of those described in the In the News box below.

((•)) IN THE NEWS | *Above and Beyond . . .*

It is important to remember amid the negative news about police officers that it is probably more common officers are engaged in going above and beyond their duties. One news item described how two Seattle police officers, Jeremy Wade and Ryan Gallagher, responding to a call, discovered that two little girls slept on the floor of the family's home. On their day off and using their own money, they bought a set of twin beds, returned and set up the beds for the family. Then, realizing that the problem was widespread, they set up the "Beds for Kids Project," which enlists sponsors and conducts fundraisers to provide beds for children in need. These officers, and their willingness to engage in supererogatory duties, represent the side of policing that is not presented in the media as often as it should be.

Source: Heffernan, 2014.

◼ Crime Fighter or Public Servant?

We will approach these chapters with an underlying premise that what drives individual decisions on the part of law enforcement officers and society's reactions to them is derived from a perception of the law enforcement mission. Two different missions—crime fighting and public service—can be identified as having quite different implications for decision making. We do not, of course, mean to say that these missions are necessarily contradictory or exclusive; however, it is important to note the history and present-day influence of these different roles.

Crime Fighter

When one asks most people what the role of policing is in society, the response is some version of "catch criminals" or "fight crime." If one views police as crime control agents, the presumption is that criminals (who are different from the rest of us) are the enemy and police officers are soldiers in a war on crime. This model is based on Herbert Packer's (1968) crime control model (which he contrasted with the due process model discussed next). According to Packer, the crime control model operates under the following principles:

1. Repression of criminal conduct is the most important function.
2. Failure of law enforcement means the breakdown of order.
3. Criminal process is the positive guarantor of social freedom.
4. Efficiency is a top priority.
5. Emphasis is on speed and finality.
6. A conveyor belt is the model for the system.
7. There is a presumption of guilt.

Police perception of their role as crime fighters will lead to certain decisions in their use of force, their definition of duty, and their use of deception and coercion. Public perception of the police mission as primarily crime fighting leads to a willingness to accept certain definitions and justifications of behavior: that drug addicts are unworthy of protection, that individuals who are beaten by police must have deserved it, that all defendants must be guilty, and so on.

Typically, members of the public who have a crime control outlook show outrage only when police accidentally violate the rights of the "good" guys instead of the "bad" guys: when the victim of deadly force turns out to be a middle-class insurance agent, when the evening news shows police officers hitting someone who doesn't look like a criminal, or when an innocent person is exonerated. In most cases, police actions are rationalized or excused by the belief that people "get what they deserve."

Public Servant

public servants
Professionals who are paid by the public and whose jobs entail pursuing the public good.

If one views police as **public servants**, presumptions are different and include the idea that criminals are not so different from us and, in fact, may be our sons or daughters. As public servants, police officers serve all people and owe everyone the duty of civility and legality. Finally, there is the idea that police actually have limited ability to affect crime rates one way or the other because crime is a complex social phenomenon.

Under Packer's (1968) due process model, the following principles stand out in contrast to those in the crime control model:

1.   There is a possibility of error.
2.   Finality is not a priority.
3.   There is insistence on prevention and elimination of mistakes.
4.   Efficiency is rejected if it involves shortcuts.
5.   Protection of process is as important as protection of innocents.
6.   The coercive power of the state is always subject to abuse.

Packer's original model of due process that he contrasted with his crime control model is somewhat different from our description of the public service mission. Rather than just an emphasis on rights as in the due process model, under the public servant model, law enforcement is perceived as "owned" by all people, so service is foremost. Police must respond to all constituencies, including groups that may be less supportive of the police than white middle-class communities. It is an enlarged view of the police officer role in society. Rather than simply catching criminals, officers are perceived to be crime preventers, peace keepers, and service providers.

A perception of the police officer as public servant implies a much more restrictive view of the use of force and police power. The utilitarian idea that the "end" (crime control) justifies almost any "means" is rejected in favor of an approach that is more protective of due process and equal protection. In the public service mission, law enforcement, above all, protects the rights of every citizen and—only in this way—escapes the taint of its historical role as a tool of oppression for the powerful.

Currently, there is a focus on moving the perception of policing from a "warrior" model to that of a "guardian." This is extremely consistent with the discussion above in that the warrior approach views police as soldiers engaged in a battle. The emphasis is on danger and force. The guardian model sees the officer as primarily a protector; of the citizenry, but also of democratic values. In academy training, the warrior mindset of power, control, battle, and survival is deemphasized with a greater focus on other values such as service and democracy (Rahr and Rice, 2015).

A precursor to the current national discussion of the warrior versus guardian model is the observation that police have become increasingly "militarized" over the last 30 years. Peter Kraska (an academic researcher) and Radley Balko (a journalist) are the two most prolific researcher/writers who have identified and discussed this trend. Kraska (1999, 2001, 2007; Kraska and Cubellis, 1997; Kraska and Kappeler, 1997; Kappeler and Kraska, 2014) has for decades noted with alarm the increasing number of Special Weapons and Tactics (SWAT) teams even while the crime rate declined dramatically, the use of SWAT teams for non-hostage situations (e.g., execution of search warrants), military imagery and training, and the merging of police officer/soldier role-sets.

Balko (2013a, b) has more recently achieved a much wider audience for the idea that policing has swung too far toward a military model with his book *The Rise of the Warrior Cop*, and his regular articles in the *Washington Post*. In his book, he described the origins of the SWAT model in Los Angeles, spurred by (then-inspector) Darryl Gates' belief that LAPD officers needed a military model to respond to events such as the Watts Riot and incidents with the Black Panthers. The SWAT team model became interconnected with the War on Drugs and drug raids. Now there are thousands of such squads in the United States (no one knows how many) conducting tens of thousands of raids each year. Federal agencies have their own SWAT teams—even the Department of Education has a SWAT team. These units use military tactics, including flash-bang grenades and battering rams. They are dressed in camouflage or black uniforms, often masked, and heavily armed. Because the crime rate is half what it was in the 1980s, there is little need for such units and critics point out that they are being used for increasingly inappropriate operations, such as licensing and gambling raids when there is no evidence that police officers will be met with force. An ACLU study found that 79 percent of SWAT team deployments were for executing a search warrant, and only 7 percent of deployments were for hostage, barricade, or active shooter scenarios (Peralta and Eads, 2015).

Balko (2013a) also focused on the dangers of the rise in the use of no-knock warrants and the dubious constitutional analysis extended by the Supreme Court in approving of heavily armed state agents bursting into private homes without announcing their presence. Balko provides a number of truly shocking examples where homeowners have been shot by police or have ended up in prison for shooting police officers whom they believed were armed intruders. Some of these raids were conducted on the wrong house against completely innocent homeowners; others were to execute arrest or search warrants for minor and/or nonviolent crimes. In one case, for instance, John Stewart, a military veteran with PTSD, was awakened by such a raid after his girlfriend reported he was growing marijuana. Believing he was under attack he fired and killed a police officer. Prosecutors sought the death penalty but Stewart hanged himself in his cell. Police found 16 marijuana plants in his basement. Other cases where SWAT raids resulted in needless death include Katherine Johnston, a 92-year-old woman killed in Atlanta in 2006; Alberto Sepulveda, an 11-year-old accidentally shot by a California SWAT officer in 2000 (Balko, 2013a); and, Aiyana Stanley-Jones, a 7-year-old shot in a Detroit raid where the SWAT team used a flash-bang grenade (perhaps to show off for the television crew that was accompanying them) and an officer accidentally discharged his weapon (Abbey-Lambertz, 2015).

Balko also was one of the first to draw attention to the 1033 program under which local police departments could receive military equipment no longer needed as the military ratcheted down its presence in Afghanistan and Iraq. Local departments now own armored vehicles, aircraft, and even grenade launchers, even if they have a homicide rate that is less than 1 per year (Apuzzo, 2014).

Balko (2014) urges a response to recent shootings by not faulting the individual officer, but by recognizing that officers today are socialized by their training and culture to be suspicious of all citizens and to be constantly wary of danger—even though that is not the reality of policing in many locales. He points to the shooting of Levar Jones by former South Carolina state trooper Sean Groubert after pulling him over for a seatbelt violation, and the shooting of John Crawford in a Walmart because he was carrying a BB rifle. Balko notes that Jones and Crawford were shot most probably because police officers were acting in conformance with their socialization that every black man is a potential threat and every day has a high probability of death—despite the falseness of these perceptions. Officers experience in-service "active shooter training," they see videos of officers killed in the line of duty, and they are exposed to a mindset that policing is getting more dangerous. It is not and police fatalities have declined since the mid-1990s. Studies indicate that in the years since the 1980s with the highest number of officer shootings, the risk of a traffic stop resulting in a shooting incident is about 1 in 4.6 million stops and the average risk is more like 1 in 10 million, but police officers are trained that traffic stops may result in violent shootouts, and a police supplier of law enforcement training targets sent targets appearing as children, pregnant women, and the elderly with the justification that they can be violent too (Balko, 2014). Balko (2014) also reports that some police officials feel that training has moved away from deescalation and conflict resolution, and instead, it teaches police officers how to legally justify force when it is used.

Since the events in Ferguson, the 1033 program has been the subject of criticism and, recently, it was announced that President Obama has issued an executive order restricting some of the types of military equipment (tracked armored vehicles, weaponized aircraft and high-caliber weapons) that can be distributed to local police departments (Peralta and Eads, 2015). This was in response to the disquieting realization that small town and university police departments possessed armored vehicles and grenade launchers. Grovum (2015) quotes both Democrat and Republican senators who believe that such heavy armaments are unnecessary and inappropriate for local law enforcement. Some legislation was written in the aftermath of Ferguson to provide oversight and/or prevent local police departments from obtaining some types of military equipment, but in the intervening months and after public outcry has decreased, such legislation seems to have stalled. In any event, there would be no way to retract the $5.4 billion worth of equipment that has already been distributed since the program began in 1997. It should be noted that the vast majority of the equipment donated to local police departments is not armaments but clothing, office supplies, exercise equipment, and appliances. However, a Stateline study of distributions showed that law enforcement in Florida received 47 mine-resistant vehicles, 36 grenade launchers, and more than 7,540 rifles. In Texas, there are 73 mine-resistant vehicles and a $24.3 million aircraft (Grovum, 2015).

Law enforcement calls the program a vital resource. Spokespeople say that the armored vehicles are used in severe weather, and such equipment is necessary because any small town may be the target of terrorism. Because of strong law enforcement opposition, legislation to restrict the program is unlikely to be successful (Tau, 2014). Peralta and Eads (2015) point out that the recent executive order does not reach most of the equipment local law enforcement receives (although grenade launchers are now prohibited), and it does not prevent law enforcement from buying prohibited equipment from private vendors.

What type of policing do we want: crime fighters or public servants? Those who value the crime fighter/warrior role are more tolerant of police error in use-of-force incidents and "overpolicing." Those who believe that police should emphasize their public servant/guardian role are much less tolerant of inappropriate uses of power. Police officers, too, tend to perceive one role as dominant over the other and this perception shapes their daily behavior. These two models are better understood if we take a brief look at the history of law enforcement in the United States.

History of Policing: From Public Servant to Crime Fighter

Kappeler, Sluder, and Alpert (1984/1994) have discussed the early origins of law enforcement as a model of service. Police were involved in social service activities: they ran soup kitchens, provided lodging for indigents, and spurred moral reform movements against cigarettes and alcohol. Of course, early law enforcement personnel were also involved in social control and employed utilitarian violence—that is, they acted as the force for power holders in society and were union busters and political-machine enforcers. Such force was frequently used against immigrants, labor organizers, and the poor (Alpert and Dunham, 2004; Harris, 2005). Researchers note that early law enforcement even used undercover agent provocateurs in the 1800s, placing them in anarchist groups to incite violence in order to justify using official violence against them. Two incidents of this are the 1874 Tompkins Square riot, where 7,000 were injured, and the Haymarket incident in 1886 (Donner, 1992: 13).

Early police departments also were marred by frequent graft and other forms of corruption. Crank (2003), for instance, discusses how police were involved in local political machines. They stuffed ballot boxes and coerced votes. Their graft was widely tolerated because of their meager salaries. Donner (1992: 62) called this the "dialectic of the bargain," referring to police pursuing and harassing dissenter groups in exchange for the power holders' toleration of police corruption.

The move toward police "professionalism," starting in the 1920s, was spurred by several factors, one of which was to improve the image of police as *objective* enforcers of the law rather than enforcers for whomever happened to be in power. In effect, there was a real or perceived shift of police loyalty from political bosses to the law itself (Kappeler et al., 1994: 49; Fogelson, 1977). Part of this transformation involved the idea that police were crime fighters—professional soldiers in the war on crime—a concept that implies objectivity, professional expertise, and specialized training. This role deemphasized the social service role and ultimately led to policing characterized by detachment from the community being policed instead of being a part of that community. In this new role, police were proactive rather than simply reactive to public demands (Payne, 2002; Crank and Caldero, 2000/2005).

Even though the professional crime fighter role of the police officer has been well established for more than 70 years, we can see remnants of the legacy of both the early political enforcer role and the public service role. Some continue to see the police as enforcers for those who hold financial and political power and point to their continuing role in investigating and monitoring dissident groups. The so-called "Red Squads" in some police departments infiltrated and spied on organizations believed to be sympathetic to socialism from the 1930s to the 1960s (Donner, 1992). Then, in the 1960s and 1970s, police turned their attention to antiwar groups and others that expressed opposition to the government. At one point the Chicago police department had files on 117,000 individuals and 14,000 organizations (Donner, 1992: 92), and J. Edgar Hoover kept his secret files on many Americans, including Martin Luther King, Jr. In fact, these activities were what led to the Church Committee (headed by Senator Frank Church that investigated the government's activities in "spying" on Americans) and more stringent wiretapping laws and legal decisions that ruled such activities improper infringements on citizens' privacy rights (Donner, 1992: 103).

After 9/11, these laws were seen as impediments in the efforts to find who was responsible and guard against another terrorist attack, and the Patriot Act and other laws have removed some restrictions to law enforcement surveillance actions. We will discuss more current developments in governmental wiretapping and the Patriot Act in Chapter 14.

Police are still sometimes seen as enforcers for the powerful in society, especially when public protests become unruly. Examples of this include the mass arrests during the Republican convention in 2004; a 2007 protest in support of illegal immigrants in Los Angeles that resulted in injuries to demonstrators when LAPD officers used rubber bullets and batons; the Occupy Protests that began in 2011 and continue sporadically in various cities; and the Ferguson and Baltimore protests in 2014 and 2015.

In other countries, the image of police as corrupt and serving the interests of the powerful is much more pronounced. Semukhina and Reynolds (2013) discuss the widespread distrust of police in Russia along with a short history of their role vis-à-vis the citizenry and the state. Before the fall of the Iron Curtain, police were viewed as the enforcers for the totalitarian government. When the government loosened its hold on Russian society (perestroika), organized crime filled the void and police came to be seen as corrupted by powerful crime figures. These researchers note that the cost of police bribery has reached an amount equivalent to the entire police system's budget. Police are described as refusing to take crime reports unless bribed, refusing to arrest a suspect if a bribe is received, and acting as protectors for organized crime. Between 1989 and 2010, opinion polls showed police trust never rose higher than 50 percent and, in some years, distrust rose as high as three-quarters of respondents, although Semukhina and Reynolds' own study showed lower levels of mistrust (35 percent believed an officer can never, or rarely, be trusted).

A new code of conduct was established and circulated to all police in Russia in 2008; however, trust in police is still very low (Wendle, 2009). Police have even been implicated in the unsolved murders of crusading journalist Anna Politkovskaya, human rights lawyer Stanislav Markelov, and journalist Anastasia Baburova. Most recently, in February 2015, Boris Nemtsov, a political opponent of Vladimir Putin, was shot dead near the Kremlin. Putin immediately ordered an investigation, but some believe that police cooperated in the assassination since surveillance cameras in that block were mysteriously inoperable on the night of the murder.

Law enforcement, if it is lawful, objective, and professional, is part of the foundation of a stable government and a hallmark of democratic societies. Banks (2014) points out the elements of democratic policing include responsiveness, accountability, defense of human rights, and transparency. She discusses how the convergence of police and the military are seen when regime protection eclipses public safety even if military dictatorships are replaced with elected governments. Other impediments to a free society include toleration for corruption in public offices, lack of political commitment to police reform, patterns of patronage, and rule by fiat. Pino and Wiatrowski (2006: 83–86) argue that democratic policing includes the rule of law, legitimacy (consent of the governed), transparency, accountability, and subordination to civil authority.

The historical social service role of police was resurrected in the **community policing** movement, which involved having officers develop closer relationships with community leaders to help them solve some of the social problems that are believed to be associated with the development of disorder and lead to crime. In community policing initiatives, police officers were involved in cleaning up parks and graffiti, helping to raze abandoned houses, helping to start youth programs, setting up storefront locations to improve communications with community members, and having community meetings to listen to what citizens think are the problems of the community (National Institute of Justice, 1992: 3; Skogan and Wycoff, 1986). Several authors described patrol officers' resistance to community policing models and explained that

community policing A model of law enforcement that creates partnerships with the community and addresses underlying problems rather than simply enforcing the law.

such efforts were viewed as trading in the crime fighter role for a much less esteemed social worker role. However, even those who resisted the community policing model admitted that the role of law enforcement has always included community relations and community service—what some have called "order maintenance."

While some aspects of the community policing approach have been institutionalized, observers note that 9/11 led to a retrenchment in policing and a return to more traditional crime fighting elements (Murray, 2005; Brown, 2007). Harris (2005) notes that 9/11 led to sweeping reforms that changed the face of federal law enforcement and influenced changes in state and local law enforcement as well. He makes an analogy between the current shift in focus of the law enforcement mission to what occurred in the 1960s and 1970s when law enforcement became involved in counter-intelligence and control efforts against war demonstrators. Today, there is pressure for local law enforcement to involve itself in immigration control and counterterrorism efforts. Harris (2005) documents the opposition (including from local police administrators) to such demands immediately after 9/11, and discusses how such efforts damage the trust and communication between the community and the police department. He promotes the view that the centralized, top-down, "crime control" approach is counterproductive in meeting the challenges of the twenty-first century and that what law enforcement should do is improve communication and trust between the police and the community. He calls this a "preventive policing" model, which includes the concepts of community policing, problem-oriented policing, and accountability mechanisms.

Future of Policing

Today, preventive policing, problem-solving policing, predictive policing, and intelligence-led policing exist in a confused mix of approaches and terminology that indicate where policing is going in the twenty-first century. Problem-solving policing arises naturally out of community-based policing whereby neighborhood problems are identified and dealt with, often in partnership with community members. Predictive policing focuses on sophisticated data gathering and analysis; geographic analysis is used to identify where criminal events are likely to occur based on where offenders have struck in the past. Intelligence-led policing is a managerial philosophy whereby data analysis and intelligence are used for objective decision making designed for crime prevention (Ratcliffe, 2008). The approach emphasizes the use of confidential informants, offender interviews, analyzing incident reports and calls for service, surveillance, and community sources of information. Another element of intelligence-led policing is the attempt to reduce the "turf warfare" of various divisions of police departments that get in the way of information sharing, so that, for instance, cities would be broken into geographic units instead of divided into vice, organized crime, major crimes, and so on.

Some describe the approach as originating in England in the early 1990s, with the United States resisting the term and the approach because it was reminiscent of the counterintelligence debacles of the 1950s through the 1970s. Meanwhile in the United States, Compstat, geospatial analysis, and data-driven approaches to policing were also evolving. While intelligence-led policing is similar to problem solving policing, Ratcliffe (2008) distinguishes them by pointing out that problem solving policing is a bottom-up approach with patrol officers identifying community issues and developing solutions for them, whereas intelligence-led policing is top-down, with information flowing upward to assist executives who set priorities and agendas and pass them back down to line staff.

After 9/11, the move toward intelligence-led policing in the United States caught up to what was happening in England and Europe, and models of information sharing and intelligence-driven decision making evolved to their current state. Today, policing, at least in major cities, is proactive (rather than merely reactive) and highly sophisticated in the use of crime analysis (Carter and Phillips, 2013).

Larger cities, such as New York and Los Angeles, have intelligence gathering that rivals the sophistication of the federal government. New York City, for instance, was in the news in 2012 because of intelligence gathering in New Jersey, and even, allegedly, has intelligence operatives in the Middle East. Their intelligence/counterinsurgency squad was reputedly run by an ex-CIA operative. Recently, the unit, which has been the subject of federal lawsuits and protests, has been disbanded (Moore, 2014).

Intelligence-led policing was resisted in the United States because of ethical concerns born of the Red Scare in the 1950s, J. Edgar Hoover's secret files, and the agent provocateurs and informants who reported on the activities of church groups and harmless hippies in the 1960s and 1970s. There are those who argue that the government cannot be trusted because intelligence gathering is, by nature, secret and impinges on privacy. Others argue that the threat of terrorism justifies great powers to collect information and monitor the activities of citizens and noncitizens alike. Finally, there are those who say that, because we are aware of past abuses, we can correct them by rigorous policies and legal guidelines. Even if such activities are legal, there are still ethical concerns over how to employ legal tools of surveillance. We return to this discussion in Chapter 14.

Power and Discretion

Klockars (1984) describes police control as consisting of the following elements: **authority** (the unquestionable entitlement to be obeyed), **power** (the means to achieve domination), **persuasion** (signs, symbols, words, and arguments used to induce compliance), and **force** (physical domination and control). Any police officer at any time might have the need or opportunity to exercise one of these four different types of domination, from unquestioned authority to physical force. Why does law enforcement have the right to employ these types of control? "We give it to them" is the easy answer. Police power is a governmental right invested in federal, state, and local law enforcement agencies. It means that these organizations, unlike almost any other except perhaps the military, have the right to control citizens' movements to the point of using physical and even deadly force to do so.

Cohen and Feldberg (1991) developed a careful analysis of, and justification for, police power and proposed that it stems from the **social contract**. Thomas Hobbes (1588–1679) and John Locke (1632–1704) created the concept of the social contract to explain why people have given up liberties in civilized societies. According to this theory, each citizen gives up complete liberty in return for societal protection against others. Complete freedom is given up in return for guaranteed protection. Police power is part of this *quid pro quo*: we give the police these powers in order to protect us, but we also recognize that their power can be used against us.

authority
Unquestionable entitlement to be obeyed that comes from fulfilling a specific role.

power   The right inherent in a role to use any means to overcome resistance.

persuasion   The use of signs, symbols, words, and arguments to induce compliance.

force   The authority to use physical coercion to overcome the will of the individual.

social contract The concept developed by Hobbes, Rousseau, and Locke in which the state of nature is a "war of all against all" and, thus, individuals give up their liberty to aggress against others in return for safety.

This general idea has corollary principles. First, each of us should be able to feel protected. If not, we are not gaining anything from the social contract and may decide to renegotiate the contract by regaining some of the liberties given up. For instance, vigilante movements arise when the populace thinks that formal agents of social control do not protect them, and isolationist groups "opt out" of most traditional societal controls because they believe that they can create a better society.

Second, because the deprivations of freedoms are limited to those necessary to ensure protection against others, police power should be circumscribed to the minimum necessary to meet the goals of protection. If police exceed this threshold, the public rightly objects.

Third, police ethics are inextricably linked to their purpose. If the social contract is the basis of their power, it is also the basis of their ethics. Cohen and Feldberg (1991) propose five ethical standards that can be derived from the social contract:

- Fair access
- Public trust
- Safety and security
- Teamwork
- Objectivity

These are not that different from the procedural justice elements discussed in a previous chapter (voice, neutrality, respect, and trustworthiness), and the hallmarks of democratic policing cited in an earlier section in this chapter.

Delattre (1989b) approaches police authority and power from a slightly different point of view. He asserts that police, as public servants, need those qualities that one desires in any public servant. He quotes James Madison, who stated that essential to any public servant are these characteristics: wisdom, good character, balanced perception, and integrity. Only if the person entrusted with public power has these qualities can we be assured that there will be no abuse of such authority and power.

Discretion and Duty

Discretion The authority to make a decision between two or more choices.

Discretion can be defined as having the authority to choose between two or more courses of behavior. Law enforcement professionals have a great deal of discretion regarding when to enforce a law, how to enforce it, how to handle disputes, when to use force, and so on. Every day is filled with decisions—some minor, some major. Discretion allows officers to choose different courses of action, depending on how they perceive their duty. **Duty** can be defined as the responsibilities that are attached to a specific role. In the case of police officers, myriad duties are attached to their role; however, there is a great deal of individual variation in how officers perceive their duty and, in a few cases such as those detailed in the news box, officers shirk their duties.

Duty Required behavior or action, that is, the responsibilities that are attached to a specific role.

One way researchers have described how discretion is utilized is through typologies of police. For instance, Wilson (1976), in one of the classic typologies, described policing styles as follows:

- The *legalistic* style of policing is described as the least amenable to discretionary enforcement. Officers enforce the law objectively without making exceptions.

(•) IN THE NEWS | *Nonfeasance of Duty*

We like to think that detectives work tirelessly to find the perpetrators of crime and officers never shirk their duty, but in rare circumstances, nonfeasance does occur. A Nassau, New York, police officer, Michael Tedesco, married father of two, pleaded guilty to 75 counts of official misconduct after it was proven that he visited two mistresses while on duty instead of responding to calls. He had been with the police department for 18 years and earned $182,748 per year. It was shown that he spent up to six hours a day with one or the other woman between 2010 and 2011. He falsified police records showing he was on calls when he was not and delayed reporting back in-service. The court ruled he has to forfeit $195,000 in termination pay, do 100 hours of community service, and pay $3,700 in restitution; in return, 29 felony counts were dropped. The investigation began when a citizen reported that his police cruiser was parked for long periods of time at a house that was out of his patrol sector. In spite of the conviction, Tedesco will still receive his pension.

Serious consequences are possible when duty is ignored. A Boston detective, Jerome Hall-Brewster, was demoted to patrol from his detective rank. A rape victim had given him the wallet of her assaulter identifying him as Edwin Alemany. The detective did nothing with it, and Alemany went on to assault two more victims and probably murder another woman, Amy Lord, who was kidnapped, beaten, forced to withdraw money from her ATM, and then stabbed to death. That lapse of duty, along with other misconduct, led to a decision to demote him back to patrol.

In New Orleans, five detectives and their two supervisors in a special victims unit were investigated for not doing their job investigating child abuse and sexual assault cases. An Inspector General's report prompted the department to transfer the identified detectives to other units during the internal investigation that ensued. The report detailed a pattern of discounting victim reports, misclassifying crimes, and leaving cases uninvestigated. In one case, detectives knew a toddler had tested positive for a sexually transmitted disease and detectives did not pursue an investigation. In another, a child complained of sexual abuse and a registered sex offender was living in the home, yet the detectives did nothing.

The report also described a "culture of indifference" toward rape victims, which seems to have been present since at least 2009, when a Time-Picayune investigation found that the NOPD classified 60 percent of rape reports as "miscellaneous" with no follow-up. In 2010, it was found that there were at least 800 backlogged rape kits in storage, untested. More recently, the investigation found that there were at least 53 outstanding DNA matches that NOPD detectives failed to follow up on to start the process of finding the suspects. The Inspector General's investigators found the detectives had misclassified 46 percent of 90 rapes they investigated.

The NOPD has evidently had a longstanding reputation for problematic rape investigations, and victims reported that detectives did not believe them or did not seem to care about their victimization. The report described one detective who told people that nonconsensual sex with an intoxicated victim should not be a crime and in 11 of those cases she was assigned, only one was presented to the DA. In several other cases, detectives never sent rape kits to the state police lab for testing even though victims' injuries were documented and evidence was collected by hospital nurses.

The absence of oversight and pervasiveness of the problem prompted some observers to note that it was a systemic problem, not just individual officers or their supervisors. The Inspector General's report indicated that the detectives wrote no investigative reports for 86 percent of the 1,290 sexual-assault or child abuse calls they were assigned from 2011 through 2013. In 65 percent of the cases reviewed by the Inspector General's investigators, detectives classified the cases as "miscellaneous" incidents that did not merit any documentation at all. In over half of the cases where there was an initial incident report, there was no supplemental follow-up report. Only 105 of the total number of cases were presented to the district attorney's office and only 74 were prosecuted, but only after the DA's office did their own investigation.

The police department established a task force to review the cases and have reopened a large number of them. The detectives have been reassigned to patrol and are under internal investigation.

Sources: CBSLocal.com, 2013; Murphy, 2014; Martin 2014.

- The *watchman* style describes police who define situations as threatening or serious depending on the groups or individuals involved, and act accordingly.
- The *caretaker* style treats citizens differently, depending on their relative power and position in society. Some people get breaks, others do not.

Muir's typology (1977: 145) included the *professional* (balancing coercion with compassion), the *reciprocator* (who had citizens solve problems and made deals to keep the peace), the *enforcer* (who used coercion exclusively), and the *avoider* (who avoided situations where they might be challenged). Finally, Brown (1981: 224) presented a typology that shared some of the same elements as those above:

- *Old-style crime fighters* are concerned only with action that might be considered crime control.
- *Clean-beat officers* seek to control all behavior in their jurisdiction.
- *Service-style officers* emphasize public order and peace officer tasks.
- *Professional-style officers* are the epitome of bureaucratic, by-the-book policing.

Each of these descriptions is obviously more detailed than the binary model of the crime control versus public servant mission that opened this chapter. However, all illustrate that different beliefs about their mission and their role in society will affect officers' use of their discretion.

Patrol officers are the most visible members of the police force and have a duty to patrol, monitor, and intervene in matters of crime, conflict, accident, and welfare. Patrol officers possess a great deal of discretion in defining criminal behavior and deciding what to do about it. When police stop people for minor traffic violations, they can write tickets or give warnings. When they pick up teenagers for drinking or other delinquent acts, they can bring in the teens for formal processing or take them home. After stopping a fight on the street, they can arrest both parties or allow the combatants to work out their problems. In many day-to-day decisions, police hold a great deal of decision-making power over people's lives because of their power to decide when to enforce the law. Studies indicate that police do not arrest in a large number of cases where they legally could. For instance, Terrill and Paoline (2007) found that officers in their sample made arrests in less than a third of the cases where an arrest was legally possible. The decision to arrest was influenced by seriousness of the offense, the city (there were two cities in their sample), whether they were responding to a citizen call for service, suspect resistance, suspect disrespect, and suspect intoxication (2007: 319). What is clear from many studies focused on police discretion is that police do not arrest, nor do they ticket, in every case where they have a legal right to do so.

Discretion also comes into play when the officer is faced with situations that have no good solutions. Many officers agonize over family disturbance calls where there are allegations of abuse, or when one family member wants the police to remove another family member. Other calls involve elderly persons who want police to do something about the "hoodlums" in the neighborhood, homeless people with young children who are turned away from full shelters, and victims of crime who are left without sufficient resources with which to survive.

A very problematic call is when family members call concerned over a mentally ill person. In these cases, officers often face extremely difficult decisions, which sometimes result in violence when the mentally ill person attacks the officers (Wells and Schafer, 2006; Finn and Stalens, 2002). Current news events illustrate several cases where officers are called to help with a mentally ill person and end up killing the individual. Crisis Intervention Training (CIT) teaches officers about how mental illness presents itself, and how to deescalate and communicate with a mentally ill person. Generally, the command language and intimidating approach of police officers is extremely counterproductive when an individual is in mental distress and can lead to violence. In situations where lethal force is used, such force is almost always legally justified; however, the actions of the officer leading up to the threat may have exacerbated the situation rather than helped to avoid the need for the use of force.

Police officers perceive their duty in different ways. Officers may respond to a domestic dispute and find a wife who is not seriously injured, but is bruised, upset, and without money or resources to help herself or her children. One officer may ascertain that departmental policy or law does not dictate any action and that the woman is afraid to press charges, so the officer can leave with a clear conscience that official duties have been completed. However, another officer might take the woman to a shelter, drive her to a relative's home, or wait with her until friends or family members arrive. Historically, law enforcement's response to domestic violence was noninterference, with the perception that domestic violence was not a crime control matter unless it involved injury amounting to felony assault. This situation is personified most dramatically by *Thurman v. City of Torrington*, 595 F. Supp. 1521 (D. Conn. 1984), which involved a woman who was beaten, stomped, and stabbed by her ex-husband on the front steps of her mother's house while a police officer sat in a car and watched. One would think that police today are more aware of domestic violence and sensitive to victims' needs; however, a $1.1 million judgment was upheld against the Federal Way, Washington, police department in 2013 by the daughters of a murdered woman. The victim had obtained an anti-harassment order against her abusive husband and the police officer served the order on the husband in the home with the wife present, leaving the husband there with her without making any attempt to ensure her safety. She was stabbed shortly after the officer left (Clarridge and Sullivan, 2013). Lapses in gender-neutral policing in cases of sexual assault and domestic violence led to a joint statement issued by the Department of Justice Community Oriented Policing Services office (COPS) and the Office of Victim Services, which urged police to appropriately respond to and investigate crimes against women (see www.justice.gov/ovw/blog/joint-statement-office-community-oriented-policing-services-office-victims-crime-and-office).

Discretion is by no means limited to law enforcement. In subsequent chapters, we will see that discretion is an important element in every subsystem, from lawmaking to the courts and corrections. Discretion in criminal justice has been attacked as contributing to injustice. A long line of researchers has explored the parameters of discretion (McAnany, 1981; Davis, 1980), concluding that the presence of discretion creates the opportunity for power to be abused, with certain groups (the poor, the powerless, and minorities) more likely to be subject to discriminatory treatment. In the next two sections, we will look at how individual officers are influenced by both the formal ethics of the agency and the informal culture that exists. These two sources arguably promote somewhat different views of the mission, values, and ethical actions for individual officers, and these views affect how they utilize their discretion.

Formal Ethics for Police Officers

A professional code of ethics exists for most professions. For instance, doctors pledge allegiance to the Hippocratic Oath, lawyers are taught their professional code of responsibility, and psychiatrists subscribe to the code promulgated by their professional organization. In fact, having a professional code of ethics seems to be part of the definition of a profession, along with some form of self-regulation (Sykes, 1989).

A code of ethics helps engender self-respect in individual officers; pride comes from knowing that one has conducted oneself in a proper and appropriate manner. Further, a code of ethics contributes to mutual respect among police officers and helps in the development of an *esprit de corps* and common goals. Agreement on methods, means, and aims is important to these feelings. As with any profession, an agreed-upon code of ethics is a unifying element. A code can help define law enforcement as a profession, for it indicates a willingness to uphold certain standards of behavior and promotes the goal of public service, an essential element of any profession.

Recent research indicates that codes of ethics are more effective in influencing behavior when they are familiar to the members of the organization, and when they are written and are perceived as useful. The code must be in the "fabric" of the organization and part of the socialization. Principles in the code must be strictly enforced (Klaver, 2014).

Police officers generally pledge an oath upon graduation from an academy, and many police agencies have adopted a code of ethics. Other agencies accomplish the same purpose by a value or mission statement that identifies what values are held to be most important to the organization. These documents may be mere wall hangings, forgotten once an officer has graduated from the academy, or they might be visible and oft-repeated elements in the cultures of the agencies, known by all and used as guides for behavior by administrators and officers alike.

The Law Enforcement Code of Ethics

The International Association of Chiefs of Police (IACP) promulgated the Law Enforcement Code of Ethics and the Canons of Police Ethics, and many departments have used these or adapted them for their own agencies. More recently, the IACP has endorsed the Oath of Honor (displayed in the Quote and Query box). This oath, developed by a committee of the IACP, is offered as a shortened version encapsulating the contents of the Code of Ethics.

The IACP code or other codes of ethics for law enforcement have at least four major themes. The principle of justice or *fairness* is the single most dominant theme in the law enforcement code. Police officers must uphold the law regardless of the offender's identity. They must not single out special groups for different treatment. Police officers must not use their authority and power to take advantage, either for personal profit or professional goals. They must avoid gratuities because these give the appearance of special treatment.

A second theme is that of *service*. Police officers exist to serve the community, and their role appropriately and essentially concerns this idea. Public service involves checking on the

---

QUOTE & QUERY

IACP Oath of Honor
On my honor,
I will never betray my badge,
my integrity, my character,
or the public trust.
I will always have
the courage to hold myself
and others accountable for our actions.
I will always uphold the Constitution,
my community, and the agency I serve.

—*International Association of Chiefs of Police, 2008*

? Does this oath emphasize a crime fighter or public service mission?

elderly, helping victims, and, in the community service model, taking a broad approach to service by helping the community deal with problems such as broken street lights and dilapidated buildings.

Still another theme is the *importance of the law.* Police are protectors of the Constitution and must not go beyond it or substitute rules of their own. Because the law is so important, police not only must be concerned with lawbreakers, but also their own behavior must be totally within the bounds set for them by the law. In investigation, capture, and collection of evidence, their conduct must conform to the dictates of law.

The final theme is one of *personal conduct.* Police, at all times, must uphold a standard of behavior consistent with their public position. This involves a higher standard of behavior in their professional and personal lives than that expected from the general public. "Conduct unbecoming" is one of the most often cited discipline infractions and can include everything from committing a crime to having an affair or being drunk in public (Bossard, 1981: 31).

The emphasis on service, justice for all groups, and higher standards for police behavior is consistent with the public service mission more so than the crime fighting mission. One might also argue that while the code promotes a public servant ideal, police are, for the most part, socialized and rewarded for actions consistent with the crime fighter role.

The Police Subculture

Research has described an occupational culture that is at odds with the formal ethics and values of the police organization, as well as the larger society. Scheingold (1984) described the factors that lead to the extreme nature of the police subculture:

- Police typically form a homogenous social group.
- They have a uniquely stressful work environment.
- They participate in a basically closed social system.

Paoline (2003) also described how certain elements of the law enforcement environment create elements of the subculture. He described a framework whereby the occupational environment created coping mechanisms and outcomes. The perception of danger leads to suspiciousness. The duty to employ coercive authority leads to "maintaining the edge" (which refers to the idea of officers always being in control over their surroundings). Supervisor scrutiny leads to a lay-low or CYA approach to performance. Finally, role-ambiguity is related to investing in the crime-fighter orientation. Social isolation and loyalty are described as outcomes of the environment officers work in.

Themes and Value Systems

In one of the classic pieces of research on the police subculture, Van Maanen (1978) discussed how police operate with stereotypes of the people with whom they come into contact. The individual who does not recognize police authority is "the asshole." Other names for this type of person include creep, animal, mope, rough, jerk-off, clown, wiseguy. The idea is the same—that some individuals are troublemakers, not necessarily because they have broken the law, but rather, because they do not recognize police authority (1978: 227). Others have identified the same concept in terms such as bad guy, punk, idiot, knucklehead, terrorist, and predator (Herbert, 1996). Herbert further points out the problem whereby officers are so quick to identify these types of individuals as threats to safety that they may overgeneralize and identify, for instance, everyone living in a neighborhood in the same way.

Van Maanen (1978: 226) observed that "certain classes in society—for example, the young, the black, the militant, the homosexual—are . . . 'fixed' by the police as a sort of permanent asshole grouping." He argued that the professionalism movement of law enforcement widened the distance between the police and the community they served, and further allowed them to be "moral entrepreneurs" who were even more likely to define some groups as bad simply because they did not conform to some preconceived standards of behavior (1978: 236).

Sherman (1982: 10–19) also described some common themes running through police attitudes and values of the police culture. First, loyalty to colleagues is essential; second, the public, or most of it, is the enemy (echoing, to some extent, van Maanen's research). Sherman explained that police use their discretion in a way that takes into account the identity of the victim and offender (attitude, class, and race impact decisions of how to enforce the law). Disrespect for the authority of police (POPO or "pissing off a police officer") is especially important in how police choose to deal with situations. Further, Sherman argued that police officers believe in the use of force for those who deserve it. Other elements described by Sherman include disparagement of due process as a barrier to doing the job and the value of deception and lying, even on the witness stand, if it means getting a bad guy. Finally, Sherman described a priority of "real" policing (crime control) over "garbage calls" (social service; 1982: 10–19). Scheingold (1984: 100–104) highlighted: police cynicism (the idea that everyone is weak or corrupt), the use of force (as justified in the face of any opposition), and the idea of the police officer as a victim (of low pay and public antipathy).

Herbert (1996) discusses six concepts or what he calls "normative orders" of policing: law, bureaucratic control, adventure/machismo, safety, competence, and morality. The normative concept of morality is related to the idea that police draw on moral definitions to justify their actions. Herbert's observational study allowed him to draw on field experiences to present examples whereby officers would continually be told and express the view that they were the "good guys" against the "evil out there." Other researchers have described "themes" of policing, such as territorial control, force, illicit coercion, the importance of guns, suspicion, danger, uncertainty, "maintaining the edge," solidarity, masculinity, excitement, and crime (Crank, 1998). Zhao, He, and Lovrich (1998) found that police exhibited similar value preferences across time (comparing 1961 to 1997) and across place. In their study, they found that police rated equality significantly lower than did the general public and, in general, were more conservative than the general public in their viewpoint. Crank and Caldero (2000/2005) also have discussed the values of police, reporting on other research showing that police officers place less emphasis on independence and more emphasis on obedience.

The Cop Code

Many authors present versions of an informal code of conduct that new officers are taught through informal socialization that is quite different from the formal code of ethics described above. Reuss-Ianni (1983: 14) presented the most complete "cop code" that included principles to watch out for partners, never "give up" another cop, be aggressive, don't implicate any other cop, and don't leave work for other cops. The informal code also specified conduct indicating that management was not to be trusted. Those code rules that are specific toward management included: protect your ass, don't make waves, keep out of the way, don't do the bosses' work, and don't trust the bosses (Reuss-Ianni, 1983: 14).

What is obvious is that the informal code of behavior, as described above, is different from the formal principles as espoused by management. Some principles of the informal code directly contradict the elements in formal codes of ethics.

Scheingold (1984: 97) described the police subculture as no more than an extreme of the dominant U.S. culture and argued that it closely resembles a conservative political perspective. In other words, we all agree with certain elements of the police value system and, if the general public is less extreme in its views, it is only because we have not had a steady diet of dealing with crime and criminal behavior as have the police.

Police Culture and "Noble Cause"

One aspect of police culture that has received recent attention is what has been called noble-cause corruption. This refers to the utilitarian concept that the "end" of crime fighting justifies "means" that might otherwise be illegal, unethical, and/or against rules or regulations (such as lying on an affidavit or the witness stand or planting evidence). Arguably, the police culture, at least in some locales, endorses or tolerates this type of activity. Cooper (2012) discusses this phenomenon as a type of role conflict, noting that officers feel torn between their "protector" role and agent of the state, which appears to be similar to our discussion of Packer's crime control versus due process model.

Klockars (1983) presented us with a type of noble-cause corruption in the "Dirty Harry problem" (from the Clint Eastwood movie), asking whether it was ethically acceptable for a police officer to inflict pain on a suspect in order to acquire information that would save an innocent victim. Various other sources also describe situations where police officers practice an "ends justify the means" approach (Moskos, 2009). Crank and Caldero (2000/2005) are noted for their expanded discussion of noble-cause corruption. They argue that practices such as "testilying" (lying to get a warrant or a conviction) are not caused by selfishness, but rather, by ends-oriented thinking. McDonald (2000) offers a detailed study of the practice of "testilying," which includes reordering facts, adding details, or omitting information. It is also referred to as shading, fluffing, firming up, or shaping and occurs in sworn affidavits for arrest or search warrants, in reports, or in testimony. In McDonald's study of one police department, he found that testilying was more likely to occur when there was a differential emphasis on the goal (crime control) over means (2000: 13). McDonald notes that, according to his sample, police perceive that some prosecutors "wink at" deception or encourage it to get a win (2000: 28). Studies show that about 60 percent of rookies support mild lies to achieve a conviction (Crank and Caldero, 2000: 157).

The most notorious example of exposed testilying is the O. J. Simpson case. The defense attorney used a tape of LAPD officer Mark Fuhrman saying 17 times that he and other police officers "regularly" manufactured and planted evidence, and when asked if he had done so in the Simpson case, he pleaded the Fifth Amendment (refusing to answer because it might incriminate him; McDonald, 2000: 3, 9).

(((•))) IN THE NEWS | *Testilying and Other Events in San Francisco*

A scandal emerged in 2011 in San Francisco when a defense attorney released a video of officers barging into private rooms in a transient hotel. The events portrayed in the videos were in direct contrast to the officer's official reports and affidavits in support of arrest warrants. In short, they lied. A wide-ranging investigation of testilying uncovered dozens of cases where officers' statements were proven to be untrue. The district attorney dismissed charges in dozens of cases and asked the FBI to investigate. The U.S. Attorney's office has also reportedly dismissed 137 cases. Eventually, in 2015, one detective was found guilty of four federal counts of conspiring to carry out illegal searches and violating the civil rights of the occupants. Another was acquitted.

In another case, Sgt. Ian Furminger and Officer Edmond Robles were convicted of charges related to stealing money and property seized during searches in 2009. Their convictions included conspiracy to violate civil rights, wire fraud, and theft from a federally funded program. The actions of the officers resulted in the dismissal of 119 drug and attempted robbery cases of people who had been arrested by the involved officers (Cheever, 2015). In the investigation and trial of former sergeant Ian Furminger, text messages between him and other officers were received by the U.S. Attorney's office and released publicly in March of 2015. The text messages were racist and included derogatory language toward members of the public and police colleagues. The text messages discussed lynching African Americans and proposed that African Americans "should

be spayed." Other texts denigrated gays, Mexicans, and Filipinos (Williams, 2015).

The exposure of the messages led to the announcement that three retired judges would be working with San Francisco prosecutors to review roughly 3,000 criminal cases that have potentially been tainted by the 14 involved officers. The cases represent the officers' cases over the last 10 years and will be examined for bias and evidence tampering. If the evidence is questionable, the task force will provide that information to defense attorneys. The task force will also identify officers and policies that create a biased culture within the police force (Albarazi, 2015). In addition to the text messages, the task force will also investigate gladiator-style fights forced on San Francisco jail inmates by sheriff's deputies. The guards allegedly bet on the fights and punished inmates who would not participate. Another area being examined by the task force is the possibility that hundreds of convictions in criminal cases may have been compromised due to improper handling of DNA samples in the police crime lab (Williams, 2015).

After the announcement of the task force, the San Francisco police union attacked George Gascon, the district attorney, for political grandstanding and not uncovering the misconduct during his tenure as police chief from 2009 to 2011. Gascon, in turn, criticized the union for looking the other way when officers commit misconduct. The police chief, Greg Suhr, also said the task force was political and that the district attorney was not responsible for handling police misconduct. He indicated that he would fire seven officers involved in the text messaging.

Sources: Lamb, 2015; Cheever, 2015; Williams, 2015; Albarazi, 2015.

In McDonald's study, the two most frequently given reasons for testilying were that legal technicalities made their job impossible to do, and the belief that the offender was guilty. The least most common reason was "pressure for productivity" (2000: 106). When asked how often do police officers they know personally engage in testimonial deception, the majority indicated they did not know anyone, but substantial numbers admitted that they knew officers who rarely or sometimes used deception when testifying (2000: 114). McDonald concluded that police officers from large agencies were more likely to use testimonial deception, as were police officers who perceived their jurisdiction as having high crime and officers who believed there were too many legal technicalities (2000: 238–239). Alexander (2013) opines that pressure for numbers does act as an incentive to lie. Police officers today, she writes, are evaluated solely by their productivity and this demand eclipses any other mission or value of police work. Federal grants based on drug confiscation levels, asset forfeiture, and quotas all are pressures to lie in order to make arrests and/or seizures.

Crank and Caldero (2000: 9) would argue that the motivation is not quotas, but the noble cause of getting an offender off the street, even if means employing a "magic pencil"—that is, making up facts on an affidavit to justify a warrant or to establish probable cause for arrests. Arguably, they are inclined to behave this way because we hire those who have values that support such actions, train and socialize them to internalize these values even more deeply, and then put them in situations where their values dictate doing whatever it takes to "make the world safe" (2000: 88). Ironically, exposure leads to the dismissal of hundreds of cases and the inability of officers involved to be police-officer witnesses because their credibility has been destroyed. Alexander (2013) and others present depressing numbers of these incidents across the country.

The occupational subculture of policing is not supportive of egoistic corruption like bribery or abuse of authority, such as when officers engage in sexual misconduct, but it may be supportive of "catching the criminal—whatever it takes." If we want to change this attitude, we must address it directly. Further, Crank and Caldero argue that such an attitude must change because we are increasingly living in a world where pluralism is the reality and the values of the police organization may not be reflective of the citizenry they police. As multiculturalism becomes the dominant reality, police must learn to adapt and accommodate the needs and priorities of different groups.

Police Culture, Loyalty, and the Blue Curtain of Secrecy

Another element of the police code is absolute loyalty to other officers, even if it means not coming forward to expose a wrongdoer. Variously described as the **code of silence**, **blue curtain of secrecy**, or other terms, it refers to the subcultural code of "Don't give up another cop" (Skolnick, 2001). This phenomenon has been recognized in academic literature, first-person accounts by former officers, and even cited in court holdings (e.g., *Jones v. Town of E. Haven*, 493 F. Supp. 2d 302 [D. Conn. 2007]). It should also be noted that a code of silence is present in other occupations and groups as well, even when members engage in incompetent or corrupt activities.

The book *Serpico* (Maas, 1973) describes how Frank Serpico became a whistle-blower against the NYPD officers who were involved in the "pad" (graft). He was shot in a drug raid and believes that fellow officers conspired to kill him. He went on to testify against corruption but never again was a NYPD cop and his name is used as an epithet by many NYPD officers today. In the Quote and Query box, Serpico's statement to the Knapp Commission illustrates the problem of police loyalty when officers are willing to cover up corruption. The later statement indicates that nothing much had changed in the decades between the Knapp Commission and the Mollen Commission.

QUOTE & QUERY

Police officer perjury in court to justify illegal dope searches is commonplace. One of the dirty little not-so-secret secrets of the criminal justice system is undercover narcotics officers intentionally lying under oath. It is a perversion of the American justice system that strikes directly at the rule of law. Yet it is the routine way of doing business in courtrooms everywhere in America.

Peter Keane, a former San Francisco police commissioner, in an article in The San Francisco Chronicle, quoted in Alexander, 2013

 Is lying in official reports ever justified?

code of silence
The practice of officers to not come forward when they are aware of the ethical transgressions of other officers.

blue curtain of secrecy Another name for the code of silence.

QUOTE & QUERY

The problem is that the atmosphere does not yet exist in which honest police officers can act without fear of ridicule or reprisal from fellow officers....

—*Frank Serpico, Knapp Commission, 1971, as reported in Hentoff, 1999*

Cops don't tell on cops.... [I]f a cop decided to tell on me, his career's ruined.... [H]e's going to be labeled as a rat.

—*Police officer testimony, Mollen Commission, 1992, as reported in Walker, 2001*

 How would you create an atmosphere in a police department wherein officers would feel more comfortable reporting the misdoings/criminality of other officers? Or would you even want to?

These quotes are old but still resonate today. In fact, Frank Serpico is involved in the case of Adrian Schoolcraft, a cop who exposed the quota system of his precinct by secretly taping his watch commander and then handing the tapes over to a journalist. In retaliation, he was hounded and intimidated. Police officials even orchestrated his involuntary commitment in a mental hospital. In his $50 million lawsuit against the city, the NYPD, and the hospital, the hospital's defense is that his commitment was warranted because he appeared paranoid (Brown, 2015). One might note, however, that when your superiors and coworkers appear at your apartment and forcibly take you to a mental hospital, there may be legitimate reasons for your paranoia.

Quinn (2005) argues that good officers are sucked into the corrupt cover-ups because of the nature of policing. Every officer does something wrong, and the most common mistake, perhaps, is using too much force. When an officer has just experienced a life-threatening event, such as a high-speed chase, a foot chase, or a fight for his weapon, the adrenalin "hijacks" reason, according to Quinn, and some officers overreact. When coworkers cover for the officer, the officer who made the mistake is indebted and trapped in a situation where the officer thinks he or she must do the same. Even if the offending officer would have told the truth about his or her mistake, the officer who covered up has lied and, therefore, it is almost impossible to "sacrifice" that loyal officer by churlishly telling the truth and calling him or her a liar.

Weisburd and Greenspan (2000) discovered that, although 80 percent of police officers did not think that the code of silence was essential for police trust and good policing, fully two-thirds reported that a whistleblower would encounter sanctions. Further, more than half agreed that it was not unusual for police to ignore improper conduct on the part of other officers, and 61 percent indicated that police officers do not always report even the most serious violations/crimes of other officers. In another study using hypotheticals, about one-third of officers responded that they would not report an incident depicting a clear case of excessive force. In this study, newer officers, supervisors, and those with many years of experience were more likely to report other officers, while those least likely to report were mid-career officers (Micucci and Gomme, 2005: 493, 499).

The code of silence can be considered on a continuum where observing and not coming forward is on one side of the continuum, representing a passive position toward the misconduct of others. More serious actions occur when officers actively lie to supervisors, or perjure themselves in the effort to cover up wrongdoing. The most serious forms of cover-up are when officers involve themselves in manufacturing evidence or intimidate witnesses. Cooper (2009) discusses a case in which officers shot an unarmed suspect 16 times. In their statements regarding the events, several officers described how the victim ran over an officer, which prompted the lethal use of force. The problem with their narrative was that forensics showed the officer's pants with the tire tracks were empty when it happened, meaning that they had put the pants on the road and drove the car over them in an effort to concoct a story to justify the shootings.

Cooper (2009) notes that all prosecutors should be familiar with the literature on the blue curtain of secrecy in order to judge police officer narratives and be aware of the possibility of cover-ups. As support for this, he utilizes a civil case in which two ATF officers sued the city of Chicago and the Chicago Police Department because when they had reported the probable illegal activities of a Chicago police officer, instead of investigating, the information was leaked to the officer, who attempted to have the two ATF officers murdered. The city's case was based on the idea that the blue code of secrecy was a myth, but the jury returned a $9.75 million judgment to the targeted ATF officers. In the dilemma that follows, the values of loyalty and honesty are in conflict.

ETHICAL DILEMMA

You are approached by internal affairs to make a statement concerning what you saw on a particular night concerning an alleged beating that occurred in a patrol car before the suspect was taken up to the jail for booking. You did see the two officers use their flashlights to hit the suspect on the head and shoulders. As they dragged the man out of the car they told you that he had been kicking at them through the grille and vomited all over the back of the patrol car. The suspect ended up being admitted to the hospital with a skull fracture. What would you do?

Law

The relevant law at issue is perjury if you lie on the witness stand or in a formal, legal document. Official oppression or obstruction of justice is sometimes also used as a charge against officers who do not tell the truth in official investigations if proof exists that they are lying about what they saw. Generally, those who merely say nothing are internally sanctioned or fired rather than criminally prosecuted; however, if they are actively involved in a cover-up, more serious charges can be filed. On the other hand, it is difficult to prove the opposite when an officer makes a statement that he didn't see anything.

Policy

Recall that the IACP Code of Ethics specifically dictates that officers who are aware of wrongdoing have the duty to do something about it. All police departments have value statements, mission statements, or codes of ethics that support exposing wrongdoing of fellow officers, but, generally, subcultural codes oppose any form of whistleblowing or "ratting" on a fellow officer.

Ethics

Teleological ethical rationales are concerned with the consequences of an action. Egoism may support not coming forward because it may not be in one's best interest. An officer might say, "I don't want to get involved," "I don't want to go against everyone," or "It's the sergeant's (or lieutenant's or captain's) job, not mine." These are all egoistic reasons for not coming forward. Utilitarian reasons to keep quiet also look at the consequences (or utility) of the action. If one engaged in "the end justifies the means" thinking, described above as noble-cause corruption, some activities that are labeled corrupt may actually further the ends of justice, at least in the short term. Even when the corrupt action cannot be labeled as noble-cause corruption, the loss of a skilled police officer—even though that officer may have committed some form of misconduct—is a loss to society. One may believe that the harm to the police department in exposing the deviance of one officer is greater than the harm to society created by what that officer is doing, or that there is greater utility in stopping the officer without making the issue public. For any of these arguments to be legitimate, the utility of not exposing the wrongdoing must outweigh the utility for everyone if the wrongdoing was exposed.

There are also teleological arguments for coming forward. Egoism may dictate that an individual has to come forward to protect himself from being accused of wrongdoing. The police officer may also endure such a crisis of conscience or fear of being punished that he or she can attain peace of mind only by "coming clean." Utilitarian arguments for coming forward are offered as well. The harm that comes from letting the individual carry on his or her misdeeds or not forcing the individual to a public punishment may be greater than the harm that would come from the scandal of public exposure. This is especially true if one is forced to either tell the truth or lie; in this case, the harm to police credibility must be taken into account.

(continued)

Recall that deontological arguments look at the inherent nature of the act. Arguments against exposing other officers include the idea that one's duty is to the police force and one's fellow officers so one should protect them from exposure. Arguments for coming forward are much stronger, including the argument that a police officer has a sworn duty to uphold the law. Also, one cannot remain silent in a particular situation unless one could approve of silence in all situations (Kant's categorical imperative), and one must do one's duty, which involves telling the truth when under an oath (Wren, 1985: 32–33). It should be noted that, in general, deontological ethics support whistleblowing because it is a higher duty to uphold the law than it is to defend one's fellow officers.

When one considers whether to come forward to expose the wrongdoing of others, external moral philosophies, such as utilitarianism, are rarely articulated. What tends to be the impetus for covering up for other officers is an internal mechanism—loyalty. While the prime motivator for coming forward and/or truth-telling is personal integrity and duty, the individual often feels great anguish and self-doubt over turning in or testifying against friends and colleagues. That is understandable because "a person's character is defined by his commitments, the more basic of which reveal to a person what his life is all about and give him a reason for going on" (Wren, 1985: 35). Loyalty is a difficult concept that others have written about extensively; it can be a vehicle of both ethical and unethical behavior (Fletcher, 1993).

Loyalty in police work is explained in that police depend on one another, sometimes in life-or-death situations. Loyalty to one's fellows is part of the *esprit de corps* of policing and is an essential element of a healthy department. Richards (2010) describes how it is part of the socialization process of the academy and infused in the rituals, routines, symbols, stories, and rites of the informal culture. If things go well in this process, an individual officer will view fellow officers as family and feel a sense of duty toward all members of the same family.

Ewin (1990) writes that something is wrong if a police officer doesn't feel loyalty to fellow officers. Loyalty is a personal relationship, not a judgment. Therefore, loyalty is uncalculating. We do not extend loyalty in a rational way or based on contingencies. Loyalty to groups or persons is emotional, grounded in affection rather than reflection. Loyalty refers to a preference for one group over another (Ewin, 1990: 13). Loyalty always involves some exclusion: one is loyal to X rather than to Y, so Y is thus excluded. At times the reverse can also be true: If a group of people is excluded (whether or not they are properly excluded), they can feel a common cause in response to what they see as oppression, which can result in the growth of loyalty among them. That loyalty, provoked by a dislike and perhaps distrust of the other group, is likely to be marked by behavior that ignores legitimate interests and concerns of the other group.

The application to policing is obvious. If police officers feel isolated from the community, their loyalty is to other police officers and not to the community at large. If they feel oppressed by and distrust the police administration, they draw together against the "common enemy." To address abuses of loyalty, one would not want to attack the loyalty itself because it is necessary for the health of the organization. Rather, one would want to encourage loyalty beyond other officers to the department and to the community. Permeability rather than isolation promotes community loyalty, just as the movement toward professionalism promotes loyalty to the principles of ethical policing rather than to individuals in a particular department.

Wren (1985) believes that police departments can resolve the dilemma of the individual officer who knows of wrongdoing by making the consequences more palatable—that is, by having a fair system of investigation and punishment, by instituting helping programs for those with alcohol and drug problems, and by using more moderate punishments than dismissal or public exposure for other sorts of misbehavior. This is consistent with the ethics of care, which is concerned with needs and relationships.

Delattre (1989a) handled the problem differently, but came to somewhat similar conclusions. He turned to Aristotle to support the idea that when a friend becomes a scoundrel, the moral individual cannot stand by and do nothing. Rather, one has a moral duty to bring the wrongdoing to the friend's attention and urge him or her to change. If the friend will not, then he or she is more scoundrel than friend, and the individual's duty shifts to those who might be victimized by the person's behavior. We see here not the ethics of care, but rather, a combination of virtue-based and deontological duty-based ethics.

Souryal (1996, 1999b) discussed loyalty to superiors or to fellow officers as misplaced. He argued that there are different kinds of loyalty: personal loyalty, institutional loyalty, and integrated loyalty (which relates to the ideal values of the profession). Loyalty to superiors is traced back to *divine right*—the idea that persons are indistinguishable from their office (1996b: 48). Today, however, we are governed by laws, not kings, and such loyalty should be properly placed in our laws and our values rather than an individual. Souryal noted that personal loyalties often lead to unethical actions and that loyalty to values or organizations has a stronger ethical justification. One might argue that even loyalty to a police organization may be misplaced if it leads to lying to protect the organization against scandal.

The informal practice of punishing individuals who come forward is an especially distressing aspect of loyalty and the police culture. Individual police officers have been ostracized and have become the target of a wide variety of retaliatory gestures after "ratting" on another officer. Reports include having equipment stolen, threats made to the officer and his family members, interfering with radio calls and thereby jeopardizing his safety, scrawling the word "rat" on his locker, putting cheese or dead rats in his locker, vandalizing his patrol car, or destroying his uniform.

As can be seen in the news stories provided, administrators are often the ones who retaliate against whistleblowers, telling the accused officer who informed on them, or supporting implicitly or explicitly the retaliation against the officer who came forward. Instead of rewarding officers who expose wrongdoing, administrators sometimes punish them by administrative sanctions, transfers to less desirable positions, or poor performance reports. This retaliation is not just true of law enforcement agencies. Sanctions against whistleblowers are so common that most states and the federal government now have laws designed to protect whistleblowers.

Police Culture Today

Our descriptions of the police culture date back more than 40 years and so a legitimate question is whether or not modern police officers subscribe to the same set of values and whether the "cop code" still exists. Arguably, the subculture and the values described above may be breaking down in police departments today. Several factors contribute to the possible weakening of the subculture:

- *Increasing diversity* of police recruits has eliminated the social homogeneity of the workforce. Many diverse groups are now represented in police departments, including African Americans, Hispanics, people of other ethnicities, women, and college-educated recruits. These different groups bring elements of their own cultural backgrounds and value systems into the police environment.

(⁙) IN THE NEWS | *Protecting Whistleblowers*

News stories across the country indicate that officers who violate the blue curtain of secrecy may still face informal sanctions by both peers and supervisors. Generally, these stories appear when the officer files a whistleblower lawsuit seeking protection or compensation. Examples include the following:

Chicago: Laura Kubiak alleged she was abruptly reassigned from the Office of News Affairs to a beat patrol in retaliation for complaining of another officer with a history of brutality complaints who allegedly (according to Kubiak and witnesses) ran up to her and screamed: "Who the f–do you think you are, you stupid b–?" "berating" and "intimidating" her to the extent that the witness believed he would use violence. When she complained to internal affairs, both she and the witness were transferred out of the news office. (Mitchell, 2014)

Florida: Florida Highway Patrol trooper Donna Watts pulled over a fellow cop in his patrol car for going over 120 miles per hour. When she approached his car and handcuffed him, she started a saga of retaliation that led to her filing a federal lawsuit. In the filing she reported that more than 88 officers from 25 jurisdictions accessed her private information using police computers. The officer she pulled over evidently regularly drove over 100 miles an hour between his home in a neighboring town and Miami where he worked. He was fired. In the months after the incident, officers looked up Watts' home address, Social Security number, and license plate in police computers and then proceeded to intimidate her through threatening phone calls and cars that would stop in front of her house for periods of time for no purpose. Reportedly her supervisors did not feel it was safe for her to return to patrol because she may not have received backup from other officers in emergencies. She is suing individual officers and also their agencies because of a lack of supervision and training. Only a few officers received letters of reprimand for their actions. Watts reported experiencing anxiety-related physical symptoms and moved from the area and no longer drives patrol. (Huriash, 2012)

Oakland: The court-appointed monitor for Oakland's Police Department reported to a federal judge that the department had not put in place protections for whistleblowers leading to retaliation. One example was Sgt. Charles O'Connor who took medical leave after experiencing retaliation for reporting his partner for beating a drunk and handcuffed suspect. (Associated Press, 2013a)

Baltimore: An officer who reported a fellow officer for beating a handcuffed suspect in 2012 endured months of retaliation leading to a federal lawsuit. He said he and fellow officers chased a drug suspect who kicked in the door of an apartment and was captured. The homeowner was a girlfriend of another officer and this officer arranged for the suspect to be returned to the scene and then beat him requiring a trip to the hospital. No one came forward to report the incident except Joseph Crystal. Afterward he was threatened by supervisors, reassigned and given confusing, against-policy, or misleading orders which he believed were attempts to "set him up." He found a rat on the windshield of his personal car parked outside his house, he did not receive backup when he called dispatcher requesting it, he was told no one wanted to ride with him, and he was asked if he liked cheese because rats like cheese. He has since quit the Baltimore Police Department and has filed a lawsuit. The officer, Anthony Williams, who beat the suspect, was convicted of assault and battery and served a 45-day jail sentence and is still on the force.

Source: Krayewski, 2014; Smith, 2014

- *Police unions*, with their increasing power, formalize relationships between the line staff and the administration. Subcultural methods for coping with perceived administrative unfairness are giving way to more formal rather than informal means of balancing different objectives of management and line staff.

- *Civil litigation* has increased the risk of covering for another officer. Although police officers may lie to internal affairs or even on a witness stand to save a fellow officer from sanctions, they may be less likely to do so when large monetary damages may be leveled against them because of negligence and perjury.

One might add that many of the authors who described the police culture did so in the 1970s and 1980s, during a time of great social change when the Supreme Court recognized groundbreaking due process protections. Older police officers who had not been socialized to give *Miranda* warnings or obtain search warrants were understandably slow to adapt to the new order. Today's recruit officers were born after the *Miranda* warning was institutionalized as a standard arrest element and have never known a time when police did not need a search warrant. Today's recruit is also more likely to have been exposed to community policing and its tenets of community–police partnership and other progressive police practices through television, education, or other means. Thus, for younger police officers, these due process protections may be seen as normal and expected elements of the job rather than barriers to good police work.

However, even recent research shows that there is still some support among even recruits for certain aspects of the informal value system of the police subculture. Phillips (2013) in a small and nonrepresentative, but interesting, study of academy recruits showed that there was already some predisposition to harbor the informal occupational value of not reporting a fellow officer for an inappropriate use of force.

There is also no doubt that the police subculture varies from department to department. Size, regional differences, and management may influence the strength of the subculture. The makeup of the department, its relationship with the community, and training may also influence the type of occupational culture found in any department.

In an incomplete measurement of police subculture, Paoline, Myers, and Worden (2000) found that the police subculture is by no means monolithic. They found substantial variation among the officers and differences in their cultural views. Further, no factors emerged as strong predictors of officers' values. There were weak and inconsistent associations between sex and cultural values. As expected, minority officers had more positive orientations than white officers toward order maintenance and community policing concepts; however, the association was not strong. The association between aggressive patrol and race was stronger, with minority officers displaying less support than white officers for aggressive patrol. In general, most of the associations were of small magnitude. The authors conclude that the police culture may be less uniform and less powerful than other researchers have portrayed. They admit, however, that their measures did not directly or comprehensively measure police culture as described in earlier research. Paoline (2003) described how organizational values, rank, and individual officers' styles could affect adherence to the occupational subculture.

Greene et al. (2004: 60–63) examined attitudinal data from a sample drawn from the Philadelphia police department. A series of questions measured their attitudes toward ethics and some elements of the police culture. More than half of the officers thought gratuities were acceptable, directives sometimes needed to be subverted to make an arrest, would not report a fellow police officer even if they knew of misconduct, and would extend professional courtesy to other officers (ignore minor violations of the law). The majority of officers did not support testilying, exaggerating probable cause, or "street justice."

Research continues to support the idea that there is a police culture, albeit one that is more fragmented and weaker than in earlier decades (Murray, 2005; Conti, 2006; Loftus, 2010). Regarding the "blue curtain of secrecy," research indicates that this practice may be breaking down. Barker (2002), for instance, reported on some research indicating that the addition of minorities and women has led to a less homogenous force and a weaker subcultural norm of covering up wrongdoing, as evidenced by the proliferation of complaints against fellow officers. Barker notes that there were more than 30 cases in Los Angeles where officers were the primary witnesses against other officers. Rothwell and Baldwin (2007a, b) found that police respondents were *more* likely to report misdemeanors and felonies of their fellow officers than were civilian employee-respondents in other agencies. These researchers also found that reporting was positively related to the agency having a mandatory reporting policy. The other factor associated with reporting misconduct of fellow officers was supervisory status. Other researchers have found that police officers were more likely to report wrongdoing of other officers if it involved acquisition of goods or money (except for gratuities) rather than excessive force or bending rules (Westmarland, 2005; Gottschalk and Holgersson, 2011). In the Walking the Walk box, the experiences of one officer who exposed wrongdoing are described.

WALKING THE WALK

Walter Harris is a big, quiet man, a college football star and an ex-NFL football player. He joined the Bloomington police department in 1991. He is not a weak man, nor a fearful one, but he admits he was scared during a time when his actions created a threat to his family. When his character made him stand up for what was right, he had to take steps to protect those he loved.

Harris was doing well in the Bloomington Police Department but decided to move to Detroit and joined the Detroit Police Department. He was quickly tagged to join the mayor's executive protection unit (EPU), and was an executive protection officer for Detroit mayor Dennis Archer until 2001, when Kwame Kirkpatrick was elected. Harris stayed on the detail after Kirkpatrick became mayor but began to notice changes in the EPU. The new mayor immediately appointed two patrol officers to head the unit, promoting them above seasoned commanders. Harris later found out that one of these officers had been in trouble before, but somehow the trouble had been swept under the rug. The other was a boyhood friend of the mayor.

Harris was proud of his credentials for executive protection from the FBI academy, and the accolades received from the FBI and other cities as to the professionalism of the EPU. He was uncomfortable with some of the new patterns of behavior, including eating and drinking with the mayor while on duty, and a lax manner toward protection protocols. Part of the problem seemed to be the two leaders, who were entirely too familiar with the mayor and casual about their formal duties. The other problem, however, was the mayor himself, who liked to go into bars to drink, and it became increasingly apparent to Harris that the mayor was also engaged in an extramarital affair with his administrative assistant and probably other women. In Washington, D.C., during a mayor's conference, he insisted on going to a bar that had been blacklisted by the local police. Unable to refuse, the officers went along, but when Harris refused to surrender his gun to the bouncer, he stayed outside while other protection officers went inside unarmed with the mayor. As they came out, there was an altercation that had the potential to turn into serious trouble, but luckily was averted. The D.C. police department informed them after that evening, they would only provide courtesy protection to the Detroit mayor while he was on official business.

As time went on, Harris became more and more uncomfortable with the behavior of the EPU leaders and the mayor himself. On at least one occasion, the mayor had his protection officers drive him to a rendezvous with a woman in an apartment building, and he sometimes disappeared from the mayor's mansion, taking one of the cars himself and leaving his protection officers behind. Due to a number of troubling incidents, Harris decided he had to quit.

Another officer had already quit and had gone to internal affairs about the problems with the EPU, including some officers padding their overtime records and drinking on duty. Harris was asked to back up this officer's allegations; otherwise, the officer would probably be made out to be a liar. This other officer had already filed a whistleblower suit, alleging retaliation for his speaking out. There was also a rumor floating around that there had been a party at the mayor's mansion with three strippers, one of whom was injured when the mayor's wife returned unexpectedly. As the story went, the woman was taken to the hospital, but somehow the hospital records disappeared.

Harris had a dilemma. If he supported this officer's allegations, he could be targeted for retaliation; if he didn't, he'd be going against everything he believed in. From the beginning of his law enforcement career he had avoided any hint of corruption; he had even turned down offers from officers when he first joined the force to fudge arrest reports to make himself look better. He told the truth and immediately began getting phone calls where the caller would hang up. He believed he was being followed by other police, and there were three separate incidents that he thought were attempts to set him up. The last was when he and his partner were told by the duty officer to take a call of a robbery, and he discovered the car they had been assigned had no camera in it. He insisted on a camera and by the time his angry superior put one in, they were still expected to go to the scene, which was strange because the dispatcher should have sent another patrol unit by then, but the call evidently hadn't been dispatched to another unit. They took the complaint from an individual in a car with several other people and thought no more of it until they were called in because of a report that Harris had robbed the complainant. This was the third citizen complaint that was completely unfounded and, if he hadn't insisted on the camera, or his partner hadn't walked to the car and taken the complaint so the man couldn't even describe Harris, he would have been facing very serious charges with very little ability to defend himself. He realized his vulnerability as a patrol officer and immediately took a stress leave, then fought with the departmental psychologist, who seemed to be committed to putting him back on the street despite what his personal doctor advised. This tenuous situation went on for months, until his family was threatened. Harris then realized that his whistleblowing had endangered his family and they moved in the middle of the night back to Bloomington, where his previous chief was happy to have him back.

The whistleblower case eventually ended Mayor Kirkpatrick's term of office, exposing him as a liar and a corrupt politician. He ended up in federal prison. When the case finally went to trial, Harris returned to Detroit to testify. His testimony was instrumental in setting the foundation for the hundreds, if not thousands, of text messages that the mayor had sent to his administrative assistant. Since they had lied on the stand about their affair, the text messages were evidence of perjury. Harris and the others won their case, although Harris did not even recover the costs involved in abandoning his house in Detroit and moving to Bloomington. However, if he had it to do over again, he would—because it was the right thing to do.

Source: Harris W., 2011.

Researchers who have studied police values find that they remain fairly consistent over time and police values are slightly different (more conservative) than the general population (Caldero and Larose, 2001). In a small sample of sheriffs' deputies, the researchers found that there were wide variations in support for noble-cause statements and that adherence to noble cause did not seem to be related to a perception of level of crime (Crank, Flaherty, and Giacomazzi, 2007).

Finally, Loftus (2010) reviews the research on police culture, adding a small study of a police department in England. The conclusion reached by this author was that the recurring elements of police culture (noted both in the United States and England), including an "exaggerated sense of mission," masculinity, force, suspiciousness, isolation, solidarity, conservativism, cynicism, and pessimism are still present. Even though community policing concepts and changing demographics have changed the police culture somewhat, these themes were prevalent and Loftus concludes that the inherent elements of policing are responsible for the stability over time of the police culture elements.

Generally, police, like any occupational group, are socialized to some type of informal value system that guides and provides a rationale for decision making. This value system may be as—or in some cases, more—influential than the police rulebook or code of ethics. It is also true that the police culture is not now, or perhaps never was, as monolithic as early writers indicated and the strength of it is affected by the size of the department and other variables.

Conclusion

Whereas the formal code of ethics emphasizes the public servant role of law enforcement, the informal subculture emphasizes the crime fighter role. The public expects the police to live up to the crime fighter role, but also expects more. The public expects the police to be problem solvers and supermen (and superwomen). From noisy neighbors to incest, we expect the police to have the answers to our problems—to be the one-stop shop for solving problems. The surprising thing is that the police do so well at this impossible task.

The Gallup Poll has measured respect for police since 1965. In a 2010 poll, 57 percent of Americans, when asked about a profession's honesty and integrity, rated police as "high" or "very high." This is down from about 68 percent in 2001, but up from 1995 when only 41 percent of the population rated police integrity and honesty as high or very high (Jones, 2010). In the 2014 poll 48 percent of respondents rated police integrity and honesty as high or very high (Gallop, 2015).

Public perceptions of police misconduct influence the public's trust in the police and the recognition of police as agents of legal and moral authority (Tyler, 1990; Tyler and Wakslak, 2004). Interestingly, at least one study found that while extensive media coverage of a police scandal influenced the public's belief about the guilt of the officers involved, it did not seem to affect the public's general perceptions of respect for the agency (Chermak, McGarrell, and Gruenewald, 2006). Another study found that public attitudes about police misconduct are separate and distinct from their attitudes about police effectiveness. The most influential factors on public attitudes about police misconduct were personal experiences of self, family and friends, neighborhood characteristics, and media coverage, while public attitudes of police effectiveness were influenced by other factors (Miller and Davis, 2007).

It is important for police departments to set and maintain high standards of conduct not only for their own professional pride, but also because it seems that police ethics impact public safety in a more general sense. Police officers who ignore the law evidently give others the green light to do so as well.

In this chapter, we have identified two "missions" of law enforcement: crime fighting and public service. We looked at the parameters of police discretion and how researchers have drawn typologies to describe the way individual police officers navigate their multifaceted role by emphasizing certain duties over others. Officers' discretion is controlled and guided by both formal ethics and the informal culture of law enforcement officers. The police subculture is not monolithic and may be different from when the early researchers described it. There does seem to be some continued support for what has been called "noble-cause corruption" and "the blue curtain of secrecy." Throughout this discussion and the chapters to follow, the mission and role of police as crime fighters or public servants is a pervasive theme.

Chapter Review

1. **Describe the two different missions of law enforcement in a democracy.**

    The two missions of law enforcement are crime fighting and public service. Under the crime fighting mission, criminals are the "enemy," and fundamentally different from "good" people. Police are the "army" that fights the enemy, and various means that might otherwise be illegal or against the rules are excused or justified because of the importance of the mission of crime fighting. Under the public service mission, police are seen as serving the needs of all the public. This role is more expansive than the crime fighter role and includes other types of public service. Furthermore, it involves the idea of public service to all people, not just law-abiding "good" citizens.

2. **Explain the types of control that police have at their disposal.**

    Authority is the unquestionable entitlement to be obeyed that comes with certain roles, such as police officer. We do what they tell us because of their uniform. Power is also inherent in the role but implies that force will be used against resistance. Persuasion uses signs, symbols, words, and arguments (and possibly deception) to induce action. Force is the use of physical coercion to subdue the will of the individual.

3. **Provide the justification for police power and the basic ethical standards that derive from this justification.**

    The social contract is the basis of police power. We basically give up some rights in return for protection (by police). Part of that agreement is that they have the right to utilize power in order to protect the populace against aggressors. The social contract is also the basis of police ethics. Cohen and Feldberg (1991) propose five ethical standards that can be derived from the social contract: fair access, public trust, safety and security, teamwork, and objectivity.

4. **Identify the differences between the formal ethics of law enforcement and the values of the police subculture.**

    Formal law enforcement ethics promote the principles of fairness, service, the importance of the law, and upstanding personal conduct. The police subculture, on the other hand, has been described as endorsing stereotyping ("assholes"), absolute loyalty to colleagues (blue curtain of secrecy), the use of force for those who don't respect police authority, and noble-cause corruption (testilying and other bad "means" to achieve the good "end" of convicting criminals).

5. **Describe recent research findings on the police subculture.**

    In a research study, two-thirds reported that a whistleblower would encounter sanctions, more than half agreed that it was not unusual for police to ignore improper conduct on the part of other officers, and 61 percent indicated that police officers do not always report even the most serious violations/crimes of other officers. About 60 percent of rookies support mild lies to achieve a conviction. However, substantial variation exists among officers in their cultural views, according to survey studies. Current researchers conclude that the police culture is not monolithic and is perhaps more fragmented today than in the past.

Study Questions

1. What are Klockars's descriptions of police authority, power, persuasion, and force?

2. Describe Wilson and Brown's typologies of police, and explain how each might use discretion.

3. Describe the elements of the formal code of ethics, and contrast them with the values of the police subculture.

4. Describe Sherman's police "values" and Herbert's normative orders.

5. Explain why some people think the police subculture is breaking down.

Writing/Discussion Exercises

1. Write an essay on (or discuss) discretion in policing. In this essay, define discretion, give examples, and discuss unethical and ethical criteria for the use of discretion. Find newspaper articles illustrating police use of discretion. Analyze the officer's use of discretion in relation to the ethical systems described in earlier chapters.

2. Write an essay on (or discuss) community policing and whether it is likely to reduce or to encourage unethical actions by police officers. Utilize current research to illustrate whether or not community policing is growing or declining in popularity.

3. Write an essay on (or discuss) the two perceptions of the police officer—crime fighter or public servant. Consider various police practices and innovations as supporting one or the other role.

Key Terms

authority	discretion	power
blue curtain of secrecy	duty	public servants
code of silence	force	social contract
community policing	persuasion	

ETHICAL DILEMMAS

Situation 1

As a patrol officer, you are only doing your job when you stop a car for running a red light. Unfortunately, the driver of the car happens to be the mayor. You ticket her anyway, but the next morning you get called into the captain's office and told in no uncertain terms that you screwed up, because of an informal policy extending "courtesy" to city politicians. Several nights later, you observe the mayor's car weaving erratically across lanes and speeding. What would you do? What if the driver were a fellow police officer? What if the driver were a high school friend?

Situation 2

There is a well-known minor criminal in your district. Everyone is aware that he is engaged in a variety of crimes, including burglary, fencing, and drug dealing. However, you have been unable to make a case against him. Now he is the victim of a crime—he reports that he is the victim of theft and that his neighbor stole his riding lawnmower. How would you treat his case?

Situation 3

You are completing an internship with a local police agency. The officers you ride with are great and let you come along on everything they do. One day, the officer you are riding with takes you along on a drug raid. You are invited to come in when the house is secure, and you observe six young men sitting on two sofas in the living room. The officers are ransacking the house and asking the young men where they have hidden the drugs. Four of the youths are black and two are white. One of the officers walks behind the sofa where the black youths are sitting and slaps each one hard on the side of the head as he walks past. He ignores the two white youths sitting on the other sofa. You are shocked by his actions, but you know that if you say anything, your chance of being hired by this agency will be very small. You desperately want a good recommendation from the officers you ride with. What would you do?

Situation 4

You are a police officer in New Orleans. During the flood following Hurricane Katrina, you are ordered to patrol a section of the downtown area to prevent looting. The water is waist high in some places, and sections of blocks are, for the most part, inundated with floodwater. You come upon one shop where the plate-glass window has been broken, and about a dozen people are coming out of the shop with clothing in their arms. The stores' contents will be written off anyway by the owners and covered by insurance. Should that make a difference in your decision? What if the store was in an area of the city that wasn't flooded and the contents were not ruined? What if the people said they were desperate and didn't have any clothes because their belongings were under water? What if the items being taken were televisions and other electronics?

Situation 5

You and your partner have been working together for more than five years. He has seen you through the serious illness of your young child, and you have been there for him during his divorce. After the divorce, though, you have become increasingly anxious about him. He is obviously not taking care of his health, he drinks too much, and he has been consistently late to roll call. Now you can smell alcohol on his breath during the day and suspect that the ever-present cup of coffee he carries has more than a little whiskey in it. You've tried talking to him several times, but he just gets angry and tells you to mind your own business. Today, when the two of you responded to an accident scene, a witness drew you aside and said, "Aren't you going to do something about him?" pointing to your partner. Unfortunately, you knew what she meant, for he was literally swaying, trying to keep his balance in the hot sun. To make matters worse, he insists on driving. What would you do?

Police Discretion
and Dilemmas

A conducted energy device (CED), also known as a Taser.

© Howard Sayer/Alamy

I n this chapter, we will focus more closely on how police officers utilize their discretion. Recall that discretion is the power to make a choice of action from a number of alternatives. Police decisions dramatically affect the lives of those they come into contact with. As noted before, even the youngest and newest patrol officer has an awesome power over the rest of us. This is the reason why we should be concerned with every aspect of policing. While the vast majority of police officers are respectful of the dignity of those they come into contact with and abide by the law; if they do not, there is little immediate recourse; if you refuse or resist, you may be subject to physical force. If a police officer insists you stop your car, you must. If they ask to search your car, you may say no, but they can then make you wait a "reasonable" amount of time for a drug-sniffing dog or arrest you for a minor traffic violation. If an officer insists you sit down on the curb, you must; if he insists you leave the area,

Chapter Objectives

1. Provide any evidence that exists that law enforcement officers perform their role in a discriminatory manner.

2. Present information concerning the prevalence of and factors associated with the use of force by police officers.

3. Enumerate predictors associated with the use of excessive force.

4. Present the ethical issues involved in proactive investigations.

5. Present the ethical issues involved in reactive investigations.

you must; and, in a few troubling cases across the country, if an officer insists you submit to a body cavity search on a public street, people do. While officers who perform unconstitutional searches may be punished at a later time and victims may receive large settlements (paid by the taxpayers, not the offending officers), the fact remains that, at that moment, the individual officer's power is supreme. The fact that unreasonable and/or illegal applications of such power are more likely to be visited upon the poor and disenfranchised in this country is a truism that should not be ignored. Police officers don't police Wall Street like they police Watts; perhaps if they did, we would see a stronger reaction to police abuse of power. It is also true that the vast majority of officers use their discretion wisely, ethically, and for the good of the community.

Obviously the events described in the news box are extremely rare. Most police officers would never think about abusing their power; however, the point is that, even with the laws in place and policies of the department supposedly in conformance with the law, officers have a great deal of discretion over the decisions that they make every single day. In fact, most ethical dilemmas that police officers face derive from their powers of discretion. Muir (1977) describes moral dilemmas of the police officer as frequent and unavoidable, always unpopular with some groups, usually resolved quickly, dealt with alone, and involving complex criteria. Police officers are trained in the law and they know departmental policy, but that still leaves a wide range of possible

(•) IN THE NEWS | *That Can't Happen Here, Can It?*

One suspects that most people, if told that police officers performed searches of peoples' genitals on the side of the road in full public view, would not believe it. Unfortunately, it has happened—more than once, in more than one state. In Texas, two women filed a federal lawsuit against the Texas Department of Public Safety troopers after they were subjected to a "cavity search" during a traffic stop. They were pulled over for tossing cigarette butts out of the window of their vehicle. The trooper believed he smelled marijuana coming from the vehicle and performed a consensual search of the vehicle finding nothing. He then called for a female trooper, who, after putting on gloves, used her fingers to search their anuses and vaginas, using the same latex glove on both women. The search was performed on the side of the road in full view of other passing vehicles (CBSDFW.com, 2012). The women settled their lawsuit for $185,000. However, a similar search also happened near Houston. Two women were stopped for speeding by a state trooper who called for a female trooper to search the women for drugs. These women also claimed that the trooper used the same gloves on both women and that they were groped in full view of passing traffic. Drug paraphernalia was found in the car, but

no drugs were found. Newspaper reports indicate that, in the second case, the female trooper was fired and the male trooper was suspended over the incident (NBC.com, 2013).

One shouldn't think it could only happen in Texas either. A large number of similar searches were reputedly performed against black men in inner-city neighborhoods in Milwaukee between 2008 and 2013; 60 people have claimed such encounters on public streets in full view of witnesses (McNally, 2014; Barton, 2014). The police chief blamed the behavior on "overzealous" policing, but eventually one officer, Michael Vagnini, pleaded guilty to four felonies and is serving 26 months in prison and three others pleaded to misdemeanors. A larger number of officers were investigated for impeding the inquiry and/or lying; however, none were charged or disciplined (Barton, 2014) One of the victims received a half-million-dollar settlement from a disgusted jury that sent a strong message that such humiliation and degradation would not be accepted even to further the mission of drug enforcement. The man testified that police stopped him in his mother's driveway and groped his penis and then felt between his buttocks (McNally, 2014).

alternatives when arriving on any scene. Should they pull over a driver who forgot to signal? Should they ask a group of black youths clustered in a park entrance what they are doing? Should they leave a domestic violence victim alone or convince her to seek shelter outside the home? An officer makes hundreds if not thousands of decisions a week. We discussed police officer discretion in the last chapter, but in this chapter we will focus on discretion as it relates to three topics: race and ethnicity, the use of force, and investigative practices. Each of these topics has been the source of controversy.

Discretion and Discrimination

When individuals have discretion, individual prejudices and perceptions of groups such as women, minorities, and homosexuals can influence their decision making. Officers' views of the world affect the way they do their job. If these views include prejudicial attitudes toward groups, and such prejudices affect decisions, those groups may not receive the same protections as "good" citizens. The point is not that police officers are more prejudiced than the rest of us; it is that their special position creates the possibility that their prejudices could cause a citizen to be treated differently than others. This becomes even more of a problem when the law enforcement agency's occupational culture reinforces prejudicial views. Essentially, when police act on prejudices while performing their jobs, discrimination takes the form of either enforcing the law differentially or withholding the protections and benefits of the law (Kappeler, Sluder, and Alpert, 1994: 175). As the In the News box illustrates, some police officers may

(•) IN THE NEWS | *Off the Record?*

In several police departments around the country, embarrassing and troubling exposure of texts and e-mails between officers have occurred that call into question the ability of police officers to police all citizens fairly. San Francisco's texting scandal came about after a prosecutor obtained them during the prosecution of one officer. Racist and homophobic messages sent during 2011 and 2012 included one where the officers discussed getting a gun and "putting down" the "monkey" (a black man involved with a relative of one of the officers). An investigation ensued and some officers resigned and others were fired (Williams, 2015a).

Similar patterns of racist messaging or forwarded jokes have taken place in Ferguson, Missouri, exacerbating the tensions there; Edison, New Jersey; Seattle, Washington; Baton Rouge, Louisiana; and Miami Beach and Fort Lauderdale, Florida. In the Miami Beach case, after racist jokes and texts were exposed, prosecutors reviewed more than 100 cases for evidence of bias. In the Fort Lauderdale incident, prosecutors dropped 11 felony and 23 misdemeanor cases of the involved officers. In that case, officers made a video featuring Ku Klux Klan imagery (Wood, 2015; Robles, 2015).

Some argue that the internet is full of racist, sexist, homophobic rants. Since the messages were private, officers have a First Amendment right to say anything they want, as long as they do not act in a discriminatory manner. The reality is that police officers do not have the same freedom on social media as the rest of us, if they can be identified as an officer. Some officers have been fired for what they post on their Facebook page because racist, homophobic, or sexist commentary can be defined as conduct unbecoming an officer. It is also extremely important to be aware of the power of implicit bias. Even if officers do not feel they are treating African Americans differently, they may be, especially if their worldview includes viewing African Americans as monkeys and seeing humor in lynching.

express extremely negative stereotypes of certain groups. Administrators cannot take the chance that such views may translate into differential enforcement of the law.

There is a longstanding, pervasive belief that police treat African Americans, and, to a lesser extent, Hispanics, more harshly, than whites. In this section, we will examine the evidence as to whether blacks are treated differentially, always with the recognition that one cannot discuss the 12,000 police agencies in the country as a monolithic unit. We will also focus specifically on racial profiling. Finally, we will examine the evidence as to whether blacks are more likely than whites to be shot by police officers.

A Racial Divide

There is a pervasive belief among minority groups in the United States that law enforcement is fundamentally racist. Some argue that this perception is based in reality. It is true that, historically, law enforcement has been involved in slave patrols, enforcing white power in late-nineteenth-century and early-twentieth-century race riots, and, more recently, using the legal force inherent in the institution of law enforcement to intimidate and abuse civil rights protestors in the 1960s. It should also be strongly emphasized that the charge of racism is not limited to law enforcement, but rather has been leveled against the whole legal system. The system of laws and punishment, the courts that administer the laws, and the corrections system that makes decisions regarding the liberties of those convicted have all been described as agencies that systematically and pervasively discriminate against minority groups. Police, in this view, are just one element in systematic, even institutional, racism. The In the News box describes the Department of Justice report of Ferguson, Missouri, after the Michael Brown shooting, which details problems that go well beyond the police department.

Most studies indicate that blacks express more distrust of police than whites or Hispanics. In the latest Pew Research Center (2014) public opinion report (conducted via a telephone survey with 1,501 adults) overall perceptions of police only modestly changed from the last poll five years before, except that the share of blacks saying they have "very little" confidence in their local police to treat blacks and whites equally has

---

((•)) IN THE NEWS | *No Charges for Officer, but Systemic Racism in Ferguson, Missouri*

Officer Darren Wilson was no-billed by a grand jury after the Michael Brown shooting, and some individuals took that to mean that the charges of racism in Ferguson were unfounded until the Department of Justice completed their investigation and released their report. The report documented widespread discriminatory practices directed toward the black community. The report put into context the violent reaction of the community to the Brown shooting, explaining that there had been years of distrust and resentment because of illegal and unethical practices by the police and justice officials in the town and county. Some of the findings indicated that the city depended on revenue generated from fines and late charges, differentially paid by the poor community. Late charges increased rapidly so that a traffic fine might end up costing thousands and inability to pay would result in jail. African Americans constituted 67 percent of the population but accounted for 93 percent of arrests and all arrests for resisting arrest were of black citizens between 2012 and 2014. Officers were encouraged to make arrests to generate revenue rather than public safety.

Source: Berman, 2015.

increased, from 34 percent five years ago to 46 percent. The group expressing the most negative views toward police were under-50, black Democrats.

The finding that young black men have the most negative views of police is supported by qualitative research. Brunson (2007), using a small (40) sample of young black men (ages 13–19) and in-depth interviews, found that 83 percent had experienced what they believed to be harassment, and almost all said they knew of others who had been the victim of police harassment. The interviews illustrated that the men reacted not just to being stopped, but also to being forced to sit or lie down on the ground and being spoken to in a derogatory manner.

In the Pew study, younger adults of all races had a more negative view of police, by more than two to one. Over two-thirds (68 percent) of those under 50 said police departments do an only fair or poor job using appropriate levels of force. The table below shows some selected responses:

Public Perception of Police

Ratings (Excellent to Poor) for Police

Police use of the right amount of force in each situation?	Excellent	Poor
Black	0%	57%
White	9%	23%
Police do good job holding police officers accountable?		
Black	3%	70%
White	9%	27%
Police treat the races equally		
Black	3%	70%
White	9%	25%

Source: Pew Research Center/*USA Today* Survey, 2014.

Hispanics also have a more negative view of police than do whites. A nationwide poll of 1,000 Hispanics, underwritten by the W.W. Kellogg Foundation and reported in the popular press, found that two in three Hispanics fear police use of excessive force, even though 84 percent agreed that police were there to protect them. About 18 percent reported that they had friends or family members who had suffered police brutality (Planas, 2015).

Academic research supports these findings. In a 33-city sample, it was found that race and age were strong correlates of distrust of police, with the level of distrust of blacks two to five times higher than whites across cities. What was interesting about this study was the variation across the cities. For instance, 32 percent of blacks in New York City as opposed to 7 percent of whites expressed distrust of police, but the differences were less pronounced in Birmingham, Alabama, with a much smaller percentage of both blacks and whites expressing distrust (8.9 percent compared to 2.08 percent; Sharp and Johnson, 2009: 166).

Studies show that civil rights complaints against police are correlated positively to the percentage of minorities in the population (Holmes, 2000), that more than twice as many lower-class African Americans as whites report disrespectful language or swearing by police officers (Weitzer, 1999), and that middle-class African Americans express more negative attitudes than do lower-class African Americans (Weitzer, 1999: 838). Age, income, sex, and education; living in metropolitan areas; and experiences with police all have been shown as influencing attitudes toward police; however, race remains a key variable even after controlling for other factors, arguably because blacks report having more negative interactions with police, are more likely to be exposed to negative media portrayals of police misconduct, and are more likely to live in high-crime areas where police employ a more combative style (Weitzer and Tuch, 2004; Reisig and Parks, 2000).

It is important to understand that the variables of citizen "disrespect" and non-compliance / resistance confound the correlation between minority status and police actions. Older research shows blacks are less likely than whites to experience initial disrespect from officers when controlling for these variables (Mastrofski, Reisig, and McCluskey, 2002). The videos one sees on YouTube show terrible examples of police officers who are rude and abusive to the citizenry, but academic studies using observers indicate that residents (both black and white) are initially disrespectful to police *three times* as often as police are initially disrespectful to residents (15 percent compared to 5 percent). Factors associated with being disrespectful include heightened emotion, number of bystanders, presence of intoxicants, being mentally impaired, and being in a disadvantaged neighborhood (Reisig et al., 2004; Mastrofski, Reisig, and McCluskey, 2002: 534; Engel et al., 2011). Engel and colleagues, after an exhaustive review of prior studies, concluded that being a resident of a disadvantaged neighborhood was a stronger predictor of police "disrespect" to citizens than race. In their own study, they utilized officer perceptions of citizen disrespect rather than observer data, noting that the officer perception was more relevant in consequences than the perception of outsiders to the interaction. In traffic stops, both black and white officers were significantly more likely to perceive black drivers as disrespectful, noncompliant, and/or resistant (Engel et al., 2011). One assumes that these perceptions (note that perceptions are not necessarily reality) affect the way that officers deal with the subjects.

Does this mean that minority residents' perceptions of unfair and differential policing are inaccurate? Not at all; it just means the situation is more complicated than a portrayal of racist cops and passive victims. Some research indicates insensitivity of police officers to how their actions, specifically, minor traffic violation stops to search the car for drugs while the driver and passengers are made to sit on the curb, appear to minority residents. (Whitehead, 2015). While legal, this heavy-handed police action performed probably hundreds of times a day across the country in minority communities is likely to result in resentment. Even if police aren't initially more disrespectful to African Americans, consistent research across many studies shows that blacks are stopped and searched more often than whites (Mastrofski, Reisig, and McCluskey, 2002: 543). A Bureau of Justice statistics study utilizing an addendum to the National Crime Victimization survey showed that more black drivers than white or Hispanic (13 percent versus 10 percent) were pulled over for traffic stops, but, interestingly, no difference existed for "street stops" (individuals stopped while walking). Blacks were less likely to believe that police acted appropriately in the stops. White drivers were searched and ticketed at a lower rate than black drivers (Langton and Durose, 2013).

If one perceives that a police stop or an order to move is discriminatory, being disrespectful or noncompliant may be the result; thus, the correlations between disrespect

QUOTE & QUERY

You have officers there that have questionable integrity, and they should not be wearing the badge, and they should not be out there policing people.... You can't change a person's heart. And you can't make a person do the right thing and be moral.

(Ex-police chief speaking of the beating of Floyd Dent by an Inkster police officer after a traffic stop that was believed to be the result of racial profiling.)

Source: Dalbey, 2015.

 Do you think that the race issue is purely a problem of biased police officers, a more systemic problem with how police are taught and socialized, or only a problem in the perceptions of minority residents?

consent decree
The legal agreement between the Justice Department and a police department whereby the police department agrees to perform specified activities and submit to monitoring to ensure that the department meets the terms of the agreement in order to avoid a lawsuit.

racial profiling
Basing a decision solely on the race/ethnicity of the other party (i.e., to stop and question).

or noncompliance and officer actions does not resolve the question as to whether blacks are unfairly treated. Some research has also shown that race was a predictor in the use of verbal and physical coercion by officers (Terrill, 2001; Terrill, Paoline, and Manning, 2003). Another study done in San Francisco covering the years 2010 to April 2015 showed that African Americans were cited for resisting arrest at a rate eight times higher than whites. The study reported that of 9,633 arrests for resisting, not accompanied by a felony, blacks (making up just 6 percent of the population) accounted for 45 percent of the arrests. Suspects can be convicted of resisting arrest, punishable by up to a year in jail and up to a $1,000 fine, even when the underlying offense is minor, such as not complying with an order to move one's car. Critics of police say the charge is used to cover up cases of police brutality (Green, 2015).

African Americans are not the only minorities who suffer from differential enforcement patterns. Perhaps some of the most egregious cases of discriminatory law enforcement occur on this nation's southern borders (Crank, 2003; Huspek, Martinez, and Jiminez, 2001). Many Hispanics are legal residents of the United States yet are treated abusively and told they should go back to Mexico. Huspek, Martinez, and Jiminez (2001: 185) argue that border agents act this way because they are encouraged by the "rhetoric of fear" and tacit acceptance of any means necessary to reduce or discourage illegal immigration.

Sheriff Arpaio in Maricopa County (Phoenix) has been engaged in a longstanding fight with the Department of Justice over his practices regarding the treatment of Hispanics in his jurisdiction. Section 14141 of the Violent Crime Control and Law Enforcement Act of 1994 grants the Justice Department a cause of action to sue a state or local government for equitable and declaratory relief when a governmental authority engages in a pattern or practice of conduct by law enforcement officers that deprives persons of rights, privileges, or immunities secured or protected by the Constitution. Generally, the Justice Department and city agree to mandated changes leading to what is called a **consent decree**. If the city and police department do not agree with the Justice Department's demands, they can be sued which is what occurred in Maricopa County as described in the In the News box.

Racial Profiling

Racial profiling occurs when a police officer makes a stop based entirely on race or ethnicity. When a young black man is seen, for instance, driving a newer-model, expensive car, police officers suspect that the vehicle is stolen and/or that the man is holding drugs. A "pretext stop" refers to the practice of police officers to use some minor traffic offense to stop the individual and in the course of the traffic stop look for other evidence of wrongdoing, specifically by a search, usually a consent search. The Supreme Court has upheld the legality of such stops in *Whren v. U.S.* (517 U.S. 806, 1996). In general, minorities are targeted because of a belief that they are more likely to be criminal.

Racial profiling began when federal agents developed a profile of drug smugglers to assist border patrol and custom agents in airports. The list of indicators included travel

(•) IN THE NEWS | *Maricopa County and the "Toughest Sheriff"*

Maricopa County Sheriff Joe Arpaio has been engaged in a long battle with the Department of Justice over treatment of Hispanic residents. Arpaio has a national reputation and been called America's "toughest sheriff" in news stories for his treatment of jail prisoners.

A federal lawsuit was filed against Maricopa County, Arizona, and Sheriff Joe Arapaio after a Department of Justice investigation, begun in 2008, found there was a pattern and practice of discrimination against Hispanics. The records showed that Hispanic drivers were four to nine times more likely to be stopped, and one-fifth of the traffic stops appeared to be unconstitutional (with no reason to stop) from a review of incident reports. Records indicated that police were dispatched when the report was only that there were "people of dark skin" or "people speaking Spanish" in an area. Findings also indicated that jail officers punished Hispanic inmates for not understanding English, refused to accept forms written in Spanish, and pressured inmates to sign forms waiving rights in English without a translation. Most announcements about programs and services were made in English, denying Spanish-speaking inmates from accessing them. Another finding was that there was a general culture of bias against Hispanics, including the use of excessive force against Latinos, a reduction of policing services to the Latino community, and a gender and/or national origin bias by failing to adequately investigate sex crimes. Relevant to this last finding, it was noted that there were 432 cases since 2007 of sexual assault and child molestation that were not properly investigated, with most victims being Hispanic.

In May 2012, Arpaio lost the federal lawsuit filed against him by the Department of Justice. U.S. District Judge Murray Snow issued a ruling that required cameras in every deputy's car, increased data collection and reporting, a community-advisory board, and a court-appointed monitor to ensure the agency is taking steps to prevent discrimination. The ruling banned "pretextual" traffic stops (stopping cars for minor traffic violations) purely to question the driver and passenger about their immigration status by a roving task force. The Sheriff's Office appealed the ruling.

In 2015, Arpaio admitted violating the order by allowing the roving patrols to continue past the judge's ruling. It had been previously reported that Arpaio allowed the patrols to continue 18 months after the judge ordered them to cease. Arpaio and his top deputy offered to personally pay $100,000 for the violation. Observers suspect that the combative sheriff admitted fault only in order to forestall an evidentiary hearing which would have required him to present data on stops and other information related to the alleged wrongdoing of some of those involved in the immigration patrols (Parvini, 2015). One deputy (who later killed himself) was arrested for "shaking down" illegal immigrants and IDs, evidence, and drugs were found at his home. Another ex-deputy allegedly protected drug shipments by finding out from his former co-workers where they were working on particular days. Other deputies were under investigation for "pocketing" items found in drug busts rather than submitting them as evidence (Billeaud, 2015).

---

patterns and behavior as well as demographic indices, such as race. The concept was expanded to highway drivers by state patrol officers who were attempting to stem the flow of drugs up through the interstates in Florida, Georgia, Texas, and other southern states (Harris, 2004; Crank, 2003). Observers contend that what eventually happened is that the behavioral and other indices of profiling were abandoned, so that decisions to target suspected drug-involved individuals were reduced purely to race. Racial profiling became known as the practice of officers stopping blacks for minor traffic violations, for example, failing to use a turn signal, in order to search the car for drugs.

Studies on racial profiling show that minorities may be stopped in numbers far greater than their proportion of the population would indicate; however, the methodology of some racial profiling studies is problematic (Smith and Alpert, 2002; Engel, Calnon, and Bernard, 2002). Comparing stops to simply the percentage of population is not very accurate because it does not take into account the percentage of non-white drivers, the percentage of non-white drivers who engage in traffic offenses, or the percentage of minorities in the geographic area that is being targeted by heavier patrols (which would result in more stops regardless of the race/ethnicity of the driver). Most of the earlier studies used percentage-of-population figures, but other researchers are highly critical of this rough approximation of the base rate. There is also no clear proof that the stops are due to prejudicial views toward those stopped. Most critics blame the individual officer, but it is important to note organizational influences, especially because studies show that black officers are just as likely as white officers to stop blacks in disproportionate numbers (Engel, Calnon, and Bernard, 2002).

In a study of what the researchers called "traffic stops" and "investigatory stops," a distinction was made between police stops that occur because the driver commits a clear violation and those where the officer is using the stop for investigatory purposes. The first stop is short and results in a ticket; the second kind of stop is longer and always includes a request for a consent search. There is little racial difference in those stopped for the first type of search but there is in the second type. In the study, 60 percent of all stops for whites were for traffic safety, versus 35 percent for blacks; however, 52 percent of all stops for blacks (versus 34 percent for whites) were for such minor reasons that the stop was coded as investigatory. In these types of searches, individuals are stopped for driving too slowly, broken lights, failure to signal, and other pretexts to initiate a search for drugs (Epp, Maynard-Moody, and Haider-Markel, 2014). The second kind of stop is proactive policing for crime (mostly drug) control. It is a cost/benefit question as to whether the benefit gained is worth the cost in the antipathy it generates among those who are stopped. The individual officer's decision to stop minority individuals can be analyzed as an ethical dilemma.

ETHICAL DILEMMA

Should you stop a late model car driven by two young Hispanic men because you suspect they cannot afford it and may have evidence of criminal activity in the car? You believe it's possible they may be illegal immigrants as well. The driver then makes a right turn without signaling as you watch. Should you stop the car (even though you wouldn't bother in other circumstances)? Should you ask for evidence that the men are legal residents of the United States?

Law

What does the law say about racial profiling? In cases such as *United States v. Martinez-Fuerte* (425 U.S. 931, 1976), the U.S. Supreme Court has basically legitimized the use of race as a criterion in profiles (although lower courts are not in agreement when race seems to be the sole or primary reason for the stop). Further, pretext stops (where police stop a driver because of some minor traffic violation, but the real reason is to investigate suspected criminal activity) have been accepted by the Court in *Whren v. United States*

(517 U.S. 806, 1996), in effect allowing the police to use their discretion to enforce minor laws as a tool to implement race-based stops. Generally, the law allows the use of race as one element in the decision to stop, but does not allow it to be used as the sole element in the decision to stop or for profiling purposes.

In May 2010, Arizona passed HB 2162, an anti-immigration law that included a section requiring law enforcement officers in the state to ask for proof of citizenship or residency if there was reasonable suspicion that the person was an illegal immigrant. The inquiries about immigration were to be initiated only after a lawful stop, detention or arrest, and stops could not be made merely because of ethnicity, race, or national origin. In June of 2012, the Supreme Court upheld this section of the law (*Arizona v. United States*, 567 U.S. ___, 2012). Police officers still have discretion in whether or not to stop for the initial traffic violation even in Arizona.

Policy

Police policies have definitely undergone dramatic change in the last 20 years regarding racial profiling, largely as a result of public concern. In 1999, President Bill Clinton condemned the practice, and congressional hearings were held to investigate how widespread the practice was. Most people objected to racial profiling as used in the "war on drugs" in the 1980s and 1990s (Weitzer and Tuch, 2002). Many states passed legislation requiring police departments to collect demographic information on police stops to determine whether racial profiling was an issue, and many departments instituted these collection procedures and training to sensitize officers to the possibility that their discretion was being used in a racial or ethnic discriminatory manner.

Ethics

Do ethical rationales help us determine whether or not racial profiling, if legal, is ethical? A utilitarian argument for racial profiling would be that the "end" of drug interdiction justifies the "means" of harassing and inconveniencing a group believed to be disproportionately responsible. However, it appears that the end is not well served. The "hit rate" for finding drugs is lower for African Americans than it is for other racial groups (Cole and Lamberth, 2001). Harris (2004) proposes the idea that when officers use race in decision making, they become less effective, not more effective, because they do not concentrate on what is important for investigation—behavior, not demographics. There is no research at this point of the effectiveness of using ethnicity to discover immigration violators.

An ethical formalist system would probably not support profile searches for drugs or immigration violations because this approach is treating those individuals as a means, and it is probably contrary to the universalism principle unless everyone would agree that they should be stopped in the same manner. Because most of us would object to numerous stops every week by police who have no reason to be suspicious other than the color of our skin, it violates the first part of the categorical imperative.

After 9/11, those who looked like they were Middle Eastern were subject to increased scrutiny before they boarded airliners. In some cases, individuals were denied entry to airplanes when other passengers complained that they would not fly with men who looked like they might be suicide bombers. Interestingly, many people who are opposed to racial profiling of blacks for drug interdiction agree that it is a necessary and ethical response to terrorism. Arguably, the reason is that the "end" of protecting us from a terrorist attack is greater than the "end" of protecting us from drug smuggling or other crime. Deontological ethical systems would arrive at a different answer because they are not consequentialist and no "end" would justify treating people as a means or in a way that could not be universalized. The ethics of care would not endorse a racial profiling policy because it would not be meeting the needs of all concerned and would place some people's needs above others; however, there might be an argument when the threat is specific and extreme and the inconvenience minor.

(⚬) IN THE NEWS | *New Rules on Profiling*

The Department of Justice issued new federal guidelines (mandatory for DOJ agents but only advisory for state law enforcement or other federal agencies) in December 2014. The rules added national origin, gender, gender identity, religion, and sexual orientation to characteristics for which profiling has been prohibited since 2003. Agents are prohibited from using these categories as the sole reason to investigate a target. They also eliminate the broad national security exception to profiling restrictions if for terrorism investigations. Critics argue that federal rules do not provide much protection against profiling, however, because they do not change the way the FBI uses nationality to map neighborhoods, recruit informants, or look for foreign spies. Relations between Muslim communities and the FBI have been strained, because of the intelligence-gathering activities conducted. Supporters argued that the new rules were a compromise between the rights of targeted groups (e.g., Muslims) and national security (Doyle, 2014; Apuzzo, 2014b).

Ultimately, there are three questions concerning racial profiling that must be considered separately. There is a question of fact: What is the most efficient and effective method to identify a drug smuggler, illegal immigrant, or terrorist? This is different from the question of law: What is the legal duty of an officer and what are the civil rights of an individual in any interaction between them? Both of these questions are different from the question of ethics: Should an officer act upon a belief and suspicion created by nothing more than an individual's membership in a minority or ethnic group? Recently, federal guidelines were promulgated for federal agents regarding racial profiling described in the In the News box.

Evidence indicates that racial profiling doesn't occur necessarily because officers are racist. It is an entrenched part of policing because there is a suspicion of blacks (men in particular) held by all police officers, whether black or white, combined with the pressure to conduct investigatory stops to obtain drugs and other contraband. Unfortunately, this pattern of enforcement leads to a script of resistance and "disrespect" on the part of those stopped, which, in turn, incites some officers to ratchet up the force used so that a simple stop ends up in a resisting arrest charge, or, worse—the use of lethal force (Bouie, 2014, 2015).

Police Shootings of Blacks

Statistics indicate black men are disproportionately the victims of police shootings. Studies show that the minority percentage of a city's population is predictive of the number of police shootings. According to another study, young black males aged 15–19 are 21 times more likely to be shot and killed by police than their white counterparts (reported in Bouie, 2014). The explanation that blacks are shot more often because they are disproportionately involved in violent crime or that they are disproportionately more likely to assault police officers (both true in some studies) explains this disproportional reality only partially (Bowes, 2015). From what we know, police shootings are more likely to occur in certain areas of the city, and these areas are more likely to be minority neighborhoods; thus, it may be that the disproportion is due primarily to living in the wrong place rather than solely because of doing something wrong.

It is possible that police officers are more likely to perceive blacks as a greater threat, even controlling for other elements of the situation. Evidence for this lies only in anecdotal data from open-carry states, where white men seem to be able to approach officers carrying visible weapons without raising the officers' alarm compared to incidents where minority children are shot for having toy guns (Tamir Rice, Andy Lopez), and black men are shot merely for holding a gun that is merchandise in a store (John Crawford, III) (Jonsson, 2014; Wines, 2014). Laboratory findings are mixed. Some research shows that individuals participating in a shoot/don't shoot scenario were slower to shoot when the suspect was black than when the suspect was white, and there were more errors of not shooting an armed black suspect. These results indicate that police officers are aware of and compensate for bias, although it is possible that the findings are an artifact of the research itself (James, Vila, and Daratha, 2014). The implicit bias studies conducted at the Kirwan Institute for the Study of Race and Ethnicity at Ohio State University (http://kirwaninstitute.osu.edu/research/understanding-implicit-bias) have been accumulating research findings for years showing how implicit bias affects perceptions of and probably actions toward members of minority groups.

In order to understand whether there is racial bias in officers' decisions to shoot, it is important to have all the facts. Unfortunately, in the area of police shootings, we do not have accurate national statistics. Police departments are not required to report shootings to any central database. It is very important to have a base number (of all shootings) before we can understand the factors that affect the decision to shoot. It would be even more beneficial to have data regarding all the situations where an officer was legally allowed to shoot with information on whether the decision was to shoot or not. Unfortunately, that type of data will probably never be available which is why researchers use shoot-don't shoot scenarios in a laboratory setting. The media stories of black men shot by police in the last several years do illustrate a problem of race relations we cannot ignore, but it is also important to remember that these media stories are a distorted reality because we do not know of all the other shootings (of black, Hispanic and white men and women) that have taken place (and the many situations where officers had a legal authority to shoot and chose not to). It is not a good comparison to simply look at percentage of population figures when evaluating whether there is a racial component to police officer decisions to shoot because there are important factors we must control for, not the least of which is whether the target is shooting at police.

Discretion and the Use of Force

Police have an uncontested right to use force when necessary to apprehend and/or subdue a suspect of a crime. They have a right to use lethal force only if they believe that the suspect poses a threat to the officer or others (*Tennessee v. Garner*, 471 U.S. 1105, 1985). When their use of force exceeds that which is necessary to accomplish their lawful purpose, or when their purpose is not lawful apprehension or self-defense, but rather personal retaliation or coercion, it is defined as excessive force and is unethical and illegal (*Graham v. Connor*, 490 U.S. 386, 1989).

In *Graham v. Connor*, Graham needed orange juice to forestall a diabetic episode. When the line was too long he ran out of the store to where his friend waited in the car. Officers stopped him, suspecting that he was somehow involved in a crime. The incident escalated and officers grabbed him and slammed him into the car hood, then threw him in the back of the police car, breaking his foot, and inflicting cuts, bruises, and injuring his shoulder. Under the Supreme Court holding from this case, officers have the right to use "reasonable" force in any interaction with the public, as determined by the facts and circumstances. They are not obligated to use the least possible force as long as the force used would be used by another officer in the same situation.

Recently, there has been attention to the fact that police officers are rarely indicted by grand juries for criminal charges after a lethal shooting. The *Graham* test allows officers to use force when they perceive a threat, and, as long as the perception is reasonable, they may make an error in their assessment and not be legally culpable. Grand juries and trial juries generally give officers the benefit of the doubt in their assessment of a reasonable threat. Other uses of force are similarly evaluated; thus, officers are given a great deal of leeway in deciding the range of force used.

In this section, we will first discuss the absence of an accurate national databank on police-caused fatalities or any national source of use-of-force statistics. What figures we do have of police shootings will be presented as well as the number of officers killed. Next, a review of research identifying factors involved in the use of force (of the target, situation, and officer) will be offered. A special section on Tasers focuses on the use of that device. Finally, current approaches to reduce the number of police shootings will be reviewed.

Probably the most well-known use of force incident in this country was that by law enforcement officers against Rodney King, revealed by the amateur video and widely disseminated. This can still be seen on YouTube even though the event occurred in 1991. In the Rodney King incident, an initial act of passing a police vehicle and leading officers in a chase led to the involvement of 12 police cars, one helicopter, and up to 27 officers. The incident resulted in King being struck at least 56 times, with 11 skull fractures, a broken cheekbone, a fractured eye socket, a broken ankle, missing teeth, kidney damage, external burns, and permanent brain damage (Kappeler, Sluder, and Alpert, 1994: 146).

This use of force probably was prosecuted (unsuccessfully) only because of the existence and widespread dissemination of the videotape. The King incident is an example of lawful force or excessive force, depending on one's perception. In the video, King clearly continued to try to rise and the officers continued to use their conducted energy devices (CEDs), kick, and hit him with their batons as long as he kept trying to rise. Some argue that the officers continued to hit him because he continued to resist; others argue that he continued to resist because he was disoriented and was trying to escape the injuries being inflicted upon him. The law allows "reasonable force," and policy interprets reasonable as proportional to the level of resistance; however, that leaves a large area of discretion for the individual officer. It is for this reason, that use of force is a legal issue, a training issue, and, also, an issue of ethics.

What We Know and Don't Know

As stated before, the events in Ferguson, North Charleston, and Baltimore brought a great deal of public scrutiny to police use of deadly force. Many were surprised to find that there is no good national statistic as to how many people are killed by police each year, and certainly we have no way to know how many people are shot each year by police and do not die. Nor is there any national database of other nonlethal uses of force.

The supplemental homicide reports provided by the FBI include a category of justifiable homicide (a legal killing almost always performed by a law enforcement officer). However, it has been known for quite some time that the number reported is a woeful undercount of the true number of homicides because police departments are not obligated to provide statistics (Hickman, Piquero, and Garner, 2008). Klinger (2012) compared internal reports from the Los Angeles Police Department to FBI numbers and found that the 184 homicides by police in the FBI report was 46 percent lower than the 340 uncovered in internal reports.

The FBI reports show that the number of individuals killed by police has been increasing even while the crime rate has declined. According to official reports, there were 461 justifiable homicides by law enforcement officers in 2013; 426 in 2012; 404 in 2011; 397 in 2010 and 414 in 2009 (reported in Schmidt, 2015). This compares to averages in the 200s in the 1960s–1970s and an average of 350 in the 1980s–early 2000s. Thus, the number of officer-caused fatalities seems to be increasing. Even more troubling, independent estimates of the number of recent killings based on other sources put the average number per year at double the official number and closer to 1,000

(Wines and Cohen, 2015). Reports also indicate that blacks are disproportionately represented in the numbers of individuals shot and killed by police. The explanation for the increasing numbers reflected in the FBI report may be simply that more incidents are being formally reported (Johnson, 2014), or it may mean something else. It is also important to note that these are raw numbers, not rates per 1,000. Obviously, the population of the country is greater in recent years than in past decades; therefore, one cannot compare across time logically without constructing a rate that takes the population base into consideration. Even if rates are computed, it doesn't tell us much because we don't know if there are more people with guns. The majority of those killed by police are armed. In some studies it has been found that at least 80 percent of individuals killed had weapons (reported in Philly.com, 2014; Kindy, 2015). If there are more guns in society, there will be more incidents where officers feel threatened. In short, we don't really know whether shootings are an increasing problem or not.

Statistics of the numbers of officers killed in the line of duty are easier to come by. An annual report by the nonprofit National Law Enforcement Officers Memorial Fund found that 50 officers were killed by guns in 2014. In 2013, 32 officers were shot and killed, and 50 were killed in 2012. In 2011, 73 officers were killed in gunfire, the most in any year in the past decade. The average since 2004 is 55 police deaths annually. The highest number of deaths was 156 in 1973 and the 1970s averaged about 140 officer deaths per year. It is important to note that these are not rates per 1,000, so the 1973 number would have been from a much smaller total number of police officers in the country. The reduction in numbers of police officers killed is probably due to the advent of body armor and better training, now required in most departments. Before one is tempted to compare these numbers to those of police-caused deaths, note that the numbers say nothing about the number of police officers shot at. That is also a number we do not have as context for the numbers of citizens killed by police. Officers Wenjian Liu and Rafael Ramos were assassinated as they were sitting in their patrol car in New York City in December 2014, supposedly as a "revenge killing" for Eric Garner and Michael Brown by a man with mental health issues. In 2009, four Lakewood, Washington, officers were shot and killed while drinking coffee in a diner. Every officer in the country must experience a sense of dread when these cases arise knowing that it could happen to them. It is true, as some point out, that statistically policing is safer than several other occupations when looking at on-the-job mortality rates; however, there must be some difference in how one experiences the risk of work-related deadly accidents compared to being the victim of an intentional assassination. There seems to be a heightened sense of risk among officers, brought about by the "militarization" of policing, but also, by several targeted fatal shootings of police officers in the summer of 2015.

There are major efforts underway to obtain better statistics. Some states have pursued legislation to require police departments to report shooting data to a central source. The national bar association recently announced it was filing open records requests in the largest 25 cities in an effort to develop a database of deaths of unarmed citizens by police. In addition, they are requesting that police departments preserve all police officers' raw notes of statements, observations and data collected from the scene of any incident where a resident is injured or killed. This request will also require information on the primary officer involved and all responding officers, as well as the officers' detail logs from the crime scene, and video and photographic evidence related to any alleged and/or proven misconduct by current or former employees.

In 1994, the Violent Crime Control and Law Enforcement Act was passed requiring the attorney general to acquire data about the use of excessive force by law enforcement officers and publish yearly reports. The annual reports required by Congress in the 1994 law were never produced (Doyle, 2014b). Estimates of the use of force come from other sources, such as the Police-Public Contact Survey and single-city studies (Hickman, Piquero, and Garner, 2008).

Factors in the Use of Force

The most important thing to know is that use of force seems to be present in a very small percentage of the total encounters between police and citizens and *excessive* force (force not justified by law or policy) occurs in less than 1 percent of interactions with the public. Second, research indicates that a small percentage of officers seem to be responsible for a disproportionate percentage of the force incidents. Finally, some studies do find an association between force and race or socioeconomic status, but other factors, such as demeanor, seem to be even more influential.

Worden and Catlin (2002) reported that the use of force occurs in 1.3 to 2.5 percent of all encounters. A Bureau of Justice Statistics (BJS) study reported that force was used in about 1.6 percent of all police–citizen interactions (Ducrose, Langan, and Smith, 2007). Another report indicated that in about 44.6 million contacts with the public, only 1 percent involve use of force; and use of force is present in about 20 percent of arrests although it is usually just grabbing and holding (Gundy, 2003: 60). However, use of force seems to vary depending on the city. Garner, Maxwell, and Heraux (2002) found in their study that use of force ranged from 12.7 percent of encounters in one city to 22.9 percent of encounters in another city. In addition, a national survey of law enforcement agencies found that the rate of use-of-force events varied by region, with the highest in the South (90 incidents per 100,000), followed by the Northeast (72), the Midwest (68), and the West (50) (Terrill, 2005). It is also important to note that the figures above are describing use of force, not excessive force. Excessive force is estimated to occur in a miniscule portion of total encounters with the public—estimated at one-third of 1 percent (Micucci and Gomme, 2005: 487).

Studies exploring use of force date back to Friedrich's (1980) now classic study that examined how individual, situational, and organizational factors have been offered as explanations to the decision to use force. In his study, however, he identified only the behavior of the offender and the visibility of the encounter as predictive of the decision to use force.

Characteristics of the target that seem to be correlated with use of force include: race, sex (male), disrespectful demeanor, emotionality, mental illness, intoxication, presence or perception of a weapon, the suspect's violent criminal record (knowledge of), suspect's use of force, gang membership, and socioeconomic status.

Situational characteristics correlated with use of force include: the number of citizens present (positive association), the number of police officers present (positive association), and whether the encounter involved a car or foot pursuit.

Characteristics of the officers involved in use of force include sex (male), age (younger), and ethnicity (being Hispanic). Psychological traits of the officer have been identified as well, including lack of empathy, antisocial and paranoid tendencies, inability to learn from experience, a tendency not to take responsibility for actions, and cynicism. Officers who use force have also been found to have a stronger identification with the police subculture. Another factor in the tendency to use force was being involved in a traumatic event or prior injury (thus, use of force would be a type of posttraumatic stress behavior; Garner, Maxwell, and Heraux, 2002; Alpert and MacDonald, 2001; Terrill and Mastrofsky, 2002; Alpert and Dunham, 2004; Worden and Catlin, 2002, Terrill, Paoline, and Manning, 2003).

Alpert and MacDonald (2001) found that agencies that required supervisors to fill out use-of-force forms had lower levels of use of force than did agencies that allowed officers to fill out their own forms. It should be emphasized that these studies and the factors identified are associated with the use of force, not necessarily *excessive* force. Also, some studies have reported findings inconsistent with others. Because there is no national database, studies were obtained in various cities and using other datasets that have their own problems (e.g., victim reports, incident reports, and/or newspaper reports).

Even though force is rare in terms of the percentage of times used of the total number of interactions between police and citizens, that does not mean it is not a problem. In past research, surveys of officers indicated that up to a quarter of officers have at least "sometimes" used more force than necessary (Weisburd and Greenspan, 2000). Even one video of excessive force can poison the relationship between a police department and its citizenry.

Use of Tasers (CEDs)

The Taser is one type of conducted energy device (CED), but the word *Taser* has come to be used in common language to refer to any CED. The devices use electrical stimuli to interfere with the body's nervous system, impairing the muscular control of the target. While the use of the CED has become popular among law enforcement agencies, it has also created controversy.

Generally, research indicates that CEDs seem to be associated with a decrease in the number of deaths of suspects, a decrease in the number of injuries to suspects, and a decrease in the number of injuries to officers (Williams, 2010, National Institute of Justice, 2008; Dart, 2004: A14; White and Ready, 2009). Supporters allege that CEDs are safe in the vast majority of cases and are potentially dangerous only when there is some underlying medical condition. One study found that death was more likely in cases where the target was under the influence of drugs or mentally ill and when the device was used more than once (White and Ready, 2009: 883); another study found that there was evidence high risk groups (drug intoxicated or those experiencing excited delirium) were vulnerable (Williams, 2013).

Amnesty International (2007) has alleged that police use CED or stun guns in hundreds of cases in which their use is unjustified and "routinely" inflict injury, pain, and death. Its investigation uncovered the fact that the CEDs were used on unarmed suspects 80 percent of the time and for verbal noncompliance in 36 percent of the cases. CEDs allegedly have been used on "unruly schoolchildren," the "mentally disturbed or intoxicated," and those who do not comply immediately with police commands. Amnesty International's report indicates that there have been at least 300 CED-related deaths (Amnesty International, 2007).

There is no doubt that injury can occur when the person falls and/or where the probes enter the body. In a study of CED injuries, researchers looked at 14,000 use-of-force incidents across seven agencies, 2,600 involving the use of CEDs. They found that injuries occurred in 32 percent of cases where force was used. Looking more closely, they found that injuries occurred in 41 percent of cases where CED only was used, 47 percent when CED plus another form of force was used, and 30 percent of the cases where the CED was not used. The only cases where the use of the CED resulted in fewer injuries was when weapons (baton) were used (Terrill and Paoline, 2011). The researchers concluded that, contrary to the premise of the CED manufacturers and law enforcement community, the CED may not be associated with fewer injuries for suspects at all. The study has been criticized, however, for using only incident reports of officers since they may not be reliable. There is also some concern that the definition of injury is too broad since CEDs, inherently, will result in puncture wounds and burns.

In December 2009, the Ninth Circuit Court of Appeals ruled that a police officer could be held liable when a CED is used on a person who poses no immediate threat (*Bryan v. McPherson*, 590 F.3d 767, 2009). In the case, Carl Bryan was stopped for speeding and stepped out of his car visibly angry. There is disagreement between the officer involved and Bryan as to whether he stepped toward the officer, but there is no question that he was unarmed and the officer used the CED within seconds of approaching him. Bryan fell to the ground and fractured four teeth, and a doctor had to remove one of the CED probes with a scalpel. There have been hundreds of federal lawsuits against municipalities and even against CED companies for alleged abuses (Plohetski and Dexheimer, 2012). Department of Justice reports on use-of-force patterns in some cities have noted improper and abusive uses, including on handcuffed suspects who were nonresisting (Kim and Leonard, 2010). In many problematic instances, officers use CEDs on individuals who pose no threat but are noncompliant. For instance, in Syracuse, a man refused to sit down on a city bus because he said standing was better for his back. The bus driver called police and when he would not get off the bus, an officer lifted the man's shirt and used his CED directly on the man's skin, then dragged him off the bus. His hip was broken in the process and he was charged with resisting arrest and disorderly conduct (O'Brien, 2013).

In another case, Georgia officers repeatedly used their CEDs on a man who was handcuffed. Gregory Towns had initially run from police who were responding to a domestic violence call, but the 281-pound man had stopped running and was sitting down when police caught up to him and handcuffed him. He asked officers to let him catch his breath before going with them. Instead they used their CEDs 14 times over 29 minutes pressing the prongs directly into his skin. The police chief asked the Georgia Bureau of Investigation to conduct the review of the incident. The Fulton County medical examiner said Towns' death was a homicide due to hypertensive cardiovascular disease exacerbated by "electrical stimulation" (Cook, 2014).

CED use, like use of force in general, varies dramatically from city to city. It was reported that in North Charleston (where Walter Scott was shot in the back by ex-officer Michael Slager in the spring of 2015) Tasers were employed 825 times from 2010 to 2014. In Tyler, Texas, a city about the same size but with 150 fewer officers, Tasers were used only 65 times. North Charleston has faced several lawsuits from Taser use, including incidents involving Slager (Binder, Fernandez, and Mueller, 2015).

Departmental policies also seem to play a role in CED use, with those departments having flexible or vague policies also being the ones with more use of CEDs by officers. Most departments utilize a continuum-of-force approach that allows proportional force to the suspect's resistance, with increasing levels of force by the officer in direct response to escalating resistance of the suspect (Walker, 2007). Policies

(•) IN THE NEWS | *Albuquerque, New Mexico*

In March 2014, Albuquerque police officers shot a mentally ill man (James Boyd, 38) who was illegally camping in the woods. A video of the incident received widespread coverage and resulted in public protests. The video showed Boyd seemingly about to follow the officers' directions to come down off a hill, but defenders of the officers argue that he had a knife out and he was unstable. Some of the officers involved have recently been criminally charged (Contreras, 2015). The event brought national attention to the police department; however, the department was already the subject of a federal investigation even before Boyd's death because of its disproportional use of force and, in 2014, the DOJ found a pattern and practice of excessive force. Since 2010, Albuquerque police have been involved in more than 40 shootings—27 of them deadly (although another source reports the numbers as 37 shot and 24 fatally).

The city and U.S. Justice Department agreed to a settlement in October 2014, although the police union contested it (Claytor, 2014). The city has appointed an independent monitor and agreed to a number of reforms in the use of force, specialized units, crisis and mental health intervention, recruitment, and community engagement. For instance, officers will have 72 hours to document the use of force to a new "force review board" (made up of bureau managers, a training director, and a legal advisor). The department will disband the Repeat Offender Project Team. More use-of-force training will be given to officers. Other changes include major changes in SWAT team protocols, a ban on chokeholds, auditing the use of every Taser, and the creation of a civilian review agency and a mental health advisory board designed to improve police response to the mentally ill as well as assigning more trained officers to a crisis intervention unit (Gallagher, 2014; Sanders, 2015). In addition to the costs to meet the settlement requirements (which will run in the millions), Albuquerque taxpayers also paid more that $12 million to settle lawsuits in 2013. Most of it was to settle a $10 million settlement to the family of Iraq War veteran Kenneth Ellis, III, who was shot when he had a gun to his own head threatening suicide (Associated Press, 2013b).

regarding Tasers have been suggested by the International Association of Chiefs of Police. Such policies recommend that a CED not be used on juveniles, the elderly, or pregnant women, and should not be used repeatedly or by multiple officers. Unfortunately, conflicting findings from research do not give us clear answers to the question as to whether the benefits outweigh the risks of CED use. Like any use of force, CEDs can play an important role in law enforcement and are certainly a preferred alternative to lethal force; however, it is possible that they should be moved up the continuum of force in training to equate to close-to-lethal force options. In the case described in the In the News box, Tasers might have been a better alternative than what occurred.

Responses to Uses of Force

It is inevitable that police officers will need to use some level of force in response to noncompliant and resisting suspects. In almost all cases, their actions are supported by the law and policy. Cases where officers' uses of force meet the definition of a crime are extremely rare, such as the Abner Louima case who was sodomized with a broomstick in a NYPD precinct bathroom by Justin Volpe. In the Louima case, ex-officers Justin Volpe received 30 years; Charles Schwarz, 15 years; and Thomas Weise and Thomas Bruder received 5 years each. A civil rights suit against the police department and the city was settled for $7.125 million and, in a rare event, the Police Benevolent Association also paid out $1.625 million for its role in assisting the officers in the cover-up after the assault. The case also resulted in policy changes, including initiating a civilian review panel for excessive force complaints and phasing out the so-called 48-hour rule whereby police officers didn't have to talk to internal affairs about any use of force for 48 hours and after they had conferred with union lawyers (Skolnick, 2001: 17).

In most cases of lethal and non-lethal uses of force, officers are not indicted or charged (and in most cases, no doubt rightfully so). A major report from South Carolina showed that officers fired at 209 suspects in the last five years, killing 79, but only 3 were accused of misconduct, and no officer has ever been convicted of any crime. In that same time period 4 police officers were killed. At least 101 African American suspects were shot at, and 34 died. At least 67 white suspects were shot at, and 41 died. Five were either Latino, Asian, or Native American, and four died. In the rest of the cases, race/ethnicity was not available (LeBlanc, 2015).

An investigation by a newspaper in New York City found that at least 179 people were killed by on-duty NYPD officers (and 43 by off-duty officers) over the past 15 years, and just three of the deaths led to an indictment in state court (but 10 of the off-duty killings led to convictions). Findings also included that since 1999, roughly 27 percent of people killed by NYPD officers were unarmed, 86 percent were black or Hispanic (when race/ethnicity was known), and 2012 had the highest number of killings (21). Roughly 20 percent involved people who were emotionally disturbed (Marzulli and Gregorian, 2014).

One would expect that most officers shoot only in those situations where they are legally justified, therefore, there should be few, if any, prosecutions of officers for their use of force. However, some argue that prosecutors are unwilling to pursue charges against officers because of the close working arrangements between prosecutors and police officers and/or that police cannot conduct such investigations fairly and objectively. Juries are also unlikely to believe that officers would use illegal force.

Civil suits are more likely to be successful than criminal prosecutions. The reason is that the level of proof necessary to show legal liability is lower. Also, suits are often settled by cities before even reaching trial. Supporters of police argue that cases are inappropriately settled since the officer did nothing wrong. No good case analysis exists to explore this question, especially since such settlements often have gag orders attached to them prohibiting either side from disclosing any information.

Officers may not be criminally charged but might still face discipline for violating policy. The reason is that although an officer may have been compelled to utilize lethal or nonlethal force given the resistance or threat presented by the suspect, the officer may have created the situation by his or her precursor actions. If such actions violate policy, then they might be disciplined.

Recently, the Department of Justice has become more aggressive in investigating and identifying problematic use-of-force patterns in several cities. More than 20 cities have been the target of DOJ attention with either a judicially approved consent decree or joint memorandums of agreement the result. Seattle, Los Angeles, New Orleans, and Phoenix, and more recently Ferguson and Baltimore, have been investigated. In most of these investigations, use of force is one of the elements of concern, with findings often including: failure to implement a use-of-force policy, failure to train, failure to monitor, failure to adequately investigate, and/or failure to discipline. Generally, such investigations point to the culture of force, lack of training (and/or lack of clear, coherent use-of-force policies), and lack of discipline as contributing to systemic problems.

The culture of force refers to the situation where officers are not sanctioned and, in fact, are informally rewarded for uses of force that might have been avoided (Skolnick and Fyfe, 1993; Micucci and Gomme, 2005). Sometimes the culture of force is limited to specialized units; sometimes a whole department might be implicated. Certain cities seem to have a problematic reputation as using force in a manner that creates controversy.

Inadequate training has also been identified as a problem. Obviously, first, policies must be clear and comprehensive, and then training should disseminate the policy in a way that supports and does not denigrate it. Many departments use a continuum of force policy that instructs the officer as to what force is appropriate relative to the level of resistance of the suspect. Other departments, however, have a one-sentence policy that basically says the officer should conform to the law.

Recently, a small set of law enforcement officials are calling for new approaches in training and an renewed emphasis on how to defuse situations in order to avoid the use of force. It has been reported that 58 hours of training is given recruits in the use of firearms and 49 hours in defensive tactics, but only eight hours in deescalation techniques (Apuzzo, 2015). If the public wants fewer shootings by police, then training will have to improve in order for them to develop the skills necessary to accomplish their job without the need for force in some situations. Critics of this position argue that police officers already avoid force when possible and second-guessing their use of force is likely to result in more police fatalities.

Another factor in use of force patterns is whether policies are enforced and officers are disciplined. News reports of incidents paint a troubling picture across the country of officers who have multiple uses of force incident complaints and receive little if any punishment. One has only to track the cases documented in videos on Youtube.com or the Cato Institute's website documenting police misconduct to see that some departments "wink" at excessive force by a few individual officers. One report indicated that out of 10,000 abuse complaints in Chicago between 2002 and 2014, only 19 resulted in any discipline (Kristian, 2014).

Past history indicates that police departments can change their level of use of force. The District of Columbia, for instance, after being put under a court order with a monitor, went from 32 police shootings (with 12 deaths) in 1998 to only 17 in 2001 with three deaths (C. Murphy, 2002).

Whether it be lethal force, a Taser, or physical blows, officers have been given the discretion to employ force that, if performed by citizens, would be illegal. We expect them to use such power wisely, and they have a legal duty to do so—that is, they must make reasonable decisions based on the facts and circumstances of each case. Officers are trained in the law and departmental policies, but both by necessity require the application of individual discretion to determine reasonableness. Further, as we have discussed, sometimes what officers have a legal right to do may not be wise or ethical, given other alternatives.

Discretion and Criminal Investigations

How officers use discretion in their interactions with minority members and decisions to use force are the hot button topics of the time; however, discretion is an issue pervasive in all policing. In this last section, we will focus on issues related to what will be called proactive investigations and reactive investigations.

Proactive Investigations

In proactive police investigations, police officers initiate investigations rather than simply respond to crimes. Drug distribution networks, pornography rings, and fences of stolen property all tend to be investigated using methods that involve undercover work and informants. In this type of undercover operation, deception is recognized as an integral part of police work.

According to one author, "Deception is considered by police—and courts as well—to be as natural to detecting as pouncing is to a cat" (Skolnick, 1982: 40). Offenses involving drugs, vice, and stolen property are covert activities that are not easily detected. Prior research has described the types of deception engaged in by police. Klockars (1984) described *placebos* (lies in the best interest of those being lied to), *and blue lies* (used to control the person or to make the job easier in situations where force could be used). Barker and Carter (1991, 1994) described *accepted lies* (used during undercover investigations and sting operations), *tolerated lies* ("necessary evils," such as lying about selective enforcement), and *deviant lies* (used in the courtroom to make a case or to cover up wrongdoing). As discussed in Chapter 5, these lies, sometimes called "testilying," can be extremely detrimental to the police officer's credibility and his or her department. If an officer has a reputation for untruthfulness in any venue, his or her value as a witness is extremely diminished. The In the News box discusses

(°) IN THE NEWS | *Brady Lists*

The term "Brady list" refers to *Brady v. Maryland* (373 U.S. 83,1963), a case that resulted in the requirement of prosecutors to disclose potentially exculpatory information to the defense. Recent cases have made clear that officer witnesses' potential credibility problems must be disclosed to the defense who will challenge their credibility if they testify. Such lists are compiled by prosecutors in order to make sure not only to provide the information to the defense, but also, to avoid those officers as witnesses.

Broward County, Florida's, list included 137 officers in 2012 who had been arrested or convicted of crimes or who were under investigation for falsification of records, perjury, or theft. The Broward County public defender disclosed that the public defenders' office kept its own list of potentially untruthful officers (Christensen, 2012).

Los Angeles County kept a database called the Brady Alert System, but only disclosed the information to defense attorneys when there was "clear and convincing evidence" of the misconduct and that the prosecutor believed that such evidence would affect the outcome of the case. New rules in 2013 were announced that require prosecutors to turn over all "favorable" information to the defense, which includes any information that goes to the credibility of the police officer witness (Leonard, 2013).

There evidently is no standard procedure for when or how prosecutors in the 58 counties in California put officers on such lists, and the powerful officers' union has objected to disciplining an officer who appears on the list. They argue that sometimes off-duty behavior is the reason officers are placed on the list, such as DWIs or misdemeanor arrests that do not lead to charges. The union proposed protection for officers so that they could not be fired, reassigned, or denied a promotion solely for being on the list and it was agreed to in 2013. The union also wants prosecutors to wait until internal discipline procedures are complete and charges are founded before the officer is placed on the list. An opposing argument is that prosecutors are legally obligated to provide any information that goes to the credibility of the officer, not just "founded" complaints, and law enforcement agencies cannot keep officers who have no credibility when they testify in court proceedings (Gutierrez and Minugh, 2013).

Across the country, prosecutors' offices are developing procedures and policies for such lists.

the use of "Brady lists" by prosecutors. These are lists of officers that prosecutors prefer not to or outright refuse to use as witnesses—most often because of lies.

Before an undercover operation is begun, targets must be identified. Arguably, the selection should be based on reasonable suspicion. However, Sherman (1985b) reported that "tips" are notoriously inaccurate as a reason to focus on a certain person. To the targets of an FBI sting, it may appear that they have been unfairly targeted and, especially when targets are political figures, the charge of improper target selection is easy to make.

Police operations that provide opportunities for crime change the police role from one of discovering who has committed a crime to one of discovering who might commit a crime if given a chance. For instance:

- A fake deer placed by the side of the road is used to entice overly eager hunters, who are then arrested for violating hunting laws.
- Police officer decoys dress as drunks and pretend to pass out on sidewalks with money sticking out of their pockets.
- Undercover officers, posing as criminals, entice doctors to prescribe unneeded medications that are controlled substances, such as Percocet and Oxycontin.
- Police undertake various stings in which they set up fencing operations to buy stolen goods.

Asset Forfeiture

Some critics of police allege that, because of asset forfeiture laws, police target individuals for investigation based more on what assets they can seize rather than other variables (Balko, 2011). Federal and similar state asset forfeiture laws allow the federal and state police and prosecutors to confiscate and keep assets associated with illegal enterprises. Most property is seized through civil asset forfeiture actions, which require less due process than criminal procedures. It is reported that 80 percent of property forfeitures now are not even associated with arrests (Worrall and Kovandzi, 2008: 221). It is not an understatement to say that many law enforcement agencies depend on forfeiture proceedings to fund their operations, leading one to wonder whether this financial incentive influences their decision making on proactive investigations.

Researchers who have looked at this issue have not found that there are more forfeiture actions in those jurisdictions that are allowed to keep all the proceeds versus those who have to turn the money or properties over to the state general fund. However, they did find that there were more "adoptive forfeitures" in restrictive states, where local law enforcement handed over arrests to federal law enforcement who then shared the proceeds with the local law enforcement agency (Worrall and Kovandzi, 2008). This program, called "Equitable Sharing" accounted for $1.5 billion in cash, cars and other property in 2012. It has been the target of critics who argue that it encourages departments to pursue forfeitures and skirt state laws requiring arrests to be made before forfeitures can take place or that funds be funneled through the state general fund.

A series of newspaper exposes (e.g., *Washington Post*, *Orlando Sentinel*) and private think-tank reports (e.g., *Policing for Profit* by the Institute for Justice) on forfeiture patterns showed clear cases of abuse whereby individuals lost their houses when a family member was involved in drugs, or lost their car for a small amount of marijuana (Williams, Holcomb, Kovandzic, and Bullock, 2010). Law enforcement in some locales are reportedly trained to stop motorists for minor traffic violations solely to gain consent to search and then to seize any large amounts of cash as evidence of drug trafficking (O'Harrow, Horwitz, and Rich, 2015). Most troubling is that in many cases, no charges are ever filed. Narcotics units sometimes obtain the property directly without much oversight from cities or even police department officials and the money spent is unmonitored. Individuals do have due-process rights to go to court to convince a judge to give them their property, but it is expensive and time-consuming. Attorneys cost thousands of dollars sometimes exceeding the amount taken.

Reports indicate that seizures occur in patterns not tied to level of crime. One news article reported on small California communities that seized more property than much larger cities. California's rules on asset forfeiture are fairly strict requiring a conviction be obtained first before seizures of property up to $25,000, and, for higher amounts, clear and convincing evidence that the property was connected to drug sales or manufacturing. Forfeitures under state law go to the general fund and law enforcement is given 65 percent of any seized assets. Under the federal Equitable Sharing program, law enforcement needed only probable cause, no conviction, and they were able to keep 80 percent, thus about six times more money came to California law enforcement agencies through the federal program than through state asset forfeiture laws (Kim, 2015).

Recently the Equitable Sharing program has been revised and restricted by the Department of Justice (O'Harrow, 2015). Law enforcement officials strongly objected to any changes in the forfeiture program; however, in 2015, Attorney General Holder issued new rules limiting the federal program. The new rules bar local law enforcement from using federal law to seize property without warrants or criminal charges, although exceptions included the confiscation of illegal firearms, ammunition, explosives and property associated with child pornography. It is reported that for hundreds of police and sheriffs' departments, such seizures account for 20 percent or more of their budget so the rule change has few supporters in law enforcement (O'Harrow, Horwitz, and Rich, 2015). Others, such as the Drug Policy Alliance, say the changes don't go far enough because many of the seizures are done by joint federal-state task forces, which are not touched by the new rules (Kim, 2015).

The Use of Informants

informants
Civilians who are used to obtain information about criminal activity and/or participate in it so evidence can be obtained for an arrest.

Informants are individuals who are not police officers but assist police by providing information about criminal activity, acting as buyers in drug sales or otherwise setting up a criminal act so police may gather evidence against the target. Informants perform such services for a reward: for money, to get charges dropped or reduced, or—in some documented cases—for drugs supplied by an officer. They may inform on former associates to get back at them for real or perceived wrongs or they may cooperate with police to get rid of criminal rivals. They may also cooperate because they are being coerced by police to do so, by threats of arrest or arrests of their loved ones. Little academic attention has been directed to the use of informants except for Miller (2011) who documents the strange role of the informant in that he or she is viewed as essential to law enforcement even while being detested since law enforcement shares the antipathy toward snitching as their criminal targets.

Informants often have been or are probably engaged in criminal activities themselves. In a recent news report, it was revealed that according to FBI's own records, agents allowed informants to commit 5,648 crimes in a single year. Most were for the controlled buy-bust operations, but agents also allowed other types of crimes to occur (Heath, 2013). In some instances, the police handlers protect the informant from prosecution (Scheingold, 1984: 122). In one case that is reputed to be the basis for the 2006 movie *The Departed*, it came to light that the FBI protected two mob informers, James "Whitey" Bulger and Stephen Flemmi, even after they had committed murders. John Connolly, an FBI agent, was convicted of obstruction of justice and is serving a 10-year prison sentence for protecting Bulger and Flemmi, who were implicated in 18 murders during the time they worked for the FBI. Connolly was also indicted and tried for second-degree murder. Allegedly, he tipped off Bulger and Flemmi about a man who was informing on them and about to give testimony to a grand jury. They had this man killed as a result (Lush, 2007). Connolly received a 40-year sentence in that murder trial, which means he will probably spend the rest of his life in prison (Anderson, 2010).

The federal witness protection program has provided new identities for some witnesses after they have accumulated bad debts or otherwise victimized an unwary public. The rationale for informant protection is that greater benefit is derived from using them to catch other criminals than their punishment would bring. This also extends to overlooking any minor crime they engage in during the period of time they provide information or afterward if that is part of the deal (Marx, 1985a: 109). This is clearly a utilitarian rationale and, as with all utilitarian justifications, it only makes sense if the math is correct; that is, whether greater benefits are indeed created. One of the problems in using informants is that it presents temptations for police officers to slide into unethical acts as a result of their relationships with informants. In a Baltimore case, it came to light that Officer Mark Lundsford, who was part of a DEA task force, was putting his informant's name on drug cases he was not involved in, recommending the informant be paid bonuses for the arrests, and then splitting the money with the informant. It also was discovered that their relationship was so close that the informant had installed flooring and an air conditioner in the officer's house (Hermann, 2009).

Obviously informants' reliability is highly questionable. Rewards are contingent upon delivering some evidence of crime to law enforcement; therefore, there is an incentive to lie. The Dallas "sheetrock" scandal involved arrests based on an informant who was lying about buying drugs and using sheetrock dust as the supposed cocaine he purchased. Defendants spent months in jail protesting their innocence before charges were dropped. He earned $200,000 before his lies were finally discovered (Curry, 2002). Several recent cases also illustrate the possibility that informants lie about purchasing drugs and/or plant drugs on victims in order to earn rewards. Prosecutors in Lowell, Massachusetts dropped 17 cases and helped to overturn two convictions after two informants were exposed. The discovery has prompted a federal investigation and a civil lawsuit (Rezendes, 2014). In an article in the *New York Times*, an informant details his involvement in a long line of cases related to the ill-famed Kenmore Hotel, a hotbed of vice and drug use in the 1980s. He now says that he was as likely to plant drugs and lie about crimes as he was to provide accurate information and he took part in framing over 150 people. He also alleges that police officers and prosecutors knew what he was doing and didn't care, but then, once someone exposes themselves as a liar, how do you know when they are telling the truth? (Powell, 2014).

In Colorado, Steffen and Osher (2015) describe how a probation officer was arrested after a confidential informant told them that she was dealing heroin and methamphetamine. The seven-year employee was charged with four felony drug counts and lost her job. The informant earned $3,085. It turned out that the informant made up the story to get back at the probation officer who had supervised the informant in the past. Informants rarely face any penalties for lying, even when the consequences for the target are devastating. A newspaper's report indicated that, from 2009 to 2014, Denver paid informants $213,987.

The Pittsburgh *Post Gazette* did an extensive series of the use of informants in federal and local drug cases in Pittsburgh in 2014 (Lord, 2014). In the series, it was revealed how widespread the use of informants was and that, often, their identity remained secret (because most cases don't go to trial). Informants were often recruited by threatening them with prosecution; if they did not inform on others, they would face charges themselves, leading to allegations of coercion.

Another concern in the use of informants is the danger posed if they are discovered. Thompson (2015) described a number of cases where informants and witnesses to a crime in the District of Columbia, were killed. They were not under police protection and some had refused relocation. The dangers of being an informant against dangerous offenders should be clear, but, often informants are not given the protection that undercover officers would receive.

Sometimes officers are tempted to manufacture informants. When writing affidavits for search warrants, officers may use information supplied by a "confidential informant" without having to name the informant. All the officer has to do is to state that the informant has given good information in the past and that it would be dangerous to reveal his or her identity. This boilerplate language is routinely accepted, so information is used to establish probable cause that cannot be verified or challenged (Barker and Carter, 1991). The temptation to do this lies in the pressure to make arrests. Strict protocols for the use of informants would prevent the use of unreliable informants as well as guard against the temptation to manufacture informants. Fitzgerald (2009) offers a standard practice template in the use of informants, including identifying and documenting the informant, strict accounting of funds, having two officers present in interactions with informants, monitoring any buys, obtaining a written statement, and other procedures to ensure chain of custody. The Commission on Accreditation for Law Enforcement Agencies (CALEA) has also developed such standards. There is also a manual from the U.S. Attorney General's office on how informants should be legally and ethically used, including how to properly register them (Hermann, 2009). Some officers openly admit that they could not do their job without informants. There is conflicting information regarding the value of informants and whether they are essential (Dunningham and Norris, 1999). South (2001) summarizes the ethical issues with using informants as follows:

- Getting too close and/or engaging in love affairs with informants
- Overestimating the veracity of the information
- Being a pawn of the informant who is taking advantage of the system for money or other reasons
- Creating crimes by letting the informant entrap people who would not otherwise have committed the crime
- Engaging in unethical or illegal behaviors for the informant, such as providing drugs
- Letting the informant invade one's personal life
- Using coercion and intimidation to get the informant to cooperate.

The Use of Undercover Officers

Undercover officers may pretend to be drug dealers, prostitutes, johns, crime bosses, friends, and—perhaps—lovers in order to collect evidence of crime. They have to observe or even participate in illegal activities to protect their cover. Undercover work is said to be a difficult role for individual officers, who may play the part so well that they lose their previous identity. Marx (1985a: 109) cited examples of officers who became addicted to drugs or alcohol and destroyed their marriages or careers because of undercover assignments. He noted a disturbing belief system among undercover officers that laws don't apply to them or that they are exempt from the law because of their assignment. It has been found that undercover officers possess high levels of neuroticism and low levels of impulse control, and that there are adverse psychological effects from the experience of being undercover (Mieczkowski, 2002: 162).

Conlon (2004), a Harvard-educated New York City police officer, described how undercover officers entered a no-man's land in the department, where they were treated almost more like informants than fellow cops. Those who were successful at setting up buys were treated like "star performers," and some developed "prima donna" attitudes. In general, they were treated and they behaved in a way that made it hard for them to maintain relationships with other police, and very probably created issues with their families.

On a continuum of intimacy, at one end is a brief buy-bust incident wherein the officer pretends to be a drug addict and buys from a street dealer, and moments later an arrest is made. At the other end of the continuum is a situation in which an undercover officer engages in a long relationship with and pretends to be romantically involved with a target of an investigation to maintain his or her cover. The second situation violates our sense of privacy to a much greater extent. It is not only criminal enterprises that are targeted. It was reported that New York City undercover officers, a year before the 2004 Republican convention, began to infiltrate activist groups that they believed might be a problem during the convention. Officers attended meetings, made friends, signed petitions, and then reported on the activities to supervisors. In the records of the NYPD's "Intelligence Squad" are hundreds of reports on people who had no clear criminal plan, including church groups, antiwar organizations, and anti-President Bush groups. Reports were evidently shared with police departments in other cities (Dwyer, 2007). This activity is reminiscent of the undercover operations during the antiwar activist era of the 1960s and early 1970s, which led to strict controls on police powers to engage in undercover investigations absent probable cause that a group was planning to commit a crime.

More generally, the use of undercover officers who pretend to be someone they are not in order to catch criminals is a power that should be used with caution and with sensitivity to the damage it does to individual relationships and public trust. There are greater moral duties present in intimate relationships than in public ones.

There is damage to all when personal relationships are used deceptively; in fact, some argue that an intimate relationship may take precedence over a concern for social well-being generally (Schoeman, 1985: 144). This comes from an ethics-of-care

QUOTE & QUERY

Sometimes you develop these relationships with these traffickers.... You know, they're stone psychopathic killers, but they have great personalities. So, it's very difficult when you have to arrest them and put them in prison for a number of years.... It is a moral dilemma, because, again sometimes these guys become your family. (Michael Vigil, retired undercover agent)

Source: Martin, 2015.

 How would you resolve the moral dilemma?

position. In this ethical system, the relationship of two people is more important than rights, duties, or laws. There is no forfeiture of rights in the ethics-of-care position; thus, one can't say that the suspect deserves to be deceived.

entrapment

When an otherwise innocent person commits an illegal act because of police encouragement or enticement.

Another issue concerning undercover operations is entrapment. **Entrapment** occurs when an otherwise innocent person commits an illegal act because of police encouragement or enticement. Currently the Supreme Court looks at the defendant's background, character, and predisposition toward crime (a subjective test) rather than the objective test that evaluated whether or not police actions provided essential elements to the crime (*United States v. Russell*, 411 U.S. 423, 1973).

Recent examples of police undercover operations raise issues of entrapment. Critics argue that when undercover police officers suggest robberies of drug dealers to residents of poor communities, as they did in Baltimore in 2013 netting 17 convictions, they created crime because the temptation of the offer swayed those who would not have committed the crime themselves. Because the targets had prior records, the subjective test resulted in a finding that they were predisposed to crime and no case was lost to an entrapment defense (Duncan, 2013). However, a federal case based on a similar "stashhouse sting" was thrown out by a judge in Los Angeles for "outrageous government conduct." The judge described the government's actions as "trawling" for crooks in seedy neighborhoods without any level of suspicion. Of concern to the judge evidently was that 9 of 10 of those convicted in the stings were black or Hispanic. The government strongly objected to the characterization of the stings as racially motivated and argued that targets generally come to their attention through others; however, in 2015, the U.S. Attorney quietly dropped the most serious charges against 27 of the defendants in the Chicago series of stings (Eckholm, 2014, 2015).

Generally, undercover actions are analyzed under utilitarian ethics. Marx (1985a: 106–107) proposed a set of questions to ask before engaging in any undercover operation, that are consistent with utilitarianism:

- How serious is the crime being investigated?
- How clear is the definition of the crime—that is, would the target know that what he or she is doing is clearly illegal?
- Are there any alternatives to deceptive practices?
- Is the undercover operation consistent with the spirit as well as the letter of the law?
- Is it public knowledge that the police may engage in such practices, and is the decision to do so a result of democratic decision making?
- Is the goal prosecution, as opposed to general intelligence gathering or harassment?
- Is there a likelihood that the crime would occur regardless of the government's involvement?
- Are there reasonable grounds to suspect the target?
- Will the practice prevent a serious crime from occurring?

Thus, utilitarianism may justify undercover operations or condemn them depending on the utility derived and the harm done to all parties involved. Act utilitarianism would probably support deceptive practices, but rule utilitarianism might not, because the actions, although beneficial under certain circumstances, might in the long run undermine and threaten our system of law. Under act utilitarianism, one would measure the harm of the criminal activity against the methods used to control it. Deceptive practices, then, might be justified in the case of drug offenses but not for business misdeeds, or for finding a murderer but not for trapping a prostitute, and so on.

The difficulty of this line of reasoning, of course, is to agree on a standard of seriousness. I might decide that drugs are serious enough to justify otherwise unethical practices, but you might not. Pornography and prostitution may be serious enough to some to justify unethical practices, but to others only murder or violent crime would justify the practices. Religious ethics would probably condemn many kinds of police actions because of the deceptions involved. Ethical formalism would probably also condemn undercover operations where innocent people are deceived because the actions could not be justified under the categorical imperative. Recall that you cannot use people as a means to an end, therefore, if innocent people would be used, it would violate the categorical imperative. Egoism might or might not justify such actions, depending on the officer involved and what his or her maximum gain and loss were determined to be.

Many people see nothing wrong—certainly nothing illegal—in using any methods necessary to catch criminals. But we are concerned with methods in use before individuals are found guilty. Can an innocent person, such as you, be entrapped into crime? Perhaps not, but are we comfortable in a society where the person who offers you drugs or sex or a cheap way to hook into cable television turns out to be an undercover police officer? Are we content to assume that our telephone may be tapped or our best friend could be reporting our conversations to someone else? When we encounter police behavior in these areas, the practices have been used to catch a person who, we realize after the fact, had engaged in wrongdoing, so we believe that police officers are justified in the deception and invasion of privacy. What protectors of due process and critics of police investigation practices help us to remember is that those practices, if not curbed, may be used just as easily on the innocent as on the guilty.

These investigative techniques are unlikely to be eliminated. Perhaps they should not be, as they are effective in catching a number of people who should be punished. Even if one has doubts about the ethics of these practices, it is entirely possible that there is no other way to accomplish the goal of crime control. However one decides these difficult questions, there are no easy answers. Also, we must realize that for us these questions are academic, but for thousands of police officers they are very real.

Reactive Investigations

In reactive investigations, a crime has already occurred and the police sift through clues to determine the perpetrator. When police and other investigators develop an early prejudice concerning who they believe is the guilty party, they look at evidence less objectively and are tempted to engage in noble-cause corruption in order to convict. This can take the form of ignoring witnesses or evidence or even manufacturing evidence to shore up a case against an individual.

Rossmo (2008) brings together descriptions of several investigations that failed because of the human tendency to ignore evidence that does not fit preconceived notions. In these cases, the true criminal was not discovered and others were suspected, and sometimes charged and convicted, because police officers did not follow proper protocol in the collection and interpretation of evidence. Protocol is necessary to avoid errors in judgment when a criminal investigator who "knows" someone is guilty happens to be wrong. Good investigators do not let their assumptions influence their investigations, because assumptions jeopardize effectiveness. Unfortunately, Rossmo's examples show that proper investigative methods are sometimes discarded when police officers think they know who committed the crime.

This tendency to slant the evidence is not limited to police investigators. FBI lab examiners have compromised cases by completing shoddy work and misrepresenting

WALKING THE WALK

Dr. Frederic Whitehurst joined the FBI in 1982 after earning a PhD in chemistry. He was also a decorated war veteran, serving three tours in Vietnam, earning four Bronze Stars and being offered (but not accepting) the Purple Heart. Between 1986 and 1998, he was associated with the FBI's highly acclaimed crime lab, becoming an international expert in explosives. During his association with the FBI, he became increasingly troubled by the practices of lab personnel. His concerns involved shoddy procedures as well as a tendency to take a pro-prosecution stance when examining evidence rather than maintaining scientific objectivity. He complained to the FBI Office of Professional Responsibility and the director of the FBI, but nothing happened. Eventually he took his concerns to the Department of Justice and the Office of the Inspector General, and his criticisms led to a 517-page Inspector General's report after an 18-month investigation, the first time ever that the highly esteemed lab had received any external review.

The report was damning, indicating that FBI examiners had given inaccurate testimony or overstated scientific findings, altered lab reports, failed to document procedures, and hidden exculpatory evidence from defense attorneys. Further, there was evidence of shoddy management and record keeping and a failure to investigate allegations of incompetence. The report, however, examined only three of the seven units that comprised the FBI lab and only investigated Whitehurst's specific allegations. Still, it led to congressional hearings, a dramatic overhaul of the lab, and, more recently, independent accreditation.

It also derailed Whitehurst's career. Shortly before the report was released in 1997, he was put on administrative leave and criticized for violating policy. In response, he argued that he was following Executive Order 12731, which required federal employees to report fraud, waste, abuse, or corruption to the proper authorities. He was eventually demoted and sanctioned, but ultimately won a whistle-blower lawsuit against the FBI. His whistleblowing led to a review by the Department of Justice of hundreds of cases where FBI examiners gave testimony. It seemed clear that there were people in prison who were there based on flawed evidence, but these individuals were never told their convictions could be challenged.

In 2007, the FBI was criticized in investigative reports by the television show *60 Minutes* and by the *Washington Post* for continuing to withhold the names of about 2,500 defendants who were convicted partially based on the results of examiners' testimony. In response, FBI officials stated that the public announcements of the faulty tests should have been notice enough to these individuals and their lawyers to pursue any appropriate appeals. In November 2007, the FBI spokesperson finally agreed that the FBI would send letters to the prosecutors in these cases to notify them that the testimony was based on faulty science. Unfortunately for many of these defendants, it may have come too late to file an appeal.

Since leaving the FBI, Whitehurst earned a law degree and is now the executive director of an independent organization called the Forensic Justice Project, which collects and disseminates information about controversial forensic science. He continues to investigate some of the cases from his days in the FBI to try and identify any innocent people that might have been affected by inaccurate scientific testimony. He is largely forgotten even though his actions led to a seismic shift in the faith placed in the FBI lab and forensic science more generally. As news stories about shoddy practices in labs continue to chronicle problems, he prefers the focus stay on the topic rather than about him. In response to a reporter's queries recently about yet another crime lab scandal and his role in improving the field, he said, "We have made the justice system question itself and that is what is important. Let the ... [attention] remain about injustice ... not about Frederic Whitehurst."

Sources: Kohn, 1997; Solomon, 2007b; Kelly and Wearne, 1998; Stein, 2010.

their findings, evidently to support police theories regarding the guilty party. In effect, they were not objective scientists, but rather, co-conspirators with police. This led to overstating their findings on the witness stand and covering up tests that were done improperly. A whistleblower exposed these practices and was suspended for his efforts. His story is presented in the Walking the Walk box. Ultimately, 13 examiners were implicated, although only two were ever formally censured (Sniffen, 1997; Serrano and Ostrow, 2000).

Crime labs across the country have been implicated in either shoddy practices or actively slanting evidence to convict the defendant. "Drylabbing" is a term for making up scientific results without running any tests. Such scandals have forced prosecutors' offices to reexamine hundreds, if not thousands, of cases across the country to determine if wrongful convictions have occurred (Axtman, 2003; Hays, 2005, Reimer, 2015; Gass, 2015). This problem seems to be more pronounced when labs are part of the law enforcement organization rather than independent from law enforcement.

The problem is that once investigators decide who the guilty party is, they may ignore evidence that doesn't fit with their idea of who did it and how it was done. It is human nature to complete the puzzle—to see things that conform to one's way of looking at the world. Good police work doesn't close the door to contrary evidence, but human nature does. Utilitarian ends-oriented thinkers may be more likely to ignore contrary evidence or overstate existing evidence if they believe they have the guilty party. Ethical formalism, however, emphasizes duties, not the end result, so those whose ethical values lean toward ethical formalism may be less likely to slide into the types of behavior that have put these forensic professionals under scrutiny.

Interrogation

Interrogating a person one believes to be guilty of a crime is probably an extremely frustrating experience. How do you get someone to confess? In past eras, the infamous "third degree" (beating) or threats of force were used to get a confession, but the use of physical force to obtain a conviction has been illegal for quite some time (*Brown v. Mississippi*, 297 U.S. 278, 1936). Legal proscriptions against torture are based on the belief that torture renders a confession unreliable. Tortured victims might confess to stop their suffering; thus, the court would not get truthful information. Many would argue that whatever information is gained from an individual who is physically coerced into confessing or giving information is not worth the sacrifice of moral standards even if the information is truthful. Human rights treaties signed by the majority of free countries condemn such practices, regardless of the reason for the interrogation.

Recently, we have come to find out how illegal interrogations have led to wrongful convictions. Extremely coercive interrogations have occurred in Chicago (recall from an earlier chapter the John Burge scandal) and New York City with prosecutors re-examining hundreds of cases where a conviction was obtained based on the investigation and/or interrogation by Detective Louis Scarcella. The discovery of his problematic methods occurred after several men were exonerated and released from prison (O'Brien, 2013).

In many cases, those who give false confessions are mentally handicapped or are juveniles, like Anthony Caravella who was a mentally challenged 15-year-old when he gave a false confession after being interviewed by police officers as a witness to a crime (McMahon, 2013; Elinson, 2013). The infamous case of the Central Park 5 (who falsely confessed to rape and assault) were all teenagers when interrogated (Tanner, 2002, Getlin, 2002). Burge's and Scarcella's tactics are aberrations today, but officers do use persuasion and deception. The classic father confessor approach (a sympathetic paternal figure for the defendant to confide to) or "good cop/bad cop" (a nice guy and a seemingly brutal, threatening officer) are ways to induce confessions and/or obtain information without using force (Kamisar, LeFave, and Israel, 1980). Evidence indicates that deception and skill work more effectively than physical abuse in getting suspects to confess. Skolnick and Leo (1992) have presented a typology of deceptive interrogation techniques. The following is a brief summary of their descriptions of these practices:

- Calling the questioning an interview rather than an interrogation by questioning in a noncustodial setting and telling the suspect that he [or she] is free to leave, thus eliminating the need for *Miranda* warnings
- Presenting *Miranda* warnings in a way designed to negate their effect, by mumbling or by using a tone suggesting that the offender had better not exercise the rights delineated or that they are unnecessary
- Misrepresenting the nature or seriousness of the offense—for instance, by not telling the suspect that the victim has died
- Using manipulative appeals to conscience through role playing or other means
- Misrepresenting the moral seriousness of the offense—for instance, by pretending that the rape victim "deserved" to be raped—in order to get a confession
- Using promises of lesser sentences or nonprosecution beyond the power of the police to offer
- Misrepresenting identity by pretending to be lawyers or priests
- Using fabricated evidence such as polygraph results or fingerprint findings that don't really exist

The trouble is that these interrogative techniques can be so effective they result in false confessions. While the Supreme Court has ruled that physical coercion used to obtain a confession is unconstitutional, there is no such proscription against deception (see, for instance, *Frazier v. Cupp*, 394 U.S. 731, 1969). In fact, 92 percent of police said they have lied about evidence to induce a confession (Forrest and Woody, 2010: 8). This is despite the fact that laboratory findings show that people will falsely confess when faced with fake evidence (Forrest and Woody, 2010).

Challenges to convictions based on confessions obtained when police interrogators deceive the defendant are based on voluntariness—and the test used by lower courts at this point seems to be whether or not police deception would induce an innocent person to plead guilty. An example of such a case occurred in 1989 when 17-year-old Marty Tankleff confessed to killing his parents. Even though there was no physical evidence to link him to the crime, interrogators told the teenager that hairs found on his mother pointed to him, that they had obtained a spot of blood from his shoulder that was matched to his mother, and that his father had emerged from a coma long enough to tell them that Marty had attacked them. All of this was untrue, but it convinced the teen to confess. He served 19 years in prison before having the conviction dismissed and charges vacated (Kassin et al., 2010: 18).

Courts may also employ a "shock the conscience" standard. If what the officers do seems to be too egregious, any evidence obtained will be excluded (*Moran v. Burbine*, 474 U.S. 412, 1986). Of course, this raises the question as to what shocks one's conscience. In practice, the lower courts have interpreted the Supreme Court's reluctance to place any restrictions on deception during interrogation as a green light to allow most forms of deception (Magid, 2001). Some state courts, however, have ruled as inadmissible confessions obtained by using faked physical evidence, such as fake lab reports or fingerprint analysis results (*Florida v. Cayward*, 522 So. 2d. 971, 1989; Kassin et al., 2010: 13), as opposed to merely lying about the presence of such reports. In one case, police used what they called "an investigative prop," which was a faked crime lab DNA report. The interrogators had been told by lab examiners that the DNA of the suspect matched the sample from the crime scene, but they didn't have the report, therefore, they faked one to use in the interrogation. The prosecutor who was present during this interrogation was so troubled by the actions of the officers that he notified his superiors and the district attorney's office notified the defense attorney. There was no confession, therefore, no legal ramifications occurred, but the incident did appear to raise legal questions since a state appellate court had ruled that confessions obtained with manufactured evidence were inadmissible (Plohetski, 2012). Courts may draw the line at this type of deception for two reasons. First, some argue that there is too great a possibility that such evidence may somehow find its way into the courtroom, which would be perpetrating a fraud upon the court; and, second, the use of manufactured evidence has a much greater possibility of inducing a false confession from a person who knows they did not do the crime, but assumes they cannot convince a jury if there is a positive DNA match, so they confess to get a plea deal.

Trainum (2008) notes how he never would have believed that an innocent person would confess to a crime they didn't commit until he reviewed a videotaped interrogation that he had conducted on a female suspect accused of murder. After a long interrogation, the woman confessed to the crime, even describing how she dumped the body. There was some evidence to tie her to it as well, including an ATM video of a person who resembled her using the victim's ATM card and a handwriting analyst who said it was her signature. However, she had an alibi and officers found she was telling the truth about being somewhere else when the crime occurred. Trainum writes how he reviewed the interrogation videotape and realized that he had unconsciously fed her information about the crime.

Some researchers estimate that about five percent of confessions are false (Kassin et al., 2010: 5). Such confessions are one of the leading causes of false convictions (along with faulty eyewitness identification and mishandling of evidence). Research indicates that suspects don't always understand their *Miranda* rights, and juveniles are especially prone to psychological manipulation. There are attempts to reduce false confessions by requiring corroborating evidence before the confession can be used in court, and several jurisdictions now require confessions (at least of serious crimes) to be videotaped (Kassin et al., 2010). Alaska, Minnesota, Illinois, Washington, D.C., Maine, New Mexico, Wisconsin, and North Carolina now require videotapes of interrogations of serious crimes. There is no evidence that it has resulted in reduced numbers of confessions (Alpert and Noble, 2009). However, Forrest and Woody (2010) point out that when expert testimony is used to educate the jury about the dangers of manufactured evidence and the fact of false confessions, convictions go down.

It is certainly much easier to justify deception than physical coercion and intimidation during an interrogation. The justification is the same: Deception is an effective and perhaps necessary means to get needed information from a resisting subject. Deontological ethics would focus on the duty of the officer. Because an officer has a duty to follow the law, any form of deception that has been ruled illegal would not be ethically justified. Do the actions conform to the categorical imperative? If the officer had a brother or mother who was accused of a crime, or was accused themselves, would they believe their actions justified? If not, then they cannot be supported by ethical formalism.

Under utilitarianism, there may not be any utility in such actions because they may result in false confessions. Keith Longtin was held by Prince George County, Maryland, police detectives for 38 hours after his wife was raped and stabbed to death. He alleges that during this time, police officers accompanied him to the bathroom, would not let him call an attorney, and continually questioned him (employing different teams of interrogators). Finally, they said that he told them what happened, but he remembers it as them telling him what happened to his wife and asking him to speculate about how the murder occurred.

A sex crimes investigator noticed the similarity between the attack and other rapes in the area, and after the rape suspect was arrested, a DNA test proved that this man killed Longtin's wife. Longtin was freed after eight months in jail, and all charges were dropped; however, if it had not been for the other investigator's actions, Longtin's confession would have most probably led to a conviction. Longtin's case and four other homicide confessions that were thrown out because other evidence proved they were false confessions led to a federal monitor for this law enforcement agency (Witt, 2001).

It is important to note that police officers do not intend for innocent people to go to prison; what occurs can be considered noble-cause corruption in that the officers believe the defendant to be guilty and utilize otherwise unethical means to obtain a confession. The trouble is that sometimes they are so effective they make innocent people falsely confess. The rationale is purely utilitarian, but the actual utility of the actions are miscalculated.

Conclusion

In this chapter, we explored some of the ways that police use of authority, power, persuasion, and force have created ethical dilemmas and sparked controversy. It seems that every few decades we enter into a period of intense scrutiny of law enforcement: The 1960s Civil Rights era led to increased diversity; the Rodney King incident led to better use-of-force policies, as well as public opinion shifting against racial profiling and discriminatory enforcement. The Ferguson and Baltimore protests may now lead to more scrutiny of policing again and this should not be condemned since constant vigilance may be (as they say) the price of freedom.

For most of us, controversial issues regarding police methods are abstract, but for individual officers who are faced with dilemmas regarding what they should do in certain situations, the questions are much more immediate. To resolve them, the individual should look to legal holdings, departmental policies, and, finally, ethical rationales. Utilitarian reasoning is used to justify many actions, but the question remains whether it is ever ethical to achieve a good end through bad acts. It seems clear that how one resolves the dilemmas involved in policing has everything to do with whether law enforcement officers are seen fundamentally as crime fighters or as public servants.

Chapter Review

1. **Provide any evidence that exists that law enforcement officers perform their role in a discriminatory manner.**

   Minorities express less satisfaction with police than do whites and report they experience more disrespect. Studies show that minorities are not more likely to experience disrespect per incident, but they are stopped 1.5 times as often as whites. Many racial profiling studies indicate that blacks are stopped disproportionately; however, the early studies suffer from methodological problems.

2. **Present information concerning the prevalence of and factors associated with the use of force by police officers.**

   The use of force seems to be present in only about 1.6 percent of all encounters with the public; however, it takes place more often in certain cities and during certain types of encounters. It is also true that some officers seem to be involved in uses of force more often than others. Correlates of uses of force have been identified including sex of officer and target (male), age of officer and target (20s–30s), presence of alcohol and/or mental illness, noncompliance, and officer personality traits.

3. **Enumerate predictors associated with the use of excessive force.**

   There seems to be evidence that excessive force occurs in certain types of calls (pursuits) and with certain groups (minorities). Female officers are less likely to use excessive force; however, any correlations should be viewed with caution since the sample size is so small. The legal standard for what is appropriate force is reasonableness, but it is somewhat problematic to review an officer's behavior after the fact and without knowing or perceiving the circumstances in the same way as the officer on the scene. Present the ethical issues involved in proactive investigation.

4. **Present the ethical issues involved in proactive investigations.**

   Ethical issues concern how the targets of undercover investigations are chosen, whether informants are reliable, whether informants are protected from sanctions for their own criminal behavior, whether such operations create crime or entrap individuals, and whether undercover operations violate the privacy rights of individuals who are deceived.

5. **Present the ethical issues involved in reactive investigations.**

   Ethical issues concern the tendency of police investigators to not remain objective in their interpretation and collection of evidence if they believe they know a suspect is guilty. Also, the use of physical coercion during interrogation is clearly illegal, but deception is not and is perhaps just as powerful. There is a possibility that such tactics may lead to false confessions.

Study Questions

1. What factors were associated with citizens' experiences of "disrespect" from police officers in the research described in the chapter.

2. What are some of the methods of interrogation according to Skolnick and Leo?

3. Describe Barker and Carter's typology of lies.

4. List the questions posed by Marx that police should use before engaging in undercover operations.

5. What factors are associated with the use of force?

Writing/Discussion Exercises

1. Write an essay on (or discuss) whether you think it is ever right for a police officer to make a decision to stop someone based on race or ethnicity. Do you think that it is ethical for police to enforce immigration laws by asking whether suspects, witnesses, and/or victims are legal residents?

2. Write an essay on (or discuss) appropriate tools in interrogation. For this essay, you should review important court cases and research typical police practices. Should interrogations be videotaped? Should attorneys always be present? Should juveniles ever be interrogated without their parents? Should deception be used? If so, what kinds?

3. Write an essay on (or discuss) the best explanation for excessive force. If you could be a change agent in a police department, describe the changes or procedures you would institute that you believe would reduce the incidence of excessive force.

Key Terms

consent decree   informants
entrapment   racial profiling

ETHICAL DILEMMAS

Situation 1

You are a rookie on traffic patrol. You watch as a young black man drives past you in a brand new silver Porsche. You estimate the car's value at around $50,000, yet the neighborhood you are patrolling in is characterized by low-income housing, cheap apartments, and tiny houses on the lowest end of the housing spectrum. You follow him and observe that he forgets to signal when he changes lanes. Ordinarily you wouldn't waste your time on something so minor. What would you do?

Situation 2

You are a homicide investigator and are interrogating someone you believe picked up a 9-year-old in a shopping mall, and then molested and murdered the girl. He is a registered sex offender, was in the area, and although he doesn't have any violence in his record, you believe he must have done it because there is no other suspect who had the means, opportunity, and motive. You have some circumstantial evidence (he was seen in a video following the child) but very little good physical evidence. You really need a confession in order to make the case. You want to send this guy away for a long time. After several hours of getting nowhere, you have a colleague come in with a file folder and pretend that the medical examiner had obtained fingerprints on the body that matched the suspect's. You tell him that he lost his chance to confess to a lesser crime because now he is facing the death penalty. He says that he will confess to whatever you want him to if the death penalty is taken off the table. Do you tell him what you did? Do you tell the prosecutor?

Situation 3

You are a federal agent and have been investigating a major drug ring for a long time. One of your informants is fairly highly placed within this ring and has been providing you with good information. You were able to "turn" him because he faces a murder charge: there is probable cause that he shot and killed a coworker during an argument about five years ago, before he became involved in the drug ring. You have been holding the murder charge over his head to get him to cooperate and have been able, with the help of the U.S. District Attorney's office, to keep the local prosecutor from filing charges and arresting him. The local prosecutor is upset because the family wants some resolution in the case. You believe that the information he is able to provide you will result in charges of major drug sales and racketeering against several of the top smugglers, putting a dent in the drug trade for your region. At the same time, you understand that you are constantly risking the possibility that he may escape prosecution by leaving the country and that you are blocking the justice that the family of the murdered victim deserves. What would you do?

Situation 4

You are a rookie police officer who responds to a call for officer assistance. Arriving at the scene, you see a ring of officers surrounding a suspect who is down on his knees. You don't know what happened before you arrived, but you see a sergeant use a Taser on the suspect, and you see two or three officers step in and take turns hitting the suspect with their nightsticks about the head and shoulders. This goes on for several minutes as you stand in the back of the circle. No one says anything that would indicate that this is not appropriate behavior. What would you do? What would you do later when asked to testify that you observed the suspect make "threatening" gestures to the officers involved?

Situation 5

You are a male suspect in a murder case. You were drunk the night of the homicide and did meet and dance with the victim, a young college girl. You admit that you had a lot to drink, but are 99 percent sure that you didn't see her except in the bar. The trouble is that you drank way too much and passed out in someone's apartment close to the bar rather than drive home. The girl was found in an apartment in the same complex. Police are telling you that they have forensic evidence that ties you to the murder. They say that they have her blood on your clothes and that it is your DNA in the sperm found in her body. They have been interrogating you now for several hours, and you are beginning to doubt your memory. You are also told that if you plead guilty, you would probably get voluntary manslaughter and might get probation, but if you insist on your innocence, you will be charged with first-degree murder and face the death penalty. What would you do?

(Obviously, this situation shifts our focus from the criminal justice professional's dilemma. If you decided earlier that the police tactic of lying about forensic evidence is ethical, this hypothetical illustrates what might happen when innocent suspects are lied to—assuming you are innocent!)

7

Police Corruption and Responses

Frank Serpico

F rank Serpico is arguably the most famous police officer in the United States, even though he hasn't worked in law enforcement since 1972. After serving in Korea, he became a New York City police officer in 1959. He realized that the "pad" (payments by store owners to the cops) was widespread, and when he refused to take the money he earned the distrust of those who did. Over 12 years, he rose to the rank of detective and never participated in the pad. After repeated attempts to get supervisors to do something, in 1970–1971, he and David Durk, a fellow officer, went to the *New York Times* and participated in an exposé of police corruption. The series of stories led to the Knapp Commission.

Serpico and Durk continued to work even though rumors that they were the "rats" were widespread and there was a real danger that corrupt police officers would retaliate against them. Before he had a chance to testify, Serpico was shot in the face at point-blank range in a drug bust while his fellow officers stood behind him. The

Chapter Objectives

1. Describe the types of police corruption (economic corruption and abuse of authority).

2. Describe individual explanations of corruption and potential solutions.

3. Describe organizational explanations of corruption and potential solutions.

4. Describe societal explanations of corruption and potential solutions.

183

shooting was suspected of being a setup, especially since the "officer down" call never was issued. However, no officer was investigated or charged with any wrongdoing in relation to the shooting. Serpico survived and went on to testify before the Knapp Commission. The name Serpico continues to elicit two different reactions. For some, it represents the epitome of an honest and brave man who stood against corruption at great risk to self. For others, it represents a "rat," a man who turned his back on his friends, and, for some officers, to be called a "Serpico" is a serious insult.

Why we still talk about Frank Serpico is that his story includes all the elements of the problem of police corruption. From what we know, the problem is "vertical" in that supervisors and administrators are either involved, have been involved, or, more often, actively try to cover up or ignore the corruption. Secondly, the problem is known to many officers even if few are involved, but the "blue curtain" shields the corrupt few. Finally, whistleblowers that expose the corruption are considered traitors and, sometimes, serious retaliation occurs.

There is no doubt that most police officers are honest and strive to be ethical in all they do; however, examples of corruption and graft in law enforcement agencies are not difficult to find. In this chapter, we provide a more detailed discussion of misconduct. For our purposes, we divide misconduct into two broad categories: economic corruption and abuse of authority. Economic corruption can be defined as the use of one's position to obtain improper financial benefit. Abuse of authority is when the power and authority of the office is misused. First, we discuss prevalence, then we provide examples. Finally, individual explanations for corruption are presented, followed by organizational and societal explanations. This same order is followed when discussing responses and potential solutions.

Since the very beginning of organized police departments, various investigative bodies have documented cases of corruption. Fyfe and Kane (2006), for instance, provide a long list of commissions and task forces that investigated police corruption scandals in a number of cities, including the Chicago Police Committee (in 1931), the Knapp Commission (New York City in 1972–1973), the Kolts Commission (Los Angeles County in 1992), the Mollen Commission (New York City in 1993), the Philadelphia Police Study Task Force (in 1987), the Christopher Commission (Los Angeles in 1996), the New Orleans Mayor's Advisory Committee (in 1993), the Royal Commission (Sydney, Australia, in 1997), and the St. Clair Commission (Boston in 1992), to name only a few. Bayley and Perito (2011) analyzed 32 different commissions that investigated police corruption; thirteen were in the United States, six in Australia, three in the United Kingdom, four in Canada, and one each in a number of other countries, including India, Ireland, Kenya, and Israel.

Even though there is a large body of literature on police corruption, few studies have been able to measure its extent and prevalence. An obvious barrier to discovery is getting police officers to admit to wrongdoing. One early study reported that, by officers' own accounts, 39 percent of their number engaged in brutality, 22 percent perjured themselves, 31 percent had sex on duty, 8 percent drank on duty, and 39 percent slept on duty (Barker and Carter, 1994). Barker (1983) reported that between 9 and 31 percent of officers who had been employed for 11 months or less reported observing corrupt practices.

In a sample of narcotics officers, Stevens (1999) reported that 63 percent said they had very often heard of narcotics officers using more force than necessary to make an arrest, 26 percent had often heard of other officers personally consuming and/or selling drugs, and 82 percent had very often heard of other narcotics officers violating the civil rights of suspects. These numbers must be interpreted carefully in that they do not mean that large numbers of officers were corrupt, only that a fairly large number of officers were aware of at least one officer's misconduct.

Fyfe and Kane (2006; also see Kane and White, 2009) studied police officers in New York City who were terminated for cause and found that only 2 percent of officers in the 22 years under study (1975–1996) were terminated for misconduct. This study's findings must also be interpreted with caution since the number of officers who come to the attention of supervisors and are officially sanctioned by termination is probably quite a bit lower than the numbers who commit corrupt acts. Further, officers are sometimes terminated for rule breaking that does not fit into any category of corruption.

In 2011, 23 Washington, D.C. officers (out of 3,818) were arrested on charges from sexual assault to murder. One officer allegedly fired into a car of transgendered people. Another had sex with a teenager. Yet another lied about a murder to protect her boyfriend. Police Chief Cathy Lanier defended the department, stating that many of the arrests were due to internal investigations; at least four of the officers were detected in a departmental audit and sting operation. We have no way of knowing whether this rate of officers committing misconduct is higher than in other departments, especially because in many states, personnel records of police officers are not subject to open records requests (McCabe, 2011).

In 1977, 37 percent of the public rated police integrity and ethics as high or very high, and 12 percent rated police integrity as low or very low. In 2011, 54 percent of the public rated police integrity as high or very high and 11 percent of the population rated police integrity as low or very low (*Sourcebook of Criminal Justice Statistics*, 2007, 2011). Of course, perceptions are not necessarily reflective of reality, so the fact is that, other than the corruption scandals that occur periodically, we really do not have any good data on the prevalence of economic corruption or abuse of authority.

Space prohibits any description of corruption in other countries. Suffice to say that the same types of scandals and examples of corruption that we see in the United States exist across the world in developing and developed countries. Transparency International charts corruption worldwide, ranking more than 90 countries. This agency defines corruption as abuse of public office (including police) for private gain (e.g., bribe taking). The countries with the highest scores for honesty typically are first-world countries, while poorest countries produced very low scores. In the latest rankings available from Transparency International, which used polls to rank 180 countries, New Zealand was ranked first in the public's trust in the honesty of their public officials, followed by Denmark, Finland, Sweden, Singapore, Norway, the Netherlands, Australia, Switzerland, and then Canada in the tenth position on the list. The United States followed the United Kingdom in rankings of 18 and 17, respectively, in 2009. In the 2011 rankings, the United States had dropped to 24, but returned to the 17th spot in 2014. At the bottom of the current rankings were countries such as Uzbekistan, Afghanistan, Myanmar, North Korea, and Somalia (Transparency International, 2011, 2014).

Before one can begin to research prevalence, it would be necessary to have some shared understanding of a definition of corruption. There are many definitions and typologies in the literature. Fyfe and Kane (2006: 37–38), for instance, reviewed the literature, and then identified a long list of types of misconduct:

- Profit-motivated crimes (all offenses with the goal of profit except those that are drug-related)
- Off-duty crimes against persons (all assaultive, non-profit-related crimes off-duty)
- Off-duty public-order crimes (not including drugs, and most commonly DWI [driving while intoxicated] and disorderly conduct)
- Drugs (all crimes related to possession, sale, conspiracy, and failing departmental drug tests)
- On-duty abuse (use of excessive force, psychological abuse, or discrimination)
- Obstruction of justice (conspiracy, perjury, official misconduct, and all other offenses with the goal of obstructing justice)
- Administrative/failure to perform (violating one or more departmental rules, policies, and procedures)
- Conduct-related probationary failures (simple failure to meet expectations).

In the discussion to follow, we will offer a much simpler typology of simply economic corruption and abuse of authority.

Economic Corruption

Corruption has been described as "acting on opportunities, created by virtue of one's authority, for personal gain at the expense of the public one is authorized to serve" (Cohen, 1986: 23). *Baksheesh*, a euphemism for graft, is endemic in many developing countries where officials, including law enforcement officers, expect *baksheesh* before doing the job they are supposed to do; alternatively, they extort money in exchange for not doing their job. "It's just the way it is" is the explanation for why such corruption exists. Obviously the problem is not systemic in this country; however, one can find many examples of police officers using their position to acquire unfair benefits.

In 1973, the Knapp Commission detailed its findings of corruption in the New York City Police Department. The terms *grass eaters* and *meat eaters* were used to describe New York City police officers who took advantage of their position to engage in corrupt practices. Accepting bribes, gratuities, and unsolicited protection money was the extent of the corruption engaged in by grass eaters, who were fairly passive in their deviant practices. Meat eaters participated in shakedowns, "shopped" at burglary scenes, and engaged in more active deviant practices. The Mollen Commission, which investigated New York City Police Department corruption 20 years later (1993), concluded that meat eaters were engaged in a qualitatively different kind of corruption in more recent times. Beyond just cooperating with criminals, the corrupt cops were active criminals themselves, selling drugs, robbing drug dealers, and operating burglary rings.

Economic corruption includes gratuities (when they conflict with law and policy), kickbacks (e.g., from towing companies), overtime schemes (e.g., such as a 2014 scandal in Houston where officers made up tickets in order to create the need to appear and earn overtime), misuse/appropriation of departmental property, payoffs (payment for shifts, promotions, or other benefits), ticket "fixing," bribery/extortion (shakedowns of storeowners or protection money to drug dealers), and theft from burglary scenes. The more serious acts in this list are also crimes. An important distinction that should be made is between crimes and ethical transgressions. It is an insult to law enforcement officers when certain actions, such as stealing from a burglary scene or taking money from a drug dealer to guard a shipment of drugs, are discussed as if they were ethical dilemmas in the same category as whether to avoid responding to a minor traffic accident or whether an officer should call in sick so he can go fishing. Stealing from a burglary scene and conspiring to protect drug dealers are crimes. The officers who engage in such acts are criminals who are quite distinct from officers who commit ethical lapses akin to other workers who do so within the parameters of their particular professions or jobs.

Gratuities

Gratuities are items of value received by an individual because of his or her role or position rather than because of a personal relationship with the giver. The widespread practices of free coffee in convenience stores, half-price or free meals in restaurants, and half-price dry cleaning are examples of gratuities. Frequently, businesspeople offer gratuities as a token of sincere appreciation for the police officers' work. Although the formal code of ethics prohibits accepting gratuities, many officers believe there is nothing wrong with businesses giving "freebies" to police officers. They see these as small rewards indeed for the difficulties they endure in police work.

> **gratuities** Items of value received by an individual because of his or her role or position rather than because of a personal relationship with the giver.

Justifications for gratuities include the idea that some businesses need (and should pay for) extra protection; that they are no different than the perks of other occupations; that they compensate for poor pay; and that they cement community relations (when the officer stays and drinks coffee with the storeowner; Prenzler, 1995; Kania, 1988).

Research indicates that people do not support gratuities, but do not think they are very serious either, especially when the items were infrequent, food, or inexpensive (Prenzler, 1995; Lord and Bjerregaard, 2003). Critics of gratuities argue that they "erode public confidence in law enforcement and undermine our quest for professionalism" (Stefanic, 1981: 63). Cohen (1986: 26) believes that gratuities violate the social contract because citizens give up their liberty to exploit only to be exploited. Critics (Ruiz and Bono, 2004; Coleman, 2004a, 2004b) argue against gratuities for the following reasons:

- Police are professionals, and professionals don't take gratuities.
- Gratuities are incipient corruptors because people expect different treatment in return.
- Gratuities are an abuse of authority and create a sense of entitlement.
- Gratuities add up to substantial amounts of money and can constitute as high as 30 percent of an officer's income.
- Gratuities can be the beginning of more serious forms of corruption.
- Gratuities are contrary to democratic ideals because they are a type of fee-for-service for public functions that are already paid for through taxes, such as police protection.
- Gratuities create a public perception that police are corrupt.

Kania (1988, 2004) argues that only when either or both the giver and taker (officer) have impure intent are gratuities wrong. For instance, it would be an unethical exchange if the intent of the giver was to give in exchange for some future service, not as reward for past services rendered. Another unethical exchange would be when the intent of the police officer taking the gratuity was not to receive unsolicited but appreciated gifts, but rather, to use the position of police officer to extort goods from business owners. A third type of unethical exchange would occur if both the giver and the police officer's motives were unethical: if the giver expected special treatment *and* the officer's intent was to take the gratuity in exchange for performing the special service. In Kania's scheme, ethical exchanges are only when true rewards or gifts with no expectation of future acts are offered and received with no expectations. Unethical exchanges are when either the giver or receiver expects something in return, such as understandings, bribes, arrangements, and shakedowns.

Where should one draw the line between harmless rewards and inappropriate gifts? Is a discount on a meal okay, but not a free meal? Is a meal okay, but not any other item, such as groceries or tires or car stereos? Do the store or restaurant owners expect anything for their money, such as more frequent patrols or overlooking sales of alcohol to underage juveniles? Should they expect different treatment from officers than the treatment given to those who do not offer gratuities? Suppose that an officer is told by a convenience store owner that she can help herself to anything in the store—free coffee, candy, cigarettes, chips, magazines, and the like. In the same conversation, the store owner asks the officer for her personal cellphone number "in case something happens and I need to get in contact with you." Is this a gift, or is it an exchange? Should the officer accept the free merchandise?

Many merchants give free or discount food to officers because they like to have police around, especially late at night. The question then becomes the one asked frequently by citizens: Why are two or three police cars always at a certain restaurant? Police argue that they deserve to take their breaks wherever they want within their patrol area. If it happens that they choose the same place, that shouldn't be a concern of the public. However, an impression of unequal protection occurs when officers make a habit of eating at certain restaurants or congregating at certain convenience stores. Free meals or even coffee may influence the pattern of police patrol and, thus, may be wrong because some citizens are not receiving equal protection.

The extent of gratuities varies from city to city. In cities where rules against gratuities are loosely enforced, "dragging the sack" may be developed to an art form by some police officers, who go out of their way to collect free meals and other gifts. Ruiz and Bono (2004) describe when a restaurant owner, who had been giving free meals to officers stopped doing so. Officers then engaged in a ticket-writing campaign, targeting his customers who double parked. After several weeks of this, the restaurant owner changed his mind and began giving free meals to officers again. Those authors also mentioned a type of contest whereby officers competed to see how many free bottles of liquor they could collect; the winning team collected 50 bottles from the bars and businesses in one district on a single shift. "The blue discount suit," according to the authors, was a term that indicated how officers felt about gratuities. Some other terms described businesses that offered free or discounted goods; these establishments were said to "show love" or give "pop"—hence the saying, "If you got no pop, you got no cop."

Officers in some departments are known for their skill in soliciting free food and liquor for after-hours parties. In the same vein, officers also solicit merchants for free food and beverages for charity events sponsored by police, such as youth softball leagues. The first situation is similar to individual officers receiving gratuities, but the second situation is harder to criticize. Officers bring up the seeming hypocrisy of a departmental prohibition against individual officers accepting gratuities, yet at the same time there may be an administrative policy of actively soliciting and receiving donations from merchants for departmental events, such as pastries, coffee, or more expensive catering items.

MacIntyre and Prenzler (1999) conducted a survey of officers to see if they would be influenced by gratuities. They asked officers what they would do if a café owner who gave them free coffee and meals was stopped for a traffic violation. The researchers found that supervisory officers were more likely than rookies to give a ticket. Although only 15 percent would not write the ticket and would continue to go back for meals, an additional 41 percent would also not write the ticket but would give the owner a warning and not go back for free meals. The remaining officers would write the owner a ticket. Another study evaluated police coverage in a medium-sized U.S. city, taking into account whether or not the businesses gave gratuities, food quality, cost, convenience, and location and found that gratuities increased coverage (DeLeon-Granados and Wells, 1998). These studies indicate that gratuities do influence officers' decisions both in how they patrol and what they might do when they have to make a decision about a giver of gratuities. More research is needed to see if these findings would be replicated.

ETHICAL DILEMMA

You are a police officer who, after eating at a new restaurant, is told that the meal is "on the house." You did not go to that restaurant knowing the owner gave free meals to police officers. Should you accept the offer?

Law

While bribery laws punish taking or receiving something of value in return for a specific act of omission or commission related to one's office, conflict-of-interest laws punish merely taking something of value prohibited by the law when one holds a public office, with no necessity to show that a specific vote or decision was directly influenced by receipt of the valued items or services. Conflict-of-interest laws recognize the reality that public official's discretion is compromised after receiving things of value from stakeholders, even if there is no way to prove a direct connection. Recently, in *Skilling v. U.S.* (130 S. Ct. 2896, 2010), the Supreme Court invalidated a federal "honest services" law as being vague. The law (18 U.S.C. Sec. 1346) made it a crime to deprive someone of honest services. The federal prosecutor did not have to prove a specific bribe or kickback, but only that there was some loss of honest services from the suspect to their clients or fiduciaries (because of private dealing or conflict of interest). The holding makes it more difficult for federal prosecutors to pursue those suspected of corruption, but it is unclear at this point whether

or not the holding implicates state conflict-of-interest laws. Even conflict of interest laws would probably not apply to a free meal.

Policy

Many departments have policies that say "no gratuities," while others specify some nominal value of goods that may be received. Gratuity policies are often the most ignored of all policies and considered to be hypocritical by the rank and file since the administration often solicits goods from the same type of vendors that might offer gratuities to individual officers. Policies that are not enforced and prevalently ignored are problematic in the organization.

Ethics

Professional ethics discourages gifts or gratuities when the profession involves discretionary judgments about a clientele (i.e., judges, professors, appraisers, and inspectors). Whether gifts are unethical relates to whether one's occupation or profession involves judgments that affect the gift givers. The police obviously have discretionary authority and make judgments that affect store owners and other gift givers. This may explain why some think it is wrong for police to accept gifts or favors. It also explains why so many other people do not see anything wrong with some types of gratuities, for police officers in most situations are not making decisions that affect the giver and, instead,

(continued)

are simply providing a service, such as responding to a burglary or disturbance call.

Ethical formalism would indicate that we must be comfortable with a universal law allowing all businesses to give all police officers certain favors or gratuities, such as free meals, free merchandise, or special consideration. However, such a blanket endorsement of this behavior would probably not be desirable. The second principle of ethical formalism indicates that each should treat every other with respect as an individual and not as a means to an end. In this regard, we would have to condemn gratuities in cases where the giver or receiver had improper motives according to Kania's typology. This also explains why some gifts seem acceptable. When something is given freely and accepted without strings, there is no "using" of others; therefore, it might be considered an innocent, honorable act by both parties.

If utilitarian ethics were used, one would have to weigh the relative good or utility of the interaction. On one hand, harmless gratuities may create good feelings in the community toward the officers and among the officers toward the community (Kania's "cementing the bonds" argument). On the other hand, gratuities often lead to perceptions of unfairness by shopkeepers who feel they are being taken advantage of, or those who feel they are not receiving the appropriate police protection because they don't give gratuities, by police who think they deserve rewards and don't get them, and so on. Thus, the overall negative results of gratuities, even "harmless" ones, might lead a utilitarian to conclude that gratuities are unethical.

The ethics of virtue would be concerned with the individual qualities or virtues of the officer. A virtuous officer could take free coffee and not let it affect his or her judgment. According to this perspective, no gift or gratuity would affect the judgment of the virtuous officer. However, if the officer does not possess those qualities of virtue, such as honesty, integrity, and fairness, even free coffee may lead to special treatment. Further, nonvirtuous officers would seek out gifts and gratuities and abuse their authority by pursuing them.

Graft

graft Any exploitation of one's role, such as accepting bribes, protection money, or kickbacks.

Graft is the exploitation of one's role by accepting bribes or protection money. Graft also occurs when officers receive kickbacks from tow truck drivers, defense attorneys, or bail bond companies for recommending them. In Klockars, Ivkovic, and Haberfeld's (2004) international comparison of officers' views regarding hypotheticals drawn to illustrate various forms of corruption, officers in the United States rated bribery as the second most serious offense. Only theft from a crime scene was rated as more serious.

Examples of graft involve a range of seriousness from "cheating a little" on overtime to sophisticated schemes that utilize police powers for private gain. For instance, a former Savannah-Chatham police chief was convicted for running interference for a gambling operation headed by Randall Roach for 10 years, earning payoffs to protect him (Skutch, 2014).

In Baltimore, 17 officers were indicted for conspiracy to commit extortion in a scheme whereby they received $300 for each time they had a car towed to a particular repair shop that was not on the city's approved list of towing companies. The repair shop paid the officers to have vehicles towed, even if they were not disabled. In one case, the officer earned $14,400 from such payments over a two-year period (CNN. com, 2011).

In Stoughton, Massachusetts former police officers pleaded guilty to federal obstruction charges and to making false statements in an investigation of corruption. The officers were accused of trading information obtained through official police computers for stolen goods, such as large screen televisions, and gift cards from Home Depot. It turned out to be an FBI sting operation, though, and the officers were caught on tape and video making the arrangements and accepting the goods (Guilfoil, 2010; Saltzman, 2010).

At the most serious end of the economic corruption continuum is blatant theft. In 2010, a Miami police officer was convicted and sentenced for theft. The officer responded to a traffic accident and drove the victim home. Later he found her ATM card in his patrol car and called her to get her PIN number, telling her it was for an investigation. He then stole $440 from her account (Moskovitz, 2010). A Suffolk County, New York, officer was arrested for stopping Hispanic drivers who he believed to be illegal immigrants and stealing from them (Cergol, 2014). More commonly, news items appear regularly that describe police officers who pick up items from stores or burglary scenes and are caught on camera doing so. Economic corruption covers a wide range of activity, some of which is similar to what occurs in other occupations and professions, and some which is unique to law enforcement.

Abuse of Authority

Abuse of authority involves officers' misuse of the power and authority inherent in their positions. Barker and Carter (1994) and Fyfe and Kane (2006) discuss police abuse of authority which can be summarized as follows:

- Physical abuse—excessive force, physical harassment, retaliatory brutality
- Psychological abuse—disrespect, harassment, ridicule, excessive stops, intimidation, deception in interrogation
- Legal abuse—unlawful searches or seizures, manufacturing evidence, perjury, planting evidence, hiding exculpatory evidence

Professional Courtesy and Ticket Fixing

One practice not included in the typologies above is called "professional courtesy," which refers to the practice of not ticketing an officer who is stopped for speeding or for other driving violations. Obviously officers do not ticket everyone they stop. They often give warnings instead, and that is a legitimate use of their discretion. Whether to ticket or give a warning should depend on objective criteria, such as the seriousness of the violation. If the officer would let another person go with a warning in the same situation, there is no ethical issue in giving a warning to a fellow officer. However, if *every other person* would have received a ticket, but the officer did not issue one *only because* the motorist was a fellow officer, that is a violation of the code of ethics ("enforce the law . . . without fear or favor"). It is a violation of deontological universalism as well as utilitarianism. Under deontological ethics, it is the officer's duty to enforce the law against everyone, including officers. Under utilitarianism, the fact that the speeding officer can cause an accident means that the utility for society is greater if the ticket is issued, for it might make the officer slow down, and by doing that, accidents can be avoided.

Justifications for not ticketing other officers are diverse and creative. For instance, some honest justifications are purely egoistic: "If I do it for him, he will do it for me one day." Other justifications are under the guise of utilitarianism: "It's best for all of us not to get tickets, and the public isn't hurt because we're trained to drive faster." One troubling aspect of professional courtesy for traffic offenses is that the practice has a tendency to bleed over into other forms of misconduct. Officers who are stopped for driving while intoxicated are sometimes driven home rather than arrested, but this application of discretion is less likely to be afforded to any other citizen. In some cases of domestic violence, victims of police officer husbands or boyfriends describe how the responding officers do nothing or take their complaints more lightly than they would if the alleged perpetrator were not a police officer.

The idea that officers are above the law is insidious. Officers who believe that they should not have to follow the same laws they enforce against others may be more prone to other forms of abuse of authority as well. It should also be noted that many officers think that they are held to a higher standard of behavior than the public. Officers point out that a domestic violence, DUI, or any other arrest may cost them their job, which may not be the case for others. The argument against this position is that perhaps one who has taken an oath to uphold the law but is engaged in unlawful behavior should not have the job.

One step more serious than not ticketing an officer (or anyone) solely for preferential reasons is "fixing" a ticket that has already been written. The reason is that such acts could be considered and charged as "tampering with official documents." A major ticket-fixing scandal in New York City is ongoing, involving a widespread practice in one precinct of "fixing" tickets for friends and family. A former lieutenant has been fired and convicted of obstruction for tipping the officers to the investigation. Indictments have been handed down for 16 police officers and 5 civilians. The Bronx district attorney's office has estimated that ticket-fixing cost the city more than $1 million in ticket revenue (Hu, 2014).

On-Duty Use of Drugs and Alcohol

Carter (1999) discussed the extent of on-duty drug use, citing previous research that found up to 20 percent of officers in one city used marijuana and other drugs while on duty. That seems to be a high figure; in other surveys, about 8 percent of employees reported drug use and only 3 percent of all workers in a "protective services" category reported drug use. In a more recent survey, protective service employees were the least likely to report any drug use (Mieczkowski, 2002: 168). It could be that the decrease seen in the use of drugs by the general population is reflected in police officer samples. As well, the sources are not exactly comparable. Thus, it is impossible to determine which source is more accurate.

Certain circumstances are present in law enforcement that, perhaps, create more opportunities for drug use. Elements of police work (especially undercover work) that can lead to drug use include exposure to a criminal element, relative freedom from supervision, and uncontrolled availability of contraband. Drug use by officers creates the potential for even more serious misbehavior, such as stealing evidence, being blackmailed to perform other unethical or illegal actions, and being tempted to steal from drug users instead of arresting them. This, of course, is in addition to the obvious problem of compromising one's decision-making abilities by being under the influence of any drug while on duty.

■ **((•)) IN THE NEWS** | *FBI Agent Convicted*

A veteran FBI agent was investigated, tried, and convicted of theft of drugs from an evidence property room. He worked on a task force focusing on heroin traffickers along the borders of the District, Maryland, and Virginia, and his thefts went on for 14 months before being discovered when he was found incoherent in a bureau car surrounded by open, empty evidence bags of heroin along with a shot-gun and a derringer pistol seized during a drug raid but never logged into evidence. The agent said he began using heroin after becoming addicted to prescription painkillers. He would check out drugs from the evidence room and say he was taking them to be tested, but before bringing them in for testing or returning to the property room, he would take out some of the heroin and replace it with a filler. He would forge signatures of supervisors and other agents in order to make the evidence bags appear untouched. At least 28 cases against defendants had to be dropped because of the agent's thefts of drugs.

Source: Hermann, 2015.

In a study of drug use, it was found that officers used drugs to relieve stress and for social reasons. No predictors emerged as to which officers were more likely to be drug users. The study results also noted other crimes that were associated with drug use, including giving drugs to others, providing confidential information to suppliers and theft (Gorta, 2008).

The use of drug tests during the hiring process is longstanding, but periodic and/or random drug testing of employed officers is a more recent policy. Generally, courts have upheld the right of law enforcement agencies to employ drug testing, applying the balancing test between a compelling governmental interest and individual privacy rights. Officers have some due process rights, however, and they must be notified of the policies and procedures involved in the agency's drug testing, have access to the findings, and have available some sort of appeal process before sanctions are taken (Mieczkowski, 2002: 179). In Fyfe and Kane's (2006) study of police officers termi-nated for cause in New York City, the most common reason for termination was a failed drug test.

Alcohol use is more socially acceptable than drug use, and it has also been cited as a problem. In one survey, it was found that about 8 percent of those in protec-tive services occupations (which include police officers) reported heavy alcohol use. This compared to 12 percent of construction workers and 4 percent of sales workers (Mieczkowski, 2002: 179). Barker and Carter (1994) indicated that 8 percent of officers reported drinking alcohol on duty. The problem of drinking on duty does not involve the vulnerability to blackmail that drug use does, but there are obvious problems, and officers who are aware of another's on-duty intoxication are faced with an ethical dilemma of whether or not to take official action. Officers may choose to informally isolate themselves from drinking officers by refusing to partner with them or avoid working calls with them.

Sexual Misconduct

It is a sad reality that a few police officers use their position of authority to extort sex from female citizens (there doesn't seem to be the parallel situation of female police officers extorting sex from male victims). Amnesty International documented widespread mistreatment of women by police around the world. Egregious cases in the United States include rapes by officers on duty and by jailers in police lockups, and a few instances where the sexual misconduct of police officers was widespread and protected by departmental supervisors, such as in Wallkill, New York. In that town, the 25-member police department evidently engaged in numerous instances of sexual intimidation of citizens before being investigated by the state police and sued in a federal civil rights lawsuit (reported in McGurrin and Kappeler, 2002: 133).

Kraska and Kappeler (1995) looked at a sample of 124 cases of police sexual misconduct, including 37 sexual assaults by on-duty officers. These authors challenged earlier studies that found sexual misconduct of officers occurred most often when women traded sexual favors for lenient treatment. This study's authors concluded that norms in a police department that ignored or condoned the exchange of sex for favored treatment opened the door to officers who used more aggressive tactics to coerce sex from citizens. Kraska and Kappeler (1995: 93) proposed a continuum of sexual invasion that ranged from some type of invasion of privacy to sexual assault. This range of behavior includes the following:

- Viewing a victim's photos or videos for prurient purposes
- Field strip searches
- Custodial strip searches
- Illegal detentions
- Deception to gain sex
- Provision of services for sex
- Sexual harassment
- Sexual contact
- Sexual assault
- Rape

Sapp's (1994) inventory of sexual misconduct includes the following:

- Nonsexual contacts that are sexually motivated (non-valid traffic stops)
- Voyeurism (e.g., patrolling lovers' lanes to watch sexual activity)
- Contact with crime victims (excessive call-backs that are not necessary for investigative purposes)
- Contact with offenders (sexual demands or inappropriate frisks)
- Contacts with juvenile offenders (sexual harassment and sexual contact)
- Sexual shakedowns (demanding sex from prostitutes or the homeless)
- Citizen-initiated sexual contact (an officer is approached by a citizen because of his officer status)

Even the most innocuous of contacts between female citizens and officers—whereby an officer might ask a woman he has stopped for a date—involve issues of power and coercion. In Kraska and Kappeler's study, police described how they routinely went "bimbo hunting," which involved sexual harassment of women out drinking (1995: 104). Maher (2010) interviewed female officers who described how this type of sexual misconduct by their male colleagues was very common.

(((•))) IN THE NEWS | *Sexual Misconduct*

Cases of police officers who commit sexual harassment or abuse can easily be found in the news:

Craig Nash was fired from the San Antonio Police Department and indicted for sexually assaulting a transgender prostitute. In 2009, San Antonio fired 18 officers over various forms of misconduct, including sexual assaults and indecent exposure (Holley, 2010).

In New York, an officer was convicted for extorting sex from an 18-year-old girl and two other women. A Brooklyn officer extorted oral sex from a woman in a precinct bathroom. This officer is also facing rape charges in a separate case (Sulzberger and Eligon, 2010).

In San Diego, Christopher Hayes was fired and received a felony conviction for forcing women to perform sex acts. Anthony Arevalos was convicted in 2011 of extorting sex acts from women and is serving eight years in prison (Davis, 2014).

In Tennessee, a police officer was acquitted of rape but convicted of official misconduct and decommissioned. He received a 12-count indictment involving demanding sex from prostitutes while on duty. The officer had already been acquitted of a prior similar sexual battery and official misconduct charge (Allyn, 2013).

Prostitutes and homeless women are populations that are extremely vulnerable to sexual extortion by police officers, because people tend not to believe them. But women who have been subject to intimidation and outright assault come from all social classes (McGurrin and Kappeler, 2002). The defense of officers is usually that, if sex occurred, it was consensual. The problem is that when officers acting in their official capacity meet women (as victims, witnesses, defendants, or suspects), the power differential makes consent extremely problematic.

McGurrin and Kappeler's (2002) research on sexual misconduct describes sexual assault, rape, and even murder by police officers in and out of uniform. Rape charges commonly were downgraded to a conviction of "official oppression" in a plea agreement, or the officer was not punished at all. Also, these researchers found that some officers who had criminal records for sexual offenses simply moved and obtained law enforcement positions in other jurisdictions.

The Cato Institute sponsors the National Police Misconduct Reporting Project, which acts as a clearinghouse for misconduct reports across the nation. It was reported that 9.3 percent of all civilian complaints on police involved sexual misconduct, the second most common form of misconduct after excessive use of force. About 354 of the 618 officers under investigation for sexual offenses involved nonconsensual sexual acts, and 51 percent, or 180, of these 354 acts involved minors (Packman, 2011).

Stinson, Brewer, and Mathna (2015) analyzed 771 sex-related arrest cases from 2005 to 2008 of 555 sworn officers at 449 non-federal law enforcement agencies in 44 states. Less than 1 percent of the offending officers were female; most were patrol officers. The modal time in service was 1 to 5 years. On-duty and off-duty offenses were about equally divided. A majority (70 percent) of the victims were minors (under 18). Most of the cases involving a child victim occurred when the officer was off duty and most of the cases involving an adult victim occurred when the officer was on duty. Forcible fondling was the most serious offense charged in the majority of cases, followed by forcible rape, statutory rape, and forcible sodomy. This study and others like it show that sexual misconduct of officers is not a negligible problem and involves more serious crimes and victimization than previously believed.

Sexual harassment of fellow officers is also a problem. In one research study, 70 percent of female officers reported being sexually harassed by other police officers (Kraska and Kappeler, 1995: 92). In another study, 75 percent said they have been sexually harassed but only 2 percent reported it (Maher, 2010). It may be that the culture of policing is particularly conducive to sexual harassment. It has been described as a "macho" or "locker room" culture even though women have been integrated into patrol since the early 1970s. Female officers today do not encounter the virulent harassment and hostility that was present in the 1970s when patrol forces were first integrated, but some remnants of that culture remain. More research is needed to update older studies of the prevalence of sexual harassment. One study reported that while 50 to 58 percent of women in the general workforce have experienced sexual harassment, 69 to 77 percent of women in male-dominated professions (like policing) experience sexual harassment (reported in Maher, 2010: 266).

Female officers who in undercover work pretend to be prostitutes are especially targeted for sexual innuendos, jokes, and other forms of comments about their body and dress, and behavior from other officers that could be considered sexual harassment, such as betting which female officer would receive more sexual offers or throwing money at her in the squad room. While some research indicates that many female officers consider such work degrading and humiliating (Nolan, 2001; Maguire and Nolan, 2011), other research found that the female officers who participated found the work exciting and fun and the joking harmless (Dodge, Starr-Gimeno, and Williams, 2005). It is interesting to note that, in these studies, it was found that male officers were never asked to pose as homosexual prostitutes even though one might argue that was also a crime problem in these areas.

There have been other cases where officers may receive administrative punishments for "conduct unbecoming to an officer" related to their sexual activity or other off-duty conduct. For instance, in a few cases officers have posed nude, participated in sexually explicit videos, or, in one case, an officer posted nude pictures of his wife on the Internet (Egelko, 2007). In the cases where these officers have been fired, courts have generally upheld the department's right to fire, although the First Amendment rights of officers is still an unsettled area of law.

In other cases, officers who have affairs with supervisors, coworkers, or wives of coworkers sometimes get sanctioned for "conduct unbecoming" (Martinelli, 2007). The fact of the matter is that officers are held to a higher standard of behavior, and even when no laws are broken, the behavior may be unethical in that it brings discredit or embarrassment to the department.

Criminal Cops

Some of the acts discussed above are crimes, for example, theft, sexual assault, official oppression. Other examples can be found where a very few officers enter into a realm that can only be described as criminal cops. These are instances where the transgressions that officers engage in become patterns of brutality and other abuses of authority, racketeering, and even armed robberies. Very often drugs are involved.

In the 1980s, the "Miami River Rats" committed armed robberies of drug deals, collecting cash and drugs. These robberies by a small group of police officers eventually led to at least one homicide (Dorschner, 1989; see also Rothlein, 1999). More recently, a Miami internal affairs officer was investigated by federal authorities who alleged he participated in aiding in the distribution of cocaine, organizing a murder-for-hire plot, providing firearms and sensitive law enforcement information to drug traffickers, and facilitating the transport of drug proceeds (Golgowski, 2014).

In the early 1980s, the "Buddy Boys" in New York were able to operate almost openly in a precinct rife with lesser forms of corruption. Ultimately, 13 officers in a precinct of only a little over 200 were indicted for crimes ranging from drug use to drug sales and armed robbery (Kappeler, Sluder, and Alpert, 1984/1994). In the early 1990s, Michael Dowd testified to the Mollen Commission that he and other officers accepted money for protecting illegal drug operations, used drugs and alcohol while on duty, robbed crime victims and drug dealers of money and drugs, and even robbed corpses of their valuables (Kappeler, Sluder, and Alpert, 1994: 201–202).

Other cities have had their own criminal cops. In 1996, seven Chicago cops were indicted for conspiracy to commit robbery and extortion for shaking down under-cover agents they thought were drug dealers (Crank and Caldero, 2000). In 2009, a similar scandal occurred and seven officers pleaded guilty to felony theft or official misconduct. The alleged ringleader, ex-cop Jerome Finnigan, was charged in a murder-for-hire plot aimed at a fellow officer who was thought to be cooperating with investigators (Meincke, 2009).

Indianapolis police officer Robert Long also ran a corrupt ring of officers. Six incidents involving thefts of drugs and money formed the case against the officers, who were under surveillance by the FBI from March to June 2008. Long was sentenced to 25 years. The prosecutor had to dismiss 26 pending cases where the involved officers were witnesses (Murray, 2009).

New Orleans police officers have also been linked to drugs, robberies, and attempted murder when a police officer was overheard in a federal wiretap of hiring someone to kill a female witness against him (Human Rights Watch, 1998). Other locations where police officers have been linked to drug dealers and evidently provided protection to them, or actually stole drugs and engaged in drug dealing themselves, include Prince George's County, Maryland (Valentine, 2009); Boston (Vaznis, 2008); and Philadelphia (Graham and Gormisky, 2010).

Costs of Corruption

We have examined a range of corruption, from the arguably trivial (gratuities) to criminal acts that include murder. The costs to communities are considerable. First, there is the cost of lost prosecutions. Literally thousands of cases across the country have had to be dismissed because prosecutors could not trust that the evidence provided by police officers was legitimate or the officer had lost credibility as a witness for any case because of his or her wrongdoing.

Many cities and police departments have also faced large judgments in response to the wrongdoing of officers. These lawsuits are most often claims of police brutality, traffic accident claims, or wrongful death suits due to police shootings. There is no way to know the total amount of money taxpayers pay across the nation in any given year because of police misconduct. Some specific localities do not even keep tallies of how much is spent in judgments or in settling lawsuits, but news reports are beginning to appear that call attention to the costs of misconduct:

Cleveland—The city has spent $8 million between 2003 and 2013 on claims related to police misconduct.

Minneapolis—A 2013 examination of city payouts for alleged police misconduct found $14 million in payments in the previous seven years; in 95 payouts between 2006 and 2012, only eight led to officers being disciplined (McKinney, 2015).

Chicago—The city paid nearly $5.4 million just to settle three cases of misconduct in 2012–2013; more than a half-billion dollars to resolve police brutality cases over the last decade (Dardick, 2013; Wallack, Ransom, and Anderson, 2015).

Boston—The city spent more than $36 million to resolve 2,000 legal claims and lawsuits against the police department over the past decade (mostly brutality and wrongful death claims); $31 million was paid in 22 cases worth $100,000 or more, including nine awards for well over $1 million (Wallack, Ransom, and Anderson, 2015).

New York City—Just in fiscal year 2013, New York paid out more than $138 million; in fiscal year 2014, it paid nearly $217 million for claims of false arrest, excessive force, and civil rights violations (Hennelly, 2015).

Despite the costs to the city of such lawsuits, there is no evidence to indicate that they are a deterrent to errant police officers. In fact, one study showed that there is no follow-up generally with the police officers involved. The lawsuit doesn't appear in the officers' personnel records, nor does anyone keep track of patterns or problem officers. In some cities, an incident is not investigated by internal affairs once it becomes the subject of a lawsuit; instead, the investigation proceeds out of the city's legal department. Police officials sometimes don't even know when the city settles because it is a decision made by city officials outside the police department. Police officers believe that city lawyers are too quick to settle "nuisance" claims, where the officer is not at fault; however, when such cases do go to trial, there is the risk of a much larger judgment (Schwartz, 2010). The important point to note though is that civil lawsuits seem to be independent from the department's own discipline system and, rarely, is there the mechanism to take note of when officers become the target of lawsuits multiple times.

Sometimes lawsuits are brought by officers themselves against the department, usually by whistleblowers for retaliation or by minority officers who are successful in showing discriminatory practices; for example, Minneapolis, Minnesota had to pay $740,000 to five African American officers who convinced a court they were discriminated against by the department (Williams, 2009).

Consent Decrees

In addition to possible lawsuits and settlement costs, police departments face the possibility of being a target of the Department of Justice. Because of the Rodney King incident, Congress in 1994 passed the Violent Control and Law Enforcement Act (42 U.S.C. Sec. 14141), which authorizes the Department of Justice to investigate and bring a lawsuit for "equitable remedies" against police departments that are found to have a "pattern or practice" of unconstitutional actions. From 1994 to 2009, there were over 70 preliminary investigations, 33 full investigations, seven consent decrees, and seven memorandums of understanding (Harmon, 2009).

Between 2009 and 2015, there have been proportionally even more. Cities such as Spokane, Seattle, Portland, Miami, Pittsburgh, Washington, D.C., Detroit, Oakland, and Los Angeles have been the target of the Justice Department's investigations. Even smaller cities like East Haven, Connecticut, have been subject to decrees. Recently, Ferguson, Missouri, and Baltimore, Maryland, were the subject of a federal investigation due to recent events.

Sometimes a police chief or mayor asks for an investigation and review. Mayor Mitch Landrieu asked the Justice Department to investigate the New Orleans police department. In March 2011, the Justice Department issued a report that detailed a pattern of misconduct that included racial profiling, not investigating police shootings, allowing extra jobs to corrupt the chain of command, and having procedures that served to intimidate citizens not to file complaints on officers, among other findings. Landrieu then reversed his support for the reform efforts demanded by the Justice Department, arguing that they were too expensive (Winston, 2013).

Consent decrees focus on the department itself rather than the individual officer and involve changes in policies or procedures, and they may require hiring more officers and/or increasing training for officers. The most common targets for change involve policies concerning use of force, citizen complaint procedures, in-car video use, racial profiling, data collection, early identification systems, and training.

Compliance with consent decrees is expensive for cities and police departments. Ross and Parker (2009) report that the Los Angeles Police Department spent $30–$40 million annually to reach compliance after the department became the object of a consent decree. Sometimes monitoring drags on for years as the city struggles to meet the reform goals. Police chiefs argue that monitoring has become a "cottage industry" with monitors' pay sometimes running into millions of dollars with no incentive to end the supervision (Goode, 2013).

Other costs include damage to the department's reputation, and a reduction in morale and potentially the loss of good officers (Ross and Parker, 2009). For instance, the LAPD was required to have officers in narcotics and gang divisions file annual individual financial reports to ensure they were not receiving illegal income. While most officers complied, in a few gang units, the majority of officers in the unit refused, requiring the department to dismantle the unit until new officers could be transferred and trained. There were also reports of intimidation and threats by those who refused to officers who did comply (Rubin and Gold, 2011).

An alternative to costly consent decrees with external monitoring is a voluntary agreement entered into where collaboration between the city and Justice Department replaces an adversarial relationship. These agreements are not externally monitored and the Justice Department provides technical assistance rather than acts as an enforcer (Goode, 2015). Arguably, because the patterns of identified issues and required reforms are so similar in the dozens of cities that have undergone or are under consent decrees, there is really no excuse that a police department doesn't know what best practices are or how to avoid being targeted by such investigations.

Before we leave this discussion of examples of police corruption, it is important to note that most officers in this country are honest and strive to do their best every day. Also, officers who engage in rule breaking or types of unethical behaviors that are not criminal should not be in the same discussion as "criminal cops" whose pattern of wrongdoing and criminality is much more serious. However an environment where minor transgressions flourish leads to the possibility that truly rogue cops feel free to engage in criminality with all officers then engaged in a conspiracy of silence. The Walking the Walk box illustrates how difficult it is to come forward in an atmosphere where even criminal cops are sometimes protected.

WALKING THE WALK

In the movie *Training Day*, a new recruit is "schooled" in the methods of a veteran, decorated cop that included brutalizing suspects, planting drugs, and generally committing crimes to catch the criminals. In a real-life version of *Training Day*, Keith Batt earned a criminal justice degree at California State University at Sacramento and fulfilled his life's dream by being hired by the Oakland Police Department. He graduated at the top of his recruit class and became an Oakland police officer in 1999.

Batt was assigned to Clarence Mabanag as his field training officer. Almost from the first day, Batt says, he was told to falsify offense reports and to use force on suspects. Batt did as he was told for two and a half weeks, including hitting a suspect and lying on an offense report, because he knew that he would be retaliated against if he did not. Then he decided that he could not continue to be a police officer if it meant violating the law he was sworn to uphold. He quit the Oakland force and turned in his FTO and the other officers to internal affairs.

Mabanag and other officers, including Matt Hornung, Jude Siapno, and Frank (Choker) Vazquez, were known as the "Riders." According to testimony, they patrolled their western poverty-stricken district of Oakland with an iron fist and used excessive force, planted drugs, and intimidated witnesses as the means to keep the peace. Partly as a result of Keith Batt's report, all four officers were fired and charged with a range of offenses including obstruction of justice, conspiracy to obstruct justice, filing false police reports, assault and battery, kidnapping, and false imprisonment. Even before these charges, the four had records of misconduct. The department had paid $200,000 to settle suits involving Siapno and Mabanag, and other lawsuits existed against Vazquez and Hornung.

Not everyone believes the foursome's culpability or applauds Keith Batt's decision to testify against them. According to one fellow officer at the time, "These guys are awesome cops, they never did anything to anybody who was innocent, just pukes, criminals, see? They just got a little too intense and went over the line." Even residents had mixed feelings, with some arguing that it took a tough cop to police a tough street. As one resident said, "The only thing the bad people understand is force." Sometimes, however, their activities evidently were not limited to just drug dealers and other criminals. One witness testified that he called police to report a stolen stereo, and when his dog wouldn't stop barking and Mabanag threatened to shoot the dog, his angry response resulted in Mabanag's choking him and ordering Batt to lie on the offense report to cover the use of force.

In the course of the ensuing scandal, Oakland paid out $11 million to settle civil suits from 119 victims of police officers (including the Riders) and ended up under a court-ordered federal consent decree. Hornung, Mabanag, and Siapno were prosecuted in two lengthy trials between 2000 and 2005. Vazquez is a fugitive of justice, believed to be in Mexico. Perhaps he should have waited to have his day in court, too, as all three escaped guilty verdicts. Hornung was acquitted of all charges, and the jury deadlocked in two trials on Mabanag and Siapno. The police chief has refused to reinstate them, and they have sued for back pay and reinstatement.

The fired officers and their attorneys say that the deadlocked jurors exonerated them. The prosecutor is convinced of their guilt, but decided not to seek a third trial because he believed that he could not get a jury to convict them. Batt has been honored as a courageous whistleblower who stood up to the "blue curtain of secrecy," but also has been vilified as a liar who feared a negative evaluation. He became a respected police officer in Pleasanton, California, and received an award for "ethical courage." But Clarence Mabanag is also a police officer in a different department in southern California, which hired him after the deadlocked jury verdict. In February 2009, in response to their appeal, an independent arbitrator ruled that the city was justified in dismissing Mabanag and Siapno.

Sources: Institute for Law Enforcement Administration, 2008; Lee, 2004; Zamora, Lee, and van Derbeke, 2003; Bay City News, 2007.

Explanations of Deviance

Explanations of corruption can be categorized into individual, organizational, and societal, based on the identified factors. These factors then provide an avenue for how to reduce misconduct. It is important to note at the outset that there is rarely only one factor or group of factors responsible for corruption scandals. Generally, a constellation of factors is present.

Individual Explanations

The most common explanation of police officer corruption is the **rotten-apple argument**—that the officer alone is deviant and that it was simply a mistake to hire him or her. This argument has been extended to describe *rotten bushels*—groups of officers banding together to commit deviant acts. The point of this argument is that nothing is wrong with the barrel, that deviance is individual, not endemic.

Sherman explained that deviant officers go through what he called a "moral career" as they pass through various stages of rationalization to more serious misdeeds in a graduated and systematic way. Once an individual is able to get past the first "moral crisis," it becomes less difficult to rationalize new and more unethical behaviors. The previous behaviors serve as an underpinning to a different ethical standard, for one must explain and justify one's own behaviors to preserve psychological well-being (Sherman, 1982). While it seems to be true that corrupt officers who come to the attention of authorities engage in a range of minor misconduct to serious behavior, there is no good evidence to indicate that something like taking gratuities inevitably leads to more serious forms of misconduct. Many police officers have clear personal guidelines on what is acceptable and not acceptable. Whereas many, perhaps even the majority of, police see nothing wrong with accepting minor gratuities, few police would accept outright cash, and fewer still would condone thefts and bribes.

Sherman also described a signification factor, or labeling an individual action that is acceptable under a personal rationale (Sherman, 1985a: 253). Police routinely deal with the seamier side of society—not only drug addicts and muggers but also middle-class people who are involved in dishonesty and corruption. The constant displays of lying, hiding, cheating, and theft create cynicism, and this, in turn, may develop into a vulnerability to temptation because officers may redefine them as acceptable behaviors.

Following are some rationales that police might easily use to justify unethical behavior (Murphy and Moran, 1981: 93):

- The public thinks every cop is a crook, so why try to be honest?
- The money is out there; if I don't take it, someone else will.
- I'm only taking what's rightfully mine; if the city paid me a decent wage, I wouldn't have to get it on my own.
- I can use it because it's for a good cause—my son needs an operation, or dental work, or tuition for medical school, or a new bicycle.

Greene, Piquero, Hickman, and Lawton (2004) examined predictive variables related to those who received citizen complaints or departmental discipline in the Philadelphia police department. In their study, they utilized background and file information on about 2,000 officers and obtained attitudinal survey results from a random sample of 500 officers. They collected data on citizen complaints, internal investigations, departmental discipline incidents, and police shootings. About a third of the sample had received departmental discipline (2004: iii). They found that 15 characteristics were significantly related to receiving departmental discipline, including being younger, being previously rejected for hire, experiencing military discipline, scoring low on some sections of academy training, and receiving academy discipline. Officers having six or more of these risk factors were 2.5 times more likely to

rotten-apple argument The proposition that the officer alone is deviant and that it was simply a mistake to hire him or her.

receive departmental discipline (2004: iv). The research found that 22 factors were significantly related to receiving a citizen complaint of physical abuse, including being younger, receiving military discipline, having one's driver's license suspended, having ever been placed under arrest, and having had one or more deceptive polygraph results (2004: v). They found, using a cynicism scale, that higher levels of cynicism predicted disciplinary actions, shootings, and other misconduct. They also found that officers who worked in districts with lower ethics scores were more likely to be involved in shootings, but no other relationships were found (2004: 65). Note that this study did not collect the data in a way that would allow them to match the actions and attitudes of individual officers; instead they had to aggregate ethics scores by district level.

Greene and his colleagues also utilized hypotheticals, finding that officers expressed a fair amount of "ethical ambiguity." Findings also indicated that where an officer was assigned was associated with the likelihood of receiving discipline, complaints, or becoming involved in police shootings. The authors indicated that there seemed to be a district culture that affected officer behavior, and the better way to look at risk factors is to see individual factors interacting with organizational elements. This is an important finding and is related to the "bad barrel" research reviewed below. The researchers emphasized that it seemed to be both individual and environmental factors that led to the likelihood of misconduct (2004: 48).

Fyfe and Kane (2006; also see Kane and White, 2009) identified correlates related to termination in their study:

1. Women were *more* likely than male officers to be terminated during their probation. They also found that, although male officers were more likely to be terminated for brutality and bribery, there was no difference in all other profit-oriented misconduct. Other research provides mixed findings regarding whether women are less likely than male peers to engage in misconduct. As more women enter policing, more examples of misconduct have emerged. Some studies examine female officer misconduct, but few carefully controlled studies exist to determine if gender differences exist (Pogarsky and Piquero, 2004; Stinson, Todak, and Dodge, 2013).

2. Younger officers (those under 22 years of age when appointed) were more likely to be terminated during probation. However, they also found that these young officers were no more likely than older officers to be terminated for any form of misconduct after probation. Past research has indicated that college-educated officers receive fewer citizen complaints and in this study, those with more years of education upon hire were less likely to be terminated for misconduct.

3. Blacks (but not other minorities) were more likely to be terminated. Prior research indicates that black officers were more likely than whites to be disciplined for misconduct. A possible explanation might be differential rule enforcement or differential assignments and vulnerability to situations where use of force, for instance, was necessary.

4. Those who had prior negative employment histories, dishonorable discharges, and/or did poorly in the academy were more likely to be terminated for misconduct. Other factors associated with high risk included prior citizen complaints, prior criminal history, and history of a public-order offense. Non-individual factors included being assigned to posts with low supervision and high citizen contact (Fyfe and Kane, 2006: xxvi–xxviii).

These findings must be viewed with caution, however, as they are only from one department, they utilize only official reports of misconduct, and they do not control for other variables. Manning (2009) criticizes Kane and White's (2009) description of the study's findings as complicating the variables of misconducts like administrative rule-breaking with much more serious deviance such as lawbreaking, not providing ethnographic data to enrich the quantitative findings, and not taking into account in their analysis of factors such as race, and the changes over time in the size and composition of the department. These are valid concerns, but arguably there is nothing in their findings regarding individual characteristics that seem to contradict earlier studies. What is more problematic is the relative weight of individual factors as compared to organizational factors that influence the presence and degree of deviance.

It should also be noted that identifying correlates of misconduct is atheoretical. It is interesting to note that, with a few exceptions, researchers have not attempted to test traditional criminological theories to see if they explain police deviance, or develop original theories. One example of applying a criminological theory to police deviance is Hickman and colleagues' (2001) use of the data from the Philadelphia study to test Tittle's control balance theory and social learning theory. These researchers found that officers with a control deficit were more likely to report fellow officers engaged in misconduct. The Philadelphia data was also used to test social learning theory to see if it was helpful in understanding police deviance, and researchers concluded that the data did support the social learning theory (Chappell and Piquero, 2004). Once again, using the Philadelphia data, Pogarsky and Piquero (2004) tested deterrence theory. They found that the threat of extra-legal and legal sanctions did potentially deter misconduct and that the trait of impulsivity tended to reduce the effect of such threats.

Harris (2010a, 2010b) adds to this discussion by offering a life-course perspective to officer misconduct. He used citizen complaints as a measure of misconduct, acknowledging that this is a somewhat problematic measure. He found that being female, having a higher education, and not being a minority are related to lower levels of receiving citizen complaints. Other findings were that officers tend to receive citizen complaints early in their career and there is a desistance over the course of the career; however, most officers in his sample had fewer than three complaints over their entire career. There was a group of officers who received a higher level of citizen complaints, and the number did not decline as dramatically as all other officers after the sixth year. This small group of officers (5 percent) received 20 percent of all complaints. He also found, contrary to other researchers, that productivity measures were not related to the number of citizen complaints. He also analyzed internally generated complaints and these showed a somewhat different pattern. They were more likely to be substantiated in formal disciplinary proceedings, and officers did not show a clear age desistance pattern as they had for citizen complaints (Harris, 2012).

One emerging individual explanation for some types of police misconduct is post-traumatic stress disorder (PTSD). Researchers have found that about 14 percent of military veterans may experience some symptoms of PTSD and other research indicates that between 3 and 17 percent of police officers experience these symptoms as well. Of course a not insignificant percentage of police officers are military veterans also. Other research indicates that 7 to 35 percent of all police officers display some PTSD symptoms, or what is called subclinical PTSD. Symptoms include hypervigilance, trouble sleeping, anger control issues, and flashbacks. Factors involved in developing PTSD symptoms include:

- Witnessing the death of a law enforcement officer or viewing the body at the scene, especially when the victim was a friend or partner
- Accidentally killing or wounding a bystander, especially if the victim is a child
- Failing to stop a perpetrator from injuring or killing someone
- Killing or wounding a child or teenager, even if the life of the officer was threatened by the person injured or killed
- Viewing the body of a child victim, particularly if the officer has children (especially if the officer's child is the same age and sex as the victim)
- Interacting with grieving family members or friends of homicide victims
- Feeling caught in a violent riot, especially if the officer cannot use deadly force to defend him- or herself for fear of hurting children in the mob
- Viewing particularly bloody or gruesome scenes
- Observing an event involving violence or murder, but not being able to intervene
- Being undercover and constantly "on guard" because of the likelihood of being hurt, killed, or discovered
- Being threatened by suspects who have been indicted, are being tried, or are incarcerated (Haidi and Koga, 2014)

Other research shows that PTSD symptoms are correlated to family violence and alcohol abuse (Haidi and Koga, 2014). More research is needed to determine if officers who engage in drinking on duty, excessive force, and other forms of misconduct may also display PTSD symptoms.

In addition to individual factors, it is important to look at organizational factors as well.

Organizational Explanations

Various elements of the organization can breed misconduct. Recall from Chapter 4 that organizational factors may include small work-group influences. Isolated work groups develop their own micro-climate which can be one that does not conform to organizational ethics. Other organizational elements include perverse incentives and a culture that does not emphasize integrity.

Small work groups

Small work groups are exemplified by special units and narcotics task forces. There seems to be a pattern in news stories of such small work groups developing a micro-culture of unethical behavior. The most famous example of this is the Ramparts scandal in Los Angeles, but other examples across the country exist as well. For instance, six Tulsa police officers and an ATF agent pleaded guilty or were convicted of charges ranging from theft of federal property to civil rights violations. They evidently planted evidence on individuals and/or used faked informant testimony to engineer false arrests and convictions, stole drugs seized as evidence, and lied in court proceedings against individuals they wrongfully accused. Sentences ranged from four months to 10 years in prison (Barber and Lassek, 2010; Newson6.com, 2011).

In Philadelphia, patterns of misconduct (theft from drug dealers, sales of drugs, falsifying evidence) in narcotics squads date back to the early 1980s, including the "One Squad" scandal, the "Five Squad" scandal, an unnamed scandal in the early 1990s involving five narcotics officers, and another scandal in 2000 with officers accused of using false information to get search warrants, planting evidence and committing perjury, and stealing drugs, cash, and valuables from drug dealers (Slobodzian, 2009).

Most recently, a newspaper series spurred an internal investigation of a Philadelphia narcotics squad who were accused by Latino bodega owners of raiding their stores, turning off the security cameras, and then (allegedly) stealing money and goods from the stores. The squad was also accused of planting drugs, falsifying warrant affidavits, and stealing from drug dealers, and one of them was accused of sexual assault by several women. Recently, it was reported that neither the U.S. attorney nor state prosecutors were going to pursue charges because the witnesses were not credible. The one fired officer obtained his job back in arbitration (Newall and Whelan, 2014). However, the city also quietly settled 21 of the civil rights cases stemming from the officers' actions (Faziollah, Slobodzian, and Steele, 2012).

Perverse Incentives

As noted in Chapter 4, organizational incentives may encourage unethical behavior. When there is pressure to achieve a goal without a corresponding message that ethical means are just as important, organizational actors are tempted to take shortcuts. The best example of how good practices can result in bad outcomes is the Compstat program, a computerized crime-counting method that emphasizes accountability of middle managers. William Bratton is credited with beginning the program in New York City. He also brought it with him to Los Angeles in 2002 when he took over as police chief of Los Angeles.

Back in New York, the program continued but became the center of a scandal when it was alleged that some precincts were routinely downgrading crime reports, even calling victims to encourage or coerce them to withdraw the report or change the facts. Adrian Schoolcraft, an officer in the 81st precinct, first reported the practice to the Quality Assurance division of the NYPD with examples of victims whose crimes were misrecorded, but nothing was done. Then he went to the media. He also had secretly recorded tapes of roll calls where supervisors urged the officers to make arrests, regardless of whether there was probable cause, and employ a very aggressive style of policing in one particular housing project, telling officers to make the arrest and think of a reason later. After the news broke, Schoolcraft was retaliated against and even, at one point, under the orders of high-level police supervisors, was forcibly taken to a mental ward in a Queens hospital, supposedly because he left work early the day before and was not answering his phone. It took him six days to obtain his release. Schoolcraft was suspended from the NYPD and now lives in upstate New York. He reports that he is still harassed by NYPD officers and has filed a $50 million lawsuit against the NYPD, the city, and the hospital (Rayman, 2010a, 2010b; S. Brown, 2015).

In 2012, a report by the NYPD Quality Assurance Division supported Schoolcraft's claims (Parascandola, 2012). Academic research also supported the allegations that midlevel managers felt great pressure and crime reports were routinely downgraded in NYPD (Eterno, Verma, and Silverman, 2014).

Arguably, Compstat can be an effective tool for improving the accountability of middle managers and ultimately improve police services for the community, or it can become a pressure for "making the numbers" that causes police to downgrade serious crime reports and increase stops and arrests. William Bratton has recently been appointed NYPD commissioner again. It will be interesting to see how Compstat evolves under his command.

Organizational Culture

Crank and Caldero's (2000, 2005) "noble-cause" explanation of some types of deviance (described more fully in Chapter 5), whereby officers lie or commit other unethical acts to catch criminals, is an organizational explanation of corruption. Whenever deviance is explained as being supported by the organizational culture—whether that be the formal culture or the informal culture—it falls into the organizational level of explanation.

Gilmartin and Harris (1998) also have discussed why some officers become compromised and argue that it is because the law enforcement organization does not adequately train them to understand and respond to the ethical dilemmas they will face. They coined the term *continuum of compromise* to illustrate what happens to the officer. The first element is a "perceived sense of victimization," which refers to what happens when officers enter the profession with naïve ideas about what the job will be like. Citizen disrespect, bureaucratic barriers, and the justice system's realities sometimes make officers cynical, feeling that no one cares and that they are needlessly exposed to danger. Cynicism leads to distrust of the administration and the citizenry. At that point, the officer is alienated and more prone to corruption. Gilmartin and Harris also talk about the officers' sense of entitlement and how that can lead to corruption. There is a sense that the rules don't apply to them because they are different from the citizenry they police. This leads to the "blue curtain of secrecy," discussed more fully in Chapter 5, when officers believe it is more ethical to cover up for other cops than it is to tell the truth.

Crank (1998: 187) and others have noted that there is a pervasive sense among rank-and-file police that administrators are not to be trusted: "Officers protect each other, not only against the public, but against police administrators frequently seen to be capricious and out of touch." The classic work in this regard is Reuss-Ianni's (1983) study of a New York City precinct in the late 1970s. She described the "two cultures" of policing—street cops and management cops. She observed that law enforcement managers were classic bureaucrats who made decisions based on modern management principles. This contrasted with the street-cop subculture, which still had remnants of quasi-familial relationships in which "loyalties and commitments took precedence over the rule book" (1983: 4). The result of this conflict between the two value systems was alienation of the street cop. Despite the gulf between management and line staff, most agree that employee behavior is influenced directly by the behavior of superiors. One might note that most large-scale police corruption that has been exposed has implicated very high level officials. Alternatively, police departments that have remained relatively free of corruption have administrators who practice ethical behavior on a day-to-day basis.

Research reveals that close supervision, especially by midlevel managers such as sergeants, reduces the use of force and incidents of misconduct by officers (Walker, 2007). Huberts, Kaptein, and Lasthuizen (2007) obtained measures of corruption (or what they called integrity violations) by asking officers to report what they knew was happening. The independent variable was leadership style. Findings indicated that role modeling was significant in limiting unethical conduct of an interpersonal nature (sexual harassment, discrimination, bullying), while strictness in supervision seemed to be more important in controlling the misuse of resources, fraud, and other forms of financial corruption. A third component of leadership was described as openness and referred to leaders encouraging subordinates to talk to them about ethical dilemmas. This was associated with fewer violations in a number of areas, especially in favoritism and discrimination. Interestingly, this study of more than 6,000 police officers found that strictness had no effect on reducing the gratuitous use of violence, but that role modeling and openness did.

As discussed in previous chapters, the concept of organizational justice has been advanced by the pioneering work of Tom Tyler (1990) who distinguished procedural justice (whether people feel the process is fair) and outcome justice (whether they think the decision is fair). There has been a growing body of literature that explores how these concepts affect citizenry and employees (for instance, Tyler and Wakslak, 2004; Tyler and Huo, 2002). DeAngelis and Kupchik (2007) found that officers' satisfaction with the discipline system was more influenced by procedural justice elements (perceptions of fairness in the process) than outcome. Wolfe and Piquero (2011) found that police officers' beliefs about organizational justice were associated with the likelihood of ethical misconduct. Those who believed their organization was fair were less likely to engage in the code of silence or believe in noble-cause corruption. Further, these researchers found lower levels of police misconduct among those who more strongly agreed that the organization was just. Other researchers have also identified a correlation between the perception that the organization is unfair and negative behavior (Reynolds, 2015).

Societal Explanations

Murphy and Caplan (1989) argue that lax community standards over certain types of behavior (gambling, prostitution) and lack of support from prosecutors and the courts (or corruption at that stage of the system) leads to police corruption. Police hear mixed messages from the public regarding certain types of crime. They are asked to enforce laws against gambling, pornography, and prostitution, but not too stringently. They are expected not only to enforce laws against drunk driving but also to be tolerant of individuals who aren't really "criminal." They are expected to uphold laws regarding assault unless it is a family or interpersonal dispute that the disputants want to settle privately. In other words, we want the police to enforce the law unless they enforce it against us. Also, rationalizations used by some police when they take bribes or protection money from prostitutes or drug dealers are made easier by the public's tolerant stance toward certain areas of vice; for example, to accept protection money from a prostitute may be rationalized by the relative lack of concern that the public shows for this type of law breaking.

We also ask the police to take care of social problems, such as the homeless, even if they have to step outside the law to do so. Extra-legal means are acceptable as long as they are not used against us. Citizens who want police to move the transients out of a park or get the crack dealers off the corner aren't concerned with the fact that the police might not have the legal authority to do so. If a little "informal" justice is needed to accomplish the task, that is fine with some people, as long as it is used against those we don't like.

When we accept and encourage such extra-legal power in some situations, we shouldn't be surprised when it is used in other situations as well. The police role as enforcer in a pluralistic society is problematic. The justification for police power is that police represent the public: "The police officer can only validly use coercive force when he or she in fact represents the body politic" (Malloy, 1982: 12). But if the police do not represent all groups, their authority is seen as oppressive. Police take their cue from the community they serve. If they serve a community that emphasizes crime control over individual rights or other public service, we will see the results of that message in the way laws are enforced. The point is that, to a large degree, the community creates the police department by what it demands and what it is willing to overlook.

Reducing Police Corruption

Comprehensive lists of suggestions to reduce police misconduct and corruption have been proposed (Malloy, 1982; Metz, 1990; Carter, 1999; Wood, 1997; Prenzler and Ransley, 2002). Some date back decades but that doesn't mean they have been implemented. Such lists include:

- Increase the salary of police
- Eliminate unenforceable laws
- Establish civilian review boards
- Improve training in ethics (including specific training for supervisors)
- Set realistic goals and objectives for the department
- Provide ethical leadership
- Perform audits (of resources and funds paid to informants)
- Have financial disclosure rules
- Provide a written code of ethics
- Provide a whistleblowing procedure that ensures fair treatment
- Improve internal affairs units
- Rotate staff in some positions
- Have better evidence handling procedures
- Employ early warning systems
- Use video cameras in patrol cars
- Use covert high-technology surveillance
- Employ targeted and randomized integrity testing
- Conduct surveys of police and the public
- Decriminalize vice crimes

Note that the majority of these suggestions target administrative changes rather than identifying the individual officer as the problem. In more recent years, body cameras, requiring police to carry their own insurance, docking pensions for misconduct, and other suggestions have been offered to reduce the costs of misconduct. In the next sections, we take a closer look at some of these means to reduce corruption and improve the ethical climate of police agencies.

"Rotten Apple" Responses

The mechanisms discussed next address the "rotten apple" idea that misconduct is due to the wrong individuals being hired.

Improving Screening

Background checks, interviews, credit checks, polygraphs, drug tests, and other screening tools are used to eliminate inappropriate individuals from the pool of potential hires. The extent of screening varies from department to department, but generally has become more sophisticated, especially in the use of psychological testing and interviews. Sanders (2008) argues that the process is more "weeding out" than selecting in those candidates best suited to policing and points out that it is hard to develop tools to identify traits that are associated with successful police performance when, in fact, there is no consensus on what makes a good police officer. Most research on the effectiveness of screening tools utilizes academy test scores or firings as the measure of good (or failed) performance.

The most common pre-employment screening tool that is used by law enforcement agencies is the Minnesota Multiphasic Personality Inventory (MMPI or its subsequent versions); (Arrigo and Claussen, 2003; Dantzker and McCoy, 2006). The Inwald Personality Inventory (IPI) was developed to measure personality characteristics and behavioral patterns specific to fitness for law enforcement. Researchers have found that the IPI more accurately identifies individuals who are unsuccessful in law enforcement (terminated) (cited in Arrigo and Claussen, 2003). The so-called "Big Five" (extroversion, neuroticism, agreeableness, conscientiousness, and openness) have been the target of enough studies to indicate that they are reliable measures of personality and, of those, conscientiousness seems to be the most relevant to job performance. Conscientiousness is related to the degree of organization, control, and motivation one has and has been related to being organized, reliable, hard working, self-governing, and persevering. There has been very little research done to determine if the trait accurately measures police performance success, and research has produced mixed results (Arrigo and Claussen, 2003; Claussen-Rogers and Arrigo, 2005; Sanders, 2008).

Education and Training

Education has been promoted as a necessary element to improve the ethics of policing; however, education itself is certainly not a panacea. Many of the unethical officers described in this book have been college graduates. Fyfe and Kane (2006) did find a correlation between education and reduced risk of terminations for cause in the New York Police Department; however, it is by no means clear that education by itself increases the ethics of police officers.

Ethics training in the academy, and in in-service courses, is common and is recommended for all police departments today. Reuss-Ianni (1983) described how, after the Knapp Commission uncovered wide-ranging corruption in the New York Police Department, ethical awareness workshops were begun. Unfortunately, they have not stopped the periodic corruption scandals that have occurred since that time.

The International Association of Chiefs of Police (2008) found that about 80 percent of responding agencies said they committed resources to ethics instruction. Most of the courses were lecture (78 percent), followed by readings and discussion (67 percent), videotapes (53 percent), and video scenarios (49 percent). Other methods (role playing, computers, or games) were used less often. Most (70 percent) reported that the course was four hours or less. In terms of content, 81 percent discussed gratuities, 76 percent discussed conflicts of interest, 90 percent discussed abuse of force, 80 percent discussed abuse of authority, 69 percent discussed corruption, and 71 percent discussed off-duty ethics. The major recommendations of the IACP based on this study were to provide job-specific training on ethics and to differentiate training for recruits, in-service, and management, as well as other units. Another recommendation was that ethics training begin with recruits and be an integral part of the departments' structure and policies. The IACP also recommended enhancing content and using appropriate learning styles. A final recommendation was that departments concentrate more on ethics training for field-training officers (IACP, 2008).

Various models of ethics training exist but there is not enough data to understand the most effective approaches. Moran (2005) described several models of police ethics training, including a view of ethics as a "shield" to protect officers from trouble, as a programmed element in the officer's training "hardwire," as a mission or crusade, or as a "command from on high," along with the sanctions for disobeying. Conti and Nolan (2005: 167) found that ethics training typically is structured in such a way to encourage conformity to the "traditional image and identity of police officers." Martinelli (2000) argues that some of the law enforcement code provisions are ambiguous to officers and require explanations—such as keeping one's private life "unsullied."

Integrity Testing

integrity testing
"Sting" operations to test whether or not police officers will make honest choices.

Integrity testing occurs when a police officer is placed in a position where he or she might be tempted to break a rule or a law and monitored to see what he or she will do. New York City has used integrity testing since the late 1970s, after the Knapp Commission exposed widespread corruption. Field associates were recruited straight from academies to investigate suspected officers (Reuss-Ianni, 1983: 80). Integrity testing is like undercover work in that officers are tempted with an opportunity to commit an illegal or corrupt act, such as keeping a found wallet or being offered a bribe (Marx, 1991). It is reported that almost 30 percent of officers have failed this type of honesty test (Prenzler and Ronken, 2001a: 322). After the Mollen Commission in the mid-1990s, the integrity testing program in New York City was expanded. In one report, in 355 tests involving 762 officers, no criminal failures were reported, and only 45 procedural failures were reported (Prenzler and Ronken, 2001a: 322).

Needless to say, most police officers have highly negative attitudes about integrity testing. Spokesmen argue that "testing raises serious issues regarding privacy, deception, entrapment, provocation, and the legal rights of individuals" (Prenzler and Ronken, 2001a: 323–324). There is a widespread belief that such testing is unfair, overly intrusive, wasteful of resources, and detrimental to morale. One study of opinions of police managers found that the majority agreed that targeted integrity testing had a place in the investigation of wrongdoing, but that random testing was ill-advised (Prenzler, 2006).

Early Warning or Audit Systems

Research indicates that a small percentage of officers often accounts for a disproportionate number of abuse or corruption complaints (Barker, 2002; Walker and Alpert, 2002). Therefore, the practice of identifying these officers through some form of early warning system seems logical. Early warning systems look at number of complaints, use-of-force reports, use-of-weapon reports, reprimands, or other indicators to identify officers. Intervention may include more supervision, additional training, and/or counseling. In one city's program, the officer's supervisor is alerted that the system has tagged the officer; the supervisor may then counsel the officer, engage in other responses, or do nothing. In Miami's early warning system, officers identified by the early warning system may be subject to the following: reassignment, retraining, transfer, referral to an employee assistance program, fitness for duty evaluation, and/or dismissal (Walker and Alpert, 2002). These programs have been endorsed by the National Institute of Justice and have been incorporated into several consent decrees between cities and federal courts to avert civil rights litigation. By 1999, about 27 percent of all police agencies had early warning systems in place (reported in Walker and Alpert, 2002: 220).

Walker (2007) reports that early warning systems vary in the elements they count and where they set the threshold of concern. The systems also have various objectives: some departments use them to provide assistance and additional training, others utilize them for punishment, and still others use them to target high achievers. One cannot simply count the number of incidents or complaints, because the officer's shift and duty, length of service, types of calls responded to, and other factors affect the number of complaints (Walker, Alpert, and Kenney, 2000; Walker and Alpert, 2002). Also, some researchers have found that simply counting use-of-force reports does not capture problematic officers without further identifying those who exceed the ratio of reasonable force in response to the resistance of the subject. To only count uses of force falsely tags some officers as problematic (Bazley, Mieczkowski, and Lersch, 2009). Hassell and Archbold (2009) argued that using citizen complaints as a proxy for bad officers is problematic because, in their study, citizen complaints were associated with officer productivity, but not with any individual characteristics. That is, officers who were more active in making arrests and stops also received more citizen complaints.

These programs are only as effective as the interventions that are triggered by the identification of a problem. Walker and Alpert note that such systems are as much a reflection of management as of individual officers. Supervisors are put on notice that they may have a problem officer and, thus, are more responsible if nothing is done and the officer engages in serious forms of misconduct.

Body Cameras

The nation has seemingly become enamored with the idea of all police officers wearing body cameras that would record every interaction with a citizen. The Obama administration has allocated $263 million for a three-year program to expand training for local police departments, including $75 million that would purchase 50,000 cameras through a matching program (Wilson, 2015).

Video has been an incredibly powerful tool to support citizens who allege brutality and show how some officers abuse their authority. Critics argue that misbehaving police officers could simply turn off the camera when they wanted to, although procedures in place create disincentives for officers to do so.

Another, more unresolvable criticism is that the cost of the cameras and storing the unimaginable amount of video that would be collected make widespread use unfeasible. Another major criticism is the invasion of privacy such cameras may create. Should officers ask for permission before filming in private homes? Should officers be able to turn off the cameras as they talk to citizens who may turn into confidential informants? Should cameras be turned off when victims or intoxicated individuals are unclothed? Rules regarding whether and when police officers should turn off the cameras is being worked out in those jurisdictions that have purchased or are making plans to purchase them.

Preliminary studies show amazing results. In San Diego, an internal report showed that citizen complaints decreased by 40 percent, use of "personal body" force by officers was reduced by 46.5 percent, and use of pepper spray was reduced by 30.5 percent (Perry, 2015). Academic studies also show major reductions in citizen complaints and use of force. In Rialto, California, in a controlled study, complaints against officers fell by 88 percent and use of force by 60 percent (Farrar, 2013). Cameras protect both citizens and police officers since a citizen cannot file a complaint and lie about what the police officer did or did not do. That is why the initial resistance of police to the use of cameras has faded in light of the benefits that have come to light.

Public Databases of "Bad" Cops

This controversial attempt to expose officers who engage in a pattern of wrongdoing stems from the public's inability to trust police departments to root out individuals who should not have the power and authority inherent in the position. Developers of such lists or databases argue that the position of police departments has always been that instances of serious wrongdoing are rare and problem officers who have a pattern of wrongdoing are rarer still. The collection of instances in some cities, however, shows that instances of wrongdoing are not rare. The Cato Institute's National Police Misconduct Reports present daily updates of news items drawn from media across the country. One can scroll through the reports and find reported misconduct for any given day or month since the reports began several years ago. The author presents the "worst case" of officer misconduct every month (www.policemisconduct.net). This is a privately funded attempt by a libertarian-leaning organization to provide the public with information that cannot be obtained through any public source but there is no way to know if the reports are an unbiased collection and there is little analysis, simply a presentation of unedited news items although one descriptive analysis was done several years ago.

Professor Philip Stinson has also been collecting misconduct reports through the media in a similar way, but entering them into a database for study. His database allows one to examine the thousands of misconduct instances to explore patterns of officer characteristics, victim characteristics, and regional characteristics (Stinson, Brewer, and Mathna, 2015; Stinson, Todak, and Dodge, 2013).

The New York Legal Aid Society, the largest organization of public defenders in the country with over 650 lawyers, has also been developing a "cop accountability" database. Over 3,000 officers and their reputed misconduct have been entered thus far. The project was created to help defense attorneys question the credibility of police officers in court. They share the information with non–Legal Aid attorneys as well (Neyfakh, 2015). Finally, the American Civil Liberties Union has begun a database project by filing open records requests in seven selected cities requesting all discipline and citizen complaint information about officers who have been the subject of alleged police brutality.

Such efforts are designed to bring light to the subject of police misconduct. They are based on a supposition that the strongest predictor of police misconduct is prior misconduct. Ironically, even police departments may not have information about an officer's prior misconduct. There is no national database for police departments to discover when an officer has been in trouble and been decertified which means losing one's license to be a police officer. The National Decertification Index reports records from 38 states but reporting is voluntary and therefore no assumption should be made as to the completeness or accuracy of the records (www.iadlest.org/projects/ndi20.aspx). There is no consistency in decertification across states anyway. While in some states, police departments are obligated to report misconduct that is serious enough to disqualify an individual from being a police officer and the state commission then will investigate and possibly decertify the officer; in other states, the state commission has no authority to decertify, or only felony criminal convictions are sufficient for a state commission to decertify. The lack of consistency in laws, policies, and procedures make any comparison across states of rates of decertification very difficult (Atherley and Hickman, 2013).

"Rotten Barrel" Responses

Organizational explanations address elements of the police organization, including such things as improving investigation and disciplinary procedures.

QUOTE & QUERY

Compiling a list of police officers who are alleged to be 'bad' based upon newspapers stories, quick-buck lawsuits, and baseless complaints—many of which are lodged in revenge by criminals seeking to punish an arresting officer—does nothing more than soil the reputation of the men and women who do the difficult and dangerous job of keeping this city and its citizens safe.

(Pat Lynch, head of the NYPD police officers' union.)

Source: Reported in Neyfakh, 2015.

 Does this quote convince you that databases of misconduct are a bad idea?

Internal Affairs Model, Civil Service, and Arbitration

In one sense, the **internal affairs model** is also a rotten-apple approach to reducing corruption since the model provides the mechanism whereby the department investigates and punishes the miscreant officer. One could also, however, see the internal affairs model as a rotten barrel approach in that if a department did not have an internal affairs function or it was widely seen as toothless, then the message to individual officers would be that the department did not care about wrongdoing. Unfortunately, internal affairs units are perceived as ineffective (by the public) and biased (by police officers). It is also the case that civil service protections in many cities mandate that if an officer is disciplined, he or she can request the case go to arbitration, which often results in reducing the level of punishment (Stephens, 2011).

internal affairs model A review procedure in which police investigators receive and investigate complaints and resolve the investigations internally.

In one Toronto study, 70 percent of those who filed complaints were not confident with the process, and only 14 percent thought their complaint was handled fairly (Prenzler and Ronken, 2001b: 180). There is no research that evaluates the actual effectiveness of internal affair models (Walker, 2007), only many news reports of citizen dissatisfaction and tallies of the number of complaints versus the number of complaints founded or the number that result in any form of discipline.

Part of the problem with the internal discipline model is that citizens may be discouraged from reporting misconduct of police to other police; especially if the process is complicated or intimidating. In recent years, both the San Antonio police department and many police departments in Nebraska were criticized for the way the citizen complaint processes were handled. In San Antonio, an investigation indicated that the police departments discouraged civilians from filing complaints, argued with them, and accused them of lying. In the Nebraska review, the threat of being prosecuted for perjury on the complaint form itself was not uncommon, and critics argue that this statement intimidates people, as does the requirement that they must talk to an internal affairs investigator. Website instructions were often absent or confusing and anonymous complaints were not accepted (Texas Civil Rights Project, 2011; Skelton, 2014). National standards for civilian complaint processes encourage police departments to accept anonymous complaints since many people are too intimidated to complain openly.

Ironically, officers don't seem to trust the internal discipline mechanisms any more than citizens do. While citizens feel that complaints are ignored and officers are protected, officers feel that some of their peers get special treatment and the purpose of such systems is purely "gotcha" rather than a constructive process of improving performance (Stephens, 2011).

Recall the horrible events in California in 2013 when Christopher Dorner issued his "manifesto" and shot the daughter of police captain Randal Quan and her fiancé, which began a series of shootings that included the deaths of two law enforcement officers at the hands of Dorner as well as critically wounding several others. Ultimately, the unprecedented manhunt for him ended in a mountain cabin where he shot himself. Dorner most probably suffered from mental issues that spurred him to such extreme measures, but the trigger for his actions was reported to be a perceived unfair discipline hearing that resulted in his termination. He was terminated for lying after he reported that his FTO kicked a mentally ill man in the face. He believed he was terminated for going against the blue curtain of secrecy and to protect the other officer. During the massive manhunt and amid public questions as to whether the charges Dorner made against the unfairness of the disciplinary procedures had any degree of truth, LAPD Chief Beck promised that Dorner's case would be reopened and an investigation would take place. Several months later, a report was released written by a special assistant to the chief that concluded that the firing was justified. Findings indicated that Dorner had experienced problems beginning in the academy that made his success as a police officer unlikely. The report concluded he used the complaint process for his own agenda; he complained about his FTO 13 days after the event and immediately after he was told he would be given an unsatisfactory rating; and, that the kick could not be substantiated due to the mental illness of the individual and the lack of witness reports (Leonard, Rabin, and Blankstein, 2013; Orlov, 2013). The importance of Dorner's case is not that he was or was not telling the truth about his FTO's use of excessive force or the fairness of the discipline; it was the fact that the possible truth of this serial killer's "manifesto" resonated with the public and, evidently, some officers as well who spoke anonymously about their suspicions that his description of favoritism and racism in the department had some elements of truth.

The New York Police Department Internal Affairs Bureau was completely revamped in 1993 after a scandal prompted then commissioner Raymond Kelly to overhaul the department. Since then, internal affairs has generated an annual report, albeit going from 81 pages in 1993 to only 15 pages in 2007 and 2008. The annual reports, released via a Freedom of Information request by the ACLU, chronicle the changes that have taken place over the last 17 years. Critics contend that the bureau has drastically reduced the number of cases it investigates, even though tips have tripled since 1992, and has become more secretive about corruption, as contrasted with the years following 1993. NYPD officials point out that the budget for IA has increased from $43 million in 2000 to $61.8 million in 2010 and there are 650 officers who investigate wrongdoing (Baker and McGinty, 2010).

Even when internal affairs and police department administrators decide to punish an officer with a suspension or termination, arbitrators often reverse the punishment. Studies have shown that arbitrators routinely "split the difference" and reduce the punishment assessed by the chief, sometimes requiring the errant officer to be rehired (Iris, 1998, 2002; Stephens, 2011). The explanation some give as to why this pattern exists, even for what seem to be egregious acts of misconduct, is that arbitrators must be selected with the agreement of both parties and those who routinely upheld the chief's punishments would not be approved by the officer or union.

Another explanation (from the arbitrators and union representatives who support the process) is that departments often have such poorly written or nonexistent policies that it would not be fair to punish officers without adequate due process (Horn, 2009).

Stephens (2011) presents a number of suggestions for improving the internal discipline process, including discipline matrixes (similar to sentencing guidelines) that spell out in advance what the range of punishment might be for types of misconduct. This would tend to reduce the feelings of officers that there is unfairness in the process. Another improvement would be to tie education and training to the discipline process so that the focus shifts from punishment to improving performance. Mediation between the citizen complainant and officer might be a better solution than punishment. Peer review has not been used but is an intriguing possibility for reducing the perception of unfairness in the process.

Some departments have enlarged the mission of internal anti-corruption units. These units, especially in other countries, now undertake a mission of not only investigation and punishment but also deterrence and prevention. Such units may undertake integrity testing, promote awareness, improve selection and screening procedures, develop performance standards, and in other ways "police" the police to minimize corruption (Moran, 2005). This may represent the future of internal anti-corruption models.

ETHICAL ISSUE

Should Disciplinary Records Be Secret and Exempt from Public Records Requests?

In the national discussions that followed the events of Ferguson and Baltimore, many people were surprised to discover that some states kept police disciplinary records secret. While in 27 states disciplinary records are open to the public; the rest have some level of exemption from public disclosure. New York offers some of the strongest protections to officers. A 1976 state law requires such information to be kept secret to the extent that it is difficult to even find names of officers involved in shootings. The law was passed in response to the 1974 Freedom of Information law that opened public records to public view through open records requests. The law was passed evidently specifically to shield disciplinary records from defense lawyers, who would use the information in court to attack the credibility of officers (ironically exactly what is required in Brady rules which require prosecutors to share such information). According to New York's civil rights code, section 50-a, incident reports involving police, disciplinary records, evaluations, and personnel records are secret, not subject to open records requests, and may not even be cited in court without judicial approval. Over time, the protection was extended to correctional officers and firefighters. The protection is so complete that the civilian review board has had

trouble accessing information to investigate cases, leading to the creation of a new inspector general position with subpoena power. Even when disciplinary proceedings are public, the transcripts of such hearings are subject to the law. Several open-government groups are targeting this New York civil service law for reform.

California has similar protections. In *Copley Press, Inc. v. Superior Court of San Diego County* (S128603, 2006), the state supreme court interpreted civil service laws to protect from public disclosure any public documents regarding police discipline involving actions taken under color of authority. An attempt to pass legislation to overturn the effect of the holding and open discipline records to the public was met with strong resistance from police unions who appeared *en masse* during the legislative hearing on the issue and were successful in scuttling the proposed change.

Supporters of such secrecy argue that police do not give up their right of privacy by virtue of being employed as a police officer, that they would be subject to harassment and potentially threatening public actions if their identities and disciplinary proceedings were revealed, and that the media or public have free access to speak with witnesses or complainants in instances of alleged misconduct and other avenues of investigation. Critics of secrecy argue

(continued)

that police officers are public servants, and, as such, the public has a right to know when an officer has a pattern of misconduct.

Law

As stated above, whether there is disclosure or not in each state depends, first, on enabling legislation and, then, on the court's interpretation of such laws. States can have different legal rights recognized until or unless there is a Supreme Court decision that has legal authority over all 50 states.

Policy

In those states where disciplinary investigations and records are secret, police departments can tightly control that information. The officer may have a legal action against the department if they do not. Departments can release aggregate numbers (how many officers have been disciplined), but if they released information protected by civil service laws, they could be sued. Thus, policy follows law.

Ethics

Utilitarian ethics would weigh up the costs and benefits of disclosure versus secrecy for the officers involved, the department, and the community. Negative effects of such secrecy are that errant police officers are protected. Even if they are fired from one department they can go on to be hired by others and do. When a person has been victimized by a police officer, they are prevented from finding out that the officer has a record of similar actions. When communities want to understand what kind of police force they have, they are restricted from important information. Benefits from the secrecy are mostly for the individual officer and department. Individual officers and their families can be targeted. When Darren Wilson's name (the officer who shot Michael Brown in Ferguson, Missouri) was revealed, he and his family were subjected to such a barrage of death threats that they were placed in hiding for their own safety.

Often, disciplinary proceedings are conducted over technical rule violations, not actions that victimize the public in any way, yet those proceedings would also be exposed to the officer's detriment. Disciplinary proceedings often result in finding the officer was innocent of the alleged wrongdoing, but that finding would probably be less prominently reported than the allegations, leading to unfairness in shaping public perceptions.

Ethics of care would attempt to meet the needs of both parties in arriving at a resolution; therefore, the safety of officers and residents would be paramount. The community's need to know is probably dependent on how well the discipline system deters officers' transgressions. Remember that the ethics of care is not concerned with rights but, instead, focuses on needs. So there is a need to deter or get rid of problem officers, but if the department does that effectively, there is less or no need to know how and when they do it or who is a problem officer. Ironically, however, without such information being public, it is impossible to know if problem officers are being dealt with appropriately.

Is such secrecy consistent with ethical formalism? It would be if someone could be in favor of the policy regardless of who they were in the situation (officer, other officers, chief, journalist, victim of police brutality, citizen). This is the first element of the categorical imperative.

As with many other policy decisions, attempting to determine an ethical policy depends on facts that we often do not have. For instance, there is no study available that examines the 27 states with open disclosure to determine if it has led to officers being victimized. There is no real evidence on either side to support the position, thus the language is of "rights" rather than the utilitarian's emphasis on utility.

Sources: Romero, 2013; Goodman & Baker, 2015; Greenhut, 2015; Wilson, 2015.

Civilian Review/Complaint Boards

Civilian review boards have been in existence since the mid-1960s in some cities yet police unions continue to strongly oppose them. The civilian review model monitors and reviews internal investigation and discipline of officers. Kansas City created one in 1970 and Berkeley's Civilian Review Board began in 1973 (Attard, 2010). Walker (2001) reviewed the range of civilian review models, but did not find that any one model seemed to be better than any other. Prenzler and Ronken (2001b) argue that it is difficult to analyze the success of such bodies because a high level of complaints may mean that there is greater trust in the process, not necessarily an increase in misconduct. Worrall (2002) found this as well.

In the **civilian review/complaint model**, an independent civilian agency audits complaints and investigations. The board may also respond to appeals and act in an

civilian review/ complaint model The use of an outside agency or board that includes citizens and monitors and/or investigates misconduct complaints against police.

advisory role in investigations. Police still investigate and conduct the discipline proceedings. Other models may involve an external board, but without any powers of subpoena or oversight (Prenzler and Ronken, 2001b; Ferdik, Rojek, and Alpert, 2015). Prenzler and Ronken (2001b) reported that external review models have about the same substantiation rate as do internal affairs models—about 10 percent of all complaints filed. The major criticism of such models centers on the idea that they are not truly independent, for police still conduct the investigations and sometimes even sit on the board. Prenzler (2000) argues that the "capture" theory is operative in civilian review models. This occurs when the regulatory or investigative body is "co-opted" by the investigated agency through informal relationships.

Even if civilian review agencies find an officer responsible for misconduct, they usually have no independent power to punish and simply refer the case back to the police department for discipline. Of 439 cases handled by the Minneapolis civilian review office, not one resulted in discipline of a police officer (Furst, 2013).

New York City's civilian review board was established in 1992 in response to a widespread belief that the police department could not adequately respond to civilian complaints. Complaints are investigated by the board and then referred to the police department for formal disciplinary action. In 2005, the police department declined to prosecute 2 percent of the cases referred by the civilian review board, but in 2008, 33 percent were declined, and in 2009, about 40 percent were declined. In response, the department points out that the conviction rate has increased from 30 to 60 percent, indicating that the decision to prosecute is based on which cases will lead to success. (Hauser, 2009). In 2012, an agreement was reached with the NYPD whereby lawyers for the board were given the power to undertake the disciplinary hearings of officers accused of misconduct, although the administrative judges will still be police employees and the police commissioner will still have the ultimate authority over decisions. There has been a widespread perception that the board was a "toothless tiger" since, from 2002 to 2010, of the 2,078 officers the board recommended be terminated, police decision makers terminated only 151 officers (Baker, 2012).

One problem with civilian review boards is that, as noted above, in some states all disciplinary records are considered outside the scope of public records and exempt from open records requests (Ivers, 2015). In states like California and New York, even the civilian review board has difficulty accessing disciplinary records and the media have no access at all. Critics object that this is highly inconsistent with transparency and democratic policing. The public literally does not know if the police officer they are dealing with has had no complaints filed against him or her or has been the subject of 100 previous complaints.

Changing the Culture

If the police culture influences the level of police misconduct, it is important to change it. Harris (2005) discusses the difficulty of changing an entrenched negative police culture, but offers examples of how it can be done. He argues that in successful change efforts, the department has reconceptualized its mission, developed measurements of what matters most, improved recruiting, changed training to emphasize human rights at least as much as crime fighting, and changed the incentive and reward structure to encourage service-oriented policing as much as crime control. He argues that change occurs as generations of new police officers take over.

As mentioned in Chapter 5, current efforts to shift the culture away from a military model with an emphasis on force (warrior model) to one more protective of civil rights (guardian model) are under way (Rahr and Rice, 2015). The descriptions of the warrior and guardian models are very similar to our crime control and public servant models and will face the same resistance that community policing efforts experienced in the 1980s. Procedural justice efforts are a part of this trend and have the potential to improve officer-citizen interactions as well as fairness for the officer in the organization (Reynold, 2015).

Ethical Leadership

We have discussed the role of ethical leadership generally in Chapter 4. Improving leadership is an essential element of improving the ethical climate of any organization. Research shows that supervisors shape the attitude of line officers toward wrongdoing. When misconduct is punished, it is perceived as more serious; if it is treated lightly, the opposite occurs (Lee, Lim, Moore, and Kim, 2011).

Even if leaders are not directly involved in corruption, encouraging or participating in the harassment and ostracism directed at those who expose wrongdoers supports an organizational culture that punishes whistleblowers. In some departments, there is a perception that favored cliques are not punished for behaviors for which others would receive punishment. This climate destroys the trust in police leadership that is essential to ensure good communication from the rank and file.

The practice of administrators to cover up wrongdoing is arguably an even more insidious problem than individual officer misconduct. In Los Angeles, Detective Russell Poole, a robbery-homicide detective, uncovered the activities of the anti-gang task force in the Ramparts Division, but his investigation was shut down by his superiors. A year later, the Ramparts scandal exploded. Evidence indicated that between 1995 and 1998 the officers lied, planted evidence, beat suspects, and shot unarmed suspects. Officers also evidently held parties to celebrate shootings, gave out plaques when one killed a gang member, and spread ketchup at a crime scene to imitate blood. Hundreds of cases had to be reviewed by the staff in the prosecutor's office to evaluate whether there was a possibility of manufactured evidence. Some evidence indicates at least 99 people were framed by Ramparts officers. The city had to use $100 million from tobacco settlements to cover anticipated lawsuits. Eleven officers were fired, and 40 convictions were overturned (Glover and Lait, 2000; Lait and Glover, 2000; Jablon, 2000; Sterngold, 2000; Deutsch, 2001; Golab, 2000). The LAPD came under a federal court monitor because of the scandal, although it has since been released from the consent decree.

This case study, along with others, shows that attempts to cover up scandals are often unsuccessful and, arguably, only make the situation worse when the corruption is inevitably exposed. In order to combat police corruption, it seems clear that the key is to have leadership that is not afraid to expose the "skeletons in the closet" and deal with problems openly without attempting to hide them from the public.

Societal Responses

It is difficult to conceive of how society can affect police corruption; however, it is possible that this is the most important part of the discussion. As noted repeatedly within these chapters, recently we have seen a new era of scrutiny regarding what is occurring in American policing. There is a saying that a community gets the government they deserve, and the same may be said for policing.

One thing that is not helpful is to paint all police as evil or brutal or any other adjective. The numbers indicate that corruption lies with an extremely small number of officers. The blue curtain of secrecy (refusing to expose peers' misconduct) is more pervasive; however, even that is beginning to change and most substantiated discipline cases are when fellow officers report misconduct.

All too often, society is not concerned when uses of excessive force are directed to the "criminal element" in society and the general feeling is that "those types" of people deserve it. The problem is once policing jumps the track of legality, there is no longer any control on the power and coercive force police officers use. Extra-legal "street justice" may be used on a drug dealer or serial rapist, but it might also be used against a law-abiding neighbor who uses his or her cellphone to record an arrest. Further, the heavy-handed policing that targets so-called "quality-of-life" issues, referring to minor ordinances such as sign placement and prohibitions on roller-skating on sidewalks, but does so solely through arrests and citations rather than efforts to improve the community leads to excessive monitoring and, some would say, harassment in certain neighborhoods. The emphasis on arrests and stops, rather than public satisfaction with police, leads to negative community perceptions, distrust, and lack of cooperation when police need to investigate serious crimes. It also provides more opportunity for police officers to stray into unethical uses of their power.

It is also important to truly understand what police officers face on the street and not succumb to knee-jerk responses that if police shoot someone, it must be a bad shooting; or if citizen complaints are not founded, there must have been collusion to protect the officer. The fact is that a miniscule number of police *ever* use their guns and when they do, most do so reflexively and suffer psychological trauma afterward. No one defends the horrible cases in the news like the killing of Walter Scott, but let us not forget there are 12,000 to 17,000 agencies (evidently no one really knows given the range of numbers in various sources) with approximately a half-million officers. The vast majority of complaints against police officers are for rudeness, thus, pretty much impossible to determine with accuracy on whose side fault lie. It is highly misleading on the part of journalists to discuss a case of excessive force and then juxtapose that with numbers of citizen complaints, leading to the assumption that the majority of complaints are for brutality. The point is that rhetoric creates heat but no light—what we need is data. We need to know how many shootings there are, the pervasiveness of different types of misconduct, what factors are associated with misconduct, and which solutions are most effective.

President Barack Obama created the Task Force on Policing in the 21st Century composed of a mix of academics and police professionals. They held hearings across the country and heard from stakeholders from all sides. In March 2015, they issued their interim report and the list of recommendations to improve policing covered many of the responses described here. The report detailed a comprehensive list of needed changes in policing (www.cops.usdoj.gov/pdf/taskforce/interim_tf_report.pdf). The changes proposed include training to deescalate violence and further study on the use of body cameras. There is a recognition that the culture of policing needs to change to deemphasize the "war" culture and replace it with messages more in keeping with the role of policing in a democratic society. It is important to note that the 21st Century Panel on Policing included police leaders as well as members of the public, aided by experts. The report makes it clear that police officers' discretion must be guided by a strong understanding of their purpose and an ethical code. To improve the ethical climate of policing, societal demand for no less is the first step; ethical leadership is the second.

Conclusion

In this chapter, we reviewed a wide range of corruption, categorized into economic corruption and abuse of authority. Explanations of law enforcement deviance can be categorized into individual, organizational, and societal explanations. We also examined a wide range of suggestions for combating police corruption, categorized into these same levels, for example, individual (education and training), organizational (civilian review), and societal (community involvement).

Chapter Review

1. **Describe the types of police corruption (economic corruption and abuse of authority).**

    Economic corruption includes any activity wherein a police officer uses his or her position to acquire economic benefit illegally or against policy. Gratuities can be a minor form of economic corruption if they are against policy. Graft includes bribery, kickbacks, and "pads." The Knapp Commission identified grass eaters (police who passively take advantage of opportunities) and meat eaters (police who actively commit crimes). Abuse of authority is not for economic gain. It includes physical or psychological abuse of the citizenry or violations of policy and/or law in the performance of one's duties (e.g., excessive force, ignoring evidence, coercive interrogation).

2. **Describe individual explanations of corruption and potential solutions.**

    Individual explanations target the individual officer, such as identifying personality characteristics that predict either misconduct or successful performance of the job. Suggestions to reduce corruption include improved screening and psychological testing, training, integrity testing, early warning systems, the use of body cameras, and databases of misconduct.

3. **Describe organizational explanations of corruption and potential solutions.**

    Organizational explanations look at factors that encourage or support misconduct, such as the police subculture or an ineffective discipline system. Proposed responses include improving internal affairs units, civilian review boards, changing the culture, and improving the leadership.

4. **Describe societal explanations of corruption and potential solutions.**

    Societal explanations focus on what messages society sends to their police department that might encourage lawlessness. Proposed solutions include re-examining these messages to law enforcement and changing the emphasis to the elements that are important for policing in a democratic society.

Study Questions

1. What countries score high in integrity according to Transparency International? Provide some examples of worldwide police corruption.
2. List and describe Kane and Fyfe's types of police corruption.
3. What are the arguments for and against the acceptance of gratuities?
4. List and describe the three types of explanations for police deviance.
5. Describe the benefits and disadvantages of body cameras.

Writing/Discussion Exercises

1. Write an essay on (or discuss) gratuities. Provide a persuasive argument as to whether or not gratuities should be acceptable. If you are arguing that they are ethical and should be acceptable, discuss what limits, if any, should be placed upon them.

2. Write an essay on (or discuss) the potential disciplinary sanctions that should be taken against officers who commit legal, policy, and/or ethical transgressions. What is the rationale for the administration of punishment? Which acts warrant more severe sanctions? What should be done with an officer who has a drinking or drug problem? Taking a bribe? Stealing from a crime scene? Hitting a handcuffed suspect? Having checks bounce? Being disrespectful to a member of a minority group? Sexually harassing a coworker?

3. Write an essay on (or discuss) the best methods to reduce noble-cause corruption among officers. Are they the same methods as those that should be used to reduce egoistic corruption for pecuniary gain? Explain why or why not. Also explain why you think the selected methods would work.

Key Terms

civilian review/complaint model	gratuities	internal affairs model
graft	integrity testing	rotten-apple argument

ETHICAL DILEMMAS

Situation 1

You are a rookie police officer on your first patrol. The older, experienced officer tells you that the restaurant on the corner likes to have you guys around, so it gives free meals. Your partner orders steak, potatoes, and all the trimmings. What are you going to do? What if it were just coffee at a convenience store? What if the owner refused to take your money at the cash register?

Situation 2

There is an officer in your division known as a "rat" because he testified against his partner in a criminal trial and a civil suit. The partner evidently hit a handcuffed suspect in the head several times in anger, and the man sustained brain injuries and is now a paraplegic. Although none of the officers you know supports the excessive use of force, they are also appalled that this officer did not back up his partner's testimony that the suspect continued to struggle, in an attempt to justify his use of force. After all, punishing the officer wasn't going to make the victim any better. Now no one will ride with this guy, and no one responds to his calls for backup. There have been incidents such as a dead rat being placed in his locker, and the extra uniform in his locker was set on fire.

One day you are parking your car and see your buddies in the employee parking lot moving away from his car; they admit they just slashed his tires. Each officer is being called into the captain's office to state whether he or she knows anything about this latest incident. Your turn is coming. What are you going to do?

Situation 3

You are a waitress (or waiter) in an all-night diner and are not too happy about pulling the midnight shift. Every evening, luckily, police officers drift in for their coffee breaks. You have been told that the diner does not offer gratuities and that you are not to give free coffee or meals to anyone, including police officers. But it's 2:00 a.m., and there are a lot of scary people out there. You figure that the pot of coffee might cost only a couple of bucks, so it's worth it to keep officers coming in. You suspect that the owner of the diner wouldn't be happy (because he doesn't like police), but he's not here, so you fall into the habit of giving all the officers free coffee. It then escalates to free pie (it was going to be thrown out anyway), and now when no one is around, you'll let the officers go without paying for their meal. Do you see a problem with your actions? Who should make the decision—the owner or the employee who is on site? If you were to stop giving free coffee and pie, do you think the officers would stop coming in?

Situation 4

You are a police officer testifying in a drug case. You have already testified that you engaged in a buy-bust operation, and the defendant was identified by an undercover officer as the one who sold him a small quantity of drugs. You testified that you chased the suspect down an alley and apprehended him. Immediately before you caught up with him, he threw down a number of glassine envelopes filled with what turned out to be cocaine. The prosecutor finished his direct examination, and now the defense attorney has begun cross-examining you. He asked if you had the suspect in your sight the entire time between when you identified him as the one who sold to the undercover officer and when you put the handcuffs on him. Your arrest report didn't mention it, but for a couple of seconds you slipped as you went around the corner of the alley and fell down. During that short time, the suspect had proceeded a considerable distance down the alley.

You do not think there was anyone else around, and you are as sure as you possibly can be that it was your suspect who dropped the bags, but you know that if you testify to this incident truthfully, the defense attorney might be able to argue successfully that the bags were not dropped by the suspect and get him acquitted of the much more serious charge of possession with intent to distribute. What should you do?

Situation 5

You (a female police officer) have been working in a small-town police department for about six months. During that time you have been dealing with a fellow police officer who persists in making comments about how pretty you are, how you don't look like a police officer, how you shouldn't be dealing with the "garbage" out on the streets, and so on. He has asked you out more than a dozen times even though you have told him every time that you are not interested and that you want him to stop asking you out and to stop making comments. Although he hasn't made any derogatory or offensive comments, his constant attention is beginning to make you not want to go to work. You have a romantic partner, and you are definitely not interested in your fellow officer. You have mentioned it to your FTO, who is a sort of father figure, but he likes the guy and tells you that you should be flattered. You want to file a sexual harassment charge against him but hesitate because, although you do feel harassed, you don't feel especially threatened; further, you know that you would encounter negative reactions from the other officers in the department. What should you do?

Law and Legal Professionals

Protesters against Arizona's immigration law.

MARK RALSTON/AFP/Getty Images

Michael Morton went to work in the early morning hours of 1986 never realizing that his life, as he knew it, was over. He had left his wife sleeping. After work, he drove to the babysitter's to pick up his son, but he wasn't there, so he called home. The person who answered told him to come home immediately. Upon arriving, he found crime tape, police officers, and crime-scene investigators. A neighbor had found his three-year-old son wandering the street covered in blood. His wife was dead, bludgeoned to death. Morton was charged and convicted, the only evidence being a note he left taped to the bathroom mirror that rebuked her for not having sex with him the night before. For 24 years he was incarcerated in Texas prisons fighting his conviction. Finally in 2011, a hearing in a Williamson County courtroom resulted in a dramatic close to his nightmare. The judge ordered him to be immediately released because DNA evidence proved that he was innocent and another man guilty of his wife's death.

Chapter Objectives

1. Understand the justifications for law, including protections against harm to others, offensive conduct, harm to self, and harm to societal morals.

2. Explain the role of law in society and the paradigms that have developed to understand how law is formed and enforced.

3. Compare the idea of our criminal law system as an adversarial system to other descriptions of how the courtroom works and the relationships between the legal professionals.

4. Present the controversy concerning the role of advocate as legal agent or moral agent.

5. Describe the history and source of legal ethics for attorneys and judges. Explain the types of ethical rules that exist and compare them to the subculture of winning.

Later, it was learned that Ken Anderson, the prosecutor during the original trial (who went on to become a judge), did not provide the defense with evidence of a bloody bandana found near the home or the statement of Morton's son, who reportedly told his grandmother that a "monster" hurt his mommy and that his daddy was not at home. The district attorney (John Bradley), who had been an assistant district attorney at the original trial, fought the requested DNA testing of the bandana for six years, delaying the exoneration of Morton. When it was finally tested, the blood on the bandana turned out to be Christine Morton's and DNA found on it was matched to another man. Even then, Bradley fought against a new trial for Morton. The Innocence Project of New York assisted Morton in his defense along with Houston attorney John Raley, who contributed thousands of hours *pro bono* to the case. When a prosecutor in neighboring Travis County and the Innocence team members noticed similarities between the murder of Christine Morton and an unsolved murder that took place two years after the Morton murder, they had the unknown DNA compared and it matched. Further, the murders were eerily similar in that household objects were piled on the bodies. Mark Alan Norwood has since been convicted of both murders and received a life sentence.

The Morton case is unusual in that Ken Anderson, the county's district attorney for 16 years and district judge for 10, was investigated in a unique "court of inquiry" and, ultimately, pleaded guilty to contempt for withholding evidence and received a 10-day jail sentence and forfeited his law license. Critics argued that it was a light punishment for being instrumental in a man's wrongful imprisonment for 25 years, especially since he did not have to forfeit his judicial pension (Colloff, 2013; Lindell, 2012b).

The Michael Morton case is only one case of many where innocent people have been exonerated, usually based on DNA. The National Registry of Exonerations, a project of the University of Michigan Law School, currently lists 1,609 exonerations (www .law.umich.edu/special/exoneration/Pages/about.aspx). The Innocence Project (www .innocenceproject.org) identifies 329 cases where DNA exonerated an individual. It seems every week a new case in covered by the media of an individual who spent decades in prison for a crime he or she did not commit. The most common factor in these wrongful convictions is mistaken eyewitness testimony, but the unethical acts of police and prosecutors also often play a role.

Just as Ferguson, Missouri, and Baltimore, Maryland, have triggered a national conversation about police, so, too, have highly publicized exonerations like Michael Morton's triggered a national consciousness that the justice system sometimes results in injustice. Also, just as with law enforcement, the focus has targeted the actions of prosecutors, judges, and defense attorneys, since it is they who are instrumental in making sure the system works. In other ways besides wrongful convictions, individuals in the system dramatically affect individuals' lives. In the In the News box on the next page, for instance, it is unclear why an unknown number of prosecutors, defense attorneys, and judges did not recognize, as the months and years went by, that there was something wrong with the system and it was their duty to fix it.

In this chapter and the next two chapters, we will discuss the ethics of legal professionals. These three chapters are set up in a similar way as the three chapters on law enforcement. In this first chapter, we will examine some basic issues concerning the role of the law in society in the same way that we explored the history of policing. In this first chapter on legal professionals, we also present the formal and informal ethical codes that guide legal professionals' actions, again similarly to the discussion in Chapter 5 where the law enforcement code and subculture was discussed. In Chapter 9, we will examine the discretion of legal professionals and how such discretion creates ethical

(◉) IN THE NEWS | *Kalief Browder*

We would like to think that the criminal justice system provides due process and works the way it should. Unfortunately that is not always the case. Kalief Browder was only 16 years old when he was arrested and charged with second-degree robbery. He was remanded without bail after being indicted because he had been on probation at the time of the charges. He spent three years in Rikers Island jail waiting for a trial. Because the Bronx courts are so overcrowded, every time the prosecutor asked for a week's continuance, the delay would turn to six weeks. There is a speedy trial guarantee, but as long as the prosecutor says they are ready for trial, scheduling delays are not counted. Once, after two years had elapsed, a judge offered to let him go with time served if he would plead guilty to two misdemeanors, but he refused because he wasn't guilty. Finally, in 2013 at over the 37th time he appeared in court, the judge told him that the prosecutor's office was not able to proceed to trial because the man who had claimed Browder had taken his backpack

(creating the alleged crime of robbery) had moved away. In Rikers Island, housed with 600 other boys 16 to 18 years old, he experienced physical and emotional abuse and spent the equivalent of two years in solitary confinement. While at Rikers, he attempted suicide at least six times. After his release, he attempted to begin his life again. He had missed his high school graduation, and all of his friends had moved on and began their lives. He began attending a community college and maintained a 3.5 GPA but struggled with depression and paranoia. He attempted suicide six months after his release. The story generated a great deal of interest in Browder's case, and he met celebrities and an anonymous donor paid for his community college tuition. Still, he struggled. In June 2015, his name was again in the news when he committed suicide by hanging himself. His attorney said that he never overcame the jail experience. The publicity has made many ask, how many more Kalief Browders are there in our nation's jails?

Sources: Ford, 2015; Gonnerman, 2013; Gonnerman, 2015.

dilemmas, which is similar to how discretion in law enforcement was the theme in Chapter 6. Finally, in Chapter 10, we will examine cases of misconduct and corruption and responses to them, just as we did in Chapter 7 for law enforcement professionals.

The Role of Law

Our **laws** serve as the written embodiment of society's ethics and morals. Laws are said to be declarative as well as active; they declare correct behavior and serve as a tool for enforcement. While **natural law** refers to the belief that some law is inherent in the natural world and can be discovered by reason, **positivist law** refers to those laws written and enforced by society. This type of law is of human construction and, therefore, fallible (Mackie, 1977: 232).

We can trace the history of law back to very early codes, such as the Code of Hammurabi (ca. 2000 BCE), which mixed secular and religious proscriptions of behavior. These codes also standardized punishments and atonements for wrongdoing. Early codes of law did not differentiate between what we now distinguish as public wrongs (criminal law) and private wrongs (torts). Criminal law is more closely associated with enforcing the moral standards of society, yet it is by no means comprehensive in its coverage of behavior.

Laws, in the form of statutes and ordinances, tell us how to drive, how to operate our business, and what we can and cannot do in public and even in private. They are the formal, written rules of society. Yet, they are not comprehensive in defining moral behavior. There is a law against hitting one's mother (assault), but (in many states) no

laws Formal, written rules of society.

natural law The idea that principles of morals and rights are inherent in nature and not human-made; such laws are discovered by reason but exist apart from humankind.

positivist law Human-made law.

law against financially abandoning her, yet both are considered morally wrong. We have laws against bad behavior, such as burglarizing a house or embezzling from our employer, but we have few laws prescribing good behavior, such as helping a victim or contributing to a charity. The exception to this consists of **Good Samaritan laws**, which are common in Europe. These laws make it a crime to pass by an accident scene or witness a crime without rendering assistance. Some states do have laws called Good Samaritan laws, but they are civil and protect medical professionals who stop at an accident scene and administer aid to the victims from being sued. These laws provide some level of immunity to those who stop and render aid, but they do not require helping as the Good Samaritan laws in Europe do.

Good Samaritan laws European legislation that prohibits passing by an accident scene or witnessing a crime without rendering assistance; can also refer to laws that provide protection from civil suits for individuals who stop and render aid.

Law controls behavior by providing sanctions but also, perhaps even more important, by teaching people which behaviors are acceptable and which behaviors are not. Thus, academics argue whether, for instance, *Brown v. Board of Education* (347 U.S. 483, 1954) came after a shift in people's values and attitudes toward segregation or whether the legal holding that ruled segregation was illegal was the change agent in transforming values and attitudes. Probably both statements are true. There is a dynamic between the law and public opinion, and the power of law is most noticeable "at the margins" where it heralds social change or, to the contrary, acts as a resistant force to evolving belief systems. Laws at the margin are those where strong opposing positions exist (e.g., same-sex marriage, drug laws, gun-control laws). Law is the final word, but it is also dynamic, shifting to reflect changing belief systems.

Just as important as a tool of behavior control and change, the law provides a blanket of protection for individuals against the awesome power of the state. We cherish our Constitution and the Bill of Rights because we understand that in those countries that do not have our legal traditions, citizens have no protection against tyranny and oppression. We know that our bedrock of rights set down by our founding fathers ensures, to some extent, that even if government officials wanted to do us harm or treat us in a way that offends the concept of due process, they could not do so without violating the law. Thus, the law is our social contract. It dictates limits on our own behavior, but also provides protection against governmental violations. Legal professionals are supposed to ensure that this contract is enforced, even though cases such as the Michael Morton case, which opened this chapter, show that sometimes this does not happen. Before we focus on legal professionals, however, it is necessary to take a step back and examine law itself.

Justifications for Law

The major justification for corrective (criminal) law is prevention of harm. Under the **social contract theory**, law is a contract; each individual gives up some liberties and, in return, is protected from others who have their liberties restricted as well. Thomas Hobbes's (1588–1679) claim that self-preservation (the law of the jungle) is paramount, and John Locke's (1632–1704) view that property is a natural right created the foundation for the social contract theory. According to this theory, members of society were originally engaged in a "war of all against all." According to Hobbes (1651), each individual has chosen to "lay down this right to all things; and be contented with so much liberty against other men, as he would allow other men against himself." Hobbes said that in order to avoid this war of all against all, people needed to be assured that people will not harm one another and that they will keep their agreements. But how much liberty should be restricted, and what behaviors should be prohibited? Rough formulas or guidelines indicate that the law should interfere as little as possible with natural liberties and should step in only when the liberty in question injures or impinges on the interests of another. The justifications for law most often cited are: preventing harm to others, preventing offensive behavior, preventing harm to self, and protecting societal morals. Each of these will be discussed next.

Preventing Harm to Others

John Stuart Mill (1806–1873) proposed the "harm principle," which basically is the idea that every individual should have the utmost freedom over their own actions unless they harm others. In this view, the law would restrict only those actions that can or do cause harm to others, such as assault, attempted murder, or theft. Most of our criminal laws are created to punish individual harms. The least controversial are those which we have inherited from the common law; however, legislators continue to add new laws all the time, supposedly in order to prevent harm.

Preventing Offensive Behavior

There are some actions that do not exactly harm others, but give rise to disgust or offense. Such actions as public lewdness, disturbing public behavior, noise, or other actions that infringe on the quality of life of others can be the subject of laws, and individuals who flaunt such laws may be fined or punished in some way. These laws are sometimes controversial because there is an argument that no law should restrict an individual's behavior that may create merely inconvenience or disgust, but that does not damage others' interests. For instance, many cities control the population of homeless people and beggars by a variety of laws because their presence and their actions upset and frighten tourists and downtown workers. Some of these laws, such as vagrancy laws, have been overturned by the Supreme Court for unduly infringing on personal liberties (*Papachristou v. Jacksonville*, 405 U.S. 157, 1972), but others have been upheld, such as "no camping" ordinances to dissuade the homeless from congregating in a downtown area. These laws have been used, for instance, to oust Occupy movement demonstrators who took over downtown parks and city centers in many locations several years ago.

Preventing Harm to Self (Legal Paternalism)

Many laws can be described as examples of **legal paternalism**—laws in which the state tries to protect people from their own behavior. Examples include seat belt laws, motorcycle helmet laws, speed limits, drug laws, licensing laws, alcohol consumption and sale laws, smoking prohibitions, and laws limiting certain types of sexual behavior. The strict libertarian view would hold that the government has no business interfering in a person's decisions about these behaviors as long as they don't negatively affect others. The opposing view is that as long as a person is a member of society (and everyone is), he or she has a value to that society, and society is therefore compelled to protect the person with or without his or her cooperation.

legal paternalism
Refers to laws that protect individuals from hurting themselves.

It may also be true that there are no harmful or potentially harmful behaviors to oneself that do not also hurt others, however indirectly, so society is protecting others when it controls each individual. Speeding drivers may crash into someone else, drug addicts may commit crimes to support their habit, gamblers may neglect their families and cause expense to the state, and so on. Some believe that government can justify paternalism only with certain restrictions. These rules try to create a balance between an individual's liberty and government control (Thompson, 1980):

- The decision-making ability of the person may be somehow impaired by lack of knowledge or competency (e.g., tobacco and alcohol prohibitions for minors).
- The restriction should be as limited as possible (e.g., DUI laws state a legal limit that is when someone is likely impaired).
- The laws should seek only to prevent a serious and irreversible error.

Paternalistic laws can be supported by an ethics of care. Remember that in this framework, morality is viewed as integral to a system of relationships. The individual is seen as having ties to society and to every other member of society. Rights are less important in this framework; therefore, to ask whether society has a right to intervene or an individual has a right to a liberty is not relevant to the discussion. Current debates regarding laws that attempt to influence people's lifestyle choices (such as smoking and eating) illustrate this debate. A large segment of the public become outraged whenever legislation is proposed that is perceived to control private decisions of eating, drinking, smoking, or other activities of adults or their children. Many also believe that government has a moral and legal duty to provide healthcare. Expensive healthcare is made necessary, to some extent because of people's lifestyle choices; therefore if government takes a larger role in providing healthcare, should it also have a larger say in lifestyle?

Preventing Harm to Societal Morals (Legal Moralism)

legal moralism
A justification for law that allows for protection and enforcement of societal morals.

The law also acts as the moral agent of society, some say in areas where there is no moral agreement. This rationale is called **legal moralism**. Some sexual behaviors, gambling, drug use, pornography, and even suicide and euthanasia are defined as wrong and are prohibited. The laws against these behaviors may be based on principles of harm or paternalism, but they also exist to reinforce society's definitions of moral behavior. For example, consensual sexual behavior between adults arguably harms no one, yet the Georgia state law prohibiting sodomy was upheld by the U.S. Supreme Court in *Bowers v. Hardwick* (478 U.S. 186, 1986), although later effectively overturned in *Lawrence v. Texas* (539 U.S. 558, 2003). More recently, there has been a great debate over whether the law ought to recognize and legitimize same-sex marriages. The underlying justification that both sides employ is legal moralism.

Pornography (at least that involving consenting adults) that is defined as obscene is prohibited arguably because of moral standards, not harmful effect. Under the legal moralism rationale, obscenity is prohibited simply because it is wrong. The issue has become even more complicated with the increasing use of the Internet and the ease with which individuals may obtain pornographic materials from anywhere in the world. Privacy rights conflict with the government's right to enforce morality.

((•)) IN THE NEWS | *Same-Sex Marriage*

In the last several years, the country has seen a sea change toward same-sex marriage with public opinion shifting to support and state laws following. As of April 2015, 30 states had legalized same-sex marriage, either by statute or case law. The Supreme Court, in *United States v. Windsor*, (570 U.S. __, 2013), heard a challenge to the federal Defense of Marriage Act and held § 3 of the Act (that defined marriage as solely between a man and a woman) a violation of the Fourteenth Amendment. Then, in January 2015, the Court consolidated cases from four different states to consider the legality of bans on same-sex marriage. On June 26, 2015, in *Obergefell v. Hodges*, the Supreme Court held that the right to marry is a protected liberty interest and all states must license and recognize same-sex marriages.

Source: CNN.com, 2015.

It should also be noted that whether an action is moral or immoral is a different question than whether there should be laws and governmental sanctions regarding the behavior. In some cases, individuals may agree that a particular action is immoral, but at the same time may not believe that the government should have any power to restrict an individual's choice. We do not have a legal system that completely overlaps our moral code, and some would argue that it would be impossible in a society as heterogeneous as ours for this to occur.

Drug laws can be justified under preventing harm to others, preventing harm to self, or legal moralism. Public opinion has shifted in this area as well and now a slim majority of Americans favor legalizing marijuana. While only 34 percent of those polled by the Gallup organization supported legalization in 2004, a high of 58 percent supported it in 2013, falling slightly to 51 percent in 2014 (Saad, 2014). Several states (Washington, Colorado, Alaska, and Oregon) have legalized small amounts of marijuana. The changes in drug laws and same-sex marriage laws show that public views on issues of morality shift. Laws against adultery used to be very common and are nonexistent today. Other crimes that existed in the 1700s are no longer crimes today (e.g., blasphemy, being a "common scold").

Some propose that only those actions that violate some universal standard of morality, as opposed to merely a conventional standard, should be criminalized. This "limited legal moralism" would prevent the situation of some groups forcing their moral code on others. Of course, this begs the question of what behaviors would meet this universal standard. Even child pornographers argue that their behavior is unfairly condemned by a conventional, rather than a universal, morality. The vast profits that are made by producing and distributing child pornography indicate that many people buy such products. Does this mean that it is simply a matter of choice and not some universal moral sense that should influence whether children should be seen as objects of sexual gratification?

The types of laws justified by moralism have also been called the "gray" area of crime in that the wrongness of such actions are not black and white, and there is disagreement that some actions (prostitution, gambling, drug use) are wrong at all. It is not surprising that law enforcement professionals often engage in ethically and legally questionable behavior in these "gray" areas. Police will ignore prostitution, for instance, until the public complains, and police may routinely let petty drug offenders go rather than take the trouble to arrest. Prosecutors may let gamblers go with a warning if no publicity is attached to the arrest. Decision makers in criminal justice use discretion in this way partly because these behaviors are not universally condemned. Consider, for instance, the argument that organized crime grew tremendously during Prohibition and that an unknown number of law enforcement officers, prosecutors, and judges accepted bribes or were involved in protection rackets. Some argue that the same scenario has occurred during the war on drugs and many of the misconduct examples presented in the last chapter involved drugs. The rationalization of authorities who are inclined to accept protection money or bribes is that offenders are engaged in providing a commodity that the public desires. Also, one might note that legal professionals may feel hypocritical enforcing laws against gambling, for instance, when there is a state lottery. These same criminal justice professionals who ignore or provide special treatment for victimless crime offenders would never consider ignoring a child molester or murderer.

Paradigms of Law

Our understanding of the law's function in society is informed by more fundamental views of the world around us, called paradigms. Basically, paradigms are models of how ideas relate to one another, forming a conceptual model of the world around us. A paradigm helps us organize the vast array of knowledge that we absorb every day. We see the world and interpret facts in a way that is influenced by our paradigms—for example, if we have a paradigm that government is corrupt, everything we read and hear will be unconsciously scanned for facts that fit our paradigm, and inconsistent or contrary facts will be ignored and/or forgotten. If our paradigm is that the system is racist, then news stories and statistics that support that notion will be remembered better than information that is not consistent; contrarily, if our paradigm is that the system is fair, the same would apply in reverse. Paradigms aren't bad or good; they are simply a function of how the human mind works. Our paradigms can shift, of course, when we are confronted with overwhelming facts that come from trusted sources or personal experiences that are contrary to our paradigm.

The three paradigms that might affect our view of the law, whether we are legal professionals, legislators, or citizens are the consensus paradigm, the conflict paradigm, and the pluralist paradigm.

Consensus Paradigm

consensus paradigm The idea that most people have similar beliefs, values, and goals and that societal laws reflect the majority view.

The **consensus paradigm** views society as a community consisting of like-minded individuals who agree on goals important for ultimate survival. In the consensus paradigm, law serves as a tool of unification. Emile Durkheim (1858–1917) viewed criminal law as a manifestation of consensual norms; we define an action as criminal because the majority of the populace holds the opinion that it is wrong (Durkheim, 1969).

Law contributes to the collective conscience by showing us who is deviant. The consensus view would point to evidence that people agree on, for the most part, what behaviors are wrong and the relative seriousness of different types of wrongful behavior. Criminology, except for critical or radical criminology, holds a consensus paradigm in that theory construction generally does not question the law itself. In the consensus paradigm:

- *Law is representative.* It is a compilation of the dos and don'ts that we all agree on.
- *Law reinforces social cohesion.* It emphasizes our "we-ness" by illustrating deviance.
- *Law is value-neutral.* It resolves conflicts in an objective and neutral manner.

Conflict Paradigm

The **conflict paradigm** views society as being made up of competing and conflicting interests. According to this view, governance is based on power; if some win, others lose, and those who hold power in society promote self-interest, not a greater good. This perspective sees law as a tool of power holders to maintain and control the status quo: those who control major social institutions determine how crime is defined (Sheley, 1985; Quinney, 1974; Reasons, 1973).

Those holding a conflict paradigm would point to laws against only certain types of gambling as evidence that the ruling class punishes the activities of other classes more severely than their own activities (e.g., numbers running is always illegal, yet some states have legalized horseracing, dog racing, and/or casinos). The Quote and Query box illustrates that the belief that law is used by the powerful against those without power is longstanding.

It is true that the definition of what is criminal often excludes corporate behavior, even though they may be just as harmful to the public as street crime. The *regulation* of business, instead of the *criminalization* of harmful business practices, is seen as arising from the ability of those in powerful positions to redefine their activities to their own advantage. The obvious example to support this view of law is that not a single banking or investment company executive has been prosecuted for activities related to the catastrophic 2007–2008 collapse of the U.S. economic system and resulting recession that has forced millions out of work and/or out of their homes. It is clear that fraudulent mortgage practices went on, banks dealt in improper and risky derivative trading, and CEOs continued to receive large bonuses, telling shareholders the companies were profitable, even while they were falling into bankruptcy. The Troubled Asset Relief Agency distributed billions (provided by taxpayers) to banks that were deemed "too big to fail." The loss and damage done to the country was immeasurable, yet the lack of punishment led some pundits to say that the bankers at the top were "too big to jail." At this point, the statute of limitations has run out for the types of financial fraud that might have been charged.

The Safety and Health Administration, the Food and Drug Administration, the Federal Aviation Administration, and other similar governmental agencies are charged with the task of enforcing regulations governing business activities in their respective areas; however, regulatory sanctions are not as stigmatizing or painful as criminal convictions. Critics also argue that the relationships between the watchdog agencies and those they watch are frequently incestuous: Heads of business are often named to

QUOTE & QUERY

Laws are just like spiders' webs, they will hold the weak and delicate who might be caught in their meshes, but will be torn to pieces by the rich and powerful.

Anacharsis, 600 BCE

The more mandates and laws which are enacted, the more there will be thieves and robbers.

Lao-Tze, 600 BCE

 What do these statements mean? Is it true that laws are manipulated by the powerful and oppress the weak?

conflict paradigm
The idea that groups in society have fundamental differences and that those in power control societal elements, including law.

watchdog agencies, and employees of these agencies may move to the business sector they previously regulated. The latest example of this is the tragedy of the Deep Water Horizon oil spill in the Gulf of Mexico. It is the worst oil spill in history, and some allege that it occurred because of the oil company's (BP) focus on profit over safety. There are also allegations that the federal agency employees responsible for overseeing deep sea drilling and monitoring safety procedures accepted expensive trips and engaged in personal relationships with oil executives (CNN.com, 2010).

Generally, in the conflict paradigm:

- *Law is repressive.* It oppresses the poor and powerless by differential definitions and/or enforcement.
- *Law is a tool of the powerful.* Those who write the laws do so in a way to promote their economic and political interests.
- *Law is not value-neutral.* It is biased and bent toward the interests of the powerful.

Pluralist Paradigm

pluralist paradigm
The concept that there are many groups in society and that they form allegiances and coalitions in a dynamic exchange of power.

The **pluralist paradigm** shares the perception that society is made up of competing interests; however, pluralism describes more than two basic interest groups and also recognizes that the power balance may shift when interest groups form or coalitions emerge. These power shifts occur as part of the dynamics of societal change.

Pluralism views law as influenced by interest groups that are in flux. Some interests may be at odds with other interests, or certainly the interpretation of them may be. For instance, conservation of natural resources is a basic interest necessary to the survival of society, but it may be interpreted by lumber companies as allowing them to harvest trees in national forests as long as they replant; alternatively, interpreted by conservation groups as mandating more wilderness areas. According to the pluralist paradigm, laws are written by the group whose voice is more powerful at any particular time.

The definition of crime may change, depending on which interest groups have the power to define criminal behavior and what is currently perceived to be in the best interests of the most powerful groups. For example, Federal Sentencing Guidelines mandated punishment for crack cocaine in a way that was 100 times more harsh (based on quantity) than powder cocaine, even though they were chemically the same substance. Conflict theory would have explained such a discrepancy by noting that poor people use crack and rich people use powder cocaine; however, it cannot explain why the 100:1 ratio has been addressed with judicial efforts to reduce the disparity, and why, in the summer of 2010, Congress reduced the disparity between the two types of cocaine to about 18 to 1 with new legislation. A pluralist paradigm would point to the growing public sentiment that the sentencing guidelines were unfair. Diverse groups such as the ACLU, Families Against Mandatory Minimums, and other interest groups do have power to affect law when they garner a certain level of public support. Recently, politicians as diverse as Rand Paul and Bernie Sanders have advocated eliminating or reducing the draconian drug sentences. This political shift indicates the pluralist view that law is dynamic and changes to reflect public sentiment.

Another example where interest groups' power seems to shift bank and forth is immigration law. Although there is a contingent in the country who strongly advocates more severe sanctions and harsher laws against illegal aliens, there are other vocal groups who advocate amnesty, worker permits, the Development, Relief, and Education for Alien Minors Act (DREAM Act), which would award citizenship to college graduates or those who enter the military, or other solutions. The federal government has indicated shifts in policy from time to time, signaling, for instance, that they will not devote resources to identifying and deporting illegal aliens who do not come to the attention of authorities because of other crimes. This results in criticism, of course, because it is a decision to not enforce existing law.

These examples illustrate that law is always dynamic and even existing law is fluid in that enforcement practices shift from time to time. Legal professionals, then, become not mere robots who enforce all laws, all the time, but, rather, interpreters of law who apply it dynamically, influenced by shifting economic, social, and personal factors.

First, Let's Kill All the Lawyers

Public perceptions of lawyers indicate that the public has little confidence in their ability to live up to ideals of equity, fairness, and justice. In 2014, respondents in a Gallup Poll rated their level of trust in the integrity of attorneys. Only about 21 percent indicated that attorneys possessed "high" or "very" high standards of honesty and ethics. Only a few professions were rated lower than lawyers, including car salespeople and members of Congress (Gallup Poll, 2014).

In the 1980s, the law scandal was the savings and loan fiasco, in which the greed and corruption of those in the banking industry were ably assisted by the industry's attorneys, and the taxpayers picked up the bill for the bankrupt institutions and outstanding loans. The scandal of the 1990s was the Bill Clinton–Monica Lewinsky investigation, with opinions mixed as to which set of lawyers was more embarrassing—those who could coach the president that oral sex wasn't technically "sexual relations" or the special prosecutor, Kenneth Starr, and his assistants, who spent millions of dollars in an investigation that centered on semen stains and the definition of sex. The new century brought us the debacle of WorldCom and Enron, and, again, lawyers played a central role, along with business executives and accountants.

After 9/11 and the War on Terror, we had the situation of the White House counsel parsing the definition of torture in secret memoranda. Then we had a virtual meltdown of our national economy fueled largely by Wall Street, again aided ably by their highly paid attorneys. After the Enron bankruptcy and other blatant acts of crime by CEOs and CFOs in the early 2000s, Congress passed the Sarbanes-Oxley Act, which created culpability for CEOs, who could no longer plead ignorance when a pattern of blatant criminality was within the scope of their responsibility. The act also required standards for attorneys appearing and practicing before the SEC that allowed for permissive disclosure of client's confidences to prevent fraud or other financial crimes. This response still did not stop the lending frenzy, the derivatives market, and the subsequent dissolution of AIG and the need to bail out the big banks in 2008–2009. For many, it seemed a virtual replay of the savings and loan scandal of the 1980s, and many wondered how it could have happened again. For every CEO and bank official who skirted the finer points of law and ethics, there was an attorney by his or her side.

This passage is humorous, but the underlying problem is not. Why do people have such low opinions of lawyers?

Finally, it seems every day there is another news story of a person who has been exonerated by Innocence Projects nationwide, reportedly because of egregious errors and/or unethical behaviors on the part of police, prosecutors, defense attorneys, and judges. It seems to be only a matter of time before the next big scandal concerning attorneys will emerge. The Quote and Query box puts the problem in a humorous light.

Perhaps the best explanation for the longstanding distrust of lawyers is that they typically represent trouble. People don't require a lawyer unless they believe that a wrong has been done to them or that they need to be defended. In fact, let us not forget the full context of the quote, "The first thing we do, let's kill all the lawyers," widely used as a stab at attorneys. In Shakespeare's *Henry VI, Part 2*, the scene involves a despot who, before making a grab for power, argues that the first thing he must do is kill all the lawyers, for it is lawyers who are the guardians of law. However, the reason the existing power holders in the play were vulnerable to an overthrow in the first place was that they were using the law to oppress the powerless. And so it is today. The law can be either a tool of oppression or a sword of justice, with lawyers and judges as the ones who wield its power. Unfortunately, there are all too many examples of attorneys and judges who do not uphold the standards of their profession.

Law and the Legal Professional

The perception of the lawyer as an amoral "hired gun" is in sharp contrast to the ideal of the lawyer as an officer of the court, sworn to uphold the ideals of justice declared sacrosanct under our system of law. Interestingly, but perhaps not surprisingly, a large percentage of elected officials are lawyers, and 25 of 44 presidents have been lawyers. Our nation's leaders and historical heroes have just as likely been lawyers (Abraham Lincoln, for example) as military generals, and our nation's consciousness is permeated with the belief in law and legal vindication.

On the one hand, the public tends to agree with a stereotype of lawyers as amoral, motivated by money, and with no conscience or concern for morality. On the other hand, the first response to any perception of wrong is to find a legal advocate and sue, with the belief that a lawyer will right any wrong and solve any problem. From ancient times, the ethics of those associated with the legal process has been suspect. Plato and Aristotle condemned advocates because of their ability to make the truth appear false and the guilty appear innocent. This early distrust continued throughout history. Early colonial lawyers were distrusted and even punished for practicing law. For many years, lawyers could not charge a fee for their services because the mercenary aspect of the profession was condemned (Papke, 1986: 32). Gradually, lawyers and the profession itself were accepted, but suspicion and controversy continued in the area of fees and qualifications. Partly to counteract public antipathy, lawyers formed their own organization, the American Bar Association (ABA), in 1878. Shortly afterward, this professional organization established the first ethical guidelines for lawyers; these became the Model Code of Professional Responsibility, discussed later in this chapter.

Apparently, even lawyers don't think much of their profession. A *National Law Journal* study found that over 50 percent of lawyers described their colleagues as "obnoxious" (reported in Krieger, 2009: 882). In a 2006 poll, about 60 percent of those in the practice of law for six to nine years were dissatisfied with their career, although the percentage went down to 40 percent for those practicing more than 10 years. Overall, only about 55 percent of attorneys were satisfied with their career. Only about a third of lawyers practicing six to nine years would recommend law as a profession to young people, and only 44 percent of all lawyers would recommend it as a career (S. Ward, 2007).

Thus far in our discussion, we have been discussing the law as an abstraction, however, it should be understood that the law is a reality created by legal professionals—legislators who pass new laws, prosecutors who decide who and how to prosecute, defense attorneys who do their duty (or don't), and judges who protect the sanctity of the process are all important actors in creating this reality. The In the News box illustrates what might happen when system actors substitute different goals.

The ideal of the justice system is that two advocates of equal ability will engage in a pursuit of truth, guided by a neutral judge. The truth is supposed to emerge from the contest. Actual practices in our justice system may be quite different. Does the "best" opponent always win? If a powerful and rich defendant is able to hire the best criminal lawyer in the country, complete with several assistants and investigators, the prosecutor

(⟨⟩) IN THE NEWS | *Legal Extortion?*

There has been growing concern about asset forfeiture (sometimes called civil forfeiture because there is no criminal conviction necessary to seize property). The legal action is taken, in essence, against property that is believed to be associated with criminal activity. Concerns have increased because of the aggressive, unfair, but legal (although that has been subject to debate) seizures described below:

The small town of Tenaha, Texas, was in the news in 2009 when news stories described how black and Hispanic motorists passing through the town were stopped by police and threatened with jail or the loss of their children if they did not hand over their money and other valuables. One man was carrying $8,500 to buy a new car and was pulled over for going a couple miles per hour over the speed limit. He was taken to jail and told that he would be charged with money-laundering, but he could leave with no charges if he would sign over the cash to the city. The district attorney reputedly threatened people that if they contested the seizures, she would have a grand jury indict them and their children would be taken by Child Protective Services (CPS).

It turns out that the "Tenaha operation," as one defense attorney who helped in a class action suit against the town described it, was the model for similar practices across the country in communities large and small. In West Philadelphia, Mary and Leon Adams' house was seized because their son sold several $20 bags of marijuana to an informant. The majority of actions are not against the drug kingpins that were the target of such laws. Targets are often minority and/or low or middle class people who have no resources to fight the seizure. Seizures are not large either; one study estimated that the average seizure was around $600.

Law enforcement must have the cooperation of prosecutors to complete seizure actions. In Tenaha, law enforcement, the prosecutor, and the city shared the profits derived from the seizures. Similar to other locales, even when drugs and cash clearly were associated with illegal operations, individuals were not charged and allowed to disappear as long as they left their property behind. Another disturbing element of the asset forfeiture patterns in some locales was that law enforcement officers earned personal "bonuses" from seizures and, because few restrictions are in place in some states on how asset forfeiture money can be used, it has been used for parties, trips, and, other questionable expenditures.

The Tenaha case resulted in a settlement where the county agreed to a set of reforms designed to put in place more controls over the practice. The prosecutor retired. The Texas legislature, stung by the negative attention, passed legislation that restricted how such funds could be used. But asset forfeiture continues.

Sources: Tuchman and Wojleck, 2009; McCollum, 2011; Stillman, 2013.

(who is typically overworked and understaffed) may be overwhelmed. Of course, this is the exception. More commonly a defendant must rely on an overworked and probably inexperienced public defender or an attorney who can make criminal law profitable only by high caseloads and quick turnover. The national scandal in underfunded indigent legal defense has reached crisis proportions with public defenders carrying caseloads of over 300 in many jurisdictions across the country (Lefstein, 2011) leading the American Bar Association and other public advocacy groups to demand more funding. In most cases, the defense is outmatched by a prosecutor in a public office with greater access to evidence and investigative assistance. Unfortunately, poverty affects a wide range of judicial processing decisions (Heffernan and Kleinig, 2000).

Blumberg (1969) and Scheingold (1984) refer to the practice of criminal law as a *confidence game* because the prosecutor and the defense attorney conspire to appear as something they are not—adversaries in a do-or-die situation. What is more commonly the case is that the prosecutor and the defense attorney will still be working together when the client is gone. Attorneys may display adversarial performances in the courtroom, but the "show" lasts only as long as the jury is in the room, and sometimes not even then. Defense attorneys, prosecutors, and judges work together every day and often socialize together; they may even be married to each other. Many defense attorneys are ex-prosecutors. In some respects, this is helpful to their clients because the defense attorneys know how the prosecutor's office works and what a reasonable plea offer would be. But one must also assume that the prosecutorial experience of these attorneys has shaped their perceptions of clients and what would be considered fair punishment.

bureaucratic justice The approach in which each case is treated as one of many; the actors merely follow the rules and walk through the steps, and the goal is efficiency.

Another perspective describes our courts as administering **bureaucratic justice**. Each case is seen as only one of many for the professionals who work in the system, and the actors merely follow the rules and walk through the steps. The goal of the system—namely, bureaucratic efficiency—becomes more important than the original goal of justice. Also, because each case is part of a workload, decision making takes on more complications. For instance, a defense lawyer may be less inclined to fight hard for a "loser" client if the lawyer wants a favor for another client later in the week. The prosecutor may decide not to charge a guilty person in order to get him or her to testify against someone else. In this sense, each case is not tried and judged separately, but is linked to other cases and processed as part of a workload.

The bureaucratic system of justice is seen as developing procedures and policies that, although not intentionally discriminatory, may contribute to a perception of unfairness. For instance, a major element in bureaucratic justice is the presumption of guilt, whereas the ideal of our justice system is a presumption of innocence. District attorneys, judges, and even defense attorneys approach each case presuming guilt and place a priority on achieving the most expeditious resolution of the case. This is the basic rationale behind plea bargaining, whether it is recognized or not: the defendant is presumed to be guilty, and the negotiation is to achieve a guilty plea while bargaining for the best possible sentence. The lowest possible sentence is the goal of the defense, whereas the highest possible sentence is the goal of the prosecutor. Plea bargaining is consistent with the bureaucratic justice system because it is the most efficient way of getting maximum punishment with minimum work.

wedding-cake illustration The model of justice in which the largest portion of criminal cases forms the bottom layers of the cake and the few "serious" cases form the top layer; the bottom-layer cases get minimal due process.

One other perception of the criminal justice system is that of Samuel Walker's (1985) **wedding-cake illustration**, based on a model proposed by Lawrence Friedman and Robert Percival. In this scheme, the largest portion of criminal cases forms the bottom layers of the cake and the few "serious" cases form the top layer. The top layer is represented most dramatically by cases such as the murder trials of O. J. Simpson and Casey Anthony, or the criminal trial of Bernard Madoff. In these highly publicized cases, defense attorneys are extremely skilled (and highly paid). They employ trial consultants, investigators, and public relations specialists. Prosecutors match these resources. However, the bottom of the cake is represented by the tens of thousands of cases that are processed every year in which defendants may meet with an attorney only once or twice for a few minutes immediately before agreeing to a plea arrangement.

Because the public is exposed only to the top of the wedding cake, people develop a highly distorted perception of the system. The U.S. public may be disgusted with the multitude of evidentiary rules and the Byzantine process of the trial itself. However, these concerns are valid for only a very small portion of criminal cases. In the vast majority of cases, there is no trial at all and the process is more of an assembly line. What happens to individuals is largely determined by the courtroom work group (composed of all the actors in the court process, including defense attorneys, prosecutors, and judges).

According to Walker's wedding-cake analysis, the courtroom work group is believed to share definitions of seriousness and operate as a unit to keep the dynamics of the courtroom static despite changes that are forced upon it. Changes in the justice system that have occurred over time, such as the exclusionary rule and determinate sentencing, have had surprisingly little impact on court outcomes because of a shared perception of serious crime and appropriate punishment. The vast majority of crime is considered trivial, and the processing of these cases involves little energy or attention from system actors (Walker, 1985).

Dershowitz's view of the criminal justice system, as displayed in the Quote and Query box, is obviously (as Dershowitz admits) an exaggeration, but he does touch on some aspects of the system that many people agree with, such as a widespread perception of guilt and a general view that case processing is routine for everyone except the individual at risk of conviction. The major ethical problem with this view (if it does represent reality) is that innocence, truth, and due process are perceived as inconvenient and expendable.

QUOTE & QUERY

Alan Dershowitz, a well-known defense attorney and law professor, presents the "rules" of the courtroom:

Rule I: Almost all criminal defendants are, in fact, guilty.

Rule II: All criminal defense lawyers, prosecutors, and judges understand and believe Rule I.

Rule III: It is easier to convict guilty defendants by violating the Constitution than by complying with it, and in some cases it is impossible to convict guilty defendants without violating the Constitution.

Rule IV: Almost all police lie about whether they violated the Constitution in order to convict guilty defendants.

Rule V: All prosecutors, judges, and defense attorneys are aware of Rule IV.

Rule VI: Many prosecutors implicitly encourage police to lie about whether they violated the Constitution in order to convict guilty defendants.

Rule VII: All judges are aware of Rule VI.

Rule VIII: Most trial judges pretend to believe police officers whom they know are lying.

Rule IX: All appellate judges are aware of Rule VIII, yet many pretend to believe the trial judges who pretend to believe the lying police officers.

Rule X: Most judges disbelieve defendants about whether their constitutional rights have been violated, even if they are telling the truth.

Rule XI: Most judges and prosecutors would not knowingly convict a defendant whom they believe to be innocent of the crime charged (or a closely related crime).

Rule XII: Rule XI does not apply to members of organized crime, drug dealers, career criminals, or potential informers.

Rule XIII: Nobody really wants justice.

Source: Dershowitz, 1982: xxi.

 Do you believe this is more accurate than the idealized vision of the adversarial system of justice?

Legal Agent or Moral Agent?

Many lawyers believe that loyalty to the client is paramount to their duties as a professional. This loyalty surpasses and eclipses individual and private decision making, and the special relationship said to exist between lawyer and client justifies decisions that otherwise might be deemed morally unacceptable. Others argue that an attorney must never abandon his or her own moral compass and if the client desires some action that

238 PART III Law

the attorney would not countenance, ethics demand that he or she convince the client not to do so or withdraw. Historians indicate that this dilemma has been problematic for lawyers since the first ethics codes were written. In writings in the 1800s, lawyers were admonished not to "plate sin with gold," (defend a wrong action by finding a legal justification for it), but others wrote that "a lawyer is not accountable for the moral character of the cause he prosecutes, but only for the manner in which he conduct it" (reported in Ariens, 2008: 364, 367).

The conundrum of what to do when a client wants you to commit some act contrary to good conscience occurs in both civil and criminal law. The following are the types of positions described and defended.

- *Legal agent.* One position is that the attorney is no more than the legal agent of the client. The lawyer is neither immoral nor moral, but merely a legal tool. This position is represented by the statement, "I am a lawyer, first and foremost."
- *Special relationship.* A more moderate position is that the loyalty to the client presents a special relationship between client and lawyer, similar to that between mother and child or with a trusted friend. This protected relationship justifies fewer actions than the legal agent relationship. The lawyer is expected to dissuade the client from taking unethical or immoral actions, but loyalty would preclude absolutely going against the client's wishes.
- *Moral agent.* The third position is that the lawyer is a moral agent who has to adhere to his or her own moral code. The client's interests come first only as long as they do not conflict with the lawyer's morality and ethical code. If there is a conflict, the lawyer follows his or her conscience.

Shaffer and Cochran (2007) offer a slightly different typology, describing the *godfather* (promotes clients' interests above all others), the *hired gun* (does whatever the client wants), the *guru* (controls the client with his own moral compass as guide), and the *friend* (engages the client in moral dialogue and tries to convince the client of a proper course of action and refuses only after the client insists). The hired gun and guru are similar to the legal agent and moral agent roles described above.

Some critics of the legal agent approach reject perspectives that discount the lawyer's responsibility as an individual to make his or her own moral decisions. In this view, lawyers should be the legal *and* moral agents of their clients rather than merely legal agents (Postema, 1986: 168). This position is represented by the statement, "I am a person first, a lawyer second." In essence, the argument is that one cannot be virtuous when pursuing a client's evil objectives (Cohen, 1991).

Cohen (1991: 135–136) suggests some principles for attorneys to follow to be considered moral:

- Treat others as ends in themselves and not as mere means to winning cases.
- Treat clients and other professional relations who are relatively similar in a similar fashion.
- Do not deliberately engage in behavior that is apt to deceive the court as to the truth.
- Be willing, if necessary, to make reasonable personal sacrifices—of time, money, popularity, and so on—for what you justifiably believe to be a morally good cause.
- Do not give money to, or accept money from, clients for wrongful purposes or in wrongful amounts.

- Avoid harming others in the process of representing your client.

- Be loyal to your clients, and do not betray their confidences.

- Make your own moral decisions to the best of your ability, and act consistently upon them.

The rationale for these principles seems to be an amalgamation of ethical formalism, utilitarianism, and ethics of care in that a lawyer should be concerned when the other side may be victimized or harmed by the actions of one's client (Cohen, 2002; Vogelstein, 2003). Some of the principles may seem impossible to uphold and may be subject to bitter criticism, especially on the part of practicing civil attorneys. For instance, how does one avoid harming the other side in a civil dispute when compromise is impossible and one side will be a winner and the other the loser?

The legal agent position is that it is impossible and unethical to substitute one's own moral code for one's clients (Memory and Rose, 2002). This position would point to rules already in place already prevent unscrupulous acts, e.g., the Model Rules of Professional Conduct. Arguably, decisions regarding justice and morality are so subjective that it is unnecessary and unwise to substitute a lawyer's morals for the client's (Memory and Rose, 2002). The only thing that would be accomplished would be the loss of the clients' trust in lawyers.

In general, Cohen (1991) and Memory and Rose (2002) seem to be in agreement that the Model Rules should prevent the most egregious misconduct of lawyers. Their disagreement comes from the value they place on rules versus individual responsibility for more ambiguous moral judgments. One need not take either position to note that training and socialization into the culture of criminal law may encourage a type of noble-cause corruption similar to what we discussed in Chapter 5 for police officers. In the legal profession, the noble cause is winning a case (at all costs). In a culture that supports "ends" thinking (winning) over "means," rules are no more likely to control misconduct by lawyers than they do some police officers.

Research indicates that the position taken by attorneys depends partially on whom they represent. On the one hand, public defenders take a more authoritarian role and seem to support the attorney as a "guru" or moral agent who tells the client what to do; attorneys for corporations, on the other hand, are apt to follow a more client centered approach (Mather, 2003).

It should be noted that the Model Rules do show glimmers of the moral agent idea. For instance, Model Rule 2.1 states that "a lawyer may refer not only to law but to other considerations such as moral, economic, social, and political factors" in making decisions. This indicates that the rules do encourage attorneys to look to the ethical systems to resolve problems. Again, though, the rules are not much help when the client and the attorney strongly disagree over what is the right thing to do.

Ethics for Legal Professionals

Formal ethical standards for lawyers and judges were originally promulgated by the American Bar Association in the *Model Code of Professional Responsibility*. The original canons, adapted from the Alabama Bar Association Code of 1887, were adopted by the ABA in 1908 and have been revised frequently since then. In 1983, the ABA switched its endorsement of the Model Code as the general guide for ethical behavior to the *Model Rules of Professional Conduct*. The Model Rules continue to be revised periodically, responding to changing sensibilities and emerging issues. Today's Model Rules cover many aspects of the lawyer's profession, including areas such as client–lawyer relationships, the lawyer as counselor, the lawyer as advocate, transactions with others, public service, and maintaining the integrity of the profession (ABA, 2015).

The rules require that attorneys zealously protect and pursue a client's interest within the boundaries of the rules while maintaining a professional and civil demeanor toward everyone involved in the legal process. Critics charge that the rules have replaced earlier ethical codes that expressed ethical norms based on a moral tradition with regulatory, some might say, picayune prohibitions (Ariens, 2008). Others argue that by placing pure client interest ahead of a transcendent professional ethos, lawyers have lost the meaning and value that used to be associated with the practice of law, and this lack of professional purpose undercuts public confidence and is the cause of a "cycle of cynicism" (Kreiger, 2009).

Section 1 of the rules is titled "Client–Lawyer Relationship." This section offers rules that require the attorney maintain a level of competence in his or her field and not take cases that are beyond his or her expertise. Rules in this section also govern the relative power between the attorney and client—in other words, who should make decisions regarding the legal strategy to pursue the client's interest. The rules mandate that attorneys, once they take a case, practice due diligence, communicate with their client, and assess appropriate fees. A controversial rule demands attorneys maintain confidentiality regarding information obtained in their representation of a client. We will discuss client confidentiality as a dilemma in Chapter 9. There are also rules that guide the attorney when there are conflicts of interest, such as the attorney should not have two clients who have competing interests or take on clients whose interests may conflict with the attorney's interests. These protections extend to former clients as well.

Section 2 offers rules concerning the lawyer's role as counselor, and Section 3 covers those situations where the attorney is pursuing the client's interest as an advocate. The Model Rules require that the attorney only pursue legitimate claims (Rule 3.1), and not engage in needless delays (Rule 3.2). Further, the attorney has an ethical obligation of "Candor Toward the Tribunal" (Rule 3.3), which means, for instance, that when presenting a legal argument, the attorney must present opposing case law as well. There are additional rules that cover fairness, decorum, trial publicity, and when the lawyer is a witness.

The Model Rules have been written for all attorneys and, thus, most of them are not directly relevant to criminal defense or prosecutors. However, Rule 3.8, "Special Responsibilities of a Prosecutor," is directed to the prosecutor. Two provisions were added to the rule in 2008, which put an affirmative duty on the prosecutor to do something when there is reason to believe a wrongful conviction has occurred (Mulhausen, 2010; Saltzburg, 2008):

> *(g) When a prosecutor knows of new, credible, and material evidence creating a reasonable likelihood that a convicted defendant did not commit an offense of which the defendant was convicted, the prosecutor shall: (1) promptly disclose that evidence to an appropriate court or authority, and (2) if the conviction was obtained in the prosecutor's jurisdiction, (a) promptly disclose that evidence to the defendant unless a court authorizes delay, and (b) undertake further investigation, or make reasonable efforts to cause an investigation, to determine whether the defendant was convicted of an offense that the defendant did not commit.*

(h) When a prosecutor knows of clear and convincing evidence establishing that a defendant in the prosecutor's jurisdiction was convicted of an offense that the defendant did not commit, the prosecutor shall seek to remedy the conviction.

These provisions were in response to the growing number of cases where innocent people have been released from prison after being exonerated, often by DNA evidence. New York was the first state to revise its state ethics rules to assign these duties to prosecutors, and the ABA began discussing such a rule in 2000. While critics argued that prosecutors are too overworked already to consider post-conviction claims of innocence and that the rules may serve as a bar to the finality of criminal convictions, proponents successfully argued that the number of exonerations and the fact that the duty of a prosecutor is to seek justice, not secure convictions, supported the inclusion of the new provisions. Thus far, however, states have not been as supportive of the rules. According to the ABA website, only Idaho, West Virginia, and Wyoming have adopted the rule substantially unchanged, six other states have modified it, and the rest of the states have not adopted the (g) and (h) additions.

ETHICAL DILEMMA

You are a prosecutor who is tasked with responding to a prison inmate's request for post-conviction DNA testing. The inmate has spent 10 years in prison for a rape and murder. DNA testing was done at the time but was inconclusive because of the degradation of source material; however, new techniques have been developed that potentially could create more accurate results. The inmate claimed innocence, but you have two eyewitnesses and a jail informant who all testified as to the defendant's guilt. Your boss, the district attorney, is against post-conviction DNA testing because he believes that inmates will "game" the system and delay their execution by requesting it. You must respond to the motion within five days. How will you decide whether to contest or agree to the testing?

Law

The Supreme Court has ruled that there is no constitutional right to post-conviction DNA testing (*District Attorney's Office for the Third Judicial District v. Osborne*, 557 U.S. 52, 2009). On the other hand, Supreme Court justices have recognized an "actual innocence" defense that would trump procedural errors in habeas corpus filings and, presumably, override the *Osborne* decision as well if the petitioner had a strong case of actual innocence (*McQuiggin v. Perkins*, 569 U.S. __, 2013). In most cases, however, especially where there is eyewitness testimony, the weight of evidence may not be sufficient to show actual innocence. Certain states have recognized a state right to post-conviction DNA testing, although usually they also attach restrictions, such as

the defendant did not have an opportunity to seek the testing at the time of trial or there has been new techniques developed that would warrant retesting.

Policy

Craig Washington, former district attorney of Dallas County, Texas, set up the first conviction integrity unit and many locales have created similar units since the first. These units analyze cases (under varying procedures that identify likely cases) for potential wrongful convictions. Post-conviction testing requests may be met with more favor in prosecutors' offices that have such units, although DNA testing is expensive and there is still probably strong pressure to protect convictions. For instance, in the Michael Morton case that opened this chapter, the evidence had not been tested at all, yet the prosecutor fought post-conviction testing for years before the appellate court overruled him.

Ethics

It would seem that all ethical systems would support post-conviction DNA testing when there is any evidence that a wrongful conviction might have occurred. However, prosecutors believe the petitioner is guilty. Therefore, they weigh the cost of the DNA testing as a potential release of a guilty person, not freeing a potentially innocent person. Given this mindset, utilitarianism would justify blocking the request. On the other hand, ethical formalism and ethics of care would support agreeing to testing requests since the ethical duty of the prosecutor is to seek justice, not convictions.

Another section of the Model Rules is titled "Transactions with Persons Other than Clients." In this section, rules require the lawyer to maintain truthfulness in statements to others, and not communicate with opposing parties except through their attorneys. Other rules cover practices concerning unrepresented persons and the rights of third persons. In a section that covers how law firms should operate, there are many rules concerning the relationships between attorneys in firms, between firms, and with other non-lawyer associates. One rule, for instance, bars attorneys from using "runners," which are non-attorneys who find cases by following up on accidents or finding victims of torts or defective merchandise.

The section on public service mandates that lawyers provide some *pro bono* (free) legal service, and otherwise contribute to the legal community and society in general. It also cautions against acting against clients' interests in one's activities in public service. Another section covers how the attorney may advertise and communicate with prospective clients. There are also rules about how to advertise specialties or being board certified (passing a special examination in a particular area of law). Section 8 is titled "Maintaining the Integrity of the Profession" and covers bar admission and discipline. Rule 8.2 is directed specifically to "Judicial and Legal Officials." Rule 8.3 dictates that attorneys have an ethical obligation to reporting professional misconduct. Rule 8.4 more specifically details misconduct, and the final rule covers the authority to enact discipline (Martyn, Fox, and Wendel, 2008).

In addition to the Model Rules, there is also the American Law Institute's Restatement of the Law Governing Lawyers (Martyn, Fox, and Wendel, 2008). Developed in 2000, the Restatement provides guidelines and commentary covering most of the same issues that the Model Rules cover. Some of the sections of the Restatement are:

- Admission to Practice Law
- A Lawyer's Duty of Supervision
- A Lawyer's Duties to a Prospective Client
- Client–Lawyer Contracts
- Duty of Care to a Client
- A Lawyer's Duty to Safeguard Confidential Client Information
- Using or Disclosing Information to Prevent Death or Serious Bodily Harm
- Client Crime or Fraud
- Falsifying or Destroying Evidence

The Restatement has eight chapters and 135 different sections. Note that the ABA and American Legal Institute (ALI) promulgate these ethical codes, but state bar associations must adopt them or adapt them to have any effect. It is the state bar associations (and the federal bar) that have the power to discipline attorneys, the most serious punishment being disbarment. Finally, it should be noted that the Model Rules and the Restatement cover the practice of law generally; thus, most of the commentary and elements relate to civil practice. Because our discussion focuses exclusively on criminal defense attorneys, prosecutors, and criminal court judges, we will be referring to the *ABA Criminal Justice Standards*, as developed by the American Bar Association in 1991–1992 and recently revised (ABA, 2015b). These standards offer guidelines and commentary directed specifically to the practice of criminal law. Ethical issues in criminal law may involve courtroom behavior, perjury, conflicts of interest, use of the media, investigation efforts, use of immunity, discovery and the sharing of evidence, relationships with opposing attorneys, and plea bargaining.

Standards relating to ethical obligations of defense attorneys appear in Chapter 4, "The Defense Function" and cover a multitude of issues, such as these:

- Function of defense counsel
- Punctuality
- Public statements
- Duty to the administration of justice
- Access and the lawyer–client relationship
- Duty to investigate
- Control and direction of litigation
- Plea bargaining
- Trial conduct
- Appeal

Chapter 3 of the *ABA Criminal Justice Standards* covers the prosecution function. There are also *National Prosecution Standards* promulgated by the National District Attorneys Association. Recall that Model Rule 3.8, described in preceding paragraphs, also covers the duties of a prosecutor. Ethical guidelines for prosecutors make special note of the unique role of the prosecutor as a representative of the court system and the state. Some of the sections of the *ABA Standards for Prosecutors* cover:

- Working with police and other law enforcement agents
- Working with victims, potential witnesses, and targets
- Contact with the public
- The decision to initiate or to continue an investigation
- Selecting investigative techniques
- Use of undercover law enforcement agents and undercover operations
- Use of the investigative powers of the grand jury
- The prosecutor's role in addressing suspected law enforcement misconduct
- The prosecutor's role in addressing suspected judicial misconduct
- Illegally obtained evidence
- Responding to political pressure

These standards for legal professionals in the criminal justice system are much more specific than the Law Enforcement Code of Ethics. Instead of being aspirational, the standards are specific guidelines for behavior.

Ethical Guidelines for Judges

To help guide judges in their duties, the *Model Code of Judicial Conduct* was developed by the American Bar Association. The latest revision was undertaken beginning in 2003, with the final document submitted to the membership in 2007. This code identifies the ethical considerations unique to judges. It is organized into four canons, which are overriding principles of ethical behavior, and under each canon there are more specific rules. The four canons of the code are as follows (ABA, 2007):

1. A judge shall uphold and promote the independence, integrity, and impartiality of the judiciary, and shall avoid impropriety and the appearance of impropriety.

2. A judge shall perform the duties of judicial office impartially, competently, and diligently.

3. A judge shall conduct the judge's personal and extra judicial activities to minimize the risk of conflict with the obligations of judicial office.

4. A judge or candidate for judicial office shall not engage in political or campaign activity that is inconsistent with the independence, integrity, or impartiality of the judiciary.

The primary theme of judicial ethics is impartiality. We must be confident that the judge's objectivity isn't marred by any type of bias. Judges should not let their personal prejudices influence their decisions. To avoid this possibility, the ABA's code specifies that each judge should try to avoid all appearance of bias as well as actual bias. To this end, the rules prohibit a judge from engaging in speeches or activities that indicate a particular bias. Such ethical rules, however, cannot impinge on the right of free speech. In *Minnesota v. White* (536 U.S. 765, 2002), the Supreme Court held that Minnesota's rule prohibiting judges from making speeches violated the First Amendment.

We expect judges, like police officers and prosecutors, to conform to higher standards of behavior than the rest of us. Therefore, any hint of scandal in their private lives also calls into question their professional ethics. Judges must be careful to avoid financial involvements that may threaten their objectivity. Of course, the elephant in the living room is that many judges are elected, thus there is a perception that those who contribute to the election campaigns receive special treatment. Almost 90 percent of voters and even 80 percent of judges believe that campaign contributions of interest groups are used to try and shape judicial opinions and 76 percent of voters and 46 percent of judges believe that contributions have at least some influence on judges' decisions (Shepherd, 2013: 1).

For state supreme court positions, nine states use partisan elections, 12 states use nonpartisan elections, and in 29 states, the governor or legislature initially appoints (called a merit or appointment plan) with a "retention" election that follows. Of those states, five use partisan elections and 14 use nonpartisan elections; generally the judge runs unopposed and simply needs to win majority approval from the voters. The other states utilize reappointment by either the governor or judicial nominating committee. For trial and appellate level judges, 19 states use partisan elections and 21 states use nonpartisan elections for at least some judicial positions, thus the majority of states utilize some form of election process for at least some of their judicial positions (Sheperd, 2013).

When judges are elected, they must solicit campaign contributions. There has been recent attention to the vast sums that have flowed to judicial campaigns in recent years. In some cases, large corporations and special interest groups fund judicial campaigns. During 2000–2009, business groups contributed over $62.6 million, or 30 percent of the total contributions to state supreme court justices, and lawyers and lobbyists contributed $59.3 million, or 28 percent of the total campaign fundraising (Shepherd, 2013: 1). Campaign financing has dramatically increased, from $83.3 million in 1990–1999 to $206.9 million in 2000–2009 (an average of $23 million per year) (Shepherd, 2013: 1). In 2011–2012, it increased to $33.7 million (Bannon, Velasco, Casey, and Reagan, 2013). Much of the money spent is "dark money," contributed by political action committees (PACs) that are not required to disclose donors. The money is used most often for "issue ads" that attack opponents. Donors may, and probably are, individuals and/or companies who have had or will have cases in front of the judges. In *Citizens United v. FEC* (558 U.S. 310, 2010), the Supreme Court infamously held that corporations were people, or at least had the same rights as people; specifically, a First Amendment right to spend as much money as they wanted. States, since that holding, have been prohibited from limiting corporate spending on elections.

One might expect that judges would recuse themselves when these corporations have cases before the judge, but this does not always happen. Brent Benjamin ran for the West Virginia Supreme Court funded by $3 million from Massey Energy, a coal company. The amount far exceeded the total of all other contributions in his campaign. When an appeal of a case came before the court involving the company, he did not recuse himself, and he, along with the majority of the court, overturned a $50 million judgment against the company. In an appeal to the U.S. Supreme Court concerning the refusal of the judge to recuse himself, the Court held that the facts of the case violated a proportionality standard to be used to determine when a single contribution to a campaign might give rise to a conflict of interest. The Supreme Court sent the case back to the West Virginia courts for rehearing and, with only one original judge sitting, the West Virginia court ruled 4 to 1 again in favor of the coal company (*Caperton v. Massey*, 129 S. Ct. 2252, 2009), which some people took to mean that the coal company was faultless and some people took to mean that the coal company had exerted financial pressure on those judges also. The Massey Coal Company was in the news again in the spring of 2010 when 29 miners died in an explosion, and a subsequent investigation showed hundreds of violations, and a pattern of ignoring safety regulations and cover-ups. A settlement agreement was reached where the new owners of the mine agreed to pay $210 million to compensate survivors and family members of the dead, institute safety measures, and pay outstanding fines (Yost, 2010; Reuters, 2011). Don Blankenship, the former CEO, was indicted by a federal grand jury in West Virginia for a number of charges related to lying to federal investigators, ignoring safety violations, and conspiring to cover up conditions from federal inspectors (Sullivan, 2014). The outcome of that case will be interesting to follow considering past history. Sheperd (2013) found a clear relationship between contributions and judicial decisions. The more campaign contributions from business interests justices receive, the more likely they were to vote for business litigants. The relationship held only for partisan and nonpartisan election systems. There was no statistically significant relationship between contributions and decisions in retention election systems. The study also discovered that the relationship was stronger in the period 2010–2012 compared to 1995–1998 (Shepherd, 2013).

The study described above was concerned with civil business-related judicial decision making not criminal law; however, the same concerns would apply. Corporations are sometimes the subject of criminal investigations, and business executives sometimes find themselves the target of criminal investigation and prosecution. Even in local races, bias is introduced when local attorneys are the largest donors to judicial campaigns. The question as to whether judges are influenced by campaign contributions seems to have been answered, the only remaining question is to what extent in each case.

Culture and Ethics

The Model Code of Professional Responsibility dictated that lawyers should be "temperate and dignified" and "refrain from all illegal and morally reprehensible conduct." The Model Rules require that "a lawyer's conduct should conform to the requirements of the law, both in professional service to clients and in the lawyer's business and personal affairs." These prescriptions are similar to those found in the Law Enforcement Code of Ethics. Both groups of professionals are expected to uphold a higher standard of behavior than the general public. These professionals have chosen to work within the legal system and help to enforce the law; thus, it is not unreasonable, perhaps, to expect that they provide a model of behavior for the rest of us. However, similar to our discussion of law enforcement officials, it seems to be true that the real world of lawyers is sometimes quite different from the vaunted ideals of the Model Rules.

Law schools have been criticized for being singularly uninterested in fostering any type of moral conscience in students. Law schools purport to be in the practice of reshaping law students so that when they emerge "thinking like a lawyer," they have mastered a type of thinking that is concerned with detail and logical analysis. Others argue this is done at the expense of being sensitive to morality and larger social issues (Spence, 1989; Stover, 1989).

Patrick Fitzgerald (2009), a well-known and highly respected U.S. attorney (federal prosecutor), in an essay concerning ethics in the prosecutor's office, identified office culture as an important component to ensure that prosecutors acted ethically. He also identified a "good" office as one that hires not just smart people, but individuals who express values conducive to public service and integrity. It seems to be probable that just as police departments each have their own culture that supports or discourages ethical decision making, prosecutors' offices also have different cultures.

In a highly critical overview of the legal profession, Glendon (1994) proposed that the legal profession has changed in dramatic ways, not all of which have been for the better. Although the practice of law was once governed by rules of ethics and etiquette, and lawyers acted like gentlemen (literally, because the profession was for the most part closed to women, minorities, and the lower class), since the 1950s, it has become increasingly open to those excluded groups. Although the inclusion of these groups is a step forward, at the same time, law practice has become less of a "gentlemen's club," where the majority followed written and unwritten rules of conduct, and more of a world of "no rules" or, more accurately, only one rule: "Winning is everything."

The other major theme in the culture of the criminal justice legal world is that described above in the bureaucratic justice system. There is a pervasive sense that all defendants are guilty and this attitude leads to cynicism and unethical behaviors on

WALKING THE WALK

Charles Swift is from a small town in North Carolina. He is an unlikely hero. He entered the United States Naval Academy in 1980 and graduated with undistinguished marks after having second chances after several close calls of being dismissed. He served seven years as a surface-warfare officer and then decided to go to law school. He graduated from Seattle University School of Law in 1994 and returned to active duty as a member of the Judge Advocate General's Corps (JAG). In March 2003, he was assigned to the defense counsel's team for the Office of Military Commissions, set up to provide a unique form of due process for Guantanamo detainees. Lt. Commander Swift was assigned to defend Salim Ahmed Hamdan, a Yemeni who at one time had been Osama bin Laden's driver.

One of the first things Swift was told in the case was that he could have access to his client only on the condition that he attempt to negotiate a guilty plea from him. When Swift decided that it was clear that there was no real due process in the so-called military commissions process, as it did not follow the Uniform Code of Military Justice, the Geneva Conventions, or any rule of law recognized in 250 years of U. S. jurisprudence, he sued his chain of command, including the commander in chief, President George W. Bush. Swift says:

> [In most countries] . . . when a military officer openly opposes the president, it is called a coup. In the United States, it is called *Hamdan v. Rumsfeld*. After the Supreme Court's decision . . ., the world was rightly in awe of our system. . . . [W]e proved once again that we are a nation of laws and not of men.

Hamdan's defense team eventually included Swift, Neal Katyal, a law professor who volunteered his services, and a private law firm in Seattle (chosen because that was the federal jurisdiction required). The exhaustive and fearless defense of Hamdan, a defense that basically challenged the military commissions as constructed by the Bush administration, resulted in the Supreme Court ruling 5–3 that the president had exceeded his power in ignoring the Geneva Conventions, the Uniform Code of Military Justice, and Congress in creating the tribunals. In an irony that was not lost on any observer, Swift was passed over for promotion and was forced to retire from the navy shortly after the Supreme Court decision was handed down. His superiors said they had submitted exemplary reports on his performance, but that promotions are granted for "breadth," not just "depth," and therefore, even though he obviously deserved excellent marks as a lawyer, he would not be rewarded with a promotion.

Because of the navy's up-or-out promotional policies, Swift had to leave the navy at the age of 44 and was not around for further developments, such as the Military Commissions Act of 2006, when Congress put the military commissions back in play by providing the legal imprimatur for them. In June 2007, the Supreme Court refused to hear two court challenges to the congressional act's military commissions but then reversed its decision and heard *Boumediene v. Bush* (553 U. S. 723, 2008). Their final ruling was that the military commissions, without any *habeas corpus* protection, did not meet minimum due process requirements and were therefore unconstitutional. Since then, however, President Obama oversaw changes to the military commissions that remedied the due process concerns of the Court. Hamdan was eventually convicted of only material support, not the more serious charges and, because of time served, spent only five more months in Guantanamo after the final verdict, before being released to his native Yemen.

Would Swift do it differently if he had it to do over? He says, "If we are to be a great nation, then we must be willing to be a nation bound by the rule of law in our treatment of all people."

Sources: Swift, 2007; Shukovsky, 2006; Mahler, 2009.

the part of both prosecutors and defense attorneys. Defense attorneys are the most important actors in preventing miscarriages of justice, yet there is pressure to cooperate with the "system" of moving individuals through rapidly and efficiently. The defense attorney may also believe in the guilt of the accused, so personal belief systems may also encourage shortcuts and less than zealous defense. In the Walking the Walk selection for this chapter, Charles Swift's commitment to the law changed his career.

Conclusion

In this chapter, we have explored the role and justification for law, and also how our paradigms affect how we see it function in society. While some view law as enforcing the will of the majority, others see law as a tool of oppression by those in power. The justification for law is primarily prevention of harm, including paternalistic laws that seek to protect individuals from themselves, and laws that enforce society's morals. The attorney and judge are the human embodiments of the law. They create the reality of how law operates. Rules defining ethical conduct for legal professionals come from their state bar, but the ABA has promulgated Model Rules that most state bar associations either adopt completely or adapt. Similar to our discussion concerning law enforcement professionals' noble-cause corruption, we note that there is a subculture of winning that competes with, and sometimes eclipses, the ethical standards that attorneys learn in law school. Also, the justice system has a pervasive culture that induces cynicism in those who are a part of it, with an attendant belief system that all defendants are guilty.

Chapter Review

1. **Understand the justifications for law, including protections against harm to others, offensive conduct, harm to self, and harm to societal morals.**

   The primary justification for law is the social contract—we each give up the right to do whatever we want in return for protection. John Stuart Mill advocated the "harm principle," which justified laws only when they prevented harm (i.e., assault, murder). Other justifications include preventing offensive conduct (i.e., lewd behavior, public disturbance). Another justification is to prevent harm to self. Legal paternalism refers to laws in which the state tries to protect people from their own behavior (i.e., seat belt laws, motorcycle helmet laws). Finally, laws prevent harm to societal morals (legal moralism), but these laws are often controversial because we don't all agree on right and wrong behaviors (i.e., pornography, gambling).

2. **Explain the role of law in society and the paradigms that have developed to understand how law is formed and enforced.**

   Basically, paradigms are models of how ideas relate to one another, forming a conceptual model of the world around us. In the consensus paradigm, law is seen as enforcing the will of the majority, and most people agree on what should be illegal. In the conflict paradigm, law is seen as a tool of the power holders to control the powerless. In the pluralist paradigm, law is seen as dynamic and changeable depending on coalitions of various interest groups.

3. **Compare the idea of our criminal law system as an adversarial system to other descriptions of how the courtroom works and the relationships between the legal professionals.**

   The ideal of the justice system is that two advocates of equal ability will engage in a pursuit of truth, guided by a neutral judge. The truth is supposed to emerge from the contest. The system has also been described as a "confidence game" where the prosecutor and the defense attorney conspire to appear as adversaries when, in fact, they will still be working together when the client is gone. Another view is that of bureaucratic justice, where the goal is efficiency, not truth or justice. One other view is that of a wedding-cake model, in which a few celebrated cases receive the vast majority of attention and resources, a middle group of cases receive a moderate amount of resources, but the vast majority of cases are processed through the system with minimal energy and minimal due process.

4. **Present the controversy concerning the role of advocate as legal agent or moral agent.**

   The legal agent is a position where the attorney is no more than the legal tool of the client and does his or her bidding as long as it is not illegal. The moral agent approach is that the lawyer has to adhere to his or her own moral code. The client's interests come first only as long as they do not conflict with the lawyer's morality and ethical code. A third position is that of a "special relationship" where the attorney attempts to convince the client to do what is right, but the position is not clear on what the course of action would be if the client refuses.

5. **Describe the history and source of legal ethics for attorneys and judges. Explain the types of ethical rules that exist and compare them to the subculture of winning.**

   The Model Code of Professional Responsibility was adapted from the Alabama Bar Association Code of 1887 and adopted by the American Bar Association in 1908. In 1983, the ABA switched its endorsement of the Model Code as the general guide for ethical behavior to the Model Rules of Professional Conduct. The Model Code of Judicial Conduct was adopted by the American Bar Association in 2007 to provide ethical standards for judges. Each state, however, must have its own model rules or ethical code to use as a vehicle of discipline. The ethical code has the force of law in each state, and lawyers may face a range of sanctions up to disbarment for violating the rules. On the other hand, disciplinary proceedings are fairly rare, and there is a subculture in the law that promotes putting the client's interests ahead of everything, and winning is valued over all else. This leads to the possibility of behavior that violates the formal Model Rules.

Study Questions

1. List some laws justified by legal paternalism. Provide the rationale for such laws, as well as opposing arguments. Discuss some types of laws that are justified by legal moralism. What are the major arguments for and against such laws?

2. Discuss how pluralism differs from the conflict paradigm and provide examples to support the view.

3. Describe in detail the evidence for and against the bureaucratic justice model of the system.

4. Describe the recent additions to Rule 3.8 for prosecutors and why they were adopted.

5. Provide some examples of the types of issues covered in Chapter 3 (for prosecutors) and Chapter 4 (for defense attorneys) of the *ABA Criminal Justice Standards*.

Writing/Discussion Exercises

1. Write an essay on (or discuss) how the conflict and consensus paradigms would interpret the following: decriminalization of marijuana for medical purposes, stem cell research, passage of hate-crime legislation, prohibiting the use of race in admissions procedures in universities and in competitions for state scholarships, and laws prohibiting racial profiling in police stops.

2. Write an essay on (or discuss) the legitimate functions of law in society. Do you agree with laws that prohibit gambling? Drinking while driving? Underage drinking? Prostitution? Liquor violations? Drugs? Helmet laws for bicycles or

motorcycles? Leash laws? Seat belts? Smoking in public places? Can you think of any paternalistic laws not mentioned above? Analyze pornography, gambling, homosexuality, and drug use under the ethical systems discussed in Chapter 2. What other laws have limited Americans' (or certain groups') freedoms? Can they be justified under any ethical rationale?

3. Write an essay on (or discuss) whether or not the justice system is simply a bureaucratic assembly line that does not promote justice as much as it simply ensures its own survival, with an emphasis on production. What should be the professional goals of the various actors in the system (judges, prosecutors, defense attorneys)?

Key Terms

bureaucratic justice
conflict paradigm
consensus paradigm
Good Samaritan laws

laws
legal moralism
legal paternalism
natural law

pluralist paradigm
positivist law
wedding-cake illustration

ETHICAL DILEMMAS

Situation 1
You ride a motorcycle, and you think it is much more enjoyable to ride without a helmet. You also believe that your vision and hearing are better without a helmet. Your state has just passed a helmet law, and you have already received two warnings. What will you do? What if your child were riding on the motorcycle? Do you think your position would be any different if you had any previous accidents and had been hurt?

Situation 2
You are a legislator who believes absolutely and strongly that abortion is a sin. You have polled your constituents and are surprised to find that the majority do not believe that the government should legislate the private decision of a woman to have an abortion. Should you vote your conscience or the will of the majority of your constituents?

Situation 3
You are a district attorney prosecuting a burglary case. The defendant is willing to plead guilty in return for a sentence of probation, and you believe that this is a fair punishment because your evidence may not support a conviction. However, the victims are upset and want to see the offender receive prison time. They insist that you try the case. What should you do?

Situation 4
You are a prosecutor with the unwelcome task of prosecuting a 12-year-old for a particularly brutal assault. You personally believe that the child basically went along with his older brother in the assault, and you think that he should have been left in the juvenile system. However, the juvenile court judge waived him to the adult system, and the media and the victim's family are demanding that he be tried as an adult. You have to decide whether to try him for attempted murder, assault, or some lesser crime. You

could deny the waiver and send the case back to juvenile court. What will you do? How do you determine your duty? Is it to the victims, to society, or to your own conscience?

Situation 5

You are a judge who believes that individuals should be allowed to choose when to die. You personally had to watch both your parents die long and agonizing deaths because your state does not have a right-to-die statute. Before you is a doctor who is being prosecuted for giving a lethal dose of morphine to a patient dying of terminal cancer. The family of the patient did not want the prosecution, the majority of the public is not in favor of the prosecution, but the prosecutor believes that if there is a law in place, it should be enforced. The doctor has opted for a bench trial. What would you do?

Discretion and Dilemmas in the Legal Profession

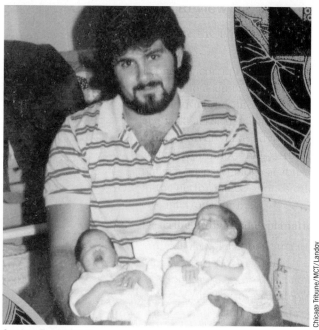

Cameron Todd Willingham.

Chapter Objectives

1. Describe the ethical issues faced by defense attorneys.
2. Describe the ethical issues faced by prosecutors.
3. Describe some of the areas of forensic science that have been challenged by opponents.
4. Describe the ethical issues faced by judges.
5. Describe how federal sentencing guidelines have changed due to Supreme Court decisions.

Cameron Todd Willingham was not someone who was ever going to be very successful in life. Raised in foster care, he drank and smoked too much, used drugs more than occasionally, and never had much of a plan about how to get ahead. Still, most people said he was a fairly decent father to his three daughters. Living with his wife in Corsicana, Texas, in 1991, the 23-year-old struggled to make ends meet. On the morning of December 23, his wife left the house to go buy Christmas presents. Describing the events later, he said he was sleeping when his 2-year-old daughter woke him up and said the house was on fire. Willingham said he told her to leave the house and he tried to get to his 1-year-old twins, but couldn't find them in the smoke and the fire forced him to run outside. All three children died in the fire. Neighbors reported that he was extremely distraught, and firemen had to hold him back from trying to break through the window and crawl into the house even though it was fully engulfed by that time. However, later, when investigators began to focus on Willingham himself as a suspect of arson, they also remembered that he wanted to move his car from the driveway, which they thought was strange for a distraught father.

Willingham was arrested for arson, and the prosecutor sought and obtained the death penalty because of the tragic deaths of the three little girls. The case theory was that Willingham was tired of the responsibilities of fatherhood and was a sociopath who was acting when he appeared to be trying to rescue his girls. The main evidence came from two senior fire investigators who testified that the fire was definitely arson. They reported that they discovered pour marks indicating an accelerant, and the heat of the fire, as measured by the spidery cracks in the glass, could only be from a fuel source. Further, they found a pour mark immediately outside the front door, indicating that he had poured an accelerant there to block escape.

Willingham steadfastly maintained his innocence and would accept no plea deal. His wife remained convinced of his innocence through the first trial and first appeal, but eventually stated that he told her he had killed their daughters (Willingham denied that he did). Dr. Gerald Hurst, who was asked to review the case file, immediately found statements from the fire investigator that had no basis in fact and had been discounted in the early 1990s when Willingham was on trial. A well-respected scientist, Hurst had conducted experiments in other arson cases that proved that "flashovers" can cause scorch patterns that look like pour marks. He discovered that the positive trace of mineral spirits at the front door was probably due to a small grill and bottle of lighter fluid that had been on the front porch, seen in a photograph from the first pictures taken of the fire, but removed in the cleanup. Hurst had been instrumental in freeing Ernest Willis, who had also been on death row in Texas for a fire that killed his children, but had been exonerated by Hurst's evidence that the fire was not arson.

The report Hurst wrote detailing his findings was finished quickly because Willingham's execution date was rapidly approaching. The Texas Board of Pardons and Paroles reviews death sentences and can recommend clemency to the governor. They had Hurst's report indicating that the most likely explanation was that the fire was set by candles or a space heater in the girls' room. It is unknown how much weight was placed on the report by the board, or if they read it at all, because they did not recommend the execution be stayed. In the state of Texas, the final decision is up to the governor, and Governor Rick Perry ordered that the execution proceed. Cameron Todd Willingham was executed on February 17, 2004 (Mills, 2005).

In 2005, Texas established a commission to investigate cases where forensic science used in criminal prosecutions might have been faulty. One of the first cases reviewed by the Texas Forensic Science Commission was the Willingham case. A fire scientist, Craig Beyler, completed his investigation in 2009 and issued a scathing report concluding that the arson investigators' testimony had no basis in fact and they should have known it at the time. Before the commission had a chance to hear the testimony of Dr. Beyler, Governor Rick Perry dismissed the chairman and another member and reorganized the board under the chairmanship of John Bradley, a "law-and-order district attorney" from Williamson County (subsequently in the news for being the prosecutor who fought DNA testing in the Michael Morton case). Bradley canceled the meeting. Finally, in the summer of 2010, the group issued a preliminary finding that the state deputy fire marshal and assistant fire chief based their testimony on flawed science, but they also found that the men were not negligent or guilty of misconduct in any way (Lindell and Embrey, 2009; Lindell, 2009; Turner, 2010). The final report had nothing to say about Willingham's guilt or innocence, just that flawed science was used as evidence.

(¡¡) IN THE NEWS | *Justice Delayed, Justice Denied*

In February 2009, Charles Baird, a criminal district court judge in Austin, Texas, ruled that Timothy Cole, a military veteran and Texas Tech student, was innocent and wrongfully convicted of the 1986 rape of a fellow student. Nine years earlier, 39-year-old Cole had died of asthma in prison. He had served 14 years of a 25 year sentence. DNA evidence was matched to the real killer, who also had written letters to prosecutors about a decade earlier confessing to the crime and explaining that Cole was innocent. Judge Baird filed an order to have the conviction expunged. Governor Rick Perry also issued a posthumous pardon for Cole. Cole had always maintained his innocence and his family had fought for years to clear his name. In 2013 a 14-foot statue of Cole was placed in Lubbock with the words "Lest we forget . . ." near the site of the rape. In 2009, Perry signed the Tim Cole Act into law. It increased compensatory payments to those imprisoned wrongfully to $80,000 a year. The Timothy Cole Advisory Panel on Wrongful Convictions was also created to study ways to prevent wrongful convictions.

Source: www.star-telegram.com/news/local/community/fort-worth/article3873738.html

Charles Baird, a district judge in Austin, opened an unusual inquiry as to whether or not Willingham was wrongfully executed, but the original prosecutor filed a motion for him to recuse himself as biased since he had been on the court of appeals when they refused to hear Willingham's appeal and Baird's public comments indicated he was not neutral. Baird eventually issued a finding that Willingham was innocent and then was rebuked by the state appellate court for exceeding his authority. The In the News box describes a similar inquiry by Baird.

In Chapter 6, we described ethical dilemmas for police officers as inevitable because of the discretion inherent in the role. The same is true of legal professionals. Although the roles and duties of a defense attorney, prosecutor, and judge are very different, what they do have in common is a great deal of discretion. Similar to all other criminal justice professionals, the power of discretion inherent in each of these roles affects individuals' lives in dramatic ways. As the Willingham case illustrates, it is entirely possible that the actions of the defense attorneys, prosecutors, and judges in a criminal case can set in motion events that can take the life of an innocent man.

Ethical Issues for Defense Attorneys

Due process, including notice, neutral fact finders, cross-examination, and presentation of evidence and witnesses, is supposed to minimize mistakes in judicial proceedings that might result in the deprivation of life, liberty, or property. The defense attorney is there during the important steps of the process to ensure that these rights are protected. For instance, defense attorneys present during interrogation can make sure no coercion is used, at lineup they make sure it is fair and unbiased, and during trial they ensure adequate cross-examination and presentation of evidence. This pure role of advocate is contradictory to the reality that the defense attorney must, if he or she is to work with the other actors in the court system, accommodate their needs as well as those of clients.

Many defense attorneys in private practice started out as prosecutors. This sometimes causes problems when they have trouble making the transition from "good guy battling evil" to the more subtle role of defender of due process. If the attorney cannot make the transition from prosecution to defense and feel comfortable in the role, it is difficult to offer a zealous defense (R. Cohen, 2001). Some argue that the system tends to operate under a presumption of guilt. Indeed, defense attorneys are often in the position of defending clients they know are guilty. The rationale for defending a guilty person is that everyone deserves due process before a finding of guilt and punishment. If defense attorneys are doing their job, we can be more confident that justice has been served. If they are not doing their job, we have no system of justice, and none of us is safe from wrongful prosecution and the awesome power of the state to investigate, prosecute, and punish. In the Quote and Query box, one lawyer decided that justice demanded that he subvert the role of the defense attorney. What is the attorney's responsibility to the client when he or she knows the client is guilty of a horrible crime?

QUOTE & QUERY

"I decided that Mr. Tucker deserved to die, and I would not do anything to prevent his execution." This statement was made by defense attorney David Smith of Greensboro, North Carolina, who accepted a capital appeal case and then admitted that he "sabotaged" the appeal of his client because he believed the man deserved execution. The attorney went through a moral crisis afterward and confessed to the state bar what he did.

Source: Rimer, 2000.

 Would you be able to defend a clearly guilty defendant? Why or why not?

Responsibility to the Client

[A defense attorney's duty is] to serve as the accused's counselor and advocate with courage and devotion (Standard 4-1.2[b]).

The *ABA Criminal Justice Standards*, 4th edition (ABA, 2015b), will be used to highlight selected ethical issues for defense attorneys and prosecutors. In the first standard we will discuss, defense attorneys are exhorted to serve as counselor and advocate; however, they are always in the position of balancing the rights of the individual client against their overall effectiveness for all their clients. Extreme attempts to protect the rights of one person will reduce the defense attorney's ability to advocate effectively for other clients. Furthermore, defense attorneys must balance the needs and problems of the client against their ethical responsibilities to the system and the profession.

A lawyer is supposed to provide legal assistance to clients without regard for personal preference or interest. Once he or she takes a case, a lawyer is not allowed to withdraw except:

- If the legal action is for harassment or malicious purposes
- If continued employment will result in violation of a disciplinary rule
- If discharged by a client, or
- If a mental or physical condition renders effective counsel impossible

In other cases, a judge *may* grant permission to withdraw when the client insists on illegal or unethical actions, is uncooperative and does not follow the attorney's advice, or otherwise makes effective counsel difficult. In general, judges are loath to allow a defendant to proceed with a *pro se* defense (defending oneself) because of the risk that the conviction will be overturned on appeal. Nor are judges likely to allow withdrawal if it will delay ongoing proceedings. Legal ethics mandate that people with unpopular causes and individuals who are obviously guilty still deserve counsel and that it is the ethical duty of an attorney to provide such counsel.

Indigent Defense

Many people are firmly convinced that the quality of legal representation is directly related to how much money the defendant can pay. The Sixth Amendment guarantees that indigent (poor) criminal defendants receive legal representation. Funded either by the state or county (or federal government for federal defendants), jurisdictions use either public defender offices or court appointed attorneys (private attorneys who receive individual cases from the court and also maintain their own private practice), or a combination of the two. About 22 states administer and fund at the state level; 18 rely primarily on county funding; the remaining states have some hybrid system (Mariano, 2015).

Research, unfortunately, supports the proposition that those who can afford private retained attorneys receive "better" representation as measured by conviction and length of sentence (Martinez and Pollock, 2008). It appears that court appointed attorneys may be the worst option. A Harvard study found, in reviewing federal criminal cases between 1997 and 2001, that lawyers who were appointed to represent indigent clients were less qualified than federal public defenders, took longer to resolve cases, with worse results for clients, including sentences that were, on average, eight months longer. The private-appointed attorneys also cost the public $61 million more than the public defenders. Evidently, these findings were due to inexperience, as public defenders practiced federal criminal law full time. In the federal system, roughly three-fourths of all defendants are represented by publicly funded attorneys; about half are public defenders and the other half are appointed (Liptak, 2007). Another study found that about 29 percent of cases with private attorneys resulted in a prison sentence, 32 percent with a public defender did so, but 46 percent of cases with appointed counsel did, indicating that there was a lower standard of representation with appointed counsel. Interestingly there was little difference in the likelihood of pleading guilty (3 to 4 percent across all groups) (Cohen, 2011).

About 80 percent of all criminal defendants are indigent and require publicly funded defense. Studies have shown how chronically underfunded the system of indigent defense is in this country which may have something to do with the number of wrongful convictions (Lefstein, 2009). In one study of how states spent their Byrne Justice Assistant Grant funds from the Department of Justice, it was found that in fiscal year 2009, $20.8 million went toward prosecution, and only $3.1 million went to public defense. A total of $1.2 billion was allocated for all programs, meaning that the public defense allocation amounted to roughly one-quarter of 1 percent (Mariano, 2015).

In 2012, Eric Holder, the U.S. attorney general, announced that significant new resources would be directed to indigent aid. A number of private and public advocacy groups (Sixth Amendment Center, Brennan Center, The Constitution Project, the Gideon at 50 Project, the American Bar Association) have brought attention to the fact that indigent legal aid is so overburdened that representation likely falls below Constitutional requirements. Studies show that standards for defense indicate caseloads should be no more than 150 felonies per year, but in some jurisdictions, public defenders carry at least twice that number (Mariano, 2015).

In 2012, the American Bar Association's Standing Committee on Legal Aid and Indigent Defendants and the National Association of Criminal Defense Lawyers completed an examination of indigent defense and produced five core principles to improve indigent defense:

- Reclassify petty and nonviolent offenses to reduce "overcriminalization" that leads to unmanageable caseloads
- Ensure counsel is provided to defendants at all initial court appearances, particularly when it comes to decisions about bail, to cut down on cost of detaining, especially those charged with minor offenses
- Ensure access to *effective* counsel
- Consult with defense bars before new law enforcement initiatives are launched . . ., and
- Foster greater private–public involvement in indigent defense under a structured system (reported in Mariano, 2015).

The problem of indigent defense exists in immigration law as well. A study by Cardozo Law School's Immigration Justice Clinic has been released regarding adequacy of counsel for indigent defendants in immigration proceedings. The study found that 33 percent of cases in deportation hearings received inadequate legal assistance (Markowitz, 2011).

Eldren (2013) writes that cognitive biases operate to make public defenders (and logically court appointed lawyers as well) unaware that they provide a lower level of representation than indigent clients deserve. The argument is that with such high caseloads, attorneys are incapable of investigating, conducting legal research, and doing the proper amount of preparation for each case; psychological mechanisms exist to reduce stress, including confirmation bias, motivated reasoning, and overconfidence bias. Confirmation bias (similar to how it was described in Chapter 3 and 6) results in the brain remembering information that fits with preconceived ideas, therefore if a public defender remembers only the pieces of evidence that lead to a belief that the defendant is guilty, it becomes easier to cajole him or her into a plea agreement. Motivated reasoning occurs when defense attorneys have to "triage" cases (ignoring some or giving them the least possible amount of time in order to save time and energy for the "winnable" ones). There is an unconscious pressure to find reasons that it is acceptable to do so (e.g., "most defendants are guilty anyway"). Finally, there is a tendency of all of us to inflate our abilities and competence. Some argue that it is ethically acceptable to triage cases because plea agreements may actually be favorable to defendants (Carroll, 2015), which is true, but it also is the case that many are victim to an assembly line of justice with mere minutes spent with a defense attorney.

Observers also note that public defenders do not ordinarily complain about excessive caseloads because they do not want to antagonize their politician funders. Court appointed attorneys have an even greater motivation to keep quiet since, if they complain that they must take too many appointments to competently defend the clients in order to make it financially feasible, they would probably be told that other attorneys would be happy to take such appointments (Carroll, 2015).

Specialty Courts

A more recent issue has emerged with the rise of specialty courts, the most common being drug courts. In such courts, defense attorneys, prosecutors, and judges take on quite different roles from the more typical adversary approach in regular criminal courts. There is an emphasis placed on the actors as a team, and the judge plays a much more active role, interacting with the defendant and monitoring progress. In these courts, the defense attorney appears almost redundant since the court's goal is to do what is best for the client/defendant.

In fact, Meekins (2007) argues that defense attorneys face sensitive and serious ethical challenges in such courts because they should not forget that their primary responsibility is to the client, just as in a criminal trial, even if it means objecting to and arguing against treatment options. There is a tendency for defense attorneys in such courts to influence clients to accept treatment, even in post-adjudicative systems, where the client has to plead guilty in order to obtain treatment. Then the defense attorney faces issues involving communication with clients and confidentiality, because of the monitoring that such courts undertake while the client is in treatment and under supervision. Even though drug courts are set up to promote the best interest of the client, the defense attorney's role as advocate should not be sacrificed, and the individual lawyer should not forget his or her role in the desire for such courts to be successful.

Conflicts of Interest

> *Defense counsel should not permit their professional judgment . . . be adversely affected by loyalties or obligations to other . . . clients . . . or other interests or relationships (Standard 4-1.7[b]).*

This standard, along with Model Rules 1.7, 1.8, 1.10, and 1.11, covers conflicts of interest. Attorneys are supposed to avoid any conflicts of interest when defending clients. For instance, an attorney may not represent a client who owns a company that is a rival to one in which the attorney has an interest. The attorney also must not represent two clients who have opposing interests—for instance, codefendants in a criminal case—for one often will testify against the other. The attorney would find it impossible in such a situation to represent each individual fairly. Disciplinary rules even prohibit two lawyers in a single firm from representing clients with conflicting interests.

Although attorneys may not ethically accept clients with conflicting interests, there is no guidance on the more abstract problem that all criminal clients in a caseload have conflicting interests if their cases are looked upon as part of a workload rather than considered separately. Many defense attorneys make a living by taking cases from people with very modest means or taking court-appointed cases with the fee set by the court. The defense attorney then becomes a "fast-food lawyer," depending on volume and speed to make a profit. However, quality may get sacrificed along the way.

plea bargain
Exchange of a guilty plea for a reduced charge or sentence.

The vast majority of cases in the criminal justice system are settled by a **plea bargain**, an exchange of a guilty plea for a reduced charge or sentence. The defense attorney's goal in plea bargaining is to get the best possible deal for the client—probation or the shortest prison sentence that the prosecutor is willing to give for a guilty plea. The defense attorney is aware that he or she cannot aggressively push every case without endangering an ongoing relationship with the prosecutor. A courtroom appearance may be an isolated event for the client, but for the defense attorney and prosecutor it is an ongoing, weekly ritual; only the names of the defendants change. Because of the nature of the continuing relationship, the defense attorney must weigh each case against the continuing relationship with the prosecutor.

Another conflict of interest may arise if the attorney desires to represent the client's interests in selling literary or media rights. Standard 4-3.6 specifically forbids entering into such an agreement before the case is complete. The temptations are obvious: If the attorney hopes to acquire financial rewards from a share of profits, his or her professional judgment on how best to defend the client may be clouded. It is debatable whether putting off signing such an agreement until the case is complete removes the possibility of unethical decisions. The potential for biased judgments is obvious. For instance, if an attorney has a client who has committed a particularly spectacular crime, there is the potential for celebrity status only if the case comes to trial, so a plea bargain—even if it is in the best interest of the client—may be considered less carefully by the attorney. Today, it seems as if criminal cases have become the new soap operas with 24-hour news coverage and endless analysis (consider the Casey Anthony or Jodi Arias case, for example). In these cases, there is a tornado of media coverage and lawyers may be influenced by the celebrity that comes with being in the center of the storm.

Zealous Defense

> *. . . Defense counsel should act zealously within the bounds of the law and . . . . may not, execute any directive of the client which violates the law . . . . (Standard 4-1.2[d]).*

Few would challenge the idea that all people deserve to have their due process rights protected. However, what many people find unsettling is the zeal with which some defense attorneys approach the courtroom contest. How diligent should the defense be in protecting the defendant's rights? A conflict may arise between providing an effective defense and maintaining professional ethics and individual morality. Lawyers should represent clients zealously within the bounds of the law, but the law is sometimes vague and difficult to determine.

Ethical standards and rules forbid some actions. The lawyer may not:

- Engage in motions or actions to intentionally and maliciously harm others
- Knowingly advance unwarranted claims or defenses
- Conceal or fail to disclose that which he or she is required by law to reveal
- Knowingly use perjured testimony or false evidence
- Knowingly make a false statement of law or fact
- Participate in the creation or preservation of evidence when he or she knows or it is obvious that the evidence is false
- Counsel the client in conduct that is illegal
- Engage in other illegal conduct

The attorney is also expected to maintain a professional and courteous relationship with the opposing attorneys, litigants, and witnesses and to refrain from disparaging statements or badgering conduct. The defense attorney must not intimidate or otherwise influence the jury or trier of fact or use the media for these same purposes.

Despite these ethical rules, practices such as withholding evidence, manufacturing evidence, witness badgering, and defamation of victims' characters are sometimes used as tactics in the defense arsenal. For instance, the practice of bringing out the sexual history of rape victims is done purely to paint her as a victim who deserved or asked for her rape. Even though rape-shield laws prohibit exposés of sexual history solely to discredit the reputation of the victim-witness, attorneys still attempt to bring in such evidence. Destroying the credibility of honest witnesses is considered good advocacy. For instance, if a witness accurately testifies to what he or she saw, a good attorney may still cast doubt in the jurors' minds by bringing out evidence of the use of eyeglasses, mistakes of judgment, and other facts that tend to obfuscate and undercut the credibility of the witness. Attorneys will do this even when they know that the witness is telling the truth. An ethical defense may include questioning the credibility of all prosecution witnesses, it is the zealousness by which it is done that defines the actions as ethical or unethical.

Most ethical conflicts arise over subtle questions of how far one should go to provide a zealous defense. It is sometimes difficult to determine when a defense attorney's treatment of a witness is badgering as opposed to energetic cross-examination, or when exploring a witness's background is character assassination as opposed to a careful examination of credibility. Some attorneys focus attacks on opposing counsel. For example, female attorneys have reported that opposing male attorneys attempt to infantilize, patronize, or sexualize them in front of the judge and jury, as a tactic to destroy their credibility. Young attorneys encounter condescending treatment by opposing counsel, with comments such as, "What my young colleague here has evidently not learned yet . . ." designed to persuade the jury that the older attorney is wiser, more honest, or more mature than the younger attorney. Whispering during opposing counsel's opening or closing, rolling one's eyes in response to a statement or question, or making other verbal or physical gestures indicating disbelief, amusement, or disdain are part of the arsenal of the trial attorney. They are considered by some to be fair and within the rules of the "game."

Jury Consultants

Attorneys often contend that a trial has already been won or lost once they have selected the jury. Whether or not this is true, attorneys are increasingly using psychologists and other experts to help them choose which members of a jury panel would make good jurors. A good juror for a defense attorney (or prosecutor) is not someone who is unbiased and fair, but rather, someone who is predisposed to be sympathetic to that attorney's case. Jury experts, through a combination of nonverbal and verbal clues, identify those jury panel members who are predisposed to believe the case presented by the attorney. Some allege that jury consultants can help to stack juries with the least sophisticated or most educated group, or any other type of group desired by the attorney.

Some lawyers survey a large sample of the population in the community where the case is to be tried to discover what certain demographic groups think about issues relevant to the case so these findings can be used when the jury is selected. Another method uses a **shadow jury**—a panel of people selected by the defense attorney to represent the actual jury. This shadow jury sits through the trial and provides feedback to the attorney on the evidence being presented during the trial. This allows the attorney to adjust his or her trial tactics in response.

shadow jury
A panel of people selected by the defense attorney to represent the actual jury; sits through the trial and provides feedback to the attorney on the evidence presented during the trial.

Attorneys have always used intuition and less sophisticated means to decide which jury members to exclude, but the more modern tactics are questioned by some as too contrary to the basic idea that a trial is supposed to start with an unbiased jury (Smith and Meyer, 1987). Consultants also provide services such as

- Preparing witnesses
- Assisting with mock trials
- Developing desirable juror profiles
- Conducting phone surveys on public attitudes about a case
- Analyzing shadow juries
- Giving advice on effective posture, clothing choice, and tone of voice

Can our ethical systems help determine what actions are ethically justified in defending a client zealously? Utilitarianism and egoism would probably allow a wider range of actions, depending on the particular interests or rewards represented by the case. Ethical formalism and religion might restrict the actions of a defense attorney to those allowed by a strict interpretation of the Model Rules. Ethics of care seems inconsistent with the advocacy role of the defense attorney since his or her role is to pursue the best interests of the client, which may come at the expense of others; however, ethics of care is consistent with specialty courts and restorative justice programs. In these situations, a defense attorney may ethically consider the needs of all concerned in arriving at a resolution.

Confidentiality

[Defense counsel has] a duty of confidentiality regarding information relevant to the client's representation . . . (Standard 4-1.3[a]).

The **attorney–client privilege** refers to the inability of authorities to compel an attorney (through subpoena or threat of contempt) to disclose confidential information regarding his or her client. The ethical duty of confidentiality prohibits an attorney from disclosing to any person, or using for one's own gain, information about one's client obtained through the attorney–client relationship. Any attorney who breaches confidentiality may face disbarment.

Confidentiality is inherent in the fiduciary relationship between the client and the attorney, but more important is that the client must be able to expect and receive the full and complete assistance of his or her lawyer. If a client feels compelled to withhold negative and incriminatory information, he or she will not be able to receive the best defense; thus, the lawyer must be perceived as a completely confidential agent of the client. Parallels to the attorney–client relationship are relationships between husband and wife and between priest and penitent. In these cases, the relationship creates a legal entity that approximates a single interest rather than two interests, so a break in confidentiality would violate the Fifth Amendment protection against self-incrimination (Schoeman, 1982: 260).

attorney–client privilege The legal rule by which an attorney cannot disclose confidential information regarding his or her client except in a very few specified circumstances.

According to Model Rule 1.6, the only situations wherein a lawyer can ethically reveal confidences of a client are these:

- When the client consents
- When disclosure is required by law or court order
- When one needs to defend oneself or employees against an accusation of wrongful conduct
- To prevent reasonably certain death or substantial bodily harm
- To prevent the client from committing a crime or fraud that is reasonably certain to result in substantial injury to the financial interests or property of another and the lawyer's services have been used to accomplish that end
- To prevent, mitigate, or rectify substantial injury to the financial interest or property of another that is reasonably certain to result or has resulted from the client's commission of a crime or fraud when the lawyer's services have been used

One of the most debated portions has been the part of this rule that specifies what type of crime justifies divulging the confidences of a client. The Model Code (used before the Model Rules) allowed disclosure to prevent *any* crime. An earlier version of the Model Rules dictated that an attorney could ethically violate a client's confidence only to prevent a future crime involving imminent death or grievous bodily harm. Many state bar associations refused to adopt the restrictive rule or enlarged it to include any crime. The current version requires disclosure of financial crimes if there is substantial injury, but it also allows disclosure to mitigate or rectify a financial crime. The Enron and WorldCom situations, in which CEOs defrauded shareholders while their accountants and lawyers remained quiet, no doubt influenced the committee that updated this rule (Ariens, 2009).

Neither the restrictive rule nor the inclusive rule regarding disclosing a client's future crime applied to the Garrow incident (described in the Walking the Walk box), so the lawyers felt ethically bound to withhold the location of two bodies from the family of the victims. Do the ethical systems support keeping the client's confidences in a situation such as the one faced by Frank Armani when defending Robert Garrow?

It should be noted that the rule of confidentiality does not apply to physical evidence. Anything that is discoverable in the possession of a client is equally discoverable if in the possession of an attorney. Therefore, an attorney must hand over files or other incriminating evidence subject to a valid search warrant, motion, or subpoena. If the attorney is merely told where physical items may be found, he or she is not obliged to tell the authorities where they are. For instance, if a client tells an attorney that a murder weapon is in a certain location, the attorney cannot divulge that information to authorities. However, if the client drops a murder weapon in the attorney's lap, the lawyer runs the risk of being charged with a felony if it is hidden or withheld from the police. If the attorney is told where a murder weapon is and goes to check, that information is still protected; however, if the attorney takes the weapon back to his or her office or moves it in any way, then the attorney may be subjected to felony charges of obstruction of justice or evidence tampering. Belge was charged in the Garrow case because he moved the body, although he was never convicted.

The confidentiality rule seems to be justified by utilitarianism because society benefits in the long run from the presence of attorney–client confidence. Therefore,

WALKING THE WALK

Frank Armani may be one of the most revered, and also hated, lawyers in the past century. In 1973, Armani was asked to represent Robert Garrow, accused of murder and attempted murder. Garrow, who had already served eight years in prison for rape, was identified as the man who tied up four college students and brutally stabbed one to death, although luckily the other three got away. Because of the similarity of the attacks, Garrow was also suspected of being responsible for another murder of a young man. The man's companion was missing, and authorities were desperate to either find her alive or find her body. One other young woman was also missing, and Garrow was suspected of being responsible for her disappearance as well.

Armani took the case because he had previously represented Garrow on a minor charge. Armani brought in Francis Belge, a criminal defense attorney. During their questioning of Garrow, he confessed to the murders of the two missing women and told the lawyers where the bodies were hidden. The two lawyers confirmed that the bodies were where Garrow said they were, and they even took pictures. In one location, the girl's head was 10 feet away from her torso, and Belge moved the head closer to the body before he took the picture. In the other case, the body was in an abandoned mine shaft, and the lawyers lowered each other down to take pictures.

The lawyers believed that attorney–client confidentiality prevented them from revealing the location of the bodies or even that Garrow had confessed to being involved. They did, however, imply to the district attorney that Garrow might reveal the location in a plea agreement. They were trying to get the prosecutor to agree to an insanity plea with commitment to a mental hospital. The prosecutor refused the deal, and before the case could come to trial for the first murder, the two girls' bodies were found. Garrow was the prime suspect.

In the small town where the trial was held, the two attorneys were shunned, vilified, and threatened. Both of the missing girls' families had pleaded with the attorneys to tell them if their daughters were alive or dead, and the families had no doubt that the attorneys knew more than they would reveal. Their suspicions became clear because after Garrow was convicted, Armani and Belge admitted in a press interview that they had known about the bodies all along.

The enraged prosecutor charged Belge with the crime of "failure to give a proper burial" and threatened both with obstruction of justice. The criminal charges were dropped, as were the state ethics charges, but both attorneys endured threats and the virtual loss of their law practices. One newspaper editorial at the time called Armani "a malignant cancer on the society that fostered him" and "less than useless to the human race." Belge left the practice of law entirely, and Armani was forced to build up his practice again after most of his clients left him. His marriage almost failed, and he flirted with alcoholism and suffered two heart attacks during the long ordeal.

When asked why he kept the murderer's secrets, Armani explained that civil rights are for the worst of us because, only then, are they there for the best of us. Eventually he was recognized for his ethical courage, but many still disagree on his stand that the client's confidentiality rights are more important than "common decency." One thing that no one can dispute, however, is that he paid a high price for his ethical principles.

Sources: Zitrin and Langford, 1999; Hansen, 2007: 28–29.

this confidence should be sacrificed only when it endangers a life, which would be a greater loss than the benefit of client–attorney trust (Harris, 1986). Religious ethics might condemn the attorney's actions because withholding information—for instance, the location of the bodies in the Garrow case described in the Walking the Walk box—was a form of deception. In the Roman Catholic religion, however, a similar ethical dilemma might arise if someone were to confess to a priest. In that case, the priest could not betray that confession no matter what the circumstances.

Under ethical formalism, the lawyer's actions must be such that we would be willing for all others to engage in similar behavior under like circumstances. Could one will that it become universal law for attorneys to keep such information secret? What if you were the parents in the Garrow case who did not know the whereabouts of their daughter, or even if she was alive or dead? It is hard to imagine that you would be willing to agree with this universal law. If you were the criminal, however, you would not want a lawyer to betray confidences that would hurt your case. If you were a lawyer, you would want a rule encouraging a client to be truthful so you would be able to provide an adequate defense. Ethical formalism is also concerned with duty; it is obvious that the duty of an attorney is always to protect the interests of his or her client. However, there are also larger duties of every attorney to protect the integrity of the justice system.

The ethics of care would be concerned with the needs of both the client and the parents in the Garrow case. This ethical system might support a resolution in a less absolutist fashion than the other rationales. For instance, when discussing the Garrow case in a college classroom, many students immediately decide that they would call in the location of the bodies anonymously, thereby relieving the parents' anxiety and also protecting, to some extent, the confidential communication. One could make the same type of phone call in the case of the wrongfully convicted, if an attorney had evidence that could help the person prove his or her innocence. However, this compromise is unsupported by an absolute view of confidentiality because it endangers the client, but it does protect the relationship of the attorney and the client and still meets the needs of others concerned.

While the attorney–client privilege is sacrosanct, some argue that there should be some exceptions when keeping quiet harms third parties. It is quite troubling, for instance, to ponder how many people are in prison for crimes they did not commit and somewhere an attorney for the real criminal knows, but cannot do anything about it.

Duty Regarding Perjury

Defense counsel should not knowingly offer false evidence . . . (Standard 4-7.6[b])

A defense attorney's ethics may also be compromised when a client insists on taking the stand to commit perjury. Model Rule 3.3 specifically forbids the lawyer from allowing perjury to take place; if it happens before the attorney realizes the intent of the client, the defense must not use or refer to the perjured testimony (Freedman, 1986; Kleinig, 1986). The quandary is that if the attorney shows his or her disbelief or discredits the client, this behavior violates the ethical mandate of a zealous defense, and to inform the court of the perjury violates the ethical rule of confidentiality.

Pellicotti (1990) explains that an attorney should first try to dissuade the client from committing perjury. If the client persists in plans to lie, the attorney then has an ethical duty to withdraw from the case, and there is some authority that the attorney should disclose the client's plan to the court. Withdrawal is problematic because it will usually jeopardize a case, and disclosure is even more problematic because, arguably, it will affect the judgment of the hearing judge.

In *Nix v. Whiteside* (475 U.S. 157, 1986), the Supreme Court held that it did not violate the defendant's Sixth Amendment right to counsel for the attorney to refuse to help the defendant commit perjury. In this murder case, the defendant told his lawyer that he had not seen a gun in the victim's hand. At a later point, he told his attorney that if he didn't testify that he saw a gun, he would be "dead" (lose the case). The attorney told him that if he were to testify falsely, he would have to impeach him and would seek to withdraw from the case. The defendant testified truthfully, was found guilty, and then appealed based on ineffective counsel. The court found that the right to effective counsel did not include the right to an attorney who would suborn perjury.

Pellicotti (1990) describes the *passive* role and the *active* role of an attorney with a client who commits perjury. In the passive role, the attorney asks no questions during direct examination that would elicit untruthful answers and may make a statement that the client is taking the stand against the advice of an attorney. The attorney does not refer to perjured testimony during summation or any arguments. The active role allows for the attorney to disclose to the court the fact of the perjured testimony. There is no great weight of authority to commend either approach, leaving attorneys with a difficult ethical dilemma. The best defense of some attorneys is not to know about the lie in the first place.

If the attorney is not sure that the client would be committing perjury, there is no legal duty to disclose. The weight of authority indicates that the attorney with doubts should proceed with the testimony; any disclosure of such doubts is improper and unethical. Thus, some attorneys tell a client, "Before you say anything, I need to tell you that I cannot participate in perjury, and if I know for a fact that you plan to lie, I cannot put you on the stand," or they ask the client, "What do I need to know that is damaging to this case?" rather than ask if the client is guilty of the crime. Further, many attorneys argue that all defendants lie about everything and they can't be believed anyway. If this is true, some attorneys may conclude that since they don't know with certainty that the defendant is lying, they can allow the defendant to say anything they want on the stand.

The ethical issues for defense attorneys revolve around being an advocate for the client, while at the same time, performing as an officer of the court. Zealous defense within the bounds of the law is the primary duty of a defense attorney.

Ethical Issues for Prosecutors

Prosecutors do not serve an individual client; rather, their client is the system or society itself, and their mission is justice. On the other hand, prosecutors want to win and so they are influenced by this desire, similarly to defense attorneys. The Quote and Query box provides some advice from Patrick Fitzgerald, an extremely well-respected U.S. attorney.

As the second line of decision makers in the system, prosecutors have extremely broad powers of discretion. The prosecutor acts like a strainer; he or she collects some cases for formal prosecution while eliminating a great many others. Prosecuting every case is impossible. Resources are limited, and sometimes evidence is weak, making it unlikely to win a conviction. Early diversion of such cases saves taxpayers money and saves individuals trouble and expense.

QUOTE & QUERY

There are a couple of golden rules that I have picked up over the years. . . .

First, never say anything to a witness that you would not want to see on the front page of the New York Times. . . .

The second rule . . . is to never do anything if you would not feel comfortable explaining to a Second Circuit judge why you did it.

Source: Patrick Fitzgerald, U.S. Attorney, 2009.

 Is this similar to the front page test described in Chapter 2?

Use of Discretion

A prosecutor should seek or file criminal charges only if the prosecutor reasonably believes that the charges are supported by probable cause, . . . and . . . [are] in the interests of justice (Standard 3-4.3[a]).

The prosecutor must seek justice, not merely a conviction. Toward this end, prosecutors must share evidence, exercise restraint in the use of their power, represent the public interest, and give the accused the benefit of reasonable doubt. Disciplinary rules are more specific. They forbid the prosecutor from pursuing charges when there is no probable cause. Standard 3-4.4 presents a list of acceptable factors prosecutors can use to decide whether and what to charge. They include:

- The strength of the case
- The prosecutor's doubt that the accused is in fact guilty
- The extent or absence of harm caused by the offense
- The impact of prosecution or nonprosecution on the public welfare
- The background and characteristics of the offender, including any voluntary restitution or efforts at rehabilitation
- Whether the authorized or likely punishment or collateral consequences are disproportionate in relation to the particular offense or the offender
- The views and motives of the victim or complainant
- Any improper conduct by law enforcement
- Unwarranted disparate treatment of similarly situated persons
- Potential collateral impact on third parties, including witnesses or victims; cooperation of the offender in the apprehension or conviction of others
- The possible influence of any cultural, ethnic, socioeconomic or other improper biases
- Changes in law or policy
- The fair and efficient distribution of limited prosecutorial resources
- The likelihood of prosecution by another jurisdiction
- Whether the public's interests in the matter might be appropriately vindicated by available civil, regulatory, administrative, or private remedies

((•)) IN THE NEWS | *Malicious Prosecution*

Prosecutors are rarely punished by state bar disciplinary boards, but in 2012, two county prosecutors (Andrew Thomas and Lisa Aubuchon) were disbarred for misusing their office. The case involves Sheriff Joe Arpaio (America's "toughest sheriff") in Maricopa County, Arizona, who allegedly influenced the two county prosecutors to file charges against two Maricopa County officials, and a county judge who were feuding with the sheriff. There were 33 separate allegations against the pair. The ethics panel ruled that the prosecutions were done maliciously and for harassment. The prosecutors were found to have broken criminal intimidation and perjury laws. Aubuchon appealed the ruling of disbarment, but her appeal was denied by the Arizona Supreme Court. They have since been ordered to pay restitution to one of those they had filed charges against and the Ninth Circuit Court of Appeals denied their legal defense of immunity.

Source: Kiefer and Sanchez, 2012; updated news reports.

Despite these ideals of prosecutorial duty, an unstated influence over prosecutorial discretion is that prosecutors want to and must (to be considered successful) win. A decision to prosecute is influenced by the factors above, but also political and public pressures, a "gut" feeling of guilt or innocence, prison overcrowding, and career factors. The prosecutorial role is to seek justice, but justice doesn't mean the same thing to everyone and certainly does not mean prosecuting everyone to the fullest extent of the law. Whether to charge is one of the most important decisions of the criminal justice process. The decision should be fair, neutral, and accomplished with due process, but this is an ideal that is sometimes supplanted by other considerations. The In the News box describes two prosecutors who misused their office.

Recently, there has been growing scrutiny of the Department of Justice's federal prosecutors and their decisions to prosecute. In 2012, a federal jury acquitted former presidential contender John Edwards of campaign finance law violations in a case that some observers described as weak. Other prosecutions of obscure federal laws have also been criticized. Opponents argue that federal laws have multiplied to the extent that anyone can be ensnared. There are over 4,000 criminal laws and innumerable other laws that are embedded in regulatory law, many of which do not have any *mens rea* requirements. When so many acts (e.g., interstate transport of hyacinths or trafficking in unlicensed dentures) could conceivably lead to prison terms, some argue there is too much power vested in prosecutors (Grissom, 2010). This is especially true at the federal level because sentencing guidelines reduce judges' discretion and plea bargaining is so ubiquitous that prosecutors, in effect, have more power than judges.

Prosecutors don't usually use their charging power for intimidation or harassment, but other factors may be involved in the decision to charge. For instance, a prosecutor might have a particular interest in a type of crime such as child abuse or drugs and pursue these cases more intensely. How sure should a prosecutor be that a suspect is guilty before prosecuting? Can a prosecutor threaten to prosecute the spouse or child of a defendant as pressure to get them to agree to a plea bargain? Can a prosecutor ethically prosecute one individual of a crime, obtain a conviction, and then prosecute another individual for the same crime? It has been known to happen (Zachiaras and Green, 2009). The Quote and Query box refers to the prosecutor's unique role in the criminal justice system.

As noted before, sometimes the discretion of a prosecutor should be used to temper the heavy sword of the law. Genarlow Wilson was a 17-year-old high school athlete on his way to a college scholarship. Instead, he ended up in prison because of a party in which several teenagers, including Wilson, engaged in consensual sex. One of the girls involved was 15. The evidence was incontrovertible—a videotape clearly showing Wilson with the underage girl. The prosecutor charged him with rape, and a jury convicted him, which meant a mandatory 10-year prison sentence for the 17-year-old (McCaffrey, 2007; ESPN News Service, 2007). The uproar, fueled also by a belief that the prosecutorial action was influenced by racism since Wilson was black, resulted in the legislature changing the law to make sex between teenagers a misdemeanor, but the law could not be retroactively applied to Wilson. He spent two years in prison before the Georgia Supreme Court released him on the grounds that the punishment was cruel and unusual.

QUOTE & QUERY

But while he may strike hard blows, he is not at liberty to strike foul ones. It is as much his duty to refrain from improper methods calculated to produce a wrongful conviction as it is to use every legitimate means to bring about a just one.

Justice Southerland in Berger v. United States (295 U.S. 78, 88 [1935]).

 What would be the best way to prevent prosecutors from using improper methods that lead to wrongful convictions?

(((•))) IN THE NEWS | *Justice Denied?*

In 2012, the Department of Justice initiated an unprecedented investigation in Missoula, Montana, after a scandal, widely reported in the news media, described the lack of prosecution of sexual assaults involving athletes at the University of Montana. Several female students alleged they were drugged and gang-raped by male students and the Missoula County Attorney's office did not pursue any charges. The women described how they received little support from the university, the police, or the prosecutor's office and were told that the cases couldn't go forward because rape was hard to prove. The DOJ began the investigation as a possible civil rights violation (gender discrimination). The county prosecutor filed suit against the Department of Justice arguing that they had no jurisdiction over his office, but in 2014, a settlement was reached whereby a range of reforms would ensue and the Montana attorney general would review any sexual assault case when charges were not filed. The suit against the DOJ was dropped although the county prosecutor insisted that there was no jurisdiction.

Source: Haake, 2014.

Other considerations that affect the decision to charge include pressure from law enforcement—for instance, to offer a lesser charge in return for testimony or information that could lead to further convictions. There is also the pressure of public opinion. Prosecutors might pursue cases that they otherwise would have dropped if there is a great deal of public interest in the case. The victim also affects the decision to prosecute. Some victims (the very young or old, those with criminal records, those of dubious reputations) don't make good witnesses; therefore, prosecutors are less likely to prosecute. Jurors may not believe victims with mental impairments and the prosecutor may have a harder time getting a conviction. Sexual assault cases are notoriously hard to prosecute when they involve acquaintances in "date-rape" situations. The In the News box describes one incident whereby the pattern of a prosecutor's decision not to charge caught the attention of the Department of Justice.

Prosecutors in state capitals often have "public integrity" units that prosecute wrongdoing on the part of public officials. Some prosecutors might file charges against political opponents at election time, but other prosecutors might be falsely accused of such political considerations when they do charge politicians with public-integrity violations. Inevitably, federal prosecutions of politicians are labeled as "political witch-hunts" even if the Department of Justice has an equal number of investigations against members of the opposite party.

A special case of discretion and charging is the decision to pursue a capital homicide conviction. Prosecutors have the power to decide whether to seek the death penalty or a prison term. Clearly, the decision to seek the death penalty is not made uniformly across jurisdictions. One of the biggest considerations is cost. Because capital trials are extremely expensive, counties that have bigger budgets are more likely to seek the death penalty; they have the resources and staff to handle the cases (Hall, 2002). Various studies have attempted to describe prosecutors' decision making; one cites office policy as an important influence (Jacoby, Mellon, and Smith, 1980). Some office policies emphasize legal sufficiency where cases are not pursued unless there is a strong chance of conviction. Other policies may have other priorities, such as rehabilitation. Budget cuts may influence office policy to focus only on serious cases and plead out all others.

Another study looked at the prosecutor as operating in an exchange system. The relationship between the prosecutor and the police was described as one of give and take. Prosecutors balance police needs or wishes against their own vulnerability. The prosecutor makes personal judgments about which police officers can be trusted. Exchange also takes place between the prosecutor's office and the courts. When the jails become overcrowded, prosecutors recommend deferred adjudication and probation; when dockets back up, prosecutors drop charges. Finally, exchange takes place between defense attorneys and prosecutors, especially because many defense attorneys have previously served as prosecutors and may be personally familiar with the procedures and even personalities in the prosecutor's office (Cole, 1970).

On the one hand, discretion is considered essential to the prosecutorial function of promoting individualized justice and softening the impersonal effects of the law. On the other hand, the presence of discretion is the reason that the legal system is considered unfair and biased toward certain groups of people or individuals. Even though we would not want to eliminate prosecutorial discretion, it could be guided by regulations or internal guidelines. Cassidy (2006) argues that the ethics of virtue can help determine ethical decisions for prosecutors because neither Model Rule 3.8 nor the Standards gives prosecutors much guidance. He argues that if prosecutors display the virtues of courage, honesty, justice, and fairness, they would make the right decisions when faced with dilemmas. Admitting that the virtues of courage, honesty, and prudence are only slightly more abstract than the concept of justice, Cassidy urges prosecutors' offices to seek employees who already exhibit character that displays virtue. Qualifications for hiring should include evidence that the individual is honest and sensitive to others. Further, those working in a prosecutor's office should be rewarded for virtuous behavior over and above simply winning cases.

Duty to Disclose

> *A prosecutor should make timely disclosure to the defense of information . . . that tends to negate the guilt of the accused, . . . (Standard 3.5.4[a–c]).*

The obligation to disclose exculpatory evidence was established in *Brady v. Maryland*, 373 U.S. 83, 1963, *Giglio v. United States*, 405 U.S. 150, 1972, *United States v. Agurs*, 427 U.S. 97, 1976, and *United States v. Bagley*, 473 U.S. 667, 1985. Evidence that is material (likely to change the outcome of the trial) must be disclosed. "*Brady* motions" are standard pretrial motions requesting any and all exculpatory evidence held by the prosecutor. There can be a *Brady* violation/error even if the prosecutor truly did not know or remember the evidence existed. It is unintentional error when the prosecutor should have disclosed something, mistakenly believing it was not material or not knowing it existed, and intentional misconduct when the prosecutor hid or suppressed exculpatory evidence that would weaken his or her case. In either case, if an appellate court finds a serious enough *Brady* violation, the conviction can be overturned. Whether any discipline occurs in the cases of intentional misconduct is another question.

The ABA's Standing Committee on Ethics and Professional Responsibility has concluded that a prosecutor's ethical duty to share exculpatory information exceeds even the requirements of the *Brady* holding. Prosecutors have a duty to disclose even if they don't believe it is exculpatory. Some offices have "open file" policies wherein defense attorneys can have any information about evidence or witnesses that prosecutors have. *Brady* violations are one of the most frequent forms of prosecutorial misconduct and will be discussed in Chapter 10.

Conflicts of Interest

. . . the prosecutor's professional judgment or obligations [should not] be affected by the prosecutor's . . . other interests or relationships. (Standard 3.1-7[f]).

About a quarter of chief prosecutors are part time, compared to about half in the early 1990s (Perry, 2006: 2). Obviously, this poses the possibility of a conflict of interest. It may happen that a part-time prosecutor has a private practice, and there may be situations where the duty to a private client runs counter to the duty of the prosecutor to the public. In some cases, a client may become a defendant, necessitating the prosecutor to hire a special prosecutor. Even when there are no direct conflicts of interest, the pressure of time inevitably poses a conflict. The division of time between the private practice, where income is generated by the number of cases and hours billed, and prosecuting cases, where income is fixed no matter how many hours are spent, may result in a less energetic prosecutorial function than one might wish.

It is well known that the prosecutor's job is a good steppingstone to politics, and many use it as such. In these situations, one has to wonder whether cases are taken on the basis of merit or on their ability to place the prosecutor in the public eye and help his or her career.

Populous counties have many assistant district attorneys (ADAs), perhaps hundreds, and only the district attorney is elected. Many ADAs work in the prosecutor's office for a number of years and then move into the private sector. The reason has largely to do with money. New assistant district attorneys earn a median salary of $50,000, and after 11 to 15 years of experience the median salary is still only about $81,500. The question then becomes: Does the career plan to enter private practice as a litigator affect their prosecutorial decision to take a case to trial or affect their trial tactics when they are prosecuting a case against a defense attorney who may be a future employer?

One potential conflict of interest that has been in the news recently is when law enforcement officers are accused of wrongdoing. Because so few law enforcement officers face charges for shootings or alleged abuses of force, the argument is that the local prosecutor's office is unable to use their discretion fairly in making the decision to bring charges because they work with the police officers every day and depend on them to gather evidence and provide witness testimony. Thus, just as critics maintain that police departments can't police themselves, a similar criticism is made that prosecutors can't be trusted to charge police officers since it conflicts with their working relationships. This has led to recent calls for special prosecutors or attorneys from the attorneys general offices in each state to deal with cases involving police officers. Prosecutors generally discount such claims by pointing to successful cases of prosecution and larger offices have entire divisions that target public officials (including police officers).

Asset Forfeiture

The financial resources that can be seized with minimal due process in asset forfeiture may also pose a type of conflict of interest for prosecutors. Although police are most often associated with asset forfeiture, they must depend on the prosecutor to take the legal steps of seizing property. As discussed in Chapter 6 and 8, the origins of civil forfeiture were in the Comprehensive Drug Abuse and Control Act of 1970 and the Organized Crime Control Act of 1970. Both of these laws allowed mechanisms for the government to seize assets associated with illegal activities. Eventually the types of assets vulnerable to seizure were expanded, including assets *intended* to be used as well as those gained by or used in illegal activities. All of the states have passed similar asset forfeiture laws. The "take" from asset forfeiture increased from $27.2 million in 1985 to $874 million in 1992 (Jenson and Gerber, 1996). In the intervening years, the amount has increased to the point that it has become an essential portion of some budgets. The U.S. Department of Justice's Assets Forfeiture Fund now receives close to $2 billion a year, and there are unknown millions more seized under state laws.

There are a number of problematic issues with civil asset forfeiture. The exclusionary rule does not apply to civil forfeiture proceedings, so some allege that police are now pursuing assets instead of criminals, because they do not have to worry about evidence being suppressed. Also, in a civil forfeiture proceeding, the defendant does not have a right to legal aid; and, in fact, may not even be present when a judge signs the order to seize their house or car or cash. There is also a criminal asset forfeiture law that is used much more rarely because a conviction must be obtained before the property can be seized. In civil asset forfeiture, the legal action is against the property itself. Chapter 8 presented the Tenaha, Texas example as an abuse of legal power. In that small town, drivers were stopped and coerced to sign away their money rather than be arrested or lose their children. The stops seemed to be more about making money for the town rather than addressing crime. While that may have been an extreme case, critics argue otherwise, pointing out that similar forfeitures are occurring all across the country in large cities and small towns.

Perhaps one of the most troubling aspects of civil forfeiture is that third parties are often those most hurt by the loss. For example, the spouse or parents of a suspected drug dealer may lose their home. The owner does not have to be involved in criminal activity; the property just has to be associated with it. There is no requirement for any level of criminality either so a house can be seized for one $20 drug deal. In one of the most widely publicized forfeiture cases, a man solicited a prostitute; the state instituted proceedings and was successful in seizing the car he was driving when he solicited the prostitute—which was, in fact, his wife's car! This case received so much press because the Supreme Court ruled that no constitutional violation occurred with the forfeiture, even though his wife had nothing to do with the criminal activity. Another case that received a great deal of media attention was that of a man who lost his expensive motorboat when one marijuana cigarette was found on it (Worral, 2001). These cases occurred over 15 years ago, and in the intervening years, the use of forfeiture has increased with few substantive restrictions. More recently, home seizures in Philadelphia received so much press when mothers and grandmothers had their homes taken because of minor drug sales by adult children that a Pennsylvania appellate court ruled that the seizures were a violation of due process unless prosecutors could prove that the homeowner was substantially involved in the illegal activity (Mondics, 2014).

Asset forfeiture has created strange bedfellows with conservative/libertarian groups like Right on Crime (http://rightoncrime.com/tag/civil-asset-forfeiture/) joining academic legal groups like the Brennan Center (www.brennancenter.org/analysis/anyone-not-cop-favor-%E2%80%9Ccivil-forfeiture%E2%80%9D-laws) and civil liberties groups like the ACLU (www.aclu.org/issues/criminal-law-reform/reforming-police-practices/asset-forfeiture-abuse) in their criticism. There is something fundamentally wrong, critics say, in government agents (prosecutors and police) receiving profits from the use of their powers because there is too great a temptation to have money influence the decision making.

asset forfeiture
A legal tool used to confiscate property and money associated with organized criminal activity.

Plea Bargaining

. . . The prosecutor should not set unreasonably short deadlines, . . . A prosecutor should not knowingly make false statements of fact or law. . . . the prosecutor should disclose to the defense . . . information currently known to the prosecutor that tends to negate guilt, mitigates the offense or is likely to reduce punishment. (Standard 3-5.6 [a–f]).

As discussed earlier, there are serious ethical concerns over the practice of plea bargaining. In jurisdictions that have determinate sentencing, plea bargaining has become "charge bargaining" instead of sentence bargaining. Most conclude that plea bargaining, even if not exactly in keeping with due process, is certainly efficient and probably inevitable. If the goals of the system are crime control or bureaucratic efficiency, plea bargaining makes sense. If the goals of the system are the protection of individual rights and the protection of due process, plea bargaining is much harder to justify. Arguments given in defense of plea bargaining include the heavy caseloads, limited resources, legislative over-criminalization, individualized justice, and legal problems of cases (legal errors that

ETHICAL ISSUE

Should Prosecutors Plea Bargain?

The practice of exchanging a reduced charge or a reduced sentence for a guilty plea is widespread. Although some disagree with the practice and say it leads to innocent people pleading guilty and a reduction in the integrity of the system, most argue that the system couldn't work without the practice and, in fact 95 percent of cases are resolved without a trial. Also, proponents argue that it is ethical to give the offender something in exchange for not putting the state to the expense of a trial.

Law

U.S. Supreme Court opinions have legitimated the use of plea bargaining. They have held that prosecutors and judges must abide by the agreements made and that defendants cannot turn around and claim afterward that the exchange was unfair. The Supreme Court has also allowed prosecutors to threaten harsher sentences if the defendant does not plead (*Bordenkircher v. Hayes*, 434 U.S. 357, 1978) and held that plea bargaining is a "critical stage" and that ineffective counsel, if proven, could invalidate a plea agreement (*Padilla v. Kentucky*, 130 S. Ct. 1473, 2010). The Supreme Court also held that not conveying a plea offer to the defendant was ineffective counsel and when the defendant was convicted at trial, reinstatement of the original plea offer was the appropriate remedy (*Missouri v. Frye*, 132 St. Ct. 1399, 2012).

Policy

Different prosecutors' offices handle plea bargaining differently. Some have guidelines, and others leave it to the prosecutor's discretion. In general, there are informal office policies so that some offices give more generous offers than other jurisdictions do. Plea bargaining is something that is covered in the training of new prosecutors.

Ethics

Prosecutors' ethical issues with plea bargaining revolve around what is the "right" amount of punishment to offer. Defense attorneys' ethical issues include the extent to which they will try to convince individuals to plead if they swear they are innocent. Judges have ethical issues as well, in that they do not have to accept a plea in a case where they do not believe evidence is sufficient to uphold the verdict.

As stated before, plea bargaining is justified by utilitarianism. It is efficient and benefits both the defendant and the state. There is a calculus to be made depending on how many innocent people plead guilty in order to get out of jail; if it is any appreciable number, the negative utility of punishing innocents may outweigh the benefits of an efficient sentence resolution. It may also be justified by the ethics of care if a prosecutor is seeking to meet the needs of all parties concerned (e.g., victim, offender, peripheral individuals) by coming up with a unique plea agreement. It is possible that the prosecutor can, through plea bargaining, moderate an unfair application of sentencing statutes by, for instance, reducing the charge to achieve a shorter sentence if an offender agrees to drug treatment.

would result in mistrials or dropped charges if the client didn't plead) (Knudten, 1978; Mariano, 2015). Plea bargaining continues to be prevalent across the United States; felony defendants are 20 times more likely to plead than go to trial (Hashimoto, 2008: 950). Guidelines providing a range of years for certain types of charges would help individual prosecutors maintain some level of consistency in a particular jurisdiction, yet no one knows how many offices have such guidelines or manuals in place.

Even if the practice of plea bargaining can be justified as an ethical way to reduce the number of cases going to trial, there are practices that prosecutors sometimes use within plea bargaining that are ethically questionable and the ABA's updated Standards have warned against them. Specifically, prosecutors are not supposed to overcharge—that is, charge at a higher degree of severity or press more charges than could possibly be sustained by evidence—so they can bargain down. Prosecutors should not mislead defense attorneys by inflating the amount of evidence or the kind of evidence they have before or during the plea process. Also, prosecutors should not engage in false promises, fraud, misrepresentation of conditions, deals without benefit of counsel, package deals, or threats during plea bargaining yet these tactics have been known to happen (Gershman, 1991; McKelway, 2013; Sapien and Hernandez, 2013). Critics contend that prosecutors hold all the cards in plea bargaining.

Another discussion is whether the prosecution should have to share exculpatory evidence (facts that support innocence) with the defense before or during plea bargaining. Recall that in *Brady v. Maryland* (373 U.S. 83, 1963), the Supreme Court held that the prosecution must share any exculpatory information with the defense that is material to the case (which means if it would affect the outcome of the trial) when they ask for it, but it is unclear whether such a requirement applies pre-plea or only before trial.

Note that the *ABA Criminal Justice Standards* do dictate an affirmative duty to share exculpatory information with the defense during plea bargaining, but legal observers predict that the Supreme Court would not apply *Brady* to pre-plea negotiations because the legal rationale is fairness of trial, not voluntariness of plea. In fact, U.S. attorneys and some state prosecutors routinely require the defendant to waive *Brady* rights as part of a plea arrangement. Obviously knowing about any exculpatory information is important in order to make the decision to plead guilty or not. Prosecutors resist the interpretation of *Brady* that requires them to provide the defense with exculpatory evidence before a plea because they lose bargaining power. Proponents of pre-plea discovery argue that it violates due process to allow a defendant to think there is no exculpatory evidence when, in fact, there is (Hashimoto, 2008). The In the News box describes one practice of a prosecutor's office that is ethically questionable in that the defendant is under the misapprehension that the prosecutor is there as a neutral party rather than simply to gain a conviction.

Criticism of plea bargaining extends to the federal level as well. In 2013, federal prosecutors went after the 26-year-old co-creator of Reddit and RSS and charged him with 13 felony fraud counts, which could have meant 35 years in prison. The prosecutors were accused of overcharging and heavily criticized in the news when the computer whiz committed suicide (McKelway, 2013). Critics allege that prosecutors have become accustomed to "piling on" every conceivable charge in order to coerce defendants to plead guilty. Because of federal mandatory minimum laws and enhancements, federal prosecutors have immense power to persuade defendants. For instance, a defendant often has the choice to plead guilty or go to trial where the prosecutor can invoke earlier convictions to obtain a sentence of life without parole if the defendant

((•)) IN THE NEWS | *Prosecutor Misconduct or Assistance?*

A panel of the New York Supreme Court ruled that the Queens district attorney's program of interviewing suspects while they are awaiting arraignment and without legal assistance was "misleading and deceptive" and violated New York State's Rules of Professional Conduct. The practice involved prosecutors interviewing defendants prior to arraignment and assignment of counsel. The script that prosecutors used "misleads the defendant into believing that the prosecutor is there to help him out" by suggesting that the prosecution will investigate "his side of the story." But they were gathering facts to use in the prosecution, not helping the defendant.

The district attorney vowed to appeal, arguing that since 2007, 9,382 suspects have been asked if they wished to be interviewed. Three-quarters agreed to talk without a lawyer present. No questioning was conducted of those who invoked their *Miranda* rights. Twenty percent confessed. In 84 of the cases, no charges were filed because the prosecutor was convinced the suspect was innocent.

In the appeal, the state supreme court agreed that the process undercut *Miranda* warnings by implying that defendants must talk to prosecutors to get their case investigated, and then reading them *Miranda* rights. The district attorney now vows to take the case to the U.S. Supreme Court.

Source: Wise, 2012; McKinley, 2014.

loses. Judges have publicly criticized the prosecutors' actions and argued that not even the prosecutors believe in the justness of such sentences, One judge wrote that the prosecutor's action "coerces guilty pleas and produces sentences so excessively severe they take your breath away" (quoted in McKelway, 2013).

In one study, it was found that federal prosecutors used the prior-convictions sentence multiplier in 24 percent of plea bargained sentences, but used the sentencing enhancer in 72 percent of trial convictions, leading some to question the fairness of the "trial penalty." It is not surprising then, that only 3 percent of cases go to trial (McKelway, 2013). Defense attorneys state that they have to advise their clients to plead because the potential cost of extremely long sentences is too high even in cases of weak evidence or potential innocence.

Another study found that there was a huge disparity in the use of prior-felony or gun enhancement sentences on the part of prosecutors leading to some individuals serving decades longer than others for no reason other than which prosecutor had the case (Sapien and Hernandez, 2013). In August of 2013, Eric Holder instructed federal prosecutors to stop such heavy-handed prosecution of low-level drug offenders and was widely criticized by conservatives for doing so (Eckholm, 2013).

Media Relations

> *. . . The prosecutor should not make . . . a public statement that . . . will have a substantial likelihood of materially prejudicing a criminal proceeding. . . . (Standard 3-1.10 [c]).*

The prosecutor has an important relationship with the press. The media can be enemy or friend, depending on how charismatic or forthcoming the prosecutor is in interviews. Sometimes cases are said to be "tried in the media," with the defense attorney and the prosecutor staging verbal sparring matches for public consumption. Prosecutors may react to cases and judges' decisions in the media, criticizing the decision or the sentence and, in the process, denigrating the dignity of the system. More often, the defense attempts to sway the press to a sympathetic view of the offense, which is easier to accomplish during prosecutorial silence.

In many celebrated criminal cases, the prosecutor and defense utilized the media to promote their version of events. The Sam Sheppard case (supposedly the case that spurred the idea for *The Fugitive* television series and movie) was the first one to illustrate the power of the media and related misconduct by the prosecution, such as discussing evidence with reporters that could not be admitted at trial. The media storm was actively encouraged by the prosecutor and ultimately led to the Supreme Court ruling that due process had been violated (Kirchmeier et al., 2009).

ABA Model Rule 3.6(b) is a prohibition against out-of-court statements that a reasonable person should expect would have a substantial likelihood of materially prejudicing a proceeding. Defense attorneys might be expected to make statements to exonerate their client and disparage the state's case, but prosecutors' statements have a greater ring of authority. The rule specifies that no statements should be given involving topics such as the character, credibility, reputation, or criminal record of a party, suspect, or witness, the identity of a witness, expected testimony, test results, physical evidence, or any inadmissible evidence, and other topics that may influence public opinion about the case.

The case of the Duke University lacrosse players accused of rape resulted in the prosecutor (Mike Nifong) being disbarred. In this high-profile 2007 case, a stripper alleged that she was raped by members of the lacrosse team after she was hired to perform at a party for them. Very early in the case, the district attorney made several public statements indicating that the athletes were guilty, and they weren't going to get away with the crime just because they were white and rich and the alleged victim was black and poor. No doubt the fact that the district attorney was in a hotly contested election had something to do with his decision to make such public statements so early in the case.

As the investigation progressed, the victim's story changed in substantive ways about who raped her and when it took place. Furthermore, no physical evidence substantiated her story. Despite this, the district attorney continued to make comments to the media that the players were guilty. Later, the alibi of one defendant was substantiated by an ATM camera showing that he was somewhere else when the rape was supposed to have taken place. Still Nifong did not drop the charges and in fact instructed a lab technician to drop a sentence from his report indicating that the semen found on the alleged victim contained the DNA of several unknown males, but not the accused men's.

Eventually, the state attorney general sent in a special prosecutor to handle the case, and this prosecutor promptly dropped the charges against the accused college athletes. Nifong was publicly sanctioned and was disbarred from the practice of law. The case is a good example of why public expressions of guilt are strictly prohibited: The prosecutor gets locked into a position that is difficult to back out of if exculpatory evidence emerges. After Nifong had committed himself to the conclusion that the college men were guilty, he found himself under intense pressure to pursue the case, even in the face of contradictory evidence (Jeffrey, 2007).

Expert Witnesses

A prosecutor . . . should not seek to dictate the formation of the expert's opinion on the subject (Standard 3-3.5[d]).

The use of expert witnesses has risen in recent years. Psychiatrists often testify as to the mental competency or legal insanity of an accused. Criminologists and other social scientists may be asked to testify on topics such as victimization in prison, statistical evidence of sentencing discrimination, the effectiveness of predictive instruments for prison riots and other disturbances, risk assessment for individual offenders, mental health services in prison, patterns of criminality, battered-woman syndrome, and so on (see Anderson and Winfree, 1987). A whole range of experts in the field of criminalistics also have emerged as important players in criminal prosecutions.

Expert testimony is allowed as evidence in trials when it is based on sound scientific method. The Supreme Court has defined a standard as to when scientific evidence can be admitted in a trial. Specifically, the so-called *Daubert* standard includes the idea that the judge is gatekeeper to make the determination of relevance and reliability. The judge must find it more likely than not that the expert's methods are reliable and reliably applied to the facts at hand. The expert can only testify as to scientific knowledge if the proponent can demonstrate that it is the product of sound "scientific methodology" which may include hypothesis testing using empirical methods. Other factors include whether the expert's findings have been subjected to peer review and publication, the known or potential error rate, and whether there are standards and controls concerning the research that have been followed (*Daubert v. Merrell Dow Pharmaceuticals*, 509 U.S. 579, 1993).

When experts are honest in their presentation as to the limitations and potential bias of the material, no ethical issues arise. However, expert witnesses may testify in a realm beyond fact or make testimony appear factual when some questions are not clearly answerable. Because of the **halo effect**—essentially, when a person with expertise or status in one area is given deference in all areas—an expert witness may endow a statement or conclusion with more legitimacy than it warrants.

Some expert witnesses always appear on either the defense side or the prosecution side and doing so should create questions about their credibility. For instance, a doctor who was often used by prosecutors in one jurisdiction during capital-sentencing hearings became known as "Dr. Death" because he always determined that the defendant posed a future risk to society—one of the necessary elements for the death penalty. Although this doctor was well known by reputation to prosecutors and defense attorneys alike, juries could not be expected to know of his predilection for finding future risk and would take his testimony at face value unless the defense attorney brought out this information during cross-examination (Raeder, 2007).

The use of expert witnesses can present ethical problems when the witness is used in a dishonest fashion. Obviously, to pay an expert for his or her time is not unethical, but to shop for experts until finding one who benefits the case is unethical, for the credibility of the witness is suspect. Another difficulty arises when the prosecutor obtains an expert who develops a conclusion or a set of findings that would help the defense. Ethical rules do not prohibit an attorney in a civil matter or criminal defense attorneys from merely disregarding the information; however, prosecutors operate under a special set of ethics because their goal is justice, not pure advocacy. Any exculpatory information is supposed to be shared with the defense; this obviously includes test results and may also include expert witness findings (Giannelli and McMunigal, 2007).

CSI and the Courts

For many years, forensic experts have testified regarding factual issues of evidence ranging from ballistics to blood spatter. Television shows such as *CSI* contribute to the mystique of the crime-scene investigator as a scientific Sherlock Holmes who uses physics, chemistry, and biology to catch criminals. However, the reality is that some of

halo effect The phenomenon in which a person with expertise or status in one area is given deference in all areas.

this "expert" testimony has been called "*junk science*" (McRoberts, Mills, and Possley, 2004a&b). Also, lab examiners who work for police laboratories may exhibit a heavy prosecution bias that colors their analysis and testimony.

As mentioned in Chapter 6, labs all over the country have been investigated and even shut down for shoddy practices or biased analyses. Scandals have occurred with labs in Houston, Cleveland, Chicago, Omaha, Oklahoma City, Washington, D.C., Boston, Indianapolis, and San Francisco; and, state crime labs in Virginia, Maryland, California, Illinois, Maryland, North Carolina, Oklahoma, West Virginia, Mississippi, and New York. Even the vaunted FBI lab has been the center of scandal in their faulty ballistics testing and misleading testimony in hair analysis, among other issues (Balko, 2011; Trager, 2014; Giannelli, 2012; Murphy, 2012).

While each locale had unique circumstances, there have also been patterns of problems. Shoddy practices and/or incompetent lab examiners have been found in a number of investigations. Labs have been found to practice poor procedures that allow contamination, use inadequate equipment, and have poorly trained or unqualified lab technicians (in some cases not even meeting minimal standards of knowledge). In a New York investigation, an examiner had been working for 15 years with no training and didn't even know how to use the microscope he supposedly used to conduct trace evidence and hair analysis. He evidently made up reports using a "cheat sheet" left by a former supervisor. This examiner committed suicide, but, before his death implicated many others in the lab and accused supervisors of countenancing widespread malfeasance and report-fudging to aid prosecution efforts (Balko, 2009).

In 2012, a Massachusetts forensic chemist admitted she had falsified thousands of drug tests. She was arrested and later admitted to mixing up evidence samples, fabricating results and lying about having a master's degree in chemistry from the University of Massachusetts. Over 1,000 requests for new trials were filed and around 500 defendants were released. Evidently this analyst, Annie Dookhan, manufactured test results to impress her superiors with her productivity. She was convicted and sentenced to three to five years in prison. Another Massachusetts forensic chemist was also arrested and convicted of tampering because she cut drug samples with counterfeit drugs to hide her thefts, evidently stealing the drug to feed her own drug habit (Trager, 2014). In fact, theft of portions of drug samples and replacing the stolen drugs with other substances is part of a pattern of problems in labs in several places. Once this occurs, literally thousands of criminal cases are compromised (Tobin and Spiegleman, 2013). Similar cases around the country (e.g., in South Carolina, Florida and Texas) continue to pop up around the country where analysts' training, competence, or honesty are questioned (Trager, 2014).

Another pattern of wrongdoing is when lab examiners are clearly slanted toward the prosecution in their work and overstate their findings to the jury, or even manufacture test results ("drylabbing") that benefit the prosecution. Another tactic used is to suppress any test results or findings that are exculpatory (e.g., DNA that doesn't match) (Liptak, 2003; Axtman, 2003; KTRK, 2009; Possley, Mills, and McRoberts, 2004; Tobin & Spiegleman, 2013; Trager, 2014). Critics argue that forensic examiners are too closely aligned with law enforcement and want to get the results that support the theory of the case. Carefully controlled studies have shown that forensic specialists have reversed their opinion on the same evidence when the "right" suspect was switched (Tobin and Spiegleman, 2013). In another study, forensic psychologists evaluated the risk of hypothetical subjects and were told in some cases that they were hired by the prosecution and in others they were hired by the defense. Those who were supposedly hired by the prosecution had significantly higher risk scores, indicating what the researchers called "an allegiance effect" (Murrie et al., 2013). The psychological bias inherent in the matching procedure (in hair, fingerprints, and other evidence) when one knows the suspect's sample is extremely problematic even for examiners who attempt be objective in their examination (Tobin and Spiegleman, 2013).

What happens in these scandals is that thousands of cases have to be reviewed, some retried, and some individuals have been exonerated. In some cases, millions of dollars in settlements for those falsely incarcerated have been paid by taxpayers. For instance, the Virginia State Crime Lab, upon review of many cases, excluded 76 felons as the source of biological evidence in their supposed crimes. A review of the results by the Urban Institute found that there were 37 potential wrongful convictions. Some of the defendants have died; some have already served their prison terms, but an unknown number may still be in prison (Green, 2010).

Another issue has been that when the labs or individual lab examiners have been identified as biased or incompetent, defense attorneys are not notified. The FBI was strongly criticized for abandoning the lead composition analysis but making very weak efforts to locate any individuals who had been wrongfully convicted based on their testimony.

Even when mismanagement, shoddy practices, and untrained staff aren't the issue, many areas of the science of **criminalistics** seem to be more in the nature of art than science. Criminalists have been defined as professionals who are involved in the "scientific discipline directed to the recognition, identification, individualization, and evaluation of physical evidence by the application of the natural sciences to law-science matters" (Lindquist, 1994: 59). Questions have been raised about the reliability of virtually all areas of this science:

criminalistics The profession involved in the application of science to recognize, identify, and evaluate physical evidence in court proceedings.

- *Hair analysis.* A Justice Department study of 240 crime labs found hair-comparison error rates ranging from 28 to 68 percent. Hair-comparison testimony is so suspect that it is outlawed in Michigan and Illinois (Hall, 2002). Basically hair analysis is simply an analyst visually inspecting two samples under a microscope and determining if they are "consistent." When the analyst has a pro-prosecution bias and knows that they are looking at the suspect's hair sample, the potential for misidentification is obvious. There is no such thing as "matching" samples when there is only visual inspection; however, testimony is often inflated and misrepresented to the jury as if the analyst scientifically concluded that the two hair samples came from the same source (Fisher, 2008).

    In 2013, the FBI agreed to review more than 2,000 criminal cases in which the FBI conducted microscopic hair analysis of crime-scene evidence and analysts testified about their findings to determine if the jury might have been misled. The investigation was prompted by the exoneration of three men in three different cases—Kirk Odom, Santae Tribble, and Donald Gates—by DNA testing in which FBI hair examiners had told juries that the defendants' hair matched hair at the crime scenes, based on microscopic hair analysis. In fact, subsequent DNA testing found that none of the hair samples matched the defendants and that one was from a dog. The probability of accuracy in the matches was wildly overstated.

    The FBI admitted that hair analysis was a problem years ago and, since the 1970s, had taken the position that hair analysis could not lead to a positive identification match; however, examiners regularly testified to the near certainty of matches. In fact, an Inspector General's report brought attention to the problem of the examiners' testimony in 1999 (Hsu, 2014). Only in 2013 was the first systematic review of FBI examiners' testimony begun to determine how widespread the problem was. There were over 2,500 cases identified in which hair analysis might have been offered. Only 342 have been reviewed thus far. Of these, 268 included hair analysis testimony; 35 of the cases led to an execution. Of these cases, 95 percent of the time the testimony overstated the science and 26 of the 28 examiners overstated the matches (Hsu, 2015).

- *Arson investigation.* Arson "science" started when arson investigators used their experience with thousands of fires, confessions of suspects, and crude experiments to identify burn patterns and accelerants. "Facts" such as "fires started with accelerants burn hotter" have been disproved. So-called "pour patterns" that have been used as proof of arson have now been associated with a natural phenomenon called "flashover," which occurs when smoke and gas in a room build to a point where the entire room explodes in flames, consuming everything. The flashover effect also calls into question the traditional belief that if the floor showed burning, it was arson, because heat rises and the floor shouldn't show burning unless an accelerant is used (Possley, Mills, and McRoberts, 2004; Fisher, 2008).

  In the Cameron Todd Willingham case that opened this chapter, the Innocence Project commissioned a panel to study some of the arson "facts" that were presented in the trial, and the study proved that many were not supported. For instance, glass cracking in a spidery fashion may not be because the fire was started with an accelerant; it is just as likely to be caused by water sprayed by firefighters. There also was no way to prove that the fire had multiple origins. However, fire investigators may still testify in court based on science that is called by some "a hodgepodge of old wives' tales" (Tanner, 2006).

- *Ballistics testing.* The FBI lab examiners testified in thousands of cases about lead composition analysis to tie suspects to the bullet retrieved at the crime scene. The theory was that the chemical composition of bullets in a single production batch was more similar than bullets from other batches. Bullets owned by the suspect are compared to the crime-scene bullet, and the expert testifies as to their similarity.

  Independent scientific tests by the National Research Council indicated a large margin of error; chemical compositions between batches are more similar than believed, and the chemical composition within a batch can vary quite a bit depending on a number of factors. These findings indicated that ballistics experts from the FBI lab and other labs had testified in a way that greatly overstated the importance of the chemical matches (Piller and Mejia, 2003; Piller, 2003). Although the FBI stopped comparative bullet lead analysis in 2004 in response to these findings, FBI lab experts were allowed to testify in cases that had already been analyzed through 2005. Also, the FBI was criticized for not releasing a list of cases in which lab examiners testimony was based on the faulty science. Several individuals had their murder convictions thrown out when appellate judges decided that the ballistics testimony materially affected the outcome of the trial (Post, 2005; Solomon, 2007a; Tobin and Spiegleman, 2013).

  Another type of ballistics testing is matching the marks on a bullet and a gun to determine if the bullet was used in that particular gun. Despite what the television shows portray, this matching has not proven to be successful in scientific tests. Ironically, because it has been admitted for so long in criminal cases, judges cite precedent to argue why they must allow it, even though experts in the field know the technique is highly inaccurate (Tobin and Spiegleman, 2013).

- *DNA testing.* The use of DNA evidence has risen dramatically in recent years. Based on the scientific principle that no two individuals possess the same DNA (deoxyribonucleic acid), a DNA "fingerprint" is analyzed from organic matter such as semen, blood, hair, or skin. Whereas a blood test can identify an individual only as being a member of a group (e.g., all those with blood type A positive), DNA testing can determine, with a small margin of error, whether two samples come from the same individual. This has been described as the greatest breakthrough in scientific evidence since fingerprinting, but there are problems with its use. Careless laboratory procedures render results useless, and there are no enforced guidelines or criteria for forensic laboratories conducting DNA tests.

  Labs often have only a small amount of organic matter to extract DNA. They use a procedure whereby the incomplete DNA strand is replicated using computer-simulation models. This procedure allows a DNA analysis of the tiniest speck of blood or skin, but critics argue that it opens a door to a margin of error that is unacceptable. Without vigorous investigation and examination of lab results from the opposing counsel, incorrect DNA test results or poorly interpreted results may be entered as evidence and used to determine guilt or innocence.

  A different problem has emerged when DNA testing is done and the results help the defense by excluding the defendant from possible suspects. In these cases, prosecutors have an ethical duty to provide test results to the defense; however, there are cases where this is not done.

- *Fingerprint analysis.* Most citizens assume that fingerprint analysis is infallible, that all criminals' fingerprints are accessible through computer matching technology, and that fingerprint technicians can retrieve fingerprints from almost any surface and can use partials to make a match. Unfortunately, the reality is far from what is seen on television. There have been attempts to undertake a comprehensive analysis of how much of a partial print is necessary to have a reliable match—an objective that is resisted by professional fingerprint examiners. Most fingerprints are partials and smudged. Some studies show that about a quarter of matches are false positives.

  In 2006, the federal government settled a suit for $2 million after three FBI fingerprint examiners mistakenly identified the fingerprint related to a terrorist bombing in Madrid, Spain, as belonging to an Oregon lawyer and he was detained even though he had an alibi. European fingerprint analysts discovered the error (Associated Press, 2004). Standards do not exist for determining how many points of comparison are necessary to declare a match (Mills and McRoberts, 2004). Problems with fingerprint analysis have found their way into the courtroom and there is a movement among defense attorneys to challenge fingerprint evidence under the *Daubert* standard (arguing that it has not been developed using scientific methods). This defense has been unsuccessful; however, if defense attorneys do succeed in excluding fingerprint evidence, it would be a ground-shifting event in criminalistics and criminal law (Fisher 2008; Garrett and Neufield, 2009).

- *Bite mark comparison.* There is no accurate way to measure the reliability of bite mark comparisons, yet forensic dentists have given testimony that resulted in convictions of several innocent defendants, and several individuals exonerated through DNA evidence were convicted largely on evidence of bite mark identification. Evidently, the experts sometimes can't even agree if an injury is a bite mark at all. One study indicated that identifications were flawed in two-thirds of the cases. Even their own organization cautions that analysts should not use the term "match," because the technique is not exact enough, but many do. Contrary to popular belief, a bite mark is not just like a fingerprint. Teeth change over time, and the condition of the skin or other substance holding the bite mark changes the indentation patterns of teeth (McRoberts and Mills, 2004). So-called experts have confused juries by confabulating dentition and bite marks since there is general agreement that identity can be established within reasonable parameters of error by comparing dental records to a full set of teeth (i.e., comparing dental records to a corpse). However, bite marks only typically involve the front teeth, and there is no evidence to indicate that bite marks are similar every time; furthermore, there are no standards to guide agreement that there is a match. Critics argue that bite mark testimony does not meet the *Daubert* standard (evidence must be from a reliable scientific methodology), but courts let the evidence in because it is presented as merely identification, not science (Beecher-Monas, 2009).

- *Scent identification.* A Texas deputy, Keith Pikett, now retired from the Fort Bend County Sheriff's Department, became semi-famous and in demand along with his dogs for finding and identifying criminals through "scent lineups." The dogs evidently could identify criminals through scents left at the scene or on property. In some cases, the dogs led the police from the crime scene to the home of the alleged offender, even though the house was miles away. Critics contend that Pikett gave the dogs unconscious clues to tag the suspect, and, in other cases, there was no way the dogs could do what Pikett says they did. The state's appellate court threw out the murder conviction of Richard Winfrey who was convicted of murdering his neighbor and sentenced to 75 years based almost entirely on the scent identification evidence. All other evidence at the crime scene—DNA, fingerprints, a bloody footprint, and 73 hairs—belonged to some unknown person. Winfrey's two adult children were also charged; his son (who fought and won to have the scent identification evidence excluded from trial) was acquitted, but his daughter (whose lawyer did not challenge the scent evidence) was convicted. In Winfrey's trial, the judge ruled that the scent identification evidence could not be used in court unless corroborated by other evidence (Lindell, 2010a; Lindell, 2010c).

- *Other forensic evidence.* Other types of evidence have been introduced at trials and also been subject to criticism, including handwriting analysis, boot or shoe print identification, and fiber identification.

In 2009, the National Academy of Sciences issued a 225-page report on forensics and crime labs across the country. It was a highly critical report, incorporating the descriptions of many cases of innocent people convicted because of faulty scientific evidence. The authors concluded that crime labs lacked certification and standards, and that many forensic disciplines, including most of those described above, were not grounded in classic scientific methods; DNA analysis was the exception. Much of the problem is in pattern recognition (e.g., fingerprints, bite marks, tool marks, handwriting). There is no agreed upon scientific standard for when to conclude a match. The report called on Congress to establish a national institute of forensic science to accredit crime labs and require that analysts be certified. In 2013, the National Forensic Science Commission was established although it appears that it had not been fully formed by summer 2015 since applications for commission membership were being solicited (www.justice.gov/ncfs).

Zealous Prosecution

The duty of the prosecutor is to seek justice, not merely to convict (Standard 3-1.2[b]).

Just as the defense attorney is at times overly zealous in defense of clients, prosecutors may be overly ambitious in order to attain a conviction. The prosecutor, in preparing a case, is putting together a puzzle, and each fact or bit of evidence is a piece of that puzzle. Evidence that doesn't fit the puzzle is sometimes conveniently ignored. The problem is that this type of evidence may be exculpatory, and the prosecutor has a duty to provide it to the defense.

Both defense attorneys and prosecutors sometimes engage in tactics such as using witnesses with less than credible reasons for testifying, preparing witnesses (both in appearance and testimony), and "shopping" for experts. Witnesses are not supposed to be paid, but their expenses can be reimbursed, and often this is incentive enough for some people to say what they think the prosecutor wants to hear. A tool in the prosecutor's arsenal that the defense attorney does not have is that prosecutors can make deals to reduce charges in return for favorable testimony.

Jailhouse Informants

The use of jailhouse informants is a particularly problematic issue. Jailhouse informants usually testify that a defendant confessed to them or said something that was incriminating. Often the "pay" for such testimony is a reduction in charges, but it could be reduced sentencing or being sent to a particular prison, or any other thing of value to the informant. It could even be money. Jailhouse informants' credibility should always be questioned and is one of the most frequent factors identified in wrongful convictions (Kirchmeier et al., 2009). Raeder (2007) points out that jailhouse informants not only respond to solicitations from police and prosecutors, sometimes they are entrepreneurs who are used multiple times in many prosecutions. She argues for ethical standards whereby prosecutors should use such informants only when they can point to specific factors that support the truthfulness of the testimony.

Research shows that even though jailhouse informant testimony is highly questionable, it is very effective. Respondents in one research study who decided whether to convict or acquit in hypothetical cases were given transcripts that either included a jailhouse informant's testimony that the defendant confessed or did not. Those who read the confession were much more likely to convict, and whether the informant received money or even a shortened sentence did not affect their greater likelihood of convicting if they were given the jailhouse house informant's testimony. More

---

((•)) IN THE NEWS | *Willingham Prosecutor May Be Disciplined*

The State Bar of Texas has asked a Navarro County court to discipline John H. Jackson who prosecuted Cameron Todd Willingham. Many believe that Willingham was wrongfully convicted and executed. Jackson has consistently denied any wrongdoing, but he has been charged with concealing evidence from the defense. Johnny Webb, who was in the same jail as Willingham, testified that Willingham confessed. Webb has since recanted, affirmed, and recanted that testimony. The alleged misconduct is that Webb received a deal from the prosecutor in return for his testimony and Jackson is accused of not telling the defense about it. He did help Webb get out of prison early, but claims he did so because Webb was receiving death threats, not as payment for his testimony. Recently revealed letters to Webb from Jackson show a years-long interaction where Jackson assisted Webb in numerous ways, none of which during or after the trial but before Willingham's execution, were revealed to the defense. The argument is that if they had been, Willingham's appeals might have been successful.

Source: Possley, 2014; recent news accounts.

---

troubling was that respondents were just as likely to convict even if they were told the informant had testified in previous cases and even when expert testimony was added that called into question the credibility of informants (Neuschatz et al., 2012). If true, this means that prosecutors have an immense power to shift the course of a trial with the use of jailhouse informants and to blithely say that the jury can adequately assess the credibility of the person is highly debatable.

ETHICAL DILEMMA

You are a prosecutor who is preparing a case against a defendant accused of a brutal rape and murder of a young child. The suspect lived in the same neighborhood as the child and is a registered sex offender. He says he didn't do it, of course, but has no alibi for the time in question, and you know in your gut that he did the crime. Unfortunately, you have no scientific evidence that incriminates him. You do have one witness who thinks she saw his car close to the playground where the child was taken, and you can prove he didn't show up for work the afternoon of the abduction. You are hoping that someone in the playground will be able to make a positive ID. One day you receive a call from the detective on the case. He tells you that there is a man in the jail cell with the defendant who says that the defendant confessed to him. The informant is willing to testify to it, but he wants a reduction in his own sentence. You meet with the man, who is a drug offender, and sure enough, he says that the defendant "spilled his guts" and told him that he took the little girl and killed her when she wouldn't stop screaming. You feel you've got the conviction sewn up. You proceed to trial. The second morning of the trial, you find out that your star witness had made a similar deal in his last drug case in a different jurisdiction and received probation for a substantial amount of meth. Since the trial has begun, double jeopardy applies. Do you reveal the information to the defense? Do you put him on the stand and let the jury decide whether to believe him or not?

Law

There is no law prohibiting the use of jailhouse informants, although some states have begun to restrict their use. The Model Rules, which have the force of law when adopted by a state bar, dictate that prosecutors cannot put false information on the stand, but if you were the prosecutor, would you tell yourself that you don't "know" the informant is lying and, therefore, you are not violating the rule? On the other hand, the Model Rules and *Brady* motions do indicate that the information about the prior case be given to the defense since it could be considered exculpatory as it calls into question the credibility of the witness. There may be more specific state laws that are relevant as well. For instance, Texas passed the Michael Morton Act (named after a wrongfully convicted man) in 2014, which mandates that all prosecutors in the state maintain an "open file" policy meaning defense attorneys should have access to everything prosecutors have unless there is some reason it should be secret.

Policy

Los Angeles has an office policy that discourages the use of jailhouse informants. Most jurisdictions do not, although they may have an office policy of not taking a case to trial that hinges on such testimony. All offices have policies that dictate responding to *Brady* motions, but some offices also have an "open file" policy that allows the defense to have access to any information the prosecutor has except the identity of confidential informants or other information that needs to be kept secret. It is possible that some offices will begin to have policies regarding jailhouse informants since so many of those exonerated have been convicted partially on the testimony of these witnesses.

Ethics

Utilitarian ethics tolerate actions that lead to a good end, but, in this case, there is not much evidence to indicate that the defendant is guilty so it is questionable that conviction is even a good end. Therefore, any "bad means" (such as keeping the information from the defense) may result in a bad end as well. The more difficult ethical issue is whether to continue with the trial at all. Juries are loath to let a murdering sex offender go free and are likely to believe that if someone is prosecuted, they are more than likely guilty. Therefore, even if you provide the information to the defense, it is possible that they will be unable to undercut the credibility of the informant and the defendant will be found guilty. Utilitarian ethics may support such an action if it results in the greatest benefit for the majority. Ethical formalism may not if one interprets a prosecutor's duty as pursuing justice, since a case dependent on a witness who is probably lying is contrary to due process. This explains why jurisdictions are moving away from using jailhouse informant testimony unless it can be corroborated.

Ethical Issues for Judges

Perhaps the best-known symbol of justice is the judge in a black robe. Judges are expected to be impartial, knowledgeable, and authoritative. They guide the prosecutor, defense attorney, and all the other actors in the trial process from beginning to end, helping to maintain the integrity of the proceeding. This is the ideal, but judges are human, with human failings. As mentioned in the last chapter, the potential for bias is exacerbated because judges are elected. Judicial elections are increasingly funded with huge amounts of money. Special interest groups called political action committees (PACs) fund television commercials that are supposedly issue-oriented but thinly veiled attack ads on opponents. The attention to judicial races is largely due to the impact of decisions on civil matters, but the politicalization of the bench has affected criminal law also. Judicial decision making seems to have become increasingly political. Judges are the arbitrators of law; when they are seen as merely tools of the politically powerful, then "the rule of law" is threatened.

Conflict of Interest

> *A judge shall uphold and promote the independence, integrity, and impartiality of the judiciary, and shall avoid impropriety and the appearance of impropriety. (Canon 1, Model Code of Judicial Conduct)*

One of the most commonly heard criticisms of judges is that they are not objective. If a judge has some interest in the case—financial, social, or emotional—then their decision making is questioned. Even the Supreme Court is not immune to charges of

(((ᴀ))) IN THE NEWS | *Judicial Favor?*

A 2014 study by the Center for Public Integrity examined three years of financial disclosure reports filed by federal appellate judges and found 24 cases where they ruled on cases in which they owned stock in a company that was one of the parties in the case. In all cases, the judges ruled in favor of the companies. In one case, the appellate judge owned $100,000 worth of stock in a company he ruled in favor of in a civil case. Judges typically argue that they are unaware of the companies in their portfolio but when they own individual stocks (rather than mutual funds), that ignorance is not as persuasive.

Source: O'Brien, Weir, and Young, 2014.

conflicts of interest. Justice Scalia has been criticized for several decisions in which he participated after having made public comments indicating his opinions regarding the legal issue. Justice Thomas has been criticized for not recusing himself in cases where his wife has been associated with the parties involved; for instance, in *Bush v. Gore* (531 U.S. 98, 2000) she was working with a group collecting resumes for the future Bush administration; in *NFIB v. Sebelius* (567 U.S. ___, 2012); a case challenging the Constitutionality of the Affordable Care Act, she was the head of a group fighting against the healthcare legislation. In neither case did he recuse himself. Justice Kagan had to recuse herself from 21 of the first 58 cases during her first term because she was formerly the solicitor general and was associated with the government in several cases where the United States was a party. There is even a website (FixtheCourt.com) devoted to improving the transparency and ethics of the Supreme Court since; technically, they are not bound by the Code of Judicial Conduct or any other ethics code. The news box describes a study of federal appellate judges.

McKeown (2011) notes that, in some cases, recusal motions are frivolous or border on harassment. Recusal is necessary when a judge has a financial interest in the case, but also when disability, bias, or relationship to the parties might influence the judgment or give the appearance of impropriety. Note that under federal rules, judges must recuse themselves even if there is no bias but a reasonable observer might question the impartiality of the judge. Judges make that determination themselves when a party files a recusal motion. It is also the case that they can ethically only recuse themselves for just cause, not because of any other reason (such as the case is a political minefield).

Use of Discretion

> *A judge shall uphold and apply the law, and shall perform all duties of judicial office fairly and impartially. (Rule 2.2., Model Code of Judicial Conduct)*

As we have learned in several previous chapters, discretion refers to the authority to make a choice between two or more actions. Judges have discretion in appointing guardian *ad litem* or indigent cases to attorneys. The practice of awarding indigent cases to one's friends or for reasons other than qualifications may not only be unethical but also may have serious consequences for the defendant. The Texas Bar Association (2002) reported major problems in the system of appointing attorneys for indigent defendants. The bar association's investigation found that some lawyers who received appointments had been disciplined by the state bar and there was no system for monitoring the quality of the representation. In 2006, a major newspaper ran a series of articles highly critical of the system of appointing lawyers for capital habeas corpus appeals for death row inmates. The investigation found that some lawyers turned in ridiculously short appeals that did not cover even the most obvious points and/or were poorly written and then billed the state for large sums of money (Lindell, 2006a, 2006b, 2006c). Stung by the widespread criticism, the Texas Court of Criminal Appeals has since revised the appointment system for capital cases, putting in place procedures to ensure qualified attorneys are appointed (see www.txcourts.gov/media/587369/standards.pdf). When habeas corpus appellate attorneys are competent, they may literally save the lives of innocent men and women; thus, whom the judge appoints is an extremely important decision.

Interpretation of Law and Rules

Judges are like the umpire in an athletic contest; they apply the rules and interpret them. Although rules of law are established in Rules of Criminal Procedure and case law, there is still a great deal of discretion in the interpretation of a rule—what is reasonable, what is probative, what is prejudicial, and so on. A judge assesses the legality of evidence and makes rulings on the various objections raised by both the prosecutors and the defense attorneys. A judge also writes the extremely important instructions to the jury. These are crucial because they set up the legal questions and definitions of the case.

One of the clearest examples of judicial discretion is in the application of the exclusionary rule, which basically states that when the evidence has been obtained illegally, it must be excluded from use at trial. The exclusionary rule has generated a storm of controversy because it can result in a guilty party avoiding punishment because of an error committed by the police. The basis for the exclusionary rule is the right to due process. The ideals of justice reject a conviction based on tainted evidence even if obtained against a guilty party. A more practical argument for the exclusionary rule is that if we want police officers to behave in a legal manner, we must have heavy sanctions against illegalities. Arguably, if convictions are lost because of illegal collection of evidence, police will reform their behavior. Actual practice provides little support for this argument. Cases lost on appeal are so far removed from the day-to-day decision making of the police that they have little effect on police behavior. In the succeeding years since the cases that recognized the rule, such as *Mapp v. Ohio* (367 U.S. 643, 1961), several exceptions to the exclusionary rule have been recognized. Judges can now rule that the illegally obtained evidence be allowed because of public safety (*New York v. Quarles*, 467 U.S. 649, 1984), good faith (*U.S. v. Leon*, 468 U.S. 897, 1984), or inevitable-discovery exceptions (*Nix v. Williams* 467 U.S. 431, 1984).

In addition to applying the exclusionary rule, the judge is called upon to decide various questions of evidence and procedure throughout a trial. Of course, the judge is guided by the law and legal precedent, but in most cases each decision involves a substantial element of subjectivity. For instance, a defendant may file a pretrial petition for a change of venue. This means that the defendant is arguing that public notoriety and a biased jury pool would make it impossible to have a fair trial in the location where the charges were filed. It is up to the judge, however, to decide if that indeed is true or whether, despite pretrial publicity, the defendant will be assured of a fair trial. If judges are biased either toward or against the prosecution or defense, they have the power to make it difficult for either side through their pattern of rulings on objections and evidence admitted. Even a personal dislike of either lawyer may be picked up by jury members, and it does affect their attitude toward that side's case.

Despite the belief that simply applying the rules will lead to the right conclusion or decision, the reality is that judges and justices are simply human, and biases can influence their decision making. The suspicion that some appellate court judges decide where they want to end up and make up the argument to get there is one that is hard to deny after a careful reading of some case decisions. At other times, appellate decision making seems to reflect a complete absence of "equity" thinking (basic fairness) in place of hypertechnical application of rules. Petitions that are denied because a deadline was missed or appeals denied because they were not drawn up in the correct fashion despite obvious substantive legitimacy are examples of this application of discretion.

One example of this form over fairness occurred in 2009 in Texas. The chief justice of the court of criminal appeals refused to accept an appeal on a death row case because the lawyers could not file it before 5 p.m. This was despite the fact that several justices were working late that night in case of late filings, and the attorneys had asked for permission to file it late because they were having computer problems. Sharon Keller, the chief justice, instructed her clerk via telephone to deny the request and close the office, and the prisoner was executed. The basis of the appeal was that the method of execution (lethal injection) was cruel and unusual, and the Supreme Court of the United States, only a week later, accepted a writ of *certiorari* on this very issue, indicating there was a good chance that the appeal would have resulted in at least a hearing on the merits. In fact, two days later, a second appeal by a different inmate was granted, while in the case where the appeal was denied for being late, the man was executed. This hypertechnical application of rules was considered so wrong that 19 attorneys filed an ethics complaint against Keller for her actions, alleging that she violated the bar association rules that judges preserve the integrity of the judiciary and act in ways that promote public confidence, and a rule that requires judges to allow interested parties to be heard according to law. The State Commission on Judicial Conduct issued a ruling that resulted in no sanctions for Keller, although she was admonished; however, the admonishment was thrown out by a special court of review, which ruled that the Commission on Judicial Conduct had no authority to issue a "warning," only a "censure" (which is a more serious punishment). There was no ruling as to the merits of the rebuke (Lindell, 2007b, 2010).

Because of the furor, the Court of Criminal Appeals published a rule that required attorneys to file appeals seven days before any execution. In 2015, David Dow, one of the attorneys in the 2009 case, filed a late appeal. Some argue it was 30 minutes late, others argue it was over a day late (the confusion is between the clear language of the rule and the example the court provided for it which describes an eight-day deadline because it used a close-of-business rather than a 24-hour timeline). He was admonished and sanctioned by being prohibited from bringing any cases to the court for 12 months. Again, attorneys are outraged because Dow is one of the foremost capital defense attorneys in the country, founder and co-director of the Texas Innocence Project, and carried a caseload of a dozen capital cases at the time of the sanction. It is also the case that other attorneys have filed late pleadings and not received the heavy, some might say, draconian punishment that was handed to Dow. It certainly has the appearance that the very public recriminations toward Judge Keller that led to the judicial inquiry might have something to do with his punishment (Lithwick, 2015). The fact of being 30 minutes late doesn't seem to equal removing a talented attorney's assistance from 12 people about to be executed.

QUOTE & QUERY

This Court has never held that the Constitution forbids the execution of a convicted defendant who has had a full and fair trial but is later able to convince a habeas court that he is "actually" innocent. Quite to the contrary, we have repeatedly left that question unresolved, while expressing considerable doubt that any claim based on alleged "actual innocence" is constitutionally cognizable.

Justice Scalia, dissenting in In Re Troy Davis, 557 U.S. __, 130 S. Ct. 1, 2-3, 2009.

 Is Justice Scalia saying that there is no Constitutional right for those actually innocent to be heard by the courts?

Another example of hypertechnical rules versus justice is the case of Johnny Conner, who was convicted of murder committed during an attempted robbery. His trial attorney neglected to bring forward evidence in which the witnesses described the robber as "sprinting" away from the scene, but Conner had nerve damage in his leg and could only limp. The appellate attorney brought up the issue on appeal, but he neglected to attach any medical evidence, so the appellate judges refused to consider it as new evidence. The attorney general of Texas later argued that, *regardless of the factuality of the evidence*, it should not be allowed in the federal appeal because it was not admitted in the state appeal (Lindell, 2006c). Johnny Connor was executed in August 2007.

Judges may simply apply black-and-white rules, or they may attempt to enact the "spirit of justice." In June 2010, the majority of the Supreme Court decided that basic fairness and the spirit of justice should trump rules. An inmate missed the deadline for an appeal because his attorney did not communicate with him for years despite the inmate's numerous and increasingly frantic written pleas to file the appeal. He even provided the attorney with the information necessary to file it. He also asked the Florida court to replace the attorney, but they refused, and when he filed a *pro se* brief five weeks late, they rejected it. The federal circuit court decided that the circumstances were not "extraordinary"; therefore, the missed deadline must result in rejecting the appeal regardless of its merit. The Supreme Court disagreed, arguing that due process is more important than what Justice Breyer described as "the evils of archaic rigidity" (*Holland v. Florida*, 130 S.Ct. 2549, 2010). At least in this case, basic fairness trumped hypertechnical rules.

Sentencing

Another area of judicial discretion is in sentencing. Judges have an awesome responsibility in sentencing offenders and yet receive little training to guide their discretion. It is also true that judges' decisions are scrutinized by public watchdog groups and appellate-level courts.

Evidence indicates that judges' decisions must be based at least partially on personal standards, for no consistency seems to appear between the decisions of individual judges in the same community. Hofer, Blackwell, and Ruback (1999) point out that most of the disparity in sentencing in the federal system before the advent of the sentencing guidelines occurred because of different patterns exhibited by individual judges. They cited studies that found, for instance, that judges' sentences were influenced by whether they had been prosecutors and by their religion.

federal sentencing guidelines
Mandated sentences created by Congress for use by judges when imposing sentence (recent Supreme Court decisions have overturned the mandatory nature of the guidelines).

The other extreme is when judges have *no* discretion in sentencing. **Federal sentencing guidelines** were written by Congress requiring the judge to impose a specific sentence unless there was a proven mitigating or aggravating factor in the case. The sentencing guidelines did reduce disparity among federal judges (Hofer, Blackwell, and Ruback, 1999); however, the guidelines received a great deal of criticism because of the extremely long sentences applied to drug crimes. Racial bias was alleged in that the sentence for crack cocaine crimes was 100 times longer than sentences for powder cocaine crimes, even though these two drugs are chemically exactly the same.

The argument supporting this disparity was that crack cocaine was more associated with other crimes and more addictive; however, there was a widespread belief that the disparity was simply racist. African Americans are much more likely to be convicted of crack crimes, and white Americans are more likely to be convicted for powder cocaine (Hofer et al., 1999).

Some federal judges, such as J. Lawrence Irving in 1991 and others, were so appalled by the length of drug sentences as required by the sentencing guidelines that they refused to sentence offenders. Some even quit, refusing to impose the mandated sentences, which they considered to be ridiculously long and overly punitive in certain cases (Tonry, 2005: 43). Congress continued to ignore the pleas to make the sentences more equitable, but, in a series of cases, the U.S. Supreme Court basically invalidated the mandatory nature of federal sentencing guidelines. First, they ruled that the defendant's Sixth Amendment rights were violated if the judges used elements to increase the sentence without first proving such elements in a court of law (*United States v. Booker*, 125 S.Ct. 1006, 2005). Then they ruled that judges could adjust the sentences downward if it was reasonable to do so (*Kimbrough v. United States*, 552 U.S. 85, 2007). Finally, they extended that ruling to all federal cases, not just drug cases (*Gall v. United States*, 552 U.S. 38, 2007). The standard to be used to evaluate any legal error in sentencing is an abuse of discretion test rather than if the sentence was required because of extraordinary circumstances (Barnes, 2007). Finally, in August 2010, President Obama signed into law legislation that reduced the disparity to 18:1 from 100:1. The new law also eliminated the five-year mandatory minimum sentence for crimes involving five grams of cocaine or more. However, other mandatory minimum laws continue to restrict federal and state judges' discretion in sentencing.

Conclusion

In this chapter, we examined how the discretion of defense attorneys, prosecutors, and judges leads to ethical dilemmas. There are crucial differences in the duties and ethical responsibilities of defense attorneys and prosecutors. The prosecutor's goal is justice, which should imply an objective pursuit of the truth; however, we know that sometimes the only goal seems to be winning. Judges have their own unique ethical dilemmas, and their discretion can be understood in the two areas of court rulings and sentencing.

Chapter Review

1. **Describe the ethical issues faced by defense attorneys.**

   Defense attorneys have ethical issues that arise in the areas of responsibility to the client (they must defend clients even if they believe they are guilty and whether or not the client can pay once appointed), conflicts of interest (balancing an individual client against overall effectiveness as an attorney with a caseload of many), zealous defense (determining the limits of what should be done to defend clients), and confidentiality (keeping clients' confidences even if it harms third parties).

2. **Describe the ethical issues faced by prosecutors.**

   The prosecutor must seek justice, not merely a conviction. Ethical issues may arise in the areas of use of discretion (determining whom to charge), conflicts of interest (and how they affect decision making), plea bargaining (specifically, whether to overcharge and/or hide exculpatory evidence), media relations (and how much to reveal about the case), expert witnesses (including the halo effect, discovery, and the use of forensic evidence), and zealous prosecution (what is acceptable in zealous prosecution).

3. **Describe some of the areas of forensic science that have been challenged by opponents.**

   Only DNA evidence has not received a barrage of criticism regarding the lack of scientific method involved in analysis. Hair analysis, arson investigation, ballistics, fingerprint analysis, bite mark identification, and scent identification have been criticized.

4. **Describe the ethical issues faced by judges.**

   Ethical issues for judges occur in the areas of how to interpret the law or rules (letting biases affect their judgments) and sentencing. While judges have the ability to use their discretion to sentence, they should be guided by reasonableness, not any personal or public bias.

5. **Describe how federal sentencing guidelines have changed due to Supreme Court decisions.**

   Sentencing guidelines were widely criticized as racially biased in that crack cocaine earned a punishment 100 times more serious than powder cocaine. Federal judges were hamstrung by the mandatory nature of the sentencing guidelines and could not sentence a drug offender to a shorter term of imprisonment. In *Booker v. U.S.*, the Supreme Court held that the mandatory nature of the guidelines was a violation of due process. The guidelines are now advisory.

Study Questions

1. Explain the confidentiality rules of defense attorneys, and some situations where they may be able to disclose confidential information.

2. Compare the potential conflicts of interest of defense attorneys and those of prosecutors.

3. List and describe the functions of jury consultants and why they are criticized.

4. Describe asset forfeiture and why it has been criticized.

5. List the types of information that can be disclosed to the media and the information that should not be revealed to the media.

Writing/Discussion Exercises

1. Write an essay on (or discuss) the proper role of defense attorneys regarding their clients. Should attorneys pursue the wishes of their clients even if they think it is not in the clients' best interest? What if it would hurt a third party (but not be illegal)? Do you think that attorneys should maintain confidentiality if their clients are involved in ongoing criminal activity that is not inherently dangerous?

2. Write an essay on (or discuss) what your decision would be if you were on a disciplinary committee evaluating the following case: A prosecutor was working with police in a standoff between a triple murderer and police. When the murderer demanded to talk to a public defender, the police did not want to have a public defender get involved, so the prosecutor pretended to be one. He spoke with the

suspect on the telephone and lied about his name and being a public defender. The man then surrendered to police. The prosecutor was sanctioned by the state bar for misrepresentation and was put on probation and required to take 20 hours of continuing legal education in ethics, pass the Multistate Professional Responsibility Examination, and be supervised by another attorney. In your essay, describe what you think should have occurred and why.

3. Write an essay on (or discuss) the legality/ethics of the following actions of a prosecutor:

    *   Announcing a suspect of a drive-by shooting to the media so the offender was in danger from rival gang members, and then offering protective custody only if the man would plead guilty.

    *   Authorizing the arrest of a 10-year-old boy who confessed to a crime, even though there was no serious possibility that he was guilty, in order to pressure a relative to confess.

    *   Authorizing the arrest of one brother for drugs, even though the prosecutor knew the charge would be thrown out (but the young man would lose a scholarship to college), in order to have leverage so that he would give evidence against his brother.

Key Terms

asset forfeiture	federal sentencing	shadow jury
attorney–client privilege	guidelines	plea bargain
criminalistics	halo effect	

ETHICAL DILEMMAS

Situation 1
Your first big case is a multiple murder. As defense attorney for Sy Kopath, you have come to the realization that he really did break into a couple's home and torture and kill them in the course of robbing them of jewelry and other valuables. He has even confessed to you that he did it. However, you are also aware that the police did not read him his *Miranda* warning and that he was coerced into giving a confession without your presence. What should you do? Would your answer be different if you believed that he was innocent or didn't know for sure?

Situation 2
You are completing an internship at a defense attorney's office during your senior year in college. After graduation you plan to enter law school and pursue a career as an attorney, although you have not yet decided what type of law to practice. Your duties as an intern are to assist the private practitioner you work for in a variety of tasks, including interviewing clients and witnesses, organizing case files, running errands, and photocopying. A case that you are helping with involves a defendant charged with armed robbery. One day while you are at the office alone, the defendant comes in and gives you a package for the attorney. In it you find a gun. You believe, but do not know for a fact, that the gun is the one used in the armed robbery. When the attorney returns, he instructs you to return the package to the defendant. What should you do? What should the attorney do?

Situation 3

You are an attorney and are aware of a colleague who could be considered grossly incompetent. He drinks and often appears in court intoxicated. He ignores his cases and does not file appropriate motions before deadlines expire. Any person who is unlucky enough to have him as a court-appointed attorney usually ends up with a conviction and a heavy sentence because he does not seem to care what happens to his clients and rarely advises going to trial. When he does take a case to trial, he is unprepared and unprofessional in the courtroom. You hear many complaints from defendants about his demeanor, competence, and ethics. Everyone—defense attorneys, prosecutors, and judges alike—knows this person and his failings, yet nothing is done. Should you do something? If so, what?

Situation 4

You are a prosecutor in a jurisdiction that does not use the grand jury system. An elderly man has administered a lethal dose of sleeping tablets to his wife, who was suffering from Alzheimer's disease. He calmly turned himself in to the police department, and the case is on the front page of the paper. It is entirely up to you whether to charge him with murder. What would you do? What criteria did you use to arrive at your decision?

Situation 5

You are a deputy prosecutor and have to decide whether to charge a defendant with possession and sale of a controlled substance. You know you have a good case because the guy sold drugs to students at the local junior high school, and many of the kids are willing to testify. The police are pressuring you to make a deal because the defendant has promised to inform on other dealers in the area if you don't prosecute. What should you do?

Ethical Misconduct in the Courts and Responses

Wrongfully convicted ex-inmate and Innocence Project attorney Barry Scheck (right)

CHRIS KLEPONIS/Getty Images

Clarence Brandley was a high school janitor in a small Texas town near Houston. In 1980, a young woman on a visiting girls' volleyball team disappeared while her team was practicing. The school was empty except for five janitors and the volleyball team. A search uncovered the girl's body in the school auditorium; it was later determined that she had been raped and strangled. Clarence Brandley and another janitor found the body and were the first to be interrogated by police. Brandley was black; the other janitor was white. The police officer who interrogated them reportedly said, "One of you two is going to hang for this." Then he said to Brandley, "Since you're the nigger, you're elected." Police and prosecutors then evidently began a concerted effort to get Brandley convicted, in the following ways:

- Evidence that might have been helpful to the defense was "lost." (Caucasian hairs near the girl's vagina were never tested and compared to those of the other janitors.)

Chapter Objectives

1. Detail the types of misconduct that have been associated with defense attorneys, prosecutors, and judges.

2. Explain the reasons why such misconduct occurs.

3. Describe the Innocence Projects, how many individuals have been found to be wrongly imprisoned, and why.

4. Discuss some proposals to improve the justice system and reduce ethical misconduct.

5. Describe the concepts associated with judicial activism or constructionism and how this issue relates to ethical misconduct.

293

- Witnesses were coerced into sticking to stories that implicated Brandley. (One of the janitors reported that he had been threatened with jail if he didn't promote the story supporting Brandley's guilt.)

- Witnesses who came forward with contrary evidence were ignored and sent away. (The father-in-law of one of the janitors who later became a prime suspect told the prosecutor that this man had told him where the girl's clothes would be found two days before police actually found them.)

- Defense attorneys were not told of witnesses. (A woman came to the prosecutor after the second trial and stated that her common-law husband had confessed a murder to her and ran away the same night the girl's body had been found. This woman's husband had worked as a janitor at the school, had been fired a month previous to the murder, but had also been seen at the school the day of the murder.)

What defense attorneys eventually discovered was that in all probability this man and another janitor had abducted and murdered the girl. The other janitors had seen the girl with these two men (not Brandley) but had lied during the two trials. Here are the words of an appellate judge who ruled on the motion for a new trial:

> In the thirty years that this court has presided over matters in the judicial system, no case has presented a more shocking scenario of the effects of racial prejudice . . . and public officials who for whatever motives lost sight of what is right and just. . . . The court unequivocally concludes that the color of Clarence Brandley's skin was a substantial factor which pervaded all aspects of the State's capital prosecution against him. (quoted in Radelet, Bedau, and Putnam, 1992: 134)

Even after this finding, it took another *two years* for the Texas Court of Criminal Appeals to rule that Brandley deserved a new trial. He served nine years on death row before his defense attorneys finally obtained his freedom. At one point, he was just six days away from execution (Davies, 1991).

Do people end up in prison for crimes they did not commit? The fact is that they do. James Curtis Giles was finally exonerated of a gang rape after spending 10 years in prison and 14 years as a registered sex offender. DNA analysis showed that there was no physical evidence linking him to rape, and there was evidence of another perpetrator. In 1982, a man who pleaded guilty to the rape said he did the crime along with men named James Giles and Michael Brown. James Curtis Giles lived 15 miles away from the victim and did not match her description of the attacker. He also had an alibi. Investigators ignored another man with same name who lived across the street from the victim and had been arrested with Brown on other charges. Despite this information, the wrong Giles was convicted (Garay, 2007).

While ethical misconduct on the part of legal professionals is not always the reason innocent people end up in prison, unfortunately in many cases it is.

Ethical Misconduct

In the sections to follow, it is true that more attention is given to the misconduct of prosecutors and judges than defense attorneys. This is not to say that defense attorneys are more ethical than the other two groups; however, except for public defenders, defense attorneys are not public servants as are the other two groups of legal professionals. It is a legitimate argument that prosecutors and judges have higher duties than defense attorneys because they represent the body politic. They are the public servants referred to in Chapter 4 who have immense powers of discretion but also are held to higher standards of behavior in their public and private life.

Defense Attorney Misconduct

The major complaint about defense attorneys is that they do not communicate regularly with clients. Complaints received by bar associations generally involve clients who believe that they are not getting what they paid for, in that attorneys don't return their calls, don't keep them informed about what is being done on their case, and don't seem to be putting any effort in the case after they have been paid. This is true for civil attorneys as well; however, criminal defendants are helpless since they may be in jail. Some attorneys meet with their client only before hearings or other court appearances. Such neglect occurs because of large caseloads. Many attorneys operate under a crisis management approach whereby the to-do list every week can only accommodate those tasks that are at deadline or after a deadline has passed. The consequence is that some cases do not get the attention they should—witnesses are not contacted, legal research is not conducted, and exculpatory evidence is not asked for.

Ineffective Counsel

One of the most often cited reasons for false convictions (in addition to eyewitness testimony) is ineffective assistance of counsel. The legal standard for what constitutes ineffective counsel is set quite high—so high that in the case of Calvin Burdine, whose lawyer slept through parts of his trial, the state appellate court said that if a lawyer wasn't sleeping during a *crucial* part of the trial, it wasn't ineffective counsel. After the defense attorneys appealed in federal court, the 5th Circuit decided that due process required that Burdine deserved a new trial (*Cockrell v. Burdine*, 262 F.3d 336, 2002). Other behaviors reported of lawyers in capital and other cases include the following (Schehr and Sears, 2005):

- Attorneys' use of heroin and cocaine during trial
- Attorneys letting the defendant wear the same clothes described by the victim
- Attorneys admitting that they didn't know the law or facts of the case
- Attorneys not being able to name a single death penalty case holding
- Attorneys drinking heavily each day of the trial and being arrested for a 0.27 blood alcohol level

There are also cases where the attorney has crossed the line from zealous defense to breaking the law. In a few cases, defense attorneys go to extreme lengths to change the course of testimony, such as bribing witnesses or judges, allowing their client to intimidate a witness, or instructing their client to destroy physical evidence or manufacture an alibi and then commit perjury. In San Antonio, a local attorney pled guilty to bribing a local judge for lenient sentences and other favors for his clients. In return, he paid for repairs on the judge's car. The judge did not run for reelection and eventually also pled guilty (Perez, 2015). Most misconduct by defense attorneys probably falls into the realm of negligence, not criminal behavior.

(•) IN THE NEWS | *Trading Legal Services for Sex*

News reports appear periodically describing how criminal defense attorneys offer potential clients legal services in return for sex. Typically, clients are poor and cannot afford legal representation and the attorney exploits this desperation. In a Texas case, a woman was trying to obtain legal representation for her husband. In a Georgia case, a public defender brought drugs to and represented women in jail in return for an agreement to show their breasts (in jail) and have sex with him when they were released.

Sources: various news stories: www.msn.com/en-us/sports/watch/denver-attorney-accused-of-trading-legal-services-for-sex/vp-AA6V4zy; www.chron.com/news/houston-texas/article/Lawyer-accused-of-trading-legal-services-for-sex-1657331.php; http://mdjonline.com/view/full_story/18390820/article-Attorney-accused-of-unlawful-trading?instance=special%20_coverage_right_column; www.theindianalawyer.com/lawyer-who-tried-to-trade-representation-for-sex-suspended/PARAMS/article/36713

Prosecutorial Misconduct

It is important to recall that the duty of prosecutors is to seek justice, not convictions. Even so, prosecutors want to win, and there are few checks or monitors on their behavior (Elliott and Weiser, 2004). When prosecutors forget that their mission is to protect due process, not obtain a conviction at all costs, misconduct can occur. The types of misconduct range from minor lapses of ethical rules to commission of criminal acts (such as hiding evidence).

A *Chicago Tribune* investigation found that between 1963 and 2002, 381 defendants across the country had a homicide conviction thrown out because prosecutors concealed exculpatory evidence or presented evidence they knew to be false. Of the 381 defendants, 67 had been sentenced to death and were exonerated by DNA evidence or independent investigations. Nearly 30 of the 67 on death row were freed, but they served between 5 and 26 years before their convictions were reversed. The prosecutorial misconduct included concealing exculpatory evidence (both testimonial and physical), misleading the jurors as to the meaning of evidence, suppressing expert witness reports when they were exculpatory, and even withholding evidence that pointed to the culpability of their witness as the real killer instead of the person they were prosecuting (Armstrong and Possley, 2002).

In 2000, the *Cincinnati Inquirer* published the results of an investigation where they found 14 cases where prosecutors had used various forms of misconduct in capital cases (reported in Kirchmeier et al., 2009). The Veritas Initiative was commissioned by the Northern California Innocence Project to examine cases between 1997 and 2009 in California. This study reviewed more than 4,000 state and federal rulings and identified 707 cases where courts found prosecutorial misconduct. These cases are an undercounting of what probably occurs because they came only from trials and the vast majority of cases are plea bargained. In most of the cases, courts upheld the conviction, finding the prosecutorial misconduct did not change the outcome of the case. In 159 cases, they set aside the verdict or declared a mistrial. The study also found that in the time period studied only 10 prosecutors received any form of disciplinary action from the state bar (Ridolfi and Possley, 2010).

In March 2011, an updated study found 102 cases in 2010 where prosecutors' misconduct could be identified. They detailed 130 instances of misconduct that occurred in California and federal courts. In 26 of the cases, judges set aside convictions or sentences, declared a mistrial, or barred evidence specifically because of the misconduct. Combined with their earlier study of cases from 1997 to 2010, the total number of cases where misconduct occurred was 800, and 202 resulted in some judicial response such as overturning a conviction or declaring a mistrial. The study identified 107 prosecutors who committed more than one case of misconduct, and a few were cited for misconduct four, five, and six times (Martinez, 2011).

The Innocence Project (working with the Veritas Initiative) conducted similar studies in New York, Texas, Arizona, and Pennsylvania. Researchers searched through Westlaw data base and reviewed trial and appeals court decisions addressing allegations of prosecutor misconduct between the years 2004 and 2008, and also searched through state bar disciplinary records. The reported findings were New York had 151 findings of prosecutor misconduct and 3 prosecutors were disciplined. In Texas, there were 91 findings of prosecutor misconduct and only 1 prosecutor disciplined. In Arizona, 20 incidents of prosecutor misconduct were found and 3 prosecutors disciplined. Pennsylvania had 46 findings of prosecutor misconduct with 2 prosecutors disciplined.

The California District Attorneys Association (CDAA) and the Texas District & County Attorneys Association (TDCAA) published reports strongly critical of the methodology of the research into prosecutorial misconduct. These organizations reanalyzed the cases used in the California and Texas studies. Their findings indicate that prosecutorial misconduct is extremely rare and that prior studies incorrectly and unfairly conflated unintentional error with misconduct (CDAA, 2012; TDCAA, 2012).

Kirchmeier et al. (2009) discuss four types of prosecutorial misconduct: withholding exculpatory evidence, misusing pretrial publicity, using false evidence in court, and using peremptory challenges to exclude jurors despite *Batson v. Kentucky* (476 U.S. 79, 1986), which prohibited race discrimination in jury selection. When a prosecutor violates the *Batson* ruling and uses peremptory challenges in a racially discriminatory manner, there should be some sanction; however, the prosecutor must show only that he or she had some other reason for exclusion, and the legal standard is whether there is any explanation for the exclusion, even if implausible (*Purkett v. Elem*, 514 U.S. 765, 1995). Statistics from the Equal Justice Initiative, a legal advocacy group, indicate that black jurors are dismissed at a blatantly disproportionate rate compared to white jurors. In some jurisdictions, blacks were removed three times as often as whites and, in another jurisdiction, 80 percent of blacks were struck from capital cases by prosecutors (*New York Times*, 2010c). There is really no way to know if a prosecutor uses a peremptory challenge because of the race of the potential juror, but in some cases, there are suspicious indications such as codes for racial appearance on the prosecutor's notes. Some other types of misconduct are discussed next.

Improper Conduct, Improper Relationships

Most prosecutorial misconduct occurs in the furtherance of the case; however, there are some examples where it appeared that the prosecutors involved did not take their duty as public servants seriously. For instance, the Two-Ton Contest in Illinois has been written about by several authors. It occurred when prosecutors participated in a contest to see who could convict 4,000 pounds of flesh. In the attempt to win, they vied to handle cases of the most overweight defendants and, one assumes, let their prosecutorial judgment be affected by the size of the defendant (Medwed, 2009).

(( )) IN THE NEWS | *Prosecutorial Misconduct*

In 2013, Charles Hynes lost the Brooklyn DA race to Ken Thompson, perhaps partially because of the actions of his top deputy Michael Vecchione. Vecchione's alleged misconduct, along with disgraced former police investigator Louis Scarcella, has led to an investigation of over 70 cases that might have resulted in wrongful convictions. One of the cases identified was Jabbar Collins who served 15 years in prison before he was released and settled his lawsuit against the city for $10 million. A court released him because of evidence that ADA Vecchione coerced false testimony. A federal judge called ADA Vecchione's conduct "horrific" and said that he was "disturbed" and "puzzled" that the D.A. did not punish him. A prosecution witness who has recanted from his testimony that he saw Collins run from the scene of the murder said that he testified against Collins because Vecchione threatened to hit him with a coffee table and make him stay in jail unless he testified. Vecchione was also accused of *Brady* violations, intimidating a second witness with jail, and promising a third witness that his probation violation would be cleared. There was also testimony that law enforcement officials from the Brooklyn District Attorney's Office held witnesses in hotel rooms against their will and without legal justification, and prosecutors used forged, falsely "sworn" applications to obtain warrants to arrest and detain individuals who were merely prospective witnesses.

Charles Hynes ordered the review of Scarcella's cases when the David Ranta appeal showed that Scarcella had instructed a witness on who to identify in a lineup, rewarded others by letting them out of jail, and probably made up the confession that Ranta was supposed to have given to him (because the language of many confessions was too similar to occur by chance). The DA created a unit to investigate about 50 cases, some decades old.

Hynes lost the election, probably at least partially as a result of the Scarcella scandal. When Mr. Thompson took office, he expanded the unit to ten lawyers from two, and added three detective investigators. He also added a review panel of lawyers and a law professor consultant. In each case, the ADAs gather evidence and the outside review panel weigh in before sending it to the DA for the final decision whether to initiate legal review of the conviction. The conviction integrity unit has been instrumental in releasing Jeffrey Deskovic (after serving 16 years for a rape and murder he didn't commit).

The investigations have shown that Scarcella, a detective in Brooklyn from 1973 until his retirement in 1999, engaged in practices that were likely to lead to false confessions and wrongful convictions. He possibly manufactured confessions, intimidated witnesses, let informants out of jail to visit prostitutes, and used the same drug-addicted prostitute as a witness in a number of cases where she was supposed to have been there to observe the defendant commit the crime. At least 71 cases connected to Mr. Scarcella are being or have been investigated by the conviction-review unit; the unit is also investigating about 30 other problematic cases. In at least five Scarcella cases, the individuals have been exonerated. Most of them date back to the 1980s and 1990s and observers note that the patterns do not point to simply one rogue detective, but, rather, the collusion of prosecutors and detectives to move cases through the system.

Sources: Robles, 2013; Robles, 2013b; Clifford, 2014; Saul, 2014; Marzulli, 2015.

Suborning Perjury and Jailhouse Informants

Model Rule 3.3(a) forbids an attorney from knowingly allowing false evidence to be admitted; some argue that "knowingly" is too strict a standard because prosecutors have argued that they did not "know" that the evidence was false. Some argue that an objective negligence standard should be used instead (Zacharias and Green, 2009). Similar to a defense attorney's quandary when a witness commits perjury, a prosecutor must also take steps to avoid allowing false testimony to stand. The prosecutor's role is the easier one because there are no conflicting duties to protect a client; therefore, when a prosecution witness perjures himself or herself, the prosecutor has an affirmative duty to bring it to the attention of the court.

Recall from Chapters 5 and 7 that the prevalence of "testilying" by police officers is unknown, but many believe that it is fairly widespread. Researchers, observers, and especially defense attorneys believe that testilying would not occur as much if not for the active or passive acceptance of the practice by prosecutors (Cunningham, 1999). In Tulia, Texas, a large number of black defendants were convicted based on the perjured testimony of one police investigator. The prosecutor knew that the police officer on the stand had lied about his past, yet he did not disclose that information and allowed the perjury to stand. It was also revealed that the investigator lied about the defendants as well. After the intervention of the ACLU and, eventually, the governor of Texas commuting the sentences, the dozens of people convicted were finally released. The prosecutor was sanctioned by the Texas bar and almost lost his law license. Many believe he should have, considering his role in the convictions (Herbert, 2002, 2003).

Many of the cases where an innocent person eventually is exonerated involve jailhouse informants. In these cases, the more common misconduct of prosecutors is a *Brady* violation, where they do not reveal to the defense attorney that there has been a deal made with the informant or any negative history of the informant that would affect his or her credibility. In some cases, however, the prosecutor has also allowed the informant to lie on the stand about receiving a deal for his testimony. In one case that is similar to many others reported in other sources, the informant was promised he would be sent to a federal prison instead of state prison in return for his testimony that the convicted man confessed to him while they were cellmates in jail. During the trial, when asked by the defense attorney if anything had been promised to him for his testimony, the informant committed perjury by answering that he had not been promised anything, and the prosecutor allowed the perjury to take place, knowing that he was lying (Raeder, 2007).

In 2015, Joseph Sledge was released from prison 37 years after being wrongfully convicted of murder. Evidence (hair that was believed to be the murderer's) that had been reported as lost was found years after it had been requested by the defense for DNA testing. A three-judge panel appointed by the North Carolina Supreme Court heard the DNA evidence as well as a recantation from the jailhouse informant who testified that he had lied at the trial in return for leniency on his own drug case. He testified he had been coached by the prosecutor as to what to say on the stand (Drew, 2015).

Generally, jailhouse informants rarely come forward unless there is an explicit or implicit reward. Observers point out that if the defense offered anything of value to witnesses for favorable testimony it would be considered felony bribery, but prosecutors routinely cut deals with co-crime partners, other suspects, and jailhouse informants. To have years cut off of a prison sentence or to have charges reduced is every bit as valuable as cash, so why isn't it considered bribery? In *Giglio v. United States* (405 U.S. 150, 1972), the Supreme Court said that the prosecutor had a duty to disclose any deals made with informants or any other information that would implicate the credibility of a witness. Garrett and Neufeld (2011) reported that in one locale, prosecutors did not offer deals until *after* the informant testified, allowing him to truthfully answer "no" when the defense asked if he had received anything for his testimony. Prosecutors knew that if they didn't come through with a deal afterward the jail grapevine would ensure the flow of jailhouse informants would stop so the process worked for everyone except the defendant. Raeder (2007) points out that Los Angeles had instituted a policy that dramatically restricted the use of jailhouse informants with no deterioration of its conviction rate. Illinois has passed legislation concerning the use of such testimony

| ((•)) **IN THE NEWS** | *Jailhouse Informant Scandal* |

In Spring 2015 Superior Court judge Thomas Goethals issued an order disqualifying the entire Orange County District Attorney's Office (all 250 prosecutors) from continuing to prosecute a major death penalty case. He did so after years of misconduct involving jailhouse informants, culminating in the case of Scott Dekraai who pleaded guilty to killing his ex-wife and seven other people in 2011. The case highlighted a pattern of misconduct where sheriffs' deputies placed informants in cells and prosecutors misled the court.

In the Dekraai case a public defender discovered that a jailhouse informant who had testified had done the same thing in another case. After further investigation, he found that the sheriff's deputies would deliberately place jailhouse snitches in cells next to high-value inmates awaiting trials, with instructions to collect confessions. The DA's office claimed they did nothing wrong, but it was discovered that there was a trove of potentially exculpatory information obtained through informants that the district attorney's office refused to disclose even upon receiving specific discovery requests. Allegations included the possibility that prosecutors did not charge the jailhouse informants in serious cases when there was probable cause in order to protect the secret system. It was also reported that two informants with extensive criminal records had received more than $150,000 from law enforcement agencies for obtaining information from jailed suspects awaiting trials. Luckily Dekraai already pled guilty to killing the eight people, so the misconduct will not derail his punishment. California attorney general Kamala Harris has appealed Goethals' ruling.

Source: Lithwick, 2015b.

in capital cases, and Canada has instituted stringent guidelines for the use of jailhouse informants (Garrett and Neufeld, 2011).

What's wrong with using jailhouse informants? It depends on how they are used. Testimony from informants is legal, even if the informant gets a reduced sentence or material benefits; however, if there is a system where informants are directed and guided by law enforcement, they become more like law enforcement agents and run afoul of Fifth and Sixth Amendment restrictions on interrogation. There is also a strong temptation to lie about what the targeted defendant said in order to obtain the promised reward.

Misconduct Involving Expert Witnesses

Misconduct also occurs when prosecutors intentionally use scientific evidence that they know to be false. There are proven instances where prosecutors put on the stand so-called experts that they knew were unqualified and/or their expertise was without merit (Gershman, 2003). Prosecutors may bolster a witness's credentials or allow him or her to make gratuitous and unsupported claims on the witness stand, such as to state "unequivocally" that the fingerprint, hair, or lip print was the defendant's.

Giannelli and McMunigal (2007) and Fisher (2008) describe a long list of expert witnesses who became well known for their pro-prosecution bias and outlandish testimony in the area of bite marks and other areas. So-called experts include Louise Robbins (who testified in one notorious case that a boot mark matched the defendant's even though no other forensic examiner agreed), and Michael West (who supposedly invented a way to use light to identify bite marks on murder victims and always seemed to find a match to the suspect). Joyce Gilchrist, a forensic chemist from Oklahoma, was implicated in several exonerations for her hair analysis testimony in which she overstated the accuracy of the procedure and/or simply lied (Raeder, 2007; Fisher,

2008). Fred Zain evidently systematically lied, altered lab reports, and suppressed test results favorable to the defense (Possley, Mills, and McRoberts, 2004). These experts continued to be used by prosecutors even after appellate courts had excoriated their testimony and they were widely criticized by peers (Fisher, 2008).

Prosecutors have had experts suppress information that was favorable to the defense and not put it in their report or not conduct tests that might be helpful to the defense. Sometimes expert reports are provided to the defense but delay is used to undercut the ability of the defense to use the information. In other cases, experts are asked not to write a report at all if their findings do not help the prosecution, or prosecutors have the report filed as inconclusive so that they do not have to provide it to the defense (Giannelli and McMunigal, 2007). In their closing arguments, prosecutors may overstate the expert's testimony so "is consistent with" becomes "matched" (Gershman, 2003: 36). In some egregious cases, prosecutors have simply lied about physical evidence, such as stating that the red substance on a victim's underpants was blood when, in fact, it was paint (Gershman, 2003: 36; *Miller v. Pate*, 386 U.S. 1, 1967).

Brady Violations

The most common charge leveled against prosecutors, failure to disclose evidence, stems from a duty to reveal exculpatory evidence to the defense. In Chapter 9 the obligation to disclose exculpatory evidence established in *Brady v. Maryland* (373 U.S. 83, 1963) was discussed. In the Anthony Graves case (described in the Walking the Walk box), prosecutor Charles Sebesta was recently disbarred for *Brady* violations and other

(⋅) IN THE NEWS | *Federal Prosecutor Misconduct*

Ted Stevens died in an airplane crash in August 2010. Before his death he had been convicted of conflict of interest and bribery in a federal investigation (labeled "Operation Polar Pen"). The conviction was eventually overturned because of prosecutorial misconduct. A judge threw out the conviction in 2009 after an FBI agent that had been an investigator on the case reported that prosecutors tried to hide a witness and did not share transcripts where Bill Allen, their star witness, made contradictory statements during interviews, and prior statements contradicted what he said on the stand. Justice Department prosecutors used pending charges of sexual misconduct with underage girls as leverage for Allen's testimony, a fact not shared with defense attorneys.

William Welch II, the lead prosecutor, stepped down as head of the Justice Department's public integrity section. Two of the prosecutors involved were found to have engaged in "reckless professional conduct." One was suspended without pay for 40 days and the other for 15 days. A third prosecutor committed suicide before the investigation was concluded.

In another case, federal prosecutors were admonished in 2009 by a judge in a case against Dr. Ali Shaygan who was acquitted of 141 counts of illegal prescriptions of painkillers. The prosecutors, suspecting witness tampering, evidently had informants who had been patients of the doctor, secretly tape conversations with Shaygan's lawyers. The prosecutors never disclosed the secret taping, and they put the informants on the stand as neutral, objective witnesses. The secret taping was exposed inadvertently by a witness-informant during testimony. In a 50-page order, U.S. District judge Alan Gold accused the federal prosecutors of knowingly and repeatedly violating ethical guidelines and acting in bad faith. He issued a public reprimand to them and their supervisors for failing to supervise them. In addition to the secret taping, the prosecutors were also alleged to have engaged in vengeful prosecution by increasing the original 26 counts to 141 because the defense attorney filed a motion to suppress evidence. Under the authority of the Hyde Amendment, which allows federal judges to impose financial sanctions against the government when federal prosecutors

(continues)

engage in frivolous prosecutions or bad faith, he ordered $601,795 be paid to Shaygan for his legal fees. The U.S. Attorney's office apologized and admitted that the prosecutors had not sought supervisory approval for the secret taping according to the office's policy. One prosecutor resigned and another asked for a transfer. However, they also appealed the order and the 11th Circuit ruled that Judge Gold had imposed the order with no due process for the prosecutors and that the prosecutors' actions did not amount to the kind of misconduct defined in the Hyde Amendment.

In New Orleans, federal Judge Kurt D. Engelhardt ruled that "grotesque prosecutorial misconduct" on the part of federal prosecutors left him no choice but to throw out the convictions of Robert Faulcon Jr., Kenneth Bowen, Robert Gisevius Jr., Anthony Villavaso II, and Arthur "Archie" Kaufman, the officers who had been convicted of homicide and a cover-up in the Danziger Bridge incident

after Hurricane Katrina. He ordered new trials for all of the men. According to the judge's ruling, federal prosecutors created a prejudicial atmosphere by anonymously posting comments before and during the trial at Nola.com, the website of the *New Orleans Times-Picayune*. Former federal prosecutors Sal Perricone, Jan Mann, and Karla Dobinski posted online comments under pseudonyms during the trial that were derogatory of the police department, the defendants, and the defense attorneys.

After the Ted Stevens case, the Department of Justice developed guidelines for discovery to be adapted by the U.S. Attorney's offices around the country in order to avoid *Brady* violations. Ironically, the DOJ would prefer that these guidelines for discovery remain secret. *USA TODAY* had to employ the Freedom of Information Act (FOIA) to gain access, and then it still took three years to receive them and 19 offices still had not provided them at the time of the publication of the article.

Sources: Perksy, 2009; Johnson, 2009; Savage, 2012a; Frankel, 2011; Finn, 2013; Lithwick and Heath, 2015.

misconduct during Graves' trial. The In the News box describes cases where federal prosecutors evidently committed *Brady* violations.

Prosecutors who engage in acts such as those described earlier not only risk losing the immediate case, but also lose their credibility and undercut the trust and faith we place in the justice system.

Judicial Misconduct

Public exposés of judicial misconduct are fairly rare. Operation Greylord, in Chicago, took place in the 1980s. As a result of an FBI investigation, 92 people were indicted, including 17 judges, 48 lawyers, 10 deputy sheriffs, 8 police officers, 8 court officials, and a member of the Illinois legislature, and 31 attorneys and 8 judges were convicted of bribery. Judges accepted bribes to "fix" cases—to rule in favor of the attorney offering the bribe. Not unlike law enforcement's "blue curtain of secrecy," not one attorney came forward to expose this system of corruption, even though what was occurring was fairly well known (Weber, 1987: 60).

In the infamous "kids for cash" scandal in Pennsylvania, former judges Michael Conahan and Mark Ciavarella in Lucerne County were prosecuted for almost literally "selling" youthful offenders to a private correctional facility. They were charged with racketeering, money laundering, fraud, bribery, and federal tax violations for accepting millions of dollars in return for sending juveniles who appeared before them to a private correctional facility. Conahan had earlier shut down the county-run youth corrections center, so they would have to send the kids to the private facility. The judges conducted hearings without appointing lawyers for the juveniles and then sent them to the private facility for minor offenses. The scandal led to overturning hundreds of juvenile convictions and releasing many of the juvenile offenders sent to the facility. No one can explain why the scheme had not been exposed years before and continued without prosecutors, probation officers, or defense attorneys questioning what was happening. But red flags were raised. A newspaper had done an exposé on harsh juvenile sentencing in 2004, and a defense attorney had filed a complaint with the state judicial disciplinary board in 2006, but it failed to act until after the two judges had been indicted by the federal grand jury. The investigation began after another judge in the jurisdiction went to the FBI with his suspicions. Conahan pleaded guilty to a racketeering conspiracy charge and was sentenced to 17 years in prison. Ciavarella went to trial, was convicted of racketeering, was sentenced to 28 years in prison, and must pay $965,000 in restitution.

Biased Decisions

Judges, for the most part, are like police officers and prosecutors. They strive to fulfill their role with integrity and honesty, taking care to protect the appearance and reality of justice. It is impossible to get into the mind of a judge to know whether he decides a certain way because he believes that is what the law requires or because of some bias; therefore, judicial canons require judges to avoid even the appearance of bias or impropriety. In Chapter 9 the problem of conflict of interests was discussed. Misconduct is alleged when judges do not recuse themselves and/or act in ways that give some preferential treatment.

There is a prohibition on attorneys and judges discussing a case outside the presence of the other attorney, this is called *ex parte* communication and is prohibited because it gives one side preference over the other. Because of working conditions, this is much more likely between prosecutors and judges than with defense attorneys. This rule applies to casual conversations as well as more formal interchanges or offerings of information. *Ex parte* communications create the perception (if not the reality) of bias and if a judge favors one side or the other, due process is imperiled. In a particularly obvious case of misconduct, a Houston judge has been investigated for sending text messages during the trial to the prosecutor suggesting a line of questioning to help bolster the prosecution's case. There were allegations that it was not the first time she had done so (Horswell, 2013).

In some cases neutrality is questioned when judges voice strong opinions on issues or cases. In the 2007 Model Code of Judicial Conduct, one of the most debated areas was how judges should comport themselves in terms of public speaking and political engagement. The ideal, of course, is that judges should not have any preconceived ideas of who is right or wrong in any controversy they will rule on, but the reality is that judges do not live in a vacuum and, of course, have opinions, values, and beliefs regarding the issues of our times. The rules have been changed to accommodate First Amendment challenges that were upheld in *Minnesota v. White* (536 U.S. 765, 2002; McKoski, 2008). Now judges are more free to do speaking engagements and appear at advocacy functions, but there are still ethical issues when a judge indicates a clear bias in a current issue that may come before him or her.

Talking to the media used to be rare, but now some judges have apparently decided it is acceptable to express their views, take a stand, and act as advocate. Many question this role for judges. In some cases, judges have been asked to recuse themselves because they have indicated to news media that they already had opinions on a case before it was concluded. In 2006, Justice Scalia, in a public speech, opined that giving full due-process rights to detainees in Guantanamo was "crazy" and also made remarks referring to his son, who was serving in Iraq at the time. Several groups demanded that

((ᵔ)) IN THE NEWS | *Judicial Misconduct*

Former Pennsylvania Supreme Court justice Seamus P. McCaffery abruptly resigned in 2014 immediately before an ethics investigation was to begin, which had the potential to strip him of his pension. A federal investigation into whether McCaffery's wife's referral fees paid by law firms with cases before the judge while she served as his top judicial aide ended with no charges filed. McCaffery was also accused of exchanging 234 e-mails containing pornographic materials, interfering in civil courts in cases involving individuals who paid referral fees or contributed to his campaign, and fixing a traffic ticket for his wife. Because he has retired, no investigation will be pursued and his pension is secure. Also in Philadelphia, Judge Joseph Waters pled guilty to federal corruption charges of wire fraud and honest services fraud for asking other judges to rule in favor of an acquaintance in a small claims case.

Federal District Court judge Mark E. Fuller of the Middle District of Alabama was arrested and charged with battery in early August 2014 for beating his wife. The incident occurred in a hotel when his wife called 911. The police report said that she reported being struck hard enough to fall to the floor and then kicked and dragged around the room. He entered a pretrial diversion program that required counseling and had the misdemeanor arrest expunged; however, he was already under investigation by the five-judge Special Committee convened by the 11th Circuit U.S. Court of Appeals. Other allegations against the judge were that he had also beat his first wife, had an affair with his current wife who was his court bailiff, refused to recuse himself from cases where the federal government was a party even though he received millions in federal money in his private business, and orchestrated the arrest and conviction of the former governor, refusing to recuse himself from that case even though there had been enmity between the two. He refused to step down despite calls for his resignation from politicians from both parties until June of 2015 when the panel found "grounds for impeachment." Their finding was "unanimously adopted" by the Circuit's full Judicial Council, a body of the U.S. Judicial Conference, who could decide to recommend the U.S. Congress take up impeachment proceedings. Fuller resigned and, thus, will keep his federal pension.

Sources: McCoy and Purcell, 2014; Blinder and Robertson, 2014; McQuade, 2014; Friedman, 2015.

he recuse himself from the case of *Hamdan v. Rumsfeld* (126 S. Ct. 2749, 2006) because the case was about that very subject (what, if any, due-process rights in American courts the detainees deserved). Justice Scalia did not recuse himself, and Hamdan did win his case, with the Supreme Court holding that detainees deserved some due process and that the military commissions that were created at the time were not sufficient. Scalia was in the dissent, however, so arguably one might conclude that he had already made up his mind before the case was decided (Lane, 2006).

Some question judges' motives in allowing cameras in the courtroom. Some argue that judges, as well as defense attorneys, prosecutors, and witnesses, become too interested in their appearance in the media rather than the interests of justice. There seems to be real concern that judges and lawyers play to the camera, perhaps to the detriment of swift resolution of the case. Other issues are raised with the prevalence of social media. One Texas judge has received a formal rebuke from the State Commission on Judicial Conduct for posting about an ongoing trial on her Facebook page. She argued that she was engaged in public education and information, and none of her statements indicated bias; however, the commission said that her actions discredited the judiciary. They based their decision on the fact that she posted information that she had not admitted into evidence, that she posted online yet forbid jurors from doing so, and that her actions cast reasonable doubt upon her own impartiality (BBC, 2015).

Other Misconduct

Swisher (2009) lists and discusses various forms of judicial misconduct, including failing to inform defendants of their rights, coercing guilty pleas, exceeding sentencing authority, exceeding bail authority, denying full and fair hearings or trials, abusing the criminal contempt power, ignoring probable cause requirements, denying defendants' rights, and penalizing defendants for exercising their rights. Other forms of unethical behavior are less blatant. Judges have a duty to conclude judicial processing with reasonable punctuality. However, there are widespread delays in processing, partly because of the lack of energy with which some judges pursue their dockets. In the same jurisdiction, and with a balanced assignment of cases, one judge may have only a couple dozen pending cases and another judge may have literally hundreds. Some judges routinely allow numerous continuances, set trial dates far into the future, start the docket call at 10:00 A.M., conclude the day's work at 3:00 p.m., and in other ways take a desultory approach to swift justice.

There are continual news examples of judges who evidently do not uphold the high standards of behavior that should be associated with the black robes. In Boston, an immigration judge was suspended for a year because he referred to himself as Tarzan when hearing a case involving a Ugandan woman named Jane. Another judge deported a man without bothering to check to see that his tax records and birth certificate were authentic (they were). Attorney General Alberto Gonzales wrote a strongly worded memo to all federal immigration judges at the time insisting that they abide by rules of professional decorum (Simmons, 2006).

Pimental (2009) notes that while egregious cases of judicial misconduct appear in the news (i.e., sexual misconduct or bribery), the more prevalent forms of misconduct may only be known to the attorneys who practice before the judge (i.e., favoritism, racial or gender bias, arbitrary decision making). However, it is extremely rare for attorneys to file complaints against judges. In fact, Pimental notes one case in which an attorney reported that his client bribed a judge, and, as a result, the attorney was sanctioned by the bar association for revealing client confidences. Nothing happened to the judge (2009: 938).

Judge Thomas Porteous, a former federal judge based in New Orleans, was one of the few judges who have ever been impeached by the House of Representatives in the winter of 2010 for bribery, perjury, and improper conduct even though he had been suspended from hearing cases back in 2008 (but continued to receive his annual salary of $174,000). Another federal judge, Samuel Kent of Texas, resigned before his impeachment process was completed in 2009. His misconduct involved sexual harassment and assault of female employees and obstruction of justice in the investigation that ensued when one of his victims filed complaints against him (Alpert, 2010). Mississippi judge Bobby DeLaughter pleaded guilty to obstruction of justice in 2009. DeLaughter was accused of giving a favorable ruling in a case in return for consideration for a federal judgeship. We must be careful not to paint with too broad a brush. Only a few judges are involved in the most egregious examples of unethical behavior, such as taking bribes or trampling the due-process rights of defendants, just as only a small percentage of police officers, defense attorneys, and prosecutors commit extreme behaviors. Most judges are ethical and take great care to live up to the obligations of their role. However, as with the other criminal justice professionals, sometimes there are systemic biases and subtle ways in which the principles of justice and due process are subverted.

Factors in Wrongful Conviction

Recall from Chapter 3 that wrongful convictions are increasingly appearing in the news. The factors that seem to be correlated with wrongful convictions clearly indicate that legal professionals must take responsibility for reducing the possibility of such gross miscarriages of justice. It should be recognized that while sometimes prosecutors are implicated as pivotal in a wrongful conviction (e.g., Ken Anderson in the Michael Morton case), in other cases, prosecutors have been pivotal in helping to free someone, as described in the Walking the Walk box.

WALKING THE WALK

In 1992 in Somerville, Texas, six people—a grandmother, her daughter, and her four grandchildren—were stabbed and bludgeoned to death. The house was set on fire to cover up the murders. Police quickly arrested Robert Carter, the father of one of the children. It came out that the motive for the murder was that he didn't want to pay child support. At some point during his questioning, he named Anthony Graves as the person who helped him commit the murders. Anthony Graves was 27 years old and lived 16 miles away in Brenham, Texas. He had spent the night of the murders at the home of his brother with three other people. Despite no evidence that he even knew the family killed, much less any evidence of a motive that would fuel such a homicidal rampage, he was arrested. At trial, the prosecutor used Carter's testimony, the testimony of five inmates and jailers who swore they heard Graves confess, and testimony that a knife owned by Graves was the same exact weapon that inflicted the fatal wounds. Even though his brother testified as to his alibi that night, his girlfriend refused and left the courthouse immediately before she was supposed to testify. He was convicted and sentenced to death.

In 2002, a journalism class at the University of St. Thomas in Houston, led by their teacher, began to investigate the case. They collected evidence that Carter had continued to tell anyone who would listen that he lied about Graves' involvement in the murders, right up to his execution. They also discovered that because of noisy fans and broken intercoms, it was probably impossible for the supposed overheard conversations to have occurred in the jail. Also, they found that Graves' girlfriend left the courtroom that day in tears because she had been intimidated by District Attorney Charles Sebesta, who asked the judge to read her *Miranda* rights and indicated to her that he was going to charge her with either perjury or accessory to the crime after she testified. Later she said that she felt if Anthony Graves could be convicted on virtually no evidence, even though he had been at home with three other people when he was supposed to have been committing the murders, she believed the same thing could have happened to her. The most damning piece of evidence that they discovered was that Carter told Sebesta right before he was supposed to testify that he had lied and Graves had nothing to do with it. Sebesta had, at the time, managed to get an indictment against Carter's wife and told Carter he wouldn't prosecute her if he would testify against Graves. So he did. Sebesta never informed the defense that Carter had recanted (again). That prosecutorial misconduct was enough to get Graves' conviction overturned by an appellate court years later.

The county brought in a special prosecutor from Houston, Kelly Siegler, to retry the case. She was known as a fierce victim's advocate and a fearless prosecutor, winning 19 death penalty cases, losing none. As she prepared for the case, she went over the evidence. At first, she said she thought it was going to be a difficult case to prosecute, especially since Carter had since been executed. However, as she examined the case files, things didn't seem to make sense. Carter's wife had been under indictment, but there was literally no evidence against her. More strange, she was released on a personal bond and then the charges were dropped. If she had been involved in a brutal mass murder, why were charges dropped so quickly? Another thing that stood out was that the type of knife owned by Graves (no actual murder weapon was recovered) that was supposedly used to kill the victims was obviously too flimsy to have inflicted the brutal wounds. Some of the stab wounds literally penetrated the skulls and this knife had no hilt. If someone had tried to use it, they would have inflicted wounds on themselves, but more likely the blade would have broken. Finally, Siegler could find absolutely no connection between Graves and Carter or the murdered family. As she read the numerous recantations of Carter, even immediately before he was executed, she started to shift from developing a trial strategy to a dawning realization that Graves might be innocent.

In an extremely unusual move, she met with the defense team and asked them to encourage witnesses to talk with her and the Texas Ranger investigator working with her. They interviewed 60 people, going over the same ground that the journalism students had and reaching the same conclusions. They then went to Bill Parham, the district attorney of Burleson County, and recommended that charges be dropped. In 2011, Graves was released from the county jail where he had been awaiting his new trial.

Siegler was lambasted by Charles Sebesta, the former prosecutor, who took out a full-page ad in the paper and gave interviews to numerous media outlets accusing her of dropping the case because she was afraid of ruining her perfect record. Her position was clear and with no equivocation she blamed Sebesta, calling him the "worst nightmare" of the criminal justice system. "It's a prosecutor's responsibility to never fabricate evidence or manipulate witnesses or take advantage of victims," she said. "And unfortunately, what happened in this case is all of those things." Graves' trial, she said, had been "a travesty." In June 2015, a three-person panel of the Texas State Bar Association voted to strip Sebesta of his law license.

However, it was not only the prosecutor who was at fault. The Texas Ranger who had investigated the case was criticized by later investigators, describing his investigation as sloppy and biased. Also clearly at fault were the appellate judges who, for years, rubberstamped a case that had literally no evidence other than a recanted accusation by the true perpetrator, and "junk science" evidence of scent identification that has been thoroughly discredited.

Siegler and the defense pursued a court order releasing Graves from imprisonment. Yet another miscarriage occurred when the Texas comptroller's office decided that because the order did not include an actual innocence finding, Graves would be ineligible for compensation. Texas has a compensation law that awards the wrongfully convicted $80,000 per year of wrongful imprisonment. Stung by a media storm of national criticism, the Texas legislature passed a special law allowing Graves to receive compensation and he received $1.4 million in June 2011, with annuity checks to follow.

Kelly Siegler is a prosecutor who deserves to be honored because she righted a wrong that had gone on for almost two decades. The sad fact is that her ethical actions (pursuing the prosecutor's duty to seek justice, not a conviction) were necessary. Unfortunately, she could not give back two decades of Anthony Graves' life.

Sources: 48 Hours Mystery.com, 2011; Colloff, 2011.

Many of the factors (perjury by informants, police and prosecutorial misconduct, false confessions, "junk science," ineffective assistance of counsel) have been discussed previously, a few more will be discussed here.

Mistaken Eyewitness Testimony

We know more today about the vagaries of eyewitness memory today than we have in previous years. Research shows that memory is not as accurate as some people (including jurors) believe. Mistaken eyewitness testimony may not involve any wrongdoing on the part of police or prosecutors; however, in some cases improper police or prosecutor behavior influenced witnesses to identify the wrong person. For instance, police officers may repeatedly ask victims if they were sure that the suspect was not the person, or using "show-ups" that present only one person to the witness instead of a lineup. Research shows that people are woefully poor witnesses and, more dangerous, are convinced they are right about the identification by the time of trial.

The Supreme Court recently rejected an argument that judicial review of eyewitness testimony was necessary even given the research that showed how faulty it was (*Perry v. New Hampshire*, 132 S.Ct. 716, 2012). This leaves it to prosecutors' offices to make sure such testimony is credible. Suggestions include using sequential identification (since witnesses feel pressure to pick one person from a regular lineup even if told none of the people may be the suspect), and double-blind identifications where the law enforcement official does not know which person is the suspect (to avoid giving conscious or unconscious cues). These science-based techniques to improve accuracy are only helpful if prosecutors and law enforcement investigators are motivated to use them.

False Confessions

False confessions are another important factor in wrongful convictions. Chapter 6 covered how police behavior can induce a person to confess, but prosecutors are also complicit in participating in or using false confessions. False confessions are so powerful that juries have convicted individuals even when there is exculpatory DNA evidence introduced at trial. Prosecutors explain away the DNA by saying in rape cases that the victim may have had consensual sex with someone else before the rape by the defendant, and, in murder cases, that innocent explanations exist for the presence of unknown persons. Garrett (2011), in his review of wrongful convictions, identified 40 cases of false confessions; over half were given by juveniles or mentally retarded suspects.

Eddie Lowery spent 10 years in prison for a rape he didn't commit. His confession included elements of the crime that only the perpetrator would have known. Why did he confess? Because police told him he failed a lie detector test and he believed that they wouldn't let up until he confessed. How did his confession include details of the crime scene? Because they coached him, said Lowery, correcting him on every element of his confession until he got it right. Lowery received $7.5 million in a suit against the police department in Riley County, Kansas (Garrett, 2011). Phillip Bivens falsely confessed to a rape and murder in Mississippi even though he had never even met his supposed crime partner. Three men were convicted. All have been exonerated. One of the three had implicated Bivens, who was so fearful of police (he thought they were going to kill him) he confessed even though there wasn't any evidence to tie him to the crime (Robertson, 2010b).

The "Norfolk Four" were four sailors who were convicted of rape and murder in 1997. They allege that they falsely confessed to the crime because of the coercive interrogation tactics of a police investigator. There was no other evidence to link them to the crime. Before they were brought to trial, another man, who knew the victim, confessed, admitting he did it alone, and his DNA was found at the crime scene, yet the prosecutors continued with their case against the Norfolk Four. One of the Norfolk Four served eight years before being released, but the other three were still in prison until being pardoned by Virginia's governor in August 2009. The pardon was conditional, however; the men were released on parole and had to register as sex offenders (Jackman and Kumar, 2009).

Racial Bias

Racial bias is probably a factor in some wrongful convictions. Garrett's (2011) study of 250 exonerees found that 70 percent were minorities. Whereas some of the cases probably involve pure and extreme racial prejudice, a prevalent factor in false convictions is a more subtle form of racism. Many in the criminal justice system tend to prejudge the guilt of the accused, especially if they are black men. There is a pervasive stereotypical belief that all defendants are guilty, and a disproportionate number of defendants are black. This thought pattern shapes and distorts decision making on the part of prosecutors who may sift and use evidence in a way that will support these predetermined beliefs. Also noted is a higher rate of error in cross-racial identification, stereotyping, and lack of resources among minority defendants (Schehr and Sears, 2005).

Confirmatory bias

Confirmatory bias is when someone ignores evidence that is contrary to what they believe. Confirmatory bias may lead to wrongful convictions because prosecutors ignore evidence that tends to refute their theory of the case. It might even lead to the noble-cause corruption discussed in Chapter 5. Just as police may commit misconduct when they think they have the guilty party, so, too, may prosecutors bend and even break the rules when they are sure the defendant is guilty. For instance, some prosecutors may not disclose evidence to the defense because they perceive that as possibly endangering their ability to get a murderer off the street. These individuals may be affected by confirmatory bias in that they cannot see the exculpatory nature of the evidence because they truly believe the defendant is guilty.

▍Explanations for Misconduct

The ideal, or vision, of our justice system is that it is fair, unbiased, and, through the application of due process, arrives at the truth before finding guilt and assessing punishment. The reality is that the law is administered by humans with human failings and that errors and misconduct result in innocent people being convicted, incarcerated, and sometimes executed. In this section, prosecutors get a disproportionate amount of attention because they are public servants and owe special duties to the public.

The reasons why defense attorneys and judges violate their professional responsibilities and ethical codes are probably as varied as the reasons why people commit any wrongdoing—greed, laziness, ignorance, and passion may be a start to understanding why they do what they do, but prosecutors have been the subject of more attention in the academic literature and press. One of the reasons we concentrate on prosecutors is that they have the similar powers of discretion as police officers, and they seem to also have a subculture that creates pressure to cut corners to gain a conviction. In the Quote and Query, a prosecutor explains how the mission of justice becomes subverted.

Explanations of Prosecutor Misconduct

In response to a question about why prosecutors commit the various forms of misconduct described above, one commentator explained succinctly, "Because they can." The office of the prosecutor is one of the least scrutinized in the criminal justice system and has not experienced the intense analysis directed to law enforcement or the courts. Hidden from public view are the decisions as to whom to prosecute and what charges to file. Furthermore, when wrongdoing is exposed, there is little chance of serious sanctions.

Prosecutors are immune from Section 1983 liability for their decision to prosecute or actions taken in preparation for or during trial (*Imbler v. Pachtman*, 424 U.S. 409, 1976). The Supreme Court has also ruled that prosecutors cannot be subject to civil suits against them even in cases of egregious rule breaking, if it

QUOTE & QUERY

. . . In 1984, I was 33 years old. I was arrogant, judgmental, narcissistic and very full of myself. I was not as interested in justice as I was in winning. To borrow a phrase from Al Pacino in the movie And Justice for All," *"Winning became everything." . . . After the death verdict in the Ford trial, I went out with others and celebrated with a few rounds of drinks. That's sick. I had been entrusted with the duty to seek the death of a fellow human being, a very solemn task that certainly did not warrant any "celebration."*

Marty Stroud, a New Orleans prosecutor in the Glenn Ford wrongful conviction case. Ford served 30 years before being exonerated. The quote is from Stroud's letter to the newspaper apologizing for what happened. Read his letter here: www.shreveporttimes.com/story/opinion/readers/2015/03/20/lead-prosecutor-offers-apology-in-the-case-of-exonerated-death-row-inmate-glenn-ford/25049063.

 Is it wrong for prosecutors to celebrate convictions?

concerns their adversarial function or prosecutorial decisions (*Connick v. Thompson*, 131 S. Ct. 1350 – 2011), 2011. They have limited immunity for actions taken during the investigative phase of a case and for administrative activities. Thus, lying for a warrant, coercing confessions, or making false statements to the press could expose them to liability, but rarely does (Kirchmeier et al., 2009; Zacharias and Green, 2009).

When Mike Nifong was sued by the lacrosse players for statements made to the press and other misconduct, the city refused to indemnify him and he declared bankruptcy. Thomas Lee Goldstein was more successful in obtaining damages. He was wrongfully convicted in Los Angeles County partially due to the prosecutor's misconduct. In this case, the prosecutor used a jailhouse informant who testified that Goldstein confessed, but the informant lied on the stand that he had never been an informant in the past. In fact, he had and had received money for previous testimony in another case. The prosecutor allowed the perjury to stand. Goldstein had his case overturned and was exonerated and sued on a theory of misconduct during the administrative functions of the prosecutor role. A lower court barred his suit holding that the prosecutor's actions fell under his immunity protections and he appealed that decision; however, he ended up settling with the city for $7.95 million (Zacharias and Green, 2009; Cathcart, 2010).

At this point, the Supreme Court has shown no inclination to take away prosecutors' immunity. In *Pottawattamie County v. McGhee and Harrington* (129 S. Ct. 2002, 2009), the parties settled before the Supreme Court reached an opinion. However, during oral arguments, the justices seemed concerned that reducing the immunity of prosecutors would make them more hesitant to aggressively prosecute crime and subject them to frivolous lawsuits. The case involved two men who were wrongfully convicted when they were teens and served almost 30 years in prison because a prosecutor helped assemble and present false testimony against them and hid evidence that implicated the relative of a city official. They settled for $12 million with the county before the Supreme Court made any decision whether or not the immunity of prosecutors extends to the acts of preparing false testimony to be used in court. In another case, the Supreme Court reaffirmed prosecutorial immunity even when the prosecutor violated *Brady* rules by not disclosing exculpatory information to the defense (*Van De Kamp v. Goldstein*, 129 S.Ct. 855, 2009).

In 2011, John Thompson's favorable verdict by a federal trial court awarding him $14 million for prosecutorial misconduct by the New Orleans prosecutors' office was overturned by the Supreme Court. Thompson was convicted of robbery and murder when New Orleans prosecutors withheld exculpatory test results of blood found at the crime scene that was not his. He spent 18 years in prison for a crime he did not commit. After he was exonerated he filed a Section 1983 suit against the district attorney's office, arguing there was deliberate indifference in allowing prosecutors to violate *Brady* rules (to turn over exculpatory evidence to the defense). The Supreme Court ruled 5–4 that the district attorney of New Orleans (Harry Connick, Sr.) could not be held liable for a single *Brady* violation (*Connick v. Thompson*, 131 S. Ct. 1350, 2011).

Raeder (2007) argues that one of the reasons for prosecutorial misconduct is that the Model Rules and Standards do not cover many of the activities described as misconduct, or they refer to them obliquely with no clear guidance. Furthermore, there are few complaints against prosecutors, except in high-profile cases. Gershman (1991) writes that prosecutors misbehave because it works and they can get away with it. Because misconduct is scrutinized only when the defense attorney makes an objection and then files an appeal (and even then the appellate court may rule that it was a harmless error), there is a great deal of incentive to use improper tactics in the court-room. The simple fact is that most prosecutors who commit wrongdoing are not disbarred or punished in any way and, in fact, some go on to be judges and politicians (Armstrong and Possley, 2002).

In a review of nine years of cases in New York City by Propublica, a liberal civil rights advocacy group, only one prosecutor was found to have been seriously punished for cases that were later overturned because of prosecutorial misconduct such as *Brady* violations, coaching witnesses, hiding witnesses, or lying to the judge. Their review of cases found that even serial offenders received raises and commendations and appar-ently experienced no consequences for misconduct, even in cases where appellate judges rebuked the prosecutor. If there are grievances against prosecutors investigated by the state bar's disciplinary committee, such proceedings are usually done in secret with no public access to their findings (Sapien and Hernandez, 2013).

In the discussion of wrongful convictions earlier, confirmatory bias was described as related to noble-cause corruption in that once there is a determination that the defendant is guilty (by police and prosecutors), this perception may lead to miscon-duct in order to make sure a conviction is obtained. Grometstein (2007) also applies the concept of noble-cause corruption to prosecutors, arguing that they adopt a utili-tarian ethic of using bad means to get a conviction, similar to police officers. Aronson and McMurtrie (2007), in their discussion of prosecutorial misconduct, also describe noble-cause corruption, only with different terminology. They identify the issue as "tunnel vision," arguing that prosecutors work under a bias that defendants are guilty, therefore they ignore exculpatory evidence. Similar to the problems this causes with police investigators, these authors discuss a number of psychological processes that contribute to misconduct:

- The presence of confirmatory bias (human tendency to seek to confirm rather than disconfirm)
- Selective information processing (only recognizing evidence to fit one's theory)
- Belief perseverance (believing one's original theory of the case despite evidence to the contrary)
- Avoidance of cognitive dissonance (adjusting beliefs to maintain existing self-perceptions)

Acker and Redlich (2011) also describe tunnel vision, expectancy theory, and confirmation bias as reasons for false convictions. Medwed (2009) discusses the pros-ecutor's "conviction psychology" and noted the fact that prosecutors work closely with police officers and victims and their families, and the emotional connections make it difficult to maintain professional objectivity in cases. Grometstein (2007) emphasizes the relationship between the prosecutor and the victim, arguing that the prosecutor spends even more time with the victim than do police officers, leading to pressure to convict.

Cummings (2010) used Bandura's moral disengagement theory to explain inten-tional prosecutorial misconduct, concentrating on three types most relevant to prosecutors:

- Reconstructing conduct as morally justified
- Obscuring personal agency
- Blaming or dehumanizing defendants

(☉) IN THE NEWS | *Quota for Convictions?*

A district attorney in Colorado received media attention when it was found she provided bonuses for prosecutors who achieved a set conviction rate. She defended the practice arguing that private industry used performance indicators for bonuses. Other prosecutors said that convictions should not necessarily be the measure of achievement and defense attorneys worried that it would influence prosecutors' decisions improperly. One possibility would be that prosecutors wouldn't take some cases to trial that should be because they might lose; another possibility is that they would refuse to offer a reasonable plea bargain in a case knowing they could get a conviction.

Source: Fender, 2011.

The first type refers to the idea that prosecutors (similar to police) feel they are on the side of the righteous, and so what they do can be justified. The second relates to office policies that have "batting averages" and pressure to convict that make it difficult for a prosecutor to express anything other than a strong conviction orientation. The final idea is again similar to police in that the culture of some prosecutors' offices includes an orientation toward defendants that dehumanizes them by using "scum," "slime," and similar words. In one study, it was found that there were 34 different words—all negative—that were used to refer to defendants (Cummings, 2010).

Explanations for Misconduct of Judges

The immunity of judges insulates them from the effects of their decisions, although their decisions are public and can create storms of controversy. Their case holdings can be scrutinized and their courtroom behavior may be grounds for an appeal. Even so, it is difficult for attorneys to challenge judges' actions or testify against them in disciplinary proceedings (Swisher, 2009). Thus, some judges evidently believe they are invulnerable and use the office as a personal throne. In the Pennsylvania case where two judges received kickbacks for sending kids to a private prison, employees and lawyers explained that anyone who criticized the judges, even slightly, found themselves facing retaliation. Judges have immense power and, as the saying goes, "power corrupts." Attorneys tend to keep their head down and their opinions to themselves even when judges are clearly in the wrong. State judicial commissions rarely sanction judges, and voters tend to be fairly oblivious to the reputation of judges, often voting along strict party lines, thus "bad" judges keep getting reelected.

█ Responding to Misconduct

Voters have some control over who become a prosecutor and judge, but once in office, most stay in the good graces of a voting public unless there is a major scandal or an energetic competitor. Similarly to misconduct in law enforcement, a range of potential responses to prosecutorial misconduct have been offered or implemented. Many of these have weaknesses that prevent their effectiveness. It should be noted also that prosecutors' associations believe that major changes in responses are unnecessary because they argue that prosecutorial misconduct is extremely rare.

Professional and Judicial Sanctions

To enforce rules of ethics, the ABA has a standing committee on ethical responsibility to offer formal and informal opinions when charges of impropriety have been made. Also, each state bar association has the power to sanction offending attorneys by private or public censure or to recommend a court suspend their privilege to practice law. Thus, the rules enforced by the state bar have essentially the power of law behind them. The bar associations also have the power to grant entry into the profession because one must belong to the bar association of a particular state to practice law there. Bar associations judge competence by testing the applicant's knowledge, and they also judge moral worthiness by background checks of individuals. The purpose of these restrictive admission procedures is to protect the public image of the legal profession by rejecting unscrupulous or dishonest individuals or those unfit to practice for other reasons. However, many believe that if bar associations were serious about protecting the profession, they would also continue to monitor the behavior and moral standing of current members with the same care they seem to take in the initial decision regarding entry.

Disciplinary committees investigate a practicing attorney only when a complaint is lodged against him or her. The investigative bodies have been described as decentralized, informal, and secret. They do little for dissatisfied clients because most client complaints involve incompetence and/or lack of attention; these charges are vague and ill-defined (Marks, Raymond, and Cathcart, 1986: 72). Many bar disciplinary committees are hopelessly understaffed and overburdened with complaints. Complaints may take years to investigate, and in the meantime, if prospective clients call, they will be told only that the attorney is in good standing and has no substantiated complaints. A study of attorney discipline by an organization for legal reform reported that only three percent of investigations by state disciplinary committees result in public sanctions and only one percent end in disbarment (*San Antonio Express News*, 2002).

While individuals with complaints against their lawyers in the civil arena receive little satisfaction, criminal defendants are arguably even less likely to have anyone care or rectify incompetence or unethical behavior on the part of their attorney. "You get what you pay for" may be true to an extent, but even that phrase does not truly represent the possibility of a family mortgaging its home, signing over cars, and emptying its bank account for an attorney who promises to represent a family member against a criminal charge and then finding that the attorney will not answer calls, doesn't appear in court, or is unprepared and forgets to file necessary motions. One of the most common complaints against attorneys is that they allow deadlines to pass or miss court dates. Criminal defense attorneys could face civil suits for their incompetence or poor work performance, sanctions from their bar association, and even be cited by courts for contempt, but such events are fairly rare.

It seems that prosecutors may be even less likely to be the target of bar discipline committees than criminal defense attorneys. Such information is hard to access because disciplinary proceedings may be secret, but the numbers of prosecutors investigated, much less sanctioned, seem to be very small.

Zacharias and Green (2009) proposed that Model Rule 1.1 requiring all attorneys to display a level of competency could be used against prosecutors who use evidence that they should know is false or withhold evidence from the prosecution. The advantage of using the competency rule rather than the rule prohibiting the use of false testimony is that the "knowing" standard is difficult to meet (the prosecutor has to "know" the evidence is false), but competency would be an easier standard to meet when prosecutors engage in acts that result in innocent people being convicted.

As mentioned earlier, it is extremely rare for prosecutors to be censured for misconduct; however, it has happened in a few cases. In Arizona, Kenneth Peasley, a prosecutor who was once named Prosecutor of the Year by the Arizona Bar Association, was disbarred for soliciting and using false testimony (Kirchmeier et al., 2009). Mike Nifong, in the Duke University lacrosse case, endured a highly publicized disbarment in 2007 because of his actions (described in Chapter 9). In Texas, Ken Anderson (Michael Morton case) and Charles Sebesta (Anthony Graves case) have been disbarred. These sanctions may be more likely today as the cases of wrongful convictions continue to receive widespread news coverage and bar associations feel pressure to do something.

Misconduct in the courtroom is sometimes orally sanctioned by trial judges. Perhaps an appellate decision may overturn a conviction, but prosecutors are rarely directly mentioned in holdings. Many times, when there is clear misconduct, the court rules it is harmless error and does not even overturn the conviction. Some states have created more stringent responses to prosecutorial misconduct and will overturn cases even if there is no way to prove that such misconduct affected the outcome of the case (Kirchmeier et al., 2009).

Rethinking Prosecutorial Immunity

Some have argued that the evidence of prosecutorial misconduct supports rethinking prosecutorial immunity, and perhaps employing criminal sanctions against prosecutors and establishing independent commissions to investigate innocence (Raeder, 2007). For instance, the Texas Judiciary and Civil Jurisprudence Committee has considered a bill that would establish liability for prosecutors in cases of extreme misconduct, giving them only qualified immunity (similar to police officers), rather than absolute immunity. Supreme Court Justice John Paul Stevens has also spoken out on removing the judge-made absolute immunity enjoyed by prosecutors, arguing that Congress never intended prosecutors to be immune from Section 1983 liability. Change would have to come from state legislatures and Congress (for the federal system) and then the new legislation would no doubt be challenged by prosecutors.

Better Training, Better Supervision

There is some argument that prosecutors do not get sufficient training on *Brady* obligations which then lead to some of the *Brady* violations that appear in wrongful convictions. Prosecutors' associations advocate enhanced training on *Brady* obligations to reduce violations. Some argue that requiring prosecutors to work with Innocence Commissions to counteract the psychology of conviction at all costs would be helpful. It has also been suggested that prosecutors' offices should have ethics officers and sanction employees who cross over the line. There should also be clear and public policies in each prosecutor's office concerning the use of jailhouse informants and turning over exculpatory material (Kirchmeier et al., 2009).

Scheck (2010), one of the founders of the Innocence Project, explains that the criminal justice process could learn from quality assurance programs in medicine.

He proposes that many of the mistakes of prosecutors are due to being overworked and careless. In other words, it isn't that they intend to suppress evidence from the defense, it is that they forget to disclose it; similarly, other mistakes occur because of a lack of quality control in the process. The medical establishment underwent a fundamental improvement in the quality of care when checklists were begun in operating rooms. Error rates plunged to near zero in the same hospitals that had been experiencing unacceptably high rates. Scheck says this same approach should be used in prosecutors' offices to uncover *Brady* material and make sure it gets to the defense. Other procedures should be an internal discipline review system that would undertake a systematic review of mistakes made and identify the prosecutors involved. Responses would depend on the reason for the mistake. If prosecutors erred because of overwork, then resources needed to be allocated; if a prosecutor was ignorant of his or her duties under the law, then training was necessary. If the prosecutor intentionally violated the law or ethical obligation, then discipline was necessary.

Conviction Integrity Units

While the number of Innocence Project affiliates is growing and the groups have been successful in identifying cases and prevailing in court, they can't be the only solution to the problem of false convictions. Craig Watkins, the district attorney of Dallas County, instituted the first conviction integrity unit in his office in 2007. The unit reviews DNA cases that have been identified by the Innocence Project of Texas and all cases where DNA evidence has identified unknown suspects in addition to the defendant. By 2014, the office had freed 33 people, was investigating 30 cases, and had a backlog of 200 cases (Barber, 2014). Watkins lost a reelection campaign in 2014, ironically because of a number of ethical scandals (including possible misuse of asset forfeiture funds) and political missteps, but his Republican successor promises to continue the work of the unit.

By 2014, over a dozen cities or counties had similar units, including San Francisco, Chicago, San Jose, Brooklyn, Detroit, Denver, Philadelphia, and Cleveland. Recall from Chapter 8 that the ABA added two sections to Rule 3.8 for prosecutors that concerned their ethical duty to investigate and remedy when there is a chance that an innocent person has been convicted. Even though most states have not adopted those changes, these units fulfill the spirit of the rule changes.

Sometimes a similar body is formed at the state level. The North Carolina Innocence Inquiry Commission was created in 2007 by N.C.G.S. §§ 15A-1461 through 15A-1470. The commission has the power to order a formal inquiry by a three-judge panel appointed by the chief justice of the North Carolina Supreme Court. Since 2007, the commission received 1,642 cases and 1,482 had been reviewed and closed by the end of 2014. Eight people have been exonerated. The remaining cases are under review (N.C. Innocence Commission, 2015).

Mandatory DNA Testing

As mentioned earlier, DNA has been the vehicle by which many innocent prisoners have obtained their release from prison. Even after many years, a small amount of preserved DNA evidence could exclude someone or help to identify the real perpetrator of a crime. Some states have mandated DNA testing of old cases when the inmate requests it. Still other offices, however, actively oppose retesting of DNA. In *District*

Attorney v. Osborne (129 S. Ct. 2308, 2009), the Supreme Court, in a 5–4 decision led by the conservative majority, ruled that defendants had no constitutional right to DNA evidence, even if it was still held by the state and even if they were willing to pay for its testing. In this case, the prisoner argued that the testing done in his trial matched him only to 1 in 6 black men and more advanced tests available today could determine more accurately that he was not the rapist. Alaska argued that such a right would jeopardize the finality of case decisions when the trial was otherwise fair. One wonders, however, how a trial could be thought of as fair if an innocent person was convicted. One also wonders why the Supreme Court would not consider access to such evidence a part of due process. Contrary to this decision, many states are taking steps to make mandatory the preservation of biological evidence in criminal cases and creating a state right to post-conviction DNA testing, even though such testing is prohibitively expensive and evidence must be kept in conditions sufficient to allow for later testing.

Private Crime Labs and Enhanced Due-Process Procedures

Because of the pro-prosecution bias that is said to exist in state or local police crime labs, there have been calls for private labs to test evidence. More than half of all labs in the country report directly to a law enforcement organization. Sometimes the bias is direct, but more often it is subtle and examiners may not even be aware of how they slant findings to the prosecution (cognitive bias). While there is an argument that private labs would not be subject to the same cognitive bias as employees of law enforcement agencies, a contrary argument is that examiners would still feel pressure because their continued contract would be the incentive to produce favorable results. A hybrid suggestion is that most testing would continue at state crime labs but periodically evidence would be sent to private labs for verification. Private labs could also be sued more easily than governmental entities giving them the incentive to follow proper procedures (Balko, 2011).

The research on eyewitness identification errors has led to a number of procedural suggestions that can increase the accuracy of identifications (e.g., sequential photo arrays, double-blind examiners). While the Supreme Court does not seem to be interested in mandating such procedures as essential to due process, there is no reason why states or even local prosecutors' offices shouldn't. The more safeguards there are in eyewitness identification, the less chance there is of an innocent person being convicted.

Procedures can also ensure that obtaining confessions occurs in a manner designed to minimize the potential for false confessions. While the legal standard is whether coercion was present and the bar is set very high, some suggestions to deal with false confessions have emerged. One suggestion is to videotape all interrogations (not just the confession); 18 states now require the confession to be videotaped (Garrett, 2011: 43). More generally, suggestions include the requirement that all confessions have corroborating evidence, that lawyers be required to be present, and that stricter exclusionary rule applications be applied when there is evidence of coercion.

As mentioned previously some locales have either eliminated or dramatically constrained the use of jailhouse informants because of the high probability that they are lying in order to gain some benefit.

There is new attention to and interest in addressing the weaknesses of the justice system to reduce the number of wrongfully convicted. It is important to note, however, that the new rules, sanctions, and guidelines that address jailhouse informants, confessions, eyewitness identifications, and other factors that have been identified as contributing to wrongful convictions will be effective only if there are ethical legal professionals who are committed to ensuring that there truly is justice for all.

Unfortunately, there is little reason for the prosecutor who sees injustice occur to come forward. In *Garcetti v. Ceballos* (547 U.S. 410, 2006), the Supreme Court ruled against a prosecutor who was retaliated against for trying to rectify what he saw as a violation of due process. In this case, Richard Ceballos was an attorney for the Los Angeles County district attorney's office. He submitted a memorandum to his superiors detailing his findings that a search warrant obtained by law enforcement officers had serious flaws and recommended the case be dismissed. Instead, his supervisor continued the prosecution. Ceballos, against orders, provided the defense with a copy of his memorandum and was called as a defense witness. He was subsequently passed over for promotions and sanctioned in other ways, and filed a Section 1983 claim arguing that his First Amendment rights were violated. The Supreme Court, in a 5–4 decision, held that the First Amendment did not apply to public servants in the course of their public duties. Sadly, this decision may act as a barrier to public officials who attempt to challenge what they believe to be miscarriages of justice. It is truly unfortunate that in the cases where prosecutorial and/or judicial misconduct are exposed, it is often the whistleblower who is punished.

It is important to remember that legions of police, lab examiners, prosecutors, and judges engage in the honorable profession of pursuing justice for victims of crimes without committing any of the acts described in these chapters. Just as suspects should not be deprived of due process and be the victims of "noble cause" corruption because of a belief that they are guilty, neither should prosecutors (or police officers). Obviously, just because there is an allegation in an appeal that prosecutors engaged in misconduct, does not make it so. Individuals on the side of defending the wrongfully convicted may be subject to confirmation bias as well and have their own ethical blinders on regarding what is legal and ethical when they believe that they are advocating for an innocent person in prison. There are continuing questions, for instance, about whether David Protess and his students at the Northwestern University Innocence Project were responsible for sending an innocent man to prison in their quest to get their client out as wrongfully convicted. The story is so tangled and confused at this point that it is hard to know who might have done the original murder (Siegel, 2015). In news stories, it is easy to be swayed to the belief of guilt or the belief of innocence according to which facts the journalist chooses to emphasize and which he or she neglects to mention. It is also important to remember that in many of the cases where someone has been exonerated, the original conviction took place in the 1980s when large cities were struggling with incredibly large caseloads related to drugs and crime. The crime rate is, in some categories, far less than half of what it was in the 1980s. Police and prosecutors' offices today have more resources to devote to each case.

Unfortunately, once a prosecutor has been found to have engaged in a *Brady* violation, put a questionable jailhouse informant on the stand, or winked at police perjury, anyone convicted can argue that the same misconduct occurred in his case. As more of these cases come to light, more suspicion is cast on all prosecutors whenever there are allegations of misconduct.

Unfortunately, guilty perpetrators may go free when police and prosecutors don't do their job legally and ethically. In one case where prosecutorial misconduct led to a conviction being overturned, Troy Bennett was allowed to plead guilty to a lesser charge, was released, and confessed to the murder (Sapien and Hernandez, 2013). The problem is that when there is no confidence in justice system actors, then every case needs to be relitigated. The cost to the system of misconduct is incalculable.

Judicial Independence and the Constitution

Recall that discretion is the ability to make a decision and that discretion exists at each stage of the criminal justice system. Professionals at each stage have the opportunity to use their discretion wisely and ethically, or, alternatively, they may use their discretion unethically. In the courts, prosecutors have discretion to pursue prosecution or not, defense attorneys have discretion to accept or refuse cases and choose trial tactics, and judges have discretion to make rulings on evidence and other trial procedures, as well as decide on convictions and sentences.

One view of law is that it is neutral and objective and that formal and absolute rules of law are used in decision making (Pinkele and Louthan, 1985: 9). However, the reality is that lawmakers, law enforcers, and lawgivers are invested with a great deal of discretion in making and interpreting the law. Far from being absolute or objective, the law is a dynamic, ever-changing symbol of political will. If we accept that discretion is an operating reality in the justice system, we must ask in what ways legal professionals use this discretion. If individual value systems replace absolute rules or laws, the resulting decisions may be ethical or unethical. For instance, a judge may base a decision on basic fairness (e.g., not adhering to hypertechnical applications of rules) or on prejudicial beliefs (e.g., that blacks are more criminal and deserve longer sentences, or that women are not dangerous and should get probation).

There are many other situations where one's biases and prejudices may not be so easily identified. Judges' rulings on evidentiary matters are supposed to be based on rules of evidence, but sometimes there is room for interpretation and individual discretion. While most judges use this discretion appropriately and make decisions in a best effort to conform to the spirit of the evidentiary rule, other judges use arbitrary or unfair criteria, such as personal dislike of an attorney, disagreement with a rule, or a desire for one side or the other to win the case.

In this text, we address the ethical issues in the *implementation*, rather than the *creation*, of law. As you learned in political science or government classes, the creation of law is political. Laws are written by federal and state representatives who supposedly enact the public will. One might think that once a law is created, its implementation would be fairly straightforward, but it should be clear by now that this is not the case. An appellate court can change over time and be influenced by political shifts in power. Far from being static, the implementation of law reflects political realities, in direct contrast to the ideal of judicial independence that is the cornerstone of our system of government.

If the judiciary is not independent of political powers, this calls into question the very existence of the checks and balances upon which this country's government is constructed. For instance, many Democrats suspected that the political composition of the Supreme Court had a great deal to do with its decision in the case challenging the Florida vote after the Bush–Gore presidential election in 2000. Whether or not the allegations are true, it should be obvious that the strength of the justice system rests on the independence of its judiciary.

In 2005, several leaders in Congress publicly chastised the federal judiciary because they did not like the decisions that the federal judges had been handing down, and then, in turn, were criticized by those in the legal profession who argued that the essence of separation of powers is that federal judges are not influenced, intimidated, or ordered by legislative leaders to enact anyone's political agenda. The Quote and Query box illustrates the controversy.

The political uproar over the firings of eight federal prosecutors in 2007 by the Bush administration may have seemed overblown to some people. After all, why shouldn't a president be able to hire and fire at will? However, what was at stake was the very essence of the separation of powers that is the greatest strength of our system of government. Traditionally, when a new president comes into office, he engages in a process whereby those affiliated with the old administration are removed and new employees are placed into those positions. That has been done in all sectors of executive government, including the Justice Department, by Democrat and Republican administrations alike, with very little criticism. What happened in 2007, however, was that, apparently, in the middle of the term of office, there was a "hit list" of federal prosecutors who were removed not for incompetence or poor performance, but rather, because White House aides relayed a message to Justice Department officials that these individuals should be replaced with others who were more loyal to the Bush administration.

Observers noted that the prosecutors targeted for firing were those who either pursued prosecutions against Republicans or were too slow to respond to pressure to pursue prosecutions against Democrats. In effect, the firings were politically motivated, not a "house cleaning" at the beginning of a term of office. When Attorney General Alberto Gonzales responded to the congressional inquiry in an unsatisfactory way (saying more than 70 times that he couldn't remember), he ultimately had to resign because of the scandal (Carr and Herman, 2007). In 2008, the Justice Department released a scathing 400-page report charging ethical violations in the firing of U.S. attorneys such as David Iglesias in New Mexico; however, it received very little press (Johanek, 2008). A special prosecutor (Nora Dannehy) concluded that no laws had been broken (Kreig, 2010).

If the justice system, including prosecutors and judges, is a pawn or an agent of political power, due process is a sham and the very essence of democracy is threatened. The importance of due process is that even criminals and enemies of the state are given due-process rights that protect them from errors in the deprivation of life, liberty, and property. If due process is reserved only for those who are not enemies of the state, all are threatened because anyone may become an enemy. If for some reason state power would become despotic, it would be likely to label as enemies anyone favoring open government and democracy. What this illustrates is that the law (and the nature of its

QUOTE & QUERY

[T]he time will come for the men responsible for this to answer for their behavior . . .
[I want to] look at an arrogant, out-of-control, unaccountable judiciary that thumbed their nose at Congress and the president.

Tom DeLay, U.S. House of Representatives majority leader, speaking in response to the Terri Schiavo case, May 2005, as quoted in Allen, 2005.

Attempts to intimidate judges into deciding pending cases in a particular way with threats of impeachment or investigation, as has been the recent practice of some members of Congress, have no place in a functioning democracy.

Source: American Judicature, 2005.

 Do you think that members of Congress should be sanctioned for threatening impeachment when they don't like the decisions of federal judges? If not, who does serve as oversight for judges who are appointed for life?

protections) is more important than the state and, indeed, is even more important than threats to the state. Those who are more influenced by political allegiance than allegiance to due process and civil liberties create a weak link in the mantle of protection against despotic state power.

The U.S. Supreme Court, as the ultimate authority of law in this country, decides constitutionality, and these interpretations are far from neutral, despite the myth of objective decision making. This is the reason that the selection of Supreme Court justices (as well as all federal judges) is such a hard-fought political contest. Ideological positions do make a difference, and no one is fooled that a black robe removes bias. The confirmations of John Roberts as Chief Justice (during the Bush administration) and Sonia Sotomayor and Elena Kagan (during the Obama administration) illustrate this. The most recent confirmation hearing, of Elena Kagan in 2010, was a replay of past hearings with opponents and proponents lined up predictably on ideological sides. What is interesting is that so-called liberal justices have been appointed by Republican presidents: Justices John Paul Stevens (appointed by Gerald Ford), David Souter (appointed by George H.W. Bush), and Sandra Day O'Connor (appointed by Ronald Reagan) were not considered activist or liberal when they were appointed but moved in that direction compared to the justices who have been appointed since then (Greenhouse, 2007). Today, some say Justice Kennedy is the most important man in America because he is often the swing vote that shifts the decision from 4–5 or 5–4. Justices Scalia, Roberts, Alito, and Thomas line up predictably conservative more often than not, and Justices Bader, Ginsburg, Kagan, Sotomayor, and Breyer, for the most part, return liberal verdicts. The fate of the most important social questions in this country being at the discretion of one individual is a troublesome reality.

Judicial Activism

Our law derives from the Constitution. Two basic philosophies regarding how to apply constitutional principles are at work in the legal arena. The first group might be called **strict constructionists** because they argue that the Constitution should be implemented as written, and if any changes are to take place in rights, responsibilities, or liberties, the changes should take place through the political system (Congress).

The extreme view of this position is that if a right isn't in the Constitution, it doesn't exist. So, for instance, the right to be free from state interference in the decision to abort one's fetus does not exist in the Constitution; therefore, it doesn't exist and cannot be created except through the actions of duly elected representatives. Strict constructionists argue that just because something *should* be a right doesn't mean that one can decide the framers meant for it to be a right. Judges should not create law.

Interpretationists (or activists) have a looser reading of the Constitution and read into it rights that the framers might have recognized or that should be recognized because of "evolving standards." They argue that the Constitution is meant to be a living document and that the language of the framers was intentionally written as to accommodate interpretation based on changing times and circumstances. Concepts such as due process, for instance, from the Fifth and Fourteenth Amendments, are flexible so they can be used to address new questions and new concerns. Interpretationists place less emphasis on precedent, minimize procedural obstacles (such as standing, ripeness, and federalism), and offer less deference to other political decision makers (e.g., they use the strict scrutiny test rather than the rational relationship

strict constructionists
The view that an individual has no rights unless these rights are specified in the Constitution or have been created by some other legal source.

interpretationists
An approach to the Constitution that uses a looser reading of the document and read into it rights that the framers might have recognized or that should be recognized as a result of "evolving standards."

test when evaluating governmental actions). When the Court was in its most activist phase during the Warren Court (1953–1969), it delivered broad opinions that have had dramatic effects on the political and legal landscape (Wolfe, 1991). The debate as to whether the Constitution should be strictly construed or liberally interpreted is an old one, as the Quote and Query box indicates.

Critics of judicial activism point out that just because judicial activists have been promoters of civil liberties and socially progressive causes, such as integration and free speech, there is no absolute necessity that activism would always champion such individual rights. Activism could, for instance, be just as likely to recognize greater rights of the state to restrict individual liberties (Wolfe, 1991), or invalidate congressional acts by an interpretation of the Constitution that favored restricting laws obtained through the democratic process (some say this is the case with the *Citizens United v. Federal Elections Commission* [558 U.S. 50 2010], case decision that invalidated a law putting limits on corporate campaign spending).

Proponents of activism argue that the federal government itself has not been content to stay within the boundaries of its enumerated powers as specified in the Constitution, and that proliferation of the federal government's reach into all areas of criminal and civil law through the expansive interpretation of the Commerce Clause requires greater judicial checks. Furthermore, there are limits to judicial power, including impeachment, confirmation, congressional definition of appellate powers, and the power to override a Supreme Court opinion through a constitutional amendment (Wolfe, 1991). The Warren Court was called activist or liberal because it recognized a whole range of civil liberties and due-process rights for groups that had been historically disenfranchised. The source of such rights was found in an expansive reading of the Constitution and based on the idea of "fundamental liberties"—those freedoms and protections that the framers would have recognized if they had been asked. Central to this view is the idea of **natural rights**. Recall that the natural law ethical system holds that there are natural laws of ethics that humans may or may not discover. Several of the authors of the Bill of Rights were natural law theorists; thus, taken out of the context of their time, they would probably recognize that humans have the following rights:

- To be free
- To be treated equal to other groups
- To be able to make decisions about personal matters without governmental interference
- To be free from torture and punishments that degrade the human spirit
- To have some protections against state power

In addition, there may be recognition that humans also have rights:

- To basic necessities to survive
- To avail themselves of opportunities to better themselves

The first set of rights leads to less government; the second set leads to more government. That is why the political terms *conservative* and *liberal* are not strictly

QUOTE & QUERY

When we are dealing with words that also are a constituent act, like the Constitution of the United States, we must realize that they have called into life a being the development of which could not have been foreseen completely by the most gifted of its begetters.

Sources: Oliver Wendell Holmes, Jr., Supreme Court Justice, 1902–1932, as quoted in Wolfe, 1991: 36.

 Does this quote by Holmes indicate he was a strict constructionist or an interpretationist?

natural rights
The concept that one has certain rights just by virtue of being born, and these rights are not created by humans, although they can be ignored.

comparable to "strict constructionist" and "interpretationist" and why there is such confusion when these terms are being used to describe judicial and political appointees and elected officials. "Liberals" argue that if the Warren Court hadn't interpreted the Constitution to recognize civil rights, blacks would still be eating at separate lunch counters. Constructionists argue that if interpretationists had their way, government and the courts would be involved in every decision from birth to death.

The Supreme Court's "activism" has been intimately tied to who has been on the bench. Observers note that it has moved back to a constructionist stance, because of the confirmations of John Roberts, Samuel Alito, Clarence Thomas, and Antonin Scalia. In recent holdings, the Court has restricted the coverage of the *Miranda* warnings, upheld federal antiabortion laws, cut back on free-speech rights of public school students, strictly enforced procedural requirements for bringing and appealing cases, limited the ability to use racially conscious measures to achieve or preserve integration, invalidated public corruption laws and campaign finance laws, and generally supported law enforcement powers, with some exceptions. On the other hand, the Supreme Court has also recognized unconstitutionality in capital punishment and life without parole for juveniles and ruled against the government's secret program to store electronic communication data of all Americans. Recent case decisions have recognized Fourth Amendment rights over cellphones and the Supreme Court held that warrants were required for blood draws and searches by drug dogs.

Judges' political leanings shouldn't influence these decisions, but it is hard to argue that there is no correlation. Even an analysis by the Justice Department determined that immigration judges (also called hearing examiners) who were hired by the George W. Bush White House based on a political affiliation requirement and their views on immigration and abortion were less likely to grant asylum than judges hired with politically neutral criteria. Using such criteria was determined to be illegal and abandoned, but the immigration hearing examiners continue to remain in place (Savage, 2008b).

One thing is clear: a judge is human and carries baggage of personal, political, and social bias. The importance of the foregoing discussion is to illustrate the law is not an equation that comes out with the right answer to every problem. Because there is room to interpret, individual ethics becomes extremely important. Prosecutors' and judges' ethics should lead them to use their discretion in ways that promote justice. We all, however, must be involved in a continuing, serious discussion about what justice means. For instance, should federal prosecutors "lighten up" on heavy charging of drug offenders or should they enforce the law to its full extent? Should asset forfeiture be restricted and curtailed or is it a legitimate punishment if one is involved, even peripherally, in crime? Should jailhouse informants be banned or should they be used when there is other evidence that points to guilt? Should we eliminate plea bargaining or does it resolve cases quickly helping both the defendant and the system? These are within the individual discretion of system actors but they take their cues from what the public seems to want. The focus today by legislatures on wrongful convictions and police misconduct is because there has been growing concern expressed by the public. It is important to continue these discussions in order to provide clear direction to justice professionals.

Conclusion

One might expect that the public's respect and trust for legal professionals, as guardians of the justice system, would be high, but that is not the case. Part of the reason is the ability to take either side in a controversy. We should not forget, however, that attorneys and judges protect the bedrock of our structure of laws.

In criminal justice, it is crucial that legal professionals remember and believe in the basic tenets of due process and be ever vigilant against the influence of prejudice or bias in the application of law toward the pursuit of justice. Unfortunately, there are cases where defense attorneys, prosecutors, and judges do not uphold the ethical standards of their profession and instead engage in various forms of misconduct. Although the types of misconduct vary depending on one's role in the system, each can be explained by individual enrichment (money, status, or time), or by ends/means thinking due to confirmatory bias (similar to noble-cause corruption for police officers).

There is a need to improve the ethics of the system, as evidenced by the Innocence Project's exonerations of hundreds of people who ended up in prison because of the failings of the system and system actors. Just as important is to make sure the same "rush to judgment" isn't directed to system actors when allegations of misconduct arise. Despite those who advocate strict constructionism, applying the law can never be truly objective or formulistic. Every decision is made through a reasoned and, one hopes, ethical interpretation of the law rather than by a robotic response. The law must be seen as a living entity, and legal professionals are its life's blood.

Chapter Review

1. **Detail the types of misconduct that have been associated with defense attorneys, prosecutors, and judges.**

   Misconduct by defense attorneys includes ignoring cases, incompetence, and going over the line when defending clients, including presenting false evidence. The types of prosecutorial misconduct include withholding exculpatory evidence, misusing pretrial publicity, using peremptory challenges to exclude jurors, and using false evidence in court. Misconduct by judges includes allowing bias (including bribery) to influence their decision making and acting arbitrarily and otherwise abusing their power.

2. **Explain the reasons why such misconduct occurs.**

   Misconduct occurs because the disciplinary functions carried out by the state bar associations rarely result in serious sanctions. Prosecutors experience very little oversight and seldom suffer from sanctions when violating the ethical rules in their zeal to obtain a conviction. Courts often rule such misconduct as harmless error. Judges are feared by employees and lawyers who hesitate to file complaints against them. Also, prosecutors, like police, may be prone to confirmatory bias or what we have called noble-cause corruption in prior chapters.

3. **Describe the Innocence Projects, how many individuals have been found to be wrongly imprisoned, and why.**

   These are loose associations of lawyers who identify cases where the prisoner may be innocent and investigate, often resulting in a new trial and exoneration. Thus far, Innocence Projects across the country have succeeding in obtaining exonerations for more than 250 individuals, but a recent registry indicated the figure of people falsely convicted was about 2,000.

4. **Discuss some proposals to improve the justice system and reduce ethical misconduct.**

Suggestions to improve the system have been to institute official Innocence Projects or conviction integrity units. Suggestions also include more training and ethics officers. Also, some have suggested reevaluating prosecutorial immunity and using civil and criminal sanctions against prosecutors who create and use false evidence and engage in other forms of misconduct to obtain convictions. Other proposals include using videotape confessions, restricting the use of jailhouse informants, and using sequential and double-blind identifications to avoid improper influence over witnesses.

5. **Understand the concepts associated with judicial activism or constructionism and how this issue relates to ethical misconduct.**

An activist judge is one who believes such concepts as due-process and liberty rights are evolving and the founding fathers did not mean for the rights enumerated in the Constitution to remain static throughout time. Constructionists argue that legislators should make law, not judges. One's opinion regarding this—and one's values, opinions, and biases in general—affect decision making, so judges' opinions on cases can be predicted ahead of time in many cases. This calls into question judicial neutrality and reminds us that, in the end, our system of laws is a system of people who enforce the law, and thus it is only as good or bad as the people in the system.

Study Questions

1. What is the evidence that shows the public mistrusts attorneys?

2. What are the four types of ethical violations that have been associated with prosecutors?

3. Discuss the number of innocents who may be imprisoned. What are the sources for the estimates? What are the criticisms of the sources?

4. What factors have been identified as contributing to false convictions?

5. What is the evidence to indicate a pervasive pattern of racial bias in the system?

Writing/Discussion Exercises

1. Using ethical and moral criteria, write an essay on (or discuss) courtroom practices: the use of videotaped testimony, allowing television cameras into the courtroom and jury room, victim statements during sentencing, preventive detention, neighborhood justice centers, the use of a waiver to adult court for violent juvenile offenders, and any others that have been in the news recently.

2. After watching a movie that presents a legal dilemma (e.g., *Presumed Innocent, 12 Angry Men, Philadelphia,* or *Michael Clayton*), write an essay on (or discuss) the ethical dilemmas of the characters. Use one or more of the ethical frameworks provided in Chapter 2.

3. Write an essay on (or discuss) judicial activism. Present the arguments on both sides of the question as to whether judges should interpret or simply apply the Constitution. Provide more current examples (the current Supreme Court docket) and predict how justices will decide. If one can predict the decisions of the justices on the Supreme Court, where does that leave the idea that no case is prejudged?

Key Terms

interpretationists	natural rights	strict constructionists

ETHICAL DILEMMAS

Situation 1

You are a defense attorney who is defending a man against a charge of burglary. He tells you that he was drunk on the night in question and doesn't remember what he did. He asks you to put him on the stand, and when you do, he responds to your questions by stating unequivocally that he was home watching a television show, describing the show and plotline. You understand that you cannot participate in perjury, but to call attention to his inconsistent stories would violate other rules, such as confidentiality and zealous defense. What do you do?

Situation 2

You are a member of a jury. The jury is hearing a child molestation case in which the defendant is accused of a series of molestations in his neighborhood. You have been advised by the judge not to discuss the case with anyone outside the courtroom, and especially not with anyone on either side of the case. Going down in the elevator after the fourth day of the trial, you happen to ride with the prosecutor in the case. He tells you that the man has a previous arrest for child molestation, but that it has not been allowed in by the judge, as being too prejudicial for the jury. You were fairly sure that the guy was guilty before, but now you definitely believe he is guilty. You also know that if you tell the judge what you have heard, it will probably result in a mistrial. What would you do? What should happen to the prosecutor?

Situation 3

You are a court administrator and really like Judge Sonyer, your boss. He is pleasant, punctual, and hardworking. One day, you hear him talking to the prosecutor in chambers. He is talking about the defendant in a trial that is about to start, and you hear him say that "the son-of-a-bitch is as guilty as sin." You happen to be in law school and know that, first, the prosecutor and judge should not be talking about the case without the presence of the defense attorney, and, second, the judge has expressed a preexisting bias. The judge's statement is even more problematic because this is a bench trial and he is the sole determiner of guilt or innocence. What would you do?

Situation 4

You are a federal judge and are about to start a federal racketeering trial that is quite complicated. Prosecutors allege that certain lobbyists funneled money into political campaigns by "washing" it through individual employees of a couple of large corporations. Still, the evidence seems equivocal—at least what you've seen so far. You get a call from one of your state's U.S. senators (who is not implicated in the case, although members of his party are), and the conversation is innocuous and pleasant enough until the senator brings up the case and jocularly pressures you to agree with him that it is a "tempest in a teapot." Then he mentions that a higher, appellate-level judgeship will be opening soon and that he is sure you would like his support on it. The message is not subtle. What would you do?

Situation 5

You are a defense attorney who sees a judge in your jurisdiction having dinner with a prosecutor. Both are married to other people. You happen to have a case in front of this judge and the prosecutor is your opponent. You consider that you could request the judge recuse himself from the case, but this may create animosity, and if he refuses, it could be detrimental to your client. Alternatively, you could keep quiet and use the information on appeal, but this may mean your client spends years in prison. Finally, you could do nothing and hope that the judge is not biased toward the prosecution in his rulings. What would you do?

11

The Ethics of Punishment and Corrections

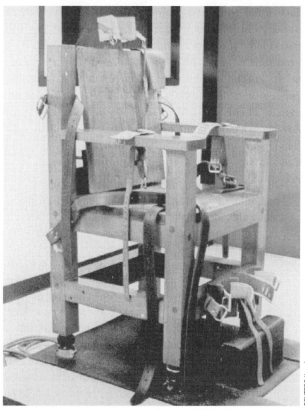

Georgia's electric chair.

REUTERS/Landov

Chapter Objectives

1. Provide the definitions of punishment and treatment and their rationales.
2. Describe how the ethical frameworks justify punishment.
3. Describe the ethical rationales for and against capital punishment.
4. Describe the ethical codes for correctional officers, treatment professionals, and probation and parole officers.
5. Explain how occupational subcultures affect adherence to professional ethics codes.

The field of corrections, which will be the topic in this next set of three chapters, encompasses county and state jails, prisons, community corrections, including probation and parole, and various forms of correctional programs. Similar to the criminal justice professionals we have discussed thus far in law enforcement and the courts, correctional professionals have a great deal of discretion and power over the lives of offenders. Also similar to law enforcement and law, we are in the midst of a national conversation questioning whether the path we have taken with long drug sentences and three-strikes laws has been effective or consistent with our national goals and identity. Reflective of this current interest, in the summer of 2015, President Obama became the first sitting president to visit a penitentiary. Recently, mass incarceration has been a topic of presidential platforms (Rand Paul), and bipartisan coalitions have been formed both by Congress (Colson Task Force on Federal Corrections) and outside of Congress (The Coalition for Public Safety). It seems that after 30 years of steadily increasing incarceration rates and exponential growth in prison populations, people are beginning to question whether it is wise or necessary to incarcerate close over two million individuals in prisons and jails.

The Coalition for Public Safety (www.coalitionforpublicsafety.org) is funded by the MacArthur Foundation as well as the conservative Koch brothers, political power brokers that generally contribute to the most conservative politicians. The Coalition states their mission is to "reform our criminal justice system to make it more just, more fair, and more effective." On their website, they advocate fair sentencing (citing research that shows long mandatory minimum sentences have no effect on recidivism), fair and appropriate use of incarceration (advocating access to mental healthcare and effective substance abuse treatment, education, and job training) at both the federal and state level, and, "fair chances" (addressing collateral consequences of a criminal conviction, including loss of civil rights and advocacy for "ban the box" campaigns to reduce the requirements to reveal or use criminal records as categorical disqualifiers from some jobs). The interesting thing about this advocacy is that it is bipartisan and both conservative and liberal advocates share the same message that our mass incarceration practices must be reexamined in light of social science and common sense.

Another similarity between corrections and law enforcement and legal professionals is that current scandals abound over ethical misconduct in the field. Joyce Mitchell, a correctional worker in New York, was charged and pleaded guilty to aiding the escape of two murderers by bringing them tools in the summer of 2015. Rikers Island has been the subject of a massive Department of Justice investigation, and the city has just entered into an agreement with DOJ that involves major changes in all aspects of the facility. Denver and Los Angeles also have had scandals in the level of abuse and misconduct in their jails, and there is an ongoing major scandal in Florida over several deaths of inmates, with some correctional workers facing criminal charges.

Two famous quotes resonate in any discussion of ethics in corrections. The first is from Dante's *Divine Comedy*: "*Abandon all hope, ye who enter here.*" This inscription at the portal to hell, often scrawled as graffiti in prisons, unfortunately encapsulates what some prisons mean to those who are sent there. Fyodor Dostoyevsky was reputed to have provided the second quote: "*The degree of civilization in a society can be judged by entering its prisons,*" which cautions that the best of us still have certain duties of respect and care toward the worst of us.

Once someone has been found guilty of a criminal offense, the type of punishment must be determined. Punishments range from a suspended sentence to death. Sometimes punishment includes treatment, at least in name. During incarceration, the wrongdoer may be required to participate in treatment programs or self-help groups such as Alcoholics Anonymous. Probationers may be required to go to drug-treatment programs; they may even be required to get their GED or obtain some type of job training. In addition to formal, legal punishments, there are informal, extra-legal punishments that should not exist, but unfortunately do exist. Inmates are raped and beaten by other inmates and sometimes even by correctional officers. Their personal property is destroyed. Some get sick or injured and receive inadequate medical treatment. Prisoner advocates maintain that these events should never be part of the formal punishment of prison, but others strongly believe that the prisoner "shouldn't do the crime if he (or she) can't do the time." Prisoners form an unsympathetic "victim" group perhaps explaining why public support for reform is usually lukewarm at best.

According to one author (Leiser, 1986: 198), five elements are essential to the definition of **punishment**:

1. There are at least two persons—one who inflicts the punishment and one who is punished.

2. The person who inflicts the punishment causes a certain harm to the person who is being punished.

3. The person who inflicts the punishment has been authorized, under a system of rules or laws, to harm the person who is punished in this particular way.

4. The person who is being punished has been judged by a representative of that authority to have done what he or she is forbidden to do or failed to do what he or she is required to do by some relevant rule or law.

5. The harm that is inflicted upon the person who is being punished is specifically for the act or omission mentioned in condition four.

> **punishment**
> Unpleasantness or pain administered by one in lawful authority in response to another's transgression of law or rules.

We also need to define **treatment**. According to correctional terminology, treatment may be anything used to induce behavioral change. The goal is to eliminate dysfunctional or deviant behavior and to encourage productive and normal behavior patterns. In prison, treatment includes diagnosis, classification, therapy, education, religious activity, vocational training, and self-help groups.

The infliction of punishment and even treatment is and should be limited. For instance, von Hirsch (1976: 5) presents the following restrictive guidelines:

> **treatment**
> Anything used to induce behavioral change with the goal of eliminating dysfunctional or deviant behavior and encouraging productive and normal behavior patterns.

- The liberty of each individual is to be protected as long as it is consistent with the liberty of others.
- The state is obligated to observe strict parsimony in intervening in criminals' lives.
- The state must justify each intrusion.
- The requirements of justice ought to constrain the pursuit of crime prevention (that is, deterrence and rehabilitation).

This chapter and the next two follow the format we have established in the previous sections on law enforcement and legal professionals. In this chapter, we will first explore relevant issues such as the various rationales for punishment, and capital punishment in particular, present the formal codes of ethics for correctional professionals and describe occupational subcultures that sometimes conflict with the formal code of ethics. In Chapter 12, we will discuss some ethical dilemmas for correctional professionals that arise because of the discretion inherent in these roles. In Chapter 13, we will review past and current instances of misconduct by correctional professionals, explanations proposed for such behavior, and suggestions for improving the ethical climate in corrections.

Rationales for Punishment and Corrections

The rationale for punishment and corrections comes from the social contract. In the same way that the social contract forms the basis for police power, it also provides a rationale for further control in the form of punishment and corrections. Recall that according to the social contract theory, we avoid social chaos by giving the state the power to control us. In this way, we protect ourselves from being victimized by others by giving up our liberty to aggress against others. If we do step outside the bounds of this agreement, the state has the right to control and punish us for our transgressions. Concurrently, the state is limited in the amount of control it can exert over individuals. To be consistent with the social contract, the state should exert its power only to accomplish the purpose of protection; any further interventions in civil liberties are unwarranted.

Corrections pursues a mixture of goals, including retribution, reform, incapacitation, deterrence, and rehabilitation. The longstanding argument between proponents of punishment and proponents of treatment reveals a system without a clear mandate or rationale for action. Garland (1990) writes that the state's goal of punishment is problematic because it is marked with inconsistencies between the intent and the implementation. The moral contradictions are that it seeks to uphold freedom by means of its deprivation, and it punishes private violence by inflicting state violence. Can treatment and punishment occur at the same time? Some argue that because punishment has the goal of inflicting pain on an individual, it is fundamentally incompatible with the goal of treatment. Others argue that there is no reason that positive change cannot occur in a correctional setting.

One of the most problematic issues in justifying what we do in the name of punishment is that what we do to offenders changes over time (and place). If what is considered to be appropriate punishment changes, how can any specific punishment be considered to be just under universalism or natural law theory? In other words, in earlier centuries we might have executed a pickpocket. Was that just, or is it just today to put that person on probation? Is it just to incarcerate 19-year-olds who had sex with 16-year-olds today when in times past (or, perhaps, in future times) they would not be

---

(((•))) IN THE NEWS | *Fair Punishment?*

In 2010 the Fair Sentencing Act was passed to reduce the disparity between federal sentencing rules for crack and powder cocaine, reducing the disparity from 100:1 to 18:1. The bill did not apply retroactively, thus, thousands in federal prisons were incarcerated only because they were sentenced before 2010 and would have received much shorter sentences if sentenced under the new law. To address this inequity, a clemency initiative was created whereby federal prisoners sentenced under the old laws could apply for clemency (length of sentence is reduced, criminal conviction remains). Stringent requirements were put in place, including:

- Their original sentence was longer than current mandatory sentences for the same offense.

- They are nonviolent, low-level offenders without "significant ties to large scale criminal organizations, gangs or cartels."

- They have served at least 10 years of their sentence.

- They do not have a "significant criminal history."

- They have demonstrated good conduct in prison.

- They have no history of violence before or during their current imprisonment.

A working group called Clemency Project 2014 was formed to provide inmates with pro bono (free) attorneys to help them with their clemency application. President Obama began approving clemency to offenders in December 2014 and by July 2015 had issued clemency orders for 89 drug offenders under the program from the 30,000 prisoners who had initially applied.

Source: Various news reports.

imprisoned at all? Prisoners in different prisons have vastly different sentences. How can the worst prison be fair if it is chance whether a prisoner ends up there or in a prison with better living conditions? Finally, at various times, courts have invalidated laws or punishments but not made their ruling retroactive; in that case, people who are already in prison stay there. Consider the states that have legalized marijuana—if individuals are in prison for possession because they were sentenced before the decriminalization occurred, can that be just? How can that be logical or fair if the punishment no longer exists? The In the News box describes one attempt to make punishment more equitable for some people.

An important question to ask is: "Whom are we punishing?" Studies show that only a small minority of individuals who commit crimes end up in prison; furthermore, we may assume that those individuals are not representative of the larger population. Those in our jails and prisons are there not only because they committed crimes, but also because they are poor, members of a minority group, or powerless. Certain types of criminals tend to avoid the more punitive sanctions of the corrections system. For instance, businesses routinely bilk consumers out of billions of dollars annually and chalk up the punitive fines imposed to operating expenses. When streams and land are polluted by industrial waste, punitive fines are the typical sanctions imposed and these are paid by company shareholders. Such costs are also typically passed on to the consumers, so taxpayers suffer the crime and then also pay the fine. Despite attempts to reduce disparity, sometimes there doesn't seem to be any logic or consistency in the amount of punishment for offenders.

Long ago, criminals were viewed as sinners with no ability to change their behavior, so punishment and incapacitation were seen as the only logical ways to respond to crime. Jeremy Bentham (1748–1832) and Cesare Beccaria (1738–1794) viewed the criminal as rational and as having free will and, therefore, saw the threat of punishment as a deterrent. Neoclassicists such as Adolphe Quetelet (1796–1874) and André-Michel Guerry (1802–1866) recognized that insane persons and juveniles could not be held entirely responsible for their actions and, therefore, believed that they should not be punished. The insane and the young were treated differently because they were considered to be moral infants, not possessing the sense to refrain from wrongdoing.

In the 1800s, the positivist school looked for differences between criminals and noncriminals. The search for differences eventually, in the 1960s and 1970s, led to the short-lived rehabilitative era and the **treatment ethic**—the idea that all criminal acts were symptoms of an underlying pathology. The treatment programs created in the last hundred years or so operate under the assumption that we can do something to offenders to reduce their criminal activity. That "something" may involve:

- Treating a psychological problem, such as a sociopathic or paranoid personality,
- Addressing physiological problems, such as alcoholism or addiction,
- Responding to social problems, such as chronic unemployment, with vocational training and job placement.

Obviously, the perception of the criminal influences the rationale for correction and punishment. The two major justifications for punishment and treatment are **retribution** and **prevention**. The retributive rationale postulates that punishment is an end in itself, whereas the prevention approach views punishment as a means of prevention rather than an end.

treatment ethic
The idea that all criminal acts are symptoms of an underlying pathology.

retribution
A rationale for punishment that states that punishment is an end in itself and should be balanced to the harm caused.

prevention
A rationale for punishment that views it as a means rather than an end and embraces any method that can avoid crime, painful or not (includes deterrence, rehabilitation, and incapacitation).

Retribution

As mentioned before, the social contract provides the rationale for punishment. The retributive rationale for punishment is consistent with the social contract theory. Simply stated, the retributive rationale is that the individual offender must be punished because he or she deserves it. Mackie (1982: 4) describes three specific types of retribution:

- *Negative retribution* dictates that one who is not guilty must not be punished for a crime.
- *Positive retribution* demands that one who is guilty ought to be punished.
- *Permissive retribution* allows that one who is guilty *may* be punished.

This formulation states that retribution may support punishment, but may also limit it. There are limits as to who may be punished (only those who commit crimes) and restrictions on the amount of punishment (only that sufficient to balance the wrong). Further, this formulation implies that punishment need not be administered in all cases. The exceptions, although not discussed by Mackie, may involve the concepts of mercy or diminished responsibility.

Another retributivist justification for punishment is that it is the only way the individual can achieve salvation. Thus, we owe the offender punishment because only through suffering can atonement occur, and only through atonement or **expiation** can the offender achieve a state of grace. Some would strongly object to this interpretation of religious ethics and argue that Christianity, while supportive of just punishment, does not necessarily support suffering as the only way to achieve a state of grace: There must be repentance, but there is also room for forgiveness.

What is an appropriate amount of punishment? This is a difficult question even for the retributivist. The difference between a year in prison and two years in prison is measurable only by the number of days on the calendar, not by how it is experienced by different people. Should this be considered during sentencing? Punishment of any kind affects individuals differently. For instance, a whipping may be worse than death for someone with a low tolerance for pain, better than prison for someone with a great need for freedom, and perhaps even pleasurable for someone who enjoys physical pain. Prison may be experienced as an inconvenience for some, and such a traumatic experience for others that it may induce suicide. Our current system of justice seldom recognizes these individual vulnerabilities or sensitivities to various punishments.

Sentencing studies routinely show little or no agreement regarding the type or amount of punishment appropriate for a wrongdoer. Disparity in sentencing led to reforms, such as determinate sentencing, that reduced judges' discretion. Yet, when legislators take on the task themselves by setting determinate sentences, their decisions are arrived at by obscure methods, probably more influenced by political pressure and compromise than by the application of fair and equitable standards.

The justice model and the just deserts model, developed in the late 1970s and early 1980s, came about partly as a backlash to the abuses of discretion that characterized the rehabilitative era of the 1970s, and led the way to the current punitive era. Basically, the **justice model** holds that individuals are rational and that, even though free will may not exist perfectly, the concept must serve as a basis for the criminal law. Punishment is to be used for retribution, not deterrence, treatment, or any other

expiation
Atonement for a wrong to achieve a state of grace.

justice model
David Fogel's conceptualization that the punishment of an individual should be limited by the seriousness of the crime, although treatment could be offered.

purpose. This model promoted a degree of predictability and equality in sentencing by reverting to earlier retributive goals of punishment and restricted the state's right to use treatment as a criterion for release. Finally, prisoners should be seen as volitional, responsible humans, not as patients (Fogel, 1975).

The **just deserts model**, appearing about the same time as the justice model, was also retributive and based punishment on "commensurate deserts" (von Hirsch, 1976, 1985; von Hirsch and Maher, 1992)). According to von Hirsch, the leading proponent of the just deserts model, crimes should be weighed in seriousness based on their recidivism potential. Offenders who commit similar crimes should be punished equally, but the rank ordering of crimes should be determined by recidivistic potential.

> **just deserts model** Von Hirsch's conceptualization that the punishment of the individual should be purely retributive and balanced to the seriousness of the crime.

Garland (1990) offered a different view, proposing that the emphasis of society should be on socializing and educating citizens. The punishment that was still necessary for those who broke the law should be viewed as morally expressive rather than instrumental and should be retributive rather than attempt prevention goals. In other words, we should punish only because the defendant deserves it and not to try and change him or her. Feeney (2005) continues this idea that sentencing should be purely retributive, and be "morally significant" in that it expresses condemnation of the behavior. Both of these writers are similar to the earlier just deserts theorists in that they believe punishment should be retributive rather than serve the goals of deterrence.

Our current time has been described as the era of **penal harm**; this refers to the idea that the system intentionally or uncaringly inflicts pain on offenders during their imprisonment. There is very little attempt to rehabilitate and no attempt to minimize punishment or its harmful effects (Clear, 1996; Cullen, 1995).

> **penal harm** The idea that the system intentionally inflicts pain on offenders during their imprisonment or punishment, because merely depriving them of liberty is not considered sufficiently painful.

No one doubts that we have become more punitive in sentencing and that offenders are serving more time in prison. The interested reader can also go to government sources, such as the Bureau of Justice Statistics, to see how imprisonment patterns have changed over the years. In 2013, one in 35 people were under some form of correctional supervision—6,899,000! This figure includes probation and parole. There were 2,220,300 prisoners in prisons and jails in 2013; 1,574,700 of those were in prison (Glaze and Kaeble, 2014).

The national incarceration rate (which includes only those in state or federal prisons, not jails) of 150 per 100,000 in the 1980s has increased to close to 500 (478). This means that we are incarcerating over three times as many people as we did in the 1980s. Incarceration rates, displayed by race and sex, tell us that certain groups have a much higher risk of being incarcerated. While the incarceration rate per 100,000 is 466 for white men, it is 1,130 for Hispanic men and an amazing 2,791 for black men. Women are incarcerated at a much lower rate: 51 per 100,000 white women are incarcerated, compared to 65 for Hispanic women and 113 per 100,000 for black women (Bureau of Justice Statistics, 2015).

Sentences of offenders (including nonviolent offenders) have increased and not because crimes have increased in severity (Raphael and Stoll, 2008). Inmates released from prison in 2009 spent an average of 2.9 years—or 36 percent—longer behind bars than offenders released in 1990; however, the increase in sentence length varied dramatically by state. In Florida, the average time served rose by 166 percent, while in New York, sentence length increased only 2 percent. Eight states showed decreases in the length of prison terms, according to the report, which analyzed data from the federal government's National Corrections Reporting Program. Variation among states seemed to follow no regional pattern (Goode, 2012). A careful analysis of sentencing patterns by Pfaff (2011) shows that the dramatic increase in incarceration rates that began in the 1980s was largely due to the decision of prosecutors to seek prison terms for convicted individuals, and, to a lesser extent, increased sentence length and changes in parole release and revocation.

The Violent Crime Control and Law Enforcement Act of 1994 provided 100,000 new jobs in policing as well as $7.9 billion for the funding of new state prisons, thus providing a strong incentive that ultimately led to more prisons and prisoners. The Violent Crime Control Act required "truth-in-sentencing" that encouraged states to reduce or eliminate the use of parole and good time, tools used to reduce sentence length. Draconian provisions also created lifetime bans from federal public housing for drug offenders, more federal death penalty statutes, and federal three-strikes sentences (Alexander, 2010).

Even after property and violent crimes began their dramatic declines in the mid-1990s, incarceration rates continued to climb. What ensued was a clash of the statisticians to determine whether or how much incarceration practices led to the crime decline. The consensus seems to be that incarceration practices were partially responsible for the dramatic decline in crime, but estimates of how much of the reduction was due to imprisonment range from one percent to a third, but even those who estimated in the higher range seem to think now that the use of prison has reached a point of diminishing returns (Raphael and Stoll, 2008). It may be that the country's thirst for retributive punishment is waning.

Recently, advocacy groups have been successful in legislative change at both the federal and state level that seems to be turning the penal harm movement around and deemphasizing the retributive rationale of corrections. There has always been a thread of academic and policy support for rehabilitation, even as prison populations grew (Listwan et al., 2008; Pollock, 2013). What seems to be new, however, is, as mentioned before, the coalition of conservative and liberal voices that advocate similar goals. While not all groups agree on all items, some of the proposals or changes that have received attention recently and briefly summarized below illustrate that the penal harm era may be giving way to a new era:

- Reducing zero tolerance policies in schools that led to suspensions for very minor acts of misbehavior
- Addressing the "school-to-prison pipeline" that has transformed school discipline into the entry into the criminal justice system through the use of municipal tickets
- Reevaluating the direct filing laws that allowed juveniles to be charged as adults (also the waiver procedures that accomplish the same thing) leading to juveniles being incarcerated in correctional facilities for adults,
- Rolling back mandatory minimum laws at both the federal and state level (these laws restrict the discretion of judges to sentence in some crime categories)
- Moving marijuana out of the Schedule 1 drug category, which is for drugs that have a high risk of addiction and no legitimate medical value
- Decriminalizing possession of small amounts of marijuana to a "ticketable" offense (or entirely as in Colorado, Washington, Oregon, and Alaska)
- Reviving or increasing the scope of pretrial release programs (Release on Recognizance) to reduce the number of people in jail simply because they can't afford bail

- Evaluating the system of fines and fees that have created new "debtors" prisons for offenders who have crushing debt they can't pay solely because of criminal justice-related fines and fees

- Specialty courts, such as drug courts, veteran's courts, and courts for the mentally ill, which divert individuals from the system at the "front end"

- Reestablishment of parole and good time in those states that had abolished one or both of these means to reduce sentences for good behavior

- Evaluation of the use of solitary confinement given findings of the pervasiveness in which it is used and the deleterious effects it has on the human psyche

- Reentry initiatives that assist offenders who are released to the community with job placement and other programs designed to reduce recidivism

- "Ban the box" initiatives that question the legitimacy of using prior arrest as a categorical disqualifier for some jobs and programs that reward employers with tax incentives for hiring ex-offenders

- Addressing collateral consequences of a criminal conviction, such as drug offenders being denied federal Pell grants or federal housing and, in some states, lifetime bans on voting

- Improvement of indigent defense so that offenders can be diverted from the system (when appropriate) sooner, rather than later, in the process

Just as there has never been a time in recent decades when police have been so heavily scrutinized, there has also never been a time in recent decades where there seems to be such an shared acceptance of and support for changing the nation's correctional system. The impetus for the change is both pragmatic (corrections costs have skyrocketed to consume ever-increasing portions of budgets) and moral (conservative rationales especially speak to the power of redemption and urge policies that support reformation). It does appear that the retributive rationale is giving way to the prevention rationale for what we do to and with offenders.

Prevention Rationale

Three common justifications or rationales for punishment can all be subsumed under a general heading of "prevention." Prevention assumes that something should be done to the offender to prevent future criminal activity. There are three possible methods of prevention: deterrence, incapacitation, and treatment. Each of these is based on certain assumptions that must be considered in addition to the relevant moral questions. For instance, it is a factual question as to whether people can be deterred from crime, but it is a moral question as to what we should do to an individual to ensure deterrence.

Deterrence

There are two types of deterrence. Specific deterrence is what is done to offenders to prevent them from deciding to commit another offense. General deterrence is what is done to an offender to prevent others from deciding to engage in wrongful behavior. The first teaches through punishment; the second teaches by example.

Our right to deter an individual offender is rooted in the same rationale used to support retribution. By virtue of membership in society, individuals submit themselves

deterrence
Specific deterrence is what is done to offenders to prevent them from deciding to commit another offense. General deterrence is what is done to an offender to prevent others from deciding to engage in wrongful behavior.

to society's controls. If we think that someone's actions are damaging, we will try various means to persuade him or her to cease that activity. The implicit assumption of a deterrence philosophy is that in the absence of controls, society would revert to a jungle-like, dangerous "war of all against all"; we need the police and official punishments to keep us in line. Under this rationale, the true nature of humankind is perceived to be predatory and held in check only by external controls. The Quote and Query box enumerates the key points of view in this justification for punishment.

The rationale behind specific deterrence depends on the effectiveness of punishment in deterring future bad acts by the individual being punished. The rationale supporting general deterrence is somewhat problematic. If we know that a term of imprisonment will not deter an offender but can deter others, can it still be justified? Under general deterrence, the offender is used as a tool to teach a lesson to the rest of us. The sociologist Emile Durkheim (1857–1917) believed that the value of criminals is in establishing the parameters of acceptable behavior. Their punishment helps the rest of us define what is "good."

If one's goal is purely general deterrence, there does not necessarily have to be an original crime. Consider a futuristic society wherein the evening news routinely shows or describes the punishments received by a variety of criminals. The crime—or the punishment, for that matter—does not have to be real to be effective. If punishing innocent people for crimes they *might* do were just as effective as punishing criminal offenders, this action might satisfy the ends of deterrence, but would obviously not be acceptable under any system of ethics—except perhaps act utilitarianism. The movie *Minority Report* presented a somewhat related ethical issue in that it portrayed a future where the government knew ahead of time when individuals would commit a crime and punished them for what they were going to do. The idea of punishing an individual for reasons other than their own acts seems wrong because it violates the retributive justification of punishment, but it certainly might be more effective to prevent crime than punish it after the fact.

Incapacitation

incapacitation
Holding an offender to prevent further crime (incapacitation is not punishment since any pain is unintended).

Another rationale is to prevent further crime through incapacitation. Strictly speaking, incapacitation does not fit the classical definition of punishment, for the purpose is not to inflict pain but only to hold an offender until there is no risk of further crime. The major issue concerning incapacitation is prediction. Two possible mistakes are releasing an offender who then commits further crimes and not releasing an offender who would not commit further crimes.

Carrying the goal of incapacitation to its logical conclusion, one would not have to commit a crime at all to be declared potentially dangerous and subject to incapacitation. We now incarcerate career criminals for life—not for their last offense, but for what they might do if released. These "habitual-felon laws" are justified by the prediction that these criminals will continue to commit crimes. Some argue that a small group of offenders commit a disproportionate share of crime and that those individuals can be identified by predictive elements such as prior convictions, prior incarcerations, juvenile convictions and detentions, use of heroin or barbiturates, and lack of employment. Selective incapacitation is a policy of incarcerating these individuals for longer periods of time than other criminals. In the past, studies indicated prediction instruments had an error of 48 percent (Auerhahn, 1999), and, more recently, with incredibly more sophisticated statistical tools (e.g., "random forest modeling"), the error rate has been reduced to 34 percent (Ritter, 2013), still a perhaps unacceptable error rate when you are discussing keeping someone in prison based on your prediction. There are grave legal and ethical issues in using any predictive devices to sentence an offender, or even to increase supervision level or make decisions about parole. The predictive tools use individual factors such as unemployment to predict recidivism, and it does not seem fair that unemployment (which may not be the offender's fault) is used to determine the level of punishment (Pollock, 2013). Former attorney general Eric Holder, in a speech to the National Criminal Defense Attorney's Association, and in a letter to the Federal Sentencing Commission, expressed his concerns over "evidence based sentencing" that used prediction tools in sentencing. The prediction tools may be racially discriminatory—not in their intent, but in their implementation since some factors will be correlated with race (Starr, 2014). In one tool used in Philadelphia, for instance, zip code of residence was used as a predictor variable in establishing supervision level. Clearly zip code in a highly segregated city like Philadelphia is an unintentional proxy for race, and, therefore, the prediction instrument can be criticized as inflicting a higher supervision level on some offenders merely because of their race/zip code (Ritter, 2013).

There are also ethical issues in how we incapacitate sex offenders. Megan's Law and Jessica's Law have mandated states to create sex offender registries and to make such registries available to the public. While states vary in the extent of the restrictions on sex offenders, typically there are housing restrictions, GPS monitoring (and requirements to pay for it), onerous filing requirements (in some states, sex offenders must be on the registry for the rest of their life no matter how young they are or how serious the crime), and work restrictions. Critics are now beginning to question whether or not the incapacitation tools have gone too far. One problematic issue in some states is that sex offenders (of all types from statutory rape to pornography) are combined with all offenders against children in one registry. This is misleading even though typically the crime descriptions are accessible through the registry as well. The most typical criticisms of sex offender registries are that:

- juveniles should be given special consideration since they may be more amenable to change,
- some offenders (such as those convicted of statutory rape when there is a small gap in age between the partners and the sex was consensual) shouldn't be on the registry at all, and
- the registries have been known to trigger vigilantism and some sex offenders have been killed by citizens.

Critics also note that the recidivism of sex offenders is no different from other offenders and, in some studies, is a bit lower. One last argument to such extreme treatment of sex offenders is that, because the offender is often a family member of the victim, the harsh sanctions lead the victim and family to hide the abuse. They do not want the offender punished so severely and/or they do not want the public shame of having a registered sex offender for the public to see (Vitiello, 2008; Pollock, 2013).

Another incapacitative tool that is being used against sex offenders is civil commitment. The Supreme Court has declared that there are no due process or Eighth Amendment violations in civilly committing a sex offender after his punishment term has expired as long as there is some due process before the decision is made (*Kansas v. Hendricks*, 521 U.S. 346, 1997; *U.S. v. Comstock*, 560 U.S. 126, 2010). This means that a sex offender may serve his sentence, and then be civilly committed for another undetermined period of time, as long as certain statutory requirements are met.

three-strikes laws Sentencing legislation that imposes extremely long sentences for repeat offenders—in this case, after three prior felonies.

Three-strikes laws are defended under an incapacitative rationale because it is argued that repeat offenders are more likely to commit future crimes, so they should be held for long periods of time. More than half of all states now have some type of three-strikes or habitual-felon laws.

California's three-strikes law has received the most attention nationally. Polly Klaas was 12 years old in 1993 when she was kidnapped out of her own home and murdered by Richard Allen Davis. That crime helped generate public support for California's three-strikes law passed the next year. The law's intent was to reduce the amount of crime by those who had prior convictions (like Davis). A prosecutor could select to apply the three-strikes provision to sentencing if the offender was facing a third felony conviction. A lesser known two-strikes provision was also part of the law that provided for a 25-year sentence to those with two felony convictions. California's law was different from most states in that it included almost all felonies while other states limited the three-strikes provision to violent felonies. The state's three-strikes law was said to be partially responsible for the exploding prison population in the state where thousands of offenders had life sentences for drug or property felonies.

Critics argued that for both practical and ethical reasons, the California three-strikes sentence was bad policy. It incarcerated past the crime-prone-age years and it incarcerated nonviolent offenders for 25 years or life. There were also wildly disparate rates of three-strike sentences across the state. Some prosecutors frequently utilized three strikes for nonviolent offenders; others never did (King and Mauer, 2001; Zimring, Hawkins, and Kamin, 2001; Leonard, 2009). Another troubling aspect of three-strikes laws was that African Americans tended to be disproportionately affected (Cole, 1999).

The U.S. Supreme Court ruled in March 2003 that California's three-strikes law was not grossly disproportionate and deferred to the state's authority in setting punishments (*Lockyer v. Andrade*, 538 U.S. 63, 2003; *Ewing v. California*, 538 U.S. 11, 2003). Various attempts to reduce the law's harshness were unsuccessful until 2012 when Proposition 36, a voter-initiated ballot, changed California's three-strikes law. Now, only certain violent felonies are eligible for the application of three strikes. A provision also allowed those in prison with life sentences to petition to have their sentence revised. The practice of incarcerating repeat offenders raises both practical and moral questions.

Treatment

If we can find justification for the right to punish, can we also find justification for treatment? Treatment is considered to be beneficial to the individual offender as well as to society. This is a very different approach from the moral rejection implicit in retributive punishment. Treatment implies acceptance rather than rejection, support rather than hatred. However, the control over the individual is just as great as with punishment; some people would say it is even greater.

ETHICAL ISSUE

Should States Utilize Three-Strikes Sentencing?

Many states have three-strikes legislation, and this type of sentencing has been around for a long time (also called habitual-felon laws). The basic assumption is that the second or third felony is more serious than the first felony and/or that punishment must be made harsher because it did not deter the first time. The first is a deontological rationale; the second is a utilitarian rationale. Opponents argue that these sentences are contrary to our justice system in that they punish the offenders twice for the same offense.

Law

With the rulings by the Supreme Court, it is clear that no federal constitutional right is violated by a state habitual-felon sentencing law. State courts could interpret state constitutional rights to be broader, and legislatures, of course, can change the law if the public pressures them to do so. In California, for instance, the law was dramatically changed due to public pressure.

Policy

Just because prosecutors have the legal authority to impose three strikes does not mean that they always do or even that they often do. It seems clear that prosecutors successfully use the threat of imposing three strikes in order to obtain plea agreements, thus those who insist on their right to trial may be more vulnerable to three-strikes sentencing. There is also disparity among jurisdictions in how prosecutors apply habitual sentencing laws (with some prosecutors using it much more than others). Thus, whether or not an offender receives a life sentence may depend, partially, on the county or state in which the crime was committed. As long as prosecutors have discretion in whether to charge under three-strikes statutes, such disparity will continue.

Ethics

Although prosecutors have discretion in whether to charge offenders under three-strikes statutes, there are ethical and unethical criteria for such decisions. Ethical criteria would be the danger posed to the public based on the felonies the offender has committed, whereas unethical criteria would include political pressure or the race of the offender. More problematic are other criteria, such as using a threat of applying a three-strikes punishment when an offender insists on a trial and won't plead guilty, or when an offender will not cooperate and testify against a crime partner. While such reasons may be justified under a utilitarian ethical system, they could not be under ethical formalism. Even under utilitarianism, it would be important to know the cost to the public of a life sentence compared to what crimes the offender might commit in the future. This calculus is subject to prediction errors, but it seems much more likely that a life sentence for a violent offender is worth the cost, while for a property or drug offender, perhaps not.

What is treatment? We sometimes consider anything experienced after the point of sentencing to be treatment, including education, prison discipline, and religious services. A court was obliged to define treatment in *Knecht v. Gillman* (488 F.2d 1136, 1973) when inmates challenged the state's right to use apomorphine, a drug that induces extreme nausea and a feeling of imminent death, as a form of aversive conditioning. In its holding, the court stated that calling something "treatment" did not remove it from Eighth Amendment scrutiny. In other words, merely labeling some infliction of pain as treatment would not necessarily render it immune from legal challenge as cruel and unusual punishment. Generally, courts have further defined treatment as that which constitutes accepted and standard practice and which could reasonably result in a "cure." It is important to note that the Supreme Court has never recognized a legal right to rehabilitative treatment on the part of most prisoners.

The Supreme Court has also ruled on whether prison officials can administer antipsychotic drugs against the will of the prisoner. Despite arguments that even prisoners have an inherent right to be free from such intrusive control, the Court held, in *Washington v. Harper* (494 U.S. 210, 1990), that an inmate's right to refuse such medication did not outweigh the state's need to administer it if there was a showing that the inmate posed a security risk.

Another question is whether or not states may administer medroxyprogesterone acetate (MPA), which is sold under the brand name of Depo-Provera, or other drugs or hormones to induce "chemical castration" in sex offenders. Punishments for sex offenders have included death, neurosurgery, and physical castration, indicating that they are an especially reviled group. More recently, chemical castration seems to have become a cautiously accepted punishment by state legislatures. California was the first state to adopt it, in 1996, making it a condition of probation for some offenders. Montana, Iowa, Wisconsin, Louisiana, Oregon, and Florida also have enabling laws. Some states mandate its use when an offender has committed multiple crimes; some when the victim is under a certain age. In some states, the treatment is voluntary (Tullio, 2009).

MPA is administered through weekly shots and reduces the offender's sexual desire by reducing the amount of testosterone in the offender's blood. Proponents claim it also makes the offender calmer and more open to treatment. Some question the effectiveness of this intervention, while others question its constitutionality. It should be noted that offenders sometimes request the drug, either because they voluntarily want to control their urges or because it is offered as a way to reduce their sentence. There are side effects, including lethargy, bone density loss, depression, weight gain, and other effects. Legal analysis indicates that the Eighth Amendment is not implicated because the treatment is reversible, it is not painful, and it is not gratuitous. Fourteenth Amendment privacy rights are outweighed by the compelling state interest of protecting children (Tullio, 2009). It is probably not effective, however, for sex offenders other than those who have compulsive sexual urges; which is why it typically is used only for pedophiles.

According to some experts, treatment can be effective only if it is voluntary; others disagree. It is true that much of the treatment that inmates and other correctional clients participate in is either implicitly or directly coerced. Providing treatment for those who want it is one thing; requiring those who are resistant to participate in psychotherapy, group therapy, or religious activities is quite another. Although a retributivist rationale would not support treatment, it is obviously consistent with a prevention rationale, as long as the results show success in reducing recidivism.

The evaluation literature on rehabilitative treatment programs could fill a room. We now have more than 50 years of evaluations, as well as dozens of meta-analyses and exhaustive reviews of the literature on rehabilitation. It is simply not true that "nothing works," as was widely believed through the 1980s and 1990s (Listwan, 2008; Pollock, 2013). However, what works is more complicated than one program for all offenders. One interesting finding that comes from evaluation research is that, evidently, sometimes a program works because of the staff characteristics, not the modality of the program. Thus, we can see again that the individual ethics and performance of public servants (treatment professionals in corrections) have a great deal to do with how well the system (in this case, treatment) works.

Ethical Frameworks for Corrections

The various rationales for punishment just described are well established and can be found in corrections textbooks. The ethical systems that were introduced in Chapter 2 are discussed less commonly in corrections texts, but they form the underlying philosophical rationale for the goals or missions of retribution and prevention (comprised of deterrence, incapacitation, and treatment).

Utilitarianism

The principle of utilitarianism is often used to support the prevention rationale of punishment: deterrence, incapacitation, and treatment. According to utilitarianism, punishing or treating the criminal offender benefits society and this benefit outweighs the negative effect on the individual offender. It is a teleological argument because the morality of the punishment is determined by the consequences derived—reduced crime. Jeremy Bentham was the major proponent of the utilitarian theory of punishment and established basic guidelines for its use.

Bentham believed that punishment works when it is applied rationally to rational people, but is not acceptable when the person did not make a rational decision to commit the crime, such as when the law forbidding the action was passed after the act occurred, the law was unknown, the person was acting under compulsion, or the person was an infant, insane, or intoxicated (Bentham, 1843; also see Beccaria, 1764/1977). The utility of the punishment would be lost in these cases; therefore, punishment could not be justified (Borchert and Stewart, 1986: 317). Bentham's basic formula for punishment provides that the utility of punishment to society (by deterring crime) outweighs the negative of the punishment itself (it is negative because it is painful). Utilitarian theory also supports treatment and incapacitation if these can be shown to benefit society. If, for instance, treatment and punishment were to have equal amounts of utility for society, treatment would be the more ethical choice because it has a less negative effect on the individual. Likewise, if incapacitation and punishment would be equally effective in protecting and providing utility to society, the choice with the least negative utility would be the ethical one.

Some argue that the harms inherent in imprisonment in either jail or prison are so extreme that they must be counterbalanced by rehabilitative programs in order to result in a greater good (Kleinig, 2001b). It is certainly true that, for minor offenders, the harm caused by incarceration far exceeds the harm they caused to a victim or society. It is also problematic when drug users (as opposed to dealers) are incarcerated because the harm caused to others by their actions may be less than the harms that they may endure in this nation's jails and prisons, such as beatings by other inmates, economic exploitation, rape, and gratuitous abuse by correctional officers.

Ethical Formalism

While utilitarianism supports prevention goals, ethical formalism clearly supports a retributive view of punishment. It is deontological because it is not concerned with the consequences of the punishment or treatment, only its inherent morality. It would support the idea that a criminal is owed punishment because to do otherwise would not be according him or her equal respect as a human. However, the punishment should not be used as a means to any other end but retribution. Treatment is not supported by ethical formalism because it can be viewed as violative of the second element in the categorical imperative (do not treat others as a means). Involuntary treatment may be seen as using the offender as a means to protect society. The Quote and Query box presents Immanuel Kant's views.

QUOTE & QUERY

Juridical punishment . . . can be inflicted on a criminal, never just as instrumental to the achievement of some other good for the criminal himself or for the civil society, but only because he has committed a crime; for a man may never be used just as a means to the end of another person. . . . Penal law is a categorical imperative, and woe to him who crawls through the serpentine maze of utilitarian theory in order to find an excuse, in some advantage to someone, for releasing the criminal from punishment or any degree of it, in line with the pharisaical proverb "it is better that one man die than that a whole people perish"; for if justice perishes, there is no more value in man living on the earth. . . .

Source: Immanuel Kant, The Science of Right, 1790.

 Do you understand what Kant was trying to say? Rephrase the passage to make it more simple and current.

Several arguments support this retributive rationale. First, Mackie (1982) discusses the universal aspects of punishment: the urge to react in a hostile manner to harm is an element inherent in human nature; therefore, one might say that punishment is a natural law. Another supporting argument is found in the principle of forfeiture, which postulates that when one intrudes on an innocent person's rights, one forfeits a proportional amount of one's own rights. By restraining or hurting a victim in some way, the aggressor forfeits his or her own liberty; in other words, he or she forfeits the right to be free from punishment (Bedau, 1982). The major point to remember about ethical formalism as an ethical rationale for punishment is that it does not need to result in any good end, such as deterrence. The offender should receive punishment because he deserves it, not because it will result in something useful for him or society.

Ethics of Care

The ethics of care would probably not support punishment unless it was essential to help the offender become a better person or help the victim become whole. This ethical system defines good as that which meets everyone's needs—victims and offenders alike. Several authors have discussed the ethics of care in relation to the justice and corrections system. For instance, Heidensohn (1986) and Daly (1989) discuss differences in the perception of justice from a care perspective versus a retributive perspective—as female and male perceptions, respectively. The female care perspective emphasizes needs, motives, and relationships, while the male retributive perspective emphasizes rights, responsibilities, and punishments.

The corrections system, ideally, is supported by a caring ethic because it takes into account offender needs. Community corrections, especially, emphasizes the relationship of the offender to the community. From this perspective, one should help the offender to become a better person because that is what a caring and committed relationship would entail. Retributive punishment and deterrence are not consistent with the ethics of care. However, some say that retribution and a care ethic are not, nor should they be considered, in opposition to each other. Restorative justice, which is discussed in more detail in Chapter 13, might be considered the merger of the two in that this approach views the offender as responsible for the wrong committed, but the responsibility is satisfied by reparation to the victim rather than by punishment and pain.

Rawlsian Ethics

John Rawls presents an alternative to utilitarianism and retributivism. Rawls's defense of punishment starts with Kant's proposition that no one should be treated as a means, and with the idea that each should have an "equal right to the most extensive basic liberty compatible with a similar liberty to others." According to Rawls, a loss of rights should take place only when it is consistent with the best interests of the least advantaged. Rules regarding punishment would be as follows (cited in Hickey and Scharf, 1980: 169):

1. We must punish only to the extent that the loss of liberty would be agreeable were one not to know whether one were to be the criminal, the victim, or a member of the general public [the veil of ignorance].

2. The loss of liberty must be justified as the minimum loss consistent with maintenance of the same liberty among others.

Furthermore, when the advantage shifts—when the offender instead of the victim or society becomes the one with the least advantage—punishment must cease. This theory leaves a lot of unanswered questions. For instance, if victims were chosen carefully (e.g., only those who would not suffer financially or emotionally) and the criminal was from an impoverished background, the criminal would still be at a disadvantage and, thus, not morally accountable for his or her actions. This rationale for punishment promotes the idea that the criminal act creates an imbalance between offender and victim, and that punishment should be concerned with regaining that balance. The utilitarian thread in this proposition is that by having this check-and-balance system in determining punishment, all of society benefits.

Punishments

We have discarded many punishments that were acceptable in earlier times, such as flogging, hanging, banishment, branding, cutting off limbs, drawing and quartering, and pillories and stocks. Although we still believe that society has the right to punish, what we do in the name of punishment has changed substantially. As a society, we became gradually uncomfortable with inflicting physically painful punishments on offenders, and as these punishments were discarded, imprisonment was used as the substitute.

Inside prison, we have only relatively recently abandoned physical punishments as a method of control (at least formally), but that is not to say that prisons are not injurious. In addition to the informal corporal punishments that are inflicted by officers and fellow inmates, prison is painful because it consists of banishment and condemnation; it means separation from loved ones and involves the total loss of freedom. More subtly, it is an assault on one's self-esteem and prevents the individual from almost all forms of self-definition, such as father, mother, professional, and so on. About the only self-definition left is as a prison "tough guy" (or woman)—a stance that destroys the spirit and reduces the individual to a baser form of humanity.

The Eighth Amendment protects all Americans from **cruel and unusual punishment**. Although what is "cruel and unusual" is vague, several tests have been used to define the terms, such as the following, discussed in *Furman v. Georgia* (408 U.S. 238 1972):

cruel and unusual punishment
Punishment proscribed by the Eighth Amendment.

- *Unusual* (by frequency). Punishments that are rarely, if ever, used thus become unusual if used against one individual or a group. They become arbitrary punishments because the decision to use them is so infrequent.

- *Evolving standards of decency.* Civilization is evolving, and punishments considered acceptable in the past century are no longer acceptable in this century.
- *Shock the conscience.* A yardstick for all punishment is to test it against the public conscience. If people are naturally repelled by the punishment, it must be cruel and unusual by definition.
- *Excessive or disproportionate.* Any punishment that is excessive to its purpose or disproportionately administered is considered wrong.
- *Unnecessary.* There must be a purpose of punishment; generally it is to deter crime. Thus we should administer only the amount necessary to do so.

These tests have eliminated the use of the whip and the branding iron, yet some say that corporal punishment, at least the less drastic kinds such as whipping, is actually less harmful than a long prison sentence. After all, a whipping takes perhaps days or weeks to get over, but a prison sentence may last years and affect all future earnings.

Some sentences given to offenders, especially some conditions attached to a probation sentence, have been criticized as being inhumane. Although typical probation conditions include performing community service, paying court costs and/or restitution, finding employment, and submitting to drug tests, other conditions are more problematic.

So-called shaming conditions include DWI offenders having special license plates that indicate to other drivers that the driver has been convicted of DWI; probation officers putting up signs in the yard or nailing them to the door of convicted sex offenders' homes, warning people that a sex offender lives there; announcing to a church congregation one's criminal conviction and asking for forgiveness; and taking out an advertisement in the town newspaper for the same purpose. These types of shaming punishments hark back to the days of the stocks and pillory, when punishment was arguably effective more because of the community scorn received than the physical pain involved. Whitman (1998) argued that the use of such penalties is contrary to a sense of dignity and creates an "ugly complicity" between the state and the community by setting the scene for "lynch justice."

stigmatizing shaming The effect of punishment whereby the offender feels cast aside and abandoned by the community.

Braithwaite (2000), Karp (1998), and others distinguish between **stigmatizing shaming** and **reintegrative shaming**. The first is a rejection of the individual and has negative effects; the second is only a rejection of the person's behavior and creates a healthier relationship between the individual and his or her community. Braithwaite (2000) is the best-known spokesperson for reintegrative shaming. He argues that shame is different from guilt because it comes from one's beliefs about how one's community feels about the crime. He argues that societies that don't have shame attached to certain crimes have a lot of that type of crime. Thus, what is necessary to reduce crime is a return to the concept of shame, but not stigmatizing shame.

reintegrative shaming Braithwaite's idea that certain types of punishment can lead to a reduction of recidivism as long as they do not involve banishment and they induce healthy shame in the individual.

Sex offender registries, discussed earlier, are incapacitative in that the public is made aware of the presence of a sex offender so they can protect their children. However, the registries are also shaming and in some cases lead to fatal results. Many offenders have been harassed and threatened, the house of one was set on fire, and garbage was thrown all over the lawn of another. A sex offender in New Hampshire was stabbed, and, in 2006, a man in Maine evidently targeted sex offenders and killed two before killing himself (Fahrenthold, 2006). A similar case occurred in Port Angeles, Washington, where two offenders on the registry were killed (Associated Press, 2012).

ETHICAL DILEMMA

You are a judge about to sentence an offender for his third DWI. He will receive a mandatory time in jail, but then he will be on probation, supervised by your court. The other district judges in your jurisdiction have begun to utilize unusual probation conditions, such as requiring the offender to go to church, put a sign on their house indicating their crime, and so on. You are urged by the prosecutor to require this DWI offender to have a special sign made for his car that indicates he is a DWI offender; this would be in addition to the ignition-lock device that will be attached to his car that prevents ignition if the driver has over the legal limit of alcohol in his or her blood.

Law

There is a question as to whether such punishments violate the Eighth Amendment. Most would argue they are not cruel and unusual, certainly not compared to a prison sentence. On the other hand, some state laws typically demand that probation conditions have a "rehabilitative function." In that case, there would have to be proof shown that these shaming punishments assisted rehabilitative goals. The other legal challenge would be a Fourteenth Amendment challenge by the offender's family who are also impacted by the punishments with no due process. For instance, a family member might drive the car with the DWI sign and be wrongly stigmatized by it. In general, judges have imposed these punishments without much serious challenge, partly because they come with probation rather than a prison sentence.

Policy

As stated in an earlier chapter, judges are not subject to any office policy. They are fiercely independent and tend to sentence and run their court in very individualistic ways. However, they are influenced by public opinion and so if there is a strong pressure to utilize some form of sentencing; if they want to be reelected, their decisions are obviously affected.

Ethics

We could also examine these conditions in light of the ethical systems discussed earlier. One issue, as noted, is the effect that shaming conditions have on family members of offenders and whether these conditions constitute a type of extra-legal punishment for them without any due-process procedures of trial and conviction. Punishments such as house signs and other public disclosures subject family members to stigma along with the offender, and, because they haven't broken any law, it would be a violation of ethical formalism (because they are being used as a means). Generally, utilitarianism would support such punishments only if it could be shown to result in a greater good. There is little research that shows they deter, but, then again, there is no evidence to indicate that they result in worse recidivism numbers than more traditional forms of punishment such as prison. The ethics of care would be concerned for all involved, so, once again, how these punishments affect family members would be an issue. In conclusion, the ethics of inflicting a punishment such as a sign on a car that the person has been convicted of DWI probably is less ethically questionable when no one else would be using the car, when the person is a multiple offender, and other methods of deterrence have been attempted first.

Sex offender registries are inclusive of individuals who may not fit the typical stereotype of a sex offender. One of the victims in the Maine case was a young man who had been convicted of statutory rape because of consensual sex with his teenage girlfriend. Even though no sex offender deserves to die at the hand of a vigilante, certainly the death of this young man, who was clearly not the predator that most people think of when they hear the term "sex offender," is a tragedy (Fahrenthold, 2006).

Supermax Prisons

The supermax prison is a type of punishment that has been challenged as unconstitutionally cruel and unusual. So-called supermax prisons hark back to the days of the Eastern State Penitentiary, with 24-hour isolation and no programs of self-improvement to salvage the waste and pain of time served (Pollock, 2013). The

((·)) IN THE NEWS | *ADX—"A Clean Version of Hell"*

ADX Florence is a "supermax" federal prison housing Ted Kaczynski (Unabomber), Terry Nichols (the Oklahoma City bomber), Eric Rudolph (the Atlanta Olympics bomber), and Zacarias Moussaoui (an Al Qaeda member that would have been part of the 9/11 attack if he hadn't been arrested). It houses organized crime figures, domestic terrorists, and serial killers, but it also houses those who rack up infractions at other prisons. Inmates spent 23 hours a day alone in their cells. Those who coped by cutting themselves were "four-pointed," where their legs and arms were restrained to their beds. In a lawsuit against the Bureau of Prisons (BOP), several years ago, the legal team met inmates who swallowed razor blades, were shackled to their beds for days and weeks at a time, ate their own fingers or feces, and, in other ways, clearly demonstrated mental problems so severe that they should have been in a psychiatric facility. Instead, they were at a supermax where, when one inmate came back from the hospital after slashing his neck in a suicide attempt, was told to mop up his blood. Their stories seemed to indicate that the prison itself may have caused at least some of their mental issues. The BOP surprisingly agreed to settle the lawsuit submitting to a list of 27 demands that required, among other things, diagnoses and a treatment plan for the mentally ill inmates. There was no financial settlement as part of the deal. The men are still in prison, but have been transferred to other prisons and are now on medication.

Source: Binelli, 2015.

criticism of these prisons has been directed both to the conditions and to the criteria and procedures used for transferring prisoners to them. Pelican Island in California, the most notorious supermax facility, was the target of a court case, *Madrid v. Gomez* (889 F.Supp 1146 [N.D. Cal. 1995]), in which the courts held the state responsible for brutality and lack of medical care. The case also exposed the practice of correctional officers covering up for each other and the power of union officials in squelching official investigations (Martin, 2003).

The other problem with supermax prisons has been who is sent there. There are allegations that the prisons are being used for troublemakers who are not especially dangerous. Some report that mentally ill offenders who cannot control their behavior are sent to supermax prisons and become even more ill because of the isolation and lack of medical services. The In the News box describes a federal lawsuit regarding this issue. Haney (2008) reports other research that indicates that 45 percent of supermax prisoners suffer from some psychological impairment—either diagnosed mental illness, severe psychiatric symptoms, psychotic or self-injurious episodes, or brain damage. Haney himself reports that he found up to two-thirds of supermax prisoners suffer psychological problems (2008: 964).

After a supermax had been built in Ohio, it was found that only half the beds could be filled with those in the prison system who met the original criteria for transfer, so officials moved death row inmates to the supermax (*Wilkinson v. Austin* et al., 125 S.Ct. 2384, 2005). The supermax in this case was similar to all the other supermaxes in having the following characteristics:

- Human contact was strictly prohibited.
- Cell lights were on 24 hours a day.
- Inmate exercise was for only one hour a day and in a small room indoors.

- The transfer was of indefinite duration and reviewed only annually.
- Transfer to supermax disqualified the inmate from parole consideration.

These prisons have been described as soul-destroying. They involve horrific deprivations of some of the most basic elements of what most people take for granted, including social support, self-esteem, and hope. Haney (2008) describes the supermax as having an "ideological toxicity," an "ecology of cruelty," and a "dynamic of desperation." He explains that the ideology of the supermax is toxic in that it is purely punishment with no redeeming elements of rehabilitation or hope. It is the "penal harm" ideology magnified. "Ecology of cruelty" refers to the architecture and policies of supermaxes that are structured to employ more and more punishment to the inmates inside. Because there are no available rewards to encourage positive behavior, the cycle of punishment spirals to horrible levels that become normal to those working within the institution. Haney describes the "dynamics of desperation" as the inevitable tension that exists between the correctional officers and guarded and the tendency for relationships between them to escalate into cruelty. Inmates react in seemingly irrational violence and/or unruliness because of the powerlessness of their environment, and officers react with greater and greater force, going through a cycle where each side's hatred of the other is reinforced. In this sense, Haney argues, the prison affects not only the inmates but also the correctional officers, who become desensitized to its violence and become cruel enforcers because the environment reinforces the notion that the inmates do not deserve to be treated as human (2008: 960). Officers are faced with moral crises when their behavior is normalized to a level of cruelty that would seem abnormal to anyone not inured to the environment of a supermax.

Haney portrays the supermax as incapable of coexisting with treatment or counseling. Treatment professionals must wear bulletproof vests and sit outside the bars of an inmate's cell with an officer standing by. In some units, he describes "programming cages" set up in a semicircle in a surreal parody of group therapy. If the inmates require such Hannibal Lector–like security, one wonders how they could ever benefit from therapy. How do treatment professionals in such environments reconcile their codes of ethics with the elements of the supermax?

There are also those who believe that the supermax violates the 1994 UN Convention Against Torture and Other Cruel, Inhuman or Degrading Treatment or Punishment. Lawsuits alleging that the supermax violates the Eighth Amendment prohibition against cruel and unusual punishment have been filed, while others argue that prisoners deserve due process before being transferred to a supermax. Generally, courts have not found the conditions of the supermax prison to constitute cruel and unusual punishment, except for the mentally ill. Some courts have required states to have policies clearly identifying which inmates can be sent to the supermax, and such policies are required to exclude the mentally ill. The court cases below are a sample of those concerning the supermax prison:

- *Madrid v. Gomez*, 889 F. Supp. 1146 (1995) (California)
- *Taifa v. Bayhm*, 846 F. Supp. 723 (1994) (Indiana)
- *Wilkinson v. Austin*, 544 U.S. 74 (2005) (Ohio)
- *Joslyn v. Armstrong*, No. 3:01-cv-00198-CFD, slip op. at 1 (D. Conn., October 17, 2001)
- *Jones 'El v. Berge*, 374 F.3d 541 (2004) (Wisconsin).

If supermax prisons must be used at all, they should be used with the greatest of care and with the greatest attention to how the environment affects the individuals housed there. Another concern is how these abnormal institutions affect those who work there.

Private Prisons

Before we leave the discussion of punishment, it is important to explore the ethics of private prisons. Opponents of privatization argue that there is something morally wrong with making a profit from incarcerating human beings. Private prisons are built and then leased to the state or, in some cases, run by the private corporation, which bills the state for the service.

Private prisons are big business bringing in over $3 billion per year (Cohen, 2015). Many have objected to the profit motive being introduced into corrections and point to a number of ethical issues raised by private "profiteers" (Pollock, 2013). First, there are potential abuses of the bidding process, as in any situation where the government contracts with a company for services or products. Money may change hands to ensure that one organization receives the contract, companies may make informal agreements to "rig" the bids, and other potentially corrupt practices may go on. Legal as well as ethical issues abound when private and public motives are mixed.

In the building phase, private corporations may cut corners and construct buildings without meeting proper standards for safety. Managing the institution also raises the possibility that a private contractor will attempt to maximize profits by ignoring minimum standards of health and safety and will, if necessary to this end, bribe inspectors or monitors to overlook the deficiencies. It has certainly happened in other areas, such as nursing homes, that those who contract with the state government and receive state monies reap large profits by subjecting clients to inhumane conditions. Some believe that punishment and profit are never compatible and that linking the two has led to a variety of historical abuses (such as the contract labor system in the South).

Private corporations argue that some state systems subject them to endless and picayune rules and continually audit them to the point where it appears that state prison officials are trying to find noncompliance in order to cancel contracts. There is

---

((•)) IN THE NEWS | *Why Prison?*

It was reported in 2014 that California contracted with the GEO Group to build and operate a 260-bed facility for female inmates in Bakersfield. Unlike the other contracts entered into with the group, this one does not have a promised quota, but will pay $94.50 per day for each prisoner (or $86.95 per prisoner if more than 260 women are sent to them). The contract specifies that only minimum and medium security women with less than 60 months left to serve will be housed in the prison and that the women not require daily nursing care, have no mental health history within the past six months, have no unresolved dental conditions, and have an anticipated need for fewer than four medical consultations per year. Critics wondered why, since the criteria for being sent to the new prison were the same as the criteria for the Alternate Custody Program that would allow women to go back to the community, that much cheaper alternative wasn't used.

Source: Law, 2014.

probably some truth that some corrections department officials are not happy to have legislators approve the use of private contractors and would like to see them fail.

Private prisons hold about 8 percent of state prisoners and 19 percent of federal prisoners (Carson, 2014: 14). Their share of prison beds continues to increase every year. Corrections Corporation of America and the GEO Group (formerly Wackenhut Corrections Corporation) are the largest players in the private prison industry, holding a little more than half of all private prison beds (more than 60,000 beds in the United States alone). In late 1998, Corrections Corporation of America (CCA) merged into the Prison Realty Trust (PRT), allowing the entity to be exempt from tax liability as long as it distributed 95 percent of its earnings to its stockholders (Geis, Mobley, and Shichor, 1999). The Realty Trust (REIT) structure requires profit be derived from passive real estate holdings, so the operational elements must be spun off into a separate company. CCA almost went bankrupt after the move but was saved by restructuring. The company ended up paying millions to shareholders to settle their lawsuit. Now both CCA and the GEO Group, another private prison company, structured themselves as realty trusts with operational portions of the enterprise separated into different companies (Stroud, 2013).

The GEO Group is considered number two among the private prison providers. It also runs mental health facilities and addiction treatment centers. Lawsuits in states concerned the use of tear gas (Louisiana), failing to prevent sexual abuse (Texas), paying $3 million to a member of the state's prison policy panel (Florida), and a murder rate higher than that of the state-run institutions (New Mexico) (Solomon, 1999; Fecteau, 1999; Greene, 2001). In addition to the "big two," more than a dozen smaller companies across the nation are competing for the private prison bids put out by the states.

In a series of news stories in Mississippi, it was revealed that nearly $60 million was spent on four private prisons. There has been a troubled history with private prison companies in Mississippi. GEO was kicked out in 2012 after a federal lawsuit over inhumane conditions. MTC, a Utah-based company, runs the four private prisons in the state and has been a target of the ACLU and Southern Poverty Law Center, who are seeking class-action certification for a lawsuit against the state Department of Corrections because of operations in one of the facilities. Complaints center around the use of solitary for mentally ill inmates and what is described as rampant abuse. A former head of corrections from another state, called in to inspect the facility, called it an extraordinarily dangerous prison "awash" in contraband and weapons. Collective violence incidents occurred in several of the privately run facilities in recent years (Mitchell, 2014).

Proponents argue that private corrections can save the state money. Private corporations are said to be more efficient; they can build faster with less cost and less red tape, and they have economies of scale (they can obtain savings because of their size). States and local governments are bound by a myriad of bidding and siting restrictions, unlike private corporations. While some studies have concluded that private prisons produce results equal to those of state institutions for less cost, others find that they are not cost-effective (Bourge, 2002; General Accounting Office, 1996; Pollock, 2013; Selman and Leighton, 2010). The problem is that many of the evaluations of private prisons are funded by private prison companies or libertarian groups that advocate private enterprise taking over government functions; thus, the objectivity of the evaluators is questionable (Bourge, 2002). At least one academic evaluator who has published articles showing private prisons are more cost-effective has owned $500,000 worth of stock in a private prison company, thus raising concern about his objectivity (Geis, Mobley, and Shichor, 1999; Mobley and Geis, 2002). Common sense would dictate that private prison companies would have a difficult time squeezing profit for shareholders out of a prison without cutting costs. While the CEOs of CCA and GEO make $2–$3 million in salary each year, correctional officers earn, on average, $10,000 less that their state-employed counterparts (Selman and Leighton, 2010: 137).

More recently, reports are published with titles that clearly indicate the conclusions, such as "Too Good to Be True: Private Prisons in America" (2012 by the Sentencing Project), and "Unholy Alliance: How the Private Prison Industry Is Corrupting Our Democracy and Promoting Mass Incarceration" (2011 by PICO National Network and Public Campaign). What these reports describe is a very troubling association between private prison companies that financially benefit from increased rates of incarceration and legislators who write laws that affect incarceration levels. Private prison companies send large sums of money to legislators' campaign funds and/or party coffers, and lobbyists for private prisons work with legislators to write laws that result in a greater likelihood of incarceration for illegal immigrants and mandatory minimum sentences that result in more incarceration for drug offenders. It is reported that private prison companies have given more than $10 million to candidates since 1989 and have spent nearly $25 million on lobbying efforts. Conservative politicians and political action committees (PACs) are the largest beneficiaries. For instance, the Republican Party of Florida PAC received nearly $2.5 million from GEO and CCA between 1989 and 2014. In 2010, GEO and its affiliates donated $33,500 to PACs benefiting Florida Republicans, including the Marco Rubio for U.S. Senate (Cohen, 2015).

In essence, many would argue that what is good for this business is bad for the country. For example, Cohen (2015) quotes from CCA's 2014 annual report to its shareholders:

> *The demand for our facilities and services could be adversely affected by the relaxation of enforcement efforts, leniency in conviction or parole standards and sentencing practices or through the decriminalization of certain activities that are currently proscribed by our criminal laws. For instance, any changes with respect to drugs and controlled substances or illegal immigration could affect the number of persons arrested, convicted, and sentenced, thereby potentially reducing demand for correctional facilities to house them. . . .*

In other words, private prison companies stand in direct conflict with (and opposition to) the trend to decriminalize, de-institutionalize, and deconstruct this nation's prison-industrial complex. Leighton (2014) describes the situation as "perverse incentives" because private prisons require contracts where governmental entities must guarantee occupancy rates of 90–95 percent. Thus, if they enter into a 20-year contract with a private prison company, they must provide those numbers of inmates or pay anyway. There is no incentive under this system to reduce prison populations. He argues that privatization does have a role in corrections, but only if there is a shift in incentives to reward rehabilitative success and prevention rather than warehousing.

The dramatic decline in crime in the last 20 years is probably why these companies have moved into housing immigration detainees. In past years, private prison company representatives were criticized for being involved in writing legislation regarding mandatory minimum sentencing. There is a troubling repetition of the practice of the lobbyists and CEOs of private corrections companies becoming involved in legislation, only this time as it concerns immigration, with the suspicion that, once again, what is good for the company (increasing numbers of illegal immigrants housed in massive detention centers) is not necessarily good for the country.

Predictably, some of the same types of allegations and sustained complaints of lack of services and abuse that was directed to private prisons are emerging relating to the immigrant detainee centers. A Freedom of Information Act request filed by the ACLU obtained a list of deaths in such facilities that uncovered troubling issues where inmates did not receive medical care and the subsequent deaths were suppressed or attempts were made to avoid news exposure. The investigation showed that officials seemed to be more concerned with keeping the deaths out of the news and avoiding scandal than trying to improve medical conditions. The ACLU also learned that more than 10 percent of deaths in immigration facilities were omitted from official lists, and alleges that the approach where Immigration and Customs Enforcement (ICE) investigates itself over allegations of abuse and medical neglect is ineffective (Bernstein, 2010).

Typically, immigrants without the proper paperwork are held by ICE until minimal due process establishes they are here illegally and then they are deported. Immigration violations are civil; however, when a person enters the country again, he or she can be criminally charged and, increasingly, they are being charged and sentenced to a term of imprisonment. After their imprisonment is complete, they are deported. These criminal aliens are held not by ICE but by the Bureau of Prisons. It has been reported that since 1999 the BOP has contracted 13 private for-profit detainee centers housing over 25,000 individuals at a cost of over $1 billion per year. In 2013, 97,384 people were prosecuted for immigration crimes in the United States, which is a 367 percent increase from 2003 (reported in Wilder and Mosqueda, 2014). Nationwide, more than half of all federal criminal prosecutions last year were for illegal entry or reentry into the United States. More people are sent to federal prison for immigration offenses than for violent crime, weapons, and property offenses combined (Wilder and Mosqueda, 2014).

A very troublesome element of privately run detainee centers and prisons is that they have been ruled exempt from open-records laws, which apply to public agencies, including departments of corrections. Shielding the inner workings of these companies is justified as protecting "trade secrets." The ACLU and other groups have difficulty gaining access and investigating private detainment facilities, but allege that shocking mistreatment and lack of medical care exists resulting in an unusually high number of deaths and riots for what should be a low-security population (Wilder and Mosqueda, 2014). Some of the detainees do not speak English or have any family to speak up for them; however, others have been in this country all of their lives and don't even speak Spanish. When they were deported (typically for drug crimes), they immediately returned to their jobs and family in this country, only to be arrested again.

One Texas facility consists of Kevlar tents, and three county commissioners were sent to prison for bribery in relation to its creation (Wilder, 2013). Originally it housed civil detainees and there were reports of beatings by correctional officers, hundreds of sexual assault allegations, prisoners being denied silverware, maggots in the food, and a dangerous lack of medical care. In response to these allegations in 2011 and just before a Frontline television expose of conditions there, the Obama administration removed the civil detainees (under the authority of ICE), transferred the facility to

(¤) IN THE NEWS | *Corrections for Sale*

A *Forbes* magazine article reported the purchase in January 2012 of a state prison in Ohio for $72.7 million as part of Governor John Kashich's (Republican) prison privatization program. The press release said taxpayers will realize an estimated $3 million in annual savings. The offer comes with a requirement the state enters into a 20-year management contract plus an assurance that the prison will remain 90 percent full over that period. The state will still be responsible for escapes and liability costs and state workers will be replaced with lower-paid private employees. Louisiana recently voted down a measure to sell three state prisons that would have paid the state $86 million. After the bill was rejected, the governor (a supporter of privatization) ordered layoffs of prison workers. The Louisiana vote that rejected increased privatization may have been motivated in part by the recent eight-part series in the New Orleans *Times-Picayune*. The article series pointed out that Louisiana's incarceration rate of 1,619 per 100,000 compares to a national rate of 730 per 100,000, and 1 in 86 adults are now in prison. The articles also showed the influence of private prisons in Louisiana and how private prison providers, who are often rural county sheriffs, lobby for harsher sentencing, arguably to keep the prisons full. Quotes likened the current private prison use to the lease labor system of the plantation era, where profits dictated policy and prisoners replaced newly freed slaves.

Sources: *Forbes*, 2012; Blow, 2012.

the Bureau of Prisons, and moved in criminal aliens, mostly convicted of immigration crimes. It was still run as a private facility by the same contractor. Once again, inmates describe overflowing toilets, insect-infested housing units, lack of recreation or jobs, and an overuse of solitary confinement (Wilder and Mosquedo, 2014).

The private facilities for criminal aliens, six of which are in Texas, are built in rural impoverished areas where the jobs provided are welcome even if they are at abysmal wages. In filings to the SEC, CCA reports that its revenues have grown 46 percent since 2005. The GEO group's revenues increased from $572 million before the criminalization of immigration violations to $975 million in 2012, a 70 percent increase (Wilder, 2013).

Private corrections is big business, and there is the potential for the large sums of money at stake to be corrupting influences on all concerned. The In the News box describes the irony of reaping profits from incarceration.

Capital Punishment

The final type of punishment we will discuss is capital punishment. Since there is a huge amount of literature on capital punishment in philosophy, law, and social science, only highlights will be touched on here. What sets capital punishment apart from all other punishments is its quality of irrevocability. This type of punishment leaves no way to correct a mistake. For this reason, some believe that no mortal should have the power to inflict capital punishment because there is no way to guarantee that mistakes won't be made. The growing number of innocent men and women who came perilously close to being executed, as described in Chapter 10, indicates that we have an imperfect system.

Public support for capital punishment has swung up and down. Public opinion polls reveal that public support for the death penalty declined gradually through the 1960s, reaching a low of 44 percent in 1966, but then increased in the next 30 years. In the late 1990s, 75 to 80 percent supported the death penalty (Britt, 1998). Public support seems to be declining in more recent years. In 2008, 63 percent of Americans supported capital punishment (Harris Poll, 2008), and in 2011, the percent dropped to a 38-year low of 61 percent, with 35 percent opposing capital punishment (Gallup Poll, 2011). In 2014, 63 percent of Americans favored capital punishment for murderers according to the Gallup poll, but the Pew Research Center presented different findings with only 56 percent of the public favored capital punishment (Gallup, 2015; Pew, 2015).

The number of executions has declined substantially from a high of 98 executions in 1999 to 43 in 2011, falling even lower to 35 in 2014. The number of death sentences handed out by judges or juries has declined from 315 in 1996 to 78 in 2011. The decline may be the result of the number of death row exonerations that have occurred, which include 23 in Florida, 20 in Illinois, and 12 in Texas (Death Penalty Information Center, 2012, 2015).

Research indicates that certain groups are more likely to favor the use of capital punishment; for instance, support is higher by 20 to 25 percentage points among whites as compared to blacks. Membership in fundamentalist Protestant churches predicts higher support for the death penalty as well. Political conservatism also predicts support. Interestingly, church activity negatively predicts support (the more active one is in one's church, the less likely one is to support the death penalty). Women are also less likely than men to support the death penalty. In one study, researchers found that black Protestant fundamentalists showed the least support for the death penalty, while white fundamentalists showed the most support (Britt, 1998).

Retentionists (who believe that we should continue to utilize capital punishment) and abolitionists (who believe that we should not execute anyone) both use utilitarianism, ethical formalism, and religion as moral justifications. Retentionists argue that capital punishment is just because it deters others from committing murder and it definitely deters the individual who is executed. This is a utilitarian argument. They also argue that capital punishment is just because murder deserves a proportional punishment. This argument is more consistent with ethical formalism. Finally, they argue that the Bible dictates an "eye for an eye." This is, of course, a (Judeo-Christian) religious justification for capital punishment.

Abolitionists argue that capital punishment has never been shown to be effective in deterring others from committing murder, and, therefore, the evil of capital punishment far outweighs any potential benefits for society because there is no proof that it actually is a deterrent. This is a utilitarian argument. Abolitionists might also utilize the categorical imperative under ethical formalism to argue that deterrence is using the individual as a means to an end. Finally, abolitionists would point to the religious command to "turn the other cheek," an argument against any Christian justification for capital punishment.

(») IN THE NEWS | *Abolishing the Death Penalty*

In May 2015 Nebraska, generally considered a conservative state, repealed the death penalty. Lawmakers voted to abolish the death penalty, but Governor Pete Rickett vetoed the bill. Lawmakers surprised pundits by overriding the governor's veto 30–19. Now there are 19 states that do not have capital punishment.

Source: various news reports.

The reason why utilitarianism can be used to justify or oppose capital punishment is that the research on deterrence is mixed. Those who have summarized the evidence marshaled on both sides of the deterrence question found little support for the proposition that executions are useful deterrents, although there are contrary findings by other researchers (Walker, 1985: 79; Kronenwerter, 1993; Land, Teske, and Zheng, 2009). Recently, the National Academy of Sciences reported that the science of death penalty deterrence research was not reliable, accurate, or valid enough to make policy decisions upon. However, despite the lack of research for general deterrence, many are still convinced that it does deter, at least the individual offender (although technically executing the offender does not result in deterrence but incapacitation). Ethical formalism supports capital punishment; however, the imperfect nature of the system is problematic. Recall that under the categorical imperative, you should act in a way that you can will it to be a universal law. In this case, knowing that innocent people may be sentenced to death, could you agree that murderers should be executed if you did not know whether you were the victim, the murderer, the judge, or an innocent person mistakenly convicted?

Religion, also, can be and has been used to support and condemn capital punishment. As with other issues, Christians have pointed to various verses in the Bible to justify their position. Kania (1999), for instance, presents a comprehensive religious justification for capital punishment, along with a social contract justification.

Questions also arise about the methods and procedures of capital punishment. Should all murderers be subject to capital punishment, or are some murders less heinous than others? Should we allow defenses of age, mental state, or reason? If we do apply capital punishment differentially, doesn't this open the door to bias and misuse? Evidence indicates that capital punishment has been used arbitrarily and discriminatorily in this country. One study, cited by the Supreme Court, indicated that minorities are more likely to be executed when their victims are white; in Georgia, black offenders charged with killing a white person were 4.3 times more likely to be sentenced to death than those charged with killing a black person. Yet the Supreme Court stated that this evidence of statistically disproportional administration was not enough to invalidate the death penalty because it did not prove that there was discrimination in the immediate case (*McClesky v. Kemp*, 481 U.S. 279, 1987).

Because our justice system is based on rationality, executions of persons with mental illness and mental retardation have been vehemently criticized. The Supreme Court has ruled that executing the mentally ill is cruel and unusual (*Ford v. Wainwright*, 411 U.S. 399, 1986). Miller and Radelet (1993) present a detailed account of the Ford case, describing the mental deterioration of Ford and the long ordeal of appeals before the Supreme Court finally ruled. They also point out the ethical issues involved when psychiatrists, other medical professionals, and psychologists participate in procedures that involve certifying someone as *death ready* and then assist in the administration of the chosen method of execution. These professions have deep and divisive arguments regarding the seeming inconsistency between identifying oneself as a helping professional and then helping someone be put to death.

In *Atkins v. Virginia* (536 U.S. 304, 2002), the Supreme Court held that a man with an IQ of 59 could not be put to death, finding that the evolution of decency and public opinion supported such a decision. The holding does not answer all the questions that it raised, however, in how serious mental retardation must be to serve as a bar to capital punishment. In *Hall v. Florida* (572 U.S. __, 2014), Florida's automatic 70 IQ test score cutoff for determining mental disability was challenged. Justice Kennedy, writing for the majority, wrote that intellectual disability was a condition, not a number. The holding specified that a cutoff score was unconstitutionally arbitrary, and a more detailed examination of the person, considering their whole history and past diagnoses was required before a sentence of death could be imposed.

In *Roper v. Simmons* (543 U.S. 551, 2005), the Court, in a narrow ruling (5–4), held that juvenile offenders could not be classified as the "worst" offenders; therefore, death sentences of juveniles would be cruel and unusual and violate the Eighth Amendment. In *Kennedy v. Louisiana* (554 U.S. 407, 2008), the Supreme Court held that the death penalty was not proportional to the crime of rape and thus would be a violation of the Eighth Amendment. Note that the question of culpability and whether or not the death sentence is a just sentence for mentally ill, retarded, or juvenile offenders, and the type of crime for which it is a just punishment, are both legal and moral questions.

The 2006 renewal of the Patriot Act added a provision that changed federal habeas corpus procedures to speed up death penalty appeals for states that are qualified. To be qualified, a state has to show that it has competent legal representation; however, it is completely up to the discretion of the U.S. attorney general as to whether or not a state is qualified. Once qualified, states can "fast track" a death penalty appeal, which means that prisoners have less time to file appeals and federal appellate judges can consider fewer issues (Copp, 2006). Critics argue that, given the woefully inadequate representation of some on death row, such a procedure is certain to result in innocent people being executed.

The Supreme Court has also ruled on a challenge to the method of execution. Opponents argued that lethal injection is cruel and unusual because the drugs administered do not prevent the sensation of pain, but they do paralyze; therefore, the individual suffers but is unable to scream or otherwise indicate distress. In *Baze v. Rees* (553 U.S. 35, 2008), the Court held that there was no evidence of substantial or an objectively intolerable risk of serious harm (pain). Recent "methods of execution" appeals are being heard in some federal circuits. Unless the Supreme Court revises its current position, which seems unlikely, the legality of executions is not in question. However, the procedures used to arrive at the decision to execute may continue to be challenged. The influential American Law Institute created the Model Penal Code in 1962, and its legal discussion of the death penalty was used by the Supreme Court to support their decision to uphold it. Now, however, the group has concluded that capital punishment in this country is "irretrievably broken" and has withdrawn their intellectual rationale for it (Liptak, 2010). The morality of capital punishment is still very much a topic of debate, and it elicits strong feelings on the part of many people. The quote illustrates a decision by a Supreme Court Justice to withdraw support for the use of capital punishment.

QUOTE & QUERY

From this day forward, I no longer shall tinker with the machinery of death. For more than 20 years I have endeavored . . . to develop . . . rules that would lend more than the mere appearance of fairness to the death penalty endeavor. . . . Rather than continue to coddle the court's delusion that the desired level of fairness has been achieved . . . I feel . . . obligated simply to concede that the death penalty experiment has failed. It is virtually self-evident to me now that no combination of procedural rules or substantive regulations ever can save the death penalty from its inherent constitutional deficiencies. . . . Perhaps one day this court will develop procedural rules or verbal formulas that actually will provide consistency, fairness, and reliability in a capital-sentencing scheme. I am not optimistic that such a day will come. I am more optimistic, though, that this court eventually will conclude that the effort to eliminate arbitrariness while preserving fairness "in the infliction of [death] is so plainly doomed to failure that it and the death penalty must be abandoned altogether." . . . . I may not live to see that day, but I have faith that eventually it will arrive. . . .

Source: Justice Harry Blackmun in a dissenting opinion in Callins v. Collins (510 U.S. 1141, 1994).

 Do you agree with Justice Blackmun? Why or why not?

Formal Ethics for Correctional Professionals

The American Correctional Association's (ACA) Code of Ethics outlines formal ethics for correctional officers and other correctional personnel. This code has many similarities to the Law Enforcement Code of Ethics presented in Chapter 5. For instance, integrity, respect for and protection of individual rights, and service to the public are emphasized in both codes, as are the importance and sanctity of the law. Also, the prohibition against exploiting professional authority for personal gain is stressed in both codes.

The ACA code indicates that members should exhibit honesty, respect for the dignity and individuality of human beings, and a commitment to professional and compassionate service. The following principles are identified:

- Protect legal rights
- Show concern for the welfare of individuals
- Promote mutual respect with colleagues and criticize only when warranted
- Respect and cooperate with all disciplines in the system
- Provide public information as consistent with law and privacy rights
- Protect public safety
- Refrain from using one's position to secure personal privileges or advantage or let these impair objectivity
- Avoid conflicts of interest
- Refrain from accepting gifts or services that appear improper
- Differentiate one's personal views from professional duties
- Report any corrupt or unethical behaviors
- Refrain from discriminating because of race, gender, creed, national origin, religious affiliation, age, disability, or other prohibited categories
- Preserve the integrity of private information; abide by civil service rules
- Promote a safe, healthy, and harassment-free workplace (the ACA Code is available at www.aca.org/pastpresentfuture/ethics.asp)

In an interesting discussion of implementing an ethics program for correctional officers, Barrier et al. (1999) described how officers presented elements of what they thought were important in an ethics code:

- Acting professionally
- Showing respect for inmates and workers
- Maintaining honesty and integrity
- Being consistent
- Acting impartially
- Being assertive but not aggressive
- Confronting bad behavior but reinforcing good behavior
- Standardizing rule enforcement
- Respecting others

- Practicing the Golden Rule
- Encouraging teamwork
- Using professional language
- Not abusing sick leave
- Telling inmates the truth
- Admitting mistakes

The American Jail Association has a similar code of ethics for jail officers. The preamble states that the jail officer should avoid questionable behavior that will bring disrepute to the agency. The code mandates that officers keep the institution secure, work with everyone fairly, maintain a positive demeanor, report what should be reported, manage inmates even-handedly without becoming personally involved, take advantage of training opportunities, communicate with individuals outside the agency in a way that does not bring discredit, contribute to a positive environment, and support professional activities (American Jail Association, available at www.aja .org/ethics.aspx).

Formal ethical guidelines for probation and parole officers are provided by the American Correctional Association Code of Ethics, and possibly by their own state ethics codes. Federal probation officers subscribe to the Federal Probation and Pretrial Officers Association's ethical code. The formal ethics of the profession is summarized by the ideal of service—to the community and to the offender. As with other codes, the federal probation officer is exhorted to:

- Maintain "decorum" in one's private life
- Avoid granting or receiving favors or benefits that are connected to the position
- Uphold the law with dignity
- Strive for objectivity in performance of duties
- "Appreciate the inherent worth of the individual"
- Cooperate with fellow workers and related agencies
- Improve professional standards
- Recognize the office as "a symbol of public faith" (Federal Probation and Pretrial Officers Association, available at www.fppoa.org/code-of-ethics)

Ethical codes exist for other correctional professionals as well. Treatment professionals typically belong to a professional organization, and this organization will have a code of ethics, such as the National Association of Social Workers Code of Ethics or, for psychiatrists, the Principles of Medical Ethics with Annotations Especially Applicable to Psychiatry. Mental health counselors adhere to the code of ethics of the American Mental Health Counselors Association, and psychologists follow the Ethical Principles of Psychologists and Code of Conduct. There are also organizations or separate divisions of professional organizations specifically for correctional workers in that profession, such as the Criminal Justice Section of the American Psychological Association. Finally, the American Correctional Health Services Association and the American Association for Correctional and Forensic Psychology also have their own ethical codes to guide their members. The American Association for Correctional and Forensic Psychology's code includes the following sections: Offender's Right to Dignity and Respect, Avoid or Minimize Harm, Maintain and Advocate for Competent Mental Health Services and Rights, and Social Responsibility. The Ethical Principles of Psychologists promote five aspirational principles: beneficence (do no harm), fidelity and responsibility (create relationships of trust), integrity (honesty and truthfulness in science and practice), justice (fairness), and respect for rights and dignity (protect privacy and self-determination) (cited and described in Bonner and Vandecreek, 2006).

The American Correctional Health Services Association is an affiliate of the American Correctional Association and has developed a code of ethics for health care providers in correctional facilities, including medical care workers as well as mental health professionals. In developing this code, they surveyed their members and consensus emerged as to the leading principles that should guide professionals in providing healthcare in corrections: respect for human dignity, beneficence, trustworthiness, autonomy, prevention of harm, and promotion of a safe environment. The code includes "should" statements such as "Respect the law and also recognize a responsibility to seek changes in those requirements that are contrary to the best interest of the patient" and "Honor custody functions but not participate in such activities as escorting inmates, forced transfers, security supervision, strip searches, or witnessing use of force" (described in Bonner and Vandecreek, 2006). All of these codes, in general or specific language, attempt to provide guidance to members who strive for ethical performance of their duties.

Occupational Subcultures in Corrections

Another similarity between the corrections field and law enforcement is that there seems to be an occupational culture that sometimes has different norms of behavior than what is described in the ethical codes. Although the ethical codes clearly call for fair and objective treatment, integrity, and high standards of performance, the actual practices found in some agencies and institutions may be quite different.

The Correctional Officer Subculture

The correctional officer subculture has not been described as extensively as the police subculture, but some elements are similar. First of all, the inmate may be considered the enemy, along with superiors and society in general. Moreover, the acceptance of the use of force, the preference toward redefining job roles to meet only minimum requirements, and the willingness to use deceit to cover up wrongdoing seem to have support in both subcultures (R. Johnson, 2002; Crouch, 1980; Grossi and Berg, 1991).

In an excellent study of the officers' world, Kauffman (1988: 85–112) notes the following norms of the correctional officer subculture:

- *Always go to the aid of another officer.* Similar to law enforcement, the necessity of interdependence ensures that this is a strong and pervasive norm in the correctional officer subculture. Kauffman describes a "slam" in Walpole Prison as when the officer slams a heavy cell door, which reverberates throughout the prison building, bringing a dozen officers to his or her aid in minutes—an obvious parallel to the "officer down" call in law enforcement.

- *Don't lug drugs.* This prohibition is to ensure the safety of other officers, as is the even stronger prohibition against bringing in weapons for inmates. The following norm against "ratting" on a fellow officer may exclude informing on an officer who is a known offender of this lugging norm.

- *Don't rat.* In ways similar to the law enforcement subcultural code and, ironically, the inmate code, correctional officers also hate those who inform on their peers. Kauffman notes two subordinate norms: Never rat out an officer to an inmate, and never cooperate in an investigation or, worse yet, testify against a fellow officer in regard to that officer's treatment of inmates.

- *Never make a fellow officer look bad in front of inmates.* This applies regardless of what the officer did, for it jeopardizes the officer's effectiveness and undercuts the appearance of officer solidarity.

- *Always support an officer in a dispute with an inmate.* Similarly to the previous provision, this prescribes behavior. Not only should one not criticize a fellow officer, but one should support him or her against any inmate.

- *Always support officer sanctions against inmates.* This is a specific version of the previous provision, which includes the use of illegal physical force as well as legal sanctions.

- *Don't be a white hat.* This prohibition is directed at any behavior, attitude, or expressed opinion that could be interpreted as sympathetic toward inmates. Kauffman also notes that this prohibition is often violated and does not have the strong subcultural sanctions that accompany some of the other norms.

- *Maintain officer solidarity against all outside groups.* Similar to police officers, correctional officers feel denigrated and despised by society at large. This norm reinforces officer solidarity by making any other group, including the media, administration, or the public, the out-group.

- *Show positive concern for fellow officers.* This norm promotes good will toward other officers. Two examples are (1) never leave another officer a problem, which means don't leave unfinished business at the end of your shift for the next officer to handle, and (2) help your fellow officers with problems outside the institution, which means lending money to injured or sick officers or helping in other ways.

If a correctional officer violates the subcultural code, the sanctions are felt perhaps even more acutely than by police officers, because one must work closely with other correctional officers all day long. Whereas police officers cite the importance of being able to trust other officers as backups in violent situations, one could make the argument that correctional officers have to trust each other more completely, more implicitly, and more frequently, given that violence in some institutions is pervasive and unprovoked, and that the correctional officer carries no weapon. An officer described to Kauffman (1988: 207) the result of violating peer trust:

> *If an incident went down, there was no one to cover my back. That's a very important lesson to learn. You need your back covered and my back wasn't covered there at all. And at one point I was in fear of being set up by guards. I was put in dangerous situations purposely. That really happened to me.*

Fear of violating the code of silence is one reason that officers do not report wrongdoing. Loyalty is another reason. Correctional officers feel a strong esprit de corps similar to the previously discussed loyalty among police. This positive loyalty also results in covering for other officers and not testifying or reporting offenses.

(((•))) IN THE NEWS | *"Rikers"*

In 2010, a correctional officer was sentenced to six years for his role in the death of a juvenile inmate at Rikers. An investigation revealed that a rogue disciplinary group of correctional officers at Rikers Island used beatings and extortion by inmate "enforcers" to keep order in a facility where young offenders, aged 16 to 18, were housed. Other correctional officers were also charged and could have spent up to 25 years in prison for what was considered to be organized crime activity; however, they entered guilty pleas and received sentences of no more than two years.

Since that case, Rikers has been the target of a major investigatory series of reports by the *New York Times*, and a two and one-half year investigation by the U.S. attorney's office of Preet Bharara into the treatment of juvenile offenders that resulted, in the summer of 2014, in a blistering 79-page report documenting pervasive abuse and cover-ups in the juvenile lock-up. The report detailed a "culture of violence" and "code of silence" of correctional officers. The U.S. attorney joined an ongoing class action lawsuit (*Nunez v. City of New York*) in December of 2014 because of the city's perceived lack of response to the report's findings. In June of 2015, a settlement agreement was announced that mandated a court-appointed monitor for the jail, a substantial increase in the number of cameras, body cameras worn by some correctional officers, use of force training, beefed up security to prevent contraband from coming in to the facility, and improved accountability measures for correctional officers who used inappropriate force. Changes in the juvenile division begun last year had already seen a reduction in the number of uses of force, improved programming for juveniles, the elimination of solitary for juveniles, and improved mental health screening.

Sources: Raftery, 2010; Weiser, 2015; Weiser, Schwirtz, and Winerip, 2014; Schwirtz, and Winerip, 2015.

McCarthy (1991) discusses how theft, trafficking in contraband, embezzlement, and misuse of authority went unreported by other correctional officers because of loyalty and subcultural prohibitions against "ratting."

A pattern of complicity also prevents reporting. New officers cannot possibly follow all the many rules and regulations that exist in a prison and still adequately deal with inmates on a day-to-day basis. Before long they find themselves involved in activity that could result in disciplinary action. Because others are usually aware of this activity and do not inform supervisors, an implicit conspiracy of silence develops so no one is turned in for anything because each of the others who might witness this wrongdoing has engaged in behavior that could also be sanctioned (Lombardo, 1981: 79).

In the years-long scandal at Rikers Island in New York referred to in the In the News box, correctional officers who used brutal retaliation against inmates were rarely punished and a conspiracy of silence ensued. Even inmates were told to "hold it down," meaning do not report beatings to outsiders. One incident was documented where two inmates in segregation threw urine or some liquid on correctional officers and they were forcibly extracted from their cells, strapped to gurneys, taken to the medical clinic (because there were no cameras there) and repeatedly beaten in the head and body to the point that blood sprayed on the walls and the medical staff pleaded with the correctional officers to stop (Winerip and Schwirtz, 2014). In the investigative reports of Rikers, many instances were detailed where correctional officers and their supervisors would lie on incident reports to justify uses of force. Staff and inmates were intimidated into silence. In the incident above, medical staff reported feeling like they had to keep quiet to avoid retaliation from correctional officers or their own superiors (medical services were provided by a private contractor) (Winerip and Schwirtz, 2014b). In the Walking the Walk box, one correctional administrator went against the pattern of cover-ups in a state system, and his actions eventually cost him his career.

The correctional officer code, and sanctions against whistleblowers, varies from institution to institution, depending on factors such as permeability, the administration, the level of violence from inmates, architecture, and the demographic profile of officers. Distrust of outsiders, dissatisfaction, and alienation are elements of both the police subculture and the correctional officer subculture. In both professions, individuals must work with sometimes unpleasant people who make it clear that the practitioner is not liked or appreciated. Further, there is public antipathy (either real or perceived) toward the profession, which increases the social distance between criminal justice professionals and all others outside the profession. The working hours, the nature of the job, and the unwillingness to talk about the job to others outside the profession intensify the isolation that workers feel.

One additional point to be made about the occupational subculture is that both law enforcement and corrections have experienced an influx of minorities, the college-educated, and women. These demographic changes no doubt have altered the dynamics of the subculture in both fields.

It should also be pointed out that some researchers believe that some of the values embedded in the correctional officer subculture may not be shared by most officers—a concept referred to as **pluralistic ignorance**. This refers to the idea that a few outspoken and visible members do not reflect the silent majority's views. In a prison, this may mean that a few officers endorse and publicize subcultural values, whereas the majority of officers, who are silent, privately believe in different values (R. Johnson, 1996: 130). Kauffman (1988: 179) found this to be true in attitudes toward the use of force

pluralistic ignorance The prevalent misperception of the popularity of a belief among a group because of the influence of a vocal minority.

WALKING THE WALK

Tom Murton found his career dramatically altered when he was hired by the Arkansas Department of Correction as its director of corrections. He had been instrumental in setting up the prison system for the state of Alaska in the late 1950s and was teaching at Southern Illinois University when he was hired by Governor Winthrop Rockefeller, who wanted to modernize the Arkansas prison system. Upon arriving in 1967 to head the Tucker prison farms, he discovered abuses and inhumane conditions, described later in several writings by Murton and immortalized in the movie *Brubaker*. The U.S. Supreme Court case of *Holt v. Sarver* (442 F.2d 304 [8th Cir. 1971]) also documented the abuses, which included subjecting prisoners to electric shocks, staff taking food meant for prisoners and feeding them a disgusting gruel, forcing inmates into a metal box for long periods of time as a punishment, allowing prisoners to guard and inflict brutal discipline on other prisoners, and other inhumane treatments. Murton began to address these issues and received information that more than 200 inmates had disappeared and were listed as escapees. Acting on the information of one informant, he dug up (on the grounds of the prison) two bodies that had injuries exactly as the inmate had described. One had been decapitated, and one had a crushed skull. Even though one of the bodies was eventually positively identified as a missing inmate, opposing testimony at the legislative hearing called in response to his investigation proposed that the bodies were from an old church cemetery. Instead of pursuing the matter further and digging up more bodies or testing them in any way for age and other identifying marks, state officials fired Murton and threatened him with prosecution as a grave robber if he didn't leave the state. He never worked in corrections again.

Sources: Murton and Hayams, 1969; Murton, 1976.

(where the silent majority did not endorse it to the extent of the verbal minority) and toward the value of treatment (which was silently supported).

Treatment Professionals

While there may be subcultural elements from correctional officers that migrate to those who work in treatment roles in correctional facilities, there doesn't seem to be much research documenting it. Thus, we can only assume that when treatment professionals such as psychologists and counselors work in a prison or other correctional facility, they are not a part of the correctional officer subculture, but they may have a different, albeit weaker subculture of their own. Similarly, correctional medical care professionals may be influenced in greater or lesser ways by the "penal harm" atmosphere that pervades some correctional institutions where inmates are seen as not deserving of the care associated with medical services outside the prison. Ethical issues exist for treatment professionals that are different from those of correctional officers, and these will be described in the next chapter.

The Probation/Parole Officer Subculture

The subculture of probation and parole officers has never been documented as extensively as that of police and correctional officers. Because of differences between these professions, the subculture of the former is not as pervasive or strong as that of the latter. Probation and parole officers do not feel as isolated as police or correctional officers do. They experience no stigmatization, they have normal working hours, they do not wear a depersonalizing uniform, and they have a less obviously coercive relationship with their clients. These factors reduce the need for a subculture. Still, one can probably identify some norms that might be found in any probation or parole office:

- *Cynicism.* They have a norm of cynicism toward clients. The subculture promotes the idea that clients are inept, deviant, and irredeemable. Probation and parole professionals who express positive attitudes toward clients' capacity for change are seen as naïve and guileless.

- *Lethargy.* There may be in some offices a pervasive subcultural norm of lethargy or minimal work output. This norm is supported by the view that officers are underpaid and overworked.

- *Individualism.* A norm of individualism can be identified. Although parole and probation officers may seek opinions from other professionals in the office, there is an unspoken rule that each runs his or her own caseload. To offer unsolicited opinions about decisions another person makes regarding his or her client violates this norm of autonomy.

Even though there does not seem to be the "blue curtain of secrecy" to the same extent as is found in policing, there no doubt is a norm against informing on colleagues for unethical or illegal behaviors. This relates somewhat to the norm of individualism, but is also part of the pervasive occupational subculture against informing on colleagues. Probation and parole officers may see and hear unethical behaviors and not feel comfortable coming forward with such information. If they work in an office where the norm against exposing such wrongdoing is strong, they may indeed suffer sanctions similar to those of police and correctional officers for exposing others' wrongdoing.

Some offices develop norms that accept unethical practices and lethargy. Once this occurs, it becomes a difficult pattern to change. If it is already present, a single officer will have a hard time not falling into the pattern. If all officers feel overwhelmed by their caseloads and their relative lack of power to do anything about failure, the result may be that they throw up their hands and adopt a "who cares?" attitude. If the supervisor does not exhibit a commitment to the goal of the organization, does not encourage workers, treats certain officers with favoritism, or seems more concerned with his or her personal career than with the needs of the office, there is an inevitable deterioration of morale. If the organization does not encourage and support good workers, it is no wonder that what develops is an informal subculture that encourages minimum effort and treats organizational goals with sarcasm and cynicism.

Conclusion

In this chapter, we have looked at some of the ethical rationales for punishment. What we do to offenders is influenced by our views on things such as free will and determinism, the capacity for individual change, and the basic nature of humankind. Punishment has always been used against those who hurt other members of society and thus might be considered consistent with natural law. However, the limits of punishment have been subject to the laws and mores of each historical era. Today, our punishments primarily consist of imprisonment or some form of restricted liberty, such as probation or parole. There are current conversations over the legality and morality of supermax prisons and the privatization of corrections. The death penalty continues to be used; however, the controversy surrounding it continues as well.

Formal ethics for those who work in corrections come from their professional organizations, such as the American Correctional Association. Common to all the codes are adherence to the law, respect for persons, and maintaining objectivity and professional standards of competence. Similar to police officers, there are elements in occupational subcultures that sometimes conflict with and subvert formal ethics.

Chapter Review

1. **Provide the definitions of punishment and treatment and their rationales.**

   According to Leiser, punishment is defined as follows: There are at least two persons—one who inflicts the punishment and one who is punished; a certain harm is inflicted; the punisher has been authorized, under a system of rules or laws; the punished has been judged by a representative of that authority by some relevant rule or law; and the harm that is inflicted upon the person who is being punished is specifically for the act or omission relevant to such law. The definition of treatment is that which may create behavioral change. The rationale for punishment and treatment is the social contract. Further, specific rationales for punishment include retribution, deterrence, incapacitation, and treatment.

2. **Describe how the ethical frameworks justify punishment.**

   Utilitarianism is often used to support the three rationales of punishment: deterrence, incapacitation, and treatment. According to utilitarianism, punishing or treating the criminal offender benefits society, and this benefit outweighs the negative effect on the individual offender. Ethical formalism clearly supports a retributive view of punishment. It is deontological because it is concerned not with the consequences of the punishment or treatment, only its inherent morality. The punishment should not be used as a means to any other end but retribution. The ethics of care would probably not support punishment unless it was essential to help the offender become a better person.

3. **Describe the ethical rationales for and against capital punishment.**

Retentionists (who believe that we should continue to utilize capital punishment) and abolitionists (who believe that we should not execute anyone) both use utilitarianism, ethical formalism, and religion as moral justifications. Retentionists argue that capital punishment is just because it deters others from committing murder and it definitely deters the individual who is executed. This is a utilitarian argument. They also argue that capital punishment is just because murder deserves a proportional punishment. This argument is more consistent with ethical formalism. Finally, they argue that the Bible dictates an "eye for an eye." This is, of course, a (Judeo-Christian) religious justification for capital punishment. Abolitionists argue that capital punishment has never been shown to be effective in deterring others from committing murder, and, therefore, the evil of capital punishment far outweighs any potential benefits for society because there is no proof that it actually deters. This is a utilitarian argument. Abolitionists might also utilize the categorical imperative under ethical formalism to argue that deterrence is using the individual as a means to an end. Finally, abolitionists would point to the religious command to "turn the other cheek" an argument against any religious (Christian) justification for capital punishment.

4. **Describe the ethical codes for correctional officers, treatment professionals, and probation and parole officers.**

Codes come from professional organizations such as the American Psychological Association, or more specific organizations for correctional personnel such as the American Correctional Association. Elements of codes for correctional officers, treatment personnel, and those who work in community corrections all seem to include the following elements: integrity, respect for and protection of individual rights and autonomy, service to the public, sanctity of the law, and prohibitions against exploiting professional authority for personal gain.

5. **Explain how occupational subcultures affect adherence to professional ethics codes.**

Subcultural elements are, in some ways, similar to those of law enforcement—the inmate is the "enemy" along with superiors and the public, acceptance of the use of force, the preference toward redefining job roles to meet only minimum requirements, and the willingness to use deceit to cover up wrongdoing for fellow officers. Treatment and probation/parole subcultures are not strong, probably because they do not share the same characteristics of the job as law enforcement and correctional officers. Generally, the major issue of these subcultures seems to be an attitude toward the client/offender that is pessimistic and cynical, with a belief that offenders are not deserving of the respect according to non-offenders.

Study Questions

1. Define punishment using the elements provided by Leiser.

2. What are the three different objectives or approaches to prevention? Explain some issues with each.

3. How would Bentham defend punishment? Contrast that position with Kant's position.

4. What are the criticisms of the supermax prison? Compare the elements of the supermax to the Supreme Court's definition of cruel and unusual punishment.

5. What are the arguments for and against private prisons?

Writing/Discussion Exercises

1. Write an essay on (or discuss) the "pains" of different types of punishment for different people, including yourself. Would you rather spend a year in prison or receive a severe whipping? Would you rather spend a year in prison or receive five years of probation with stringent restrictions? Would you rather spend a year in prison or pay a $30,000 fine?

2. Write an essay on (or discuss) your views on the justification for punishment. If you knew for certain that prison did not deter, would you still be in favor of its use? Why? If we could predict future criminals, would you be willing to incapacitate them before they commit a crime in order to protect society? Explain.

3. Write an essay on (or discuss) your views on the use of capital punishment and the reasons for your position. Now take the opposite side, and give the reasons for this view.

Key Terms

cruel and unusual punishment	justice model	retribution
deterrence	penal harm	stigmatizing shaming
expiation	pluralistic ignorance	three-strikes laws
incapacitation	prevention	treatment
just deserts model	punishment	treatment ethic
	reintegrative shaming	

ETHICAL DILEMMAS

Situation 1

A legislator has proposed a sweeping new crime and punishment bill with the following provisions for punishment. Decide each issue as if you were being asked to vote on it:

- Mandatory life term with no parole for any crime involving a weapon
- Corporal punishment (using an electrical apparatus that inflicts a shock) for all personal violent crimes
- Mandatory five-year prison sentences for those convicted of DWI
- Public executions
- Abolition of probation, to be replaced with fines and prison sentences for those who are not able to pay or are unwilling to do so

Situation 2

Another legislator has suggested an alternative plan with the following provisions. Vote on these:

- Decriminalization of marijuana
- Mandated treatment programs for all offenders who were intoxicated by alcohol or other drugs at the time of the crime
- Restructuring the sentencing statutes to make no sentence longer than five years, except homicide, attempted homicide, robbery, and rape
- Implementation of a restitution program for all victims whereby offenders stay in the community, work, and pay back the victims for the losses and/or injuries they received

Situation 3

Your state allows relatives of homicide victims to witness the execution of the perpetrator. Your brother was killed in a robbery, and the murderer is about to be executed. You receive a letter advising you of the execution date and your right to be present. Would you go? Would you volunteer to be the executioner?

Situation 4

Your house has been burglarized. Your community has a new sentencing program, and the program's directors have asked you to participate along with the offender who burglarized your house. As you understand it, this means that you would be sitting down with representatives from the police department and court system and the offender and his family. The group would discuss and come to an agreement on the appropriate punishment for the crime. Would you do it? Why or why not?

Situation 5

You are a legislator who is the chairman of a committee that is making decisions about whether to build a new prison or contract with a private prison provider. You are visited by a lobbyist for one of the companies that is being considered and he explains that the company is sponsoring a "fact finding" trip to Scandinavia and other parts of Europe to tour several prisons and meet with correctional officials. He invites you and your spouse to go with the group. You would stay in very nice hotels and have social and entertainment events as well as the official activities—everything would be paid for by the company. He explains that because it is a fact-finding or educational trip for you, it does not violate your state's laws or ethics code. Would you go?

Discretion and Dilemmas in Corrections

Correctional officer and inmate.

Image Source/Getty Images

ohn Edwards was abandoned by his parents and raised by a foster mother, but was on the streets at a young age. He turned to male prostitution and acquired HIV. His horrible childhood doesn't excuse the fact that he killed his ex-wife and another person. Edwards was convicted of the murders and incarcerated in a Florida penitentiary where, in a scuffle, he bit a correctional officer in the face. He reportedly laughed and told the officer, "Now you have it, too." That decision led to his transfer to Charlotte Penitentiary where a group of correctional officers called "The Family" used beatings and force to instill fear in the inmates. When Edwards was brought into the prison, the two transfer officers and the receiving officers kicked and punched him in the head and abdomen, slammed him into the wall, and beat him until he couldn't stand up. When he was on the floor, they continued to kick him. The beatings continued through several shift changes; each new set of officers came into the room and administered their own

Chapter Objectives

1. Describe the role conflict of correctional officers.

2. List and describe some ethical issues for correctional officers.

3. Describe the different challenges that face jail officers as compared to correctional officers in prisons.

4. Explain the role conflict of treatment professionals and provide examples.

5. Describe the ethical issues of probation and parole officers.

punishment for his assault on a fellow correctional officer. At one point, officers threw his food on the floor and made him get on all fours to eat it and then kicked him in the head when he did.

On the third day, Edwards used his identification badge and his teeth to hack open a vein in his arm. He was found lying in a pool of blood, and officers kicked him again before they dragged him to the infirmary. The nurses were told to write a report that the injuries they saw were present when he was received at the prison. They bandaged his wound, but did not stitch the open vein, then took him to a close-custody room and put him in four-point restraints (where wrists and ankles are restrained on the four corners of a cot). Edwards lay there naked and bleeding. The captain who had participated in and supervised his beatings came in again and beat him and kicked him in the genitals as he lay there. Finally, Edwards bled to death. The autopsy report indicated gross medical negligence (York, 2012).

Gary York, a former investigator for the Florida State Inspector General's office, describes the case and subsequent trial of those involved. The information about what happened came from two correctional officers who confessed and two who witnessed the abuse. Eventually, the FBI and state attorney's office joined the investigation and 10 people were arrested. Two captains, three sergeants, six officers, and three nurses lost their jobs. Of those arrested, three told the truth, pleaded guilty, and were sentenced to probation and community service. The seven who denied everything went to trial and were acquitted. It was reported that several jurors went out and celebrated with the officers and their families after the verdict. Jurors told reporters that they couldn't convict the officers because, after all, Edwards was a murderer (York, 2012).

Correctional professionals are exposed to the worst members of our society on a daily basis. Their job entails risking being punched, bitten, and spit upon; being showered with urine or feces; and being subjected to a constant barrage of profanity and aggressive commands, demands, and criticisms by some inmates. Many inmates are psychotic or have mental problems so severe that one cannot turn one's back on them for fear of being attacked. Other inmates have, for many reasons, developed into the most hardened, violent, manipulative, unremittingly unpleasant individuals to deal with that can be imagined. Correctional officers work with these individuals daily and all are changed as a result of working in the prison.

Friedrich Nietzsche said, "Whoever fights monsters should see to it that in the process he does not become a monster. And if you gaze long enough into an abyss, the abyss will gaze back into you." The descriptions of what occurs in this nation's prisons certainly give credence to that thought. There are correctional officers who have become more criminal than the criminals they supervise, and many others who pretend not to see. Inmate violence against officers spurs officer violence against inmates which, in turn, creates the probability of more violence as inmates and correctional officers alike sink into a spiral of retaliation. This does not describe all prisons or jails, but it does describe some. Similar to our discussion of law enforcement, the vast majority of correctional officers in jails and prisons do their jobs to the best of their ability and within the bounds of the law, but there are a small percentage who take it upon themselves to be judge, jury, and, in some cases, executioners of inmates.

Institutional correctional personnel can be divided into two groups: (1) correctional officers and their supervisors, and (2) treatment professionals, a group that includes educators, counselors, psychologists, and all others connected with programming and services. These groups have different jobs and different ethical issues. There are also community correctional professionals, including probation and parole officers and staff in work release and halfway houses. All correctional professionals share the two goals of protecting society and assisting in the reform of the criminal offender.

Throughout this text, discretion has been shown as pivotal in each phase of the criminal justice system. In corrections, discretion is involved when a correctional officer chooses whether to write a disciplinary ticket or merely delivers a verbal reprimand; this is similar to the discretion that police have in traffic stops. Discretion is also involved when the disciplinary committee makes a decision to punish an inmate for an infraction. The punishment can be as serious as increasing the length of a sentence through loss of good time or as minor as a temporary loss of privileges. This type of discretion is similar to the discretion of the prosecutor and judge in a criminal trial. Officers make daily decisions regarding granting inmates' passes, providing supplies, and even answering questions. Probation and parole officers have discretion in when to file a violation report or what to recommend if a client violates one or more conditions of their supervision. Halfway house personnel issue disciplinary infractions and have the authority to make recommendations whether a resident should be returned to a prison or granted early release.

As always, when the power of discretion is present, the potential for abuse is also present. Sometimes correctional professionals have the *power* to do things that they don't have the *legal authority* to do. That is, some officers can deny an inmate a pass to go to the doctor even though, according to the prison rules, the inmate has a right to go. When officers exceed their authority, inmates' only recourse is to write a grievance. Professional ethics, as provided in a code of ethics, should guide officers and other staff members in their use of discretion and power, but, as with law enforcement and legal professionals, adhering to a code of ethics is influenced by the occupational subculture and institutional values. There are also examples where correctional officers become as criminal as the inmates they are supposed to be supervising, either because of their use of illegal punishment, as the opening story describes, or because of the temptation of money that can be earned for smuggling in contraband.

Correctional Officers

Correctional officers (COs) are similar to police officers in that their uniform represents the authority of the institution quite apart from any personal power of the person wearing it. Some COs are uncomfortable with this authority and do not know how to handle it. Other COs revel in it and misperceive the bounds of authority given to them as a representative of the state. The following statement is a perceptive observation of how some COs misuse the authority they have:

> *[Some officers] don't understand what authority is and what bounds you have within that authority. . . . I think everyone interprets it to meet their own image of themselves. "I'm a corrections officer! [slams table] You sit here! [slam] You sit there!" rather than, "I'm a person who has limited authority. So, you know, I'm sorry, gentlemen, but you can't sit there. You are going to have to sit over there. That's just the rules," and explaining or something like that the reason why. (Kauffman, 1988: 50)*

This observer obviously recognizes that the uniform bestows the authority of rational and reasonable control, not unbridled domination. The power of the CO is limited. In actuality, it is impossible to depend on the authority of the uniform to get tasks accomplished, and one must find personal resources—respect and authority stemming from one's personal reputation—in order to gain cooperation from inmates. In fact, a common refrain of correctional officers is that they only control the institution because the inmates let them. While not entirely true since they do have controls and sanctions at their disposal, the idea of one correctional officer amidst 200 inmates (a typical ratio in a housing unit) does tend to support the idea that the keepers rule only with the tacit consent of the kept.

Some officers who perceive themselves as powerless in relation to the administration, the courts, and society in general may react to this perceived powerlessness by misusing their little bit of power over inmates. They may abuse their position by humiliating or disrespecting those in their control. It also may be the case, as some argue, that CO brutality stems from a fear of being victimized. The old saying "a strong offense is the best defense" describes this explanation of officer brutality.

Similar to police officers, correctional officers have a range of coercive control over inmates, from loss of liberty to lethal force, if necessary. This power may be misused. Blatant examples are an officer who beats an inmate or coerces sex from an inmate. The possibility for these abuses of power exists because of the powerlessness of the offender relative to the officer. Inmates have even less power against officer abuses than do citizens on the street against police officers' abuses of power. Inmates' powerlessness is exacerbated by public antipathy and disinterest. Sensitivity to ethical issues in corrections involves recognition and respect for the inherent powers and concurrent responsibilities of the profession.

Not surprisingly, COs and inmates tend to agree on a description of a good officer as one who treats all inmates fairly with no favoritism but who does not always follow rules to the letter. Discretion is used judicially; when a good officer makes a decision to bypass rules, all involved tend to agree that it is the right decision. A good officer is not quick to use force, or afraid of force if it becomes necessary. A good officer treats inmates in a professional manner and gives them the respect they deserve as human beings. A good officer treats inmates in the way anyone would like to be treated. If an inmate abuses the officer, that inmate will be punished, but through formal, not informal, channels. In some cases, the officer will go far outside regular duties to aid an inmate who is sincerely in need; however, he or she can detect game playing and cannot be manipulated. These traits—consistency, fairness, and flexibility—are confirmed as valuable by research (Johnson, 2002).

correctional officer The term that replaced the old label of *guard*, indicating a new role.

During the rehabilitative era of the 1970s, professional security staff in corrections exchanged the old label of *guard* for a new one—**correctional officer**. Crouch (1986) examined how changing goals (from custody to rehabilitation) in the 1970s and 1980s created role conflict and ambiguity for the correctional officer. Also in the 1970s, federal courts recognized an expanding number of prisoner rights, including the rights to exercise religious beliefs, obtain medical care, and enjoy some due process before being punished for prison infractions. The disruption in the "old way" of doing things created real chaos, and the 1970s and 1980s brought danger, loss of control, and stress for officers. In addition to increasing prisoner rights, the advent of unionization, professionalism, and bureaucratization changed the correctional officer's world (Crouch, 1980, 1986; Silberman, 1995; R. Johnson, 2002; Pollock, 2013a).

The prisoners' rights era of the 1970s gave way to the "due deference" era of today, where courts are more apt to defer to prison officials. Now, when responding to prisoner challenges, prison officials only have to prove a "rational relationship" between prison policies or procedures and the correctional goal of safety and security (Pollock, 2013a). The Prison Litigation Reform Act of 1996 (PLRA) drastically curtailed the ability of inmates to file lawsuits and made it nearly impossible for federal courts to order consent decrees or order injunctive relief. It also limited attorney's fees.

Today, the prison is not the same as it was before the rights and rehabilitation era of the 1960s and 1970s, and correctional officers probably think that inmates still have too many rights. However, the courts' retreat into due deference has arguably led to a new era of penal harm. When legal rights are limited, professional ethics must step into the breach to guide what is appropriate treatment of those in custody.

WALKING THE WALK

James Yee was raised as a Lutheran in a Chinese American family in New Jersey. He converted to the Muslim faith after graduating from West Point in 1990. Yee left the army for a short time, but then came back into the army as a chaplain. In 2002, he was sent to Guantanamo to minister to the prisoners. For 10 months, from November 2002 to September 2003, he witnessed hostile acts toward the prisoners, including beating and humiliation by military police and interrogators. He saw religion used as a weapon. Prisoners were made to bow down in the middle of a satanic circle and profess that Satan was their god, not Allah. Detainees were mocked during prayer and teased sexually by female soldiers. Detainees begged Yee to take away their copies of the Quran because, allegedly, the military police would deface the holy books.

Chaplain Yee began to be known as a prisoner advocate. He ministered to the detainees and tried to intervene to stop the abuse they endured. As he explained, "I was not willing to silently stand by and watch U.S. soldiers abuse the Quran, mock people's religion, and strip men of their dignity—even if those men were prisoners." He advocated openly for the prisoners, especially against actions that were taken against the religious practices of the Muslim prisoners. His advocacy brought him into conflict with his superiors. "I believed that the hostile environment and animosity toward Islam were so ingrained in the operation that Major General Miller and the other camp leaders lost sight of the moral harm we were doing."

He became concerned especially about the young detainees. Boys as young as 12 to 14 years old, who had been seized as they engaged in hostilities against American soldiers in Afghanistan, were detained at Guantanamo. Once there, they were held with no idea as to when they would be released, or even if they would be. They may have been interrogated with coercive measures, and they experienced day-to-day treatment by guards that is typical of the worst prisons. Yee asked himself how these young men would turn out and what they would think of America. Despite the pervasive attitudes that he experienced that discouraged any attempt to advocate for prisoners, he continued to do so.

On his first leave from Guantanamo, in September 2003, Yee was arrested at the airport coming back into the United States and accused of being a spy. He was imprisoned for 76 days under conditions of sensory deprivation and interrogated. Yee's wife and daughter were subjected to interrogation as well.

Eventually the treason and spying charges were dropped. Because Yee was carrying names of detainees and interrogators, he was charged with mishandling classified information. He was also charged with pornography because of pictures on his computer, and with adultery for an affair he had had with another officer. Even those charges were dropped in 2004. General Miller (the superior officer he had criticized at Guantanamo) was quoted as saying that the reason charges were dropped was that national security would be compromised in any prosecution; however, nothing in the record indicated that Yee was, in any way, a spy. He was never formally exonerated nor was he ever issued an apology, even though his life had been torn apart by the accusations and he ended up with $260,000 in legal bills.

Yee believes that there was a plan to discredit him (by accusing him of being a spy) in case he exposed the treatment of the Guantanamo detainees. He left the military in 2005, with an honorable discharge, and today continues to speak out against what the United States has done in Guantanamo.

Sources: Buchholz, 2008: G1, G4; Lewis, 2005; Yee and Molloy, 2005.

As discussed in the Walking the Walk box, Chaplain James Yee stood up to what he believed were abuses of power in the Guantanamo detainment facility, arguably a place where detainees had fewer rights than even the prisoners we will be discussing in these chapters. He paid a heavy price for it.

A New Era of Corrections?

It should also be noted that *Brown v. Plata* (131 S.Ct. 1910, 2011) may be signaling a new era of prisoner rights (although it was a 5–4 decision, indicating no strong consensus on the part of the justices). In this case, the Supreme Court ordered the state of California to release prisoners if they could not provide a constitutionally mandated level of medical care. The case came about because the state and lower federal courts had been in contention for years as to whether the state was obligated to improve medical care for prisoners and, if so, by how much. When the state balked at the lower federal court order to allocate huge new sums of money to improve care or release prisoners, the case went before the Supreme Court and their affirmation of the lower court's order surprised everyone.

The record indicated that the abysmal level of medical care in California prisons led directly to the death of at least 34 prisoners. The alleged deficiencies included:

- Inadequate medical screening of incoming prisoners
- Delays in or failure to provide access to medical care, including specialist care
- Untimely responses to medical emergencies
- The interference of custodial staff with the provision of medical care
- The failure to recruit and retain sufficient numbers of competent medical staff
- Disorganized and incomplete medical records
- A "lack of quality control procedures, including lack of physician peer review, quality assurance and death reviews"
- A lack of protocols to deal with chronic illnesses, including diabetes, heart disease, hepatitis, and HIV
- The failure of the administrative grievance system to provide timely or adequate responses to complaints concerning medical care

The state's response to the case decision was AB 109 and AB 117, signed into law on October 1, 2011, otherwise known as the Realignment Act, which shifted a large responsibility of corrections for nonviolent offenders to the counties. In November 2012, Proposition 30 was passed, creating permanent funding for counties to take greater responsibility for offenders. California, which had been operating its prisons at 200–300 percent over capacity, was committed to reducing its prison population to 155 percent of capacity by 2012, which it did, and to 140 percent of capacity by 2016. Within six months, the California's prison population dropped by 11,000 inmates, and the state has now decreased the prison population by about 25 percent (Simon, 2014; Salins and Simpson, 2013).

The language of the Supreme Court in the *Plata* decision focused on human rights and it appeared that the justices were literally shocked and appalled at the inhumane conditions that were tolerated in the California prisons. The decision in this case seemed to herald a shift in the penal harm era to one where evidence-based and rational correctional alternatives may take hold. The effort to change the mission and culture of corrections has been described as turning a cruise ship around—it can be done, but it isn't quick and it isn't easy.

Relationships with Inmates

One would assume that the general relationship between officers and inmates is one of hatred. That is not necessarily the case. As Martin (1993), a prisoner writer, points out, the posturing and vocalization from either side come from a small number, with the majority of inmates and officers living in an uneasy state of truce, hoping that no one goes over the line on either side. The Quote and Query box points out the extremes in relationships between convicts and correctional officers.

The majority of correctional officers and inmates prefer to live in peace and understand that they have to treat each other with some modicum of respect in order to get along. Even though prisoners have been known to come to the aid of officers in physical confrontations, in general, inmates support their fellow inmates and correctional officers support their fellow correctional officers, regardless of how little support the individual deserves. Thus, a brutal correctional officer may be protected by his fellows, and a racist correctional officer will not be informally or formally sanctioned. Likewise, an assaultive inmate will not be kept in check by his peer group unless his actions are perceived to hurt their interests.

An officer's ethics and professionalism are seriously threatened when relationships with inmates become personal. Gresham Sykes (1980) discussed the issue of **reciprocity** in supervision: Officers become dependent on inmates for task completion and smooth management of the housing unit; in return, COs may overlook inmate infractions and allow some favoritism to enter their supervision style. An example of a type of reciprocal relationship that may lead to unethical actions is that between an officer and an informant. Several authors have described how rewarding informants sometimes creates tension and trouble in a prison environment even though management often depends on the information (Hassine, 1996; Marquart and Roebuck, 1986).

reciprocity
Sykes's term denoting the situation in which officers become indebted to inmates and return favors.

COs involvement with inmates can occur because of daily contact combined with shared feelings of victimization by the administration. Officers may start to think they have more in common with inmates than with the administration, especially now that officers are more likely to come from urban areas, come from minority groups, and be more demographically similar to the inmates they supervise. This is especially true for jails. This shared identity, in addition to treatment by administration that seems arbitrary and unfair, may create bonds with inmates that interfere with professional duties. Identification and friendship may lead to unethical conduct, such as ignoring infractions or doing illegal favors for an inmate.

York (2012) provides a current description of Sykes' reciprocity concept in describing how an officer is led down a path where an inmate will first ask him or her for a piece of gum or other innocuous merchandise, then cigarettes (which are contraband in most prisons now), then information, then alcohol, and then, because at this point the officer is extremely vulnerable to

QUOTE & QUERY

Some convicts hate all prison guards. They perceive them as the physical manifestation of their own misery and misfortune. The uniform becomes the man, and they no longer see an individual behind it. . . . Many guards react in kind. The hatred is returned with the full force of authority. These two factions become the real movers and shakers in the prison world. They aren't a majority in either camp, but the strength of their hatred makes its presence known to all.

Source: Martin, 1993: 94–95.

 How would one reduce the level of hate between these small numbers of prisoners toward correctional officers and correctional officers toward prisoners?

discipline for past infractions, he is asked to bring in drugs or weapons. McCarthy (1991) points out that lack of training, low visibility, and unfettered discretion contributes to this type of exchange and a variety of other corrupt behaviors.

An extremely problematic situation arises when the officer becomes sexually involved with an inmate (or inmates). Sexual relationships run a continuum of coercion from "true love" to rape. Coercion is more likely to be present between a female inmate and a male officer rather than a male inmate and female officer (Pollock, 2013a). This special type of problematic relationship is discussed in the next section.

The subcultural norms against sympathizing with or becoming too friendly with inmates may be seen as a tool to prevent officers from becoming personally involved with inmates and compromising their professional integrity. An officer who is too close to inmates is seen by other officers as untrustworthy. The officer subculture minimizes this possibility with a view of inmates as animalistic and not worth human sympathy. Some correctional officers then treat inmates accordingly. In fact, how they are treated by COs is sometimes described by inmates as more painful than any physical deprivations. Kauffman (1988) also notes, however, that inmates themselves make it difficult for COs to continue to hold sympathetic or friendly views because of the inmates' negative behaviors.

Just as officers may act in unethical ways when they like an inmate, they also may abuse their authority with inmates they do not like. These extra-legal harassments and punishments may include "forgetting" to send an inmate to an appointment, making an inmate stay in "keeplock" longer than necessary, or pretending not to hear someone locked in a cell asking for toilet paper or other necessary items. Lombardo (1981, 1989) noted the practices of putting an inmate in "keeplock" on a Friday even without a supportable charge because the disciplinary committee would not meet until the following Monday to release the inmate, the use of profanity toward inmates even in front of families, not notifying an inmate of a visitor, and losing passes. During the time period she studied, Kauffman (1988) noted that officers sometimes flushed cell toilets to aggravate inmates, dumped good food into the garbage, withheld toilet paper or matches, made up "tips" reporting contraband in a cell that resulted in a shakedown, scratched artwork, and in other innumerable informal ways made the targeted inmate's life miserable.

Because prisoners are in a position of need, having to ask for things as simple as permission to go to the bathroom, officers have the power to make inmates feel even more dependent than necessary and humiliated because of their dependency. The relative powerlessness of officers in relation to their superiors, the administration, and society in general creates a situation where some take advantage of their only power—that over the inmate. The gulf between the status of the guards and guarded is the theme of the Quote and Query box.

For officers, the potential of injury or being taken hostage is never far from their mind, and may affect to a certain extent their supervision of inmates, for it is potentially dangerous to be personally disliked. Also, on a day-to-day basis, some inmates are friendly, some are funny, and some are good conversationalists. This strange combination of familiarity and fear results in a pervasive feeling of distrust. Officers insist that "you can be friendly with inmates, but you can never trust them." Mature officers learn to live with this basic inconsistency and are able to differentiate situations in which rules must be followed from those in which rules can be relaxed. Younger and less perceptive officers either take on a defensive attitude of extreme distrust or are manipulated by inmates because they are not able to tell the difference between good will and gaming.

Sexual Relationships and Sexual Abuse in Prison

One of the results of the gender integration of corrections that occurred in the 1980s has been the rise of sexual misconduct and sexual abuse, which is mostly heterosexual, but can also be same-sex as well.

Until the mid-1800s, female prisoners were housed together with men in jails, with predictable results. Women were raped and sexually exploited, and they sold themselves for food and other goods. Various scandals and exposés of prostitution rings led to women's reform groups pressuring legislatures to build completely separate institutions for women in the late 1800s and early 1900s. These women's prisons were staffed by female matrons. This pattern continued until the 1980s, when female correctional officers challenged the hiring patterns of state prison systems that barred them from working in institutions for men. They were successful in achieving the right to work in men's prisons. Male inmates account for 93–96 percent of the prison population, so there are more prisons for men in any state, thus making it more likely that a female correctional officer could work close to home if she could work in a prison for men.

Through the 1980s into the 2000s, the number of female correctional officers working in prisons for men rapidly increased, but so did the number of male correctional officers working in prisons for women because legal equal protection worked in both directions. Sexual abuse and sexual misconduct complaints have risen with the increased number of men in women's prisons (in some state systems male officers comprise over 50 percent of the total force in the women's prison) and, also, the number of women in prisons and jails for men (reportedly women comprised 75 percent of the correctional officer force in the state-run Baltimore jail described elsewhere in this chapter).

The idea of prison rape is pervasive in our culture and is even the source of (poor) jokes in popular culture. The problem of prison rape was largely believed to be male inmate-on-inmate violence. Added to this problem, however, was a growing realization through the 1990s into the 2000s that female inmates were being sexually coerced and/or physically assaulted by male correctional officers. The Prison Rape Elimination Act (PREA), passed by Congress in 2003, mandated that every state keep a record of prison rapes and allocated money to study the problem and develop solutions. This source of data provided surprising findings: first, there was a great deal of sexual victimization occurring between female inmates (although not violent physical assault), and, second, there was a surprising amount of sexual interaction (not necessarily coerced) between male inmates and female officers.

In the 2010 report (reporting on surveys done in prior years), BJS researchers reported that about 4 percent of prison inmates and 3 percent of jail inmates reported some type of sexual victimization in the past 12 months. Sexual victimization was

QUOTE & QUERY

I never shake hands with an inmate. . . . They neither are nor ought to be viewed as equals.

George Beto, administrator of Texas prison system, 1962–1972, quoted in Dilulio, 1987: 177.

[T]he sergeant had succeeded in making me feel even more isolated from the world that existed outside the prison walls. I was no longer so proud to be an American. I was just a convict without rights.

Victor Hassine, inmate, 1996: 52.

Because legitimate power is so unevenly distributed between the keepers and the kept, left to its own inertia abuses of that power will inevitably creep into any prison without diligent and sensitive oversight.

Source: Patrick McManus, state correctional official, reported in Martin, 1993: 333.

 Should the attitude of correctional professionals be that inmates are not worthy of a handshake, or does that isolation from the "community of man" create the potential for abuse?

defined as everything from a violent rape to unwanted touching. A little less than half of the time, the perpetrator was an inmate, and in a little more than half, the perpetrator was a staff member. The rate of victimization varied widely from prison to prison; in one prison, for instance, 11 percent of inmates reported sexual victimization by staff as compared to the 2 percent reported in most institutions (Beck and Harrison, 2010). The Bureau of Justice Statistics also has surveyed former prisoners and 9.6 reported some form of sexual victimization while in prison. Again, victimization was roughly divided between inmate and staff member perpetrators (Beck and Johnson, 2012). Juvenile institutions have also been surveyed and over 10 percent of juvenile inmates reported ever being sexual victimized by staff members (Beck, Guerino, and Harrison, 2010).

In a more recent report, the years 2011–2012 were analyzed (unfortunately, due to a lack of resources, there is a long lag time between when surveys are conducted and when BJS reports its analysis). An estimated 4 percent of state and federal prison inmates and 3 percent of jail inmates reported experiencing sexual victimization in the past 12 months. Again, less than half of incidents involved inmate perpetrators (2.0 percent) and more than half (2.4 percent) were of staff member perpetrators (some inmates reported being victimized by both inmates and staff members). Researchers reported that from 2007 to 2011–2012, reports of "willing" sexual activity with staff (excluding touching) declined in prisons and jails, while reports of other types of sexual victimization remained stable (Bureau of Justice Statistics, 2014).

Juveniles evidently are more likely to be victimized by staff than other inmates. In 2011–2012, an estimated 1.8 percent of juveniles aged 16 to 17 held in adult prisons and jails reported being victimized by another inmate, and 3.2 percent of juveniles reported experiencing staff sexual misconduct (Bureau of Justice Statistics, 2014). While about equal numbers of male and female adult inmates reported staff victimization (2.3 percent of women and 2.4 percent of men), four times as many female inmates (6.9 percent) as male inmates (1.7 percent) reported inmate perpetrators (Beck, Berzofsky, Caspar, and Krebs, 2013). Recall that the definition of sexual victimization is broader than violent sexual assault and includes unwanted touching. Female inmates report other inmates making sexually suggestive comments and pressuring them for sex along with touching their breasts and buttocks (Owen et al., 2008). As described in the In the News box on page 377, transgender and homosexual inmates are more likely to be sexually victimized as well as inmates incarcerated for sexual crimes. Another vulnerable group are those with mental health issues (Beck, Berzofsky, Caspar, and Krebs, 2013).

As noted earlier, equal numbers of male and female inmates report sexual victimization by staff members (both willing and unwilling sexual contact by staff members is defined as sexual victimization in this survey). While contact between male inmates and female correctional officers is more likely to be consensual, there are instances in women's prisons where male COs have committed violent rapes of female prisoners, and many more instances where they used threats and intimidation to coerce women to engage in sex (Henriques, 2001; Craig, 2003; Owen et al., 2008; Pollock, 2014). In one egregious case, a female inmate was raped in a federal prison when officials housed women in the segregation unit of a prison for men. Officers took money from male inmates in return for unlocking the women's cell doors so the male inmates could have sex (willing or unwilling) with them. When one female inmate fought back and reported her attempted rape, she was attacked again, raped and viciously beaten by several inmates (Siegel, 2001).

((•)) IN THE NEWS | *Vulnerable Inmates*

An especially vulnerable group to prison rape are transgender inmates who have feminine characteristics, but, because their sex-change is not complete, are housed in prisons for men. These inmates report rape and other forms of sexual victimization as well as a lack of protection by correctional authorities who don't seem to care and correctional officers who actively torment the individuals. Two transgender inmates describe what their life was like in prison in news stories and chronicle a horrifying series of physical violence. "Passion," in a Texas prison, explains that she realized she was transgender in prison although prison officials do not recognize her as such because she did not begin the transition process. Through her years in prison, she was coerced into sexual relationships with gang members for protection. When she refused sexual advances she has been choked, raped, and physically assaulted. Prison officials refused to put her in protective custody even after she reported attacks. She has been in 3 of the 10 prisons categorized as "high risk" for sexual assault by the PREA reports. Because of her reporting the attacks and filing grievances to try and get protective custody, she was attacked by gang members and slashed in the face requiring 36 stitches. She has been suicidal. After 10 years of requesting protective custody, she was finally transferred there 10 days after a *New York Times* reporter asked to interview her.

Ashley Diamond lived as a transgender woman since adolescence and had been taking hormones for 17 years, but when she went to a Georgia prison intake center in 2012, she had to strip alongside male inmates. At 33, it was her first time in prison, and her sentence was for burglary, but she was sent to a maximum security prison. She was raped seven times by other inmates, called a "he-she thing" by correctional officers, and punished with solitary confinement for "pretending to be a woman." She tried to castrate herself and attempted suicide.

She filed a federal lawsuit and in March of 2015 the Justice Department intervened on her behalf. The lawsuit asks the court to direct prison officials to provide her hormone therapy, to allow her to express her female identity through "grooming, pronoun use and dress," and to provide her safer housing. The Justice Department declared hormone therapy to be necessary medical care, and ruled that the prison must treat "gender dysphoria" like any other health condition and provide "individual assessment and care." She and her lawyers allege that prison authorities are retaliating against her for the lawsuit and there is a real concern that she will not survive her prison sentence.

Sources: Sontag, 2015; Sontag, 2015b.

Periodically, news stories report that female inmates have been coerced to have sex with prison or jail correctional officers who threaten to plant drugs on them or write them up for disciplinary infractions if they do not submit (Owen et al., 2008; Coherty, 2014; Plog, 2014; Stein, 2015). A Justice Department investigation of the Julia Tutwiler prison in Alabama found rampant sexual abuse with officers allegedly forcing women to engage in sex acts just to obtain basic sanitary supplies. Male officers openly watched women shower or use the toilet, staff helped organize a "strip show," prisoners received a constant barrage of sexually offensive language, and prisoners who reported improper conduct were punished, according to investigation findings. Allegedly, at least a third of the 99 employees at Tutwiler had sex with prisoners (Department of Justice, 2014). The federal investigators accused the highest level of administrators of knowing about the abuse and doing nothing about it: "Officials have been on notice for over 18 years of the risks to women prisoners and, for over 18 years, have chosen to ignore them" (Acting Assistant Attorney General Jocelyn Samuels, quoted in Coherty, 2014). The DOJ and Alabama entered into an agreement that included a federal monitor at the prison and a wide range of changes in the prison, including identifying vulnerable inmates, and better investigation and punishment for sexual misconduct by correctional officers (Stein, 2015).

Although in most prisons and jails only a few correctional officers sexually victimize female inmates, more allow it to happen by setting the tone of the prison. Staying silent while other officers sexualize prisoners by ribald comments, allowing officers to demean and belittle inmates, and participating in conversations where women are referred to by their body parts allow the true predators to victimize. A prison culture that disparages and demeans inmates gives the green light to brutal individuals who wear a uniform. This situation is similar to the earlier discussion about rogue police officers who come to believe drug offenders and others are fair game for victimization because they don't deserve the same rights as the rest of us.

It should be noted that female inmates may also be victimized by female officers and male inmates are victimized by male officers. In one case in south Texas, a male prison nurse used drugs to extort sex from male inmates. When an inmate reported the nurse, prison investigators had the inmate wear a wire and his offer of drugs for oral sex was caught on tape (Santo, 2015).

Female officers also engage in sexual relationships with inmates. In fact, the most recent PREA survey reported 79 percent of all instances of staff sexual misconduct were female officers having sex with male inmates (Beck and Johnson, 2012). This statistic is misleading of course because the vast majority of inmates are male and the majority of sexual interactions male inmates are having with correctional officers are heterosexual. Still, in some prisons this unethical behavior on the part of female correctional officers seems to be a growing problem. If the problem was unknown before, it certainly has hit the news in recent years. Joyce Mitchell was a civilian employee, not a correctional officer, but in the summer of 2015 admitted smuggling in tools to two inmates who used the tools to escape. She reported to police investigators that she had a sexual relationship with one of the inmates. In Baltimore, 13 female correctional officers were indicted for smuggling in contraband to the state-run jail. Many of these female correctional officers were in sexual relationships with the inmates; in fact, the ringleader, a Black Guerilla gang leader, impregnated four different correctional officers (Toobin, 2014). This case is described in the In the News box on page 379.

Academic studies also indicate that the problem of officers having sexual relationships with inmates (Marquart, Barnhill, and Balshaw-Biddle, 2001; Dial and Worley, 2008; Worley and Worley, 2011). In Dial and Worley's (2008) research, out of a sample of 367 male inmates, 14 percent reported that they had a sexual relationship with an officer. In most cases, this was with a female officer. York (2012) described numerous cases of female officers and civilian staff found to be engaged in sexual relationships with inmates. They were rarely prosecuted; instead they were dismissed and the inmate was typically transferred to a more secure facility.

Correctional officers go down a "slippery slope" of developing a personal relationship with an inmate by talking about their private life, then sharing pictures, then perhaps talking with the inmate's family outside of the prison. Even if the officer wanted to retreat from such a relationship, they cannot because they fear exposure. Many times the inmate "grooms" the officer to be a "mule" (carrying in illegal contraband) by developing the sexual relationship; in these cases, it is the officer who ends up being coerced instead of the other way around.

Beginning in the mid-1990s, many states began to change or add new laws to make even consensual sexual relationships with inmates illegal. Part of the reason for the change was the difficulty of prosecuting correctional officers whose defense was that the inmate was willing. Even if the inmate was willing to testify against the guard, jurors were not likely to believe an inmate over a guard. In 1990, just 18 states had laws expressly prohibiting sexual abuse of inmates, but by 2006, such laws existed in all 50 states. It is a felony in all states but Iowa and Maryland where it is a misdemeanor (reported in Santo, 2015).

In an analysis of what happens in staff sexual misconduct cases in Texas by a legal advocacy group (The Marshall Project), it was found that since 2000, the state prison system's inspector general has referred nearly 400 cases of staff sex crimes against inmates to prosecutors with prosecutors pursuing only about half of them. Only nine were sentenced to serve time in state jail. The majority of the rest received fines ranging from $200 to $4,000. Most received deferred adjudication (Reported in Santo, 2015).

((•)) IN THE NEWS | *Sex, Drugs, and Smuggling*

A smuggling scheme in the Baltimore City Detention Center (BCDC), a state-run jail, ended in indictments and sentences for 25 people, including 13 guards. Federal investigators uncovered widespread smuggling of cellphones and other contraband for prison gang members from the Black Guerrilla Family (BGF) back in 2009. The correctional officers were all women and many were engaged in sexual relationships with the inmates. Over a dozen cellphones were also confiscated; the phones were evidently used to manage criminal activities on the outside. Inmates paid for the drugs and other contraband by texting 14-digit numbers to load money onto Green Dot MoneyPak cards belonging to BGF members. Gang leaders, in turn, used the Green Dot cards to pay their suppliers and buy cars, jewelry, and other goods. It is reported in some sources that the ringleader bragged about making $15,000 a month by the smuggling operation.

The ringleader was Tavon Martin, a BGF gang leader. He was in the jail awaiting trial for attempted murder. He had a sexual relationship with an unknown number of female correctional officers, but at least four of them had given birth to babies by him. Another inmate had relationships with at least five female guards. Martin evidently bought diamond rings and luxury cars for the women with income earned by their smuggling. Two of the correctional officers had his name tattooed on their body—one on her neck and the other on her wrist. In addition to smuggling in prescription pills, cellphones, and other contraband, correctional officers tipped off BGF members about law enforcement "shakedowns," stood lookout while the correctional officers had sex with inmates, and facilitated BGF assaults in the prison.

The longevity of the operation as well as its pervasiveness calls into question the management of the facility. Fourteen high-ranking administrators were transferred or retired after the indictments were announced. Correctional officers were able to smuggle in contraband in their underwear because searches were cursory. They evidently carried in cellphones for inmates to use even though cellphones were prohibited. It was reported that 75 percent of the 650 correctional officers in the facility were women (BCDC houses 2,000–2,300 inmates). Many of the female correctional officers were very young, one started working when she was 18. It is possible that some were recruited by the gangs even before being hired. According to papers in the legal cases against the gang members, documents were found in one Maryland prison that detailed how new BGF recruits were taught to target female COs with low self-esteem, insecurities, and certain physical attributes because they are easily manipulated.

All involved were indicted in 2013 on charges of drug conspiracy, extortion, money laundering, and/or racketeering. The defendants faced a maximum 20-year imprisonment if convicted. Many involved pled guilty and were sentenced in 2014. After announcing the sentences, Maryland officials vowed changes, including engineering a system whereby only approved cellphones would be able to transmit in the facility. Other changes included: improved background checks for correctional officers, more polygraph tests once the correctional officers were hired, the recruitment of 100 male correctional officers, repair of surveillance cameras, new search protocols, and weekly reviews to determine if any detainee has been held longer than 18 months.

Sources: Cauvin, 2009; Fenton, 2010; Marimow and Wagner, 2013; Toobin, 2014; Gray, 2014.

PREA was supposed to not only create a national reporting system for prison rape, but also push states to enact procedures to reduce sexual assaults in prison. The Department of Justice took years to develop national standards and then instituted a process whereby states had to assure that they were meeting goals to reach standards. The only punishment for not doing so, however, is to lose five percent of federal funds going to correctional programs. Several states, led by Governor Rick Perry of Texas, refused to sign the assurance letters. Arizona, Florida, Idaho, Indiana, and Utah governors also refused to sign the assurance letters. The standards are comprehensive, covering such things as hiring and staffing levels, investigation and evidence collection, medical treatment, and rape crisis counseling. States particularly balk at limitations on cross-sex strip searches and pat downs, and sight and sound barriers between juvenile offenders and adult offenders because of staffing and housing costs (Sontag, 2015b).

In both women's and men's prisons, inmate altercations sometimes occur because they are fighting over the affections of a particular officer, who knowingly or unknowingly has encouraged the inmates' beliefs that they are a love interest. In a few instances, female officers engage in sexual relationships with more than one inmate (York, 2012); more often, female officers think they are in a committed love relationship. Male officers seem to be more likely to engage in serial or multiple relationships with inmates or engage in sexual activity without a relationship at all; it is merely a financial exchange or coerced sex. The motivations are different in these two circumstances, but the ethics of the activity are not—they are a violation of policy and law. Generally, however, correctional officers are not prosecuted; they are simply fired and lose their license to obtain a job in corrections elsewhere.

Use of Force

The use of force is a legal and sometimes necessary element of correctional supervision. Most observers say that the serious abuse that occurred in the past such as **"tune-ups"** in the Texas prisons which involved "verbal humiliation, profanity, shoves, kicks, and head and body slaps," "ass-whipping," and using blackjacks and batons to inflict injury (Crouch and Marquart, 1989: 78) simply does not take place today. Murton (1976) also described a litany of abuses that occurred in Arkansas prison farms, including the **Tucker telephone**, an electrical device that was attached to the genitals of inmates to deliver severe shocks as a form of torture.

One prison warden described hanging inmates on cell bars so their feet did not touch the floor and leaving them overnight, or making them stand on a 2 by 4 or a barrel for hours; if they fell off, the time would start again (Glenn, 2001: 25–26). This same warden described a situation in which an inmate tried to escape, was shot, and then was hung on the front gate, bleeding, for the field hoe squads to see as they came back from the fields. This was described by Glenn as an "effective . . . object lesson" rather than brutality (2001: 44). Glenn also described a prison captain who played a "game" with inmates whom he believed weren't working hard enough on the hoe squad. The captain had them tied and stripped, and then lowered his pants and threatened to sodomize them (2001: 69).

Ironically, as violence by officers decreased in the late 1970s and 1980s, it opened the door to the violence of inmate gangs and cliques. Inmates in the 1980s had less to fear from correctional officers but more to fear from one another as racial gangs and other powerful cliques or individuals solidified their control over prison black markets. There

"tune-ups"
"Lessons" taught to inmates by Texas prison guards that involved verbal humiliation, profanity, shoves, kicks, and head and body slaps.

Tucker telephone
An electrical device attached to the genitals of inmates that delivered severe shocks as a form of torture; formerly used at an Arkansas prison farm.

was a time in the 1970s and 1980s when officers described some prisons as "out of control." There were prisons where correctional officers were afraid to walk into living units, and inmates literally controlled some parts of the prison (Carroll, 1998; Taylor, 1993).

Bowker (1980), and other authors who described the victimization of inmates by correctional officers, explained the violence by the officers' pervasive sense of fear and a CO subculture that tolerated, if not encouraged, such victimization. Crouch and Marquart (1989) and Crouch (1986) also discussed the use of violence as a rite of passage for the correctional officer, a way to prove himself as competent. Today, illegal uses of force are not pervasive, but they do still exist (Pollock, 2013a; York, 2012; Prendergast, 2003).

In *Hudson v. McMillian* (503 U.S. 1, 1992), the U.S. Supreme Court dealt with a case involving an inmate who had been forced to sit in a chair while two officers hit him in the head and chest area, with a lieutenant looking on. The state argued that because there was no "serious injury," there was no constitutional violation, because cruel and unusual punishment had to involve serious injury. Although some justices agreed with this logic, the majority held that injuries need not be serious to constitute a constitutional violation, if the injury was purely gratuitous (unnecessary). As with the use of force in law enforcement, policy definitions of *necessary force* are vague. This may mean that the resort to violence is absolutely the last alternative available, or it may mean that force is used when it is the most convenient way to get something accomplished (Morris and Morris, cited in Crouch, 1980: 253).

In 1999, nine Florida correctional officers were indicted for the murder of an inmate. The inmate died from his injuries, which included broken ribs, swollen testicles, and innumerable cuts and bruises. He was on death row for killing a prison guard in a botched escape attempt in 1983. Prosecutors alleged that he was killed because he was planning to go to the media with allegations of widespread abuse in the prison and because he killed a guard. The accused guards insisted that he killed himself by flinging himself against the concrete wall of his cell or, alternatively, that he was killed by other inmates (Cox, 2000). Three officers were acquitted in the case in February 2002 (*New York Times*, 2002). The opening story for this chapter describes another case where Florida correctional officers beat an inmate until he died. Once again, jurors refused to convict despite other officers' testimony about the brutal beatings that took place. These cases illustrate the tendency for jurors to refuse to punish officers because inmates are not sympathetic victims.

Beatings of inmates who attack other correctional officers are utilitarian; they serve as warnings to all inmates that they will receive similar treatment if they attack COs. Officers might also defend the action on retributive grounds because the inmate would probably not be punished for the attack through legal channels. However, these retaliations always represent the most brutal and inhumane aspects of incarceration and damage the integrity of all correctional professionals. In addition, by allowing such activity to go unpunished, citizens are complicit in a system that withdraws basic human sympathy and civil liberties from some individuals (inmates).

The problem with not punishing officers who beat inmates as retaliation for injuring officers is this gives some COs a green light to beat inmates who talk back or who don't give them the proper respect, and, maybe, some COs feel it is also acceptable to beat inmates who are black or Hispanic or mentally ill. In fact, in the *New York Times* investigation of Rikers Island jail identifying 129 cases of inmates injured so badly in an 11-month period by officers that they required outside medical care to address organ failure or broken bones, it was reported that three-quarters had mental health issues (Winerip and Schwirtz, 2014b). As mentioned before, once rights are taken away from one group, they may not be there for others. The same jurors who believe that an inmate deserves to be beaten by correctional officers probably would not feel that their son or daughter arrested for a minor crime deserves to be beaten while in jail, but unsanctioned violence has a way of getting out of control. Recall that in Chapter 7 we made the argument that the community helps to create a corrupt police department if they allow or encourage illegal sanctions to take place against those they don't like (e.g., the homeless or rowdy youth) because once the bonds of legality are removed, the same treatment may be visited upon anyone. The same is true with corrections. There is no ethical or legal justification for punishment that is not the product of formal due process and restrained by legal guidelines regardless of what the inmate has done, even under utilitarianism, because the cost to justice and due process is just too high.

Maintaining Morality in Prison

Correctional officers report that they experience a great deal of stress, and stress-related illnesses such as hypertension are common among officers, as well as social problems such as alcoholism and divorce. Some reports indicate that these problems exist in higher numbers with correctional officers than with police officers. Correctional officers feel criticized and even scorned by many, so it is little wonder that they adapt to their role by sometimes unethical and egoistic patterns of behavior. Yet it is important to understand the consequences of such a position. Kauffman (1988: 222) talked to officers who reported that they had lost their morality in the prison:

> *These officers experienced anguish at the change that was wrought in them by the prison environment: Initially, many attempted to avoid engaging in behavior injurious to inmates. . . . As their involvement in the prison world grew and their ability to abstain from morally questionable actions within the prison declined, they attempted to neutralize their own feelings of guilt by regarding prisons as separate moral realms with their own distinct set of moral standards or by viewing inmates as individuals outside the protection of moral laws. When such efforts failed, they shut their minds to what others were doing and to what they were doing themselves.*

Without a strong moral and ethical code, correctional officers may find themselves drifting into relativistic egoism: behavior that benefits the individual is considered to be acceptable, despite long-term effects or inconsistencies with their duty and their personal value system. The result is a feeling of disillusionment and anomie, and the side effects can be serious dissatisfaction and depression. To maintain a sense of morality in an inherently coercive environment is no easy task, yet a strong personal ethical code is probably the best defense against being changed by the negative environment of the prison.

Jail Officers

Little has been written about jail officers, who may be sheriff's deputies completing their assignment at the jail before they can be "promoted" to street patrol. Sometimes jail officers are street deputies who are transferred back to the jail as punishment.

In other situations, jail officers are not deputies and have a separate title and lower pay scale. Generally, the skills associated with managing jail inmates are discounted when compared to street patrol or investigation. They shouldn't be, and some might argue that it is a much more difficult job to be a jail officer than either a sheriff's deputy on the street or a correctional officer of a prison. Jail officers deal with much more visitation (with a concomitant potential for smuggling). They deal with highly stressed individuals who are just coming in from the street or on their way to prison, and, because of the transitory nature of the population, jail officers may not know much about the inmates. In the summer of 2015, Sandra Bland was arrested and committed suicide in a Texas jail. Although some believed there was some type of law enforcement conspiracy in Bland's death, the evidence indicated that a more likely explanation was that, even after she had indicated a prior suicide attempt, she was not monitored as a suicide risk. Jail officers deal with individuals who are experiencing despair and anxiety over the legal issues and must be constantly alert to the possibility of suicide. Some jail officers, especially in urban areas, may live in the same communities as the jail inmates and their families. All this combines to create many management challenges.

There is a need for greater professionalization of jail officers. The position should not merely be a dreaded rite-of-passage assignment, a punishment, or a steppingstone to deputy status, because the body of knowledge required to perform the job well is different from that which a street deputy needs. Recently there has been an attempt to professionalize the image of jail officers, starting again with a code of ethics (discussed in the last chapter). Similar to prisons, jails are sometimes the site of illegal uses of force, as the In the News box describes on page 384.

Jail inmates include juveniles, violent criminals, misdemeanants, mentally ill, and mentally challenged. Offenders may come into jail intoxicated, have undiagnosed epilepsy or other diseases, suffer overdoses, or be suicidal. Visitation is more frequent, and family issues are more problematic in jails than prisons. The constant activity and chaotic environment of a jail often create unique ethical dilemmas.

Many jail inmates, especially those with mental illness, cannot or will not follow rules. Prisoners and correctional officers alike do not tolerate their irrational behavior very well. Jail officers tend to deal with all troublesome behavior as a discipline issue. Is throwing feces a behavioral problem or an indication of mental illness? Sometimes it is both. When the person is placed in isolation (as in segregation), the situation may bring on hallucinations, anxiety attacks, and distorted thinking (Turner, 2007). Mentally ill inmates are more likely to be charged with rule violations, including physical or verbal assaults on staff members, and more likely to be injured, yet jail officers are not trained to be mental health specialists.

Unfortunately, in jails one can find the same type of unethical behavior that one finds with police and prison officers. Jail officers can be uncaring and insensitive to human needs. A few officers use their position to bolster their own ego by abusing their power over inmates. More are probably negligent in that they simply do not care and necessary duties go undone. Then again, other jail officers may be described as human service officers, who seek to enrich their job by taking on more of a counseling role with inmates. As always, the vast majority of professionals in corrections, as in law enforcement and the courts, simply try to do their job to the best of their ability every day.

(( )) IN THE NEWS | *Denver Jail*

The report on the Denver jail issued by an outside review group in May of 2015 was the culmination of a long scandal over problems of excessive force in the Denver jail that had gone on for years. In the summer of 2014, the Denver City Council settled a federal lawsuit filed by Jamal Hunter for $3.25 million. Hunter was beaten, almost suffocated, and held down while his genitals were scalded with boiling water by a group of inmates who thought he was a snitch. He alleges that a jail correctional officer was complicit in that he lied to the inmates about Hunter being an informant, he could hear Hunter's screams and did nothing, and he turned the light out in the pod where the assault took place. Other inmates testified that Hunter's screams could be heard throughout the jail pod and security cameras show the correctional officer walking around the pod during the time of the assault. Even the inmates who assaulted him testified that the deputy knew the attack was going to take place and offered to turn off the lights. Hunter evidently had made disparaging remarks to the correctional officer regarding his drinking on the job, which is why the correctional officer sought retaliation. While he was still recovering from that incident, he was choked by deputies, including that same officer, for allegedly asking to see a nurse. Security cameras show that he was noncombative at the time.

The Hunter lawsuit is just one of a long line of incidents at the jail that eventually caused Sheriff Gary Wilson to step down in the summer of 2014. Another incident was the death of a homeless "preacher," Marvin Booker, who was allegedly choked to death after being Tased in a scuffle with jail correctional officers. Hunter's federal lawsuit described a cellblock that was run by gangs. Prison liquor "hooch" was brewed by the gallon and contraband was pervasive. The deputy who ignored his screams was allegedly drunk on the job often and instigated fights between inmates by telling them when others filed grievances and who were charged with sex offenses. The deputy denied all charges and was given a 40-day suspension. None of the inmates were charged.

It was reported that nearly $13 million of the $16.7 million paid out by the city of Denver to settle legal claims between 2004 and 2014 involved the police and sheriff departments, and 58 percent of that was for excessive force or civil rights violations. Jail inmates filed numerous claims of excessive force, sometimes the incidents certainly seemed to be gratuitous force used in full view of security cameras.

A group of task forces created in the spring of 2014 issued 40 recommendations to improve the jail, including automatic notifications of excessive force complaints, an independent monitor, a review of the Taser policy, creating a corporal position and adding more sergeant positions, Crisis Intervention Team Training (CIT), shorter work shifts and a revised break policy.

An outside review team was hired to evaluate all the procedures of the jail. Their report cost the city over $300,000 and detailed a jail that needed reform at every level. The report issued a scathing description of management and resources that were woefully lacking. The recommendations were broad (hire a new sheriff from the outside) and detailed (replace prisoners' briefs with boxers so that contraband was not so easily hidden in underwear). The group issued 14 key findings and 277 recommendations for change.

Some of the findings show that basic management practices were not followed; for example, there was no method for counting inmates who were at court or at the hospital, and correctional officers were not trained in how to monitor for contraband or other problems in the pods. Even the consultants found heroin, homemade hooch, and inappropriate photographs in the jail pods. There was no identification of gang affiliation for cell assignments. There was no staffing plan. The use-of-force investigations did not meet minimum standards of thoroughness and objectivity. Employees were not searched when they came into the jail. Deputies did not know policies and the policy handbook was out of date. Supervisory staff had difficulty taking corrective action against deputies because of the employee grievance procedures in place. The report also noted that the culture of the jail needed to change; deputies had very little training in deescalation tactics. It was also noted that deputy training was largely for patrol officers on the street, and they did not receive a skillset specific to the problems of supervising inmates in a jail. The consultants reported that jail staff seemed open to and hoped for meaningful change.

Sources: Phillips, 2015; Cotton, 2014; Gurman, 2014; Mitchell, 2014; Murray, 2014; Phillips, 2014.

ETHICAL DILEMMA

An inmate asks you to mail a letter for him because he's on daylock with no privileges. He tells you that you can open the envelope and look at it in order to make sure it is okay; it is only a birthday card for his daughter. If it doesn't get in the mail today, she will not get it in time. He is a good inmate, never gives you any trouble, and has actually helped you out a few times with more troublesome inmates. You believe that there is nothing wrong with the card, and you think the guy got a bad deal with the discipline anyway because he was only out of place and that usually gets only a warning, not daylock. You also know that if you do the favor for him, he will continue to be a help to you on the tier, and if you don't, he'll probably hold it against you. What should you do?

Law

Some acts committed by correctional officers are crimes. Obviously, smuggling drugs is a crime and an officer who smuggled would probably end up with a prison sentence himself. Taking items out of the prison is against the rules and could be considered bribery if the officer received money or anything of value for transporting the contraband. In this case, while taking the letter out is obviously against the rules, since the officer is not receiving anything of value from the inmate to do so, there may be no law involved.

Policy

Policies against taking letters out of the institution for inmates exist because such activities bypass censorship and intelligence-gathering procedures. While in this case it could be that it is only an innocent birthday card, it could also be a code for something else that gang intelligence officers would flag. It could also be a situation where the inmate was under a judicial order to not make contact with his daughter. Another consideration is that the inmate may be testing the officer to see if he may be willing to do more serious acts in the future. If he does take the letter out against the rules, the inmate has gained a little control over him because he can report the officer and get him in trouble. Next time, he may ask the officer to do something a little more serious and, then the next time, something more serious, so that the officer becomes entirely controlled by the inmate. Policies exist for a reason, even if they may not make sense in one particular case.

Ethics

An egoistic rationalization would be that a favor done for the inmate may result in benefit to the officer because the inmate owes him; however, as noted earlier, it may backfire because the officer will also "owe" the inmate in order for him to keep quiet about the rule violation. A utilitarian rationale would weigh up the costs and benefits to all concerned, but, as usual with utilitarian reasoning, there is no way to know all of the possible ramifications of the act ahead of time, or even what the true nature of the act is (innocent card or something else). An ethical formalist would abide by the duties of the role, which, in this case, is to obey the policy about not carrying out letters. Ethics of care reasoning would attempt to solve the problem so the officer may take the card and talk to his sergeant or lieutenant to see if an exception to the suspension of mail privileges could be granted. This way would meet the needs of the inmate, protect the officer from any negative effect of breaking the rule, and protect the institution since the superior officers would presume to know more about the circumstances of the inmate and whether the card was innocent or not.

Treatment Staff

A number of ethical issues that correctional treatment personnel may be faced with are similar to those experienced in a more general way by all treatment professionals, so available sources dealing with ethics in the helping professions would also be applicable to those who work in the corrections field (see, for instance, Corey, Corey, and Callanan, 1988; Braswell, Miller, and Cabana, 2006). However, the unique issues facing correctional treatment professionals derive from their dual goals of treating the individual and being an employee (or contractor) of the state with a corresponding duty to maintain safety and security (whether in an institution or community setting).

The ethical issues for treatment professionals have grown as the number of inmates in both prisons and jails with serious mental health problems has grown. A recent report noted that there are 10 times as many mentally ill in prison as in psychiatric facilities (Treatment Advocacy Center, 2014: 3). Mentally ill prisoners, who comprise at least 10 percent of the population of prisons and jails, and some estimates put it at much higher, present enormous problems for both correctional officers and treatment staff.

The professional goal of all treatment specialists is to help the client, but sometimes helping the client is at odds with the safety and security of the institution. For instance, prison psychologists may be privy to information or confessions that they feel bound to hold in confidence, even though this may jeopardize the security of the prison. Assessing risk also involves mixed loyalties. Any treatment necessarily involves risk. How much risk one is willing to take depends on whether the public should be protected at all costs, in which case few people would ever be released, or whether one thinks the public must risk possible victimization in order to give offenders a chance to prove themselves.

A basic issue is whether to provide treatment to people who do not want it. One of the elements of codes of ethics for treatment professionals is that one should respect the autonomy of individuals, and this generally is interpreted to mean no forced treatment. In corrections, however, treatment professionals are often involved in what may be considered coerced treatment. In particular, psychiatrists and psychologists have to reconcile their professional ethics in two fields—corrections and psychiatry—and at times this is hard to do. Psychiatrists in corrections, for instance, believe at times that they are being used for social control rather than treatment (Tanay, 1982). Disruptive inmates, although needing treatment, pose security risks to prison officials, so intervention, especially the use of antipsychotic drugs and barbiturates, often takes the form of control rather than treatment.

The practice of using antipsychotic drugs is especially problematic for treatment professionals. Although the Supreme Court determined in *Washington v. Harper* (494 U.S. 210, 1990) that the administration of such drugs to unwilling inmates is not unconstitutional, the practice must be scrutinized and held to due-process protections in order to uphold professional ethical standards. Some observers have alleged that inmates are being maintained on high dosages of drugs during their prison stay. Once released, they may go through withdrawal and have no assistance from community mental health facilities (Martin, 1993). On the other hand, not providing antipsychotic medication puts the individual in a downward spiral of psychosis exacerbated by the stress of the prison itself (Treatment Advocacy Center, 2014).

Psychologists in correctional settings have two ethical codes to follow: the American Psychological Association's Ethical Principles of Psychologists and Code of Conduct, and the code for the American Association for Correctional and Forensic Psychologists. Some principles of the Ethical Principles of Psychologists seem especially relevant to corrections. For instance, in Standard 3.11, psychologists who are providing services through other organizations are instructed to provide information beforehand to clients about:

- The nature and objectives of the services
- The intended recipients
- Which of the individuals are clients

- The relationship the psychologist will have with each person and the organization
- The probable uses of services provided and information obtained and who will have access to the information
- The limits of confidentiality

This obviously affects institutional psychologists, who must make clear to inmates their responsibility to custody concerns.

Other principles also reflect the reality of correctional placements. For instance, in Standard 3.10, psychologists are mandated to obtain informed consent for treatment; however, the ethical code recognizes that some activities without consent may be mandated by law or governmental regulation. The standard does state that when treatment is court-ordered, the individual must be informed of the nature of the anticipated services and any limits of confidentiality.

Haag (2006) describes some ethical dilemmas of prison psychologists in Canada, which apply to the United States as well. In his discussion, he mentions issues of:

- *Confidentiality*: The inability to keep prisoners' secrets
- *Protection of psychological records*: Whether or not psychologists should create "shadow files" that are not subject to view by other staff
- *Informed consent*: Whether consent is possible from a coerced population
- *Assessment*: What the psychologist's role is when assessment is used for correctional purposes
- *Corroboration*: The importance of not accepting everything the inmate says, as the inmate may be engaged in "impression management"
- *Refusal of services*: Whether psychologists should honor an inmate's refusal of psychological services
- *Nondiscrimination*: Treating all inmates equally regardless of group membership or individual characteristics
- *Competence*: The importance of being aware of the boundaries of one's competence
- *Knowledge of legal structure*: Being aware of the rights of the parties involved
- *Accuracy and honesty*: Making clear the limits of predictive validity of psychological assessments
- *Misuses of psychological information*: Refusing to allow file information to be misused to damage an inmate's interests
- *Multiple relationships*: Avoiding dual roles (such as assessment and treatment), which is problematic and creates confusion for the client.

Lichtenberg, Lune, and McManimon (2004) use the 1971 movie *A Clockwork Orange* to discuss issues of voluntariness and morality in treatment. The movie is a critical treatment of behavior modification and illustrates the fear that manipulating people's minds through aversive conditioning takes away, in some respects, the essence of what it means to be a free individual. Although the film is a satire and obviously an extremely drawn portrait of the power of aversive conditioning, the central idea—that when people have been conditioned, they are not rationally choosing good because they cannot freely choose evil—is relevant and important to our discussions of moral culpability, as well as the ethics of trying to change individuals who do not want to be changed.

As in the legal profession, confidentiality is an issue for psychologists. The ethical principles (Standard 4.01) address this issue. Psychologists have a primary obligation and take reasonable precautions to protect confidential information obtained through or stored in any medium, recognizing that the extent and limits of confidentiality may be regulated by law or established by institutional rules or professional or scientific relationships. Treatment professionals in corrections must inform their clients, whether they are prison inmates or on some form of supervised release in the community, of the extent or limitations of the confidentiality. It may be that there is no confidentiality at all when the counselor, psychologist, or other professional is employed by the court. In any environment, psychologists and counselors must be aware of the *Tarasoff* rule (*Tarasoff v. Regents of the University of California*, 17 Cal. 3d 425, 1975), from a case that held a psychologist liable for not warning a victim of imminent harm from one of their clients. Treatment professionals do have legal duties to third persons if they have cause to reasonably believe that one of their clients is going to harm that person.

Treatment and security concerns clash in many instances. The treatment professional must choose between two value systems. To emphasize security concerns puts the psychiatrist or counselor in a role of a custodian with professional training used only to better control inmate behavior. To emphasize treatment concerns puts the professional in an antagonistic role vis-à-vis the security staff, and he or she may be in situations where these concerns directly conflict.

In an online resource for community treatment staff, some ethical principles were presented with discussion. These included:

- *Do no harm.* The discussion brought up the point that the best thing to do in some cases is no intervention at all since the harm done in bringing an individual into the criminal justice system outweighs the benefit to society or the individual. Focus on a person's deficiencies may only exacerbate them when more supportive interventions might provide more utility. This is a utilitarian concept.

- *Respect people as ends.* The discussion concerned treating people as having intrinsic value and not just considering them numbers or diagnoses. Also, included was the idea of allowing the participants some role in determining what they need and respecting legal rights. These concepts are consistent with ethical formalism.

- *Do what is best for everyone under the circumstances.* This discussion counsels that everyone can't be helped all the time, but the treatment professionals just do the best they can to help everyone, although there was also a warning that sometimes what is best is not clear. This is consistent with the ethics of care position.

- *Don't abuse or exploit participants.* This discussion self-evidently proscribes unethical actions against participants. It is consistent with all ethical systems.

- *Don't intervene unless competent.* This discussion concerns not operating outside one's field of expertise and keeping up with professional training as an obligation. It is consistent with all ethical systems.

- *Actively strive to improve the program and community.* The discussion brings up the point that it is not clear how far one's ethical obligations carry when there are problems in the community that go well beyond one's job description. There are no easy answers to this question. It is consistent with all ethical systems, but most congruent with ethics of care.

- *Maintain confidentiality of clients.* The discussion presents the various complexities of this simple principle in that sometimes the treatment professional has other competing responsibilities, such as to funders or legal actors. This principle is consistent with all ethical systems, except for those circumstances when it does not result in the greatest amount of utility for all, in which case it would be inconsistent with utilitarianism.

- *Disclosure is important.* The discussion described different types of disclosure, such as what types of information must be shared, including how long the program would last, the cost (if any), and so on. It is important to be transparent and provide information to the clients in order that their consent is knowing and voluntary. This is consistent with all ethical systems.

- *Be concerned with conflicts of interest.* The discussion included personal, financial, political, and professional conflicts. For instance, conflicts that compromise professional judgments include having a relative in the treatment program, having a relationship with a client, having one's job or income depend on judgments rendered, engaging in a business relationship with a client, and so on. This principle is consistent with all ethical systems (Community Tool Box, 2012).

Glaser (2003) argues that the values and mission of sex offender treatment is at odds with traditional ethical codes. He notes specifically: the protection of society overriding client interest, advocacy for involuntary treatment, breaches of confidentiality, no choices for the client regarding modality or therapist, treatment programs utilizing unqualified staff, and therapy that infringes on dignity and autonomy. The concern is that therapists who work in treatment programs with the foregoing elements are in an ethical vacuum. Traditional ethical codes don't apply, but they have no code that accommodates the unique elements of sex offender treatment. The solution is to develop specific ethics codes for sex offender treatment professionals that take into consideration the special elements of such a correctional population and the concerns of treatment staff.

Faith-based treatment programs, such as the Prison Fellowship Ministries, a Washington, D.C., group created by former Watergate figure Charles "Chuck" Colson, can be found in many prisons. The program is Christ-centered, biblically rooted, and values-based, and it emphasizes family and community. Inmates volunteer for the program (see www.prisonfellowship.org). Having such programs in prison raise several issues. Some argue that the programs violate the separation of church and state and are an unconstitutional violation of freedom of religion. If a Christian program offers hope for early release or other advantages, Muslims or those following other religions may participate only if they also compromise their faith. Administrators of such programs must take care not to intrude upon the religious freedom of inmates and not use the benefits of the program to coerce religious conformity.

Probably the most prevalent issue for treatment professionals is how to maintain one's commitment to a helping profession while being in an environment that does not value the goals and mission of treatment. This dichotomy of treatment versus punishment creates a myriad of ethical issues for treatment professionals.

Another area that must be considered under the general heading of treatment is that of medical services. Recall that in *Brown v. Plata* (2011) the Supreme Court ordered California to release prisoners if they could not bring the level of medical care up to a constitutional standard. The record indicated that 34 inmates died because of lack of medical care. Court cases and exposés have documented the sometimes deadly consequences when the medical needs of inmates are ignored or not met. Vaughn and Smith (1999) described several different ways in which medical services—or more specifically, the lack of such services—created pain and suffering for inmates. Sometimes poor medical care is a result of neglect or lack of resources, but sometimes the medical staff simply did not care, believed that prisoners should suffer, and/or did not believe that inmates were sick or injured. The authors suggest that the medical staff sometimes furthers penal harm by withholding medical services and justifies such actions by a type of ethical relativism in which inmates aren't seen as deserving the same type of care as others.

Various international bodies have promulgated ethics or values statements concerning the ethics of medical professionals involved in corrections, including the United Nations (UN), the Council of Europe, the World Medical Association, the International Council of Nurses, Physicians for Human Rights, and Penal Reform International. These ethical statements consistently identify important principles of medical care for prisoners, including free access to medical care, equal healthcare to what would be available in the community, confidentiality, patients' consent, preventive healthcare, humanitarian assistance, complete professional independence, and competence. However, according to Pont, Stover, and Wolff (2012), these principles continue to be ignored across the world. The most overriding problem is dual loyalties where the health-care professional is also an employee of the correctional agency and owes a duty to that agency as his or her employer. These dual loyalties are in contravention to the principles of independent and objective medical treatment.

There have also been some cases where medical professionals tasked with providing medical care for prisoners have involved themselves in activities arguably against ethical principles, including forensic assessments, disclosure of patient-related medical data to others without consent of the patient, assisting in body searches or obtaining blood or urine for analyses for safety and security reasons, providing medical expertise for the application of disciplinary measures, and assisting or being complicit in physical or capital punishment. The reason that these ethical violations continue is that there is virtually no ethics training in correctional medical-care training, there are no sanctions for medical professionals who violate the ethical codes, and professional organizations have not directed any attention to the topic. Assisting in body-cavity searches and testing for drugs are two activities that have been raised as ethically questionable in American prisons. These control activities are not a part of the helping profession of medicine and may interfere with the medical professional–client relationship (Kipnis, 2001).

Recommendations to remove medical care from the direct authority of the correctional agency are proposed to eliminate dual loyalty pressures (Pont, Stover, and Wolff, 2012). However, there have been recurrent issues of poor medical services by contracted providers as well who absorb the "penal harm" culture of a prison or jail and/or have profit motives that conflict with a high level of service delivery.

Community Corrections

community corrections
A term that encompasses halfway houses, work release centers, probation, parole, and any other intermediate sanctions, such as electronic monitoring, either as a condition of probation or as a sentence in itself that takes place in the community rather than prison.

Community corrections has a more positive and helpful image than does institutional corrections. However, even in this subsystem of the criminal justice system, the ideals of justice and care become diluted by bureaucratic mismanagement and personal agendas. The Bureau of Justice Statistics reports that there were about 853,200 parolees in 2013 (compared to 3,910,600 probationers). That equates to about 1 in 50 people being on some sort of community correctional supervision (Glaze and Kaeble, 2014: 2). Professionals in community corrections do not have the same power as police or correctional officers to use physical force, but they do have a great deal of non-physical power over the clients they control. Similarly to other treatment personnel, ethical dilemmas for probation and parole officials often revolve around the dual goals of promoting rehabilitation for the client and safety and security for the community.

Discretion in probation exists at the point of sentencing: Probation officers make recommendations to judges concerning whether or not the offender should be sent to prison or be monitored on probation and the number of years to be served. Discretion also exists during supervision in the following ways:

- Probation officers decide when to file violation reports.
- They decide what recommendation to make to the judge during revocation hearings.
- They make numerous decisions along the way regarding the people on their caseload.

Parole board members or their designees make decisions regarding release, and parole officers have the same discretion in managing their caseload that probation officers do. What criteria are used for these decisions? Usually, the risk to the public is the primary factor for decision making on the part of probation and parole officials, but other considerations also intrude. Some of these other considerations are ethical; some might not be, such as race, type of crime, family ties, crowding in institutions, who the victim was, what the judge wants, and publicity concerning the crime.

Probation officers write presentence reports to help judges decide sentences, but research has found that there may be errors in the information presented and that some officers are not as thorough as others in gathering information. This may not make much difference if it is true, as some have found, that probation officers' recommendations and judges' decisions are determined almost completely by the current offense and prior record (Whitehead, 1991).

Probation and parole officers have the authority and power to recommend revocation. This power is also limited because probation and parole officers' recommendations can be ignored by the judge or the parole hearing officer. Yet the implicit power an officer has over the individuals on his or her caseload must be recognized as an important element of the role, not to be taken lightly or misused.

Probation and parole officers have been described as adopting different roles on the job. Recall the typologies offered to describe how police officers approached their role and how their "type" might affect their decisions; the same discussion can be applied to probation and parole officers. They have also been described by their orientation to the job and individual adaptation to organizational goals. For instance, Souryal (1992) summarizes other literature in his description of the following types:

- The punitive law enforcer
- The welfare/therapeutic practitioner
- The passive time server
- The combined model

punitive law enforcer The type of officer who perceives the role as one of enforcer, enforces every rule, and goes "by the book."

welfare/ therapeutic worker The type of officer who perceives the role as one of counselor to the offender and who helps to effect rehabilitative change.

passive time server The type of officer who does the bare minimum on the job to stay out of trouble.

Different ethical issues can be discussed in relation to each of these types. For instance, the **punitive law enforcer** may need to examine his or her use of authority. This officer may have a tendency to use illegal threats and violate the due-process protections that each client deserves. The **welfare/therapeutic worker** may need to think about natural law rights of privacy and autonomy. These officers have a tendency to infringe on clients' privacy because of their mindset that they are helping the client (and, indeed, they might be), but the client may prefer less help and more privacy. The **passive time server** may violate professional ethics in not performing duties associated with the role.

All of us may have some tendency to be a time server in our respective professions. It is important to continue to take personal inventories and ask whether we are still putting in a "day's work for a day's pay." As is the case for many of the other criminal justice professionals we have discussed in this book, parole and probation officers often have a great deal of flexibility in their day. They leave the office to make field contacts, and they often trade weekdays for weekend days because weekends are more conducive to home visits. This flexibility is necessary if they are to do the job, but some abuse it and use the freedom to accomplish personal tasks or spend time at home. Some offices have attempted to prevent this behavior by instituting measures such as time clocks and strict controls on movements, but these controls are inconsistent with professionalism and not conducive to the nature of the task.

Caseload Supervision

Discretion exists not only at the recommendation-to-release stage but also throughout supervision. Officers do not make the decision to revoke, but they do make the decision to file a violation report and make a recommendation to the judge or the parole hearing examiner to continue with supervision status (perhaps with new conditions), or recommend revocation and a prison sentence. Many do not submit violation reports automatically upon discovery of every offender infraction. In this way, they are like police officers, who practice selective enforcement of the laws. Like police officers, some of their criteria for decision making are ethical and some are not. Also like police officers, the individual officer may face ethical dilemmas when the law doesn't seem to take into account social realities, such as poverty.

The discretion to decide when to write a violation report is a powerful element in the control the officer has over the offender, but this can obviously be a difficult decision to make at times. If the officer excuses serious violations (e.g., possessing a firearm or continuing drug use) and the decision to do so is based on personal favoritism, fear, or bribery, that officer is putting the community at risk and is unethical in making the decision to do so. Situations in which the officer sincerely believes the offender made a mistake, has extraordinary excuses for such misbehavior, and is a good risk still present a danger to the community. Is the decision any more ethical because of the officer's belief in the offender? Would it be more ethical to conduct oneself "by the book" and always submit violation reports when the offender commits any violation, including a purely technical one?

Probation and parole officers are presented with other dilemmas in their supervision of offenders. For instance, the offender often acquires a job without the employer's knowledge of his or her previous criminality. Is it the duty of the officer to inform the employer and thereby imperil the continued employment of the offender? What about offenders becoming personally involved with others and refusing to tell them about their past history? Does the probation or parole officer have a duty to the unwary party, especially if the offender is on probation or parole for an assaultive offense? If the probation or parole officer knows or suspects that the offender is HIV positive and the offender begins an intimate relationship with someone, does the officer have a duty to warn the other party? Most states protect the confidentiality of victims of AIDS, and in these cases the officer has a legal duty *not* to disclose.

What is the probation or parole officer's responsibility to the offender's family? If family members are unwilling to help the offender and perhaps fear his or her presence, should the officer find a reason for revocation? Again, these questions revolve around competing loyalties to the public and client. The correctional professional must balance these interests in every decision, and the decisions are often not easy to make.

Similar to the police officer, at times the probation officer's role as a family member or friend conflicts with the professional role. Family members and/or friends may expect special treatment or expect that the officer will use his or her powers for unethical purposes, such as using official records to find out information about someone. These are always difficult dilemmas because family and friends may not be sympathetic to the individual's ethical responsibilities to the organization and to society at large. Probation and parole officers are likely to have overlapping circles of acquaintances and family connections with those on their caseloads, especially in small towns. Confidentiality and favoritism are issues that come up frequently.

The officer also has to contend with the issue of gratuities. Again, similar to the police officer, probation or parole officers may be offered special treatment, material goods, or other items of value because of their profession. In most cases, the situation is even more clearly unethical for probation and parole officers because the gift is offered by a client over whom decisions are made, as opposed to police officers who may or may not ever be in a position to make a decision regarding a restaurant or convenience store manager.

Probation departments have clear rules against any "business relationships" with probationers, and this makes sense, but probation officers in small towns ask, "How can I avoid a business relationship with a client when the only coffee shop in town is run by one of my clients? Am I never to go there during the years he is on probation?" In the same manner as police, probation and parole officers may believe that some gifts offered are given in the spirit of gratitude or generosity and not to influence decision making.

Some probation or parole officers encounter ethical conflicts when they seek part-time employment at counseling centers. They may have counseling or drug treatment licenses that allow them to run groups and engage in individual counseling to earn extra income. This becomes an ethical issue when their part-time employment may involve working with correctional clients. Because their role as private counselor would conflict with their role as professional correctional supervisor, ethics boards have ruled that such employment is acceptable only when counselors do not interact with their own clients.

Because probationers may appear to be similar to the probation or parole officer in socioeconomic status, family background, lifestyle, or personal value systems, they have a greater tendency to feel affinity and friendship for some clients. Some probation officers have been known to have clients babysit for them, to rent a room in their house, or to socialize with them and their families. Obviously, these personal relationships hinder the ability to perform one's official function as a protector of the community and enforcer for the legal system. Personal relationships of any type—romantic, platonic, or financial—are simply not appropriate or ethical for the probation and parole professional.

Parole Officers

We have been discussing probation and parole officers simultaneously earlier, but there are some important distinctions between the two. First, parolees are perceived to be more of a threat to the community, so the supervision role of parole officers is emphasized much more strongly than in probation, where supervision is balanced with a service/counseling emphasis. Further, paroled offenders are usually older and have a longer criminal record, so the relationship between supervisor and client might be different. The problems faced by parolees are quite different from those faced by probationers.

Because of the drastic increase in the number of those incarcerated during the 1980s even though the use of parole decreased, the sheer number of those eligible has been swelling the ranks of parole caseloads. Most have the same low levels of education and vocational skills that they had going into prison and have not had access to many, if any, rehabilitative programs in prison. Further, many of those newly released will be those who *maxed out*—meaning that they completed their entire sentence with no requirements to be supervised

Many of those released from prison return. A BJS study tracked 404,638 prisoners in 30 states after their release from prison in 2005. The researchers found that about two-thirds (67.8 percent) of released prisoners were rearrested within three years (not necessarily convicted); 76.6 percent were rearrested within five years of release. More than half (56.7 percent) were arrested by the end of the first year. About 82.1 percent of released property offenders were arrested for a new crime compared with 76.9 percent of drug offenders, 73.6 percent of public order offenders, and 71.3 percent of violent offenders (Durose, Cooper, and Snyder, 2014).

Our incarceration rate—currently one of the highest in the world—has had a tremendously negative impact on communities. Entire neighborhoods are affected when a large percentage of their population is sent away for years at a time. Generational effects are obvious; children of inmates are six times as likely to be delinquent (Mauer, Chesney-Lind, and Clear, 2002). More subtle effects exist as well. The economy and the social fabric of a community are also affected when large numbers of young people are removed. Community corrections professionals have some power in this scenario. They make release recommendations and affect revocation rates. They can help offenders with reentry problems, or they can blindly enforce every bureaucratic rule.

Recall that under ethical formalism, to be an ethical professional, one must do one's duty. Some officers believe that they have met their ethical duty by explaining the rules to a parolee and then catching the person if he or she "messes up." Others see a more expanded role wherein the officer has some duty to help the offender readjust to society. This may involve taking some responsibility for counseling the offender, referring him or her to services, acting as a troubleshooter or mediator in conflict with family or others, and acting as an advocate in obtaining help. In other words, this officer takes a proactive approach to the parolee's success. Is filing a violation report a success (because the offender was caught) or a failure (because the offender did not succeed)? How an officer feels about the answer to that question may indicate how they view their role.

Halfway Houses

The ethical issues concerning halfway houses are a combination of those that confront institutional corrections and those seen in community corrections. Halfway houses can be large institutions and staff may feel like correctional officers, in which case there are concerns that they will abuse their positions by exploiting the residents. However, halfway houses are in the community, often have loose security in that residents may work or have educational release during the day, and offenders are nearing their full release date. In this regard, halfway house staff members have more similar concerns to those of probation and parole officers balancing the rights of offenders against the safety concerns of the community in their use of discretion in allowing furloughs, disciplining offenders for infractions, or making a decision to send the offender back to the prison.

Because there has been a strong financial pressure to reduce the prison population in every state, there are increasing numbers of halfway houses. In some ways this is a good thing because community alternatives are probably less damaging to the individual and they certainly are less expensive for the taxpayer. On the other hand, if care is not taken and professional staff members do not treat their duties seriously, this increased use of community corrections could result in less safety for the public and more problems for the offender.

In 2012, the *New York Times* conducted an eight-week investigation into the use of halfway houses in New Jersey. The impetus for the investigation was the number of escapes from halfway houses, but the investigation also uncovered some troubling facts. One fact stood out—most halfway houses were privately owned. Community Education Centers is a for-profit agency that owns the majority of halfway houses in New Jersey and other states, receiving $71 million out of the total $105 million New Jersey allocated for halfway houses annually. Since 2005, there have been 5,000 escapes from halfway houses, 1,300 since about 2010, and 452 escapes in 2011. Escapes from halfway houses often mean the offender simply walked away from an outside job or did not return from a furlough. Halfway house staff members are not armed, and they are not expected to stop a resident if the resident is determined to leave. There are no correctional officers in these facilities. Since the *New York Times* began its investigation, the state has revised its escape numbers down, explaining that some were technical escapes only. The state also began fining private halfway houses for escapes since state resources are used to try and find absconders. One thing that seems puzzling is that very rarely are inmates prosecuted for escape from a halfway house (Dolnick, 2012a).

Halfway houses are less expensive than prisons in New Jersey (and elsewhere) with the per diem costs for halfway houses at $60 to $75 compared to $125 to $150 for prisons. However, they may not be a bargain. Critics contend that there is an unacceptable level of drugs, gang activity, violence, and even sexual assault in these facilities. In fact, some escapees have argued that these issues are the reason they didn't go back. Further criticism was that there were virtually no true treatment programs in the facilities.

The investigation also uncovered troubling relationships between the governor of New Jersey, Chris Christie, and the vice president of Community Education Centers. The executive at the halfway house is a close friend and political advisor to Governor Christie, and Christie was registered as a lobbyist for the business in 2000–2001. There may be no legal or ethical improprieties in the governor's public support for a company that absorbs the bulk of state funding for community corrections, but some object to the real or perceived pressure toward favoring the halfway houses. When a state committee on community corrections was created to help set the agenda for the future, a well-respected professor-researcher resigned in protest at what she described as undue influence from a halfway house executive on the committee (Dolnick, 2012b).

After the investigative series of articles was published, William J. Palatucci, the close friend and political advisor of Gov. Chris Christie's stepped down as a senior executive at Community Education Centers. The governor announced stronger oversight of halfway houses and the New Jersey legislature held two days of hearings. The company received a $130 million contract from Essex County putting the company in a financial healthy position despite the media coverage (Dolnick, 2012c).

Even though only nonprofit companies can receive government contracts for halfway house services, the largest (Community Education Centers) and second largest (The Kintock Group) each have a second for-profit related company. In essence, the nonprofit "hires" the second company and money flows straight through one to the other (Dolnick, 2012d).

David Fawkner, founder of The Kintock Group, reportedly received an annual salary and benefits as high as $805,000 in recent years. His daughter, brother-in-law, and son-in-law all worked for the for-profit company, and some worked for both, earning two salaries (Dolnick, 2012d). He stepped down as chief executive in 2010 to become executive chairman, and now receives a salary of $250,000. The other major nonprofit operator, Education and Health Centers of America, is essentially a nonprofit arm of Community Education Centers. Both are controlled by John J. Clancy and carry about $35 million in contracts. Critics contend that the relationship between the nonprofit and for-profit subsidiary runs afoul of IRS rules (Dolnick, 2012d).

The *New York Times* and *The Crime Report* have also published articles on an investigation of what are called "three-quarter" houses in New York City and Narco Freedom, one of the largest drug treatment providers in the northeast. Individuals who have no resources for rent either live on the street, in dangerous and drug-ridden shelters, or they have the roughly $200 per month the city will pay a "three-quarter house" operator. These are unregulated and no one knows how many there are in the city or how many individuals live in them. The investigation revealed that four men would squeeze into small bedrooms, there were rats, bedbugs and cockroaches, heat and water would be chronically broken, tenants died of overdoses, and individuals were evicted at a moment's notice if they argued or complained. Those in the three-quarter homes were told they had to go to drug treatment as a condition to stay in the facility. The reason is that allegedly the drug treatment programs received Medicaid dollars for treatment. The $200 per month was not lucrative enough to provide an incentive to run the homes; however, that $200 plus the kickbacks received from the treatment programs which billed Medicaid millions did make the schemes profitable, especially if they put the bare minimum amount of funds into the houses themselves (Barker, 2015a).

The three-quarter houses received referrals from the state parole system because parolees had literally nowhere else to go when released. Recruiters would also trawl for residents on the streets and in jails. The most attractive residents were the mentally ill or handicapped who received governmental disability checks. Because the individual had to identify a caregiver to receive the check, the house manager would be designated as such and the individual would receive a small amount of cash every week with the house keeping the rest. One of the largest operators of these homes was a Russian man with felony indictments pending against him related to a Medicaid and insurance fraud scheme from a series of medical clinics he ran with his wife. Although state officials said he was to be prosecuted, while that case stagnated, he opened up a series of three-quarter homes. Ex-residents allege he would tell them to start using drugs again if they wanted to stay in the house because, otherwise, they weren't eligible for treatment (Barker, 2015a).

Narco Freedom ran both treatment programs and houses. Being in treatment was a condition of having a bed in one of the houses, yet the houses themselves were not regulated because they were considered a housing program not a treatment program, but tenants were perceived to have no rights vis-à-vis landlords because the houses were considered a program. Thus, the facilities were in legal limbo and individuals lived in constant anxiety about being kicked out. The problem is that individuals exiting prison or those on the street have literally no choices for affordable housing; thus they are dependent on the three-quarter houses, or sober houses, as they are sometimes called. Some are run well and present a lifeline to those on the margins, but the temptation to make money often leads to decrepit and dangerous housing and coercion to participate in Medicaid-funded treatment (Seville and Gates, 2013).

After the series ran, the New York City Comptroller announced plans to stop the city practice of referring individuals to the three-quarter houses and make a stronger effort to identify and regulate such homes. A large number of homes (59) had already been identified and inspected. City officials also noted that their actions would be carried out in a way that the residents of the homes would not be left on the street if the home was closed down. The Russian owner put his $3.5 million home up for sale and closed down most of the three-quarter homes he owned, evicting the residents even though a judge ruled that the evictions were illegal (Barker, 2015b; 2015c).

Executives at Narco Freedom have been indicted and charged with money laundering, insurance fraud, commercial bribe receiving and two counts of grand larceny. They each face between eight and 25 years in prison. Both Allen Brand and his son, along with four other executives, were indicted, accused of defrauding Medicaid and siphoning revenue from the nonprofit company. Charging documents indicated that Narco Freedom received nearly $40 million annually in Medicaid funds and about $27 million of it was "stolen" by the individuals involved through a variety of schemes, including excessive services and kickbacks. The "Freedom Houses," the three quarter homes linked to Narco Freedom housed about 1500 individuals (Kates, 2014, 2015).

The Brands allegedly used the kickback money from at least two dozen three-quarter homes and exorbitant salaries to fund a lavish lifestyle with Florida condos, luxury cars, and Long Island mansions. They created at least six for-profit companies and then contracted with these for-profit companies to provide cleaning, maintenance and other tasks, paying hugely inflated fees for such services; with kickbacks directly back to them. Tax filings indicate Brand earned a salary of $386,000 in 2011. Jason Brand earned only $109,000 from Narco Freedom but paid himself $526,000 through the various for-profit companies. Similar to the Kintock Group described earlier, several family members were also employed and earned large salaries. The state attorney general is moving to seize the assets as part of its criminal action. The problem is that Narco Freedom is so large that thousands of addicts and ex-offenders would have their housing and treatment taken away from them if the operation was shut down. For now, the Brands are no longer involved in its operation and it is in receivership (Seville and Kates, 2015; Kates, 2015).

The privatization of corrections is a problematic issue because, as discussed in the last chapter, profit motives are always present. Advocating for more releases to halfway houses and three quarter houses may be the right thing to do, but when there are profits to be made, some individuals will inevitably learn how to manipulate the system. Drug addicts and the homeless are victimized by such schemes, but so, too, are the taxpayers. Caution must be taken when interpreting the results of these journalistic investigations. They clearly focus on the most egregious cases; however, clearly legitimate concerns have been raised and responded to by the states involved. One wonders, in fact, what is going on in states that have not been the target of these investigative reports. It is important that community corrections, including halfway houses, play a role in every state's correctional system, but, obviously, it is also important to address problems in their implementation. An important element of any well-run halfway house is obviously staff who are trained in and committed to an ethical code.

Conclusion

In this chapter, we touched on some of the ethical issues that correctional personnel face in institutional corrections and in the community. Discretion exists at each stage of the criminal justice system, and each of the correctional professionals we have introduced in these chapters has discretion in different ways. The difficult decisions for correctional officers arise from the personal relationships that develop with inmates, the trust that is sometimes betrayed, the favors that seem harmless, and the coercive environment that makes violence normal and caring abnormal. Correctional treatment personnel have their own problems in resolving conflicts between loyalty toward clients and toward the system. Community correctional professionals also must balance public safety with client interests. They often, especially in small towns, have difficulty in their supervisor role when it overlaps with other community relationships.

To be in a helping profession in a system geared for punishment is a difficult challenge for anyone, and the temptation to retreat into bureaucratic compliance or, worse, egoistic relativism is always present. Arguably, the criminal justice system operates as well as it does only because of the caring, committed, honest people who choose it as a career.

Chapter Review

1. **Describe the role conflict of correctional officers.**

   Prisons experienced changing goals (from custody to rehabilitation) in the 1970s and 1980s, and this created role conflict and ambiguity for the correctional officer. Also in the 1970s, federal courts recognized an expanding number of prisoner rights, including the rights to exercise religious beliefs, obtain medical care, and enjoy some due process. The disruption in the old way of doing things created real chaos, and the 1970s and 1980s brought danger, loss of control, and stress for officers.

2. **List and describe some ethical issues for correctional officers.**

   Officers' uniforms bestow authority, not unbridled domination, and each officer learns how to utilize this authority. Most do so in ethical ways, although some officers abuse their position. Relationships with inmates present other ethical issues. Officers tend to support other officers against inmates, even when the officer is wrong. However, reciprocity and personal relationships with inmates also can be an issue and potential problem for officers; officers may like an inmate too much and compromise security, or utilize their position to coerce or harass an inmate. Correctional officers report that they sometimes experience a great deal of stress from their role. They are generally disliked by inmates and scorned by society. Some lose their morality in the negative environment of a prison.

3. **Describe the different challenges that face jail officers as compared to correctional officers in prisons.**

   Jail officers have become more professional in recent years, but the position is still sometimes used as a dreaded rite-of-passage assignment, a punishment, or a steppingstone to deputy status. The jail officer deals with a transient population that includes juveniles, the mentally ill or intoxicated, and those with other health problems. There is more interaction with relatives of offenders because the jail is in the community; this also means the jail officers may know or be neighbors of offenders or relatives of offenders. Contraband is a major problem in jails and sometimes officers facilitate smuggling.

4. **Explain the role conflict of treatment professionals and provide examples.**

   Correctional treatment professionals have the dual goals of treating the individual and protecting the safety and security of the institution and/or the community. Sometimes this creates conflict—for instance, prison psychologists may be privy to information or confessions that they feel bound to hold in confidence, even though this may jeopardize the security of the prison. Treatment professionals must assess risk to the community in every decision to allocate more freedoms for clients. Allocating treatment resources is also an issue, specifically how to determine who should have access to treatment programs.

5. **Describe the ethical issues of probation and parole officers.**

   Ethical issues arise in the probation or parole officers' ability to file violation reports or (for probation officers) recommend sentencing in that there are ethical and unethical criteria for such decisions. There is also discretion in managing the caseload, including issues of gratuities, relationships with clients, and when family or friends expect special favors or treatment.

Study Questions

1. How do COs have discretion similar to police officers and court personnel?
2. Describe the role ambiguity that COs faced in the 1970s and 1980s. What are the role types of officers identified by R. Johnson?
3. What are the ethical issues identified by Haar for treatment professionals in corrections?
4. Explain the two areas where probation and parole officers have discretion.
5. What are the role types of probation and parole officers? Describe them.

Writing/Discussion Exercises

1. Write an essay on (or discuss) the range of legal rights that you believe prisoners should have. Look at international treaties on human rights, the ACA standards, and other sources before you write your essay.

2. Write an essay on (or discuss) how you would put together a policy manual for treatment professionals who work in a prison or jail. Evaluate the professional codes and identify problematic controversies, and then create a policy that can accommodate a conflict (such as confidentiality).

3. Write an essay on (or discuss) whether probation and parole officers should have the power to carry weapons (in some states they are required to, in others they are prohibited from doing so).

Key Terms

community corrections	punitive law enforcer	"tune-ups"
correctional officer	reciprocity	welfare/therapeutic
passive time server	Tucker telephone	worker

ETHICAL DILEMMAS

Situation 1
You are a prison guard supervising a tier. One of the inmates comes to you and asks a favor. He wants you to check to see why he hasn't been called down to the admin building to see a counselor, because he put in a slip to see his counselor that morning. You know that it is likely he won't be called out today, and you could tell him that, or you could make a call, or you could do neither. Which would you do? Why?

Situation 2
As a new CO, you soon realize that a great deal of corruption and graft are taking place in the prison. Guards routinely bring in contraband for inmates in return for money, food bought for the inmates' mess hall finds its way into the trunks of staff cars, and money is being siphoned from inmate accounts. You are not sure how far up the corruption goes. Would you keep your mouth shut? Would you go to your supervisors? What if, in exposing the corruption, you implicate yourself? What if you implicate a friend?

Situation 3
You are a prison psychologist, and during the course of your counseling session with one drug offender, he confesses that he has been using drugs. Obviously, this is a serious violation of prison rules. Should you report him? What if he tells you of an impending escape plan?

Situation 4
You are a parole officer whose caseload includes a single mother with three hyper-active, attention-deficit-disordered young children. She receives no support from her ex-husband. Her own mother wants nothing to do with her or the children, believing that "God is punishing her." The parolee works as a topless dancer but hates it. She continues dancing because it pays the bills so well. You know that she smokes

marijuana on a fairly regular basis in an effort to deal with stress. Obviously, this is a violation of probation. However, if you file a violation report on her, she will go back to prison. You know she is doing the best she can with her kids, she is heavily involved with their school, and they are strongly bonded to her. You worry about what will happen to the kids. What would you do?

Situation 5

You are a prison counselor and have a good relationship with the other counselors. You all go out drinking after work sometimes, and in general you like and respect everyone. Recently you've noticed that something seems to be going on with one of the other counselors. Stella is usually outgoing and cheerful, but lately she seems distracted and upset. You see her in the parking lot one evening and ask her what is wrong. She confides to you that she is in love with an inmate. She knows it is wrong, but she says that they had an instant chemistry and that he is like no man she has ever known. She has been slipping him love notes, and he has also been writing her. You tell her that she has to stop it or else quit her job. She tearfully tells you that she can't let him go, she needs her job, and you've got to keep quiet or you'll get her fired. What would you do?

Correctional Professionals: Misconduct and Responses

In Abu Ghraib prison, dogs were used to terrorize detainees.

David Armstrong was feared by inmates in the Bureau of Prison's supermax prison in Florence, Colorado. He was a part of a group of correctional officers (COs), known as the Cowboys, who worked the Special Housing Unit (SHU), the segregation unit of the prison. Allegedly, Armstrong was one of the ringleaders of the group who, after several correctional officers had been injured in 1995, got the green light from their captain to "teach some inmates a lesson" by vicious beatings. At first the group selected defiant, violent inmates for "treatments." The COs would punch, kick, and choke the inmates, or drop them, handcuffed, headfirst on the concrete floor. They would then fabricate a story about why they had to use force, even to the point of inflicting injuries on themselves to justify the use of force. From 1995 through 1997, the group conducted these systematic beatings, eventually targeting not only violent inmates but gradually including mouthy and

Chapter Objectives

1. Describe types of misconduct by correctional officers, including the typologies of misconduct by Souryal and McCarthy.

2. Describe types of misconduct by community corrections professionals.

3. Explain the Zimbardo experiment and what it might imply for correctional professionals.

4. Provide explanations for misconduct.

5. Present some suggestions to decrease misconduct by correctional professionals.

troublesome inmates as well. The Cowboys also threatened other officers, at one point promising that any officer who snitched would be taken out to the parking lot and beaten.

The group stuck together. Six of the seven were ex-military; several had gone through the Bureau of Prisons' training academy together and arrived at United States Penitentiary (USP) Florence together. Their key phrases were "Lie 'til you die" and "What happens in SHU stays in SHU." A Catholic priest and other staff members heard complaints from inmates and tried to get the warden to listen, but most believed that the inmates were lying because, after all, inmates always lied. The Cowboys eventually broke up. Some, like Armstrong, were promoted and transferred. After he left Colorado and was working in a federal prison in Pennsylvania, he evidently had trouble breaking old habits and was disciplined repeatedly for his treatment of inmates. Then, in 1998, he was visited by an FBI agent who wanted to know what had happened in Colorado.

The ensuing FBI and Department of Justice investigation took five years and resulted in a grand jury indictment that listed more than 55 acts of beatings, intimidations, and lies. A nine-week trial with more than 60 witnesses ended with two weeks of jury deliberations. Armstrong was the government's star witness, and on the stand he described beating after beating, explaining that there were so many he couldn't remember them all. Why did he violate the "lie 'til you die" command? It may have been the plea bargain the government offered him in return for his testimony, or it may have been that he had terminal cancer and sought some type of redemption for what he had done before his death. On the witness stand, he could hardly talk and required an oxygen tank to breathe.

Armstrong might have been remorseful, or he might have been trying to make the best deal for himself, but the seven accused COs denied everything. Despite Armstrong's and other correctional officers' testimony, the jury acquitted four officers of all charges and convicted three others of only some of the charges (Prendergast, 2003). The story of the Cowboys is not typical of correctional professionals today, but it does illustrate the difficulties of preventing, monitoring, investigating, and responding to correctional officer misconduct. The prison is a closed world, and outsiders may never know what happens inside the walls.

The vast majority of news items and academic attention in the area of ethics and misconduct has covered police officer misconduct; very little attention has been directed to misconduct by correctional officers in prisons and jails. Even less attention has been directed to probation and parole officers or treatment professionals in corrections. Maybe the prevalence of misconduct is much lower with these other professional groups. That seems unlikely, but until more research is conducted, it is difficult to say.

Misconduct and Corruption

McCarthy (1991, 1995) and Souryal (1999a) discuss the major types of corruption by correctional officers and other officials in institutional corrections. Categories include theft, trafficking, embezzlement, and misuse of authority. Under misuse of authority, McCarthy (1991) details the following:

- Accepting gratuities for special consideration during legitimate activities
- Accepting gratuities for protection of illicit activities

- Mistreatment/harassment or extortion of inmates
- Mismanagement (e.g., prison industries)
- Miscellaneous abuses

Souryal (1999a), in another typology, describes the types of corruption as falling into the following categories:

- Arbitrary use of power (treating workers or inmates preferentially or in a biased fashion)
- Oppression and failure to demonstrate compassion/caring
- Abusing authority for personal gain (extortion, smuggling, theft)

In a more recent typology, Souryal (2009: 28–29) describes corruption sociologically as the use of arbitrary power, legally as the use of oppression or extralegal methods, and ethically as the failure of officers to demonstrate compassion or keep a promise. He describes acts of **misfeasance** (illegitimate acts done for personal gain), acts of **malfeasance** (acts that violate authority), and acts of **nonfeasance** (acts of omission such as ignoring rule violations).

misfeasance
Illegitimate acts done for personal gain.

malfeasance
Acts that violate authority.

nonfeasance
Acts of omission.

Bomse (2001) identifies different types of prisoner abuse as follows:

- *Malicious or purposeful abuse.* This is the type of abuse inflicted by individual officers intentionally, including excessive use of force, rape and sexual harassment, theft and destruction of personal property, false disciplinary charges, intentional denial of medical care, failure to protect, racial abuse and harassment, and excessive and humiliating strip searches.
- *Negligent abuse.* This type of abuse is also inflicted by individual officers, but not intentionally, and includes negligent denial of medical care, failure to protect, lack of responsiveness; and negligent loss of property or mail.
- *Systemic or budgetary abuse.* This type of abuse is systemwide and refers to policies, including overcrowding, inadequate medical care (systematic budget cutting), failure to protect, elimination of visits or other programs, copayments and surcharges, and use of isolation units.

Although there is no research that supports this premise, a cursory reading of a wide range of news reports, both current and historical, of corruption in corrections indicates that corruption tends to occur in patterns. That is, if there is sexual misconduct, there is also smuggling. If there is physical abuse of inmates, there are also other forms of mistreatment. It also appears that corruption tends to permeate levels of supervisors who are able to protect the corrupt activities. Cover-ups at the highest levels also occur, arguably not necessarily because the highest level administrators are involved directly, but more so because of long-term friendships between those involved and those who can protect them and/or a desire to keep the illegal activities from being exposed to the public. Patterns of corruption also seem to occur when there is a deficit of resources, including understaffing, deferred maintenance leading to decrepit facilities, and a seeming lack of care and attention from the top management. In a way, one might describe it as the "broken windows" theory of corrections in that when policies and procedures are ignored, when buildings fall into disrepair, when relationships between inmates and correctional officers drift into unprofessional familiarity or animosity, then corruption/crime seems to be present as well.

Every decade there are major scandals reported in one or more prisons across the country. Sexual abuse of inmates, brutality, bribery at the highest levels, and drug smuggling all are reported with depressing regularity (Carroll, 1998; Houston, 1999; Hassine, 1996). Some scandals live in infamy, such as the gladiator fights that were orchestrated by correctional officers in Corcoran prison in California where correctional officers coerced inmates to fight in the prison yard and used shotguns from the towers to stop them. Despite the litigation and criminal prosecutions that followed, correctional officer–coerced "gladiator fights" have been alleged more recently in the Denver jail, in juvenile detention facilities in Texas, and other locations. Other scandals, such as smuggling rings where correctional officers bring in cellphones, drugs, and other contraband for inmates, are so similar when they appear in various states, that it seems only the names of the individuals and prison gangs involved are different. Officers are often tempted by the large sums of money offered to bring items into the prison (drugs, cash, cellphones) or out of the prison (notes or letters). Some correctional officers are coerced by inmates who tell the officers they know where they live or where their kids go to school, but much more often inmates find correctional officers, who sometimes make as little has $16,000 per year, willing to sell their integrity for money, or who smuggle contraband into the prison for an inmate-lover.

In the sections to follow, a brief description of the types of corruption found in prisons and jails will be offered by state. This is not to portray these states are worse than others, or that there is no corruption in states that aren't represented here. One thing that should be noted is that examples of corruption exist from the very top to the line-staff employee.

California

The gladiator fights and shootings of inmates in the yard at Corcoran led to federal indictments, and several officers were tried for a killing, but they were acquitted. Some argue that the officer union "tainted" the jury pool by running television ads before the jury selection, showing officers as tough, brave, and underappreciated (Arax, 1999; Lewis, 1999).

California's Department of Corrections has been described as corrupt "from the top down" because investigations of wrongdoing seemed to be thwarted by powerful union leaders. During legislative hearings about a Folsom riot that was said by some to have originated through correctional officers conspiring with one of the gangs, one legislator received death threats, and witnesses were put under protective custody (Thompson, 2004). The riot and its cover-up evidently led directly to the suicide of an officer who attempted to thwart the riot but was stopped by a supervisor. He left a message: "My job killed me" (Warren, 2004a). Several wardens and assistant wardens resigned, took early retirement, or were fired over the Folsom Prison riot scandal, and dozens of correctional officers were fired for wrongdoing (Warren, 2004b).

Donald Vodicka, a 15-year correctional officer veteran in California, testified in a criminal case that the code of silence was pervasive, especially at the Corcoran and Pelican Bay prisons, and that a whistleblower would not be protected by the Department of Corrections against fellow correctional officers. He described the activities of a group of officers at Salinas Valley State Prison, called "the Green Wall," in a book of the same name. His description of what he went through after daring to tell the truth about corrupt officers and supervisors is unfortunately one that has been repeated throughout this text. His story is presented in the Walking the Walk box.

WALKING THE WALK

D. J. Vodicka looks like someone you wouldn't want to anger. At six feet, six inches tall and 300 pounds, with a shaved head and an inscrutable look honed by a hitch in the military and 16 years as a correctional officer, he is definitely not the picture of a liberal do-gooder. Yet Vodicka gave up his career, and even some friends, and risked his safety when he broke rank with other correctional officers and exposed "the Green Wall" for their abuse of inmates. The phrase was adopted by a group of officers at the Salinas Valley State Prison in California after a prison disturbance on Thanksgiving Day in 1998; more than a dozen officers were injured in the melee. The prison suffered from the effects of understaffing and too many inexperienced officers combined with some of the worst offenders in the California prison system. The desire to teach the inmates a lesson and keep control of a dangerously unstable institution allegedly led to officers using illegal force, planting evidence on inmates, and utilizing a pattern of intimidation and threats on inmates. Even other officers were threatened in order to keep their activities under the radar of prison officials.

When he was asked by his superior to write a report on the activities of the Green Wall, Vodicka followed orders, as he had always done in his military career and his years with the California Department of Corrections. He did not feign ignorance, as others did, but wrote a report that detailed the green armbands, lapel pins, and ink pens used by members; the incident where one member received an engraved green-handled knife upon his promotion; the graffiti scrawled on walls and desks proclaiming the group; and the evidence that indicated that Green Wall members were

well known in the institution and even tacitly supported by the warden. Instead of dealing with the situation through proper disciplinary channels, the lieutenant who asked for the report was summarily transferred and the report was leaked to other correctional officers, leading to a situation where Vodicka was transferred for his own safety. The news that he was a "rat" traveled with him to the new prison. He encountered hostile remarks and ostracism there until the day he ran to respond to an emergency alarm, turned around and found that the officers behind him had stopped behind a gate, leaving him alone in a yard full of brawling, violent inmates. Their excuse was that they were waiting for a sergeant. Realizing his vulnerability, Vodicka left the prison that day, never to return.

In 2004, he testified before a California state senate committee about the Green Wall and how prison administrators did little or nothing to stop the illegal activities, nor did they punish those who were retaliating against him for speaking out. The hearings led to the resignation of some officials and a broad effort by the Department of Corrections to "clean house" at Salinas Valley. Eventually Vodicka won a whistleblower lawsuit against the Department of Corrections, but he continues to live in an undisclosed location because his safety is still compromised by his decision to stand up against the Green Wall. He continues to be perceived by many correctional officers in the system as disloyal. Others argue that Vodicka displays the right kind of loyalty—loyalty to the law, to the truth, and to the citizens of the state who employed him, rather than the criminals in green uniforms who forgot what it meant to be public servants.

Sources: Vodicka, 2009; Arax, 2004.

In 2007, advocates, journalists, and inmates reported systematic abuses in a California prison in Susanville. Inmates reportedly were strip searched and made to stand for hours in the snow, and correctional officers allegedly tried to provoke attacks between inmates, spread feces on cell doors, and used excessive force. Inmates who filed grievances against officers were allegedly retaliated against and threatened. Reports indicated that the Department of Corrections' own staff members sent to the prison to investigate documented some abuses, and after visiting the facility concluded that correctional officers believed they could carry out extreme forms of punishment against inmates because it was a behavioral modification unit for inmates who had been identified as disruptive in other prisons (Piller, 2010).

A California inspector general's report detailed 278 cases of alleged employee misconduct closed during the second half of 2012 (from a total of 1,074), including numerous employees having sex with inmates, including juveniles; one correctional officer having the baby of an inmate; a correctional officer challenging an inmate to a fistfight and then covering it up; and one correctional officer drinking inmate-made alcohol with the inmates. The report only reviews how the incidents were dealt with by the department of correction, not what happened to the officers involved, and criticized the internal affairs unit in one region of the state in particular for doing poor investigations (Thompson, 2013).

As described earlier, California has drastically reduced its prison population due to the court holding in *Brown v. Plata*, and the Realignment Act resulted in many more inmates in county jails. For years, the Los Angeles County Jail has been cited by advocates, inmates, attorneys, and staff members as a place where a widespread abuse of inmates occurred by officers who were immune to punishment and, arguably, encouraged by Sheriff Baca. Years ago, the Department of Justice was asked to investigate the jail in a letter signed by former California attorney general John Van de Kamp, two former U.S. attorneys, three former assistant U.S. attorneys, the Los Angeles County public defender, the former head of the Civil Rights Division of the Department of Justice several law school deans, and numerous attorneys and religious leaders (Faturechi, 2011).

The ACLU National Prison Project and the ACLU of Southern California published a report in September of 2011 detailing incidents of abuse. In the descriptions of what was happening in the jail, deputies slammed inmates' heads into walls, kicked them when they were on the floor unresisting, used Tasers on unresisting inmates, and allowed other inmates to brutalize and sexually assault victims (in one case an inmate was described as sodomized with a broom handle; in another an inmate was raped while his head was being held in a flushing toilet to stop him from screaming). Documented injuries include a fractured jaw, broken collarbone, eye damage, and numerous other injuries—all received, according to deputy reports, while the inmate was "resisting." The ACLU collected 70 sworn statements by prisoners, chaplains, teachers, other civilian staff, and other deputies to submit to the court in an ongoing court case, *Rutherford v. Baca* (begun as *Rutherford v. Block*, 2006 WL 3065781 [C.D. Cal. Oct 27, 2006]).

Some of the abuse was witnessed by civilians (chaplains and attorneys) who alleged being threatened by correctional officers if they reported what they saw. Even when the abuse was reported to administrators, nothing was done about it. A chaplain, despite being threatened, did report an incident where an unresisting inmate was being beaten and some deputies called him a "rat" and "motherf****r" when he passed them in the hallway in the days that followed. Two years passed before he heard that his report had supposedly been "resolved internally" (Faturechi, 2011).

Most of the abuse took place on the third floor of the jail, and two deputies were attacked by six third-floor deputies at a Christmas party in 2011 when one of those attacked was perceived to have criticized what happened on the floor. This group was described as "gang-like" who used gang hand signs and called themselves the 3,000 Boys (for the third floor); in later court filings, they were described as having tattoos on the back of their necks and awarding one another points for breaking prisoners' bones (Williams, 2014). The jail has had gang-like groups of officers before with names such as the Grim Reapers, Vikings, and Little Devils. The Vikings were described by a federal judge as a neo-Nazi group and, because of their actions, the county had to pay $9 million in fines and training costs in 1996 (Faturechi and Blankstein, 2011; Liebowitz and Eliasberg, 2011).

The LA jail had already been under a federal monitor for 12 years for its treatment of mentally ill inmates. In 2013, a federal judge, exasperated with what he described as recalcitrance on the part of the county and jail officials to do anything to improve conditions, went forward with a consent decree designed to force compliance. The letter to county officials cited dimly lit, vermin-infested living conditions that exacerbated mental health problems, and 10 inmate suicides in 2013 (Chang, 2013).

A county blue ribbon panel, created after the ACLU report was published, issued a report in 2012 that said Sheriff Baca and his assistants had created an environment where deputies believed it was acceptable to use physical beatings and humiliation to control inmates and to cover up such abuse. The lawsuit by the ACLU also went forward and the Department of Justice opened up a civil rights investigation (similar to those conducted in cities where there are problems with police departments) (Williams, 2014). In two separate civil lawsuits filed by inmates who had been injured in the jail, two juries found Sheriff Baca personally liable for incidents of abuse. In one of those cases the plaintiff was a man awaiting trial in 2009 in the jail when deputies severely beat him; he was punched and kicked repeatedly, shot with a Taser multiple times and struck "numerous times" in the ankle with a heavy metal flashlight, causing fractures and head injuries. The jury found in favor of the plaintiff against the deputies involved, their supervisors, and Sheriff Baca who, it was determined, failed to control violence in the jail. The jury awarded $165,000 in punitive damages to the plaintiff and the defendants agreed that Baca would pay $100,000 of it. The case was appealed (Medina, 2013; Sewell and Faturechi, 2013).

The most bizarre chapter in the saga of the LA County jail occurred in 2011 when the FBI engineered an undercover operation by paying a corrupt correctional officer to smuggle in a cellphone to a prisoner-informant, who was supposed to collect evidence of the brutality in the jail with the phone. When the cellphone was discovered and the prisoner-informant told deputies he was working for the FBI, he was prevented from communicating with his FBI handlers. The FBI filed a writ in court to produce him, but the court order "got lost" at the sheriff's department. He was successfully hidden for several weeks by deputies moving him around to different facilities under false names, until the sheriff's department was finally forced to produce him in response to a judge's order. Their explanation for secreting the inmate from his FBI handlers was that they were only trying to keep him safe. Recorded interviews between the informant and deputies, however, made it clear that they were upset about the FBI investigating "their house" and that they were attempting to persuade the informant not to tell the FBI agents anything. Two deputies also conducted surveillance on and accosted an FBI agent in her driveway and told her there was going to be a warrant for her arrest in an attempt to coerce her to tell them what the FBI knew about what was going on in the jail (Kim and Chang, 2014).

In late 2013, 18 deputies and supervisors were arrested under four different grand jury indictments on an array of charges, including civil rights violations and obstruction charges in relation to the FBI investigation (Hews, 2013). In 2014, federal prosecutors won guilty verdicts against six of these sheriff's deputies for their roles in the scheme to obstruct the federal investigation, including the two who threatened the FBI agent with arrest. The deputies were sentenced to prison terms from 21 to 41 months for their actions. The federal judge found that there was routine cover-up of inmate abuse, and an "unwritten code" taught to new jail deputies that any inmate who fought a guard should end up in the hospital (Kim, 2014). The defendants insisted they were merely following orders from Sheriff Lee Baca and Undersheriff Paul Tanaka. Sheriff Baca resigned abruptly in January of 2014, and one of those who ran for the sheriff's position was Undersheriff Paul Tanaka. He denied any wrongdoing (Medina, 2013; Kim and Chang, 2014). Tanaka lost the election to Jim McDonnell, who had been on the Citizens' Commission on Jail Violence, the blue ribbon panel formed after the ACLU report that had issued the highly critical report in 2012. Tanaka left the L.A. County Jail after losing the election, and was eventually also indicted in 2015. As of summer of 2015, former sheriff Baca had not been charged (Chang and Winton, 2015).

In 2014, the ACLU lawsuit was settled when the Los Angeles County Board of Supervisors agreed to enter into a federal consent decree. The agreement involved neither financial damages nor an admission of wrongdoing by the Sheriff's Department, but a three-person panel, appointed by a federal judge, will be responsible for overseeing the implementation of sweeping new policy changes. One of the changes is firing deputies who are guilty of illegal uses of force (Williams, 2014).

Mississippi

Mississippi has had a long history of prison brutality, and problems with private prisons in the state were described in Chapter 11. Christopher Epps, the head of Mississippi's corrections department, was an enthusiastic proponent of private prisons; however, it appears that at the time he was promoting that option he was receiving money from Cecil McCrory, an ex-sheriff's deputy who had a company that had contracts with the corrections department.

In 2014, Christopher Epps abruptly resigned and was indicted on 40 counts of bribery, money laundering, conspiracy, and tax charges after a federal investigation of his relationship with Cecil McCrory. One such deal was described whereby Epps personally urged MTC, a Utah-based private prison company that received the contract to run all the private prisons in the state, to hire McCrory and, when he was hired, they split the fee (Faussett, 2014). Epps, at the time of his resignation, was the president of the American Correctional Association and the Association of State Correctional Administrators. He was the longest-running corrections head in Mississippi's history (Pender, Gates, and Coz, 2014).

Evidently McCrory paid off Epps' $200,000 mortgage in 2008 and, later, also paid off the mortgage on a condominium. Altogether Epps may have received $2 million from McCrory in return for McCrory receiving lucrative contracts from the corrections department. Epps eventually pleaded guilty in February 2015 to filing a false tax return and two counts of conspiracy of money laundering. The federal government seized Epps' home, Florida condo, and Mercedes Benz. McCrory also pleaded guilty and will forfeit $1.2 million in cash plus property and automobiles. The men are reportedly cooperating with authorities and more indictments may follow in an investigation that federal agents have dubbed the "Mississippi Hustle." The governor has assigned a task force to investigate the practice of no-bid contracts (Mitchell and Gates, 2013). MTC still has the contract to run Mississippi prisons.

Texas

Texas has also had its share of prison scandals. In the 1990s, James A. "Andy" Collins, an ex-director of the Department of Corrections, was convicted of bribery, conspiracy, and money laundering for locking the state into a long-term contract to buy large quantities of "VitaPro," a vegetable-based protein substance that evidently tasted bad and created digestive problems, while receiving payments of $10,000. When the investigation began, he resigned and immediately became a $1,000 per day consultant for the company. Collins appealed, and in 2008 a federal judge overturned the guilty verdict (M. Ward, 2008).

In a news investigation in 2009, it was found that from 2003 to 2008, 263 employees of the Texas prison system were reprimanded for possessing prohibited items, and most (75 percent) were put on a probationary status by the department of corrections. Only 35 lost their job, and only one was formally prosecuted. It should also be noted that the contraband was most often smokeless tobacco or cigarettes, not drugs, although cellphones and alcohol were also frequent examples of contraband. A cellphone scandal erupted shortly before this investigation when a death row inmate called and threatened a legislator. A shakedown resulted in the confiscation of more than 200 cellphones. Prison officials cite low pay and high turnover for correctional officer misconduct and indicate that these issues are part of the reason why many officers who are caught are allowed to keep their job (Associated Press, 2009a).

A federal investigation called "Operation Prison Cell" resulted in 29 individuals being sentenced for a large conspiracy involving smuggling and money laundering. Fourteen were correctional officers. All but one person pleaded guilty. The smuggling ring was centered in a south Texas prison in Beeville. Those sentenced were either correctional officers, inmates, or "facilitators" in the community. Correctional officers would smuggle in the contraband (usually drugs and cellphones), and inmates would sell the contraband. Correctional officers would also smuggle cash. Federal officials described the prison as having a "culture of corruption." This was not the first time correctional officers there had been arrested for participating in smuggling rings run by the inmate gangs; corruption has been said to be rampant there since at least 2005. The current investigation was a joint operation between the Texas Office of Inspector General and the FBI and began in 2009 when a criminal car smuggling scheme was thwarted and it was discovered that members of an Aryan prison gang orchestrated the criminal enterprise with cellphones from the prison. Another prison gang was implicated in a series of violent home invasions (U.S. Attorney's Office, 2013).

Florida

With 20,000 employees and more than 100,000 inmates, Florida's prison system is the third largest in the country, after California and Texas, with one of the highest rates of imprisonment. Florida has also seen its share of scandals. The federal courts, citing the Eighth Amendment violations, oversaw the state's prisons for more than two decades starting in the mid-1970s, ordering legislators to relieve overcrowding and provide adequate medical and healthcare.

James Crosby was appointed secretary of the corrections system by Governor Jeb Bush in 2003. When he was appointed to the job of secretary of the Department of Corrections, troubling reports began to emerge about alcohol-fueled parties and cozy relationships with prison vendors who provided perks for Crosby and other high-ranking individuals. Friends of Crosby were perceived as untouchable in that no matter what allegations emerged, they would not be punished (York, 2012). Ultimately, in 2006 he was forced to resign, and Crosby and a top-ranking administrator ended up in federal prison for accepting bribes from a food vendor. Crosby evidently was pocketing over $10,000 a month in kickbacks. The 2006 investigation that led to the convictions also led to criminal charges against more than two dozen other employees, including charges related to illegal steroid use and distribution, creating phantom jobs, stealing prison equipment, and obtaining illegal services from inmates (Morgan, 2010; York, 2012).

In 2014, a *Miami Herald*'s investigative series of Florida's prison system exposed a seemingly corrupt system that was chronically underfunded and rife with abusive staff and cover-ups. In 2014, the Department of Justice indicated they would be investigating the prison system for civil rights violations.

Inmate deaths that may have been covered up are the most serious allegations. There were about 320 deaths in 2014 in the Florida prison system, most of which were probably due to the aging prison population. There had also been, however, a doubling of the use of force by correctional officers in the previous five years (Brown, 2014).

In one case in 2009, Bernadette Gregory was due to be released in eight months, was planning her wedding, and, by all accounts, seemed excited to begin a new life after prison. She was also afraid of a correctional officer and reported abuse. Four days before her death, DOC records show that Gregory filed a written complaint alleging that a Captain Greer had beaten her and bashed her over the head with a radio. When she was found hanging in her cell, Department of Corrections' records reported she tied a double knot in a sheet, twisted it around the top bunk, and hung herself. She supposedly did this in a short 11 minutes between being viewed by correctional officers, even though she was wheelchair bound and handcuffed. Prison officials reported she was handcuffed in front of her torso, and insisted her death was thoroughly investigated and two officers were disciplined for failing to follow procedure (Brown, 2014a).

Another death was of Darren Rainey, a 50-year-old mentally ill inmate at Dade Correctional Institution. Rainey died in 2012 after corrections officers locked him in a 180-degree shower, purportedly as punishment for defecating on the floor of his cell and refusing to clean it up. Witnesses said he was left in the closet-like shower for nearly two hours as he screamed in agony, then collapsed. A nurse who was on duty that night and examined Rainey's body postmortem told reporters that the corpse was so hot that it exceeded the range on her thermometer but didn't want to be identified because she feared retaliation (Brown, 2014d). After the *Miami Herald* series reported on the death three years later, police detectives finally interviewed witnesses.

Another death was ruled "natural causes," but Randall Jordan-Aparo's death occurred after he was gassed with chemical agents. In evidence "accidentally found" three years after his death, it was discovered that his medical records showed he suffered from a rare blood disorder that caused him respiratory distress, he had begged to be taken to the hospital because he felt ill and was rude to a nurse, then he was gassed so severely that the pictures show an outline of his body with the yellow chemical agent covering the wall behind the spot where his body lay. Reports written by the officers after the death falsely claimed that he had been involved in a prison disturbance. Four investigators with the Florida Department of Corrections' Inspector General's office subsequently filed a whistleblower lawsuit against the chief inspector general, Linda Miguel, claiming there was a cover-up to thwart their efforts to expose and punish the officers in 2013 (Brown, 2014f; Brown and Bousquet, 2014).

Latandra Ellington's death is also suspicious. She was found dead in October 2014 after she sent a letter to her family saying that a sergeant at Lowell Correctional was threatening to kill her. The sergeant was placed on perimeter duty pending the outcome of the investigation. Newspaper reports indicated that he had been arrested twice, for fraud in 1986 and for possession of steroids in 1994. His arrests, however, were not reported to FDLE's Criminal Justice Standards and Training Commission, which keeps track of law enforcement misconduct. Sources reported he was on vacation and not on duty when Ellington died. Her letter also named another correctional officer who threatened her. Corrections officials did not tell Ellington's family anything about her death, but the family hired an attorney and paid for a private autopsy, which showed she suffered blunt-force trauma to her stomach consistent with being punched or kicked (Brown, 2014b).

After the *Miami Herald* series on these and other inmate deaths, 32 correctional officers were fired in connection with investigations that date back to 2010 (Associated Press, 2014). Mike Crews, the head of the Department of Corrections at the time, also fired or forced into retirement several wardens and deputy wardens and attempted a series of reforms. He also asked that the Florida Department of Law Enforcement (FDLE), a separate independent investigative body that answered to the governor, take on the duty of investigating inmate deaths and correctional officer abuse. Gerald Bailey, the commissioner of FDLE, asked the legislature for an additional $8.4 million for 66 new investigators to probe prison deaths and cases involving excessive force by Florida law enforcement officers (Brown, 2014; Associated Press, 2014). Crews also created an ombudsman to monitor the care of inmates with mental illnesses and warned the health-care provider Corizon that it must rectify serious deficiencies in its medical care (Brown and Bousquet, 2014).

The correctional officer union objected to the firings, arguing they were done without due process and that Crews did not hold supervisors accountable. Eventually, most of the guards got their jobs back (Associated Press, 2014) Crews' reform of posting death investigations for access by family and outsiders was deemed virtually useless because the reports are heavily redacted and didn't include 90 percent of deaths because they were deemed "natural" (Associated Press, 2014).

One of the people forced out was Jerry Cummings. He had been with the prison system since 1974 as a corrections officer, then retired in 2000, but returned to the system in 2003 to take a warden's position at the troubled facility where Darren Rainey died in the scalding shower. After the focus on Rainey's death and other events, Cummings was removed from his post and placed on administrative leave. He retired again soon afterward. He reported to *Miami Herald* reporters that his attempts to improve the prison were thwarted and said that "the biggest challenge a warden has is to change the culture of an institution." When he made surprise visits to the prison at 2 a.m., he would see doors wide open, unstaffed stations, and sleeping guards. He described a maintenance worker that was so involved in smuggling drugs and cigarettes that he never had time to do his job. Cummings said, "It is, by far, the most dangerous prison I've ever worked in." He also said that the inmates weren't treated like human beings.

A major problem was understaffing, so much so that there was "ghost rostering"—in which guards are listed as working at a particular post but really were not there. He described the mental health unit where Rainey died: "There was no air conditioning. The doors to the control rooms were broken. The plumbing was bad, bad, bad. Water was leaking everywhere. All you could smell was urine and feces. The inmates were all in soiled clothing. . . . I would walk in there and they would beg for food, for soap, for a toothbrush. . . . The officers held all the power and if they didn't want to feed them, they wouldn't feed them." Cummings said he reported to the Inspector General's office that he found suspicious elements to the shower death of Rainey, including the facts that the officers passed by closer showers to put him in the one where the shower was hose fed from an adjacent janitor's closest and the water temperature could reach 160 degrees in that shower only. He attempted to fire the officer involved but was ordered not to do so (Brown, 2014e).

In 2014, a Florida State University group called The Project on Accountable Justice, a think tank made up of academics, judges, and law enforcement and corrections professionals, urged the legislature to conduct a complete overhaul of the prison system because of what they called mismanagement from the highest level. The report included a series of recommendations, including:

- Create a public safety oversight commission that would set policy and standards for prisons
- Raise the minimum standard for hiring corrections officers and set up educational incentives
- Separate the terms of the secretaries of the department of corrections from the governors who appoint them and have the legislature involved in the vetting and evaluation to improve independence (Brown, 2014c).

The group noted that the department's leadership had changed six times in the past eight years. In late 2014, Mike Crews quit and Julie Jones was appointed as secretary of the Corrections Department in January 2015. When asked his reasons for leaving the post, he cited a persistent budget deficit of $25 million although he denied that there was conflict with the governor due to his pushing for a budget increase (Brown and Bousquet, 2014). Later, in 2015, however, he told reporters that he was forced to cut so many correctional officers positions that the facilities were dangerously understaffed to the point that they couldn't keep adequate counts of inmates and the buildings were so deteriorated that their electrical, plumbing, and security systems were constantly failing. Contraband smuggling was widespread because guards could make $200 for a single pack of cigarettes and they were woefully underpaid. Crews said after the *Miami Herald* series started he was ordered not to create written reports detailing inmate deaths. He said that because the governor was in a reelection race, he was told he was supposed to take the blame so that it would not affect the governor. In September 2013, Crews had told a Senate committee that the DOC budget was $500 million less than it was in 2007, yet there were 9,000 more inmates in the system. He said he had to beg hotel chains for discarded sheets and pillows. Part of the budget slashing made no sense though; because as positions were cut, overtime costs increased. Overtime was dangerous though because officers working double shifts were tired and burned out. He said he was asked to slash his request for more officers and refused to agree publicly that the prisons were funded at adequate levels. He resigned in November 2014, and in January 2015 Governor Scott announced a $51.5 million increase in the prison budget; he had only asked for $37 million (Brown and Klas, 2015).

Since Julie Jones, the former head of the state highway department, took over in January 2015, she has fired 44 correctional officers and supervisors (Brown, 2015). One firing was of an assistant warden at the facility where Latandra Ellington died. He reportedly acted in such a way that most suspected he was involved with several female inmates. When officers tried to discipline some of his inmate-favorites, the women would threaten to tell "Marty" and they would be overruled. One officer went to the local police department and filed a report that said he had been threatened by the assistant warden who said he would get "his ass kicked" because he searched the property of one of the inmates and seized a large amount of contraband (Brown, 2015).

In testimony to the state legislature in early 2015, current and former prison inspectors testified that they were repeatedly ordered to ignore evidence of crimes committed by corrupt officials because doing so would give the Department of Corrections a "black eye." Three inspectors and one former inspector cited cases where they were told to withhold information from prosecutors, to close investigations into staffers who were politically connected and to avoid bringing criminal charges no matter how much evidence they had. They said they were threatened or retaliated against by their boss Jeffrey Beasley in the Inspector General's Office, especially after they spoke with *Miami Herald* reporters in the story series about mysterious inmate deaths. A former DOC inspector, now a sheriff, said that during the two years he worked in the Inspector General's Office, he was told twice not to pursue cases despite his belief that they could result in criminal charges. In one case, he believed a nurse's medical neglect led to near fatal incidents but was told to drop the investigation allegedly because the nurse was having an affair with the warden. The current Department of Corrections Secretary Julie Jones refuted the testimony and reportedly said that it was their view, it happened several years ago, and that cases were reported to the state attorney's office when "appropriate." Jones complained that IG investigators were exceeding their authority because only FDLE investigators were supposed to be investigating cases. In recent months Jones had ordered investigators and other staffers to sign confidentiality agreements prohibiting them from talking about cases under the threat of losing their job (Klas and Brown, 2015b). She backed off that plan after legislators reacted strongly to the idea that her staff was prohibited from speaking at legislative hearings about the agency (Klas and Brown, 2015a).

The legislative hearings in 2015 led to a prison-reform bill passed unanimously by the House that needs approval by the Senate. Legislators promised a joint committee to oversee the DOC and a list of reforms, including an overhaul of the IG's investigative function of the prisons, and a pilot program of putting body cameras on some correctional officers. Stricter elements of reform that had been in a Senate bill were taken out, including a provision that removed the power of hiring of the DOC secretary from the governor. One provision is to remove civil service protections from the entire staff of the Inspector General's Office, including those who testified at the legislative hearings, which concerns them greatly since they had previously testified to retaliation from supervisors for coming forward and speaking about problems in the DOC (Klas, 2015).

The changes needed in the Florida prison must be navigated through the influence of the powerful correctional officers' union, which has strong supporters in the legislature, a governor who has promised tax cuts making any expectations of increased resources problematic, and an entrenched culture that is resistant to change (Klas, 2015). A recent piece of news from Florida is that several Florida correctional officers were arrested when their plot to kill an ex-inmate was revealed. One of the officers was angry because the inmate, who had tested positive for HIV, had bitten him. The officers, reputedly members of the Ku Klux Klan, were ensnared in an FBI undercover investigation where an informant pretended to have had the inmate killed for them (Robles, 2015).

Treatment Professionals

Most news items and academic articles describe misconduct in prisons in terms of correctional officers, but there are instances where counselors and other treatment professionals also engage in misconduct. Sometimes they smuggle in contraband; sometimes they coerce or engage in consensual sex with inmates. For instance, a female mental health counselor in the Lake Correctional Institution in Florida was arrested for possession of crack cocaine in September 2009. She had been investigated for drug smuggling into the prison after a tip from an inmate (Colarossi, 2009).

Probably the most common issue for treatment and medical personnel is not providing the services that inmates are legally entitled to. As discussed in the last chapter, medical personnel sometimes adopt the "penal harm" philosophy of corrections and deprive inmates of services because of a belief that they don't deserve treatment. It is very difficult to maintain a helping profession orientation in a correctional environment. Inmates are often unpleasant individuals and sometimes violent as well. Similar to law enforcement's attitude toward certain segments of society, treatment personnel in corrections sometimes develop an attitude that all inmates are liars, crooks, and addicts and don't deserve even basic services. The trouble with this line of reasoning, besides the fact that it is contrary to professional duties, is that once some are perceived as outside the bounds of professional duties, it is easier to ignore duties and respect for all.

Community Corrections

While most news items describe misconduct in prisons, there are also examples of ethical misconduct and criminal acts by community corrections professionals. Peter Maas's (1983) book *Marie* details a scheme in Tennessee that involved selling paroles to convicts. In the early 1990s, ex-parole board members in Texas were found to have sold their services as "parole consultants" to inmates and inmates' families in order to help them obtain a favorable release decision (Ward, 2006).

More recently, a *Denver Post* review of parole records discovered "fundamental errors" in 60 percent of the cases. The review of 2,000 cases showed that parole officers left parolees on their caseload even after repeated failures to appear. In one case a parolee had missed therapy sessions or failed drug tests 49 times and was arrested twice and the parole officer had not filed a violation report. This offender ended up sexually assaulting a six-year-old and was sent back to prison. In another case, an offender tested positive for drugs 12 times and the parole officer did nothing, not even a home visit of the parolee as required for over a year. In another case, despite a string of well-publicized robberies, one parolee's supervision report included nothing about the arrests. Auditors concluded that parole officers did not respond appropriately to violations or conduct required visits in about a third of the cases. Overall 60 percent of all cases had some fundamental error in supervision. The head of the parole division was fired after a parolee murdered Tom Clements, the head of corrections in March of 2013 (Osher and Olinger, 2013).

In 2013 four Texas parole officers were arrested after a year-long investigation into parole officers taking bribes to ignore drug trafficking and other illegal activity by parolees. Federal indictments allege that the four arrested parole officers took bribes averaging $1,000, although one payoff was $3,000. Federal authorities said the four officers worked at two Houston parole offices, where allegations of bribery and exchanges of sexual favors had been the target of investigation for some time. The inspector general of the Texas Department of Corrections, the FBI, the Houston Police, and the Texas Rangers were involved in the investigation, which started when an inmate reported to a state legislator's office that he or she had been "shaken down" for money and sex (Ward, 2013).

Also in Texas, parole decision making is criticized for being secretive and arbitrary. Critics argue that the parole board operates in secrecy and makes parole decisions too quickly, on average of one every seven minutes. There are also troubling reports that the case summaries used for such decisions are often wrong, with some crimes inaccurately attributed to the wrong inmate or, in other cases, not enough detail is provided to indicate the true seriousness of the crime. Inmates and their lawyers do not have access to these case summaries, so they cannot correct any errors. Inmates have, at present, no legal right to parole or due-process rights in the parole release decision, but some argue that they should. Until then, it is an issue of professionalism and ethics as to how parole board members make release decisions (Ward, 2009). Recently a parole commissioner has been indicted for falsifying official records. Allegedly she filed paperwork that said inmates had refused to meet with her when she was at the prison doing parole release hearings, but witnesses reported that despite a number of inmates waiting for their hearings, it was she who left the prison abruptly without seeing them (Rogers, 2014).

In other states, there have been scandals regarding probation departments. In Massachusetts, probation officials have been accused of giving jobs to relatives and friends of state legislators. Also, a legislator was accused of exerting pressure on the agency to promote an officer who gave campaign contributions to the legislator, and that same probation officer wrote a letter of recommendation on probation office stationery for a convicted racketeer (Levenson, 2010).

The head of Cook County (Chicago) probation was removed after a newspaper investigation series that exposed the fact that the office had lost track of hundreds of offenders and overlooked new crimes. The chief judge, who has authority over probation, removed the acting head who had held the position since 2005 along with another responsibility of heading the social services department. He had previously complained that meeting supervision goals was difficult with 25 percent reduced staffing and antiquated technology. The news investigation showed that probation officers often did not do criminal records checks but took offenders' word that they hadn't been arrested. Violation reports were not written when offenders violated the terms of their probation, including not showing up for appointments (Dizikes and Lighty, 2014a).

Another news article described the practice of probation officers working with police officers to conduct illegal searches of probationers' homes. The chief judge hired a law firm to investigate the practice of probation officers bringing FBI agents into probationers' homes. The searches have been defended by some as legal even if there were no warrants (because probation officers have greater powers of search) and they have uncovered contraband. Defense attorneys argue the partnerships are illegal because the law enforcement agents do them as an alternative to getting a warrant. Some offenders allege that contraband was planted and they were coerced to become informants for the FBI and law enforcement (Dizikes and Lighty, 2014b).

A Dallas County audit revealed that officers mishandled 70 percent of cases, not following departmental procedures when handling technical violations. Similar to

ETHICAL ISSUE

Should Probation Officers Partner with Law Enforcement to Search Probationers' Homes?

Law

In *Griffin v. Wisconsin* (483 U.S. 868, 1987) the Supreme Court upheld warrantless searches of probationers' homes under a special needs analysis. Specifically, the Court held that probationers were under a restricted form of liberty and that probation officers had special duties of supervision that justified the intrusion of privacy. Most state corrections probation orders moot the issue anyway by requiring, as a condition of probation, that the offender allow probation officers into their home at any hour of the day or night. Some states may give probationers (or parolees) more comprehensive rights, such as requiring a probation officer to have reasonable suspicion, but there is no Fourth Amendment right recognized that a probation officer must have a warrant, even if accompanied by a law enforcement officer. Generally, bringing law enforcement officers is seen as reasonable because of safety concerns for the probation officer who may or may not, depending on the state, carry a weapon.

Policy

The policies of offices may require home visits and searches periodically in order to supervise offenders on caseloads. Probation officers may be asked to perform searches by law enforcement specifically because of suspicions that do not give rise to probable cause, and to do a search based solely on a request from law enforcement to avoid the need for a warrant may violate policy.

Ethics

As with all ethical issues, we begin by examining the issue in light of law, policy, and then ethics. If there is no law that prohibits the practice, and the policy of the agency allows it, then we look at the inherent "right or wrongness" of the action. Searches are an invasion of privacy of the offender but also the offender's family members. If he or she lives with a relative or friend, those individuals have less Fourth Amendment protections than other citizens merely because of their association with an offender. On the other hand, searches by probation officers may uncover contraband, including weapons, so one might imagine that they may prevent serious violent crimes. As we have discussed many times previously in this text, utilitarianism would weigh the costs and benefits of the practice. In this case, it seems as if the benefit of probation (over prison) for the offender outweighs the invasion of privacy. The disutility for others requires, however, that the searches are done with some form of protections, for example, only with reasonable suspicion, only with supervisor approval, only with the minimal amount of disruption (e.g., the search doesn't extend to rooms lived in exclusively by those other than the offender). While partnering with law enforcement might be perceived as skirting the Fourth Amendment requirements of a warrant, probationers are on a restricted liberty status. They have different legal protections than others in the community and, thus, just as prisoners in a prison cannot expect warrants before searches of their cell, neither can probationers expect the same degree of liberty as those who have not been convicted of crimes.

If such searches are done for other, ulterior motives, however, then their ethical justification is more suspect. If law enforcement officers use probation officers to coerce probationers to be informants, that would be using both parties and is a violation of the categorical imperative (do not treat others as a means . . .). The duty of a probation officer is to supervise and file violation reports when necessary, but it is not to help create informants for the FBI or local law enforcement. That would be using the powers invested in the role in a way that exceeds and is contrary to the duties of the role.

the Colorado audit, probation officers did not file violation reports when offenders had positive drug tests or did not pay their fees. Staff members from the probation department argue that strict policies regarding violations apply only to certain categories of offenders and that technical violations must be responded to using discretion and common sense, typically with additional conditions, not violation and revocation. The audit was requested by a judge who had not been informed of violations, such as repeated DWIs. The judge stated that if she couldn't trust that probation officers were enforcing conditions, she would disband the special DWI court. The auditors' recommendations included the following:

- Add pertinent e-mails about cases into the probationer's main file.
- Document all appearances by a probationer before a judge.
- Better inform the judges about the policies for sanctioning probationers with technical violations.
- Develop standard auditing forms and follow up with another audit when problems are found.
- Eliminate a policy that allows probation officers to work from home.
- Update probation department manual.
- Ensure probation officers' ongoing policy training is more timely (Emily, 2014).

The *New York Times* investigation of New Jersey halfway houses, described more fully in Chapter 12, detailed numerous instances of staff misconduct, including drinking on duty, notifying residents of "surprise" drug tests or forging test results completely, dealing drugs to residents, engaging in sexual relationships with residents, reading self-help books to inattentive residents instead of conducting actual group therapy, and making up case progress reports or cutting and pasting the same report in numerous case files (in one case, 30 case files had exactly the same progress report entered with just the name changed) (Dolnick, 2012b).

The unfortunate reality is that a few people can taint the entire agency or program and, even though community correctional alternatives are sorely needed, programs will be eliminated if perceived as allowing violence, drug use, or other forms of misconduct to occur. Staff members cannot be held entirely responsible for not providing good programming when they are underqualified with inadequate training, and other misconduct may be due to being overworked and stressed. Other forms of misconduct, however, such as selling drugs to residents or sexually assaulting them, are not excusable no matter how understaffed or undertrained staff members are. CEOs and administrators of private and public community correction facilities have ethical obligations to not accept more residents than the facility can safely accommodate and to maintain proper staffing levels and programming opportunities. To do less is to ignore one's ethical obligations, not to mention contractual obligations.

Explanations for Misconduct

The explanations for correctional misconduct can be described in similar ways to those in the law enforcement chapters, where they were divided into individual explanations, organizational explanations, and societal explanations.

Individual Explanations

Correctional managers attribute misconduct to low pay and poor screening during hiring (Mesloh, Wolf, and Henych, 2003). Law enforcement has made great strides in developing tools to help hire the most qualified individuals; however, corrections is decades behind in the research into and use of assessment tools. It may be that corrections will never catch up because the low pay and low status attached to the job discourage many from applying. Only in times of high unemployment do correctional agencies have no trouble finding qualified applicants. More often, they struggle to fill positions. It is no doubt the case that utilizing personality tests, more detailed background checks, and a stronger interview process would catch some individuals who go on to commit misconduct because of individual traits that make them unsuitable for the job. There is also some indication, as mentioned earlier, that some COs seek the position in a long-term plan to smuggle drugs, and one assumes that a more stringent background investigation would expose these individuals.

Another individual explanation of misconduct is PTSD. Similar to law enforcement, there is a growing recognition that some misconduct of correctional officers may be due to chronic or traumatic stress. As described earlier, correctional officers are often the victims of serious assaults by inmates; they have also been spat on and sometimes subjected to horrible working conditions. It is important to remember that when there is no air conditioning, correctional officers are also spending their day in buildings that top 100 degrees. When toilets back up, correctional officers also must put up with the stench. When inmates are screaming for hours at a time because of mental illness or just because they feel like it, correctional officers have to listen. When an inmate stabs their cellmate in the eyeball with a pencil, or disembowels a rival, or brutally rapes a snitch, correctional officers are the first on the scene. They also see their peers assaulted and suffer injuries themselves. There is virtually no research on the issue, but it is not hard to imagine that exposure to the incidents that occur in prison may create PTSD symptoms of flashbacks, hypervigilance, insomnia, alcohol or drug abuse, depression and anger issues. It is reported that the suicide rate for correctional officers is twice as high as police officers or the general public. It is possible that some of the brutality by correctional officers is due, not to sadistic people being attracted to the job, but the job changing individuals and creating symptomatology that includes brutal behavior toward inmates. As in law enforcement, admitting the need for help goes against the macho culture, and for correctional officers, there is even less awareness of the problem than in law enforcement (Lisitsina, 2015).

As in law enforcement, a few correctional professionals will be crooks first and officers second; they use the job to pursue their deviant interests. Many others, however, probably slide into corruption because of a lack of organizational support for ethical behavior. Also as in law enforcement, officers who are stressed and burned out may be the most vulnerable to ethical relativism and bad decisions. If the organization does not support and nurture ethical workers, there will inevitably be those who slide down the slippery slope.

A prison is an interesting place in that individuals work together over long periods of time, and often they live in small towns where acquaintances and family members also work at the prison. Male and female officers work together long hours and in close proximity; sometimes they engage in sexual relationships; sometimes they marry; sometimes they divorce; sometimes they have affairs with other staff members (or even inmates) while they are married. In some prison towns, everyone seems to be related to or have some type of relationship with a prison employee. While people's personal lives are their own, sometimes the personal lives of correctional officers, like police officers, influence their professional ethics. For instance, if a disciplinary sergeant is married to a CO who has written a ticket on an inmate, can that sergeant truly be objective when determining punishment? What happens when an inmate accuses an officer of sexual harassment and the grievance officer is the wife of the accused officer? Sometimes male and female COs allow a sexually charged atmosphere to develop where sexual joking and innuendos are rampant, and the atmosphere encourages officers to engage in the same type of behavior with inmates—obviously an inappropriate

ETHICAL DILEMMA

You are a correctional sergeant who is assigned as disciplinary sergeant. You process disciplinary "tickets" written by COs against inmates and determine the punishment. If the inmate appeals your decision, it goes to a lieutenant, but the vast number of cases are dealt with at your level. The disciplinary case before you is one where an inmate has been accused of having contraband in his cell, in this case a knife. This is a very serious charge and the punishment should be loss of good time and segregation. The inmate swears that the knife isn't his and it has been planted by other inmates to get him in trouble. He is a "jailhouse lawyer" who files a steady stream of lawsuits against officers and the state. You also consider the officer involved, who has stated in front of other officers that the inmate deserves to get taught a lesson and that he should be sent "down" (to segregation). The other wrinkle is this officer is your brother. You have a gut feeling that the inmate is telling the truth, but the only evidence is that the knife was found in his cell—pretty strong evidence that it was his.

Law

The Supreme Court has held that inmates must have some form of due process before a neutral hearing body before having good time taken away. The disciplinary process in place today typically utilizes correctional sergeants or lieutenants and this has been accepted as neutral even though the hearing officer may have ties to the officers who write the tickets. There is a law that makes having a knife in prison a felony, which may subject the inmate to additional charges if you find him guilty. There is also a law against correctional officers or anyone else from lying on the official documents involved in filing a disciplinary charge; however, it is extremely rare, if ever, that someone is prosecuted, even if they are found to be lying.

Policy

The formal policies of a prison are that the inmates should be given due process before being punished. The informal policies of some prisons are that the disciplinary proceedings are merely pro forma exercises in order to meet court requirements, and inmates' appearances in front of these disciplinary boards are always exercises in futility.

Ethics

In this case, the disciplinary sergeant has the duty to evaluate the facts, make a decision about guilt, and assess punishment. The weight to assign to the credibility of the inmate, the officer, and/or other inmates is discretionary. The sergeant in this case would certainly be well within the norm if he found the inmate guilty and took away good time. Under ethical formalism, however, it would be his or her ethical duty to investigate if there was any doubt, even if it meant going against one's brother. How likely this is to occur is another matter. Some disciplinary officers split the difference by finding guilt but assessing a lesser punishment. This may be personally more palatable, but doesn't meet the necessity of doing one's duty as a fact finder. Arguably it also doesn't stop the process of using the disciplinary system to informally punish certain inmates who engage in legal, but unwanted, activity by staff members. Utilitarianism would evaluate the greater good. Does it result in a greater good to ensure that the jailhouse lawyer who takes up state resources gets punished, regardless of whether he had a knife, or is the greater good to protect the integrity of the disciplinary process? Egoism would also be concerned with how the decision would affect the relationship with one's brother. Most ethical systems would support investigating to see if there were any credible witnesses to the charge of possessing contraband.

and unprofessional interaction. Correctional officers practically live with the inmates. If they pull double shifts, they may spend up to 16 or even 20 hours at a time with inmates. This familiarity with inmates sometimes tempts officers to engage in unethical behaviors.

The discretion and authority inherent in the role of correctional, probation, or parole officer takes maturity to handle as well as a strong internal ethical code. Other individual characteristics associated with misconduct have not been identified by research.

Organizational Explanations

When the abuse in Iraq's Abu Ghraib prison was exposed, many made comparisons between the behaviors of military prison correctional officers and those of correctional officers in U.S. prisons. The comparisons were hard to ignore because several of the worst abusers were correctional officers in civilian life, and the person who helped set up the Abu Ghraib prison was Lane McCotter, an ex-head of the Texas, New Mexico, and Utah prison systems (Ward, 2004). Allegations of misconduct in prisons and jails in the United States that were similar to what took place in Abu Ghraib include (Butterfield, 2004):

- Male inmates being forced to wear pink underwear as punishment (Arizona)
- Inmates being stripped as punishment (Pennsylvania)
- Inmates being made to wear black hoods (Virginia)
- Using dogs to attack inmates (Texas)

It cannot be denied that the very environment of an incarceration facility sometimes brings out the worst in people. Many people have described the culture of prison as a "jungle" where inmates and officers are affected by pervasive hopelessness and negativity. While, typically, very few officers engage in serious abuse, the culture of the institution protects them because officers are always right and inmates are always wrong.

The Zimbardo experiment of the 1970s was one of the experiments that spurred the creation of human-subjects review boards in colleges and universities. In this experiment, college men were arbitrarily assigned to be correctional officers or inmates, and a mock prison was set up in the basement of a building on the grounds of Stanford University. The changes in both groups were so profound that the experiment was canceled after six days. Zimbardo (1982) noted that about one-third of the correctional officers became brutal and authoritarian, and prisoners became manipulative and exhibited signs of emotional distress and mental breakdown. If college men who knew the experiment was artificial succumbed to the temptation to inflict their will on the powerless, the inescapable conclusion is that the environment itself causes people to act in ways that they would not otherwise.

The informal culture of a prison is created by administrators and staff. If administrators turn a blind eye to misconduct and excessive force, then COs will feel free to engage in such activity, and ethical officers will quit or succumb to temptation. If the administration of an institution pays only lip service to rehabilitation for inmates, then it should be no surprise when officers became lethargic and negative. Worse, if leaders are unethical, then it is unlikely that ethics will flourish in the organization. In many of the case studies and news stories presented in these chapters, top leaders, like Andy Collins, Christopher Epps, and James Crosby, exhibited the worst models of leadership. They were exposed for their bribery and economic corruption, but it isn't hard to imagine that they exhibited poor ethics in other ways as well. In both the Los Angeles jail scandal and the Florida scandal, top administrators seemed to focus on suppressing investigations of wrongdoing and thwart employee discipline rather than provide clear direction for those employees who tried to do their job ethically.

Unions have been seen by researchers as a force resistant to rehabilitation, concerned only with individual benefits for members rather than the mission or goal of corrections. Unions provide legal assistance to officers accused of wrongdoing and support officers who, many would argue, have no business working in corrections. This is similar to police unions that defend police officers who are guilty of using excessive force. Union representatives would argue that they only ensure that the accused receive their rightful due process after being accused, and it is certainly true that accused employees deserve due process just like everyone else. However, what has happened in some instances is that when some correctional officers come forward to testify against the accused, they are vilified and treated as enemies of the union. This one-sided position that officers can do no wrong—except for the wrong of speaking out against other officers—is problematic and a disservice to those officers who try to do the right thing.

Stohr et al. (2000) developed a survey instrument to measure the ethics of correctional workers. In their study, they could find few significant individual correlates that predicted ethical beliefs or behavior, but they did find that the type of institution affected officers' attitudes. Mesloh, Wolf, and Henych (2003) found that the existence of a deviant subculture among correctional officers affected misconduct.

The Commission on Safety and Abuse in America's Prisons (2006) also identified a "culture of violence" in American prisons. The scandal at Abu Ghraib led to this national commission tasked to examine U.S. prison conditions, chaired by a former U.S. attorney general and a chief judge of the Third Circuit. The commission spent several years holding hearings and obtained testimony from researchers, experts, prison staff members, and family members concerning the state of prisons in this country. (The entire report or an executive summary can be accessed by going to www.vera.org/project/commission-safety-and-abuse-americas-prisons.) The commission concluded that violence in prisons was partially caused by inactive and unproductive inmates and an overuse of force by officers. They also found that medical services were inadequate, and the use of high-tech segregation (supermax prisons) was counterproductive and needed to be reduced. Correctional administrators are often the most insightful observers of what occurs when the culture of a prison supports abusive behaviors, as the quote in the Quote and Query box illustrates.

The commission went on to conclude that the culture in prison was also due to underqualified and underpaid staff and that in order to reduce violence, steps needed to be taken to reduce crowding; promote productive programming; improve classification; reduce the use of pepper spray, Tasers, and other uses of force; and support community and family bonds of inmates. Their major finding was that a culture of violence needed to be replaced with a culture of mutual respect. This was necessary not only because it would make the prison a better place to live for inmates—it would also improve the working conditions of correctional staff members. As stated by a correctional official giving testimony, "When you go to work in a place that has a tendency to be condescending, negative, vulgar, that can show up in your life" (Commission. . ., 2006: 67).

In all cases of abuse in prison, the reasons seem to be a failure of leadership and lack of discipline, training, and supervision (Ward, 2004). When prison leaders ignore violations on the part of staff and do not clearly convey that the mission is to run a safe and secure prison without the corrupting presence of extralegal force, the result is more likely to be a spiral of violence where hatred grows on each side.

Another useful way to understand prison corruption by staff members is to consider the procedural justice research. Tyler's (2006) original work on the importance of believing in the legitimacy of the law has been applied to various elements of the criminal justice system, including corrections. As discussed in prior chapters, the concept of **procedural justice** (Tyler, 2006, 2010) includes the idea that the perception of legitimacy (of legal authorities) comes about when legal authorities practice fairness, participation (letting people speak), neutrality (governing by rules neutrally and consistently), treat everyone with dignity and respect, and illustrate trustworthiness (authorities are sincerely concerned with well-being) (Jackson, Tyler, Bradford, Taylor, and Shiner, 2010; Rottman, 2007). Research has shown that if legal authorities are seen as legitimate, this leads to people following the law, even without monitoring, and encourages rule following.

Several studies have explored procedural justice principles in corrections, and findings indicate that inmates' views of procedural justice lead to feelings of legitimacy of correctional authorities, while feelings of injustice seem to affect recidivism (Jackson et al., 2010; Rottman, 2007). In another study, prisoners who believed in a "just world" expressed less anger, reported greater well-being, and were less likely to have problem behaviors even after controlling for criminal and personal backgrounds (Dalbert and Filke, 2007).

What is just as important is that findings indicate that workers who have higher levels of belief in the procedural justice of their agency and believe they are being treated fairly are probably more likely to behave ethically (Pollock et al., 2012; Lambert, 2003; Lambert, Hogan and Allen, 2006; Lambert, Hogan, and Griffin, 2007). Lambert (2003) found that procedural justice perceptions had a significant positive effect on organizational commitment. Lambert, Hogan, and Allen (2006) found that both "outcome" and procedural justice were related to job stress, but procedural justice was the strongest predictor (in a negative direction) for job stress. Lambert, Hogan, and Griffin (2007), in another study, found that both outcome and procedural justice had negative relationships with job stress and organizational commitment. However, only procedural justice influenced job satisfaction (Lambert, Hogan, and Griffin, 2007). The previously mentioned studies do not prove that officers who perceive procedural justice occurs are more likely to treat inmates ethically; however, the "trickle down" theory of ethical management is that officers will treat inmates the way they perceive they are being treated by management—with fairness, compassion, and respect, or with less than fairness, compassion, and respect. It becomes easier to justify unethical actions if one feels victimized. Obviously, if employees are expected to be responsible, loyal, and treat each other and inmates with respect, administrators should practice these same behaviors (Houston, 1999; Souryal, 1999a; Wright, 2001). Furthermore, staff members who are coerced by management to do unethical or illegal actions are more likely to behave in unethical and illegal ways by their own initiative.

QUOTE & QUERY

Security and control—given necessities in a prison environment—only become a reality when dignity and respect are inherent in the process.

Source: A prison warden, cited in Commission on Safety and Abuse in America's Prisons, 2006: 15.

 Why is it so hard to run a prison where dignity and respect toward inmates exist?

procedural justice   The idea that the perception of legitimacy of legal authorities comes about when legal authorities practice fairness, participation, neutrality, respect, and illustrate trustworthiness.

Societal Explanations

As mentioned earlier, the community helps to create the correctional environment by their tacit or direct endorsement of the informal subcultural norm that inmates deserve less due process and legal protection than the rest of us. When juries acquit correctional officers solely because the victim was an inmate, this endorsement reinforces unethical subcultural norms. When criminal correctional officers are not prosecuted and simply fired, this provides a message that there are few costs involved in such misconduct. If the state doesn't care enough about corrections to allocate enough funding to provide decent programming, training, or hiring of qualified staff, it sends a message that the prison (or community correctional program) houses throw away people who fall outside legal protection. Once a group is removed from the envelope of protection of civil society, then there are no limits to the abuses that might be visited upon them, and the attitude that such conduct lies outside the bounds of law inevitably, it seems, transcends to abuses against others. If groups of correctional officers are allowed to inflict physical beatings on prisoners, often these officers also threaten physical retaliation against other correctional officers for perceived disloyalty. If no one stops widespread sexual innuendos directed to and exploitation of female inmates, then female correctional officers sometimes find themselves the victims of the same type of behavior. If inmate accounts and property are considered fair game to steal from, then it becomes more likely that state monies are also embezzled. The point is that there can be no dividing line between those whom one should treat ethically and those who do not "deserve" ethical treatment. One's behavior is either ethical or not, legal or not without regard to the target of it. If society wants an ethical correctional system, then they have to demand it and expect that even murderers will be treated according to the law.

Responses to Corruption

In Chapter 7, management efforts to respond to law enforcement misconduct and corruption were described. Surprisingly, parallel sources on correctional management efforts to respond to misconduct are fairly sparse. With some exceptions, correctional management has not developed in the way that law enforcement management has; there are fewer texts on correctional management, and those that can be found rarely mention ethics for supervisors and administrators (Wright, 2001).

Correctional managers can and should generate a strong anti-corruption policy (obviously, managers should not be engaging in corrupt practices themselves). Such a policy would include (McCarthy, 1991):

- Proactive measures such as mechanisms to investigate and detect wrongdoing
- Reduced opportunities for corruption
- Screening of employees using state-of-the-art psychological tools
- Improved working conditions
- Providing good role models in the form of supervisors and administrators who follow the appropriate code of ethics

The Commission on Safety and Abuse in American Prisons (2006) developed a comprehensive list of recommendations to reduce the "culture of violence," including the following:

- Improve staffing levels, hiring, and training
- Provide independent oversight for complaints and investigations of misconduct
- Create a national database of violent incidents and misconduct
- Increase access to the courts by repealing or amending the Prison Litigation Reform Act
- Increase the level of criminal prosecution of wrongdoers (perhaps using federal prosecutions)
- Strengthen professional standards

Souryal (2009: 33) discusses the "civility" of a correctional institution as being influenced by the level of education required for hire, the amount of in-service training officers receive, the policies regarding employees who act in unethical ways, and the presence of a professional association or union that can effectively monitor the agency's practices. He also discusses the importance of integrated thinking (use of reasoning and wisdom) and moral agility (distinguishing between moral choices). To improve the ethical climate of an agency, he advocates upgrading the quality of personnel, establishing quality-based supervisory techniques, strengthening fiscal controls, and emphasizing true ethical training.

Wright (2001) offers seven principles as a guide for how administrators and supervisors should treat employees:

- Safety
- Fair treatment
- Due process
- Freedom of expression
- Privacy
- Participation in decision making
- Information

In regard to fair treatment, not penalizing staff members who do corrupt acts is not treating honest officers fairly. As to privacy, staff members have a right to a private life, but not when the use of drugs, alcohol, or inappropriate sexual partners interferes with their job performance.

Burrell (2000) directs attention to probation and proposes that in order to prevent stress and burnout, probation (and parole) organizations should provide clear direction, manage proactively, establish priorities if there are high workloads, ensure stability and constancy, be consistent in expectations, manage with fairness, enforce accountability, delegate authority, provide proper resources, maintain communication, and allow participative decision making.

Barrier and colleagues (1999) discussed an ethics training program with correctional officers in which part of the training involved having the officers identify important elements of an ethics code. Many of the elements the officers described had to do with the practices of management rather than officers:

- Treating all staff fairly and impartially
- Promoting based on true merit
- Showing no prejudice
- Leading by example
- Developing a clear mission statement
- Creating a positive code of ethics (a list of dos, rather than don'ts)
- Creating a culture that promotes performance, not seniority
- Soliciting staff input on new policies
- Being respectful
- Getting the word out that upper management cares about ethics

As discussed earlier, correctional administrators in the 1970s and 1980s had to deal with court decisions that were decided in favor of prisoners. In response, correctional administrators sometimes barely complied with the letter of a court ruling, much less the spirit of the ruling. The career path of an administrator, with its investment of time and energy and the mandate to be a "company man," often creates an immersion in bureaucratic thinking to the point that an individual loses sight of ethical issues. For instance, protecting the department or the director from scandal or litigation becomes more important than analyzing the behavior that created the potential for scandal in the first place. If decision making becomes influenced solely by short-term gains or by avoiding scandal, decisions may be unsupported by any ethical system.

Administrators are responsible for what happens in their facility, and training, supervision, and careful attention to assignments can avoid many problems. It should go without saying that administrators and managers should take pains to avoid illegal or unethical behavior themselves. Administrators should act as role models and never engage in behavior that may be misconstrued as sexual coercion or be perceived by their employees as offensive. Supervisors have a higher duty than coworkers to set a tone for an office free from sexual innuendo that may lead to a description of the workplace as a hostile work environment. Supervisors have an ethical and legal duty to stop sexual humor, inappropriate touching, disparaging and unprofessional remarks about inmates, racial jokes, and inappropriate behavior before there is a complaint. Top administrators often have an outward orientation because their role is to communicate with legislators, the central office, and the community; however, a good administrator does not ignore his or her own backyard. Management by walking around (MBWA) and having a good sense of what is happening in the institution have always been the marks of a good administrator and are also the best defense against having the institution ending up on the front page of the newspaper.

In community corrections, there seems to be the same management tendency to hide or ignore wrongdoing on the part of individual officers. This may be a misguided utilitarianism in managers who are attempting to protect the organization from public scandal, or it may be simply self-interested egoism from managers who fear that the blame will be directed at them. For whatever reason, there seems to be a tendency to ignore officers who are obviously unable or unwilling to do the job. If this is true, it's not surprising that some probation and parole officers seem to have little moral authority over the clients they supervise.

Another way to respond to misconduct and corruption in corrections is to shift the orientation away from punishment and retribution. The high incarceration rate in the United States has led to the prison-industrial complex, which has provided jobs and profits to legions of companies and people. The penal harm movement discussed in Chapter 11 has generated a cultural message that inmates and offenders are worthless, deserving of whatever harm befalls them in the corrections systems. Unfortunately, some offenders are violent and manipulative and so all get treated as if they were. Violence in prison is often a spiral, where correctional officers (as in ADX in Florence, Colorado; the California prison where the Green Wall correctional officers operated; and the L.A. jail) decide to inflict extralegal punishment after inmates have assaulted correctional officers. The reaction is understandable but illegal. It is also the case that once such illegal violence begins, it has a tendency to spread to inmates who don't "deserve" it in any estimation of fault and, more tellingly, such violence has a way of spreading even to other correctional officers, who are threatened or sometimes even assaulted when they are perceived as rats or traitors. At that point, there truly is no difference between those who wear the correctional officer uniform and those who wear the prisoner uniform. Once one is outside the law and knows it, subsequent illegalities to cover up and protect oneself become almost inevitable.

A New Era? Procedural Justice/Restorative Justice

Recall from Chapter 11 that there seems to be a new vision of corrections that is permeating legislatures, advocates, and governmental agencies. There is a growing realization that this country incarcerates too many people and that the prisons are warehouses, not places of reform. If such a shift is strong enough to permeate the culture of corrections, then we may see fundamental changes in the ethics and expectations for correctional officers and other correctional professionals. Once again, it is important to note that the vast majority of professionals perform their jobs ethically and with integrity. What might be the result of a cultural shift is that they will feel more supported in their adherence to ethical standards of behavior.

The principles of procedural justice seem to show the most promise in reforming the prison culture. If correctional officers are managed under the principles of voice, fairness, neutrality, and trustworthiness as described in an earlier section, then they will be more likely to treat prisoners in the same way. This approach can be described as evidence-based in that there are research findings that show supervising people under these principles does achieve behavioral change.

A major shift in the ideology of punishment may be spurred by the economic burden that the penal harm era has generated, but there is also a moral element in that many advocates consider that the pendulum has swung too far toward severe prison terms, especially for drug offenders. There are alternative approaches that are not based on a punishment ideology. The restorative justice movement was mentioned briefly in Chapter 3. It is an approach that seeks to provide reparation rather than retribution (Reichel, 1997; Bazemore and Maloney, 1994).

The historical origins of and analogies to restorative justice can be found throughout recorded history. Early laws demanded victim compensation, and reparation has a much longer history than penal servitude. Many advocates (see Umbreit, 1994;

peacemaking corrections An approach to corrections that depends on care and wholesight, or looking at what needs to be done with both the heart and the head.

Umbreit and Carey, 1995; van Ness and Heetderks Strong, 1997; Perry, 2002) now believe that restorative justice appropriately places the emphasis back onto the victims and can be life-affirming and positive for the offender as well. The key is to find a method of restoration that is meaningful and somehow related to the offense instead of merely punitive labor—such as the infamous rock pile, which is devoid of worth to the victim, the offender, or society. The Quote and Query box is Braithwaite's summary of restorative justice.

Peacemaking corrections also offers an approach of care and of *wholesight,* or looking at what needs to be done with both the heart and the head (Braswell and Gold, 2002). Both restorative justice and peacemaking corrections are consistent with the ethics of care and might be considered "feminine" models of justice because of the emphasis on needs rather than retribution. It is said that a retributive, punitive orientation results in an offender's perception of unfairness (through denial of victim, denial of injury, or a belief that a more serious victimization was visited upon the offender). A different model may reduce those feelings and force the offender to squarely face his or her own responsibility. Arguably, a restorative justice program directs attention to the injuries of the victim and does not involve stigma, banishment, or exclusion for the offender. The offender then would have more difficulty generating rationalizations and excuses for his or her behavior.

Programs under the rubric of restorative justice include sentencing circles, family group counseling, victim–offender mediation, community reparation boards, and victim education programs (Umbreit, Coates, and Vos, 2002). Karp (1998) provides an interesting perspective on why restorative justice programs have received positive responses. The public may not believe that probation or other forms of alternative sanctions have the same moral condemnation that prison does; therefore, these punishments are seen as cheapening or lessening the moral blame of the offender. However, shaming penalties inherent in such programs as sentencing circles emphasize the individual's responsibility to the victim and society. Such programs instill a strong dose of morality and redemption, and the public seems to respond to that.

Forgiveness, like mercy, is an interesting concept. When a gunman killed five young girls in an Amish schoolhouse in 2006 before killing himself, the nation was appalled and grieved along with the Amish community. It was a truly horrific event, made all the more so by the gentle nature of the religious community, where violence was such a rarity. In a truly unusual and unique turn of events, the parents of the murdered children and the community immediately forgave the murderer and his family. In the Amish religion and tradition, forgiveness is said to be much more important than anger or revenge. This forgiveness was as newsworthy as the killings themselves and gave rise to many discussions about the nature of forgiveness and how it fits into religion and faith (Draybill, 2006).

Dzur and Wertheimer (2002) discuss how restorative justice can further forgiveness, but they ask the question "Is forgiveness a social good?" They argue against the idea that what is good for the individual victim is also good for everyone else. They point out that forgiving offenders may be good for the individual victim but may not be good for the "class of victims" who have yet to be victimized. They argue that utilitarianism might support punishment even if the individual victim forgives the offender because the greater good will accrue to society from deterrence. Of course, there is no empirical approach that could determine (or has yet determined) whether punishment deters more offenders than forgiveness.

Restorative justice programs are looked upon with favor by some victims' rights groups because of the idea of restoration and restitution for victims. However, the approach is oriented to meeting the needs of both victims and offenders, and in some cases it may be that the offender is needier. Would a victim reject such an approach? Should the victim be able to veto this approach and demand traditional punishment? Is it possible for a victim to be too vindictive? Other victims' rights groups tend to be cautious about restorative justice programs in general because of the focus on offenders. The anger that victims feel toward offenders and the system that ignores their needs leaves little room for forgiveness. Most groups advocate harsher punishments, not restorative justice; they discuss "rights" rather than "needs" and thus draw their moral legitimacy from retribution rather than the ethics of care. However, other sources also argue that forgiveness and restorative justice are just as beneficial to the victim as the offender (Morris, 2000).

Restorative justice programs may lead to a greater sense of mission for correctional professionals and, therefore, decrease burnout and misconduct. However, there are ethical issues with such programs. First, because such interventions are seen as benign, they have the potential to create net widening, further enlarging the scope of corrections over the citizenry. There are also questions of due process and whether restorative justice meets the traditional goals of crime prevention (Dzur and Wertheimer, 2002). Another issue is the potential privacy issues of the offender and other members who are involved. One of the strengths of restorative justice interventions is the inclusion of a number of parties, including the offender's family, coworkers, and friends, as well as the victim and the victim's support group. But what if some individuals important to the process choose not to participate? If even schools have trouble getting some parents to involve themselves in their children's progress, it is entirely possible that a juvenile who is otherwise qualified for a program would not be able to participate because of unwillingness of family members. Also, even when the process is seen as a positive intervention, whenever state actors are involved, there is a potential for coercion, and some people react strongly to that idea.

Restorative justice programs would not be appropriate for all offenders; there will always be a need for incarceration facilities for the violent, recidivistic offenders who need to be incapacitated. It does, however, offer an approach that seems to be more positive for offenders and personnel alike. It provides a more optimistic vision and mission and, one assumes, creates better relationships between correctional professionals and offenders. Thus, it might be an approach where there is less burnout, cynicism, and unethical behavior.

The idea of having a pro-social, ethical correctional institution where inmates are not coddled, but neither are they abused, seems to be a difficult goal to achieve. Scandinavian countries have long been known for humane prisons. In one Norwegian prison, residents live in attractive wooden chalets in a square mile of forest and hills. They go horseback riding, to the theatre, and ski on the prison grounds. The administrators describe it as the world's first human-ecological prison where inmates learn to take responsibility for their actions by caring for the environment. They grow their own organic vegetables, compost, and raise chickens, cows, horses, and sheep. The prison is on an island and has no fences or bars. Only five correctional officers remain on the island after 3 p.m. Thus far, the recidivism rate for this prison's releasees is about 20 percent, which is less than half the average in Norway. Even the harshest prison in the country, built for maximum security prisoners, is designed as a small village—trees obscure the perimeter wall, and the cells are similar to college dormitory rooms, with flat-screen televisions and mini fridges. Each cell has a window. The prison has a two-bedroom house on the grounds where prisoners can host family members overnight. The "normalization principle" championed by Norway's leaders proposes that offenders respond best to the message that they are still members of the community and increasing levels of trust bridge their reentry.

Of course, there are very few prisoners in Norway, compared to this country. Norway's rate of incarceration (70 per 100,000) is about a tenth of the rate found in the United States. Experts point out that Norway and other Scandinavian countries enjoy very low crime rates, possibly because they invest much more in social welfare programs. One of the important elements of Norway's prisons is that officers have an elevated status as compared to the United States. They go through one year of theoretical training and then a year of practical training at an academy. They call prisoners by their first names and play sports and eat meals with them. Evidently, some still succumb to the temptation to abuse their power, since one inmate was quoted as saying, "Twenty percent of them shouldn't work with people—or animals. But the other 80 percent think it's their mission in life to help people. I believe most of them" (Adams, 2010: 3).

The horrific massacre by Anders Behring Breivik in July 2011 has challenged the Scandinavian model of corrections. Breivik set off a car bomb in downtown Oslo, killing eight people, and then went to a holiday island where a group of teenagers were at a Labor party camp for young people. He shot and killed 69 people and wounded scores more. In June 2012, his trial was complete and prosecutors asked that he be declared insane, while his defense attorneys argued he was innocent. Norway has a maximum term of 21 years for anyone (although five-year increments can be added if there is a finding of continued danger). The case has brought a strong chorus of complaints from other countries that perhaps Norway's approach to crime and justice is not tough enough. Thus far, there does not seem to be a change in the "normalization" principles of Norwegian corrections. In August of 2012, the mass murderer was declared sane by the court and sentenced to 21 years, the maximum term allowed by Norwegian law.

Other countries also have less punitive approaches to corrections. Leighton (2014) describes a Japanese prison that combines advanced technology and a reform approach that makes the institution more livable for the inmates and staff. Research was used to design programming and the goal is to change criminal behavior patterns humanely without sacrificing the dignity of the individual. Inmates wear electronic chips to speed counts, electronic scanners (like those in airports) are used instead of strip searches, and the facility uses shatterproof glass rather than bars. There is also a focus on public-private partnerships and the community is integrated into the prison with space for community meetings and other avenues of communication.

Sadly, the concepts of individual respect, rehabilitation, and integration with the community were prevalent in American corrections in the 1970s but fell by the wayside during the ramping up of the incarceration binge in the 1980s and the punitive era of the 1990s–2000s. As the saying goes, everything old is new again, and perhaps, that will be true in corrections as well if the principles of respect and rehabilitation are regenerated in the years to come. If so, the shift in mission will affect the duties and expectations of correctional professionals.

Conclusion

In this chapter, we examined various forms of misconduct by correctional professionals. Research has indicated that the very nature of a prison may encourage an abuse of power. It was also noted that much of the misconduct may occur because of the informal subculture and a loss of a sense of mission by professionals, as well as poor management. Responses to ethical misconduct and corruption in corrections lag behind the efforts previously reported in law enforcement. Suggestions include ethics training and improving management. Procedural justice research shows that if authorities practice fairness, neutrality, and the other elements of procedural justice, there is more faith in and compliance with rules. This concept applies to prisoners and correctional officers equally. Restorative justice principles may help to improve the sense of mission and commitment to ethical behavior by correctional workers.

Chapter Review

1. **Describe types of misconduct by correctional officers, including the typology of misconduct by Souryal and McCarthy.**

   McCarthy's categories of misconduct include theft, trafficking, embezzlement, and misuse of authority. Under misuse of authority, he includes the following: gratuities (as bribes for legitimate or illegitimate activities), mistreatment/harassment or extortion, mismanagement, and miscellaneous abuses. Souryal's categories of corruption are arbitrary use of power, oppression and failure to demonstrate compassion/caring, and abusing authority for personal gain.

2. **Describe types of misconduct by community corrections professionals.**

   There are not as many news stories of corruption, but there have been instances of inappropriate influences and errors in parole release decisions, nepotism in awarding jobs in probation departments, and accepting bribes from offenders to get out of community service obligations or drug testing.

3. **Explain the Zimbardo experiment and what it might imply for correctional professionals.**

   The Zimbardo experiment of the 1970s put college men into an artificial prison as correctional officers or inmates. The changes in both groups were so profound that the experiment was canceled after six days. About one-third of the correctional officers became brutal and authoritarian, and prisoners became manipulative and exhibited signs of emotional distress and mental breakdown. It is widely used as evidence that placing people in absolute power over others is a corrupting situation.

4. **Provide explanations for misconduct.**

   Similar individual, organization, and societal explanations for misconduct exist as were described in Chapter 7. Some reasons for misconduct involve hiring those who should not be in corrections. As in law enforcement, officers who are stressed and burned out may be the most vulnerable to ethical relativism and bad decisions. Organizational explanations include a failure of leadership and lack of discipline, training, and supervision. Management practices that do not provide the direction, mission, oversight, and training needed contribute to misconduct. While there are a few correctional officers who would be deviant regardless of the environment, others probably slide into corruption because of a lack of organizational support for ethical behavior. Society is also at fault in that if we allow inmates to be mistreated because they are inmates, then that lawlessness has a tendency to spread.

5. **Present some suggestions to decrease misconduct by correctional professionals.**

McCarthy's suggestions are largely directed to management practices, including proactive measures such as mechanisms to investigate and detect wrongdoing, reduced opportunities for corruption, screening of employees using state-of-the-art psychological tools, improved working conditions, and providing good role models in the form of supervisors and administrators. Ethics training is also suggested. Finally, restorative justice is offered as a different approach to respond to criminal offenders that is more positive and less conducive to the creation of a subculture that supports mistreatment.

Study Questions

1. Describe Bomse's categories of misconduct.
2. Describe some of the reported instances of misconduct and corruption in prisons.
3. Describe some of the reported instances of misconduct in probation or parole.
4. What management practices were identified as contributing to an ethical workplace?
5. What are the principles of restorative justice? Contrast these with traditional models of justice.

Writing/Discussion Exercises

1. Write an essay on (or discuss) how you would implement an anti-corruption strategy in a prison known for brutality and other forms of corruption.
2. Write an essay on (or discuss) forgiveness. Would you want to meet with the murderer of a loved one? What would you want to ask him or her? Would you be able to forgive?
3. Write an essay on (or discuss) restorative justice. Find examples in your state. Do you agree or disagree with the philosophy of restorative justice? Why?

Key Terms

malfeasance	nonfeasance	procedural justice
misfeasance	peacemaking corrections	

ETHICAL DILEMMAS

Situation 1

You are a probation officer and have a specialized sex-offender caseload. The judge disagrees with a recommendation for a prison sentence and places an offender on probation. This man was convicted of molesting his 4-year-old niece. One of the conditions of his probation is that he notify you whenever he is around children. He becomes engaged to and moves in with a woman who has three children under the age of 12. You believe that the man is not repentant and that there is a good chance he will molest these children. Although the woman knows his criminal history, she does not seem to care and even allows him to babysit the young girls. The judge has indicated that he will not entertain new conditions or a revocation unless there is evidence of a crime, but you understand from the offender's counselor that the offender continues to be sexually aroused by children. What can you do? What should you do?

Situation 2

You are a probation officer with a DWI probationer who has not been reporting for any of the court-sanctioned programs, and a motion to revoke (MTR) was supposed to be filed. However, a high-ranking administrator in your office tells you not to file the MTR or take any other negative actions because the probationer is a personal friend and, anyway, he isn't a "serious criminal." What would you do?

Situation 3

You are the director of a restorative justice program in your community. It is set up for juvenile offenders and involves circle sentencing, in which the offender meets with family members, school officials, and the victim and the victim's relatives and friends. The circle comes up with what should be done, and often there is no punishment per se. Rather, the juvenile is connected with programs that can help him or her get back in school, get a job, or receive vocational training. In the case you are reviewing, you suspect that there are real questions as to whether the juvenile actually committed the burglary he is accused of. There is no evidence to link the juvenile with the crime, and he and his court-appointed attorney have claimed innocence. They then changed their plea and agreed to the restorative justice program, perhaps because if it is completed successfully, the juvenile will have no criminal record. Should you care whether the juvenile is innocent or not, given that the program is restorative, not punitive?

Situation 4

You are a prison warden, and a new CO comes to you and says she has been sexually harassed by the captain. You know that the captain has been with the prison for 20 years and has not had any negative reports in his record. On the one hand, you like him and think he is an excellent captain. On the other hand, this CO seems earnest and believable and is quite upset, so you believe something must have happened. What is the ethical course of action? What is the legal course of action?

Situation 5

You are a prison counselor in a co-ed prison and have some real concerns about your coworker's treatment of offenders. You hear him screaming obscenities at them in his office, and one time you saw him pat a female prisoner on the rear end and say, "Be sweet to me and I'll get you out of here." No one else seems to notice that anything is wrong. Could you have misinterpreted the exchange with the prisoner? Might it have been simply bad taste rather than sexual harassment? Should you do anything?

14

Making Ethical Choices

September 11, 2001.

Chapter Objectives

1. Identify the basic themes of the book.

2. Describe the basic elements of the "just war" debate and the "just means" discussion.

3. Describe the responses to 9/11.

4. Explain the human rights model of policing.

5. Present a method to resolve ethical dilemmas.

In this book, we have explored ethical issues in each of the subsystems of the criminal justice system. We have discovered certain themes that run through each of the subsystems:

- The presence of authority, power, force, and discretion
- Informal subcultures contrary to formal codes of ethics
- The importance of ethical leadership
- Tension between deontological ethical systems and teleological or "means–end" ethical analysis

In this final chapter, we will reiterate some of these themes and conclude with some last thoughts regarding how to behave in an ethical manner as a justice professional. We will review the basic themes of the book and the path to ethical decision making within a discussion of one of the most important ethical issues of our time—the response to terrorism.

Just Wars and Just Means

On September 11, 2001, the United States was changed forever. The terrorist attack on the World Trade Center was the single most devastating terrorist attack in this country and, indeed, the world, with almost 3,000 deaths and the complete destruction of two buildings that stood as icons of Western capitalism. Although we had experienced earlier incidents—the 1993 bombing of the World Trade Center, the Oklahoma City bombing in 1995, and numerous attacks on U.S. targets worldwide—nothing prepared the country for the severity of the attack. The event traumatized a city, affected the American psyche, led to U.S. military engagement on foreign soil in two countries, and spurred the dramatic restructuring of federal agencies with the introduction of the Department of Homeland Security. We have also seen pervasive changes in law enforcement at both the federal and the local levels, and the country is still mired in controversy over the responses taken in the "war on terror." In addition to governmental responses that took place immediately after 9/11, Edward Snowden's June 2013 exposure of NSA's domestic surveillance activities showed that the war on terror affected us in ways seen and unseen.

The controversy over what means are acceptable responses to terrorism is related to criminal justice ethics because the war on terror not only involves military and federal agencies; every law enforcement and justice agency in the land may have occasion to be involved. Targets of terrorist activity include not only buildings and bridges in big cities, but also dams, power plants, schools, government buildings, and farms in the most remote areas. The attack spurred the endorsement of intelligence-led policing and there are now over 72 "fusion centers" that gather information from law enforcement agencies and act as a resource for them. Federal courts have dealt with numerous cases involving suspects caught in foiled terrorist bombing plots. The country's continuing controversy over what to do about illegal immigration includes the fear of terrorists infiltrating the country's borders and police officers have been enlisted to identify and respond to this group even as "lone wolf" American citizen–terrorists are reputed to be a greater concern for officials.

The responses to the attack on the World Trade Center also illustrate the prevalence of means–end thinking: the idea that what would usually be wrong can be justified to achieve a good end. We see this argument over and over again in the war on terror and, surprisingly, some people seem to think it is a new argument. It isn't. Nor is terrorism a new threat.

Terrorism has been defined as the "deliberate, negligent, or reckless use of force against noncombatants, by state or non-state actors for ideological ends and in the absence of a substantively just legal process" (Rodin, 2004: 755). Terrorism has led to questions about what is appropriate or ethical in investigative techniques, individual privacy rights vis-à-vis the government, and what is legal and ethical in the detention and treatment of prisoners. However, it is important to note that these are not new questions. From the very earliest philosophers, there has been a struggle to define and agree upon when it is right to wage war and what means are acceptable to secure victory. There is no coincidence in why we use the term *war* to denote a national challenge; the language of war creates the justification for methods that might not be acceptable otherwise. We can see the same argument played out whether we are talking about the war on terror, the war on drugs, the war on illegal immigrants, or the war against crime. War implies that the normal rules don't apply and, arguably, justifies

terrorism The deliberate, negligent, or reckless use of force against noncombatants, by state or non-state actors for ideological ends.

extreme methods (e.g., "All is fair in love and war."). Interestingly, however, philosophers have concluded that rules should apply and not everything is fair — even in war.

The traditional justification for war comes from natural law, and the second comes from positivist law. Classical "just war" theorists such as Hugo Grotius (1583–1645) have held that natural law gives sovereigns the right to use force when it is necessary:

- To uphold the good of the community
- When unjust injuries are inflicted on others
- To protect the state (Grotius, 1625/2005; Bellamy, 2004)

States are justified to engage in war when any of these events exist; otherwise, the war is unjust and immoral. However, natural law has been criticized as a justification for war because of the likelihood that leaders use moral arguments to justify wars that are, in reality, initiated for other means. For instance, some people criticized the U.S. invasion of Iraq. President Bush justified it under self-defense (because of the alleged presence of weapons of mass destruction) or protection (protecting the Iraqi people from Saddam Hussein), but some believed it was only to protect American interests in the oilfields. The problem with the natural law justification for armed conflict is that there are no bright lines to distinguish when the self-defense or protection justifications become "ripe." That is, there are incipient enemies around the globe and there are dictators who oppress their people—when does it become acceptable to go to war against them?

positivist law
Human-made law.

The second, more recent, justification for war comes from **positivist law**, which is man-made law. Increasingly, this is used as the only legitimate justification for war; legal incursions into the sovereignty of other nations are justified only under the auspices of international law as provided through the United Nations and other multilateral treaties and organizations (e.g., NATO). The problem with positivist law as the basis for justifying war is that no single authoritative legal body in international relations sits above all sovereigns, and international legal bodies do not include all countries and cover all circumstances (Bellamy, 2004).

Because of the lack of complete coverage of positivist law, natural law justifications continue to be used when military action is not mandated by the United Nations. Intrusions in internal conflicts within states have been undertaken when gross humanitarian violations have occurred (such as the ethnic cleansing campaigns in Rwanda and Bosnia). Discussions occurred over whether the United States should intervene in countries involved in the Arab Spring in 2012 when citizen-led uprisings in Tunisia, Egypt, Libya, Yemen, Bahrain, Syria, and Algeria occurred. There is tension weighing whether to protect a people from violent actions from their government and respecting a sovereign state's autonomy. More recently, some argue the United States should become involved in the Ukraine after Russia took over Crimea in March of 2014 by military force and is accused of supporting and encouraging violent dissidents.

Using natural law or moral imperative justifications to engage in war can be abused and misused; therefore, limits on the moral justifications for war have been proposed, including the following (Bellamy, 2004):

- The violations must be knowable to all.
- The violations must be widespread and systematic.
- The force used must save more lives than it injures.

These are not too different from other justifications that have been offered by other writers. For instance, Crank and Gregor (2005: 230) and Hicks (2004) have offered the following justifications for war:

- The threat must be grave, lasting, and certain.
- There are no other means to avert the threat.
- There must be a good probability of success.
- The means must not create a greater evil than the threat responded to.

These justifications seem to be consistent with a utilitarian system of ethics and are not inconsistent with ethical formalism because of the principle of forfeiture, which states that someone who impinges on others' rights forfeits his or her rights to the same degree.

Even if a military action can be justified by natural or positivist law, the second question is: What means are acceptable in fighting the war? Under utilitarianism, in determining "just means," the extent of the harm is weighed against the end or injury averted, just as when one asks if the war itself is justified. Ethical formalism does not look at the consequences of an action to justify it; however, the **principle of double effect** states that if one undertakes an action that is a good, but that also results in a negative end, as long as the negative end was not the intent of the actor, the good action and the good end can be considered a good. For instance, if one bombs a military target and innocents are harmed during the bombing, the act, if otherwise considered ethical, does not become unethical because of the death of civilians.

> **principle of double effect** The concept that a means taken for a good end that results in the good end but also in an inevitable but unintended bad effect is still considered ethical.

Today the more amorphous war on terror continues to spur discussions about acceptable means. The In the News box describes drone attacks of American citizens; this has generated controversy since, some say, no government should be able to order the execution of its citizens without due process. The opposing argument is that when a citizen takes up arms (or advocates taking up arms) against his or her country, then the legal analogy is more akin to war than crime and rules of war apply.

There has been a good deal of argument and analysis over whether traditional "just war" arguments can be applied to the fight against terrorists (Crank and Gregor, 2005; Zohar, 2004). Smilansky (2004) argues that terrorists have no moral justification, and they attack democracies partially because the ethos and values of such countries prohibit taking an "any means necessary" response. However, the fact is that democratic

(⋅⋅) IN THE NEWS | *Legal Killings*

A targeted drone attack killed Anwar al-Awlaki, an American radical cleric believed to be responsible for soliciting and initiating several terror plots against the United States, including the massacre of soldiers and civilians at Fort Hood, Texas. Critics argued that no power gives the president the right to order the killing of an American citizen without due process of law. A 2010 Office of Legal Counsel memo (the so-called drone memo) provided the legal justification for lethal drone attacks, even of American citizens, arguing that due process is a flexible formula that can be met in ways other than the criminal justice process, and that threats to the United States and the authorization to use military force by Congress gave the president the legal authority to order such killings.

Source: Savage, 2012b; Savage, 2014.

governments have resorted to a variety of means in response to terrorist attacks that are arguably inconsistent with democratic values and the United States sanctioned a number of practices that many consider illegal, immoral, and contrary to our ideals.

The Response to 9/11

Since 9/11, we have seen a fundamental shift in the goals and mission of law enforcement and public safety. This shift has included an expansion of the number of law enforcement agencies and personnel, a nationalization and/or militarization of law enforcement, a reduction of civil liberties, and a merging of immigration control and traditional law enforcement. One of the most dramatic changes after 9/11 has been the creation of the Department of Homeland Security, an umbrella federal agency that has incorporated many federal law enforcement functions. Many observers note that the creation of this mammoth federal agency indicates a move toward the nationalization of our police force. Historically, a national police force has been resisted because of the origins of this country and the legacy of distrust of centralized power. The Department of Homeland Security has absorbed agencies such as Immigration and Naturalization Service and Customs, and the director is the central coordinator of all information regarding counterterrorism, even though the FBI and the CIA are not formally under the organization chart of the DHS.

Community policing, popular before 9/11, was an approach that sought to forge links between law enforcement and the community it served by having police officers take on expanded duties in helping improve quality of life for residents. Most observers agree that community policing was, for the most part, abandoned after 9/11, and federal financial support was drastically reduced. We have seen federal money directed instead to training law enforcement officers to act as "first responders" to critical events such as terrorist attacks and active shooter scenarios. There has also been more federal money available for hardware purchases and the creation of fusion centers where intelligence analysts receive and analyze information from an array of law enforcement agencies as well as open sources (e.g., newspapers). Beyond policing, since 9/11, the nation has been involved in moral debates over such responses as:

- Detainments
- Renditions and secret prisons
- Guantanamo and the military commissions
- The use of torture
- Governmental secrecy
- Wiretapping and threats to privacy
- Undercover operations

Detainments

Immediately after 9/11, hundreds of noncitizens were detained on either immigration charges or material witness warrants. The Patriot Act required that all individuals on visas report to immigration offices, and once there, many were detained for minor violations of their visa. Hundreds were held for months in federal facilities and county jails without hearings. Despite civil liberties groups pressing for the names of the detainees, it took months for the federal government to release even the numbers of individuals detained, much less their names.

The deportation hearings that were held were closed to the public and to the media, despite legal suits to open them. Individuals were deported for extremely minor immigration violations, some of whom had lived in the United States for 30 years or more. The detainment of individuals on material witness warrants seemed to be based on rumor, innuendo, and a level of proof that did not even meet reasonable suspicion (Kreimer, 2007).

While some individuals believe that nothing like the Japanese internment during World War II could happen again in this country, pundits and some politicians advocated just such a response in the fearful days following 9/11 against those of Middle Eastern descent, especially those who practiced the Muslim faith (Harris, 2006). Legal experts point out that the Supreme Court case that upheld the internment of 110,000 Japanese, *Korematsu v. U.S.* (323 U.S. 214, 1944), has never been overturned, even though Congress has issued an official apology and voted to make reparations to internees (Harris, 2006).

Renditions and Secret Prisons

Other actions that the United States has taken in response to 9/11 have occurred overseas. Officials in Canada, Sweden, Germany, and Italy have declared that the CIA kidnapped individuals in those countries and subjected them to torture to discover what they knew about terrorist activities. The practice, called rendition, is usually done with the host country's knowledge, but in some cases no notice was given or permission granted. Several countries' leaders have objected to the U.S. practice of ignoring the sovereignty of the country and its laws (Whitlock, 2005; Weinstein, 2007).

Evidently CIA operatives kidnapped a radical Egyptian cleric in February 2003 from Italy and smuggled him out on a U.S. military airplane. In an unusual turn of events, 22 CIA agents were prosecuted *in absentia* in Milan, Italy, for this kidnapping. In May 2008, the wife of Osama Moustafa Hassan Nasr, the kidnapped man, testified in an Italian court that after he was kidnapped by CIA agents in 2003, he was taken to an Egyptian prison and held for 14 months. During those months, he was beaten, shocked over all parts of his body including his genitals, and tortured in other ways. Similar to others who were subjected to rendition, he was released with no explanation of why he had been taken in the first place (Associated Press, 2008b). After years of appeals, Italy's highest court upheld the convictions.

One of the CIA agents tried *in absentia*, Sabrina De Sousa, sued in order to force the U.S. government to grant her diplomatic immunity to protect her from the Italian conviction and five-year prison sentence. The federal judge dismissed the lawsuit, agreeing with government attorneys that the granting of immunity is a foreign policy decision solely within the discretion of the executive branch, but stated that not granting immunity sends a demoralizing message to agents for the government involved in actions abroad that expose them to legal liability (Associated Press, 2012d). In 2013, the former CIA bureau chief, also convicted *in absentia*, was held briefly by Panamanian authorities on an international warrant issued by Italy, but instead of being extradited, he was released to return to the United States (Miller and DeYong, 2013).

In another rendition case, Maher Arar, a Syrian-born Canadian, was seized in an American airport after officials received information from Canada that he was involved in terrorist activities. He was taken to Syria and tortured, then released because, as it turned out, the information was incorrect. Canada has reputedly offered him $10 million in damages, but his U.S. lawsuit in the Second Circuit of Appeals was dismissed based on the threat to state secrets.

Legal activity has taken place in Germany as well regarding rendition. News reports indicated that German authorities issued arrest warrants for the CIA agents believed to be responsible for a 2003 kidnapping of Khaled El-Masri, a German

WALKING THE WALK

Mary McCarthy was born in 1945. She received a Ph.D. in history from the University of Minnesota. In 1984, she began working for the CIA as an intelligence analyst. Her specialty was Africa, and she was known as an independent-minded analyst. She was promoted to director of intelligence programs on the National Security Council staff and was appointed as special assistant to the president and senior director for intelligence programs under President Clinton. In this position, she reviewed all clandestine operations. After President George W. Bush was elected, she left that position in 2001, took a sabbatical, and obtained a J.D. In 2005, she was working for the CIA again, but in the Office of the Inspector General. That office investigates complaints about unethical or illegal actions by federal employees, and McCarthy's position involved investigating detainee treatment in Iraq and Afghanistan.

In 2006, she was castigated and fired over revealing governmental secrets. Although the whole affair continues to be murky, it seems that, weeks away from retirement, she spoke with Dana Priest, a *Washington Post* reporter who wrote a series of Pulitzer Prize–winning articles on the U.S. practice of rendition and operating "black sites," which were secret prisons in Eastern European countries. These were the places where enemy combatants picked up in Iraq, Afghanistan, and in countries all over the world were taken for interrogation.

The Bush administration and CIA director Porter Goss launched an intensive investigation concerning the leak. McCarthy reportedly failed a polygraph and then admitted she talked to the reporter, according to CIA sources. McCarthy and her lawyer deny that she gave information to Priest about the black sites, and the reporter will only say that her information came from "multiple sources." McCarthy was fired 10 days before her planned retirement. Her colleagues were surprised since she was a veteran employee with decades of service. McCarthy has been described as "engaging, charming, persistent, loud, and aggressive." She evidently could not be "snowed easily" and was, by nature, a sceptic. The reason she spoke with the reporter seemed to be, according to news stories citing her friends and colleagues, that she was disturbed that senior officials were not telling the truth to the Senate and House committees investigating CIA activities regarding interrogation. She and other CIA staff members were convinced that the interrogation tactics approved by the White House violated international treaties. Worse, congressional committees were not aware of the extent of the interrogation tactics used, at least from her perspective.

The news stories led to the decision to shut down the secret prisons and move the detainees (who were also known as "ghost detainees" since they never appeared on official lists provided to the International Red Cross) to Guantanamo. Whether Mary McCarthy is a hero or a traitor depends on one's perspective. It is still unclear whether or not she was the source for the reporter's story about the secret prisons. Some argue that her position at the Inspector General's Office would not have given her access to such information. Others argue that she would have had access to the information only if there had been internal complaints from other CIA employees that laws were being broken. To some, she betrayed the secrets of her employer and country. Most CIA agents and other observers condemned her actions, arguing that you never leak secrets, no matter what the reason. To others, once McCarthy saw that the internal processes were not going to stop what she believed was unlawful and wrong, she did something that was much more effective—bringing the white light of public scrutiny to the activities. As the events such as Abu Ghraib, the secret prisons, and Guantanamo fade into memory, it is important to understand the dilemmas faced by those who saw wrong and tried to right it. They changed the pages of history.

Sources: Smith and Linzer, 2006: A01; Smith, 2006.

citizen believed to be a terrorist, kidnapped, and sent to Afghanistan where he was allegedly tortured and then released. News reports indicate he was confused with a different man who was an al-Qaeda operative because they had a similar name. The United States exerted political pressure through diplomatic cables (later exposed by WikiLeaks) to get the legal action quashed, urging the German government to think about the foreign relation implications of pursuing prosecution (Slackman, 2010). The movie *Rendition* is a fictionalized account of El-Masri's story.

In some of the cases, the kidnapped suspects were sent to secret prisons run by the CIA in Eastern European countries. The existence of secret prisons run by the United States in formerly Soviet countries is an ironic and sad commentary on recent history. After the existence of such prisons was exposed in 2006, they were allegedly closed, with some of the detainees sent to Guantanamo (Whitlock, 2007). The Walking the Walk box describes how the secret prisons may have been exposed.

Guantanamo and the Military Commissions Act

Soon after the U.S. military initiated hostilities in Afghanistan, "enemy combatants" were captured and sent to Guantanamo Bay in Cuba, a military installation that is considered American territory. Suspected terrorists were also picked up in other countries and sent to Guantanamo or to the secret prisons. Then the Iraq War began, and enemy combatants from Iraq were also sent there. Fourteen years later, a few remaining detainees continue to be incarcerated at Guantanamo, their legal status obscure and what to do with them a problem that President Obama may leave to his successor.

The initial arguments by the federal government were that the individuals did not deserve the due-process rights granted by the American Constitution because they were not Americans and were not on American soil, and they did not deserve the due-process rights granted by the Geneva Conventions (the agreements made by all the major world powers after World War II on how to treat war prisoners) because they were defined as enemy combatants, not soldiers.

In *Hamdi v. Rumsfeld* (542 U.S. 507, 2004), the Supreme Court held that U.S. citizens could not be held indefinitely without charges even if they were labeled enemy combatants. In *Rasul v. Bush* (542 U.S. 466, 2004), the Supreme Court held that detainees in Guantanamo could challenge their detention in U.S. federal courts. A related case was *Clark v. Martinez* (125 S.Ct. 716, 2005), which involved Cubans held for years in federal penitentiaries after illegally entering the United States. In this case, the Court held that the government may not indefinitely detain even illegal immigrants without some due process. In *Hamdan v. Rumsfeld* (125 S.Ct. 972, 2005), the Supreme Court held that the military commissions, set up as a type of due process for the detainees, were outside the president's power to create (the power belonged to Congress) and were, therefore, invalid.

Congress then passed the Military Commissions Act, which set up procedures similar to those struck down by the Supreme Court. In *Boumediene v. Bush* (553 U.S. 723, 2008), the Supreme Court rejected the military commissions as a due-process substitute for federal courts and habeas corpus, and it further held that the Detainee Treatment Act with the provision of some form of appeal over the "enemy combatant" status was also not an adequate substitute for habeas corpus rights. The Court's rationale was that Guantanamo is considered to be a legal territory of the United States and therefore is subject to U.S. law. Dissents by Chief Justice Roberts and Justices Scalia, Thomas, and Alito vigorously opposed the Court's rationale and predicted "devastating" consequences (Greenhouse, 2008; Savage, 2008b).

President Obama promised that Guantanamo would be closed within the first year of his presidency, but that has not occurred and what to do with the remaining detainees continues to be problematic. The Obama administration has refined the military commissions to respond to the due-process concerns raised by the Court and now there are more due-process elements than earlier versions. The Military Commissions Act of 2009 incorporates the presumption of innocence, requires proof beyond a reasonable doubt, provides for a right to counsel and a right to present evidence and cross-examine witnesses, prohibits the use of statements obtained through torture or cruel and inhuman treatment, states that hearsay can be used by both sides as long as it is deemed reliable and relevant, and provides for a right to appeal to Article III judges. The current military commissions also allow for the protection of sensitive sources in that defense attorneys have to have secret-level security clearances. There are also no requirements for *Miranda* warnings, and interrogations must be interpreted considering "wartime realities." The commissions can only be used for al-Qaeda affiliated cases and cannot be used for American citizens, and for only specified offenses (violations of laws of war).

As of June 2015, there were 116 detainees still in Guantanamo, from a high of 779 (Human Rights First, 2015). The detainees, some of whom have been held for over a decade, have never been found guilty of any crime by a court of law, although the military commissions used as a substitute due-process mechanism continue.

Khalid Sheikh Mohammed, the alleged mastermind of 9/11, and four other detainees were brought before a military commission in May 2012, but the process was delayed over continued arguments over procedures. For instance, the military judge considered a protective order that prohibited the defendants from discussing in any way the CIA's actions during interrogation eliminating their defense that they were tortured to obtain information used against them (Fox, 2012). The prosecution of Khalid Sheikh Mohammed has been criticized as rife with legal and ethical misconduct, including the release of a half-million defense attorney e-mails to prosecutors, the discovery of hidden microphones placed by the FBI in attorney-client conference rooms, and allegations that FBI agents have been spying on defense teams. One of the JAG officers (Major Jason Wright) assigned to Mohammed's defense was summarily reassigned. Instead of abandoning the case, which he viewed as a violation of his ethical duty as an attorney, he resigned from the army (Urza, 2014). As of July 2015, Khalid Sheikh Mohammed's military commission proceeding still had not begun.

There is some indication that many who were sent to Guantanamo were innocent and either accused by others who gave names because they were being tortured, or were accused by bounty hunters simply because they received money for identifying supposed terrorists (Selksky, 2009). Some of the detainees were captured as youngsters 14 or 15 years old, sparking international outrage since treaties mandate that juveniles are not to be treated as war criminals (Williams, 2008). Some were held in the hope that they had information. Hundreds have now been released and repatriated back to their own or other countries. The military commission for Hamdan (of *Hamdan v. Rumsfeld*) ended with a sentence of 66 months, but with credit for the 61 months he had already served. He was transferred to serve the rest of his sentence in Yemen. Many others have also returned to their countries. Recent reports indicate that some of the released detainees have joined terrorist organizations.

Torture

After World War II, commanders of the Japanese and German armies were tried for war crimes that included unnecessary killings of civilians, mistreatment of civilians, and the use of torture against captured soldiers. One of the forms of interrogation used by the Japanese that was later the basis for convictions was the "water cure." We know it today as waterboarding. In the 1940s, judicial officials assessing guilt in war crime trials called it torture and convicted the military officers who ordered it or allowed it to happen; however, because of 9/11, President Bush called waterboarding legal and necessary. President Obama has said that the enhanced interrogation techniques used, including waterboarding, was torture, but has also said that no one will be prosecuted.

Torture is defined as the deliberate infliction of violence and, through violence, severe mental and/or physical suffering upon individuals. Others describe it as any intentional act that causes severe physical or mental pain or suffering. Amnesty International considers all forms of corporal punishment as falling within the definition of torture and prohibited by the United Nations Convention Against Torture (McCready, 2007).

We now know that immediately after 9/11, certain individuals suspected of being involved in the planning of the attacks or of being members of al-Qaeda were seized wherever they happened to be and taken to secret locations. At first they were sent to countries such as Egypt and Syria that used torture in interrogation. Later they were taken to secret prisons run by the CIA in Eastern Europe. Finally, some were moved to Guantanamo. Evidently, by 2002, various forms of coercive interrogation techniques were being used at Guantanamo, as well as at Bagram prison in Afghanistan. At these locations, suspects were subjected to extreme forms of coercive interrogations, including the following (Massimino, 2004: 74):

- Subjected to loud noises and extreme heat and cold
- Deprived of sleep, light, food, and water
- Bound or forced to stand in painful positions for long periods of time
- Kept naked and hooded
- Thrown into walls and slapped
- Sexually humiliated
- Threatened with attack dogs
- Shackled to the ceiling or kept in small containers

In an ironic twist, it has now been revealed that military interrogators in Guantanamo were trained in the techniques of coercive interrogation techniques with material that was originally from a 1957 Air Force study of Chinese Communist techniques used during the Korean War. The original source detailed a continuum of coercive techniques that were used to obtain false confessions from U.S. soldiers, including practices such as semi-starvation, filthy surroundings, extreme cold, and stress positions. The techniques that could "brainwash" American soldiers into falsely confessing war crimes became included in military training on how to withstand such pressures. Survival-Evasion-Resistance-Escape (SERE) training is designed and administered by the military but with the assistance of civilian psychologist contractors. While the country was still in the grip of fear expecting another attack, officials sought advice on how to obtain information from the suspected terrorists they had captured and turned to these psychologists.

What seems unbelievable now is why psychologists who had no familiarity at all with interrogation were consulted instead of intelligence and interrogation experts in the military, FBI, or other federal agencies. The psychologists from the SERE training program, Jim Mitchell and Bruce Jessen, began to train military and CIA interrogators on the techniques used in SERE training, including waterboarding. These techniques, used on American soldiers to expose them to what they might experience while in enemy hands, were supposed to "break" detainees in order to get them to talk (Shane, 2008b; Shane and Mazzetti, 2009; Eban, 2007). Reports also indicate that Mitchell was there at the first waterboarding, reportedly of Abu Zubaida (also spelled Zubahday or Zubaidah, and he is also called Zayn al-Abidin Muhammed Hussein) and that the waterboarding took place before the 2002 memo that defined it as legal (Warrick and Finn, 2009). It was the videotapes of the waterboarding and interrogation of Zubaida that the CIA destroyed in 2005. Expert interrogators argued the methods were ineffective and unnecessary, and no one seemed to know or care that the methods, especially waterboarding, had been defined as war crimes after WWII. It was reported that veteran interrogators referred to these two psychologists as the "poster boys" because it was believed that they would eventually end up on the FBI's "most wanted" list for what they were doing (Eban, 2007).

The role of these psychologists is especially controversial and has sparked disciplinary action in their respective licensing agencies. Mitchell, Jessen, and other psychologists who were present during the enhanced interrogations at Guantanamo have been the subject of lawsuits and disciplinary actions because, it has been alleged, they have violated their professional ethical code in participating in what amounts to torture. There was an action filed in Texas, for instance, since Jim Mitchell is licensed there; another psychologist was licensed in New York and a Human Rights organization filed a lawsuit against him there. It appears that the psychologists will escape any sanctions, however, since the organization's disciplinary body decided that what they were doing was not part of professional psychological services; therefore, the professional rules would not apply and the professional body had no power to discipline (Eligon, 2011). More recently, it has been revealed that there might have been coordination between officials at the American Psychological Association (APA) and CIA employees in that the APA standards covering psychologists involved in interrogation were written with the help of CIA employees. There has been an independent investigation to determine the accuracy or extent of what some call collusion between the professional association and the CIA (Risen, 2015).

In 2002, George Tenet, then director of the CIA, and his chief deputy described in great detail the techniques they sought approval for to the Principals Committee of the National Security Council. This group included George W. Bush, Condoleezza Rice, Dick Cheney, John Ashcroft, and Donald Rumsfeld. The techniques were also described to the top leaders of the Senate and House Intelligence Committees (although conflicting memories seem to exist as to what they were told).

In 2009, in response to a FOIA request, President Obama released CIA memos that were written around this same time period and graphically describe the techniques used (Miller and Meger, 2009). They were clinically specific, including how hard to slap a detainee's face, the total number of times a person could be slammed into a wall (30), and how many times someone could be waterboarded (6 times within 2 hours). The memos also discuss Zubaida's fear of insects and how that could be used to torture him (in a scenario taken straight from George Orwell's *1984*, where the interrogators determined the greatest fear of the protagonist was rats and used this fear to torture him).

These interrogation techniques were contrary to the military field manual and believed by many to be against American law. FBI agents who were at Guantanamo to assist in interrogations wrote memoranda to their superiors objecting to what they saw, as did some military lawyers and other officers. FBI officials instructed agents to leave the room when such interrogations were carried out. However, we now know that a legal memorandum authored by lawyers John Yoo and Robert Delahunty from the Office of Legal Counsel had provided a 2002 opinion that the president had legal authority to authorize waterboarding and other forms of torture based on the Authorization to Use Military Force passed by Congress and the executive power of the presidency. Yoo also wrote a 2003 memorandum with Jay Bybee that basically reiterated the justification that the president had the legal right to order torture as long as it did not result in organ failure or death. Steven Bradbury wrote a series of memos in 2005 basically endorsing the earlier memo's reasoning (Shane, 2008a).

Critics argue that these legal memoranda ignored other sources of law, including international treaties that bar such acts, including the Convention Against Torture, which the United States ratified in 1994 (Gillers, 2004). The authors, Bybee, Yoo, and Bradbury, faced an investigation from the Department of Justice's Office of Professional Responsibility and possible sanctions from their respective bar associations. However, the final report concluded that they exercised flawed legal reasoning but were not guilty of professional misconduct, and recommended that they not be referred to their state bar associations for discipline. Bybee is now a federal appeals court judge, and Yoo is a law professor (Lichtblau and Shane, 2010).

In December 2014 the Senate Select Committee on Intelligence released a massive investigative report on the activities of the CIA during the time period after 9/11, including the enhanced interrogation techniques. Most of the information in the report was already known—at least to those paying attention. The report was widely condemned by Republicans as politically motivated, except for Senator John McCain, who had been tortured as a Vietnamese prisoner of war. Findings included the following:

- There was little evidence that the torture led to useful intelligence.
- The CIA lied to Congress and even withheld full information from President Bush about the degree of torture being used and the number of detainees being tortured.
- The torture resulted in physical and psychological damage to the detainees.
- The program was mismanaged and had little oversight even by CIA bosses.
- A substantial number of lower-level employees were concerned about the enhanced interrogation but were overruled by their superiors (Ashkenas, Fairfield, Keller, and Volpe, 2014).

Ali Soufan, an FBI interrogator, has publicly stated that he had been successful in initial interrogations of Ali Zubaida, a Yemeni thought to be a high-ranking al-Qaeda official but eventually discovered to be more of a travel agent for the terrorist organization (Finn and Warrick, 2009). He practiced standard interrogation techniques that involved developing rapport; in Zubaida's case, he helped the man with wounds he had acquired during the capture and called him a nickname only used by his mother. Soufan has stated that he obtained information about José Padilla from Zubaida, not the CIA agents who later claimed credit (Eban, 2007). It was when CIA interrogators and contractors arrived and began using the enhanced interrogation techniques that Zubaida began to provide information that was later determined to be useless or inaccurate, although others insist that he provided hundreds of names of al-Qaeda's agents

(Finn and Warrick, 2009). Eventually Zubaida was waterboarded 83 times. Khalid Sheikh Mohammed was waterboarded 183 times.

Soufan and other interrogators have insisted that traditional techniques and old-fashioned "cop tricks" are effective and would have been effective in the interrogation of terrorist suspects without resorting to "enhanced" techniques (Margasak, 2009). For instance, Soufan described using the traditional method of gaining rapport and then asking the detainee if there was anything else he should tell them. He said he gained important information that he would have never obtained during questioning. Torture victims are unlikely to offer additional information and they are more likely to lie in order to stop the torture (Ghosh, 2009; Finn and Warrick, 2009). Furthermore, any information that is obtained through torture cannot be used to convict terrorist agents in military commissions or federal courts. If the only information that supports their guilt was obtained through torture, they can't be convicted and punished. The CIA and military have now attempted to reinterrogate men like Zubaida with "clean teams" (interrogators who did not participate in waterboarding or other questionable interrogation techniques), but, not surprisingly, the detainees are not very cooperative (Finn and Warrick, 2009).

By the time the Abu Ghraib prison scandal erupted in 2004, such techniques had been used in Guantanamo and in Bagram prison in Afghanistan. The pictures that Sergeant Joseph Darby (profiled in the Walking the Walk box in Chapter 2) provided to army CID showed prisoners being subjected to a range of physically painful and psychological traumatizing behaviors. Later investigations documented that the following acts occurred:

- Forcing naked prisoners to pose in humiliating, sexually oriented poses
- Forcing hooded prisoners to stand on a box and be attached to electric wires
- Threatening male detainees with rape
- Sodomizing a male detainee with a broomstick
- Threatening detainees with attack dogs
- Pouring chemicals from broken light bulbs onto detainees (Massimino, 2004)

Some bitterly criticized the fact that no higher-ranking military officers were ever punished for the Abu Ghraib incident, such as Brigadier General Janis Karpinski or Lt. Colonel Ricardo Sanchez. They argue that under the doctrine of "command responsibility" superiors are responsible for the war crimes committed by their soldiers when they either knew what was happening or should have known. Despite the fact that the United States and Allied Forces utilized the concept of command responsibility in war crimes trials after WWII to hold Japanese and German commanders responsible for the acts of others, the Uniform Code of Military Justice does not have a parallel responsibility of American commanders (Smith, 2006). General Taguba's report of Abu Ghraib indicated that the reserve soldiers assigned to be guards in the prison did not have training in the Geneva Conventions, nor were there clear directions from the commanding officers as to what was acceptable or not in the treatment of prisoners. The soldiers, such as Charles Graner, testified that they were never told not to engage in the abusive acts portrayed in the pictures and, in fact, Graner was complimented on his ability to "soften up" the prisoners for interrogation. However, when the soldiers tried to use a "superior orders defense" (which basically states that they were not guilty because they were following orders) in their courts martial, the defense was rejected (Smith, 2006).

Others argue that military commanders over Abu Ghraib and other prisons may deserve some blame, but their position was tenuous since the questioning was often done by the CIA or other contractors. Military investigations and prosecutions have exposed the fact that paramilitary units called Scorpions, which included CIA operatives, Special Forces, and civilians, used tactics in Afghanistan and Iraq that included beating prisoners (White, 2005). In fact, the blurred lines of authority, not to mention conflicting legal opinions from the Justice Department and the Pentagon, led to a situation where abuse was probably not only possible, but, in fact, probable (Swift, 2007).

In Bagram prison in Afghanistan, similar practices occurred and included the following:

- Stepping on the neck of a detainee and kicking him in the genitals
- Forcing a detainee to roll on the floor of a cell and kiss the feet of the interrogators
- Forcing a detainee to pick plastic bottle caps out of a drum mixed with excrement and water (Golden, 2005)

In one case, a detainee was stuffed in a sleeping bag, wrapped in electrical cord, and beaten to death (White, 2005). Also at Bagram, a young taxi driver was killed by interrogators who suspended him from the ceiling and beat his legs so badly that an autopsy revealed his leg bones were pulverized (see the Quote and Query box). It was discovered that Dilawar, the taxi driver, had no association at all with insurgents and that his taxi and the passengers in it had been picked at random by an Afghan guerrilla commander who told the Americans that they were responsible for bombing a U.S. camp. Later it was discovered that the commander himself was responsible for the bombing (Golden, 2005).

It seems that the worst forms of interrogation techniques were not used after 2005 although President Bush publicly continued to support waterboarding through 2008 and in his memoirs insists it was legal. In 2006, a new army field manual specified new rules of interrogation consistent with the Geneva Conventions' Article 3 (outlawing forced nudity, hooding, dogs, waterboarding, stress positions, and sleep deprivation). The military manual asks the soldier to question a method in a way reminiscent of ethical formalism and universalism: "If the proposed approach technique were used by the enemy against one of your fellow soldiers, would you believe the soldier had been abused?"

The argument that we should not use torture because our enemies then will feel free to use torture against American soldiers is a utilitarian argument (greatest benefit), but it also has elements of the categorical imperative (act in such a way that you will it to be a universal law) and the religious imperative (do unto others as you would have them do unto you). Kleinig (2001a) and others, even before the worst abuses were revealed, examined the weak justification for torture and abusive practices during interrogation and also pointed out that they have been used in Northern Ireland, Israel, South Africa, and South America, among many other countries. The so-called doctrine of necessity is purely utilitarian, as is the argument of some that there must

QUOTE & QUERY

We take this moral high ground to make sure that if our people fall into enemy hands, we'll have the moral force to say, "You have got to treat them right." If you don't practice what you preach, nobody listens.

Source: Senator Lindsey Graham, in support of an amendment banning torture to military prisoners, quoted in Galloway and Kuhnhenn, 2005: A4.

 Is this argument against torture a utilitarian argument or an ethical formalist argument?

Dirty Harry problem The question of whether police should use immoral means to reach a desired moral end (taken from the Clint Eastwood movie *Dirty Harry*).

be secrecy concerning interrogation tactics so they can be more effective. To the contrary, Kleinig (2001a: 116) points out that torture dehumanizes both victim and oppressor: "There is a loss of the moral high ground, a compromising of values that supposedly distinguish a society as civilized and worth belonging to."

The national argument as to whether torture is legally or ethically justified is no different from Klockars' (1983) **Dirty Harry problem**. This dilemma originated in a situation from the *Dirty Harry* movie where a captured criminal refuses to tell the location of a kidnapped victim. Because the victim is sure to die without help, the police officer (played by Clint Eastwood) tortures the criminal by stepping on his injured leg until he admits the location. Klockars' point was that the situation has no good solution. If the police officer behaves in a professional manner, the victim would be sure to die. If the officer behaves in an immoral manner, there is a chance he could save a life. Klockars' conclusion is that by engaging in dirty means for good ends, the officer has tainted his innocence and must be punished, for there is always a danger that dirty means will be redefined as neutral or even good by those who use them. Klockars also infers that we all are guilty in a sense by expecting certain ones among us to do the dirty work and then condemning them for their actions. In effect, police (and others such as the CIA and Special Forces) become our *sin eaters* of early folklore; they are the shady characters on the fringe of society who absorb evil so the rest of us may remain pure. These persons are depended upon to protect us, but shunned and avoided when their actions see the light of day.

The post-9/11 Harry Callahan was Jack Bauer, the hero from the television show *24*. Every season he was confronted with a variation of the "the ticking bomb scenario," specifically, whether one should use torture to find the location of a bomb that is about to go off and kill many people. While the stakes may be higher, this is the same dilemma that faced the fictional Harry Callahan, and, one might add, the same analysis may be applied: Are bad means ever justified by a good end? In the television drama, Bauer never hesitated and the show's villains were treated to a wide array of beating, cutting, burning, electrocuting, and other forms of psychological and physical torture. A group opposed to violence on television called it the worst show on the air and noted that depictions of torture in other programs increased fivefold after it began airing (Mayer, 2007).

The television show was entertainment but also a powerful argument that enhanced interrogation was the right thing to do, supporting the Bush administration's position. The show's producer was a conservative, counting Rush Limbaugh as a good friend, and President Bush, Vice President Cheney, and Homeland Security Secretary Michael Chertoff were reportedly huge fans. Even Justice Scalia made a controversial public reference to the fact that Jack Bauer was a hero who shouldn't be prosecuted. Others, however, criticized the series in that it promoted the message that torture was effective and encouraged the viewer to root for the hero who illegally tortured. In 2006, U.S. Army Brigadier General Patrick Finnegan, dean of the United States Military Academy at West Point, led a delegation of expert interrogators from the army and FBI to Hollywood to meet with producers of the show in an effort to get them to change the message that torture was good. They noted that the show was being referenced by their students at West Point as justification for why they should not have to stay within legal guidelines. The producers and actor Kiefer Sutherland insisted the show was just entertainment and no one should take it seriously, but evidently Michael Chertoff, the head of Homeland Security and part of the group that approved enhanced interrogation techniques, said in reference to the show at a public debate, "Frankly, it reflects real life." The real-life interrogators, however, as opposed to Washington bureaucrats, called the show immoral and said, "Only a psychopath can torture and be unaffected. You don't want people like that in your organization" (Mayer, 2007).

Whether torture is effective or not is a utilitarian argument. Some argue that it is not effective because people will say anything to stop the torture, and interrogators can't tell when someone is lying (Rejali, 2007). Others argue that torture does work in getting information out of individuals. Even those people, however, admit that using torture to interrogate may damage the interrogator as well as the detainee. Individuals may find the dark corners of their soul when they realize that they get some form of excitement from inflicting pain on others. They may suffer guilt that destroys their peace of mind and affects them long after the detainee's wounds have healed. It has been reported that some interrogators are suffering posttraumatic stress syndrome (Blumenfeld, 2007). Further, there is no way to tell whether torturing a suspected terrorist may create more disutility for society. In the case of waterboarding detainees after 9/11, it is very possible that such actions hardened hatred against the United States and possibly created new terrorists, resulting in a net disutility.

There is a tempting logic to the use of torture in a ticking time bomb scenario. Even Alan Dershowitz (2004), a renowned liberal defense attorney, offered a utilitarian argument as a rationale—he wrote that sometimes the greatest benefit is to torture, but that it should be limited to situations in which the benefit is so great that it overwhelms the harm to the individual. He also proposes, however, that any torture should be done under the auspices of a court or objective hearing body that issues a type of "torture warrant." Others (e.g., McCready, 2007) dispute the feasibility of this proposal, arguing that any need for torture would be immediate and, if there was time to pursue a warrant, there probably would be other ways to get that information.

When individuals such as Dershowitz and others present justifications for torture, they invariably use the most extreme situation—the "ticking bomb" scenario in which one *knows* that the person being tortured has information about a bomb that is going to go off soon, killing many people. Whether one accepts the utilitarian equation for such a scenario does not necessarily justify the actual incidents of torture that have taken place. There is a world of difference between the ticking bomb scenario that appears in a hypothetical or in a television show where viewers already know what has happened and the real life situations that occurred in Guantanamo and Bagram.

Torturing a suspect because he *might* know something about al-Qaeda, or torturing a suspect to obtain his confession so that it can be used against him are quite different. The only calculus that supports a utilitarian rationale for torture is when the person being tortured does know something, that knowledge will avert a catastrophe, and the information cannot be discovered by other means. In reality, torture occurred against innocents, like Dilawar, the taxi driver, who suffered unimaginable pain and terror because he did not know anything about the bombing he was accused of. As discussed throughout the text, utilitarianism depends on an ability to know the consequences of one's actions. In reality, the long-term utilities and disutilities of torture cannot be known. The actions of the interrogators may have saved lives but another possible consequence might lie in the horrifying specter of the rise of ISIS in the Middle East, seemingly a group so lacking in humane sympathy that they are denounced even by al-Qaeda and Hamas.

In 2009, Attorney General Holder appointed John Durham to investigate whether criminal charges should be brought against any CIA agents or other officials for their role in the enhanced interrogations that occurred, but President Obama also said they would not prosecute anyone who operated in good faith that they were following U.S. law. In 2011, the Justice Department dropped 99 of the 101 cases of alleged torture, reporting there was not enough evidence to pursue an investigation. The remaining cases concerned Manadel al-Jamadi, who died in 2003 in Abu Ghraib (he was the plastic-wrapped corpse soldiers posed next to in the Abu Ghraib pictures), and Gul Rahman, who died of hypothermia in Afghanistan shackled to a wall. In 2012, Eric Holder announced that there would be no prosecutions in these two cases either (Dilanian, 2012). This may not be the end of the story, however, since numerous legal actions are occurring around the world against American officials who are believed to have violated human rights and international law.

Governmental Secrecy

The responses to 9/11 described earlier are now part of history and the government no longer engages in wholesale roundups of visa holders, renditions, or torture (as far as we know). There are other governmental responses to 9/11 that are continuing to play out and are very much part of current national discussions about "just means" in the war on terror. Perhaps as a response to 9/11, there is less openness in governmental activities, a trend begun in the Bush administration, but continuing into the Obama administration. Specific elements of this include fewer White House briefings and punishing government employees for giving unclassified information to the press (Crank and Gregor, 2005: 223). President Obama campaigned on a promise to roll back the pattern of secrecy, but critics allege that he has, instead, continued the pattern of using executive privilege and classifying as state secrets activities of the government that should be accessible. A state secrets justification has also been used for dismissing lawsuits brought by victims of torture (e.g., Khaled al-Masri's case was dismissed) and wiretapping.

The Justice Department, under President Obama, has also been accused of using double standards when going after "leakers" who expose governmental wrongdoing such as John Kiriakou, an ex-CIA analyst who discussed waterboarding with journalists and served a 30-month prison sentence for revealing a CIA agent's name to a journalist even though the name was never published, and General Petraeus, a former CIA director, who was found to have shared secret information with his biographer-lover but was charged with only a misdemeanor of mishandling classified information. The Kiriakou case is described in the documentary "*Silenced.*" In fact, Kiriakou's prosecution—along with the prosecutions of two other whistleblowers—Thomas Drake and William Binney—was mentioned by Edward Snowden as a reason for his decision to go public with the data he stole from the NSA. Drake came forward with information about wasteful spending and Binney was threatened with, but ultimately not prosecuted for, leaking classified information about the extent of the government's surveillance capability. Snowden reported to journalists in 2013 that the government's harsh treatment of these whistleblowers indicated to him that he would be unfairly treated if he tried to work within the system or stayed within legal reach of the justice system (Savage and Shane, 2013).

Government secrecy has other effects besides harsher sanctions against whistle-blowers. Kaufman and Toomey (2015) argue that in earlier decades, Fourth Amendment law was developed because government agents gave notice to defendants of the type of surveillance that was used against them. For instance, the Supreme Court in *Katz v. United States* (389 U.S. 347, 1967) concluded that the government required a warrant before wiretapping when the target had an expectation of privacy, and, in *Kyllo v. United States* (533 U.S. 27, 2001), a warrant was deemed necessary before heat measuring devices were used to detect indoor marijuana cultivation. The resulting legal challenges to the government action were possible only because defendants *were told* that these devices had been used against them. The so-called sneak and peek provision of the Patriot Act means that the government does not have to give targets notice that they have been the object of secret surveillance, and government agents are taught "parallel construction," which means that they create a parallel track of evidence to be used in prosecution so that the secret surveillance will not be revealed (Kauffman and Toomey, 2015). What this means is that secret governmental activities do not bear the light of day and, thus, escape legal analysis.

Others argue that opponents of secrecy are naïve and that the published reports of U.S. activities against terrorists provided by WikiLeaks and other anonymous sources make it more difficult to protect America. For instance, publishing the plans leading up to the killing of Osama bin Laden has resulted in a long prison term for the Pakistani doctor who assisted the American effort, and publishing the details of a foiled terrorist plot using a double agent in May 2012 endangered that man's life and led to a reduced probability of assistance by other countries. The release of the wiretapped private conversations of political leaders in our ally countries makes it more difficult to count on their support in times of need.

It is a difficult and controversial question as to what should be public knowledge and what should not be. Edward Snowden's release of a massive treasure trove of governmental secrets to journalists at the *Washington Post* and *Guardian* newspapers and other outlets has spurred legislators to reexamine the powers that the Patriot Act gave the National Security Agency. At the same time, it has created the debate as to whether Snowden is a hero or a traitor. One thing is certain, it has made Snowden a man without a country, and his residence in Russia is an ironic consequence for someone who violated the law in order to protect what he considered to be Americans' civil liberties.

Wiretapping and Threats to Privacy

In 1978, in response to violations of privacy by our government during the 1960s and 1970s, the Foreign Intelligence Surveillance Act (FISA) was passed, which created the Foreign Intelligence Surveillance Court (FISC), consisting of seven federal district court judges appointed by the Supreme Court's chief justice. Federal agents who wanted to wiretap in this country had to go to this court and show that their target was an agent of a foreign power and that the information sought was in furtherance of counterintelligence. The FISA legislation originally approved only electronic eavesdropping and wiretapping, but was amended in 1994 to include covert physical entries and, in 1998, to permit pen/trap orders (which record telephone numbers) and business records. If the target is a U.S. citizen, there must be probable cause that his or her activities may involve espionage, and a warrant requested and obtained from the FISC was required.

The Patriot Act, passed very quickly after 9/11, created expanded powers for federal agents in search and seizure, including provisions that allowed federal agents to "sneak and peek," and to utilize national security letters instead of warrants in cases "relevant" to national security investigations. **National security letters** are subpoenas issued by the Federal Bureau of Investigation (FBI) to access private information without a warrant, typically these would be phone records or financial records. Recipients of such a letter, until later modifications of the Patriot Act, could not ever tell anyone of the letter. Thus, a librarian who received a letter demanding all Internet records for a particular patron, or a telecommunications agency that received a similar request, could not tell the target of the letter or even discuss the letter with their lawyers. Now recipients are at least allowed to confer with a lawyer.

national security letters Letters issued by the Federal Bureau of Investigation (FBI) to access private information without a warrant.

Freedom of Information Act requests showed that after the Patriot Act created the authority to circumvent warrant requirements, the FBI was issuing over 30,000 letters a year, and, in 2004, the actual number was closer to 65,000. It has also come to light that the FBI's use of such letters often broke the law by what was asked for or the level of proof they had in order to justify the letter. FBI agents invoked terrorism emergencies to obtain approval when they did not exist and it was revealed that among the telephone numbers searched for call records were telephones belonging to the *Washington Post* and *New York Times*. In one random audit of 77 letters, 22 had possible violations of law or policy (Kreimer, 2007: 1185; Solomon and Johnson, 2010).

More recently, the use of the letters has been the subject of several conflicting lower federal appellate level lawsuits including *In Re: National Security Letter, Under Seal v. Holder, Sealed*. Ironically, this court case is sealed, meaning that public access to the case records is denied. The court has set up a website for the public to access some information about the case at www.ca9.uscourts.gov/content/view.php?pk_id=0000000715.

After 9/11 President Bush authorized secret wiretapping of American citizens by the National Security Agency without going through the FISC to obtain a warrant. Evidently, only a few people knew of the wiretapping, and warrantless wiretapping of American citizens had not received the formal approval of the Justice Department or Attorney General Ashcroft (Lichtblau, 2008). After the wiretapping was exposed, civil libertarian groups tried to sue, but the Supreme Court refused to hear the case. White House lawyers argued that, first, the ACLU and other civil liberties groups who brought suit had no standing (since they had not been the ones wiretapped) and, second, that under the state secrets privilege, the plaintiffs could not get information on who had been wiretapped; therefore, it was impossible to have a court hearing on any wiretapping that might have been done (Savage, 2008a). Evidently, the Supreme Court agreed with these arguments.

In August 2007, the Protect America Act was passed, which, in effect, gave approval to the secret wiretapping program after the fact. The Protect America Act expired in 2008, but its provisions were included in the FISA Amendments Act of 2008. Legal immunity for telecommunications companies that cooperated with warrantless wiretapping was also provided. The bill also changed some elements of the FISC by expanding government's powers to invoke emergency wiretapping before approval is granted, but affirming the position that the FISC is the only legal authority to grant wiretaps; specifically opposing any presidential power in that regard (Lichtblau, 2008).

Congress passed the FISA Amendments Reauthorization Act of 2012 that extended the provisions for five more years. Basically, the government now has the power to wiretap when it is for the purpose of foreign intelligence collecting and at least one party is outside the United States. Further, even if both parties are in the United States, agents can begin a wiretap as long as they seek a warrant within 72 hours.

Targets of wiretapping have little recourse in the courts since they may not know they have been the object of wiretapping—or if they do know, courts have not been open to reviewing whether legal protections were adhered to. In 2013, the Supreme Court held that a group of lawyers, journalists and organizations couldn't sue to challenge the expansion of the FISA because they couldn't prove they were being monitored and, therefore, had no standing (*Clapper, Director of National Intelligence, et al. v. Amnesty International USA, et al.*, February 26, 2013).

The Quote and Query box illustrates the concerns of many.

The Bush administration had pushed for several data-mining programs that basically sift through large amounts of information, tagging key words for further scrutiny. For instance, the Total Information Awareness pilot program was an initiative proposed by the government to collect voluminous amounts of information about citizens through the Internet (Kravets, 2003; Moss and Fessenden, 2002). Another proposal—"Operation TIPS"—encouraged citizens to spy on one another and proposed an official identity card (Cole, 2002). These programs were rejected by Congress.

What we now know, however, is that the NSA did proceed with the technology of acquiring massive amounts of electronic data. It now makes sense, for instance, why the government issued regulations in 2010 that required all Internet service providers to create "back door" capabilities to unencrypt private communications so they would be accessible to governmental surveillance efforts (Savage, 2010). In 2012, a few news items described a major government installation in Utah that utilized the electricity of a small city and was reputed to be the repository of massive amounts of electronic communications scooped up by the NSA. The facility was reported to be able to store the equivalent of 500 quintillion pages of text. According to the reports, data would be diverted to the facility from 10 to 20 data switching stations throughout the United States and satellite monitoring stations (Bamford, 2012). Not many people paid attention until June of 2013 when Edward Snowden revealed the extent of the NSA's surveillance activities which evidently came as a great surprise to almost everyone, even Congress.

Edward Snowden, a young cyber-security contractor for the NSA, flew to Hong Kong and then released a huge trove of secrets to journalists at major newspapers. He said he did it because he was increasingly concerned about the extent of NSA's spying on Americans and lying to Congress about the extent of their capabilities and activities. He was accused of being a spy for the Chinese and then for Russia when he ended up in that country to stay out of the reach of extradition. His revelations led to embarrassment and apologies from U.S. officials to world leaders like German Chancellor Angela Merkel whose cellphone was evidently tapped with her private conversations stored in the NSA data banks and revealed, along with others, by Snowden.

Now, from Snowden's disclosures, we know that the NSA does collect all electronic transmissions and stores them to analyze "metadata." Supposedly this is not the content of the calls, but only the phone numbers (or e-mail addresses) and the length of the calls. Snowden has told journalists that NSA analysts also monitor content and

QUOTE & QUERY

We're protecting freedom and democracy, but unfortunately freedom and democracy have to be sacrificed.

Source: Jethro Eisenstein, New York lawyer, quoted in Moss and Fessenden, 2002: A18.

 Is this claim overstating the issue?

even pull nude pictures from private cellphone transmissions to share with each other. No independent corroboration exists for that allegation, but the fact that NSA officials say they do not monitor phone conversations or e-mail transmissions without court orders does not, by itself, mean that it does not happen since they also had previously testified in Congressional hearings that they did not collect metadata and that was not true. Some individuals knowledgeable about NSA's activities reported that there could have been ways to limit the collection of data, but the decision was made to capture all communications, arguably because the vast trove of information was being used to develop encryption-breaking software and, also, storing older data allowed them to retrieve it and break the encryption as their tools improved (Bamford, 2012).

Interestingly, the American public seemingly quickly lost interest in the fact that their private communications may be monitored by the government, and by 2015 less than 40 percent of respondents in one survey were concerned about the government spying on them (Raine and Madden, 2015). Legislators are more concerned, however, and they probably should be since anyone with the political power to control and utilize the governmental spying apparatus would conceivably be able to use it against their political enemies. In May of 2015, the House passed the USA Freedom Act which supposedly ends the NSA's storage of metadata, but still allows the NSA to request records from telecommunications companies with a court order. The provision of the Patriot Act (Section 215) that the NSA interpreted to give them the broad power to collect data expired June 1, 2015 without a Senate vote on the bill, but on June 2, 2015, the Senate passed the USA Freedom Act (which stands for "Uniting and Strengthening America by Fulfilling Rights and Ending Eavesdropping, Dragnet-collection and Online Monitoring Act"), and it was signed into law by the president. Proponents say it has ended the mass storage of American's data, critics say that such activities can still take place (and probably are) under Executive Order 12333 and/or FISA Court judges' generous interpretation of Section 702 of the FISA Amendments Act. These powers include the collection of the actual content of internet communications and phone calls, not just metadata.

The government is using a range of surveillance technology that citizens are only dimly aware of and sometimes that technology is used in domestic criminal cases. In fact, in one case a criminal offender was given "the deal of a century" to protect secret technology. Reportedly the offender robbed a marijuana dealer and faced four years in prison. Before trial, the defense attorneys discovered that police used a "Stingray," a cell tower simulator that hijacks all cellphone transmissions in an area. When the judge ordered the prosecutor to produce the equipment, the defendant was offered an extremely generous plea bargain. According to the ACLU, the Tallahassee police used a StingRay or similar device in more than 250 investigations between 2007 and 2014. Reportedly 48 law enforcement agencies in 20 states have purchased the device, and the FBI has a gag order to prohibit law enforcement officials from discussing it. At this point, there is no Fourth Amendment law that is related specifically to the use of the device, perhaps because when defense attorneys challenge the use of the technology, defendants are offered deals too good to pass up (Nakashima, 2015).

News reports have also revealed that the DEA worked with AT&T on an enormous database called The Hemisphere Project, which allows DEA agents, working with AT&T employees, to access phone records going back to 1987. While supposedly the NSA stores their metadata for five years, this program's data goes back over 20 years and covers every call that went through an AT&T switch. Governmental spokespeople said the program does not pose privacy concerns because the data is stored by

AT&T, not the government, and that agents go through standard due-process protections (subpoenas and warrants). The very secrecy of the program (it was revealed by a privacy advocate who had received, probably mistakenly, training slides through a FOI request) indicated that it would be considered problematic by the American public (Shane and Moynihan, 2013).

Other surveillance tools used by local law enforcement include cameras on a manned civilian aircraft for wide-scale surveillance, military-grade facial recognition software, license-plate scanners, streetlights with recording capabilities, behavioral recognition software (using camera footage, the software detects suspicious activity), and intelligence analysis software partially funded by the CIA (Chen, 2014). The problematic nature of these types of surveillance and analysis technology is not so much that law enforcement is using them, but that the public is not aware of the use, nor are there good checks and balances in place to make sure the use stays within the bounds of legality.

Undercover Operations

There were close to 500 prosecutions for terrorist-related activities between 9/11 and 2012 (Human Rights Watch, 2014). Most of these prosecutions have been for "material support" and conspiracy. Generally, a target is identified in a chat room or through contacts and evaluated as to their likely involvement. An informant or governmental agent will then develop a relationship with the person. When there has been sufficient preparatory activity for criminal liability, the plot is exposed and the would-be terrorists are arrested. Critics argue, however, that many would-be terrorists would never have been able to accomplish the tasks without the involvement of the government agent. In some cases, the targets were juveniles, still living at home. In another case, the target was mentally disturbed and was in a downward mental spiral even as the plot unfolded. In still others, informants offered the targets money to participate, therefore, making it unclear if they were motivated by jihad or purely money. These cases, which result in very long prison sentences, have enraged some in Muslim communities who wonder why the targets were selected and encouraged by government agents to participate in the plot (Human Rights Watch, 2014).

Sting operations have long been used in drug and other criminal investigations and the legal test is whether the target has a predisposition to commit the crime. Supporters of such sting operations argue that identification of the would-be terrorists in jihad chat rooms shows evidence of predisposition; therefore, no entrapment has occurred and none of the accused has been successful in an entrapment defense (Wheeler, 2012). Critics argue, however, that overly aggressive pursuit of individuals in these types of operations tend to alienate the very communities that law enforcement should be partnering with and soliciting information from. If community members believe that juveniles or vulnerable malcontents are the victims of unfair or overly punitive treatment by the government, then it will be unlikely they will go to government officials when there is knowledge of "lone wolf" terrorists inspired by ISIS or al-Qaeda. An opposing argument, however, is that the April 2013 Boston bombing by Chechen brothers Dzhokhar Tsarnaev and Tamerlan Tsarnaev show that young malcontents are very capable of harming large numbers of people without government help. Discovering these potential bombers in a chat room and targeting them for an undercover operation might have saved lives.

Not only federal agents are involved in undercover operations to combat terrorism. The New York City Police Department (NYPD) evidently had an intelligence division of about 1,000 individuals, led by an ex-CIA agent, from 2003 to 2014. The unit included two dozen civilian experts, lawyers, academics, linguists, and other specialists in addition to law enforcement investigators. Later it was revealed that at least four CIA agents were "embedded" in the NYPD; in some cases taking unpaid leave from the CIA and being paid by the NYPD. In other cases NYPD officers went to Langley for training. Privacy advocates are concerned with this overlap and merging of domestic law enforcement and a spy agency that was created and continues to have a mission to protect the nation against external threats (Savage, 2013).

The unit, called the Demographic Unit and then the Zone Assessment unit, monitored jihad websites, gathered tips regarding terrorist activity, and monitored mosques with "mosque crawlers" (agents who infiltrated mosques and neighborhoods and reported back to the police intelligence analysts) and surveillance; (Feuer, 2010; Wasikowska, 2013). Critics point out that such surveillance, if conducted solely because of one's ethnicity, race, religion or legal activities may be against the law. One informant reported that he attended and took notes on the people attending a Muslim Student Group at John Jay College. This type of focus on perfectly legal groups with no suspicion attached to them is similar to the overreach that occurred in the 1970s that led to the Church Committee, which investigated governmental surveillance abuse, and the creation of the FISA court (Wasikowska, 2013).

One such surveillance operation in Newark, New Jersey, was exposed when Newark police were called to investigate the suspicious activities of NYPD operatives. The NYPD officers were "staking out" the local mosque taking pictures of car licenses and people who attended. Citizens called police to report the suspicious activity of the officers and Newark politicians were understandably concerned to find NYPD officers conducting such an operation in their city (Apuzzo and Goldman, 2011; Associated Press, 2012b).

Privacy concerns have been raised by the ACLU and various Arab Islamic rights organizations over the activities of this NYPD unit. Critics complain that the NYPD is still under legal guidelines arising from a class action lawsuit (*Handschu v. Special Services Division*, 349 F.Supp. 766, 1972) due to alleged privacy abuses by the department's "Red Squad" back in earlier decades. In 2014, Bill Bratton, Commissioner of NYPD again, disbanded the unit and reassigned the officers (Apuzzo and Goldstein, 2014).

The New York City Police Department is obviously not the only police department that has increased its activities in the area of domestic surveillance. In fact, there has been a sea change within law enforcement that has been described as a move toward "intelligence-led" policing. Part of the emphasis on collection and analysis of "pre-reasonable suspicion" data has been the creation of "fusion centers" and joint terrorism task forces, funded by the federal government, to help local police develop the capability of identifying potential threats. A national information sharing network connecting police departments and federal agencies, known as the Information Sharing Environment (ISE) has developed the ability to coordinate and share information. According to Price (2013: 3) approximately 14,600 different sub-federal law enforcement agencies, 78 regional and state-run fusion centers, and 103 Joint Terrorism Task Forces (JTTFs) now exist in an overlapping and patchwork network of information gathering. This intelligence sharing may be helpful in improving the ability to protect national security, but it also raises important questions about what information local police collect, how long do they keep it, and who do they share it with.

Various legal and privacy advocates have concerns that the fusion centers are either violative of individual privacy in collecting information about private citizens, ineffective in the types of information it collects, or both. The federal government spends well over a billion dollars on the fusion centers, but in the only governmental audit of the centers, there was little evidence that they had helped uncover any terrorist plots and they had a troubling pattern of violating Constitutional provisions regarding privacy. In a review of fusion centers and local law enforcement's role in intelligence gathering, investigators from the Brennan Center (a law school-affiliated think tank focusing on civil liberties) reported that individuals who worked in such centers and task forces received inadequate training and oversight regarding privacy protections (Price, 2013).

Critics allege that, just as in the 1960s and 1970s, unfettered power to spy has been misused today in the indiscriminate use of national security letters and spying on groups that have no possible connection to terrorism but are merely left-leaning or are groups that disagree with the administration's actions (Harris, 2006). For instance, it has been reported that the Department of Homeland Security issued a "threat assessment" of pro-choice and anti-abortion groups for a local police department, and issued a report on a Muslim conference held in Georgia. These investigations of American citizens are outside the scope of the investigative powers of the federal government (because they do not involve espionage and terrorism) and cause concern for civil libertarians even though the reports were destroyed after concerns were raised (Savage and Shane, 2009). The Office of the Inspector General (2010) issued a report that described FBI investigations of groups that could not reasonably be considered terrorist organizations, such as the Thomas Merton Center of Pittsburgh, the People for the Ethical Treatment of Animals, Greenpeace, the *Catholic Worker*, and the Religious Society of Friends. The report concluded that the FBI activities potentially implicated First Amendment rights even though the reports were destroyed.

It was reported that the latest government report detailing the numbers of "sneak and peek" warrants (a provision of the Patriot Act) reveals that most are not used for terrorism. In 2014, the Administrative Office of the U.S. Courts finally released reports on warrants requests for 2011, 2012, and 2013. An analysis of these warrants showed that, in 2011, 6,775 requests were made with only 31 being terrorism related; in 2013, 11,129 requests were made with only 51 being terrorism-related. The majority of requests were for narcotics cases (Jaycox, 2014). Thus, a provision written to provide tools to combat terrorism is being used far more often for domestic drug offenders.

Crank and Gregor (2005) also noted cases where ordinary criminals were dealt with using tools for terrorism, such as a federal law against terroristic threats applied to a lovesick woman who wanted the cruise ship she was on to turn around, the use of a law against weapons of mass destruction against a methamphetamine "cook," and the use of federal subpoena power to investigate members of an anti-war group that sponsored a rally with signs reading "Bring the Iowa Guard Home." The pattern of federal agents sharing information with local police is a troubling overlap between the powers of the federal government to protect us against terrorism and the use of such power against the nation's citizens, even if they are law violators. As mentioned previously, once rights and liberties are taken away from some groups, they become more tenuous for us all.

Thus far, the Supreme Court has either refused to hear cases concerning governmental surveillance and undercover operations or ruled in the government's favor, meaning that, legally, there seems to be great power invested in government operatives to intrude into Americans' privacy. This greater power requires greater self-control to stay within legal and ethical boundaries.

Even more troubling than mission creep and use of surveillance tools against suspected criminals is the documented abuse of such power by NSA analysts and others. Previously top secret reports were released by the NSA in response to a records request by the American Civil Liberties Union showing that dozens of NSA agents and others misused their great powers of surveillance to spy on girlfriends, spouses and others. Workers were fired or allowed to retire rather than face criminal charges (Hensley, 2014; Walker, 2014). When the barrier between federal powers designed to protect against external threats and law enforcement's domestic powers used against citizens no longer exists we have much less legal protection against unethical abuses of such power.

▌ Utilitarianism versus Human Rights–Based Policing

Utilitarianism is the ethical justification for the counterterrorism measures we've discussed. Recall that in earlier chapters it was discussed as the justification for illegal acts taken by police officers or prosecutors to secure convictions. In this section, we argue that utilitarianism is a faulty ethical justification for what has been done in the name of security after 9/11 and point out that the internationally recognized **human rights– based policing** is more firmly grounded in ethical principles.

human rights– based policing model The policing approach that recognizes the police as servants of the public good; although crime control is important, protection of civil liberties is the fundamental mission.

Our discussions since 9/11 have always been a forced choice between safety and liberty. More surveillance, more intrusions on privacy, and more law enforcement are supposed to make us safe, so we should not complain. Some argue, however, that it is a false argument to weigh privacy or any civil liberty against security. Writing before 9/11, Alderson (1998: 23) presented a prescient argument against the "end" of security as a justification for taking away liberties:

> *I acknowledge that liberty is diminished when people feel afraid to exercise it, but to stress security to unnecessary extremes at the price of fundamental freedoms plays into the hands of would-be high police despots. Such despots are quick to exploit fear in order to secure unlimited power.*

Alderson also addressed terrorism directly: "It is important for police to maintain their high ethical standards when facing terrorism, and for their leaders to inspire resistance to any degeneration into counter-terrorism terror" (1998: 71).

The major problem of utilitarianism or means–end thinking is that we are unable to know the outcome of our actions. Justifying otherwise unethical means by arguing that these means will lead to a good end depends on the ability to know that the means will result in the desired outcome. Unfortunately, this is not possible. For instance, not respecting the rights of Muslims in this country may backfire in that the Muslim community can be a great ally to police in preventing or investigating terrorist activity. If the Muslim community is cooperative with preventive efforts, it is because this community believes in the legal system and the integrity of those within it. Observers noted that one of the reasons that British police were able to identify the subway bombers so quickly in 2005 was the cooperation of the Muslim community, but that later police actions enraged community members and hardened opinion against the police; thus, it is possible that their assistance in identifying future perpetrators might be less forthcoming (Buchholz, 2005; Emling, 2005). In 2012, the Muslim community in New York City marched against the police department in opposition to what they considered illegal surveillance of their community. It is possible that police actions in this country have made it less likely that they will receive help from the community against potential terror threats.

In our utilitarian measures to protect ourselves from terrorists, it is at least conceivable that we may create more terrorists. The current generation of Middle Eastern children may identify the United States only as an aggressor; 10-year-olds who saw the pictures of American soldiers terrorizing prisoners in Abu Ghraib are in their twenties today. How do they feel about the United States? By engaging in renditions, operating secret prisons, and defending the right to torture, we have lost allies and gained enemies around the world and, in the process, have threatened our future security. By engaging in acts that are associated with oppressive countries, such as torture and secret prisons, we make it easier for radical clerics and others to convince adherents that this country is evil and deserves to be a victim of terroristic acts. By deciding that human rights exist for some and not for others, we weaken civil liberties for all citizens. Once we start parceling out human rights and justice differentially, it opens the door to those who look for an excuse to abuse and victimize.

Human rights–based law enforcement is not utilitarian. There is recognition that some acts are never justified. No end is so important that governments can stoop to slavery, genocide, or torture. No situation ever justifies sexism, racism, murder, rape, or intimidation. There is a suspicion of state power in rights-based law enforcement and a fear that police will be used to oppress the powerless. The way to avoid this is to place the protection of rights, rather than crime control, as the central theme of policing, because the definition of crime and the identification of who is a criminal may be subverted for political ends. The United Nations' *Code of Conduct for Law Enforcement Officials* illustrates the values and premise of the rights-based approach: "In the performance of their duty, law enforcement officials shall respect and protect human dignity and maintain and uphold the human rights of all persons" (Article 2, reported in Kleinig, 1999).

Neyroud and Beckley (2001: 62) describe the police standards of the United Kingdom as reflecting an emphasis on human rights. Standards include the following provisions:

- To fulfill the duties imposed on them by the law
- To respect human dignity and uphold human rights
- To act with integrity, dignity, and impartiality
- To use force only when strictly necessary, and then proportionately
- To maintain confidentiality
- Not to use torture or use ill-treatment
- To protect the health of those in their custody
- Not to commit any act of corruption
- To respect the law and the code of conduct and oppose violations of them
- To be personally liable for their acts

QUOTE & QUERY

... more has been done in the past 25 years internationally to advance the cause of human rights than in the 400 years since Hugo Grotius first began to write about the necessity for international law.

Professor David Bayley.

Source: Bayley, 2014: 3.

 What role do police have in promoting human rights across the world?

Because European police have had a longer history of dealing with terrorism, it is interesting that the trend there evidently has been to move toward a rights-based model of policing. For instance, British police have had their share of noble-cause corruption in dealing with Irish terrorists; Spain has dealt with Basque terrorists; Germany dealt with the Baader-Meinhof gang in the 1970s and, more recently, with neo-Nazi groups; and so on.

Bayley (2014) reviewed human rights policing across the world and observed that the incredibly expensive attempt to bring policing in Afghanistan and Iraq into conformance with democratic ideals has been largely regarded as a failure. Despite major efforts from the United Nations and other bilateral organizations, police reform across the world has not been extremely successful. He argues that the principles of human rights policing, including humane treatment, due process, and justice-based interactions with the public have been disseminated widely across the world, however the implementation of actual practices is much less successful. As to dissemination, Bayley reports that the United Nations' *Universal Declaration of Human Rights* (1948) is the most translated document in history. The United Nations has several documents that present standards for human rights policing, including the *Human Rights Standards for Law Enforcement* in 1996, and the Council of Europe has published the *European Code of Police Ethics* in 2001. The United Nations also has a police unit that deploys police officers worldwide to provide technical assistance and mentoring as well as monitor international agreements. The Quote and Query box indicates that Bayley is quite positive in the success of promoting the ideals of human rights and the role of police in protecting them.

As to implementation of democratic ideals, Bayley (2014), after conducting a small survey of international police experts is less optimistic. He found that experts cited only three countries that had undertaken substantial reforms: Northern Ireland, El Salvador and South Africa. Others mentioned by some, but not most experts included: Croatia, Bosnia-Herzegovina, Kosovo, East Germany, Poland, the Czech Republic, and Slovenia. Across the world, police departments continue to reflect the problems of their respective countries. Police departments in problematic, corrupt regimes share these same qualities. Democratic policing and the rule of law is associated with higher education and higher socioeconomic standing of the citizenry. Human rights–based policing comes along with broader political reform. In his presentation of proposals to advance human-rights policing, Bayley mentions the commitment of political leaders and external accountability measures for policing. Ironically, recall that external accountability measures (e.g., civilian review boards) create raging controversy whenever they are proposed in this country.

In Chapter 10, we discussed the importance of an independent judiciary. This concept is an essential element of the discussion here as well. It is no coincidence that the United Nations and the European Union both mandate that a country have an independent judiciary in order for that nation to be considered protective of human rights and thus eligible to join the European Union. The way to freedom and democracy is through the recognition of human rights, and the way to protect human rights is through an independent judiciary (Keith, 2002: 196–197).

Several observers have noted the increased militarization of the police since 9/11, which is a trend that may not be consistent with the human rights approach described here. Police departments have increasingly taken on military characteristics, buying armored vehicles and normalizing the use of military style tactics in mainstream policing. SWAT officers wear military uniforms and use flash-bang grenades and entry explosives exactly like military commando squads. The overlap between police and the military is understandable—military veterans are physically fit, respond to authority, are trained in weapons, understand hierarchy of command, and are familiar with dangerous conditions. In other ways, however, policing and military service are not similar at all and should not be. The war analogy is especially inappropriate when dealing with citizens, and police are much more likely to violate citizens' rights when they view them as the enemy. The Quote and Query box encapsulates this view.

Human rights–based policing is consistent with the procedural justice research that has been previously described in several chapters. There are good reasons for protecting rights for everyone and the proposition that criminals are our "canaries in the coalmine" has some potency. What this refers to is the way we treat criminals may be a harbinger of things to come for us all. The Supreme Court Justices may understand this in their recent ruling that cellphones are personal and police officers must obtain a warrant to search them (*Riley v. California*, June 25, 2014). The surprising unanimous decision in this case may indicate that even the most conservative Supreme Court justices are troubled by the reach of governmental surveillance and no longer persuaded by the utilitarian argument that the end of crime control justifies incursions into the liberties that all Americans should cherish and protect.

> ## QUOTE & QUERY
>
> Since 9/11, America has experienced an arguably dangerous weakening of the traditional separation between these two occupations, a blurring of the boundary lines separating the military and the police, and a move toward rather than away from, a more authoritarian dispensation.
>
> *Source: Brown, 2011: 670.*
>
> Do you agree that law enforcement is becoming more militarized? Give examples if so.

Ethical Dilemmas and Decisions

This last chapter has focused on the war on terror because it is the greatest challenge facing this country today, but it also illustrates in dramatic ways how ethics is a largely unanalyzed but powerful element in how events unfold. This last section reiterates the idea that ultimately ethics is about facing a dilemma and making a decision. Like police officers, CIA and FBI agents may be tempted to use illegal and unethical means to accomplish their mission. Like prosecutors, lawyers in the Justice Department and the military justice system have been pressured to skirt the law to pursue a good end. Like correctional officers, personnel who worked in Guantanamo and Bagram were exposed to a subculture where prisoners were considered not worthy of basic respect and humane treatment.

The My Lai incident in Vietnam has almost passed out of this nation's consciousness, but at the time, there was great debate over whether soldiers should follow their superiors' orders blindly or make an independent assessment of the morality of the action. In this case, several officers were prosecuted by a military court for killing women and children in a village during the Vietnam War without any evidence that they were a threat to the unit's safety. The officers' defense was that their superiors gave the orders to take the village without regard to whether the inhabitants were civilians or guerrillas. The rationale was that often there wasn't time to establish whether a civilian was friendly or not, and that, in any event, civilians often carried grenades or otherwise harmed U.S. troops. There was heated public discussion in support of and against the soldiers' actions. Is an individual excused from moral culpability when following orders, or should one disobey orders that one believes to be illegal or immoral? Generally, military justice does not allow a defense of "following orders" if the order is against a treaty or law.

In the Abu Ghraib prison scandal, while soldiers argued that they were only following orders when they abused the detainees, Joseph Darby was so distressed by the pictures showing various types of abuse that he turned them in to the army's CID, and the resulting investigation led to indictments and resignations. Some, however, condemned Darby as a traitor to his country, and he and his family received death threats and were not able to return to their hometown to live because of the town's hostility to him.

A soldier's dilemma is not all that different from a police officer's dilemma in that both organizations place a great emphasis on chain of command and loyalty. It is possible that police officers may receive orders that they know to be illegal and/or unethical from their field training officer (FTO) or other supervisor. Do police officers or other criminal justice professionals have a duty to substitute their personal moral judgments when presented with an unlawful or unethical order, or is obedience to superiors mandatory? In these circumstances, one has to depend on the law rather than the chain of command. If the action is clearly illegal, there will be no defense if the individual officer follows orders; he or she will still be legally culpable. If the action is not against the law but is against policy, departmental sanctions may be applied. If the action is not against the law and not against departmental policy, does any ethical system support going against one's superior? Following appropriate grievance procedures if something seems to be wrong may be a more supportable avenue unless there is immediate harm to an innocent or a pattern of wrongful action going up the chain of command.

Some of the hardest decisions one will be faced with in the course of a career involve going against superiors or colleagues. Even if the behavior is obviously illegal, it is difficult to challenge authority. **Whistleblowers** are those who risk their career to expose wrongdoing in their organization. Of course, some may have purely egocentric reasons for exposing wrongdoing, but many whistleblowers do so because their principles and individual ethical system will not allow them to stand quiet when others in the organization are committing unethical and/or illegal acts.

In a recent Supreme Court case, Justice Sotomayor, in her holding clarified an earlier case ruling and provided greater protections to public employees who come forward to report wrongdoing in their agencies. In *Garcetti v. Ceballos* (2006), discussed in an earlier chapter, The Supreme Court held that a prosecutor was not covered under whistleblower protection because his disclosure to the defense attorney of Brady material was part of his job, not First Amendment speech. This case holding acted to freeze public employees from reporting wrongdoing because most public jobs could be interpreted as having a duty to report wrongdoing; thus, if one were fired or demoted, there would be no First Amendment challenge as a legal protection. In the more recent case, a youth worker testified that a legislator was being paid from public funds but not actually working. The legislator was convicted of bribery, but the worker who testified against her was fired. He filed a whistleblower protection suit and the state's position was that it was his duty to report, and, therefore, not First Amendment speech. The Supreme Court held that he had testified as a citizen and his testimony was on a matter of public concern. Thus, even when the testimony relates to public employment or concerns information learned during that employment it is considered First

whistleblowers
Individuals, usually employees, who find it impossible to live with knowledge of corruption or illegality within a government or organization and expose it, usually creating a scandal.

Amendment speech (*Lane v. Franks*, June 19, 2014). This case should provide some degree of comfort to whistleblowers in public agencies, although the extent of the ruling remains to be seen.

Throughout this book, the Walking the Walk boxes have presented individuals facing ethical dilemmas. Some of them were involved in the war on terror, such as Charles Swift, who was assigned to defend Salim Ahmed Hamdan against the president and the Pentagon; Mary McCarthy, who might have exposed the secret prisons; James Yee, who defended the rights of the detainees in Guantanamo and was labeled a traitor as a result; and Joe Darby, who revealed the abuses occurring at Abu Ghraib. There are also others who might be labeled whistleblowers because they came forward with information about governmental actions they believed to be wrong. Babak Pasdar, a computer security expert, was hired to conduct a security audit of a major telecommunications carrier. In the course of his audit, he found a mysterious circuit that others called the "Quantico circuit," which was sending all information about telephone and e-mail from subscribers to a government facility in Quantico, Virginia. When Pasdar asked about it and objected that it was a threat to the security of the system, he was told to forget that he ever saw it. He could not forget it, though, and, because of his concern, ended up testifying before Congress about what he witnessed and went public in March 2006. Pasdar is now affiliated with an organization that seeks to protect the privacy of Americans from secret governmental spying (Devine, 2008: 4A).

Lieutenant Commander Matthew Diaz was a JAG lawyer for the joint military task force at Guantanamo, in charge of holding and interrogating enemy combatants. He supported the 2004 Supreme Court decision *Rasul v. Bush*, granting detainees the right of habeas corpus, and thought they should be allowed lawyers to represent them. He disagreed with the government's refusal to supply the names of the detainees after a civil rights organization had filed a request under the Freedom of Information Act to obtain them. On January 15, 2005, he mailed a list of detainees to the Center for Constitutional Rights in New York. In 2006, a federal court declared that the list of names was public information, and the government released it to the Associated Press, but Diaz was still prosecuted for his disclosure with the government arguing that he exposed the United States to danger. Diaz was convicted and sentenced in May 2007 to six months' imprisonment and was given a dishonorable discharge (Wiltrout, 2007).

Coleen Rowley was the FBI lawyer who made headlines when she publicly reported that officials in Washington ignored reports from the field about Zacarias Moussaoui, who admitted conspiring with al-Qaeda. Rowley retired from the FBI in frustration over the bureaucratic practices that punished those who criticized superiors who were not doing their job in sharing and analyzing important information (Carr, 2005: A1, A6).

It is not only whistleblowers, however, who face ethical dilemmas. Sometimes, ethics simply means doing one's job. General Antonio Taguba was tasked with preparing a report on Abu Ghraib. He was criticized informally, evidently for the comprehensiveness of the report and his strong condemnation of the practices he found there. According to reports, his career was derailed by doing his job too well in investigating and chronicling the abuses at Abu Ghraib and documenting the lack of leadership that led to the abuses.

In 2014, an editorial in the *New York Times* called for "positive accountability." Noting that there were not going to be any prosecutions for torture, illegal wiretapping, or other potential illegalities that took place in the governmental response to 9/11, the writer called for publicly celebrating those who "kept their moral clarity intact" and objected to what they knew to be wrong; in some cases at great personal cost. In addition to those already mentioned earlier, they included:

> *Alberto Mora, former general counsel of the Navy, who fought against the vicious new protocols [of enhanced interrogation]; Philip Zelikow, an adviser to Condoleezza Rice who wrote an "anti-torture memo" that the White House attempted to destroy; and Ian Fishback, an infantry captain who reported widespread prisoner abuses by his own unit. Getting no clear response from his chain of command, Fishback wrote an open letter to Senator John McCain. Fishback asked: "Do we sacrifice our ideals in order to preserve security?" His answer: "I would rather die fighting than give up even the smallest part of the idea that is 'America'"* (Luban, 2014).

The author called for President Obama to praise these people, and even award some Presidential Medals of Freedom. Thus far, there is no indication that is going to happen. There are many others—some known, many more unknown—who faced difficult decisions about what was right in the days, months, and years after 9/11.

How we face and resolve dilemmas is influenced by our ethical systems and understanding that doing the right thing is not always easy, nor is it necessarily easy to determine what is right. Some of the individuals mentioned earlier were and still are criticized bitterly over their decisions. While some consider them heroes, others consider them traitors. One might agree with their goals and disagree with their actions. We cannot deny, however, that they faced their dilemma and chose to do what they considered was right, knowing they would face consequences for doing so.

In the final analysis, the approach we have taken throughout this book is perhaps the best one when faced with any type of ethical dilemma. To review, when faced with a dilemma one should consider law, policy, and then apply several ethical systems such as utilitarianism and ethical formalism in order to determine the right course of action:

- Is there relevant law? Are you being asked to do something or observe something that is contrary to state, national, or military law?
- Is there relevant policy? Does the action violate company or agency policy? If you feel the policy is wrong, can you use official channels to object?
- Finally, what do ethical systems tell you to do?

Although utilitarianism may be the most pervasive ethical system used in the war on terror and when responding to other dilemmas, there must be limits to what can be done for a "good end." Too often, the worst abuses are justified by perpetrators using a faulty utilitarian justification. Utilitarianism cannot provide a justification when there is no proof that the bad "means" was the only way to get to the good "end." More importantly, it is impossible to know the outcome of one's actions, therefore, the argument of greater good cannot be supported in many cases. Expediency and fear often are the enemies of coherent ethical analysis. It is always best to also consider ethical formalism or ethics of care when considering the right course of action along with utilitarianism, or, even the simpler "front page test," which basically just asks you to consider how you would feel if your action was described on the front page of a newspaper. If you would not want your actions exposed, there may be problems with your ethical analysis.

For the criminal justice professional who must uphold and enforce the law, the discussion of morality, justice, and law is not just academic. Line officers often face questions of individual morality versus obedience and loyalty to one's superiors or the organization. One thing that every professional must understand is that they alone are morally and ethically responsible for their own decisions and actions. It is for this reason that the study of ethics is so important. Although professionals and practitioners may get bogged down with day-to-day problems, and bureaucratic agendas may cause them to lose sight of larger goals, foremost in their minds should always be the true scope and meaning of the power inherent in the criminal justice system. It is people who make a *justice* system *just* (or corrupt). To protect the citizenry from misuse and abuse of power, personnel in the criminal justice system must have a strong professional identity. Their power must be recognized for what it is and held as a sacred trust.

Criminal justice professionals are public servants and, as such, should aspire to a higher standard of behavior. They have a duty to the citizenry they serve, but even more than that, they must possess the moral and ethical sense to prevent the power inherent in their positions from being used for tyranny. Education isn't enough. Learning a body of knowledge and acquiring essential skills do not give individuals the moral sense necessary to use those skills wisely. Witness the recurring scandals involving lawyers and business professionals. A highly educated group is not necessarily free from corruption.

Criminal justice practitioners find themselves faced with a wide spectrum of ethical choices, including:

- Balancing friendship against institutional integrity—that is, when friends and colleagues engage in inappropriate or illegal behavior or rule breaking
- Balancing community and/or client (or offender) needs against bureaucratic efficiency and institutional goals
- Balancing personal goals or biases that conflict with fair and impartial treatment of the public and the clients served

Most people in the criminal justice field (or, indeed, any profession) have basically good characters. However, it can be argued that in some situations even those who have formed habits of honesty, truthfulness, and integrity are sincerely perplexed as to the correct course of behavior. These situations arise because the behavior choice seems so innocuous or trivial (e.g., whether to accept free coffee) or so difficult (e.g., a partner or friend wants you to cover up something she did wrong). In these instances, where basically good people have trouble deciding what to do, the ethical systems might help them analyze their choices.

It must also be accepted that in some dilemmas there are going to be costs involved in making the right decision. For instance, an officer who knows it is his duty to provide evidence against his brother-in-law, who is a major drug dealer, may lose his wife's and children's love. There is no assurance that doing the right thing will not come at a high cost. The ethical person may not necessarily be honored; some have been heavily sanctioned. However, those who do not expose wrongdoing and/or go along with it in an effort not to "rock the boat" often find that their long-term peace of mind pays the price for their silence.

QUOTE & QUERY

Political liberty, which is one of the greatest gifts people can acquire, is threatened when social order is threatened. It is dismaying to see how ready many people are to turn to strong leaders in hopes that they will end, by adopting strong measures, the disorder that has been the product of failed or fragile commitments. Drug abuse, street crime, and political corruption are the expression of unfettered choices. To end them, rulers, with the warm support of the people, will often adopt measures that threaten true political freedom. The kind of culture that can maintain reasonable human commitments takes centuries to create but only a few generations to destroy.

Source: James Q. Wilson, cited in Cole, 2002: 234.

 Although Wilson's statement is discussing the sacrifice of due process in the drug war and crime control, it has incredible relevance to the issues of terrorism. Interestingly, it was made by a noted conservative. How do we meet the threat of terrorists?

Conclusion

The 9/11 attack and other assaults on U.S. targets around the world have created a sense of vulnerability and fear. The response to this fear has been to reduce civil liberties through law, policy, and individual practices. This "end justifies the means" thinking is insidious and pervasive. If utilitarianism is used as a justification for wiretapping, governmental secrecy and other actions, then one must also show what facts exist to prove that the desired end will be brought about and that negative side effects do not outweigh the good that one seeks. This step seems to be missing in many current discussions. However, ethical formalism and other systems would conclude that even if one could prove the good end outweighs the bad means, some acts cannot ever be justified. Certain human rights belong to everyone—even criminals, even terrorists. In the crime war, drug war, or war on terror, the most important element of making ethical decisions is to apply ethical reasoning and not succumb to fear. Our final Quote and Query box makes a case for political liberty.

Most of us are lucky in that we will never have to decide whether or not to participate in torture, violate laws against wiretapping, or expose secrets in a way that could be considered a threat to national security. Criminal justice professionals, however, will probably encounter at least some of the dilemmas that have been described in previous chapters. The power of discretion, authority, and the duty of protecting public safety create dilemmas for these professionals that are quite different from those that most citizens encounter. Ultimately, for criminal justice professionals as well as everyone else, the way you resolve dilemmas throughout the course of your career will constitute, in no small measure, the person you are.

Chapter Review

1. **Identify the basic themes of the book.**

   The presence of authority, power, force, and discretion exists in each of the subsystems of the criminal justice system. Informal practices and value systems among criminal justice actors may vary from formal codes of ethics. The importance of ethical leadership exists in each area of the system. The tension between deontological ethical systems and teleological or "means–end" ethical analysis also exists in each area of the system, as well as in the war on terror.

2. **Describe the basic elements of the "just war" debate and the "just means" discussion.**

   The traditional justification for war comes from natural law, and the second justification comes from positivist law. Natural law gives sovereigns the right to use force to uphold the good of the community, when unjust injuries are inflicted on others, and to protect the state. Positivist law justifies war when agreed upon by international bodies such as the United Nations.

3. **Describe the responses to 9/11.**

   Since 9/11, the nation has been involved in moral debates over such responses as detainments, renditions and secret prisons, Guantanamo and the military commissions, the use of torture, governmental secrecy, wiretapping, and threats to privacy through undercover operations.

4. **Explain the human rights–based model of policing.**

   Human rights–based policing is not utilitarian. In the human rights model, values, and ethics focus on human rights, including the right to due process, and the fundamental duty of all public servants is to protect those rights. In this approach, the protection of rights is more important than the end of crime control.

5. **Present a method to resolve ethical dilemmas.**

   The method used throughout the book has been to evaluate the choices of action based on relevant law, policy, and ethics. A short ethical test is the "front-page test."

Study Questions

1. What are some actions the federal government has taken in response to terrorism?
2. What are the arguments in support of torture? What are the arguments against torture?
3. What are some rights recognized by the United Nations and the European Union?
4. Explain why "means–end" thinking leads to criminal actions.
5. What are the two justifications for a just war?

Writing/Discussion Exercises

1. Write an essay on (or discuss) the most difficult ethical dilemma in this chapter, and try to answer it by considering law, policy, and ethics. Also, use the "front-page test." This is a quick ethics test that asks if you would feel comfortable if your action were published on the front page of the newspaper. If you would not want it to be, there may be an ethical problem with your action.
2. Write an essay on (or discuss) an ethical or moral dilemma from your own life. Try to solve it by using any guidelines derived from this book. Be explicit about the procedure you used to arrive at a decision and about the decision itself.
3. Write a code of ethics for yourself.

Key Terms

Dirty Harry problem	national security letters	terrorism
human rights–based policing model	positivist law	whistleblowers
	principle of double effect	

ETHICAL DILEMMAS

Situation 1

You are a member of Congress, and the Patriot Act is coming up for a vote to renew its provisions. What would you do, and why?

Situation 2

As a soldier in Afghanistan, you have pictures of fellow soldiers engaging in various acts of abuse and torture. What, if anything, would you do with the pictures?

Situation 3

You are a new police officer and are talking with other officers before roll call. The group is loudly and energetically proposing various gruesome torture techniques to get al-Qaeda operatives to talk. There is some hyperbole in the discussion, but also the sincere belief that torture is justified by the circumstances. What do you think about this position? If you object to torture, would you make your position known?

Situation 4

You live next door to an Arab family, and you hear the husband talking negatively about the United States. Your friends at work tell you that you should report him to the police because he might be a terrorist. What would you do? Why?

Situation 5

You are the president of the United States, and there has been another terrorist attack using passenger airplanes. One has crashed into the Pentagon, and another is heading for the White House. You have deployed fighter jets to surround the plane, and whoever is flying it refuses to acknowledge the command to turn around. Your military commanders are advising you to shoot down the plane—an act that would kill the 353 people aboard. What would you do? Would your answer be any different if it were heading toward the Statue of Liberty? Toward an athletic stadium filled to capacity?

Bibliography

48 Hours Mystery.com. 2011. "Students Help Free Wrongfully Convicted Man." 2011. *48 Hours Mystery*, April 23. Retrieved 7/30/2012 from www.cbsnews.com/2100-18559_162-20056494.html.

Aaronson, T. 2005. "Hollywood's Finest: After Even a Police Chief Called Them Unfit, These Officers Continue to Patrol Hollywood's Streets." *Broward Palm Beach.com*, June 30. Retrieved 7/29/2012 from www.browardpalmbeach.com/content/printVersion/139221.

Abbey-Lambertz, J. 2015. "Charges Dismissed Against Joseph Weekley, Cop Who Fatally Shot Sleeping 7-Year-Old." *Huffington Post.com*, January 28, 2015.

Acker, J. and A. Redlich. 2011. *Wrongful Convictions: Law, Science, and Policy*. Durham, NC: Carolina Academic Press.

Adams, S. 2014. "The Highest Paid CEOs Are the Worst Performers, Study Says." *Forbes.com*, June 18, 2014. Retrieved from http://www.forbes.com/sites/susanadams/2014/06/16/the-highest-paid-ceos-are-the-worst-performers-new-study-says/.

Adams, V. 1981. "How to Keep Em Honest." *Psychology Today*, November: 52–53.

Adams, W. 2010. "Sentenced to Serving the Good Life in Norway." *Time*. Retrieved 7/30/2012 from www.time.com/time/magazine/article/0,9171,2000920,00.html.

AFL/CIO.org. 2015. "100 Highest Paid Executives." Retrieved 7/1/2015 from http://www.aflcio.org/Corporate-Watch/Paywatch-2014/100-Highest-Paid-CEOs.

Akers, R. L. 1998. *Social Learning and Social Structure: A General Theory of Crime and Deviance*. Boston, MA: Northeastern University Press.

Albarazi, H. 2015. "DA Launches Probe Into Law Enforcement Misconduct." *SF Bay.com*, March 30, 2015. http://sfbay.ca/2015/03/30/da-launches-probe-into-law-enforcement-misconduct.

Alderson, J. 1998. *Principled Policing: Protecting the Public with Integrity*. Winchester, MA: Waterside.

Aleixo, P. and C. Norris. 2000. "Personality and Moral Reasoning in Young Offenders." *Personality and Individual Differences* 28(3): 609–623.

Alexander, M. 2010. *The New Jim Crow: Mass Imprisonment in the Age of Colorblindness*. New York City: The New Press.

Alexander, M. 2013. "Why Police Lie Under Oath." *New York Times*, February 3: SR4.

Allen, H. and C. Simonsen. 1986. *Corrections in America: An Introduction*. New York: Macmillan.

Allen, M. 2005. "DeLay Wants Panel to Review Role of Courts." *Washington Post*, April 2. Retrieved 7/30/2012 from www.washingtonpost.com/wp-dyn/articles/A19793-2005Apr1.html.

Allyn, B. 2013. "Jury Convicts Former Metro Cop of Official Misconduct, Acquits Him on Rape Charges." *The Tennessean*, July 18, 2013. Retrieved from http://archive.tennessean.com/article/20130718/NEWS/307180111/Jury-convicts-former-Metro-cop-official-misconduct-acquits-him-rape-charges.

Alpert, B. 2010. "Impeached Judge Thomas Porteous Will Be Tried by Senate Committee." *Nola.com*, March 12. Retrieved 7/30/2012 from www.nola.com/crime/index.ssf/2010/03/impeached_judge_thomas_porteou.html.

Alpert, G. and R. Dunham. 2004. *Understanding Police Use of Force*. New York: Cambridge University Press.

Alpert, G. and J. MacDonald. 2001. "Police Use of Force: An Analysis of Organizational Characteristics." *Justice Quarterly* 18(2): 393–409.

Alpert, G. and J. Noble. 2009. "Lies, True Lies, and Conscious Deception: Police Officers and the Truth." *Police Quarterly* 12(2): 237–254.

American Bar Association. 2007. *Model Code of Judicial Conduct*. Retrieved 7/30/2012 from www.americanbar.org/groups/professional_responsibility/publications/model_code_of_judicial_conduct.html.

American Bar Association. 2015a. *Model Rules of Professional Responsibility*. Retrieved 6/11/2015 from www.americanbar.org/groups/professional_responsibility/publications/model_rules_of_professional_conduct.html

American Bar Association. 2015b. *Standards for Criminal Justice*, 4th ed. Retrieved 6/11/2015 from http://www.americanbar.org/groups/criminal_justice/standards/ProsecutionFunctionFourthEdition.html.

American Judicature. 2005. "Judicial Independence." Retrieved 7/30/2012 from www.ajs.org/include/story.asp?content_id=418.

Amnesty International. 2007. *Amnesty International's Concerns About TASER Use: Statement to the U.S. Justice Department Inquiry into Deaths in Custody*. London: Amnesty International.

Anderson, C. 2010. "John Connolly Gets 40 Years in Prison." *WBZ38.com*, January 15. Retrieved 5/15/2010 from http://wbtv.com/local/john.connolly.sentence.2.909001.html.

Anderson, P. and L. T. Winfree. 1987. *Expert Witnesses: Criminologists in the Courtroom*. Albany, NY: SUNY Press.

Antes, A., S. Murphy, E. Waples, M. Mumford, R. Brown, S. Connelly, and L. Devenport. 2009. "A Meta-analysis of Ethics Instruction Effectiveness in the Sciences." *Ethics and Behavior* 19(5): 379–402.

Apuzzo, M. 2014. "Local Police Gearing Up With Tools of Combat." *The Seattle Times*, June 9: A4.

Apuzzo, M. 2014b. "Profiling Rules Said to Give F.B.I. Tactical Leeway." *New York Times*, April 10: A1.

Apuzzo, M. 2015. "Police Rethink Long Tradition on Using Force." *New York Times*, May 5: A1.

Apuzzo, M. and A. Goldman. 2011. "New York Police, CIA Team Up for Secret Anti-Terror Unit." *Austin American-Statesman*, August 25, 2011: A5.

Apuzzo, M. and J. Goldstein. 2014. "New York Drops Unit That Spied Among Muslims." *New York Times*, April 16: A1.

Arax, M. 1999. "Ex-Guard Says 4 Men Set Up Rape of Inmate." *Los Angeles Times*, October 14, 1999: A3.

Arax, M. 2004. "Guard Challenges Code of Silence." *Los Angeles Times*, January 20. Retrieved 7/30/2012 from http://articles.latimes.com/2004/jan/20/local/me-guard20.

Ariens, M. 2008. "American Legal Ethics in an Age of Anxiety." *St. Mary's Law Journal* 40: 343–452.

Ariens, M. 2009. "Playing Chicken: An Instant History of the Battle over Exceptions to Client Confidences." *Journal of the Legal Profession* 33: 239–300.

Aristotle. 2012. *Nicomachean Ethics*. Retrieved 7/30/2012 from www.cwu.edu/~warren/Unit1/aristotles_virtues_and_vices.htm.

Armstrong, K. and M. Possley. 2002. "The Verdict: Dishonor." *Chicago Tribune Reports*, November 11. Retrieved 11/11/2002 from www.chicagotribune.com/news/watchdog/chi-020103trial1,0,479347.story.

Aronson, R. and J. McMurtrie. 2007. "The Use and Misuse of High-Tech Evidence by Prosecutors: Ethical and Evidentiary Issues." *Fordham Law Review* 76: 1453–1538.

Arrigo, B. and N. Claussen. 2003. "Police Corruption and Psychological Testing: A Strategy for Reemployment Screening." *International Journal of Offender Therapy and Comparative Criminology* 47: 272–290.

Ashkanasy, N., C. Windsor, and L. Trevino. 2006. "Bad Apples in Bad Barrels Revisited: Cognitive Moral Development, Just World Beliefs, Rewards, and Ethical Decision-Making." *Business Ethics Quarterly* 16(4): 449–473.

Ashkenas, J., H. Fairfield, J. Keller, and P. Volpe. 2014. "7 Key Points From the C.I.A. Torture Report." *New York Times*, December 9: A1.

Associated Press. 2004. "FBI Apologizes to Lawyer Held in Madrid Bombings." MSNBC.com, May 25. Retrieved 7/30/2012 from www.msnbc.msn.com/id/5053007/.

Associated Press. 2008b. "Wife Says Cleric Tortured After CIA Captured Him." *Austin American-Statesman*, May 15: A4.

Associated Press. 2009a. "Probation Was Most Common Punishment for Prison Smuggling." *Austin American-Statesman*, March 15: B1.

Associated Press. 2012a. "Port Angeles: Death Penalty Option for Sex Offender Killer." *The Olympian*, June 8. Retrieved 7/30/2012 from www.theolympian.com/2012/06/08/2133098/port-angeles-death-penalty-option.html.

Associated Press. 2012b. "Records Detail Mosque Spying, NYPD Defends Tactics." *USA Today*, February 24. Retrieved 7/29/2012 from www.usatoday.com/news/nation/story/2012-02-22/newark-nypd-muslim-spying/53212918/1.

Associated Press. 2012c. "Judge Dismisses Former State Department Official's Lawsuit in Italian Kidnapping Case." *Washington Post*, January 5. Retrieved 6/15/2012 from www.washingtonpost.com/politics/courts-law/judge-dismisses-former-state-department-officials-lawsuit-in-italian-kidnapping-case/2012/01/05/gIQAMnuodP_story.html

Associated Press. 2013a. "Court-Appointed Watchdog Says Oakland Police Fails to Protect Whistleblowers." CBSlocal.com, July 20. Retrieved 8/3/2015 from http://sanfrancisco.cbslocal.com/2013/07/20/court-appointed-watchdog-says-oakland-police-fails-to-protect-whistleblowers/

Associated Press. 2013b. "Potential Taxpayer Tab for Albuquerque Police Misconduct Cases is Above $12 Million." *The Arizona Republic*, April 7. Retrieved 8/3/2015 from http://www.therepublic.com/view/story/4d19f8a524e242afa9bba91779122251/NM—Albuquerque-Police-Lawsuits.

Associated Press. 2014. "Florida Fires 32 Prison Guards After Inmate Deaths." Associated Press, September 21. Retrieved 8/3/2015 from http://www.tallahassee.com/story/news/2014/09/21/florida-fires-prison-guards-inmate-deaths/15999207/Florida fires 32 prison guards after inmate deaths

Associated Press. 2015. "Prosecutor in Texas Execution Case Accused of Misconduct." *Austin American Statesman*, March 18, 2015: A1.

Atherley, L. and M. Hickman. 2013. "Officer Decertification and the National Decertification Index." *Police Quarterly* 16: 420–437.

Attard, B. 2010. "Oversight of Law Enforcement Is Beneficial and Needed—Both Inside and Out." *Pace Law Review* 30: 1548–1561.

Auerhahn, K. 1999. "Selective Incapacitation and the Problem of Prediction." *Criminology* 37(4): 705–734.

Axtman, K. 2003. "Bungles in Texas Crime Lab Stir Doubt over DNA." *Christian Science Monitor*, April 18. Retrieved 7/30/2012 from www.csmonitor.com/2003/0418/p03s01-usgn.html.

Baelz, P. 1977. *Ethics and Beliefs*. New York: Seabury.

Baker, A. 2012. "Independent Agency Gets New Powers to Prosecute New York Police Officers." *New York Times*, March 28: A20.

Baker, A. and J. McGinty. 2010. "NYPD Confidential." *New York Times*, March 26. Retrieved 7/30/2012 from www.nytimes.com/2010/03/28/nyregion/28iab.html.

Balko, R. 2009. "Report: New York State Crime Lab Tainted by Incompetence, Corruption, Indifference." Reason.com blog, December 18. Retrieved 7/30/2012 from http://reason.com/blog/2009/12/18/report-new-york-state-crime-la.

Balko, R. 2011. "Take the Money and Run." *Slate*, February 4. Retrieved 7/30/2012 from www.slate.com/articles/news_and_politics/jurisprudence/2010/02/take_the_money_and_run.html

Balko, R. 2011b. "Private Crime Labs Could Prevent Errors, Analyst Bias: Report." *Huffington Post*, June 14, 2011

Balko, S. 2013a. *Rise of the Warrior Cop*. New York City, NY: Public Affairs.

Balko, S. 2013b. "Rise of the Warrior Cop." *Wall Street Journal*, July 19, 2013: C1.

Balko, R. 2014. "A (Sort Of) Defense of South Carolina State Trooper Sean Groubert." *Washington Post*, September 26. Retrieved 8/3/2015 from http://www.washingtonpost.com/news/the-watch/wp/2014/09/26/a-sort-of-defense-of-south-carolina-state-trooper-sean-groubert.

Bamford, J. 2012. "The NSA is Building the Country's Biggest Spy Center (Watch What You Say)." *Wired.com*, March 15. Retrieved 8/3/2015 from www.wired.com/2012/03/ff_nsadatacenter.

Bandura, A. 1964. *Principles of Behavior Modification*. New York: Holt, Rinehart and Winston.

Bandura, A. 1969. "Social Learning of Moral Judgments." *Journal of Personality and Social Psychology* 11: 275–279.

Bandura, A. 1971. *Social Learning Theory*. New York: General Learning Press.

Bandura, A. 1990. "Mechanisms of Moral Disengagement in Terrorism." In *Origins of Terrorism: Psychologies, Ideologies, Theologies, States of Mind*, ed. W. Reich, 161–191. Cambridge, England: Cambridge University Press.

Bandura, A. 1991. "Social Cognitive Theory of Moral Thought and Action." In *Handbook of Moral Behavior and Development*, ed. W. Kurtines and J. Gewirtz, 44–103. Hillsdale, NJ: Lawrence Erlbaum.

Bandura, A. 2002. "Selective Moral Disengagement in the Exercise of Moral Agency." *Journal of Moral Education* 31(2): 101–119.

Banks, C. 2014. "Implementing Law Enforcement Ethics Democratic Policing Reform: Challenges and Constraints in Three Developing Countries." In *Law Enforcement Ethics*, ed. B. Fitch, 347–385. Thousand Oaks, CA: Sage

Bannon, A., E. Velasco, L. Casey, and L. Reagan. 2013. *The New Politics of Judicial Elections, 2011-2012*. Washington, DC: Brennan Center. Retrieved from http://www.brennancenter.org/publication/new-politics-judicial-elections-2011-12.

Barber, B. and H. Lassek. 2010. "Bartlett: Judgment Protection Needed." *Tulsaworld.com*, July 25. Retrieved 7/30/2012 from www.tulsaworld.com/site/printerfriendlystory.aspx?articleid=20100725_11_A1_Financ960321.

Barber, E. 2014. "Dallas Targets Wrongful Convictions, and Revolution Starts to Spread." *Christian Science Monitor*, May 25. Retrieved 8/3/2015 from http://www.csmonitor.com/USA/Justice/2014/0525/Dallas-targets-wrongful-convictions-and-revolution-starts-to-spread.

Barker, K. 2015a. "Choice for Addicts: Use Again, or Lose Home." *New York Times*, May 31: A1.

Barker, K. 2015b. "Stringer Zeros in on 'Three-Quarter' Homes, Urging an End to City Referrals." *New York Times*, June 16: A20.

Barker, K. 2015c. "City Task Force to Investigate 'Sober' Homes." *New York Times*, June 1, 2015: A14.

Barker, T. 1983. "Rookie Police Officers' Perceptions of Police Occupational Deviance." *Police Studies* 6: 30–40.

Barker, T. and D. Carter, eds. 1994. *Police Deviance*, 3rd ed. Cincinnati: Anderson.

Barker, T. and D. Carter. 1991. "Police Lies and Perjury: A Motivation-Based Taxonomy." In *Police Deviance*, 2nd ed., ed. T. Barker and D. Carter. Cincinnati: Anderson.

Barnes, R. 2007. "High Court Reaffirms Leeway on Sentencing." *Austin American-Statesman*, December 11: A7.

Barrier, G., M. Stohr, C. Hemmens, and R. Marsh. 1999. "A Practical User's Guide: Idaho's Method for Implementing Ethical Behavior in a Correctional Setting." *Corrections Compendium* 24(4): 1–3.

Barry, V. 1985. *Applying Ethics: A Text with Readings*. Belmont, CA: Wadsworth.

Bartley, L. 2014. "ABC7 Eyewitness News Obtains Evidence Against Los Angeles County Sheriff's Department Defendants." ABC7 Eyewitness News, October 14. Retrieved 8/3/2015 from http://abc7.com/news/exclusive-abc7-eyewitness-news-obtains-lasd-trial-evidence/350453.

Barton, G. 2014. "Officers Investigated for Hampering Strip Search Inquiry Not Charged." *Milwaukee Journal Sentinel*, September 13. Retrieved 8/3/2015 from www.jsonline.com/watchdog/watchdogreports/officers-investigated-for-hampering-strip-search-inquiry-not-charged-b99345460z1-275030441.html.

Bateman, T. S. and D. W. Organ. 1983. "Job Satisfaction and the Good Soldier: The Relationship Between Affect and Employee 'Citizenship.'" *Academy of Management Journal* 26(4): 587–595.

Bay City News. 2007. "Three Oakland 'Riders' Still Seeking Arbitration." *East Bay Daily News*, February 6. Retrieved 3/28/2008 from www.ebdailynews.com/article/2007-2-6-02-06-07-bcn89.

Bayley, D. 2014. "Human Rights in Policing: A Global Assessment." *Policing and Society: An International Journal of Research and Policy*. DOI: 10.1080/10439463.2014.895352

Bayley, D. and R. Perito. 2011. *Police Corruption, What Past Scandals Teach About Current Challenges*. U.S. Institute for Peace. Retrieved from www.usip.org.

Bazelon, L. 2015. "Scalia's Embarrassing Question: Innocence is Not Enough to Get You Out of Prison." *Slate*, March 11. Retrieved 8/3/2015 from www.slate.com/articles/news_and_politics/jurisprudence/2015/03/innocence_is_not_cause_for_exoneration_scalia_s_embarrassing_question_is.single.html.

Bazemore, G. and D. Maloney. 1994. "Rehabilitating Community Service: Toward Restorative Service Sanctions in a Balanced Justice System." *Federal Probation* 58(1): 24–35.

Bazerman, M. and M. Tenbrunsel. 2011. *Blind Spots: Why We Fail to Do What's Right and What to Do About It*. Princeton, NJ: Princeton University Press.

Bazley, T., T. Mieczkowski, and K. Lersch. 2009. "Early Intervention Program Criteria: Evaluating Officer Use of Force." *Justice Quarterly* 26(1): 107–124.

BBC.news. 2015. "Judge Appeals Against Facebook Training Demand." BBC.com, April 29. Retrieved 8/3/2015 from http://www.bbc.com/news/technology-32513074.

Beauchamp, T. 1982. *Philosophical Ethics*. New York: McGraw-Hill.

Beccaria, C. 1764/1977. *On Crimes and Punishment*, 6th ed., trans. Henry Paolucci. Indianapolis: Bobbs-Merrill.

Beck, A., P. Guerino, and P. Harrison. 2010. *Sexual Victimization in Juvenile Facilities Reported by Youth, 2008–2009*. Washington, DC: Bureau of Justice Statistics, U.S. Dept. of Justice.

Beck, A. and P. Harrison. 2010. *Sexual Victimization in Prisons and Jails Reported by Inmates, 2008–2009*. Washington, DC: Bureau of Justice Statistics, U.S. Dept. of Justice.

Beck, A. and C. Johnson. 2012. *Sexual Victimization Reported by Former State Prisoners, 2008*. Washington, DC: Bureau of Justice Statistics, U.S. Dept. of Justice.

Beck, A., M. Berzofsky, R. Caspar, and C. Krebs. 2013. *Sexual Victimization in Prisons and Jails Reported by Inmates*. Washington, DC: Bureau of Justice Statistics, U.S. Department of Justice.

Bedau, H. 1982. "Prisoners' Rights." *Criminal Justice Ethics* 1(1): 26–41.

Beecher-Monas, E. 2009. "Reality Bites: The Illusion of Science in Bite-Mark Evidence." *Cardozo Law Review* 30: 1369–1410.

Bellamy, A. 2004. "Ethics and Intervention: 'The Humanitarian Exception' and the Problem of Abuse in the Case of Iraq." *Journal of Peace Research* 41: 131–145.

Bells, J. 2015. "America's Dirtiest Cops: Cash, Cocaine and Corruption on the Texas Border." *Rolling Stone*, January 5. Retrieved 8/3/2015 from http://www.rollingstone.com/culture/features/americas-dirtiest-cops-cash-cocaine-texas-hidalgo-county-20150105?page=7.

Bentham, J. 1843. "The Rationale of Punishment." In *Ethical Choice: A Case Study Approach*, ed. R. Beck and J. Orr. New York: Free Press, 1970.

Berman. M. 2015. "After the Justice Department Report, What's Next for Ferguson?" *Washington Post*. March 8. Retrieved 8/3/2015 from www.washingtonpost.com/news/post-nation/wp/2015/03/06/after-the-justice-department-report-whats-next-for-ferguson/.

Bernstein, N. 2010. "Officials Hid Truth of Immigrant Deaths in Jail." *New York Times*, January 10. Retrieved 7/30/2012 from www.nytimes.com/2010/01/10/us/10detain.html.

Billeaud, J. 2013. "Arizona County Settles 2 Lawsuits vs. Sheriff." CNS News.com, December 20. Retrieved 8/3/2015 from www.cnsnews.com/news/article/arizona-county-settles-2-lawsuits-vs-sheriff.

Billeaud, J. 2015. "Arpaio Immigration Unit Tarnished by Misconduct Allegations." Associated Press, April 19. Retrieved 8/3/2015 from www.nytimes.com/aponline/2015/04/19/us/ap-us-arizona-sheriff-smuggling-squad.html.

Binder, A., M. Fernandez, and B. Mueller. 2015. "Use of Tasers Is Scrutinized After Walter Scott Shooting." *New York Times*, June 1: A1.

Binelli, M. 2015. "Inside America's Toughest Federal Prison. *New York Times*, March 29: MM37.

Blinder, A. and C. Robertson. 2014. "Judge Pressed to Resign After Abuse Charges." *New York Times*, September 19: A21.

Blow, C. 2012. "Plantations, Prisons and Profit." *New York Times*, May 25. Retrieved 7/30/2012 from www.nytimes.com/2012/05/26/opinion/blow-plantations-prisons-and-profits.html.

Blumberg, A. 1969. "The Practice of Law as a Confidence Game." In *Sociology of Law*, ed. V. Aubert, 321–331. London: Penguin.

Blumenfeld, L. 2007. "The Tortured Lives of Interrogators." *Washington Post*, June 4: A01.

Bomse, A. 2001. "Prison Abuse: Prisoner-Staff Relations." In *Discretion, Community and Correctional Ethics*, ed. J. Kleinig and M. Smith, 79–104. Oxford, England: Rowman and Littlefield.

Bonner, R. and L. Vandecreek. 2006. "Ethical Decision Making for Correctional Mental Health Providers." *Criminal Justice and Behavior* 33: 542–578.

Borchert, D. and D. Stewart. 1986. *Exploring Ethics*. New York: Macmillan.

Boss, J. 2001. *Ethics for Life*, 2nd ed. Mountain View, CA: Mayfield Publishing.

Bossard, A. 1981. "Police Ethics and International Police Cooperation." In *The Social Basis of Criminal Justice: Ethical Issues for the 80's*, ed. F. Schamalleger and R. Gustafson, 23–38. Washington, DC: University Press.

Bouie, J. 2014. "Black and Blue: Why More Diverse Police Departments Won't Put An End to Police Misconduct." *Slate Magazine*, October 13. Retrieved 8/3/2015 from http://www.slate.com/articles/news_and_politics/politics/2014/10/diversity_won_t_solve_police_misconduct_black_cops_don_t_reduce_violence.html.

Bouie, J. 2015. "Broken Taillight Policing." *Slate Magazine*, April 8. Retrieved 8/3/2015 from www.slate.com/articles/news_and_politics/politics/2015/04/north_charleston_shooting_how_investigatory_traffic_stops_unfairly_affect.single.html.

Bourge, C. 2002. "Sparks Fly over Private v. Public Prisons." UPI. Retrieved 2/12/2002 from www.upi./com/view.cfm?storyID=20022002-064851-U221.

Bowes, M. 2015. "Blacks Disproportionately Killed by Police, Assault Police in Va." *Richmond Times-Dispatch*, January 24. Retrieved from www.richmond.com/news/article_364d9fc4-e56a-58c2-baf9-53c8b6e6f328.html.

Bowie, N. 1985. *Making Ethical Decisions*. New York: McGraw-Hill.

Bowker, L. 1980. *Prison Victimization*. New York: Elsevier.

Boyce, W. and L. Jensen. 1978. *Moral Reasoning: A Psychological-Philosophical Integration*. Lincoln: University of Nebraska Press.

Boyer, P. 2001. "Bad Cops." *New Yorker*, May 21. Retrieved 7/30/2012 from www.newyorker.com/archive/2001/05/21/010521fa_FACT.

Braithwaite, J. 2000. "Shame and Criminal Justice." *Canadian Journal of Criminology* 42(3): 281–301.

Braithwaite, J. 2002. "Linking Crime Prevention to Restorative Justice." In *Repairing Communities Through Restorative Justice*, ed. J. Perry, 67–83. Lanham, MD: American Correctional Association.

Braswell, M. 1996/2002. "Ethics, Crime, and Justice: An Introductory Note to Students." In *Justice, Crime, and Ethics*, ed. M. Braswell, B. McCarthy, and B. McCarthy, 3–9. Cincinnati: Anderson.

Braswell, M. and J. Gold. 2002. "Peacemaking, Justice, and Ethics." In *Justice, Crime, and Ethics*, ed. M. Braswell, B. McCarthy, and B. McCarthy, 13–25. Cincinnati: Anderson.

Braswell, M., B. McCarthy, and B. McCarthy. 2002/2007. *Justice, Crime, and Ethics*, 3rd ed. Cincinnati: Anderson.

Braswell, M., L. Miller, and D. Cabana. 2006. *Human Relations and Corrections*, 6th ed. Prospect Heights, IL: Waveland Press.

Britt, C. 1998. "Race, Religion, and Support of the Death Penalty: A Research Note." *Justice Quarterly* 15(1): 175–191.

Brown, B. 2007. "Community Policing in Post-September 11 America: A Comment on the Concept of Community-Oriented Counterterrorism." *Police Practice and Research* 8(3): 239–251.

Brown, C. 2011. "Divided Loyalties: Ethical Challenges for America's Law Enforcement in Post 9/11 America." *Case Western Reserve Journal of International Law* 43(3): 651–675.

Brown, J. 2014a. "After Inmate Deaths, Department of Justice to Probe Florida Prison System." *Miami Herald*, December 13. Retrieved 8/3/2015 from http://www.miamiherald.com/news/special-reports/florida-prisons/article4457578.html.

Brown, J. 2014b. "After Inmate's Death, Sergeant to be Questioned." *Miami Herald*, October 8. Retrieved 8/3/2015 from www.miamiherald.com/news/state/florida/article2628799.html#storylink=cpy.

Brown, J. 2014c. "Group Calls for Overhaul of Florida Prisons." *Miami Herald*, November 14. Retrieved 8/3/2015 from www.miamiherald.com/news/local/community/miami-dade/article3916342.html#storylink=cpy.

Brown, J. 2014d, "2 Years Later, Florida Keeps Lid On Prison Death Details." *Miami Herald*, June 11. Retrieved 8/3/2015 from www.miamiherald.com/2014/06/11/4172535/2-years-later-florida-keeps-lid.html#storylink=cpy.

Brown, J. 2014e. "Deposed Warden Says Dade Correctional Was a Dysfunctional Mess." *Miami Herald*, November 2. Retrieved 8/3/2015 from www.miamiherald.com/news/state/florida/article3527395.html#storylink=cpy.

Brown, J. 2014f. "Inmate's Gassing Death Detailed in Florida DOC Whistle-blower Complaint." *Miami Herald*, July 7. Retrieved 8/3/2015 from www.miamiherald.com/news/local/community/miami-dade/article1974526.html.

Brown, J. 2015. "'Daddy,' Womanizing Assistant Warden, Fired From Troubled Prison." *Miami Herald*, January 22. Retrieved 8/3/2015 from www.miamiherald.com/news/special-reports/florida-prisons/article7943703.html#storylink=cpy.

Brown, J. and S. Bousquet. 2014. "Amid Turmoil, Florida Prisons Boss Exits." *Miami Herald*, November 24. Retrieved 8/3/2015 from www.miamiherald.com/news/local/community/miami-dade/article4122143.html#storylink=cpy.

Brown, J. and M. Klas. 2015. "Former Florida Prisons Chief Says Gov. Rick Scott Ignored Crisis in Corrections System." *Miami Herald*, January 31. Retrieved 8/3/2015 from www.miamiherald.com/news/local/community/miami-dade/article8875121.html#storylink=cpy.

Brown, M. 1981. *Working the Street*. New York: Russell Sage Foundation.

Brown, S. 2015. "Hospital Defends NYPD Cop's Forced Stay in Psych Ward." *New York Daily News*, February 3. Retrieved 8/3/2015 from /www.nydailynews.com/new-york/exclusive-hospital-defends-nypd-psych-hold-article-1.2101357.

Brunson, R. 2007. "'Police Don't Like Black People': African-American Young Men's Accumulated Police Experiences." *Criminology and Public Policy* 6(1): 71–102.

Bryson, D. 2010. "South Africa: Mandela Marks 20 Years of Freedom." Associated Press, February 11. Retrieved 7/30/2012 from www.guardian.co.uk/world/feedarticle/8941298.

Buchholz, B. 2005. "Innocents Are Dying, in the Name of Security." *Austin American-Statesman*, September 4: HI.

Buchholz, B. 2008. "Chaplain's Guantanamo Nightmare." *Austin American-Statesman*, March 23: Gl, G4.

Buckle, S. 1993. "Natural Law." In *A Companion to Ethics*, ed. P. Singer, 161–175. London: Blackwell Publishing.

Bureau of Justice Statistics, 2014. *PREA Data Collection Activities, 2014.* Retrieved 6/28/2015 from http://www.bjs.gov/content/pub/pdf/pdca14.pdf.

Bureau of Justice Statistics. 2015. "Corrections Statistical Analysis Tool." Retrieved 6/24/2015 from http://www.bjs.gov/index.cfm?ty=tp&tid=13.

Burgess, R. L. and R.L. Akers. 1966. "A Differential Association-Reinforcement Theory of Criminal Behavior." *Social Problems* 14(2): 128–147.

Burrell, W. 2000. "How to Prevent PPO Stress and Burnout." *Community Corrections Report* 8(1): 1–2, 13–14.

Butterfield, F. 2004. "Mistreatment of Prisoners Is Called Routine in U.S." *New York Times*, May 8. Retrieved 7/30/2012 from www.nytimes.com/2004/05/08/national/08PRIS.html.

Caldero, M. and A. Larose. 2001. "Value Consistency Within the Police: The Lack of a Gap." *Policing* 24: 2162–2180.

California District Attorneys Association (CDAA). 2012. *The California Prosecutor: Integrity, Independence and Leadership*. Retrieved from http://digitalcommons.law.ggu.edu/cgi/viewcontent.cgi?article=1227&context=caldocs_agencies.

Callahan, D. 1982. "Applied Ethics in Criminal Justice." *Criminal Justice Ethics* 1(1): 1, 64.

Carr, R. 2005. "In Federal Job: Blow Whistle, Get Boot." *Austin American-Statesman*, December 11: A1, A6.

Carr, R. and H. Herman. 2007. "Attorney General Apologizes for Handling of Firings but Says He Can Do Job." *Austin American-Statesman*, April 14: A1, A7.

Carroll. D. 2015. *How Public Defenders Struggle with Ethical Blindness*. Sixth Amendement Center, February 4, 2015. Retrieved from http://sixthamendment.org/how-public-defenders-struggle-with-ethical-blindness.

Carroll, L. 1998. *Lawful Order: A Case Study of Correctional Crisis and Reform*. New York: Garland.

Carson, E. A. 2014. *Prisoners in 2013.* Washington, DC: Bureau of Justice Statistics, U.S. Dept. of Justice.

Carter, D. 1999. "Drug Use and Drug-Related Corruption of Police Officers." In *Policing Perspectives*, ed. L. Gaines and G. Cordner, 311–324. Los Angeles: Roxbury.

Carter, J. and S. Phillips. 2013. "Intelligence-Led Policing and Forces of Organizational Change in the USA." *Policing and Society: An International Journal of Research and Policy*. DOI: 10.1080/10439463.2013.865738

Cassidy, R. 2006. "Character and Context: What Virtue Theory Can Teach Us About a Prosecutor's Ethical Duty to 'Seek Justice.'" *Notre Dame Law Review* 82(2): 635–697.

Cathcart, R. 2010. "Wrongly Convicted Man Gets $7.95 Million." *New York Times*, August 13: A14.

Cauvin, H. 2009. "Inmates, Md. Prison Guards Face Drug Smuggling Case." *Washington Post*, April 17. Retrieved 7/30/2012 from www.washingtonpost.com/wp-dyn/content/article/2009/04/16/AR2009041604337.html. www.cbs2chicago.com/local/Abbate.cop.bar.2.1524014.html.

CBSDFW.com. 2012. "Irving Women Claim Assault, Humiliation After Roadside Cavity Search." CBS News, December 18. Retrieved 8/3/2015 from http://dfw.cbslocal.com/2012/12/18/irving-women-claim-assault-humiliation-after-roadside-cavity-search-by-troopers/.

CBSLocal.com. 2013. "Boston Detective Demoted After Amy Lord Murder Had Past Misconduct." CBSLocal.com, July 30. Retrieved 8/3/2015 from http://boston.cbslocal.com/2013/07/30/boston-detective-demoted-after-amy-lord-murder-had-past-misconduct/.

CBS.news.com. 2005. "Praise for Iraq Whistleblower." Retrieved 7/30/2012 from www.cbsnews.com/stories/2004/05/10/iraq/main616660.shtml.

CBS.news.com. 2007. "Exposing the Truth of Abu Ghraib." CBSnews.com. Retrieved 7/30/2012 from www.cbsnews.com/stories/2006/12/07/60minutes/main2238188_page4.shtml.

Cergol, G. 2014. Long Island Police Veteran Accused of Targeting Hispanic Drivers in Traffic Stops." 4NewYork.com, February 3. Retrieved 8/3/2015 from www.nbcnewyork.com/news/local/Suffolk-Police-Veteran-Arrested-Misconduct-Targeted-Hispanic-Drivers-Traffic-Stops-242983441.html.

Chang, C. 2013. "L.A. County Unable to Avert Federal Oversight of Jails." *Los Angeles Times*, October 3. Retrieved 8/3/2015 from www.latimes.com/local/countygovernment/la-me-1003-sheriff-consent-decree-20141003-story.html.

Chang, C. and R. Winton. 2015. "Paul Tanaka Indicted, Accused of Obstructing Federal Jail Abuse Probe." *Los Angeles Times*, May 14. Retrieved 8/3/2015 from http://touch.latimes.com/#section/-1/article/p2p-83538720/

Chappell, A. and A. Piquero. 2004. "Applying Social Learning Theory to Police Misconduct." *Deviant Behavior* 25: 89–108.

Cheever J. 2015. "Suhr: Convicted Officers Betrayed Public Trust." *Bay City News*, January 22. Retrieved 8/3/2015 from http://sfbay.ca/2015/01/22/suhr-convicted-officers-betrayed-public-trust.

Chen, K. 2014. "7 Mass Surveillance Tools Your Local Police Might be Using." *Beacon Reader*, July 29. Retrieved 7/4/2015 from https://www.beaconreader.com/the-center-for-investigative-reporting/7-mass-surveillance-tools-your-local-police-might-be-using.

Chermak, S., E. McGarrell, and J. Gruenewald. 2006. "Media Coverage of Police Misconduct and Attitudes Toward Police." *Policing: An International Journal of Police Strategies and Management* 29(2): 261–281.

Christensen, D. 2012. "TV Show Case Leads to Disclosure of Broward Cops in Trouble with the Law." *Sun-Sentinel.com*, January 3. Retrieved 7/30/2012 from http://articles.sun-sentinel.com/2012-01-03/news/fl-cops-suspect-testimony-bulldog-20120103_1_officers-and-deputies-prosecutors-tv-show.

Christianson, S. 2004. *Innocent: Inside Wrongful Conviction Cases*. New York: New York University Press.

Christie, B. and J. Billeaud. 2012. "U.S. Closes Criminal Probe Against Arizona Sheriff." *Philly.com*, September 02. Retrieved 8/3/2015 from http://articles.philly.com/2012-09-02/news/33549651_1_arpaio-critics-anti-public-corruption-squad-toughest-sheriff.

Citizens for Responsibility and Ethics in Washington (CREW). 2013. *Crews Most Corrupt*, 2013. Available via website: http://www.crewsmostcorrupt.org/mostcorrupt/entry/most-corrupt-members-of-congress-report-2013.

Clarridge, C. and J. Sullivan. 2013. "$1.1M Verdict for Victim's Family Upheld by State Supreme Court." *Seattle Times*, October 17, 2013. Retrieved from http://www.seattletimes.com/seattle-news/11m-verdict-for-victimrsquos-family-upheld-by-state-supreme-court.

Claussen-Rogers, N. and B. Arrigo. 2005. *Police Corruption and Psychological Testing*. Durham, NC: Carolina Academic Press.

Claytor, S. 2014. "Police Union Challenges Settlement Between the City of Albuquerque and the DOJ." KOB Eyewitness News, December 20. Retrieved 8/3/2015 from www.kob.com/article/stories/s3656213.shtml#.VJcFWl4AKA.

Clear, T. 1996. *Harm in American Penology: Offenders, Victims, and Their Communities*. Albany, NY: SUNY Albany Press.

Clifford, S. 2014. "14 More Brooklyn Convictions Examined." *New York Times*, July 31: A20.

Close, D. and N. Meier. 1995. *Morality in Criminal Justice*. Belmont, CA: Wadsworth.

CNN.com. 2010a. "Oil Inspectors Took Company Gifts, Watchdog Group Finds." CNN.com, May 25. Retrieved 8/3/2015 from www.cnn.com/2010/US/05/25/oil.spill.interior/.

CNN.com. 2010b. "Jihad Jane, American Who Lived on Main Street." CNN.com, March 10. Retrieved 7/30/2012 from www.cnn.com/2010/CRIME/03/10/jihad.jane.profile

CNN.com. 2011. "Baltimore Police Officers Arrested in Repair Shop Extortion Scheme." CNN.com, February 23. Retrieved 2/24/2011 from www.cnn.com/2011/CRIME/2/23/maryland.police.arrests/index.html.

CNN.com. 2015. "Same-Sex Marriage in the U.S." CNN.com, April 3. Retrieved 8/3/2015 from www.cnn.com/interactive/us/map-same-sex-marriage.

Cohen, E. 1991. "Pure Legal Advocates and Moral Agents: Two Concepts of a Lawyer in an Adversary System." In *Justice, Crime, and Ethics*, ed. M. Braswell, B. McCarthy, and B. McCarthy, 123–163. Cincinnati: Anderson.

Cohen, E. 2002. "Pure Legal Advocates and Moral Agents Revisited: A Reply to Memory and Rose." *Criminal Justice Ethics* 21(1): 39–55.

Cohen, H. 1986. "Exploiting Police Authority." *Criminal Justice Ethics* 5(2): 23–31.

Cohen, H. and M. Feldberg. 1991. *Power and Restraint: The Moral Dimension of Police Work*. New York: Praeger.

Cohen, L. and M. Felson, 1979. "Social Change and Crime Rate Trends: A Routine Activity Theory Approach." *American Sociological Review* 44(4): 588–608.

Cohen, P. 2015. "Owner of a Credit Card Processor Is Setting a New Minimum Wage: $70,000 a Year." *New York Times*, April 14: B3.

Cohen, M. 2015. "How For-Profit Prisons Have Become the Biggest Lobby No One is Talking About." *Washington Post*, April 28. Retrieved 8/3/2015 from http://www.washingtonpost.com/posteverything/wp/2015/04/28/how-for-profit-prisons-have-become-the-biggest-lobby-no-one-is-talking-about

Cohen, R. 2001. "How They Sleep at Night: DAs Turned Defenders Talk About Their Work." *American Lawyer: The Legal Intelligence*, April 9.

Cohen, T. 2011. "Who's Better at Defending Criminals? Does Type of Defense Attorney Matter in Terms of Producing Favorable Case Outcomes." Social Science Research Working Paper series. Retrieved from https://nationalcdp.org/docs/defense-counsel-and-ajudication.pdf.

Coherty, J., J. Levine, and P. Thomas, 2014. "Alabama Prison Was House of Horrors for Female Inmates, Feds Say." ABCNews.com, January 22. Retrieved 8/3/2015 from http://abcnews.go.com/US/women-universally-fear-safety-alabama-prison-feds/story?id=21627510

Colarossi, A. 2009. "Lake County Prison Official Arrested on Drug Charge." *Orlando Sentinel*, September 4. Retrieved 9/15/2009 from www.orlandosentinel.com/news/local/breakingnews/orl-bk-prison-worker-arrest-090409,0,980900.story.

Cole, D. 1999. *No Equal Justice*. New York: Free Press.

Cole, D. 2002. "Trading Liberty for Security After September 11." *Foreign Policy in Focus Policy Report*. Retrieved 7/30/2012 from www.fpif.org/articles/trading_liberty_for_security_after_september_11.

Cole, D. and J. Lamberth. 2001. "The Fallacy of Racial Profiling." *New York Times*, May 13: A19.

Cole, G. 1970. "The Decision to Prosecute." *Law and Society Review* 4, February: 313–343.

Coleman, S. 2004a. "Police, Gratuities, and Professionalism: A Response to Kania." *Criminal Justice Ethics* 23(1): 63–65.

Coleman, S. 2004b. "When Police Should Say 'No!' to Gratuities." *Criminal Justice Ethics* 23(1): 33–14.

Colloff, P. 2011. "Innocence Found." *Texas Monthly*, January 2011. Retrieved 7/30/2012 from www.texasmonthly.com/2011-01-01/feature2.php.

Colloff, P. 2013. "Jail Time May be the Least of Ken Anderson's Problems." *Texas Monthly*, November 14. Retrieved 8/3/2015 from www.texasmonthly.com/story/jail-time-may-be-least-ken-anderson%E2%80%99s-problems.

Columbia Law School. 2002. "A Broken System, Part II: Why There Is So Much Error in Capital Cases, and What Can Be Done About it." *Columbia Law School Publications*. Retrieved 7/30/2012 from www2.law.columbia.edu/brokensystem2/report.pdf.

Commission on Safety and Abuse in America's Prisons. 2006. *Confronting Confinement*. Washington, DC: Commission on Safety and Abuse in America's Prisons.

Community Tool Box. 2012. *Ethical Issues in Community Interventions*. Retrieved 7/30/2012 from http://ctb.ku.edu/en/tablecontents/sub_main_1165.aspx.

Conlon, E. 2004. *Blue Blood*. New York: Riverhead.

Conti, N. 2006. "Role Call: Preprofessional Socialization into Police Culture." *Policing and Society* 16(3): 221–242.

Conti, N. and J. Nolan. 2005. "Policing the Platonic Cave: Ethics and Efficacy in Police Training." *Policing and Society* 15(2): 166–186.

Contreras, R. 2015. "Prosecutor Avoids Grand Jury in Albuquerque Police Killing." Associated Press, January 13. Retrieved 8/3/2015 from www.valleycentral.com/news/story.aspx?id=1148596.

Cook, R. 2014. "Family Files Lawsuit Against East Point in Taser Death." *The Atlanta Journal-Constitution*, August 28. Retrieved 8/3/2015 from http://www.ajc.com/news/news/breaking-news/family-files-lawsuit-against-east-point-in-taser-d/nhBKk.

Cooper, C. 2009. "Yes Virginia, There Is a Police Code of Silence: Prosecuting Police Officers and Police Subculture." *Criminal Law Bulletin* 45(2): 277–293.

Cooper, J. 2012. "Noble Cause Corruption as a Consequence of Role Conflict in the Police Organization." *Policing and Society: An International Journal in Research and Policing* 22(2): 169–184.

Copp, T. 2006. "Renewed Patriot Act Could Limit Appeals." *Austin American-Statesman*, March 10: A1, A8.

Corey, G., M. Corey, and P. Callanan. 1988. *Issues and Ethics in Helping Professions*. Pacific Grove, CA: Brooks/Cole.

Cormier, A. 2011. Special Report: Florida's Flawed System for Policing the Police. *Miami Herald*, December 4. Retrieved 8/3/2015 from www.heraldtribune.com/article/20111204/article/111139979?tc=ar.

Cotton, A. 2014. "Denver Releases 40 Draft Recommendations for Sheriff Department Reform." *Denver Post*, August 21. Retrieved 8/3/2015 from www.denverpost.com/news/ci_26383613/denver-releases-40-draft-recommendations-sheriff-dept-reform

Cox, D. 2000. "Grand Jury Inquiry into Death of Inmate Extended." *Sun-Sentinel* (Ft. Lauderdale), January 5. Retrieved 8/3/2015 from http://articles.sun-sentinel.com/2000-01-06/news/0001051186_1_fred-griffis-valdes-death-nine-prison-guards.

Crank, J. 1998. *Understanding Police Culture*. Cincinnati: Anderson.

Crank, J. 2003. *Imagining Justice*. Cincinnati: Anderson.

Crank, J. and M. Caldero. 2000/2005. *Police Ethics: The Corruption of Noble Cause*. Cincinnati: Anderson.

Crank, J. and P. Gregor. 2005. *Counter Terrorism After 9/11: Justice, Security and Ethics Reconsidered*. Cincinnati: Lexis/Nexis Publishing.

Crank, J., D. Flaherty, and A. Giacomazzi. 2007. "The Noble Cause: An Empirical Assessment." *Journal of Criminal Justice* 35(1): 103–116.

Crouch, B. 1980. *Keepers: Prison Guards and Contemporary Corrections*. Springfield, IL: Charles C Thomas.

Crouch, B. 1986. "Guard Work in Transition." In *The Dilemmas of Corrections*, 3rd ed., ed. K. Haas and G. Alpert, 183–203. Prospect Heights, IL: Waveland.

Crouch, B. and J. Marquart. 1989. *An Appeal to Justice: Litigated Reform in Texas Prisons*. Austin: University of Texas Press.

Cullen, F. 1995. "Assessing the Penal Harm Movement." *Journal of Research in Crime and Delinquency* 32(3): 338–358.

Cummings, L. P. 2010. "Can an Ethical Person be an Ethical Prosecutor? A Social Cognitive Approach to Systemic Reform." *Cardozo Law Review* 31(6): 2139–2159.

Cunningham, L. 1999. "Taking on Testilying: The Prosecutor's Response to In-Court Police Deception." *Criminal Justice Ethics* 18(1): 26–40.

Curry, M. 2002. "Faulty Drug Cases Draw Police Inquiry." *Dallas Morning News*, February 21: 25A.

Dalbert, C. and E. Filke. 2007. "The Belief in a Personal Just World, Justice Judgments, and Their Function for Prisoners." *Criminal Justice and Behavior* 34(1): 1516–1527.

Dalbey, B. 2015. "'Robocop,' Accused of Severely Beating Black Man in Traffic Stop, Has Notorious History." *Patch*, April 3. Retrieved 8/3/2015 from http://patch.com/michigan/wyandotte/robocop-accused-severely-beating-black-man-traffic-stop-has-notorious-history-0.

Daly, K. 1989. "Criminal Justice Ideologies and Practices in Different Voices: Some Feminist Questions About Justice." *International Journal of the Sociology of Law* 17: 1–18.

Dantzker, M. and J. H. McCoy. 2006. "Psychological Screening of Police Recruits: A Texas Perspective." *Journal of Police and Criminal Psychology* 21(1): 23–32.

Dardick, H. 2013. "City Council Approves $4.1 Million Settlement of Chicago Police Misconduct Case." *Chicago Tribune.com*, February 13. Retrieved 8/3/2015 from http://articles.chicagotribune.com/2013-02-13/news/chi-city-council-approves-41-million-settlement-of-chicago-police-misconduct-case-20130213_1_police-mi.

Dart, B. 2004. "Police Use Taser Guns 'Excessively,' Rights Group Asserts." *Austin American-Statesman*, November 30: A14.

Davies, N. 1991. *White Lies*. London: Chatto and Windus.

Davis, K. 1980. *Discretionary Justice: A Preliminary Inquiry*. Santa Barbara, CA: Greenwood Press.

Davis, K. 2014. "SDPD Seeks Audit on Misconduct Cases." *San Diego Union-Tribune*, February 16. Retrieved 8/3/2015 from http://www.sandiegouniontribune.com/news/2014/feb/16/police-audit-misconduct-hays-lansdowne/.

De Angelis, J. and A. Kupchik, A. 2007. "Citizen Oversight, Procedural Justice, and Officer Perceptions of the Complaint Investigation Process." *Policing: An International Journal of Police Strategies & Management* 30(4): 651–671.

De Sousa, L. 2010. "Anti-Corruption Agencies: Between Empowerment and Irrelevance." *Crime, Law, & Social Change* 53(1): 5–22.

Death Penalty Information Center. 2012. *Fact Sheet*. Retrieved 7/30/2012 from www.deathpenaltyinfo.org/documents/FactSheet.pdf.

Death Penalty Information Center. 2015. *Fact Sheet*. Retrieved 7/4/2015 from www.deathpenaltyinfo.org/documents/FactSheet.pdf.

Del Bosque, M. 2013a. "The Shadow of the Son." *Texas Observer*, March 27. Retrieved 8/3/2015 from www.texasobserver.org/the-shadow-of-the-son.

Del Bosque, M. 2013b. "Exclusive: The Man Behind Hidalgo County's Biggest Law Enforcement Scandal." *Texas Observer*, May 28. Retrieved 8/3/2015 from http://www.texasobserver.org/exclusive-the-man-behind-hidalgo-countys-biggest-law-enforcement-scandal/.

Delattre, E. 1989a. *Character and Cops: Ethics in Policing*. Washington, DC: American Enterprise Institute for Public Policy Research.

Delattre, E. 1989b. "Ethics in Public Service: Higher Standards and Double Standards." *Criminal Justice Ethics* 8(2): 79–83.

DeLeon-Granados, W. and W. Wells. 1998. "Do You Want Extra Police Coverage with Those Fries?" *Police Quarterly* 1(2): 71–85.

Department of Justice. 2012. *Consent Decrees*. Retrieved 7/30/2012 from http://www.justice.gov/opa/pr/2012/July/12-ag-917.html.

Dershowitz, A. 1982. *The Best Defense*. New York: Vintage.

Dershowitz, A. 2004. *Rights from Wrongs: A Secular Theory of the Origins of Rights*. New York: Basic Books.

Deutsch, L. 2001. "L.A. Police Corruption Probe Set to Wrap Up." *San Jose Mercury News*. Retrieved 11/12/2001 from www.mercurycenter.com/premium/local/docs/rampart08.htm.

Devine, T. 2008. "The Need for Privacy." *San Marcos Daily Record*, March 28: 4A.

Dial, K. and R. Worley 2008. "A Quantitative Analysis of Inmate Boundary Violators in a Southern Prison System." *American Journal of Criminal Justice* 33: 69–84.

Dilanian, K. 2012. "Investigations of CIA End Without Criminal Charges." *Austin American Statesman*, August 31, 2012: A3.

Dizikes, C. and T. Lighty. 2014. "Watchdog Update: Head of Cook Co. Adult Probation Removed." *Chicago Tribune*, March 17. Retrieved 8/3/2015 from www.chicagotribune.com/news/local/breaking/chi-watchdog-update-head-of-cook-co-adult-probation-removed-20140317-story.html.

Dodge, M., D. Starr-Gimeno, and T. Williams. 2005. "Puttin' on the Sting: Women Police Officers' Perspectives on Reverse Prostitution Assignments." *International Journal of Police Science and Management* 7(2): 71–85.

Dolliver, R. H. 1981. "Reflections on Fritz Perls's Gestalt Prayer." *Personnel and Guidance Journal* 59(5): 311–13.

Dolnick, S. 2012a. "As Escapes Stream Out, a Business System Thrives." *New York Times*, June 17: A1.

Dolnick, S. 2012b. "Poorly Staffed: A Halfway House in New Jersey Is Mired in Chaos." *New York Times*, June 18: A1.

Dolnick, S. 2012c. "Executive at Company Tied to New Jersey's Halfway Houses Is Leaving." *New York Times*, November 9: A23.

Dolnick, S. 2012d. "Halfway Houses Prove Lucrative to Those at Top." *New York Times*, December 30: A1

Donner, F. 1992. *Protectors of Privilege*. Berkeley, CA: University of California Press.

Dorschner, J. 1989. "The Dark Side of the Force." In *Critical Issues in Policing*, 2nd eds. R. Dunham and G. Alpert, 254–274. Prospect Heights, IL: Waveland.

Doyle, M. 2014. "U.S. Adds New Rules to Restrict Profiling." *Austin American-Statesman*, December 9: A10.

Doyle, M. 2014b. "Data on Police Shootings is Hard to Find." McClatchy Washington Bureau, August 20. Retrieved 8/3/2015 from http://www.mcclatchydc.com/2014/08/20/237137_data-on-police-shootings-is-hard.html?sp=/99/200/365/&rh=1#storylink=cpy.

Draybill, D. 2006. "Forgiveness in the Foundation of Amish Faith." *Austin American-Statesman*, October 11: A11.

Drew, J. 2015. "After 37 Years in Prison, Innocent Man Goes Free." *Austin American Statesman*, January 24: A6.

Ducey Vetoes Bill Shielding Names of Officers. 2015. AZCentral.com. March 30. Retrieved 8/3/2015 from www.azcentral.com/story/news/arizona/politics/2015/03/30/ducey-officer-shooting-shield-sign-veto/70690552.

Ducrose, M., A. Cooper, and H. Snyder. 2014. *Recidivism of Prisoners Released in 30 States in 2005: Patterns from 2005 to 2010*. Bureau of Justice Statistics Special Report. Washington, DC: Bureau of Justice Statistics, U.S. Dept. of Justice.

Ducrose, M., P. Langan, and E. Smith. 2007. *Contacts Between Police and the Public, 2005*. Bureau of Justice Statistics Report, April 29 Retrieved 7/30/2012 from http://bjs.ojp.usdoj.gov/index.cfm?ty=pbdetail&iid=653.

Duncan, I. 2013. "Federal Authorities Ensnare Criminals in 'Reverse Stings.'" *The Baltimore Sun*, July 28. Retrieved 8/3/2015 from www.baltimoresun.com/news/maryland/baltimore-city/bs-md-ci-atf-dea-stings-20130727,0,6298276.story#ixzz2b1i1g8Bl.

Dunningham, C. and C. Norris. 1999. "The Detective, the Snout, and the Audit Commission: The Real Costs in Using Informants." *Howard Journal of Criminal Justice* 38(1): 67–87.

Durkheim, E. 1969. "Types of Law in Relation to Types of Social Solidarity." In *Sociology of Law*, ed. V. Aubert, 17–29. London: Penguin.

Dwyer, J. 2007. "New York Police Spied on Protesters." *New York Times*. Reported in *Austin American-Statesman*, March 25: A11.

Dzur, A. and A. Wertheimer. 2002. "Forgiveness and Public Deliberation: The Practice of Restorative Justice." *Criminal Justice Ethics* 21(1): 3–20.

Eban, K. 2007. "Rorschach and Awe." *Vanity Fair*, July 17. Retrieved 7/30/2012 from www.vanityfair.com/politics/features/2007/07/torture200707.

Eckholm, E. 2013. "Prosecutors Draw Fire for Sentences Called Harsh." *New York Times*, December 6: A19.

Eckholm, E. 2014. "More Judges Question Use of Fake Drugs in Sting Cases. *New York Times*, November 21: A16.

Eckholm, E. 2015. "Prosecutor Drops Toughest Charges in Chicago Stings That Used Fake Drugs." *New York Times*, January 31: A14.

Editorial Board. 2014. "How Race Skews Prosecutions." *New York Times*, July 14: A10.

Egelko, B. 2007. "Firing over Web Site of Nude Wife Upheld." *SFGate.com*, September 6. Retrieved 7/30/2012 from www.sfgate.com/news/article/Firing-upheld-for-cop-who-put-his-wife-in-porn-2523580.php.

Eldred, T. 2013. "Prescriptions for Ethical Blindness: Improving Advocacy for Indigent Defendants in Criminal Cases." *Rutgers Law Review* 65: 333–379.

Eligon, J. 2011. "Advisors on Interrogation Face Legal Action by Critics." *New York Times*, April 27: A21.

Elinson, Z. 2013. "False Confessions Dog Teens: Protocols Proposed to Protect Youth Who Admit to Crimes They Didn't Commit." *Wall Street Journal*, September 8, 2013.

Elliott, A. and B. Weiser. 2004. "When Prosecutors Err, Others Pay the Price." *New York Times*. Retrieved 7/30/2012 from www.nytimes.com/2004/03/21/nyregion/21prosecute.html.

Ellis, L. and A. Pontius. 1989. *The Frontal-Limbic-Reticular Network and Variations in Pro-Antisociality: A Neurological Based Model of Moral Reasoning and Criminality*. Paper presented at 1989 ASC conference, Reno, NV.

Emerson, T. and J. McKinney. 2010. "Importance of Religious Beliefs to Ethical Attitudes in Business." *Journal of Religion and Business Ethics* 1(2): 1–15.

Emily, J. 2014. "Dallas County Officers Mishandled 70% of Probation Violations, Initial State Audit Finds." *DallasNews.com*, May 18. Retrieved 8/3/2015 www.dallasnews.com/news/crime/headlines/20140518-dallas-county-officers-mishandled-70-of-probation-violations-initial-state-audit-finds.ece

Emling, S. 2005. "Terror Crackdown Upsets British Race Relations." *Austin American-Statesman*, August 6: A18.

Engel, R. S., J. Calnon, and T. Bernard. 2002. "Theory and Racial Profiling: Shortcomings and Future Directions in Research." *Justice Quarterly* 19(2): 249–273.

Engel, R., R. Tillyer, C. Klahm, and J. Frank. 2011. "From the Officer's Perspective: A Multilevel Examination of Citizens' Demeanor During Traffic Stops." *Justice Quarterly*, 29, 5: 574–643.

Epp, C., S. Maynard-Moody, and D. Haider-Markel. 2014. *Pulled Over: How Police Stops Define Race and Citizenship*. Chicago, IL: University of Chicago Press.

Eterno, J., A. Verma, and E. Silverman. 2014. "Police Manipulations of Crime Reporting: Insiders' Revelations." *Justice Quarterly*. DOI: 10.1080/07418825.2014.980838.

Ewin, R. 1990. "Loyalty and the Police." *Criminal Justice Ethics* 9(2): 3–15.

Fahrenthold, D. 2006. "Online Registry or Target List?" *Washington Post*, April 20: A03.

Farmer, S. J., T. A. Beehr, and K. G. Love. 2003. "Becoming an Undercover Police Officer: A Note on Fairness Perceptions, Behavior, and Attitudes." *Journal of Organizational Behavior* 24: 373–387.

Farrar, T. 2013. "Self Awareness to Being Watched and Socially Desirable Behavior: A Field Experiment on the Effect of Body Worn Cameras on Police Use of Force." *Police Foundation*. Retrieved from: http://www.policefoundation.org/content/body-worn-camera.

Faturechi, R. 2011a. "L.A. County Sheriff's Department to Dismiss 6 Deputies Involved in Montebello Assault." *New York Times*, March 23. Retrieved 7/30/2012 from http://articles.latimes.com/2011/mar/23/local/la-me-deputies-fired-20110323.

Faturechi, R. and A. Blankstein. 2011b. "L.A. County Sheriff's Department Fosters 'Gang-Like Activity' Among Jail Deputies, Suit Alleges." May 5. Retrieved 7/30/2012 from http://articles.latimes.com/2011/may/05/local/la-me-deputies-lawsuit-20110505.

Fausset, R. 2014. "Indictment of Ex-Official Raises Questions on Mississippi's Private Prisons." *New York Times*, November 16. Retrieved 8/3/2015 from http://www.nytimes.com/2014/11/17/us/indictment-of-ex-official-raises-questions-on-mississippis-private-prisons.html?_r=0.

Faziollah, M., J. Slobodzian, and A. Steele. 2012. "21 Suits Settled in Narcotics Unit Case." *Philly.com*, May 21. Retrieved 7/30/2012 from http://articles.philly.com/2012-05-21/news/31788992_1_security-cameras-surveillance-cameras-officers.

Fecteau, L. 1999. "Private Prisons Warned." *Albuquerque Journal*, August 27. Retrieved 7/30/2012 from www.albqjournal.com/news/2news08-27-99.html.

Feeney, J. 2005. "The Wisdom and Morality of Present-Day Criminal Sentencing." *Akron Law Review* 38: 853–867.

Feibleman, J. 1985. *Justice, Law and Culture*. Boston: Martinus Nijhoff.

Feinberg, J. and H. Gross. 1977. *Justice: Selected Readings*. Princeton, NJ: Princeton University Press.

Felkenes, G. 1987. "Ethics in the Graduate Criminal Justice Curriculum." *Teaching Philosophy* 10(1): 23–36.

Fender, J. 2011. "DA Chambers Offers Bonuses for Prosecutors Who Hit Conviction Targets." *Denverpost.com*, March 23. Retrieved 7/30/2012 from www.denverpost.com/news/ci_17686874.

Fenton, J. 2010. "Raid on Corrections Officer's Home Shows Links to Criminals." *Baltimore Sun*, July 9. Retrieved 7/30/2012 from http://articles.baltimoresun.com/2010-07-09/news/bs-md-bgf-search-warrant-20100709_1_corrections-officer-gang-members-criminals.

Ferdik, F., J. Rojek, and G. Alpert. 2013. "Citizen Oversight in the U.S. and Canada: An Overview." *Police Practice and Research* 14(2): 104–116.

Feuer, A. 2010. "The Terror Translators." *New York Times*, September 19: MB1.

Fink, P. 1977. *Moral Philosophy*. Encino, CA: Dickinson.

Finn. C. 2013. "New Trial for New Orleans Police Convicted of Post-Katrina Killings." Reuters, September 17. Retrieved 8/3/2015 from www.globalpost.com/dispatch/news/thomson-reuters/130917/new-trial-new-orleans-police-convicted-post-katrina-killings.

Finn, M. and L. Stalans. 2002. "Police Handling of the Mentally Ill in Domestic Violence Situations." *Criminal Justice and Behavior* 29: 278–289.

Finn, P. and J. Warrick. 2009. "Detainee's Harsh Treatment Foiled No Plots." *Washington Post*, March 29. Retrieved 7/30/2012 from www.washingtonpost.com/wp-dyn/content/article/2009/03/28/AR2009032802066.html.

Fishbein, D. 2000. *Biobehavioral Perspectives on Criminology*. Belmont, CA: Wadsworth.

Fisher, J. 2008. *Forensics Under Fire: Are Bad Science and Dueling Experts Corrupting Criminal Justice?* New Brunswick, NJ: Rutgers University Press.

Fitch, B. 2014. *Law Enforcement Ethics*. Thousand Oaks, CA: Sage.

Fitzgerald, D. 2009. "Wrong-door Raids, Phantom Informants, and the Controlled Buy." *The Champion*, November. Retrieved from www.NACDL.org.

Fitzgerald, P. 2009. "Thoughts on the Ethical Culture of a Prosecutor's Office." *Washington Law Review* 84: 11–35.

Flanagan, D. and K. Jackson. 1987. "Justice, Care, and Gender: The Kohlberg-Gilligan Debate Revisited." *Ethics* 97: 622–637.

Fletcher, G. 1993. *Loyalty: An Essay on the Morality of Relationships*. New York: Oxford University Press.

Fogel, D. 1975. *We Are the Living Proof*. Cincinnati: Anderson.

Fogelson, R. 1977. *Big City Police*. Cambridge, MA: Harvard University Press.

Foot, P. 1982. "Moral Relativism." In *Relativism: Cognitive and Moral*, ed. J. Meiland and M. Krausz, 152–167. Notre Dame, IN: University of Notre Dame Press.

Forbes. 2012. "Corrections Corp. of America on Buying Spree—State Prisons for Sale?" *Forbes*, February 14. Retrieved 7/30/2012 from www.forbes.com/sites/walterpavlo/2012/02/14/corrections-corp-of-america-on-buying-spree-state-prisons-for-sale.

Forbes. "10 Highest Paid Executives." *Forbes.com*, retrieved 7/1/2015, http://www.forbes.com/pictures/eggh45jef/highest-paid-bosses.

Ford, D. 2015. "Man Jailed as Teen Without Conviction Commits Suicide." CNN.com, June 8. Retrieved 8/3/2015 from www.cnn.com/2015/06/07/us/kalief-browder-dead/.

Forrest, K. and W. Woody. 2010. "Police Deception During Interrogation and its Surprising Influence on Jurors' Perceptions of Confession Evidence." *Trial*, November: 9–19.

Fox, B. 2012. "Security Ground Rules Considered for War Tribunals." *Austin American Statesman*, October 15: A5.

Frankel, A. 2011. "11th Cir. On Prosecutorial Misconduct." Reuters, August 29. Retrieved 8/3/2015 from http://blogs.reuters.com/alison-frankel/2011/08/29/11th-circ-on-prosecutorial-misconduct-what-does-%E2%80%98or%E2%80%99-mean.

Freedman, M. 1986. "Professional Responsibility of the Criminal Defense Lawyer: The Three Hardest Questions." In *Ethics and the Legal Profession*, ed. M. Davis and F. Elliston, 328–339. Buffalo, NY: Prometheus.

Friedman, B. 2015. "America's Most Heinous Judge Resigns." *Salon*, June 1. Retrieved 8/3/2015 from www.salon.com/2015/06/01/americas_most_heinous_judge_resigns_wife_beater_mark_fuller_leaves_the_bench_finally_but_not_easily.

Friedrich, R. 1980. "Police Use of Force: Individuals, Situations, and Organizations." *Annals of American Academy of Political and Social Science* 452: 82–97.

Fritzsche, D. 1995. "Personal Values: Potential Keys to Ethical Decision-Making." *Journal of Business Ethics* 14: 909–922.

Fuller, L. 1969. *The Morality of Law*. New Haven, CT: Yale University Press.

Furst, R. 2013. "No Minneapolis Cops Have Been Disciplined After 439 Complaints." *Minneapolis Star Tribune*, August 28, 2013: A1.

Fyfe, J. and R. Kane. 2006. *Bad Cops: A Study of Career-Ending Misconduct Among New York City Police Officers* (Document #215795). Washington, DC: U.S. Department of Justice.

Gallagher, M. 2014. "A New Chapter for APD." *Albuquerque Journal.* November 1, 2014.

Gallup Poll. 2011. "Are You in Favor of the Death Penalty for a Person Convicted of Murder? *Gallup Poll.* Retrieved 7/30/2012 from www.gallup.com/poll/1606/death-penalty.aspx.

Gallup Poll. 2014. "Americans Rate Nurses Highest on Honesty, Ethics." *Gallup Poll.* Retrieved 6/11/2015 from www.gallup.com/poll/180260/americans-rate-nurses-highest-honesty-ethical-standards.aspx.

Gallup Poll. 2015. "Honesty and Integrity of Institutions." *Gallup Poll.* Retrieved 6/24/2015 from www.gallup.com/poll/1654/honesty-ethics-professions.aspx.

Gallup Poll. 2015b. "Americans Support For Capital Punishment Remains Stable." *Gallup Poll.* Retrieved 6/25/2015 from www.gallup.com/poll/178790/americans-support-death-penalty-stable.aspx.

Galston, W. 1980. *Justice and the Human Good.* Chicago: University of Chicago Press.

Garay, A. 2007. "Man's Innocence in Gang Rape Affirmed." *Austin American-Statesman*, April 10: B5.

Gardner, H. 2007. *Five Minds for the Future.* Boston, MA: Harvard Business School.

Garland, D. 1990. *Punishment and Modern Society.* Chicago: University of Chicago Press.

Garner, J., C. Maxwell, and C. Heraux. 2002. "Characteristics Associated with the Prevalence and Severity of Force Used by the Police." *Justice Quarterly* 19(4): 705–745.

Garrett, B. 2011. *Convicting the Innocent: Where Criminal Prosecutions Go Wrong.* Cambridge, MA: Harvard University Press.

Garrett, B. and P. Neufeld. 2009. "Invalid Forensic Science Testimony and Wrongful Convictions." *Virginia Law Review* 95(1): 72–93.

Gass, H. 2015. "When Expert Testimony Isn't." *Christian Science Monitor*, May 26. Retrieved 8/3/2015 from www.csmonitor.com/USA/Justice/2015/0526/When-expert-testimony-isn-t-Tainted-evidence-wreaks-havoc-in-courts-lives-video.

Gau, J. 2014. "Procedural Justice and Police Legitimacy: A Test of Measurement and Structure." *American Journal of Criminal Justice* 39: 187–205.

Gavaghan, M., K. Alex, and J. Gibbs. 1983. "Moral Judgment in Delinquents and Nondelinquents: Recognition versus Production Measures." *Journal of Psychology* 114: 267–274.

Geis, G., A. Mobley, and D. Shichor. 1999. "Private Prisons, Criminological Research and Conflict of Interest." *Crime and Delinquency* 45(3): 372–388.

General Accounting Office (GAO). 1996. *Private and Public Prisons—Studies Comparing Operational Costs and/or Quality of Service.* Washington, DC: U.S. Government Printing Office.

German Bosque Arrested. "Florida's Dirtiest Cop' Charged With Kidnapping Man Who Wanted To File Brutality Complaint." *Huffington Post*, June 7. Retrieved 8/3/2015 from www.huffingtonpost.com/2013/06/07/german-bosque-arrested-floridas-dirtiest-cop_n_3405593.html?.

Gershman, B. 1991. "Why Prosecutors Misbehave." In *Justice, Crime, and Ethics*, ed. M. Braswell, B. McCarthy, and B. McCarthy, 163–177. Cincinnati: Anderson.

Gershman, B. 2003. "Misuse of Scientific Evidence by Prosecutors." *Oklahoma City University Law Review* 28: 17–41.

Getlin, J. 2002. "DA Suggests Overturning Convictions in Jogger Case." *Austin American-Statesman*, December 6: A16.

Ghosh, B. 2009. "After Waterboarding: How to Make Terrorists Talk?" *Time.com*, May 29. Retrieved 7/30/2012 from www.time.com/time/magazine/article/0,9171,1901491,00.html.

Giannelli, P. 2012. "The North Carolina Crime Lab Scandal." *Criminal Justice* 27(1): 1–10

Giannelli, P. and K. McMunigal. 2007. "Prosecutors, Ethics, and Expert Witnesses." *Fordham Law Review* 76(3): 1493–1537.

Gillers, S. 2004. "Tortured Reasoning." *American Lawyer*, July: 65–66.

Gilligan, C. 1982. *In a Different Voice: Psychological Theory and Women's Development.* Cambridge, MA: Harvard University Press.

Gilligan, C. 1987. "Moral Orientation and Moral Development." In *Women and Moral Theory*, ed. E. F. Kittay and D. Meyers, 19–37. Totowa, NJ: Rowman and Littlefield.

Gilmartin, K. and J. Harris. 1998. "Law Enforcement Ethics: The Continuum of Compromise." *Police Chief*, January 1998. Retrieved 3/26/2008 from www.rcmp-learning.org/docs/ecddl 222.htm.

Glaser, B. 2003. "Therapeutic Jurisprudence: An Ethical Paradigm for Therapists in Sex Offender Treatment Programs." *Western Criminology Review* 4 (2): 143–154.

Glaze, L. and D. Kaeble. 2014. *Correctional Population in the United States, 2013.* Washington, DC: Bureau of Justice Statistics, U.S. Dept. of Justice.

Glendon, M. 1994. *A Nation Under Lawyers.* New York: Farrar, Straus and Giroux.

Glenn, L. 2001. *Texas Prisons: The Largest Hotel Chain in Texas.* Austin, TX: Eakin.

Glover, S. and M. Lait. 2000. "71 More Cases May Be Voided Due to Rampart." *Los Angeles Times.* Retrieved 4/20/2000 from www.latimes.rampart/lat_rampart000418.html.

Golab, J. 2000. "L.A. Confidential." *Salon.com.* Retrieved 1/17/2003 from http://dir.salon.com/news/feature/2000/24/rampart/index.html.

Gold, J., M. Braswell, and B. McCarthy. 1991. "Criminal Justice Ethics: A Survey of Philosophical Theories." In *Justice, Crime, and Ethics*, ed. M. Braswell, B. McCarthy, and B. McCarthy, 3–25. Cincinnati: Anderson.

Golden, T. 2005. "Cruel and Unusual Punishment." *Austin American-Statesman*, May 21: A16.

Golgowski, N. 2014. "Miami-Dade Police Officer Arrested for Alleged Murder-for-Hire Plot, Aiding Drug Traffickers." *New York Daily News*, April 8. Retrieved 8/3/2015 from www.nydailynews.com/news/national/fla-arrested-murder-for-hire-plot-aiding-drug-traffickers-article-1.1750044.

Golgowski, N., M. Wagner, and C. Siemaszko. 2014. "Three Missouri Police Officers Out of Jobs in Wake of Ferguson Protests." *New York Daily News*, August 29. Retrieved 8/3/2015 from www.nydailynews.com/news/national/missouri-officers-job-ferguson-threats-article-1.1921712

Gonnerman, J. 2013. "Before the Law." *The New Yorker*, October 6. Retrieved 8/3/2015 from www.newyorker.com/magazine/2014/10/06/before-the-law.

Gonnerman, J. 2015. "Kalief Browder, 1993–2015." *The New Yorker*, June 7. Retrieved 8/3/2015 from www.newyorker.com/news/news-desk/kalief-browder-1993-2015.

Goode, E. 2012. "Average Prison Stay Grew 30 Percent in Two Decades." *New York Times*, June 6: A12.

Goode, E. 2013. "Some Chiefs Chafing as Justice Department Keeps Closer Eye on Policing. *New York Times*, July 27: A14.

Goodman, J. D. and A. Baker. 2015. "New Challenges to Secrecy That Protects Police Files." *New York Times*, February 5: A19.

Gordon, M. 2015. "Racial Disparity in Charlotte Traffic Stops Grows, Study Finds. *Charlotte Observer*, April 11. Retrieved 8/3/2015 from www.charlotteobserver.com/news/local/crime/article18289739.html#storylink=cpy.

Gorta, A. 2008. "Illegal Drug Use by Police Officers: Using Research and Investigations to Inform Prevention Strategies." *International Journal of Police Science and Management* 11(1): 85–96.

Gottschalk, P. and S. Holgersson. 2011. "Whistleblowing in the Police." *Police Practice and Research* 12(5): 397–409.

Gourevitch, P. and E. Morris. 2008. "Exposed: The Woman Behind the Pictures at Abu Ghraib." *New Yorker* (March). Retrieved 7/30/2012 from www.newyorker.com/reporting/2008/03/24/080324fa_fact_gourevitch.

Graham, T. and L. Gormisky. 2010. "Two Philadelphia Cops Charged with Robbing Undercover Investigator." *Philadelphia Inquirer*, October 5: A1.

Grasmick, H. and R. Bursik. 1990. "Conscience, Significant Others, and Rational Choice: Extending the Deterrence Model." *Law and Society Review* 24: 837–899.

Gray, M. 2014. "Racketeering, Smuggling, Sex with Guards: 25 Indicted in Massive Baltimore Prison Scandal." *Time*, April 24, 2013. Retrieved 8/3/2015 from http://nation.time.com/2013/04/24/sex-with-guards-in-baltimore-prison-scandal.

Green, E. 2015. "African Americans Cited for Resisting Arrest at High Rate in S.F." *S.F.Gate.com*, April 29. Retrieved 8/3/2015 from www.sfgate.com/bayarea/article/African-Americans-cited-for-resisting-arrest-at-6229946.php.

Green, F. 2010. "Williamsburg DNA Case Raises Question of Effort." *Richmond Times-Dispatch*, February 5. Retrieved 7/30/2012 from www2.timesdispatch.com/member-center/share-this/print/?content=ar1665060.

Greene, J. 1999. "Zero Tolerance: A Case Study of Police Policies and Practices in New York City." *Crime and Delinquency* 45(2): 171–187.

Greene, J., A. Piquero, M. Hickman, and B. Lawton. 2004. *Police Integrity and Accountability in Philadelphia: Predicting and Assessing Police Misconduct*. Washington, DC: U.S. Dept. of Justice, NCJRS. Retrieved from www.ncjrs.gov.

Greenberg, J. 2002, "Who Stole the Money and When? Individual and Situational Determinants of Employee Theft." *Organizational Behavior and Human Decision Processes* 89: 985–1003.

Greenhouse, L. 2007. "Supreme Court Took Big, Small Steps to Right." *Austin American-Statesman*, July 1: A15.

Greenhouse, L. 2008. "Justices, 5–4, Back Detainee Appeals for Guantanamo." *New York Times*, June 13: A1.

Greenhut, S. 2015. "The Sweeping Impact of Copley Decision: 2006 Decision Shielded Police Disciplinary Hearings from Public." *San Diego Union Tribune*, May 30. Retrieved 8/3/2015 from www.utsandiego.com/news/2015/may/30/sweeping-impact-copley-decision-significance.

Grissom, B. 2010. "Too Many Laws, Too Many Prisoners." *The Economist*, July 22. Retrieved 7/30/2012 from www.economist.com/node/16636027.

Grometstein, R. 2007. "Prosecutorial Misconduct and Noble Cause Corruption." *Criminal Law Bulletin* 43(1): 1–22.

Grossi, E., and B. Berg. 1991. "Stress and Job Dissatisfaction Among Correctional Officers: An Unexpected Finding." *International Journal of Offender Therapy and Comparative Criminology* 35(1): 79–110.

Grotius, H. 1625/2005. *The Rights of War and Peace*. Book 1, ed. Richard Tuck. Indianapolis: Liberty Fund.

Grovum, J. 2015. "Can States Slow the Flow of Military Equipment to Police?" *Stateline*, March 24. Retrieved 8/3/2015 from www.pewtrusts.org/en/research-and-analysis/blogs/stateline/2015/3/24/can-states-slow-the-flow-of-military-equipment-to-police.

Guilfoil, J. 2010. "Ex-officer Admits to Obstruction of Justice." *Boston.com*, February 17. Retrieved 2/22/2010 from www.boston.com/news/local/massachusetts/article.

Gundy, J. 2003. "The Complexities of Use of Force." *Law and Order* 51(12): 60–62.

Gurman, S. 2014. "Lawsuit: Denver Sheriff's Deputy Ignored Inmate's Screams in Attack." *The Denver Post*, January 30. Retrieved 8/3/2015 from www.denverpost.com/news/ci_25029462/lawsuit-denver-sheriffs-deputy-ignored-inmates-screams-attack.

Gutierrez, M. and K. Minugh. 2013. "California Police Unions Fight Discipline of Officers Under Prosecutors' Lists." *Sacramento Bee*, September 12. Retrieved 8/3/2015 from www.sacbee.com/2013/09/12/5728305/california-police-unions-fight.html#storylink=cpy.

Haag, A. 2006. "Ethical Dilemmas Faced by Correctional Psychologists in Canada." *Criminal Justice and Behavior* 33: 93–109.

Haake, K. 2014. "Missoula County, State, DOJ Sign Agreements to Improve Handling of Sexual Assault Cases." *The Missoulian*, June 10. Retrieved 8/3/2015 from http://missoulian.com/news/local/missoula-county-state-doj-sign-agreements-to-improve-handling-of/article_bb8c665a-f0c1-11e3-8689-0019bb2963f4.html.

Haederle, M. 2010. "The Best Fiscal Stimulus: Trust." *Miller-McCune Magazine*, September/October: 42–49.

Haidt, J. 2001. "The Emotional Dog and its Rational Tail: A Social Intuitionist Approach to Moral Judgment." *Psychological Review* 108(4): 814–834.

Hall, M. 2002. "Death Isn't Fair." *Texas Monthly*, December: 124–167.

Hall, M. 2010. "Trial and Error." *Texas Monthly*, September: 82–97.

Hamidi, A. and P. Koga. 2014. "Neuropsychological Correlates of Misconduct in Law Enforcement Officers With Subclinical Post-Traumatic Stress Disorder." In *Law Enforcement Ethics*, ed. B. Fitch, 209–227. Thousand Oaks, CA: Sage

Haney, C. 2008. "A Culture of Harm: Taming the Dynamics of Cruelty in Supermax Prisons." *Criminal Justice and Behavior* 35: 956–984.

Hansen, M. 2007. "The Toughest Call." *ABA Journal*, August: 28–29.

Harmon, R. 2009. "Promoting Civil Rights Through Proactive Policing Reform." *Stanford Law Review* 62(1): 1–68.

Harris Poll. 2008. "Support for Capital Punishment." Harris Opinion Poll. Retrieved 7/30/2012 from www.pollingreport.com/crime.htm.

Harris, C. 1986. *Applying Moral Theories*. Belmont, CA: Wadsworth.

Harris, C. 2010a. *Pathways of Police Misconduct*. Durham, NC: Carolina Academic Press.

Harris, C. 2010b. "Problem Officers: Analyzing Problem Behavior Patterns from a Large Cohort." *Journal of Criminal Justice* 38: 216–225.

Harris, C. 2012. "Longitudinal Patterns of Internally Generated Complaints Filed Against a Large Cohort of Police Officers." *Policing and Society: An International Journal of Research and Policy* 20(4): 401–415.

Harris, C. and R. Worden. 2014. "The Effect of Sanctions on Police Misconduct." *Crime & Delinquency* 60(8): 1258–1288

Harris, D. 2004. "Review Essay/Profiling: Theory and Practice." *Criminal Justice Ethics* 23(2): 51–57.

Harris, D. 2005. *Good Cops: The Case for Preventive Policing*. New York: The New Press.

Harris, D. 2006. "Do Something Before the Next Attack, but Not This." *Criminal Justice Ethics* 25(2): 46–54.

Harris, W. 2011. *Badge of Honor: Blowing the Whistle*. Shelbyville, KY: Wasteland Press.

Hashimoto, E. 2008. "Toward Ethical Plea Bargaining." *Cardozo Law Review* 30: 949–963.

Hassell, K. and C. Archbold. 2009. "Widening the Scope on Complaints of Police Misconduct." *Policing: An International Journal of Police Strategies and Management* 33(3): 473–489.

Hassine, V. 1996. *Life Without Parole: Living in Prison Today*. Los Angeles: Roxbury.

Hatamyar, P. and K. Simmons. 2002. "Are Women More Ethical Lawyers? An Empirical Study." *Florida State University Law Review* 31: 785–857.

Hauser, C. 2009. "Few Results for Reports of Police Misconduct." *New York Times*, October 5. Retrieved 7/30/2012 from www.nytimes.com/2009/10/05/nyregion/05ccrb.html.

Hays, K. 2005. "Report: Houston Crime Lab Was Long Neglected." *Austin American-Statesman*, July 1: B7.

Heath, B. 2013. Exclusive: FBI *Allowed Informants to Commit 5,600 Crimes. USA Today*, August 4. Retrieved 8/3/2015 from www.usatoday.com/story/news/nation/2013/08/04/fbi-informant-crimes-report/2613305/

Heffernan, E. 2014. "Police Fill a Need with 'Beds for Kids.'" *The Seattle Times*, June 26: B1.

Heffernan, W. and J. Kleinig. 2000. *From Social Justice to Criminal Justice: Poverty and the Administration of Criminal Law*. New York: Oxford University Press.

Heidensohn, F. 1986. "Models of Justice: Portia or Persephone? Some Thoughts on Equality, Fairness and Gender in the Field of Criminal Justice." *International Journal of the Sociology of Law* 14: 287–298.

Hennelly, R. 2015. "Poisonous Cops, Total Immunity: Why an Epidemic of Police Abuse is Actually Going Unpunished." *Salon.com*, May 13. Retrieved 8/3/2015 from http://www.salon.com/2015/05/13/poisonous_cops_total_immunity_why_an_epidemic_of_police_abuse_is_actually_going_unpunished/.

Henriques, Z. 2001. "The Path of Least Resistance: Sexual Exploitation of Female Offenders as an Unethical Corollary to Retributive Ideology and Correctional Practice." In *Discretion, Community and Correctional Ethics*, ed. J. Kleinig and M. Smith, 192–201. Oxford, England: Rowman and Littlefield.

Hensley, N. 2014. "NSA Analysts Spied on Spouses, Girlfriends: Documents." *New York Daily News*, December 27. Retrieved 8/3/2015 from www.nydailynews.com/news/politics/nsa-analysts-spied-spouses-girlfriends-documents-article-1.2058282.

Herbert, B. 2002. "In Tulia, Justice Has Gone into Hiding." *Austin American-Statesman*, August 13: A9.

Herbert, B. 2003. "Truth Has Been Told About Tulia, but Story Isn't Over Yet." *Austin American-Statesman*, April 29: A9.

Herbert, S. 1996. "Morality in Law Enforcement: Chasing 'Bad Guys' with the Los Angeles Police Department." *Law and Society Review* 30(4): 799–818.

Hermann, P. 2009. "The Murky World of Informants." *Baltimore Sun*, October 4. Retrieved 7/30/2012 from http://articles.baltimoresun.com/2009-10-04/news/0910030041_1_informants-fbi-agent-cops-and-crooks/3.

Hermann, P. 2015. "FBI Files Tell How Addicted Agent Was Able to Get the Drugs." *Washington Post*, January 15. Retrieved 8/3/2015 from www.washingtonpost.com/local/crime/fbi-files-tell-how-addicted-agent-was-able-to-get-the-drugs/2015/01/15/a8206bf6-8203-11e4-81fd-8c4814dfa9d7_story.html.

Hersh, F. 1979. *Developing Moral Growth: From Piaget to Kohlberg*. New York: Longman.

Hews, B. 2013. "18 Los Angeles County Sheriff Officials Indicted in Massive Corruption,Civil Rights Case." *Los Cerritos News*, December 9. Retrieved 8/3/2015 from www.loscerritosnews.net/2013/12/09/18-los-angeles-county-sheriff-officials-indicted-in-massive-corruptioncivil-rights-case.

Hickey, J. and P. Scharf. 1980. *Toward a Just Correctional System*. San Francisco: Jossey-Bass.

Hickman, M., A. Piquero, and J. Garner. 2008. "Toward a National Estimate of Police Use of Nonlethal Force." *Criminology & Public Policy* 7: 563–604.

Hickman, M., A. Piquero, B. Lawton, and J. Greene. 2001. "Applying Tittle's Control Balance Theory to Police Deviance." *Policing* 24(4): 497–519.

Hicks, W. 2004. "Constraints in the Police Use of Force: Implications of the Just War Tradition." *American Journal of Criminal Justice* 28(2): 254–270.

Hight, B. 2005. "In Atoning for Tragedy, a Former Navy Captain Finds His Voice." *Austin American-Statesman*, March 11: A11.

Hinkel, D. and P. O'Connell. 2015. "Suit: Northwestern Allowed Unethical Acts, Leading to Wrongful Conviction." *Chicago Tribune*, February 17. Retrieved 8/3/2015 from www.chicagotribune.com/news/local/breaking/chi-alstory-simon-lawsuit-northwestern-20150217-story.html#page=1.

Hinman, L. 1998. *Ethics: A Pluralistic Approach to Moral Theory*, 2nd ed. Ft. Worth, TX: Harcourt Brace.

Hirschi, T. 1969. *Causes of Delinquency*. Berkeley, CA: University of California Press.

Hobbes, T. 1651. *Leviathan*. New York: Penguin Classics, 1982.

Hofer, P., K. Blackwell, and R. B. Ruback. 1999. "The Effect of Federal Sentencing Guidelines on Inter-judge Sentencing Disparity." *Journal of Criminal Law and Criminology* 90(1): 239–321.

Holley, P. 2010. "Second Officer Fired over Alleged Misconduct." *MySANews.com*, March 20. Retrieved 4/7/2010 from www.mysanantonio.com/news/local_news/Officer_accused_of_sexual_assault_to_be_fired.html.

Holmes, M. 2000. "Minority Threat and Police Brutality: Determinants of Civil Rights Criminal Complaints in U.S. Municipalities." *Criminology* 38(2): 336–343.

Hopfe, L. 1983. *Religions of the World*. New York: Macmillan.

Hopkins, S. 2013. "How Effective are Ethics Codes and Programs?" *Financial Executives*, March: 43–45.

Horn, D. 2009. "Fired to Rehired." *Cincinnati.com*, August 25. Retrieved 8/3/2015 from www.cincinnati.com/apps/pbcs.dll/article?Dato=20080629&Kategori=NEWS01&Lopenr=108250002.

Horswell, C. 2013. "Judge Accused of Texting Prosecution From Bench to Sway Case." *Houston Chronicle*, July 14, 2013: A1.

Houston, J. 1999. *Correctional Management: Functions, Skills, and Systems*. Chicago: Nelson-Hall.

Hsu, S. 2014. "Federal Review Stalled After Finding Forensic Errors by FBI Lab Unit Spanned Two Decades." *Washington Post*, July 29, 2014.

Hsu, S. 2015. "FBI Admits Flaws in Hair Analysis Over Decades." *Washington Post*, April 18. Retrieved 8/3/2015 from www.washingtonpost.com/local/crime/fbi-overstated-forensic-hair-matches-in-nearly-all-criminal-trials-for-decades/2015/04/18/39c8d8c6-e515-11e4-b510-962fcfabc310_story.html.

Hu, W. 2014. "Ex-Lieutenant Gets Community Service in Ticket-fixing Case." *New York Times*, December 19: A27.

Huberts, L., M. Kaptein, and K. Lasthuizen. 2007. "A Study of the Impact of Three Leadership Styles on Integrity Violations Committed by Police Officers." *Policing* 30(4): 587–607.

Human Rights First. 2015. *Guantanamo By the Numbers*. Retrieved from website 7/2/2015 from www.humanrightsfirst.org/sites/default/files/gtmo-by-the-numbers.pdf.

Human Rights Watch. 1998. *Shielded from Justice: Police Brutality and Accountability in the U.S.* New York: Human Rights Watch.

Human Rights Watch. 2011. *Getting Away with Torture: The Bush Administration and Mistreatment of Detainees*. New York: Human Rights Watch.

Human Rights Watch. 2014. *Illusion of Justice: Human Rights Abuses in US Terrorism Prosecutions*. Retrieved from www.hrw.org/reports/2014/07/21/illusion-justice-0.

Hume, D. 1739. *A Treatise of Human Nature*. Retrieved from //ebooks.adelaide.edu.au/h/hume/david/h92t/B2.3.3.html.

Huriash, L. 2012. "FHPP Trooper: Illegal Police Searches Led to her Fear for her Safety." *Sun Sentinel*, December 26. Retrieved 8/3/2015 from http://articles.sun-sentinel.com/2012-12-26/news/fl-deputy-watts-lawsuit-20121224_1_law-enforcement-officers-margate-officers-police-officers

Huspek, M., R. Martinez, and L. Jiminez. 2001. "Violations of Human Civil Rights on the U.S.-Mexico Border, 1997–1997: A Report." In *Notable Selections in Criminal Criminology and Criminal Justice*, ed. D. Baker and R. Davin, 183–202. Guilford, CT: McGraw-Hill/Dushkin.

Hylton, W. 2006. "Prisoner of Conscience." *GQ.com*. Retrieved 7/30/2012 from www.gq.com/news-politics/newsmakers/200608/joe-darby-abu-ghraib.

Institute for Law Enforcement Administration. 2008. Ethical Courage Awards. Retrieved 7/30/2012 from www.cailaw.org/ilea/pastwinners.html.

International Association of Chiefs of Police (IACP). 2008. *Ethics Training in Law Enforcement*. Retrieved 7/30/2012 from www.theiacp.org.

Iris, M. 1998. "Police Discipline in Chicago: Arbitration or Arbitrary?" *Journal of Criminal Law and Criminology* 89: 215–244.

Iris, M. 2002. "Police Discipline in Houston: The Arbitration Experience." *Police Quarterly* 5:132–151.

Isikoff, M. 2008. "The Fed Who Blew the Whistle." *Newsweek* Online. December 13. Retrieved 7/30/2012 from www.thedailybeast.com/newsweek/2008/12/12/the-fed-who-blew-the-whistle.html.

Ivers, D. 2015. "Newark Police Unions Say Civilian Review Board Plans Would Violate State Law." *NJ Advance Media for NJ.com*, January 20. Retrieved 8/3/2015 from www.nj.com/essex/index.ssf/2015/01/newark_police_unions_say_civilian_review_board_pla.html

Jablon, R. 2000. "L.A. Confronts Police Scandal That May Cost Tens of Millions." *Austin American-Statesman*, February 19: A18.

Jackman, T. and A. Kumar. 2009. "3 of 'Norfolk 4' Conditionally Pardoned in Rape, Killing." *Washington Post*, August 7. Retrieved 7/30/2012 from www.washingtonpost.com/wp-dyn/content/article/2009/08/06/AR2009080602065.html.

Jackson, J., T. Tyler, B. Bradford, D. Taylor, and M. Shiner. 2010. "Legitimacy and Procedural Justice in Prisons." *Prison Service Journal* 19(1): 4–6.

Jacoby, J., L. Mellon, and W. Smith. 1980. *Policy and Prosecution*. Washington, DC: Bureau of Social Science Research.

Jaffee, S. and J. Hyde. 2000. "Gender Differences in Moral Orientation: A Meta-analysis." *Psychological Bulletin* 126(5): 703–726.

James, L., B. Vila, and K. Daratha. 2014. "Results From Experimental Trials Testing Participant Responses to White, Hispanic and Black Suspects in High-fidelity Deadly Force Judgment and Decision-making Simulations." *Journal of Experimental Criminology*, DOI: 10.1007/s11292-012-9163-y.

Jaycox, M. 2014. *Peekaboo, I See You: Government Authority Intended for Terrorism is Used for Other Purposes.* Electronic Frontier Foundation. Retrieved 7/4/2015 from www.eff.org/deeplinks/2014/10/peekaboo-i-see-you-government-uses-authority-meant-terrorism-other-uses.

Jeffrey, D. 2007. "How Prosecutors Go Bad." *Legal Times*, August 6: 1–2.

Jenson, E. and J. Gerber. 1996. "The Civil Forfeiture of Assets and the War on Drugs: Expanding Criminal Sanctions While Reducing Due Process Protection." *Crime and Delinquency* 42(3): 421–434.

Johanek, M. 2008. "Justice Department Scandal Almost Buried by Financial Crisis." *Toledo Blade*, October 10. Retrieved 7/30/2012 from www.toledoblade.com/MarilouJohanek/2008/10/10/Justice-Department-scandal-almost-buried-by-financial-crisis.html.

Johnson, C. 2009. "Justice Department Aims to Prevent Another Stevens Fiasco." *Washington Post*, October 15. Retrieved 7/30/2012 from www.washingtonpost.com/wp-dyn/content/article/2009/10/14/AR2009101403771.html.

Johnson, K. 2014. "Police Killings Highest in Two Decades." *USA Today*, November 11. Retrieved 8/3/2015 from www.usatoday.com/story/news/nation/2014/11/11/police-killings-hundreds/18818663/

Johnson, K. 2015. "DEA Chief Resigns Amid Reports of Agents' Misconduct." *USA Today*, April 21. Retrieved 6/25/2015 from www.usatoday.com/story/news/nation/2015/04/21/dea-chief-leaving-sex-parties/26129977/.

Johnson, R. 1996/2002/2006. *Hard Time: Understanding and Reforming the Prison.* Belmont, CA: Wadsworth.

Jondle, D., A. Ardichvili, and A. Mitchell. 2014. "Modeling Ethical Business Culture: Development of the Ethical Business Culture Survey and its Use to Validate the CEBC Model of Ethical Business Culture." *Journal of Business Ethics* 119: 29–43.

Jones, D. A. 2009. "A Novel Approach to Business Ethics Training: Improving Moral Reasoning in Just a Few Weeks." *Journal of Business Ethics* 88: 367–379.

Jones, J. 2010. "Nurses Top Honesty and Ethics List for 11th Straight Year." *Gallup Economy*, December 3. Retrieved 7/30/2012 from www.gallup.com/poll/145043/Nurses-Top-Honesty-Ethics-List-11-Year.aspx#2.

Jonsson, P. 2014. "Darren Wilson Testimony Raises Fresh Questions About Racial Perceptions." *Christian Science Monitor*, November 25. Retrieved 8/3/2015 from www.csmonitor.com/USA/Justice/2014/1125/Darren-Wilson-testimony-raises-fresh-questions-about-racial-perceptions-video.

Josephson Institute of Ethics. 2005. *Preserving the Public Trust.* Retrieved from www.josephsoninstitute.org.

Josephson Institute of Ethics. 2008. *The Six Pillars of Character.* Retrieved 7/30/2012 from http://josephsoninstitute.org/MED/MED-2sixpillars.html.

Kamisar, Y., W. LeFave, and J. Israel. 1980. *Modern Criminal Procedure: Cases, Comments, and Questions.* St. Paul, MN: West.

Kane, R. and M. White. 2009. "Bad Cops: A Study of Career-Ending Misconduct Among New York City Police Officers." *Criminology and Public Policy* 8(4): 737–769.

Kania, R. 1988. "Police Acceptance of Gratuities." *Criminal Justice Ethics* 7(2): 37–49.

Kania, R. 1999. "The Ethics of the Death Penalty." *The Justice Professional* 12: 145–157.

Kania, R. 2004. "The Ethical Acceptability of Gratuities: Still Saying 'Yes' After All These Years." *Criminal Justice Ethics* 23(1): 54–63.

Kant, I. 1981. "Ethical Duties to Others: Truthfulness." In *Lectures on Ethics*, ed. L. Infield, 224–232. Indianapolis: Hackett.

Kant, I. 1788/1949. *Critique of Practical Reason*, trans. Lewis White Beck. Chicago: University of Chicago Press, 1949.

Kaplan, M. 1976. *Justice, Human Nature and Political Obligation.* New York: Free Press.

Kappeler, V. and P. Kraska. 2013 "Normalizing Police Militarization, Living in Denial." *Policing and Society: An International Journal of Research and Policy.* DOI:10.1080/10439463.2013.

Kappeler, V., R. Sluder, and G. Alpert. 1984/1994. *Forces of Deviance: Understanding the Dark Side of Policing.* Prospect Heights, IL: Waveland.

Karp, D. 1998. "The Judicial and Judicious Use of Shame Penalties." *Crime and Delinquency* 44(2): 277–295.

Kassin, S., S. Drizin, T. Grisso, G. Gudjonsson, and R. Leo. 2010. "Police-Induced Confessions: Risk Factors and Recommendations." *Law and Human Behavior* 34: 3–38.

Kates, G. 2014. "NYC 'Sober Homes' Operators Accused of Fraud." *The Crime Report*, October 23. Retrieved 8/3/2015 from. http://www.thecrimereport.org/news/articles/2014-10-nyc-sober-homes-operators-accused-of-fraud.

Kates, G. 2015. "New Indictments in Narco Freedom Case." *The Crime Report*, March 2. Retrieved 8/3/2015 from www.thecrimereport.org/news/inside-criminal-justice/2015-03-new-indictments-in-narco-freedom-case.

Katz, D. 1964. "The Motivational Basis of Organizational Behavior." *Behavioral Sciences* 9: 462–466.

Kauffman, B. and P. Toomey. 2015. "The Notice Paradox: Secret Surveillance, Criminal Defendants and the Right to Notice." *Santa Clara Law Review* 54: 843–900.

Kauffman, K. 1988. *Prison Officers and Their World.* Cambridge, MA: Harvard University Press.

Keith, L. 2002. "Judicial Independence and Human Rights Protection Around the World." *Judicature* 84(4): 195–200.

Kelly, J. and P. Wearne. 1998. "Tainting Evidence: Inside the Scandal at the FBI Crime Lab." *New York Times.* Retrieved 5/15/2010 from www.nytimes.com/books/first/k/kelly-evidence.html.

Kessler, G. 1992. *Voices of Wisdom: A Multicultural Philosophy Reader.* Belmont, CA: Wadsworth.

Kiefer, M. and Y. Sanchez. 2012. "Thomas, Aubuchon to be Stripped of Legal Licenses." AZCentral.com, April 10. Retrieved 7/30/2012 from www.azcentral.com/news/politics/articles/2012/04/10/20120410thomas-aubuchon-stripped-their-legal-licenses.html.

Kim, V. 2014. "Six L.A. County Sheriff Workers Get Prison for Obstructing Jail Probe." *Los Angeles Times*, September 24. Retrieved 8/3/2015 from www.latimes.com/local/countygovernment/la-me-deputy-corruption-20140924-story.html.

Kim, V. 2015, "Report: Small L.A. County Cities Seize Large Amounts in Civil Forfeitures." *Los Angeles Times*, April 20. Retrieved 8/3/2015 from http://touch.latimes.com/#section/-1/article/p2p-83346896.

Kim, V. and C. Chang. 2014. "L.A. County Jail Verdicts Don't Let Sheriff Leaders Off the Hook." *Los Angeles Times*, July 14. Retrieved 8/3/2015 from www.latimes.com/local/countygovernment/la-me-deputies-verdict-20140703-story.html.

Kim, V. and J. Leonard. 2010. "Justice Department Seeks Police Reform in Inglewood." *Los Angeles Times*, January 11. Retrieved 7/30/2012 from www.latimes.com/news/local/la-me-inglewood11-2010jan11,0,7526464,full.story.

Kindy, K. 2015. "Fatal Police Shootings in 2015 Approaching 400 Nationwide." *Washington Post*, May 30. Retrieved 8/3/2015 from www.washingtonpost.com/national/fatal-police-shootings-in-2015-approaching-400-nationwide/2015/05/30/d322256a-058e-11e5-a428-c984eb077d4e_story.html.

King, R. and M. Mauer. 2001. *Aging Behind Bars: Three Strikes Seven Years Later*. Washington, DC: The Sentencing Project.

Kipnis, K. 2001. "Health Care in the Corrections Setting: An Ethical Analysis." *Discretion, Community and Correctional Ethics*, eds. J. Kleinig and M. Smith, 113–124. Lanham, MD: Rowman and Littlefield.

Kirchmeier, J., S. Greenwald, H. Reynolds, and J. Sussman. 2009. "Vigilante Justice: Prosecutor Misconduct in Capital Cases." *Wayne Law Review* 55: 1327–1385.

Klas, M. 2015a. "Legislators Take Ownership of Prison Reform With New Plan." *Herald Times Tallahassee*, April 25. Retrieved 8/3/2015 from http://www.miamiherald.com/news/politics-government/state-politics/article19406310.html#storylink=cpy.

Klas, M. 2015b. "Senate Committee Starts Effort to Fix Abusive Prison System." *Herald Times Tallahassee*, January 5. Retrieved 8/3/2015 from http://www.miamiherald.com/news/state/florida/article5472549.html#storylink=cpy.

Klas, M. and J. Brown. 2015a. "Florida Prisons Riddled With Corruption, Staffers Tell Senators." *Miami Herald*, March 10. Retrieved 8/3/2015 from www.miamiherald.com/news/special-reports/florida-prisons/article13200422.html#storylink=cpy.

Klas, M. and J. Brown. 2015b. "New Prison Policy Punishes Investigators Who Speak Out." *Miami Herald*, February 5. Retrieved 8/3/2015 from www.miamiherald.com/news/special-reports/florida-prisons/article9371633.html#storylink=cpy.

Klaver, J. 2014. "Research on Ethics Codes." In *Law Enforcement Ethics*, ed. Brian Fitch, 3–29. Thousand Oaks, CA: Sage.

Kleinig, J. 1986. "The Conscientious Advocate and Client Perjury." *Criminal Justice Ethics* 5(2): 3–15.

Kleinig, J. 1999. "Human Dignity and Human Rights: An Emerging Concern in Police Practice." In *Human Dignity and Police: Ethics and Integrity in Police Work*, ed. G. Lynch, 8–40. Springfield, IL: Charles C Thomas.

Kleinig, J. 2001a. "National Security and Police Interrogations: Some Ethical Considerations." In *Policing, Security and Democracy: Special Aspects of Democratic Policing*, ed. S. Einstein and M. Amir, 105–127. Huntsville, TX: Office of International Criminal Justice (OICJ), Sam Houston State University.

Kleinig, J. 2001b. "Professionalizing Incarceration." In *Discretion, Community and Correctional Ethics*, ed. J. Kleinig and M. Smith, 1–17. Oxford, England: Rowman and Littlefield.

Klinger, D. 2012. "On the Problems and Promise of Research on Lethal Police Violence: A Research Note." *Homicide Studies* 16(1): 78–96.

Klockars, C. 1983. "The Dirty Harry Problem." In *Thinking About Police: Contemporary Readings*, ed. C. Klockars and S. Mastrofski, 428–438. New York: McGraw-Hill.

Klockars, C. 1984. "Blue Lies and Police Placebos." *American Behavioral Scientist* 27(4): 529–544.

Klockars, C., S. Ivkovic, and M. Haberfeld. 2004. *The Contours of Police Integrity*. Thousand Oaks, CA: Sage.

Knudten, M. 1978. "The Prosecutor's Role in Plea Bargaining: Reasons Related to Actions." In *Essays on the Theory and Practice of Criminal Justice*, ed. R. Rich, 275–295. Washington, DC: University Press.

Kohlberg, L. 1976. "Moral Stages and Moralization." In *Moral Development and Behavior: Theory, Research and Social Issues*, ed. T. Lickona, 31–53. New York: Holt, Rinehart and Winston.

Kohlberg, L. 1983. *Essays in Moral Development, Vol. 2. The Psychology of Moral Development*. New York: Harper and Row.

Kohlberg, L. 1984. *The Psychology of Moral Development*. San Francisco: Harper and Row.

Kohn, S. 1997. "Testimony of Stephen Kohn, Attorney for Frederic Whitehurst." Retrieved 5/14/2010 from www.fas.org/irp/congress/1997_hr/h970513w.html.

Korecki, N. 2014. "Illinois Supreme Court Ruling Means Burge Can Keep His Pension." *Chicago Sun-Times*, July 3. Retrieved 8/3/2015 from http://politics.suntimes.com/article/chicago/illinois-supreme-court-ruling-means-burge-can-keep-his-pension/thu-07032014-808am.

Kottak, C. 1974. *Anthropology: The Exploration of Human Diversity*. New York: Random House.

Krajicek, D. 2015. "A Freakishly Rare Anamoly: America's Awkward Relationship with Wrongful Convictions." *The Crime Report*. February 9. Retrieved 8/3/2015 from www.thecrimereport.org/news/inside-criminal-justice/2015-02-a-freakishly-rare-anomaly.

Kraska, P. B. 1999. "Questioning the Militarization of US Police: Critical Versus Advocacy Scholarship." *Policing and Society* 9 (2): 141–155.

Kraska, P. B. 2001. *Militarizing the American Justice System: The Changing Roles of the Armed Forces and the Police*. Boston, MA: Northeastern University Press.

Kraska, P. B. 2007. "Militarization and Policing—Its Relevance to 21st Century Police." *Policing* 1 (4): 501–513.

Kraska, P B. and L. J. Cubellis. 1997. "Militarizing Mayberry and Beyond: Making Sense of American Paramilitary Policing." *Justice Quarterly* 14 (4): 607–629.

Kraska, P. B. and V. E. Kappeler. 1995. "To Serve and Pursue: Exploring Police Sexual Violence Against Women." *Justice Quarterly* 12(1): 85–111.

Kraska, P. B. and V. E. Kappeler. 1997. "Militarizing American Police: The Rise and Normalization of Paramilitary Units." *Social Problems* 44 (1): 1–18.

Kravets, D. 2003. "ACLU: Privacy Rights Diminished." *Salon.com*. Retrieved 1/16/2003 from www.salon.com/tech/wire/2003/01/16/aclu.

Krayewski, E. 2014. "Ex-Baltimore Cop Alleges Retaliation for Reporting Police Brutality." *Reason Magazine*, December 26. Retrieved 8/3/2015 from http://reason.com/blog/2014/12/26/ex-baltimore-cop-alleges-retaliation-for.

Kreig, A. 2010. "New Questions Raised About Prosecutor Who Cleared Bush Officials in U.S. Attorney Firings." Nieman Watchdog Blog (Nieman Foundation for Journalism, Harvard University), July 25. Retrieved 7/30/2012 from www.niemanwatchdog.org/index.cfm?askthisid=00469&fuseaction=ask_this.view.

Kreiger, N. 2009. "A Twenty-First Century Ethos for the Legal Profession: Why Bother?" *Denver University Law Review* 86: 865–900.

Kreimer, S. 2007. "Rays of Sunlight in a Shadow 'War': FOIA, The Abuses of Anti-Terrorism, and the Strategy of Transparency." *Lewis and Clark Law Review* 11(4): 1141–1220.

Kringen, A. L. 2014. *Understanding Barriers That Affect Recruiting and Retaining Female Police Officers: A Mixed Method Approach* (Doctoral dissertation). Retrieved from ProQuest Dissertations & Theses Global. (3681033).

Kristian, B. 2014. "7 Reasons Police Brutality Is Systemic Not Anecdotal." *The American Conservative*, July 2. Retrieved 8/3/2015 from www.theamericanconservative.com/seven-reasons-police-brutality-is-systematic-not-anecdotal/?utm_source=feedly&utm_reader=feedly&utm_medium=rss&utm_campaign=seven-reasons-police-brutality-is-systematic-not-anecdotal#ixzz36KWUbZGv.

Krogstand, J. and J. Robertson. 1979. "Moral Principles for Ethical Conduct." *Management Horizons* 10(1): 13–24.

Kroneberg, C., I. Heintze, and G. Mehlkop. 2010. "The Interplay of Moral Norms and Instrumental Incentives in Crime Causation." *Criminology* 48(1): 259–294.

Kronenwerter, M. 1993. *Capital Punishment: A Reference Handbook.* Santa Barbara, CA: ABC-CLIO.

KTRK. 2009. "Man Walks Free After 22 years." KTRK News, April 30. Retrieved 5/25/2010 from http://abclocal.go.com/ktrk/story?section=news/localandid=6789190.

Lait, M. and S. Glover. 2000. "LAPD Chief Calls for Mass Dismissal of Tainted Cases." *Los Angeles Times*. Retrieved 7/30/2012 from http://articles.latimes.com/2000/jan/27/news/mn-58195.

Lamb, J. 2015. "Gascon Draws SF Police Union Rebuke Over Officer Misconduct Investigation." *SF Examiner.com*, April 6. Retrieved 8/3/2015 from www.sfexaminer.com/sanfrancisco/gascon-draws-sf-police-union-rebuke-over-officer-misconduct-investigation/Content?oid=2925769.

Lambert, E. 2003. "Justice in Corrections: An Exploratory Study of the Impact of Organizational Justice on Correctional Staff." *Journal of Criminal Justice* 31: 155–168.

Lambert, E., N. Hogan, and R. Allen. 2006. "Correlates of Correctional Officer Job Stress: The Impact of Organizational Structure." *American Journal of Criminal Justice* 30: 227–246.

Lambert, E. G., N. Hogan, and M. Griffin. 2007. "The Impact of Distributive and Procedural Justice on Correctional Staff Job Stress, Job Satisfaction, and Organizational Commitment." *Journal of Criminal Justice* 35: 644–656.

Land, K., R. Teske, and H. Zheng. 2009. "The Short Term Effects of Execution on Homicides: Deterrence, Displacement or Both?" *Criminology* 47 (4): 1009–1039.

Lane, C. 2006. "Scalia's Recusal Sought in Key Detainee Case." *Washington Post*, March 28: A06.

Langton, L. and M. Durose. 2013. *Police Behavior During Traffic and Street Stops, 2011*. Washington, DC: Bureau of Justice Statistics, DOJ.

Larrabee, M. 1993. *An Ethics of Care: Feminist and Interdisciplinary Perspectives*. New York: Routledge.

Lau, L. and J. Haug. 2011. "The Impact of Sex, College, Major, and Student Classification on Students' Perception of Ethics." *Mustang Journal of Business Ethics* 1: 92–105.

Lavelle, J. J., D. E. Rupp, and J. Brockner. 2007. "Taking a Multifoci Approach to the Study of Justice, Social Exchange, and Citizenship Behavior: The Target Similarity Model." *Journal of Management* 33(6): 841–866.

Law, V. 2014. "California Turns to Private Prison to Address Overcrowding and Medical Care." *Truthout*, June 10. Retrieved 8/3/2015 from www.truth-out.org/news/item/24173-california-turns-to-private-prison-to-address-overcrowding-and-medical-care.

LeBlanc, C. 2015. "SC Officers Exonerated in More Than 200 Shootings." *The State.com*, March 21. Retrieved 8/3/2015 from http://www.thestate.com/news/local/crime/article15654974.html#storylink=cpy.

Lee, H. 2004. "Oakland 'Riders' Lied, Brutalized Man, Ex-Rookie Testifies." *SFGate.com* December 14. Retrieved 7/30/2012 from www.sfgate.com/bayarea/article/OAKLAND-Riders-lied-brutalized-man-2629441.php.

Lee, H., H. Lim, D. Moore, and J. Kim. 2011. "How Police Organizational Structure Correlates With Frontline Officers' Attitudes Toward Corruption: A Multilevel Model." *Police Practice and Research* 1: 1–16.

Lefstein, N. 2011. *Securing Reasonable Caseloads: Ethics and Law in Public Defense*. Washington, DC: ABA, Standing Committee on Legal Aid and Indigent Defense.

Leighton, P. 2014. "'A Model Prison for the Next 50 Years:' The High Tech Public Private Shimane Asahi Rehabilitation Center." *Justice Policy Journal* 11(1): 1–16.

Leiser, B. 1986. *Liberty, Justice and Morals*. New York: Macmillan.

Leonard, J. 2009. "Law Students Help Free Three-Strikes Offenders." *Los Angeles Times*, May 13. Retrieved 7/30/2012 from http://articles.latimes.com/2009/may/13/local/me-threestrikes13.

Leonard, J. 2013. "District Attorney Revises Policy on Police Misconduct Disclosure." *Los Angeles Times*, June 11, 2013.

Leonard, J., J. Rabin, and A. Blankstein. 2013. "Dorner's LAPD Firing Hinged on Credibility." *Los Angeles Times*, February 10. Retrieved 8/3/2015 from http://articles.latimes.com/2013/feb/10/local/la-me-lapd-dorner-20130211.

Leonnig, C. and D. Nakamaura. 2014. "Whistleblowers Tell Senate Panel of Alleged Sexual Misconduct by Secret Service Agents." *Washington Post*, November 14. Retrieved 8/3/2015 from www.washingtonpost.com/politics/secret-service-agents-and-managers-accused-of-sexual-misconduct-by-whistleblowers/2013/11/14/8d1c4750-4d6e-11e3-9890-a1e0997fb0c0_story.html.

Levenson, M. 2010. "Probation Uproar Fuels State Campaigns." *Boston.com*, May 20. Retrieved 7/30/2012 from www.boston.com/news/local/massachusetts/articles/2010/05/29/probation_department_scandal_puts_incumbents_on_defensive.

Levine, C., L. Kohlberg, and A. Hewer. 1985. "The Current Formulation of Kohlberg's Theory and Response to Critics." *Human Development* 28: 94–100.

Lewis, M. 1999. "Corcoran Guards Launch Ads." *Fresno Bee*, September 17: A1.

Lewis, N. 2005. "In New Book, Ex-Chaplain at Guantanamo Tells of Abuses." *New York Times*, October 3. Retrieved 7/30/2012 from www.nytimes.com/2005/10/03/politics/03yee.html.

Lichtblau, E. 2008. "Senate Approves Bill to Broaden Wiretap Powers." *New York Times*. July 10. Retrieved 7/30/2012 from www.nytimes.com/2008/07/10/washington/10fisa.html.

Lichtblau, E. and S. Shane. 2010. "Report Faults 2 Authors of Bush Memos." *New York Times*, February 19. Retrieved 7/30/2012 from www.nytimes.com/2010/02/20/us/politics/20justice.html.

Lichtenberg, L., H. Lune, and P. McManimon. 2004. "'Darker than Any Prison, Hotter than Any Human Flame': Punishment, Choice, and Culpability in 'A Clockwork Orange.'" *Journal of Criminal Justice Education* 15(2): 429–449.

Liebowitz, S., P. Eliasberg, M. Winter, and E. Lim. 2011. *Cruel and Unusual Punishment: How a Savage Gang of Deputies Controls LA County Jails*. Los Angeles, CA: ACLU National Prison Project.

Lindell, C. 2006a. "When $25,000 Is the Limit on a Life." *Austin American-Statesman*, October 30: A1.

Lindell, C. 2006b. "Sloppy Lawyers Failing Clients on Death Row." *Austin American-Statesman*, October 29: A1, A8.

Lindell, C. 2006c. "Lawyer's Writs Come Up Short." *Austin American-Statesman*, October 30: A11.

Lindell, C. 2007b. "Criticism Grows for Judge over Execution." *Austin American- Statesman*, October 11: B1.

Lindell, C. 2009. "Man Executed over Arson that Wasn't, Scientist Says." *Austin American-Statesman*, August 26: A1, A5.

Lindell, C. 2010a. "Ex-deputy, Dogs Facing Court Test over Scent Evidence in Murder Case." *Austin American-Statesman*, April 11: A1, A8.

Lindell, C. 2010b. "Panel Hits Judge with $100,000 Ethics Fine." *Austin American-Statesman*, May 1: A1.

Lindell, C. 2010c. "Judges Find Scent Evidence Unreliable. *Austin American-Statesman*, September 23: A1, A4.

Lindell, C. 2012b. "State Bar Dismisses Bradley Complaint." *Austin American-Statesman*, January 4: B1.

Lindell, C. and J. Embry 2009. "Governor Shakes Up Forensic Agency." *Austin American-Statesman*, October 1: A1, A8.

Lindquist, C. 1994. "Criminalistics in the Curriculum: Some Views from the Forensic Science Community." *Journal of Criminal Justice Education* 5(1): 59–68.

Liptak, A. 2003. "Houston DNA Lab Worst in Country, Experts Say." *Austin American-Statesman*, March 11: B1.

Liptak, A. 2004. "Study Suspects Thousands of False Convictions." *New York Times*, April 19. Retrieved 7/30/2012 from www.nytimes.com/2004/04/19/national/19DNA.html.

Liptak, A. 2007. "Study Reveals Gap in Performance of Public Defenders." *Austin American-Statesman*, July 14: A7.

Liptak, A. 2010. "Group Gives Up Death Penalty Work." *New York Times*. January 5. Retrieved 7/30/2012 from www.nytimes.com/2010/01/05/us/05bar.html.

Lisitsina, D. 2015. 'Prison Guards Can Never Be Weak': The Hidden PTSD Crisis in America's Jails." *The Guardian*, May 20. Retrieved 8/3/2015 from http://www.theguardian.com/us-news/2015/may/20/corrections-officers-ptsd-american-prisons.

Listwan, S., C. Johnson, F. Cullen, and E. Latessa. 2008. "Cracks in the Penal Harm Movement: Evidence from the Field." *Criminology and Public Policy* 7(3): 423–465.

Lithwick, D. 2015a. "Revenge, Not Justice." *Slate*, March 12. Retrieved 8/3/2015 from www.slate.com/articles/news_and_politics/jurisprudence/2015/03/david_dow_suspended_by_texas_court_death_penalty_defense_lawyer_s_conflicts.html

Lithwick, D. 2015b. "You're All Out: California Prosecutors and Police Engaged in Massive Misconduct—and Finally Got Caught." *Slate*, May 28. Retrieved 8/3/2015 from www.slate.com/articles/news_and_politics/jurisprudence/2015/05/orange_county_prosecutor_misconduct_judge_goethals_takes_district_attorney.html.

Lithwick, D. and B. Heath. 2015. "Rules to Keep Federal Prosecutors in Line Revealed." *USA Today*, March 3. Retrieved 8/3/2015 from www.usatoday.com/story/news/2015/03/03/justice-department-discovery-policies-released/24239225.

Loftus, B. 2010. "Police Occupational Culture: Classic Themes, Altered Times." *Policing and Society: An International Journal of Research and Policy* 20(1): 1–20.

Lombardo, L. 1981/1989. *Guards Imprisoned: Correctional Officers at Work*. New York: Anderson (Elsevier).

Loo, R. 2003. "Are Women More Ethical than Men? Findings from Three Independent Studies." *Women in Management Review* 18(4): 169–181.

Lord, R. 2014. "Confidential Informants Are An Integral But Problematic Part of Federal Law Enforcement." *Pittsburg Post Gazette*, October 19. Retrieved 8/3/2015 from www.post-gazette.com/local/region/2014/10/19/

Confidential-informants-are-an-integral-but-problematic-part-of-federal-law-enforcement/stories/201410190076.

Lord, V. and B. Bjerregaard. 2003. "Ethics Courses: Their Impact on the Values and Ethical Decisions of Criminal Justice Students." *Journal of Criminal Justice Education* 14(2): 191–211.

Luban, D. 2014. "Celebrate the Ones Who Stood Up for What Was Right." *New York Times*. December 10. Retrieved 8/3/2015 from. http://www.nytimes.com/roomfordebate/2014/12/09/a-tortured-accounting/celebrate-the-ones-who-stood-up-for-what-was-right.

Lucas, J. 1980. *On Justice*. Oxford, England: Oxford University Press.

Luscombe, B. 2001. "When the Evidence Lies." *Time.com*, May 13. Retrieved 7/30/2012 from www.time.com/time/magazine/article/0,9171,999906,00.html.

Lush, T. 2007. "The G-Man and the Snitch." *MiamiNewTimes.com*, February 8. Retrieved 4/26/2008 from www.miaminewtimes.com/2007-02-08/news/the-g-man-and-the-snitch/print.

Lutwak, N. and J. Hennessy. 1985. "Interpreting Measures of Moral Development to Individuals." *Measurement and Evaluation in Counseling and Development* 18(1): 26–31.

Lynch, T. 2013. Police Misconduct: The Worst Case in November. Cato Institute website, December 6, 2013. http://www.policemisconduct.net.

Maas, P. 1973. *Serpico*. New York: Viking.

Maas, P. 1983. *Marie*. New York: Random House.

MacIntyre, A. 1991. *After Virtue*. South Bend, IN: University of Notre Dame Press.

MacIntyre, A. 1999. *Dependent Rational Animals: Why Human Beings Need the Virtues*. Chicago: Open Ct.

MacIntyre, S. and T. Prenzler. 1999. "The Influence of Gratuities and Personal Relationships on Police Use of Discretion." *Policing and Society* 9: 181–201.

Mackie, J. L. 1977. *Ethics: Inventing Right and Wrong*. New York: Penguin.

Mackie, J. L. 1982. "Morality and the Retributive Emotions." *Criminal Justice Ethics* 1(1): 3–10.

Mador, C. 2014. "Why It's Impossible to Indict a Cop : It's Not Just Ferguson—Here's How the System Protects Police." *The Nation*, November 25. Retrieved 8/3/2015 from www.thenation.com/article/190937/why-its-impossible-indict-cop.

Maestri, W. 1982. *Basic Ethics for the Health Care Professional*. Washington, DC: University Press.

Magid, L. 2001. "Article: Deceptive Police Interrogation Practices: How Far Is Too Far." *Michigan Law Review* 99(5): 1168–1210.

Maguire, M. and T. Nolan. 2011. "Faux Hos: Women Police Attitudes About Decoy Sex Work." *Police Practice and Research: An International Journal* 12(3): 209–222.

Maher, T. 2010. "Police Sexual Misconduct: Female Police Officers' Views Regarding Its Nature and Extent." *Women and Criminal Justice* 20: 263–282.

Mahler, J. 2009. *The Challenge: How a Maverick Navy Officer and a Young Law Professor Risked Their Careers to Defend the Constitution and Won*. New York: Farrar, Straus and Giroux.

Malloy, E. 1982. *The Ethics of Law Enforcement and Criminal Punishment*. Lanham, NY: University Press.

Manning, P. 2009. "Bad Cops." *Criminology and Public Policy* 8(4): 787–794.

Margasak, L. 2009. "Harsh Methods Useless, Ex-interrogator Says." *Austin American-Statesman*, May 14: A4.

Mariano, N. 2015. "Justice Denied: The High Price of Justice." *The Southern.com*, April 19. Retrieved 8/3/2015 from http://thesouthern.com/news/local/justice-denied/the-high-price-of-justice-sixth-amendment-guarantee-deteriorating-under/article_2992e476-c4ca-5124-a433-23a025a26bf8.html.

Maril, R. 2014. "Violence and Corruption by Drug Cartels Hits Homeland." *Homeland Security Newswire*, April 24. Retrieved 8/3/2015 from www.homelandsecuritynewswire.com/dr20140424-violence-and-corruption-by-drug-cartels-hits-homeland.

Marimow, A. and J. Wagner. 2013. "13 Corrections Officers Indicted in Md., Accused of Aiding Gang's Drug Scheme." *Washington Post*, April 24: A1.

Markowitz, P. 2011. *Accessing Justice: The Availability and Adequacy of Counsel in Immigration Proceedings*. Available through Cardozo Law School. Retrieved 7/30/2012 from www.cardozolawreview.com/content/33-2/NYIRS%20Report.33-2.pdf.

Marks, F., F. Raymond, and D. Cathcart. 1986. "Discipline Within the Legal Profession." In *Ethics and the Legal Profession*, ed. M. Davis and F. Elliston, 62–105. Buffalo, NY: Prometheus.

Marquart, J., M. Barnhill, and K. Balshaw-Biddle. 2001. "Fatal Attraction: An Analysis of Employee Boundary Violations in a Southern Prison System, 1995–1998." *Justice Quarterly* 18(4): 877–911.

Marquart, J. and J. Roebuck. 1986. "Prison Guards and Snitches." In *The Dilemmas of Corrections: Contemporary Readings*, ed. K. Haus and G. Alpert, 158–176. Prospect Heights, IL: Waveland.

Martin, D. 1993. *Committing Journalism: The Writings of Red Hog*. New York: Norton.

Martin, M. 2003. "Corrections Director Summoned to Testify: Federal Inquiry Seeks Pelican Bay Answers." *SFGate.com*. Retrieved 7/30/2012 from www.sfgate.com/news/article/Corrections-director-summoned-to-testify-2579360.php.

Martin, N. 2014. "Allegations of Bungled Rape, Child Abuse Cases Latest for Troubled NOPD Unit." *The Times-Picayune*, November 12. Retrieved 8/3/2015 from www.nola.com/crime/index.ssf/2014/11/nopd_rape_problems.html#incart_m-rpt-2.

Martin, R. 2015. "For Undercover Agents, On-The-Job Adrenaline Can Be Addictive." National Public Radio website, March 29. Retrieved 8/3/2015 from http://www.npr.org/2015/03/29/396071802/for-undercover-agents-on-the-job-adrenaline-can-be-addictive.

Martinelli, T. 2000. *Combating the Charge of Deliberate Indifference Through Police Ethics Training and a Comprehensive Risk Management Policy*. Paper presented at the Annual Meeting of the Academy of Criminal Justice Sciences, New Orleans, LA.

Martinelli, T. 2007. "Minimizing Risk by Defining Off-Duty Police Misconduct." *Police Chief*, June: 40–45.

Martinez, M. 2011. "Calif. Study: Prosecutors' Misconduct Reverses 18 Convictions in 2010." CNN.com. Retrieved 7/30/2012 from www.cnn.com/2011/CRIME/03/30/california.prosecutors.misconduct/.

Martinez, P. and J. Pollock. 2008. "The Impact of Type of Attorney on Criminal Sentencing." *Criminal Law Bulletin* 5(44): 1–22.

Martyn, S., L. Fox, and W. Wendel. 2008. *The Law Governing Lawyers: 2007–2008 Edition*. New York: Aspen Publishers.

Marx, G. 1985a. "Police Undercover Work: Ethical Deception or Deceptive Ethics?" In *Police Ethics: Hard Choices in Law Enforcement*, ed. W. Heffernan and T. Stroup, 83–117. New York: John Jay Press.

Marx, G. 1985b. "Who Really Gets Stung? Some Issues Raised by the New Police Undercover Work." In *Moral Issues in Police Work*, ed. F. Elliston and M. Feldberg, 99–129. Totawa, NJ: Rowman and Allanheld.

Marx, G. 1991. "The New Police Undercover Work." In *Thinking About Police: Contemporary Readings*, ed. C. Klockars and S. Mastrofski, 240–258. New York: McGraw-Hill.

Marzulli, J. 2015. "Brooklyn Prosecutor Loses Warrant to Arrest Witness in Murder Case, Finds it 7 Years Later." *New York Daily News*, May 11. Retrieved 8/3/2015 from www.nydailynews.com/new-york/nyc-crime/exclusive-da-finds-warrant-murder-case-7-years-article-1.2217479.

Marzulli, J. and D. Gregorian. 2014. "In 179 Fatalities Involving On-Duty NYPD Cops in 15 years, Only 3 Just 1 Conviction." *New York Daily News*, December 8. Retrieved 8/3/2015 from http://www.nydailynews.com/new-york/nyc-crime/179-nypd-involved-deaths-3-indicted-exclusive-article-1.2037357.

Massimino, E. 2004. "Leading by Example? U.S. Interrogation of Prisoners in the War on Terror." *Criminal Justice Ethics* 23(1): 2, 74–76.

Mastrofski, S., M. Reisig, and J. McCluskey. 2002. "Police Disrespect Toward the Public: An Encounter-Based Analysis." *Criminology* 40(3): 519–551.

Mather, L. 2003. "Ethics Symposium: What Do Clients Want? What Do Lawyers Do?" *Emory Law Journal* 52: 1065–1088.

Mauer, M., M. Chesney-Lind, and T. Clear. 2002. *Invisible Punishment: The Collateral Consequences of Mass Imprisonment*. New York: The Sentencing Project.

Mayer, J. 2007. "Whatever It Takes: the Politics of the Man Behind 24." *New Yorker*, February. Retrieved 7/30/2012 from www.newyorker.com/reporting/2007/02/19/070219fa_fact_mayer.

Mazerolle, L., S. Bennett, J. Davis, E. Sargeant, and M. Manning, 2013. "Procedural Justice and Police Legitimacy: A Systematic Review of Research Evidence." *Journal of Experimental Criminology* 9: 245–274.

McAnany, P. 1981. "Justice in Search of Fairness." In *Justice as Fairness*, ed. D. Fogel and J. Hudson, 22–51. Cincinnati: Anderson.

McCabe, S. 2011. "23 DC Cops Charged with Crimes in 2011." *Washington Examiner*, September 6. Retrieved 7/30/2012 from http://washingtonexaminer.com/23-d.c.-cops-charged-with-crimes-in-2011/article/118035.

McCaffrey, S. 2007. "Release of Sex Video Draws Fire." *Austin American-Statesman*, July 13: A6.

McCarthy, B. 1991. "Keeping an Eye on the Keeper: Prison Corruption and Its Control." In *Justice, Crime, and Ethics*, ed. M. Braswell, B. McCarthy, and B. McCarthy, 239–253. Cincinnati: Anderson.

McCarthy, B. 1995. "Patterns of Prison Corruption." In *Morality in Criminal Justice*, ed. D. Close and N. Meier, 280–285. Belmont, CA: Wadsworth.

McCollum, D. 2011. "Nacogdoches Attorney Responds to Class Action Certification on Tenaha Lawsuit." KTRE.com, August 30. Retrieved 7/30/2012 from www.ktre.com/story/15355047/federal-judge-rules-in-favor-of-plaintiffs-in-lawsuit-against-tenaha.

McCoy, C. and D. Purcell. 2014. "In Stepping Down, McCaffery Moved to Save Pension, Avoid Ethics Inquiry." *Philly.com*, October 28, 2014. Retrieved from http://www.philly.com/philly/news/politics/20141028_In_stepping_down__McCaffery_moved_to_save_pension__avoid_ethics_inquiry.html.

McCready, D. 2007. "When Is Torture Right?" *Studies in Christian Ethics* 20: 393–398.

McDonald, W. 2000. *Testilying: The Psychological and Sociological Determinants of Police Testimonial Deception*. Dissertation. City University of New York. Ann Arbor, MI: University of Michigan Dissertation Abstracts.

McGurrin, D. and V. Kappeler. 2002. "Media Accounts of Police Sexual Violence." In *Policing and Misconduct*, ed. K. Lersch, 121–142. Upper Saddle River, NJ: Prentice Hall.

McKelway, D. 2013. "Win at all Costs? Suicide of Computer Whiz Prompts Look at Federal Prosecutors' Tactics." FoxNews.com, February 15. Retrieved 8/3/2015 from www.foxnews.com/politics/2013/02/15/win-at-all-costs-suicide-computer-whiz-prompts-look-at-federal-prosecutors.

McKeown, M. 2011. "To Judge or Not to Judge: Transparency and Recusal in the Federal System." *Review of Litigation* 30(4): 653–669.

McKinley, J. 2014. "Court Rules Against Queens District Attorney." *New York Times*, October 29: A25.

McKinney, M. 2015. "Minneapolis Police Officer With Two Costly Lawsuits Has Record of Complaints." *Minneapolis Star Tribune*, May 15. Retrieved 8/3/2015 from www.startribune.com/minneapolis-police-officer-with-two-costly-lawsuits-has-record-of-complaints/258717081/.

McKoski, R. 2008. "Charitable Fundraising by Judges: The Give and Take of the 2007 ABA Model Code of Judicial Conduct." *Michigan State Law Review* 2008: 769–841.

McMahon, P. 2013. "Caravella Case Not Deputy's First Link to Wrongful Convictions." *Sun-Sentinel*, March 14. Retrieved 8/3/2015 from http://articles.sun-sentinel.com/2013-03-14/news/fl-tony-fantigrassi-bso-sued-20130314_1_anthony-caravella-caravella-case-lie-detector-test.

McNally, J. 2014. "A Big Boot Drops on Police Misconduct." *Express Milwaukee*, August 12. Retrieved 8/3/2015 from http://expressmilwaukee.com/article-permalink-23799.html.

McQuade, D. 2014. "Philadelphia Judge Joseph C. Waters, Jr. Pleads Guilty to Federal Corruption Charges." *Phillymag.com*, September 24. Retrieved 8/3/2014 from www.phillymag.com/news/2014/09/24/philadelphia-judge-court-cases-fixed/.

McRoberts, F. and S. Mills. 2004. "From the Start, a Faulty Science." *Chicago Tribune* Online Edition. Retrieved 7/30/2012 from www.chicagotribune.com/news/watchdog/chi-041019forensics,0,7597688.story.

McRoberts, F., S. Mills, and M. Possley. 2004. "Forensics Under the Microscope." *Chicago Tribune* Online Edition. Retrieved 7/30/2012 from www.chicagotribune.com/news/watchdog/chi-forensics-specialpackage,0,7787855.special.

Medina, J. 2013. "Arrests Challenge Los Angeles County Sheriff's 4-Term Tenure." *New York Times*, December 15: A24.

Medwed, D. 2009. "The Prosecutor as Minister of Justice: Preaching to the Unconverted from the Post-conviction Pulpit." *Washington Law Review* 84: 35–66.

Meekins, T. 2007. "Risky Business: Criminal Specialty Courts and the Ethical Obligations of the Zealous Criminal Defender." *Berkeley Journal of Criminal Law* 12: 75–135.

Meincke, P. 2009. "Cops Plead Guilty, Sentenced in Corruption Cases." ABC.com. September 25. Retrieved 10/1/2009 from www.abclocal.go.com/wls/story?section=news/local andid=7033273andpt=print.

Meisner, J. 2013. "City OKs $10 Million Payment Over Coerced Guilty Plea." *Chicago Tribune*, July 24. Retrieved 8/3/2015 from http://articles.chicagotribune.com/2013-07-25/news/ct-met-chicago-police-brutality-burge-20130725_1_eric-caine-city-oks-police-misconduct.

Memmott, M. 2011. "Justice Dept Drops Probe of Leaker Who Exposed Bush-era Wiretapping." National Public Radio, April 26. Retrieved 8/3/2015 from http://www.npr.org/sections/thetwo-way/2011/04/26/135735752/report-justice-drops-probe-of-leaker-who-exposed-bush-era-wiretapping.

Memory, J. and C. Rose. 2002. "The Attorney as Moral Agent: A Critique of Cohen." *Criminal Justice Ethics* 21(1): 28–39.

Mesloh, C., R. Wolf, and M. Henych. 2003. "Perceptions of Misconduct: An Examination of Ethics at One Correctional Institution." *Corrections Compendium* 28(5): 1–19.

Metz, H. 1990. "An Ethical Model for Law Enforcement Administrators." In *Ethics in Criminal Justice*, ed. F. Schmalleger, 95–103. Bristol, IN: Wyndam Hall.

Micucci, A. and I. Gomme. 2005. "American Police and Subcultural Support for the Use of Excessive Force." *Journal of Criminal Justice* 33: 487–500.

Mieczkowski, T. 2002. "Drug Abuse, Corruption, and Officer Drug Testing." In *Policing and Misconduct*, ed. K. Lersch, 157–192. Upper Saddle River, NJ: Prentice Hall.

Milgram, S. 1963. "Behavioral Study of Obedience." *Journal of Abnormal and Social Psychology* 67: 371–378.

Miller, G. and K. DeYong, 2013. "Panama Releases Former CIA Operative Wanted by Italy." *Washington Post*, July 19. Retrieved 8/3/2015 from www.washingtonpost.com/world/national-security/panama-releases-former-cia-operative-wanted-by-italy/2013/07/19/c73ebc12-f083-11e2-a1f9-ea873b7e0424_story.html.

Miller, G. and J. Meyer. 2009. "Obama Discloses Memos Outlining CIA Torture Tactics." *Austin American-Statesman*, April 17: A3.

Miller, J. M. 2011. "Becoming an Informant." *Justice Quarterly* 28: 203–220.

Miller, J. and R. Davis. 2007. "Unpacking Public Attitudes to the Police: Contrasting Perceptions of Misconduct with Traditional Measures of Satisfaction." *International Journal of Police Science and Management* 10(1): 9–22.

Miller, K. and M. Radelet. 1993. *Executing the Mentally III*. Newbury Park, CA: Sage.

Mills, S. 2015. "Burge Reparations Deal a Product of Long Negotiations." *Chicago Tribune*, May 6. Retrieved 8/3/2015 from http://my.chicagotribune.com/#section/-1/article/p2p-83469100.

Mills, S. 2005. "Texas May Have Put Innocent Man to Death." *Chicago Tribune*, April 20: A7.

Mills, S. and F. McRoberts. 2004. "Critics Tell Experts: Show Us the Science." *Chicago Tribune*, October 17: A18.

Mitchell, J. 2014. "Private Prisons Face Suits, Federal Probes." *The Clarion-Ledger*, October 15. Retrieved 8/3/2015 from http://www.clarionledger.com/story/news/2014/10/11/private-prisons-face-suits-federal-probes/17122977

Mitchell, J. and J. Gates. 2015. "Chris Epps, Cecil McCrory Plead Guilty to Corruption" *Clarion-Ledger*, February 25. Retrieved 8/3/2015 from www.clarionledger.com/story/news/2015/02/25/epps-pleads-guilty/23990739.

Mitchell, K. 2014. "Jamal Hunter Contemplates Future Both With Scars and $3.25 Million." *The Denver Post*, July 23. Retrieved 8/3/2015 from http://www.denverpost.com/news/ci_26205168/jamal-hunter-contemplates-future-both-scars-and-3

Mitchell, M. 2014. "Former CPD News Affairs Officer Sues City, Former Supervisors." *Chicago Sun Times*. February 19. Retrieved 8/3/2015 from www.suntimes.com/news/mitchell/25702732-452/former-cpd-news-affairs-officer-sues-city-former-supervisors.html.

Moll, J., R. Zahn, R. de Oliveira-Souza, F. Krueger, and J. Grafman. 2005. "The Neural Basis of Human Moral Cognition." *Nature* 6: 799–809.

Mondics, C. 2014. "Court Restricts City's Ability to Seize Homes Used by Drug Dealers." *The Philadelphia Inquirer*, December 29. Retrieved 8/3/2015 from www.philly.com/philly/business/20141230_Appeals_court_restricts_use_of_civil_forfeiture_to_seize_homes_used_by_drug_dealers_.html#31JFZbubbeEKAP1F.99.

Moore, T. 2014. "NYPD Commissioner Bill Bratton Disbands Unit Responsible for Spying on Muslim Communities." *NY Daily News.com*, April 16. Retrieved 8/3/2015 from www.nydailynews.com/new-york/bratton-disbands-nypd-muslim-spying-unit-article-1.1757446.

Moran, J. 2005. "'Blue Walls,' 'Grey Areas' and 'Cleanups': Issues in the Control of Police Corruption in England and Wales." *Crime, Law and Social Change* 43: 57–79.

Morgan, L. 2010. "Two Florida Businessmen Indicted in Prison Kickback Case." *Tampa Bay Times*, July 16. Retrieved 7/30/2012 from www.tampabay.com/news/politics/two-florida-businessmen-indicted-in-prison-kickback-case/1109244.

Morgenson, G. 2015. "Comparing Paychecks With C.E.O.s." *New York Times*. April 12: BU1.

Morris, R. 2000. *Stories of Transformative Justice*. Toronto: Canadian Scholars Press.

Moskos, P. 2009. *Cop in the Hood: My Year Policing Baltimore's Eastern District*. Princeton, NJ: Princeton University Press.

Moskovitz, D. 2010. "Police Officer Sentenced in Identity Theft Case." *Miami Herald*, September 20. Retrieved 8/3/2015 from http://triallawmiami.com/2010/10/02/a_miami_police_officer_sentenc/.

Moss, M. and F. Fessenden. 2002. "War Against Terrorism Stirs a Battle over Privacy." *Austin American-Statesman*, December 11: A17–A19.

Muir, W. 1977. *Police: Streetcorner Politicians*. Chicago: University of Chicago Press.

Mulgan, R. and J. Wanna, 2011. "Developing Cultures of Integrity in the Public and Private Sectors." In *Handbook of Global Research and Practice in Corruption*, Vol. 1, ed. A. Graycar and R. G. Smith, 416–429. Northampton, MD: Edward Elgar Publishing, Inc.

Mulhausen, M. 2010. "A Second Chance at Justice: Why States Should Adopt ABA Model Rules of Professional Conduct 3.8(g) and (h)." *University of Colorado Law Review* 81(1): 309–341.

Murphy, B. 2014. "Michael Tedesco, Ex-Nassau Cop Visited Mistresses on Duty, Pleads Guilty." *Newsday*, May 12. Retrieved 8/3/2015 from www.newsday.com/long-island/nassau/michael-tedesco-ex-nassau-cop-who-visited-mistresses-on-duty-pleads-guilty-1.7999192.

Murphy, C. 2002. "Monitor Gives DC Police Mixed Review." *Washington Post*. August 6. Retrieved 7/30/2012 from www.washingtonpost.com/ac2/wp-dyn?pagename=article&contentId=A52807-2002Aug6.

Murphy, J. 1985/1995. *Punishment and Rehabilitation*. Belmont, CA: Wadsworth.

Murphy, J. 1988. "Forgiveness, Mercy, and the Retributive Emotions." *Criminal Justice Ethics* 7(2): 3–15.

Murphy, M. 2012. "Crime Lab Scandal Puts 34,000 Cases Under Review." *Statehouse News.com*, September 6. Retrieved 7/20/2012 from www.com/dpp/news/massachusetts/crime-lab-scandal-puts-34000-cases-under-review.

Murphy, P. and D. Caplan. 1989. "Conditions that Breed Corruption." In *Critical Issues in Policing*, ed. R. Dunham and G. Alpert, 304–324. Prospect Heights, IL: Waveland.

Murphy, P. and K. Moran. 1981. "The Continuing Cycle of Systemic Police Corruption." In *The Social Basis of Criminal Justice: Ethical Issues for the 80's*, ed. F. Schmalleger and R. Gustafson, 87–101. Washington, DC: University Press.

Murray, J. 2005. "Policing Terrorism: A Threat to Community Policing or Just a Shift in Priorities?" *Police Practice and Research* 6(4): 347–361.

Murray, J. 2009. "Ex-drug Cop's 25-year Sentence Among Longest for Local Police." Indystar.com, September 24. Retrieved 7/30/2012 from www.indystar.com/article/20090924/NEWS02/909240450/Ex-drug-cop-s-25-year-sentence-among-longest-local-police.

Murray, J. 2014. "Denver Pays Millions to Settle Abuse Claims Against Police and Sheriff." *Denver Post*, August 3. Retrieved 8/3/2015 from www.denverpost.com/politics/ci_26266070/denver-pays-millions-settle-abuse-claims-against-police.

Murrie, D., D. Boccaccini, L., Guarnera, and K. Rufino. 2013. "Are Forensic Experts Biased by the Side That Retained Them?" *Psychological Science*, DOI: 10.1177/0956797613481812.

Murton, T. 1976. *The Dilemma of Prison Reform*. New York: Irvington.

Murton, T. and J. Hyams. 1969. *Accomplices to the Crime: The Arkansas Prison Scandal*. New York: Grove.

Nakashima, E. 2015. "Secrecy Around Police Surveillance Equipment Proves a Case's Undoing." *Washington Post*, February 22. Retrieved 8/3/2015 from www.washingtonpost.com/world/national-security/secrecy-around-police-surveillance-equipment-proves-a-cases-undoing/2015/02/22/ce72308a-b7ac-11e4-aa05-1ce812b3fdd2_story.html.

National Conference of State Legislators. 2015. *Minimum Wage Rate Table*. Retrieved 4/24/2014 from www.ncsl.org/research/labor-and-employment/state-minimum-wage-chart.aspx.

National Institute of Justice. 1992. "Community Policing in the 1990s." *National Institute of Justice Research Bulletin*, August: 2–9.

National Institute of Justice. 2008. *Study of Deaths Following Electro Muscular Disruption*. Washington, DC: Office of Justice Programs.

National Registry of Exonerations. 2015. *Exonerations in 2014*. Retrieved from http://www.law.umich.edu/special/exoneration/Documents/Exonerations_in_2014_report.pdf.

NBC.com. 2013. "Houston Women Sue DPS for Intrusive Cavity Search." NBC.com, October 29. Retrieved 8/3/2015 from www.nbcdfw.com/news/local/Houston-Woman-Sues-DPS-for-Intrusive-Cavity-Search-214326731.html.

Neuschatz, J., M. Wilkinson, C. Goodsell, S. Wetmore, D. Quinlivan, and N. Jones, 2012. "Secondary Confessions, Expert Testimony, and Unreliable Testimony." *Journal of Police and Criminal Psychology* 27: 179–192.

New York Times. 2002. "Three Guards Acquitted in Death of Inmate." February 16: A13.

New York Times. 2010b. "Justice in the Jury Box." June 4. Retrieved 7/30/2012 from www.nytimes.com/2010/06/06/opinion/06sun2.html.

Newall, M. and A. Whelan. 2014. "Credibility Issues Undermined Case Against Philadelphia Narcotics Squad, Files Show." *Philly.com*, May 15. Retrieved 8/3/2015 from http://articles.philly.com/2014-05-15/news/49849543_1_search-warrants-thomas-tolstoy-documents.

Newport, F. 2014. "Gallup Review: Black and White Attitudes Toward Police." *Gallup.com*. Retrieved from www.gallup.com/poll/175088/gallup-review-black-white-attitudes-toward-police.aspx.

Newson6.com. 2011. "Four Convicted in Tulsa Police Corruption Trial Sentenced Tuesday." *Newson6.com*, December 6. Retrieved 7/30/2012 from www.newson6.com/story/16198390/sentencing-set-for-3-tulsa-police-officers-atf-agent.

Neyfakh, L. 2015. "The Bad Cop Database: A Radical New Idea for Keeping Tabs on Police Misconduct." *Slate.com*, February 13. Retrieved 8/3/2015 from www.slate.com/articles/news_and_politics/crime/2015/02/

bad_cops_a_new_database_collects_information_about_cop_misconduct_and_provides.html.

Neyroud, P. and A. Beckley. 2001. *Policing, Ethics and Human Rights.* Devon, England: Willan.

Noddings, N. 1986. *Caring: A Feminine Approach to Ethics and Moral Education.* Berkeley: University of California Press.

Nolan, T. 2001. "Galateas in Blue: Women Police as Decoy Sex Workers." *Criminal Justice Ethics* 20(2): 2–67.

North Carolina Innocence Commission. 2015. *Annual Report, 2014.* Available via website, www.innocencecommission-nc.gov/Forms/pdf/gar/2014%20Annual%20Report%20(sent%20to%20General%20Assembly%20in%202015).pdf.

O'Brien, J. 2013. "Centro Bus Video Shows Syracuse Police Tasering Disabled Man." *Syracuse.com*, August 5. Retrieved 8/3/2015 from http://www.syracuse.com/news/index.ssf/2013/08/disabled_man_plans_to_sue_syracuse_police_over_tasering_for_standing_on_a_bus.html.

O'Brien, R., K. Weir, and C. Young. 2014. "Federal Judges Plead Guilty." Public Integrity.org, Retrieved 4/28/2014 from www.publicintegrity.org/2014/04/28/14630/federal-judges-plead-guilty.

Office of the Inspector General. 2010. *A Review of the FBI's Investigations of Certain Domestic Advocacy Groups.* Washington, DC: Office of the Inspector General.

O'Harrow. R. 2015. "Lawmakers Urge End to Program Sharing Forfeited Assets with State and Local Police." *Washington Post*, January 9. Retrieved 8/3/2015 from www.washingtonpost.com/investigations/lawmakers-urge-end-to-program-sharing-forfeited-assets-with-state-and-local-police/2015/01/09/8843a43c-982f-11e4-8005-1924ede3e54a_story.html.

O'Harrow, R., S. Horwitz, and S. Rich. 2015. "Holder Limits Seized-Asset Sharing Process that Split Billions with Local, State Police." *Washington Post*, January 18. Retrieved 8/3/2015 from www.washingtonpost.com/investigations/holder-ends-seized-asset-sharing-process-that-split-billions-with-local-state-police/2015/01/16/0e7ca058-99d4-11e4-bcfb-059ec7a93ddc_story.html.

Olivo, A. 2015. "Long Delays in John Geer Shooting Probe Leave Fairfax County Board Seeking Changes." *Washington Post*, February 2. Retrieved 8/3/2015 from www.washingtonpost.com/local/virginia-politics/long-delays-in-john-geer-shooting-probe-leave-fairfax-county-board-seeking-changes/2015/02/02/0ad2000a-ab14-11e4-9c91-e9d2f9fde644_story.html

Orlov, R. 2013. "Chris Dorner Firing Review Officially Complete, LAPD Defends Termination." *Huffington Post*, June 22. Retrieved 8/3/2015 from www.huffingtonpost.com/2013/06/22/christopher-dorners-firi_n_3483056.html.

Osher, C. and D. Olinger. 2013. "Colorado Parole Audits Find Fundamental Errors 60 Percent of Cases." *Denver Post*, November 17. Retrieved 8/3/2015 from www.denverpost.com/news/ci_24539737/colorado-parole-audits-find-fundamental-errors-60-percent#ixzz2lDL53VUV.

Owen, B., J. Wells, J. Pollock, B. Muscat, and S. Torres. 2008. *Gendered Violence and Safety: A Contextual Approach to Improving Security in Women's Facilities.* Washington, DC: National Institute of Justice.

Packer, H. 1968. *The Limits of the Criminal Sanction.* Stanford, CA: Stanford University Press.

Packman, D. 2011. 2010 *NPMSRP Police Misconduct Statistical Report.* Cato Institute. Retrieved from http://www.policemisconduct.net/2010-npmsrp-police-misconduct-statistical-report.

Paoline, E. 2003. "Taking Stock: Toward a Richer Understanding of Police Culture." *Journal of Criminal Justice* 31: 199–214.

Paoline, E., S. Myers, and R. Worden. 2000. "Police Culture, Individualism, and Community Policing: Evidence from Two Police Departments." *Justice Quarterly* 17(3): 575–605.

Papke, D. 1986. "The Legal Profession and its Ethical Responsibilities: A History." In *Ethics and the Legal Profession*, ed. M. Davis and F. Elliston, 29–49. Buffalo, NY: Prometheus.

Parascandola, R. 2012. "NYPD Report Supports Claims by Adrian Schoolcraft, Cop Whistleblower." *New York Daily News.* March 7.

Retrieved 7/30/2012 from http://articles.nydailynews.com/2012-03-07/news/31134075_1_officer-adrian-schoolcraft-deputy-inspector-steven-mauriello-jon-norinsberg.

Parvini, S. 2015. "Sheriff Arpaio Admits Violating Court Order in Profiling Suit." *Los Angeles Times*, March 18. Retrieved 8/3/2015 from http://touch.latimes.com/#section/-1/article/p2p-83093795.

Pastor, K. 2014. "Will New York Follow Texas in Criminal Justice Reform? *Citylimits.com*, April 2. Retrieved 8/3/2015 from www.citylimits.org/news/articles/5095/will-new-york-follow-texas-in-criminal-justice-reform.

Paul, R. and L. Elder. 2003. *The Miniature Guide to Critical Thinking: Concepts and Tools.* Dillon Beach, CA: The Foundation for Critical Thinking.

Payne, D. 2002. *Police Liability: Lawsuits Against the Police.* Durham, NC: Carolina Academic Press.

Pellicotti, J. 1990. "Ethics and the Criminal Defense: A Client's Desire to Testify Untruthfully." In *Ethics and Criminal Justice*, ed. F. Schmalleger, 67–78. Bristol, IN: Wyndam Hall.

Pender, G., J. Gates, and E. Coz. 2014. "Epps, McCrory Arraigned on Federal Indictment." November 6. Retrieved 8/3/2015 from www.clarionledger.com/story/politicalledger/2014/11/05/epps-resigning-corrections/18538947/bcb7e3_story.html?hpid=%5B%27z3%27%5D.

Peralta, E. and D. Eads. 2015. "White House Ban on Militarized Gear for Police May Mean Little." National Public Radio, May 21. Retrieved 8/3/2015 from www.npr.org/sections/thetwo-way/2015/05/21/407958035/white-house-ban-on-militarized-gear-for-police-may-mean-little.

Perez, N. 2015. "Former Bexar County Judge Expected to Plead Guilty in Court Today." KSAT12.com, April 10. Retrieved 8/3/2015 from www.ksat.com/content/pns/ksat/news/2015/04/10/former-bexar-county-judge-expected-to-plead-guilty-to-bribery-ch.html.

Perksy, A. 2009. "A Cautionary Tale: The Ted Stevens Prosecution." *Alaska Bar Rag* 33: 1–8.

Perry, J. (Ed.). 2002. *Repairing Communities Through Restorative Justice.* Lanham, MD: American Correctional Association.

Perry, S. 2006. *Prosecutors in State Courts, 2005*. Washington, DC: Bureau of Justice Statistics, U.S. Dept. of Justice.

Perry, T. 2015. "San Diego Police Body Camera Report: Fewer Complaints, Less Use of Force." *Los Angeles Times*, March 18. Retrieved 8/3/2015 from. http://touch.latimes.com/#section/-1/article/p2p-83088560.

Peterson, R. 2012. "The Central Place of Race in Crime and Justice." *Criminology* 50(2): 303–327.

Pew Research Center/USA Today. 2014. *Few Say Police Forces Nationally Do Well in Treating Races Equally*. Retrieved from 6/25/2015 http://www.people-press.org/2014/08/25/few-say-police-forces-nationally-do-well-in-treating-races-equally.

Pew Research Center. 2015. American Support For Death Penalty Declining. Retrieved 6/25/2015 from www.people-press.org/2015/04/16/less-support-for-death-penalty-especially-among-democrats.

Pfaff, J. 2011. "The Micro and Macro Causes of Prison Growth." *Georgia State University Law Review* 28(4): 1237–1272.

Phillips, N. 2015. "Consultants Uncover Deep Problems Within Denver Sheriff Department." *Denver Post*, May 21. Retrieved 8/3/2015 from www.denverpost.com/news/ci_28159042/consultants-uncover-deep-problems-within-denver-sheriff-department.

Phillips, N. 2014. "Denver Mayor Calls for Outside Review of Sheriff Department, Jail." *Denver Post*, July 28. Retrieved 8/3/2015 from www.denverpost.com/news/ci_26232974/denver-mayor-calls-outside-review-sheriff-department-jail.

Phillips, S. 2013. "Police Recruit Attitudes Toward the Use of Unnecessary Force." *Police Practice and Research: An International Journal*. DOI: http://dx.doi.org/10.1080/15614263.2013.845942.

Philly.com. 2014. "Report: Police Gun Deaths Up, Still Below Average." *Philly.com*, December 30. Retrieved 8/3/2015 from http://www.philly.com/philly/news/nation_world/20141230_ap_3ed5 14f2eb674d2fab8a6c4d14d62481.html#6HXcZiHeE1lrlGTL.99.

PICO. 2011. "Unholy Alliance: How the Private Prison Industry is Corrupting Our Democracy and Promoting Mass Incarceration." Retrieved 7/30/2012 from http://publicampaign.org/reports/unholyalliance.

Piller, C. 2010. "Prison Officials Open 'Full Investigation' into Abuse Claims." *Sacramento Bee*, May 10: 1A.

Piller, C. and R. Mejia. 2003. "FBI's Bullet Analysis Method Is Flawed, Studies Suggest." *Austin American-Statesman*, February 4: A8.

Pimentel, D. 2009. "The Reluctant Tattletale: Closing the Gaps in Federal Judicial Discipline." *Tennessee Law Review* 76: 909–957.

Pinkele, C. and W. Louthan. 1985. *Discretion, Justice and Democracy: A Public Policy Perspective*. Ames: Iowa State University Press.

Pinker, S. 2002. *The Blank Slate: The Modern Denial of Human Nature*. New York: Viking.

Pino, N. W. and M.D. Wiatrowski. 2006. "Implementing Democratic Policing and Related Initiatives." In *Democratic Policing in Transitional and Developing Countries*, ed. N. W. Pino and M. D. Wiatrowski, 99–128. Burlington, MA: Ashgate Publishing.

Planas, R. 2015. "Poll Reveals Widespread Fear Of Police Among Latinos." *Huffington Post*, November 12. Retrieved 8/3/2015 from www.huffingtonpost.com/2014/11/12/poll-police-brutality-latinos_n_6147162.html.

Plog, K. 2014. "Two Fife Corrections Officers Resigned—Weeks Apart—Amid Claims of Sexual Misconduct, Records Show." *The News Tribune*, December 6. Retrieved 8/3/2015 from www.thenewstribune.com/news/local/crime/article25901554.html.

Plohetski, T. 2012. "Police Use of Doctored DNA Report Prompts Legal Questions." *Austin American-Statesman*, January 29: A1.

Plohetski, T. and E. Dexheimer. 2012. "Austin's Taser Policy Is Less Restrictive than Others." March 11: A4.

Pogarsky, G. and A. Piquero. 2004. "Studying the Reach of Deterrence: Can Deterrence Theory Help Explain Police Misconduct?" *Journal of Criminal Justice* 32: 371–386.

Pollock, J. 2004/2013a. *Prisons and Prison Life: Costs and Consequences*. Los Angeles: Roxbury (Oxford University Press).

Pollock, J. 2013b. *Criminal Law*. Cincinnati, OH: Anderson Publishing Company.

Pollock, J. 2014. *Women's Crimes, Criminology and Corrections*. Prospect Heights, IL: Waveland Press.

Pollock, J., N. Hogan, E. Lambert, J.I. Ross, and J. Sundt. 2012. "A Utopian Prison: Contradiction in Terms?" *Journal of Contemporary Criminal Justice* 28: 60–76.

Pont, J., H. Stover, and H. Wolff. 2012. "Health Policy and Ethics." *American Journal of Public Health* 102(3): 475–480.

Possley, M. 2014. *The Prosecutor and the Snitch*. The Marshall Project, August 3. Available on website: www.themarshallproject.org/2014/08/03/did-texas-execute-an-innocent-man-willingham.

Possley, S., S. Mills, and F. McRoberts. 2004. "Scandal Touches Even Elite Labs." *Chicago Tribune*, October 21. Retrieved 7/30/2012 from www.chicagotribune.com/news/watchdog/chi-041021forensics,0,3075697.story.

Post, L. 2005. "FBI Bullet Test Misses Target: Court Rejects Test." *Whistleblowers.org*. Retrieved 7/30/2012 from www.whistleblowers.org/storage/whistleblowers/documents/fbi_bullet_test_misses_target.pdf.

Postema, G. 1986. "Moral Responsibility in Professional Ethics." In *Ethics and the Legal Profession*, ed. M. Davis and F. Elliston, 158–179. Buffalo, NY: Prometheus.

Poveda, T. 2001. "Estimating Wrongful Convictions." *Justice Quarterly* 18(3): 689–708.

Powell, M. 2014. "Takeover of Hotel: Informer Recalls His Complicity." *New York Times*, July 3:A19.

Power, C. and L. Kohlberg. 1980. "Faith, Morality, and Ego Development." In *Toward Moral and Religious Maturity*, ed. J. Fowler and C. Bursselmans, 311–372. Morristown, NJ: Silver Burdett.

Prendergast, A. 2003. "Cowboy Justice." *Denver Westword*, June 26. Retrieved 7/30/2012 from www.westword.com/2003-06-26/news/cowboy-justice/4.

Prenzler, T. 1995. "Police Gratuities: What the Public Thinks." *Criminal Justice Ethics* 14(1): 15–26.

Prenzler, T. 2000. "Civilian Oversight of Police: A Test of Capture Theory." *British Journal of Criminology* 40: 659–674.

Prenzler, T. 2006. "Senior Police Managers' Views on Integrity Testing, and Drug and Alcohol Testing." *Policing: An International Journal of Police Strategies and Management* 29(3): 394–407.

Prenzler, T. and J. Ransley. 2002. *Police Reform: Building Integrity*. Sydney, Australia: Hawkins.

Prenzler, T. and C. Ronken. 2001a. "Police Integrity Testing in Australia." *Criminal Justice* 1(2): 319–342.

Prenzler, T. and C. Ronken. 2001b. "Models of Police Oversight: A Critique." *Policing and Society* 11: 151–180.

Price, M. 2013. *National Security and Local Police*. New York City, NY: Brennan Center.

Prior, W. 1991. "Aristotle's Nicomachean Ethics." In *From Virtue and Knowledge: An Introduction to Ancient Greek Ethics*, ed. W. Prior, 144–193. New York: Routledge, Kegan Paul.

Putman, Y. 2008. "Retired Navy Officer Reflects on Honesty, Responsibility." *Chattanooga Times Free Press*, February 27. Retrieved 7/30/2012 from www.timesfreepress.com/news/2008/feb/27/retired-navy-officer-reflects-honesty-responsibili.

Quinn, M. 2005. *Walking with the Devil*. Minneapolis: BooksbyQuinn.

Quinney, R. 1974. *Critique of the Legal Order*. New York: Little, Brown.

Radelet, M., H. Bedau, and C. Putnam. 1992. *In Spite of Innocence: Erroneous Convictions in Capital Cases*. Boston: Northeastern University Press.

Raeder, M. 2007. "See No Evil: Wrongful Convictions and the Prosecutorial Ethics of Offering Testimony by Jailhouse Informants and Dishonest Experts." *Fordham Law Review* 76: 1413–1452.

Raftery, I. 2010. "6-Year Sentence for Guard in Rikers Island Beatings." *New York Times*, August 6. Retrieved 7/30/2012 from www.nytimes.com/2010/08/07/nyregion/07guard.html.

Rahr, S. and S. Rice. 2015. "From Warriors to Guardians: Recommitting American Police Culture to Democratic Ideals." (New Perspectives in Policing Series). Washington, DC: U.S. Department of Justice, National Institute of Justice, 2015. NCJ 248654.

Raine, L. and M. Madden. 2015. "Americans' Views on Government Surveillance Programs." *Pew Research Center*. Retrieved 7/4/2015 from http://www.pewinternet.

org/2015/03/16/americans-views-on-government-surveillance-programs.

Ramirez, C. 2014. "On Your Side Investigates Traffic Stop Nightmare." *Gawker.com*, November 4. Retrieved 11/4/2014 from http://gawker.com/routine-traffic-stop-leads-to-anal-probe-nightmare-agai-1460304269.

Ramsey, R. 2007. "Perceptions of Criminal Justice Professionals Regarding the Frequency of Wrongful Conviction and the Extent of System Errors." *Crime and Delinquency* 53(3): 436–470.

Raphael, D. 1980. *Justice and Liberty*. London: Athlone.

Raphael, S. and M. Stoll. 2008. *Do Prisons Make Us Safer? The Benefits and Costs of the Prison Boom*. New York: Russell Sage Foundation.

Rashbaum, W. 2011. "8 City Officers Charged in Gun Smuggling Case." *New York Times*, October 26: A1.

Rashbaum, W. and T. Kaplan. 2015. "U.S. Says Assembly Speaker Sheldon Silver Took Millions in Payoffs, Abusing Office." *New York Times*, January 23: A1.

Ratcliffe, J. 2008. *Intelligence Led Policing*. Cullompton, Devon: Willan Publishing.

Rawls, J. 1971. *A Theory of Justice*. Cambridge, MA: Belknap.

Rayman, G. 2010a. "The NYPD Tapes: Inside Bed-Stuy's 81st Precinct." *Village Voice*, May 4. Retrieved 7/30/2012 from www.villagevoice.com/2010-05-04/news/the-nypd-tapes-inside-bed-stuy-s-81st-precinct/5.

Rayman, G. 2010b. "The NYPD Tapes, Part 2: Bed-Stuy Street Cops Ordered: Turn This Place into a Ghost Town." *Village Voice*, May 11. Retrieved 7/30/2012 from www.villagevoice.com/2010-05-11/news/nypd-tapes-part-2-bed-stuy.

Reasons, C. 1973. "The Politicalization of Crime, the Criminal and the Criminologist." *Journal of Criminal Law, Criminology and Police Science* 64(March): 471–477.

Reeves, B. 2015. *Local Police Departments, 2013: Personnel, Policies, and Practices*. Washington, DC: Bureau of Justice Statistics, OJP, USDOJ. Available via website.

Reichel, P. 1997. *Corrections*. Minneapolis: West.

Reiman, J. 1984/2005/2007. *The Rich Get Richer and the Poor Get Prison: Ideology, Class, and Criminal Justice*. Boston, MA: Allyn & Bacon.

Reiman, J. 1990/2004. *Justice and Modern Moral Philosophy*. New Haven, CT: Yale University Press.

Reimer, N. 2015. "Flawed Forensics: The Story Behind An Historic FBI Review." *The Crime Report*, April 30. Retrieved 8/3/2015 from www.thecrimereport.org/viewpoints/2015-04-flawed-forensics-the-story-behind-an-historic-fbi-re.

Reisig, M. and R. Parks. 2000. "Experience, Quality of Life, and Neighborhood Context: A Hierarchical Analysis of Satisfaction with Police." *Justice Quarterly* 17 (3): 607–630.

Reisig, M., J. McCluskey, S. Mastrofski, and W. Terrill. 2004. "Suspect Disrespect Toward the Police." *Justice Quarterly* 21(2): 241–268.

Rejali, D. 2007. "What Torture Tells Us (And What It Doesn't)." *Washington Post*. Reprinted in *Austin American-Statesman*, December 23: Gl, G4.

Reuss-Ianni, E. 1983. *Two Cultures of Policing: Street Cops and Management Cops*. New Brunswick, NJ: Transaction.

Reuters. 2011. "Settlement Reached in Massey Mining Disaster." *Reuters News.online*. Retrieved 7/30/2012 from www.reuters.com/article/2011/12/06/us-masseyenergy-mineaccident-idUSTRE7B507V20111206.

Reynolds, P. 2015. *The Impact of Fairness, Organizational Trust, and Perceived Organizational Support on Police Officer Performance* (Unpublished doctoral dissertation). Texas State University.

Reynolds, P. and J. Hicks 2014. "There is No Justice in a Police Department: A Phenomenological Study of Police Experiences." *Police Practice and Research: An International Journal*. DOI: 10.1080/15614263.2014.931229.

Rezendes, M. 2014. "Feds Probe Use of Informants in Lowell." *The Boston Globe*, September 19, 2014.

Richards, N. 2010. "Police Loyalty Redux." *Criminal Justice Ethics* 29(3): 221–240.

Ridolfi, K. and M. Possley. 2010. *Preventable Error: A Report on Prosecutorial Misconduct in California 1997-2009*. Santa Clara, CA: Northern California Innocence Project. Retrieved from http://law.scu.edu/ncip.

Rimer, S. 2000. "Lawyer Sabotaged Case of a Client on Death Row." *New York Times*, November 24. Retrieved 7/30/2012 from www.nytimes.com/2000/11/24/us/lawyer-sabotaged-case-of-a-client-on-death-row.html.

Risen, J. 2015. "Report Finds Collaboration Over Torture." *New York Times*, May 1: A1.

Ritter, N. 2013. "Predicting Recidivism Risk: New Tool in Philadelphia Shows Great Promise." *NIJ Journal (February)*. Retrieved 6/24/2015 from http://www.nij.gov/journals/271/pages/predicting-recidivism.aspx.

Robertson, C. 2010. "30 Years Later, Freedom in a Case with Tragedy for All Concerned." *New York Times*, September 17: A18.

Robles, F. 2013. "Scrutiny of Prosecutors After Questions About Brooklyn Detective." *New York Times*, May 2: A3.

Robles, F. 2013b. "In Review of Brooklyn Cases, So Many Obstacles." *New York Times*, May 24: A1.

Robles, F. 2015. "Racist Police Emails Put Florida Cases in Doubt." *New York Times*, May 16: A10.

Robles, F. 2015b. "Florida Officials Say Guards Who Are in Klan Plotted to Kill An Ex-Inmate." *New York Times*, April 3: A13

Rodin, D. 2004. "Terrorism Without Intention." *Ethics* 114: 752–771.

Rogers, B. 2014. "Texas Parole Board Member Indicted." *Houston Chronicle*, October 3. Retrieved 8/3/2015 from www.houstonchronicle.com/news/houston-texas/houston/article/State-parole-commissioner-indicted-5799025.php.

Rokeach, M. 1973. *The Nature of Human Values*. New York: Free Press.

Romero, G. 2013. "Open Up Police Discipline Records." *Sacramento Bee*, February 18. Retrieved 8/3/2015 from www.ocregister.com/articles/police-496339-public-misconduct.html.

Rosenbaum, D. and D. Lawrence. 2012. "Teaching Respectful Police-Citizen Encounters and Good Decision-Making: Results of a Randomized Control Trial with Police Recruits." National Police Research Platform Report. Washington, DC: National Institute of Justice.

Ross, D. and P. Parker. 2009. "Policing by Consent Decree: An Analysis of 42 U.S.C. § 14141 and the New Model for Police Accountability." *Police Practice and Research* 19(3): 199–208.

Rossmo, K. 2008. *Criminal Investigative Failures*. Boca Raton, FL: Taylor and Francis.

Roth, A. and J. Roth. 1989. *Devil's Advocates: The Unnatural History of Lawyers*. Berkeley, CA: Nolo.

Rothbart, M., D. Hanley, and M. Albert. 1986. "Differences in Moral Reasoning." *Sex Roles* 15(11/12): 645–653.

Rothlein, S. 1999. "Policy Agency Efforts to Prevent Abuses." In *Human Dignity and the Police: Ethics and Integrity in Police Work*, ed. G. Lynch, 15–27. Springfield, IL: Charles C Thomas.

Rothwell, G. and J. Baldwin. 2007a. "Ethical Climate Theory, Whistle-blowing, and the Code of Silence in Police Agencies in the State of Georgia." *Journal of Business Ethics* 70: 341–361.

Rothwell, G. and J. Baldwin. 2007b. "Whistle-Blowing and the Code of Silence in Police Agencies: Policy and Structural Predictors." *Crime and Delinquency* 53(4): 605–632.

Rottman, D. J. 2007. "Adhere to Procedural Fairness in the Justice System." *Criminology and Public Policy* 6: 835–842.

Rubin, J. and S. Gold. 2011. "LAPD Gang Units Dismantled in Some High Crime Areas." *Los Angeles Times*, February 2. Retrieved 7/30/2012 from http://articles.latimes.com/2011/feb/02/local/la-me-lapd-gangs-20110202.

Ruggiero, V. 2001. *Thinking Critically About Ethical Issues*, 5th ed. New York: McGraw-Hill.

Ruiz, J. and C. Bono. 2004. "At What Price a 'Freebie'? The Real Cost of Police Gratuities." *Criminal Justice Ethics* 23(1): 44–54.

Ryan, H. 2015. *Unequal Treatment: Mobilizing the Private Bar to Fight Mass Incarceration*. New York: Lawyers Committee for Civil rights Under the Law.

Saad, L. 2014. "Majority Continues to Support Pot Legalization in U.S." *Gallup.com*, November 6. Retrieved 8/3/2015 from www.gallup.com/poll/179195/majority-continues-support-pot-legalization.aspx.

Salins, L. and S. Simpson. 2013. "Efforts to Fix a Broken System: *Brown v. Plata* and the Prison Overcrowding Epidemic." *Loyola University of Chicago Law Journal* 44: 1153–1200.

Saltzburg, S. 2008. "Changes to Model Rules Impact Prosecutors." *Criminal Justice* 23: 1–36.

Saltzman, J. 2010. "Former Stoughton Detective Pleads Guilty to Lying to FBI Agents." *Boston.com*, January 6. Retrieved 7/30/2012 from www.boston.com/news/local/breaking_news/2010/01/former_stoughto_2.html.

San Antonio Express News. 2002. "Lawyers Should Not Aid, Abet Wrongdoers." December 29: 2H.

Sandel, M. 2009. *Justice: What's the Right Thing to Do?* New York: Farrar, Straus and Giroux.

Sanders, B. 2008. "Using Personality Traits to Predict Police Officer Performance." *Policing: An International Journal of Police Strategies and Management* 31(1): 129–147.

Sanders, S. 2015. "Albuquerque Selects Independent Monitor To Oversee Police Reforms." National Public Radio, January 20. Retrieved 8/3/2015 from www.npr.org/sections/thetwo-way/2015/01/20/378694515/albuquerque-selects-independent-monitor-to-oversee-police-reforms.

Santo, A. 2015. *Preying on Prisoners*. The Marshall Project, June 17. Retrieved from, www.themarshallproject.org/2015/06/17/preying-on-prisoners?utm_medium=email&utm_campaign=newsletter&utm_source=opening-statement&utm_term=newsletter-20150617-203.

Sapien, J. and S. Hernandez. 2013. "Who Polices Prosecutors Who Abuse Their Authority? Usually Nobody." *Propublica*, April 3. Retrieved 8/3/2015 from www.propublica.org/article/who-polices-prosecutors-who-abuse-their-authority-usually-nobody.

Sapp, A. 1994. "Sexual Misconduct by Police Officers." In *Police Deviance*, 3rd ed., ed. T. Barker and D. Carter, 187–200. Cincinnati: Anderson.

Saul, J. 2014. "DA Planning to Overturn Another of Scarcella's Murder Convictions." *New York Post*, November 5. Retrieved 8/3/2015 from http://nypost.com/2014/11/15/da-planning-to-overturn-another-of-scarcellas-murder-convictions.

Savage, D. 2008a. "High Court Won't Hear Surveillance Program Challenge." *Austin American-Statesman*, February 20: A10.

Savage, D. 2008b. "Court: Detainees Have Rights." *Los Angeles Times*. Reprinted in *Austin American-Statesman*, June 13: A1, 13.

Savage, C. 2012a. "Prosecutors Suspended in '08 Trial of a Senator." *New York Times*, May 25: A22.

Savage, C. 2012b. "U.S. Law May Allow Killings, Holder Says." *New York Times*, March 6: A18.

Savage, C. 2012c. "Justice Inquiry Faults Its Own in Guns Fiasco." *New York Times*, September 20: A1.

Savage, C. 2013. "C.I.A. Report Finds Concerns With Ties to New York Police." *New York Times*, June 26: A1.

Savage, C. 2014. "Justice Department Memo Approving Targeted Killing of Anwar Al-Awlaki." *New York Times*, June 23. Retrieved 8/3/2015 from http://www.nytimes.com/interactive/2014/06/23/us/23awlaki-memo.html.

Savage, C. and S. Shane, 2009. "Intelligence Improperly Collected on U.S. Citizens." *New York Times*, December 16. Retrieved 7/30/2012 from www.nytimes.com/2009/12/17/us/17disclose.html.

Savage, C. and S. Shane. 2013. "N.S.A. Leaker Denies Giving Secrets to China." *New York Times*, June 17: A1.

Schafer, J. 2002. "Community Policing and Police Corruption." In *Policing and Misconduct*, ed. K. Lersch, 193–217. Upper Saddle River, NJ: Prentice Hall.

Schafer, J. 2010a. "The Ineffective Police Leader: Acts of Commission and Omission." *Journal of Criminal Justice* 38: 737–746.

Schafer, J. 2010b. "Effective Leaders and Leadership in Policing: Traits, Assessment, Development, and Expansion." *Policing: An International Journal of Police Strategies and Management* 33(4): 644–663.

Schaper, D. 2007. "Former Illinois Gov. George Ryan Heading to Prison." National Public Radio. Retrieved 7/3/2012 from www.npr.org/templates/story/story.php?storyId=16051850.

Scheck, B. 2010. "Professional and Conviction Integrity Programs: Why We Need Them, Why They Will Work, and Models for Creating Them." *Cardozo Law Review* 31(6): 225–256.

Schehr, R. and J. Sears. 2005. "Innocence Commissions: Due Process Remedies and Protection for the Innocent." *Critical Criminology* 13(2): 181–209.

Scheingold, S. 1984. *The Politics of Law and Order*. New York: Longman.

Schmadeke, S. 2015. "Inmates Who Allege Police Abuse by Burge May Get Hearing on Innocence Claims." *Chicago Tribune*, March 26. Retrieved 8/3/2015 from http://my.chicagotribune.com/#section/-1/article/p2p-83148566.

Schmidt, M. 2015. "Scant Data Frustrates Efforts to Assess Number of Shootings by Police." *New York Times*, April 9: A16.

Schoeman, F. 1982. "Friendship and Testimonial Privileges." In *Ethics, Public Policy and Criminal Justice*, ed. F. Elliston and N. Bowie, 257–272. Cambridge, MA: Oelgeschlager, Gunn and Hain.

Schoeman, F. 1985. "Privacy and Police Undercover Work." In *Police Ethics: Hard Choices in Law Enforcement*, ed. W. Heffernan and T. Stroup, 133–153. New York: John Jay Press.

Schuck, A. and D. Rosenbaum. 2011. *The Chicago Quality Interaction Training Program: A Randomized Control Trial of Police Innovation*. National Police Research Platform Topical Report. Washington, DC: National Institute of Justice.

Schwartz, J. 2010. "Myths and Mechanics of Deterrence: The Role of Lawsuits in Law Enforcement Decisionmaking." *U.C.L.A. Law Review* 57:1023–1070.

Schweigert, F. 2002. "Moral and Philosophical Foundations of Restorative Justice." In *Repairing Communities Through Restorative Justice*, ed. J. Perry, 19–37. Lanham, MD: American Correctional Association.

Schwirtz, M. and M. Winerip. 2015. "Correction Commissioner Calls Overhauling Rikers a 'Long, Heavy Lift'". *New York Times*, June 5: A19.

Schwirtz, M. and M. Winerip. 2015. "De Blasio, at Rikers, Unveils a Plan to Reduce Violence and Smuggling." *New York Times*, March 13: A22

Seiler, S., A. Fischer, and Y. Ooi. 2010. "An Interactional Dual-process Model of Moral Decision Making to Guide Military Training." *Military Psychology* 22: 490–509.

Sekerka, L. 2009. "Organizational Ethics Education and Training: A Review of Best Practices and Their Application." *International Journal of Training and Development* 13(2): 77–95.

Selksky, A. 2009. "Many Guantanamo Detainees Innocent, Ex-Bush Official Says." *Austin American-Statesman*, March 20: A5.

Selman, D. and P. Leighton. 2010. *Punishment for Sale: Private Prisons, Big Business, and the Incarceration Binge*. Boston, MA: Rowman & Littlefield Publ.

Semukhina, O. and K. M. Reynolds. 2013. "Russian Citizens' Perceptions of Corruption and Trust of the Police." *Policing and Society: An International Journal of Research and Policy* DOI: 10.1080/10439463.2013.784290

Sentencing Project. 2012. *Too Good to Be True: Private Prisons in America*. Washington, DC: Sentencing Project.

Serrano, R. and R. Ostrow. 2000. "Probe of FBI Lab Reviews 3,000 Cases, Affects None." *Los Angeles Times*. August 17. Retrieved 7/30/2012 from http://articles.latimes.com/2000/aug/17/news/mn-5863.

Seville, L. and G. Kates. 2013. "A Home of Their Own." *The Crime Report*, July 8. 2013. Retrieved 8/3/2015 from www.thecrimereport.org/news/inside-criminal-justice/2013-07-a-home-of-their-own.

Seville, L. and G. Kates. 2015. "The Narco Freedom Case: Who's Watching the Caregivers?" *The Crime Report*. January 5. Retrieved 8/3/2015 from www.thecrimereport.org/news/inside-criminal-justice/2015-01-the-narco-freedom-case-whos-watching-the-caregivers.

Sewell, A. and R. Faturechi. 2013. "L.A. Sheriff Baca Held Liable for $100,000 in Inmate Abuse Case." *Los Angeles Times*, October 17. Retrieved 8/3/2015 from www.latimes.com/local/lanow/la-me-ln-baca-inmate-abuse-damages-20131017,0,2160426.story.

Shaffer, T. and R. Cochran. 2007. "'Technical' Defenses: Ethics, Morals, and the Lawyer as Friend." *Clinical Law Review* 14: 337–353.

Shakespeare, W. *The Merchant of Venice*, Act 4, Scene 1.

Shane, J. M. 2012. "Police Employee Disciplinary Matrix: An Emerging Concept." *Police Quarterly* 15(1): 62–91.

Shane, S. 2008a. "Waterboarding Inquiry Focuses on Legal Advice." *Austin American-Statesman*, February 23: A10.

Shane, S. 2008b. "China Inspired Interrogations at Guantanamo." *New York Times*, July 2. Retrieved 7/30/2012 from www.nytimes.com/2008/07/02/us/02detain.html.

Shane, S. and S. Mazzetti. 2009. "In Adopting Harsh Tactics, No Look at Past Use." *New York Times*, April 22. Retrieved 7/30/2012 from www.nytimes.com/2009/04/22/us/politics/22detain.html.

Shane, S. and C. Moynihan. 2013. "Drug Agents Use Vast Phone Trove, Eclipsing N.S.A.'s." *New York Times*, September 2: A1.

Sharp, E. and P. Johnson. 2009. "Accounting for Variations in Distrust of Local Police." *Justice Quarterly* 26 (1): 157–182.

Shaw, A. 2014. "City Pays Heavy Price for Police Brutality." *Chicago Sun-Times*, April 13. Retrieved 8/3/2015 from http://chicago.suntimes.com/chicago-politics/7/71/167182/city-pays-heavy-price-for-police-brutality.

Sheley, J. 1985. *Exploring Crime*. Belmont, CA: Wadsworth.

Shelton, L. 2013. "Exonerated Man Sues Burge, Others Over Police Beating, Wrongful Conviction. *Chicago Tribune*, May 30, 2013: A1.

Shepherd, J. 2013. *Justice at Risk: An Empirical Analysis of Campaign Contributions and Judicial Decisions*. Washington, DC: American Constitution Society.

Siegel, J. 2015. "The Innocence Project May Have Framed a Man For a Crime He Didn't Commit." *The Daily Beast*, February 22. Retrieved 8/3/2015 from www.thedailybeast.com/articles/2015/02/22/the-innocence-project-on-trial-in-chicago.html.

Sherman, L. 1981. *The Teaching of Ethics in Criminology and Criminal Justice*. Washington, DC: Joint Commission on Criminology and Criminal Justice Education and Standards, Law Enforcement Assistance Administration.

Sherman, L. 1982. "Learning Police Ethics." *Criminal Justice Ethics* 1(1): 10–19.

Sherman, L. 1985a. "Becoming Bent: Moral Careers of Corrupt Policemen." In *Moral Issues in Police Work*, ed. F. Elliston and M. Feldberg, 253–273. Totawa, NJ: Rowman and Allanheld.

Sherman, L. 1985b. "Equity Against Truth: Value Choices in Deceptive Investigations." In *Police Ethics: Hard Choices in Law Enforcement*, ed. W. Heffernan and T. Stroup, 117–133. New York: John Jay Press.

Shermer, M. 2004. *The Science of Good and Evil: Why People Cheat, Gossip, Care, Share, and Follow the Golden Rule*. New York: Times Books, Holt and Co.

Shukovsky, P. 2006. "Gitmo Win Likely Cost Navy Lawyer His Career." *Seattle Post-Intelligencer*, July 1. Retrieved 4/2/2008 from http://seattlepi.nwsource.com/national/276109_swift01.html.

Siegal, N. 2001. "Sexual Abuse of Women Inmates Is Widespread." In *How Should Prisons Treat Inmates? Opposing Viewpoints*, ed. M. Wagner, San Diego: Greenhaven Press.

Silberman, M. 1995. *A World of Violence: Corrections in America*. Belmont, CA: Wadsworth.

Simmons, A. 2006. "Immigration Judges' Abusive Antics Prompt Review." *San Antonio Express News*, February 12: 6A.

Simon, J. 2014. *On Trial: A Remarkable Court Decision and the Future of Prisons in America*. New York: The Free Press.

Skelton, A. 2014. "ACLU Report Criticizes Nebraska Law Enforcement's Citizen Complaint Procedures." *Omaha.com*, August 13. Retrieved 8/3/2015 from www.omaha.com/news/nebraska/aclu-report-criticizes-nebraska-law-enforcement-s-citizen-complaint-procedures/article_8fa0f534-40cf-5984-9c71-ce9fefa8acd4.html.

Skutch, J. 2014. "Former Savannah-Chatham Police Chief Fall Mirrors Department Ills." November 29. Retrieved 8/3/2015 from *Savannahnow.com*, http://savannahnow.com/news/2014-11-29/lovetts-fall-mirrors-department-ills-shame.

Skogan, W., M. Van Craen, and C. Hennessy. 2014. "Training Police for Procedural Justice." *Journal of Experimental Criminology*, December 2014. DOI: 10.1007/s11292-014-9223-6.

Skogan, W. and M. Wycoff. 1986. "Storefront Police Officers: The Houston Field Test." In *Community Crime Prevention: Does It Work?*, ed. D. Rosenbaum, 122–126. Beverly Hills, CA: Sage.

Skolnick, J. 1982. "Deception by Police." *Criminal Justice Ethics* 1(2): 40–54.

Skolnick, J. 2001. "Corruption and the Blue Code of Silence." *Police Practice and Research* 3(1): 7–19.

Skolnick, J. and J. Fyfe. 1993. *Above the Law: Police and the Excessive Use of Force*. New York: Free Press.

Skolnick, J. and R. Leo. 1992. "Ideology and the Ethics of Crime Control." *Criminal Justice Ethics* 11(1): 3–13.

Skutch, J. 2014. "Former Savannah-Chatham Police Chief's Fall Mirrors Department Ills." *Savannahnow.com*, November 29. Retrieved 8/3/2015 from http://savannahnow.com/news/2014-11-29/lovetts-fall-mirrors-department-ills-shame.

Slackman, M. 2010. "Officials Pressed Germans on Kidnapping by C.I.A." *New York Times*, December 8. Retrieved 8/3/2015 from http://www.nytimes.com/2010/12/09/world/europe/09wikileaks-elmasri.html?_r=0.

Slobodzian, J. 2009. "FBI Report Finds Pattern of Police Misdeeds." *Philly.com* April 25. Retrieved 4/28/2009 from www.philly.lcom/philly/news/homepage/20090425_FBI_report_finds_pattern_of_police_misdeeds.html.

Smilansky, S. 2004. "Terrorism, Justification and Illusion." *Ethics* 114: 790–805.

Smith, M. and G. Alpert. 2002. "Searching for Direction: Courts, Social Science, and the Adjudication of Racial Profiling Claims." *Justice Quarterly* 19(4): 673–703.

Smith, R. 2006. "Fired Officer Believed CIA Lied to Congress." *Washington Post*, May 14. Retrieved 7/30/2012 from www.washingtonpost.com/wp-dyn/content/article/2006/05/13/AR2006051301311.html.

Smith, R. and D. Linzer. 2006. "CIA Officer's Job Made Any Leaks More Delicate." *Washington Post*, April 23: A01.

Smith, S. and R. Meyer. 1987. *Law, Behavior, and Mental Health*. New York: New York University Press.

Smith, V. 2014. "Whistle-blowing Former Baltimore Police Detective

Sues Department for Retaliation." *City Paper*, December 30. Retrieved 8/3/2015 from www.citypaper.com/news/mobtownbeat/bcp-whistleblowing-former-baltimore-police-detective-sues-department-for-retaliation-20141230,0,7758822.story#sthash.cy3Bp3uR.dpuf.

Sniffen, M. 1997. "FBI Suspends Agent Whose Charges Led to Critical Report." *Austin American-Statesman*, January 28: A5.

Solomon, A. 1999. "Wackenhut Detention Ordeal." *Village Voice*, August 8. Retrieved 7/30/2012 from www.villagevoice.com/1999-08-31/news/wackenhut-detention-ordeal.

Solomon, J. 2007a. "Former N.C. Chief Justice Takes Up Prisoner's Case." *Washington Post*, November 28: A07.

Solomon, J. 2007b. "FBI Fails to Tell Convicts of Ruling that Could Help Their Cases, Investigation Finds." *Washington Post*, reprinted in *Austin American-Statesman*, November 18: A11.

Solomon, J. and C. Johnson. 2010. "FBI Broke Law for Years in Phone Record Searches." *Washington Post*, January 19. Retrieved 7/30/2012 from www.washingtonpost.com/wp-dyn/content/article/2010/01/18/AR2010011803982.html.

Sontag, D. 2015. "Push to End Prison Rapes Loses Earlier Momentum." *New York Times*, May 13: A1.

Sontag, D. 2015b. "Every Day I Struggle: Transgender Woman Cites Attacks and Abuse in Men's Prison." *New York Times*, April 6: A1.

Sourcebook of Criminal Justice Statistics. 2007. "Respondents' Ratings of the Honesty and Ethical Standards of Police, Table 2.20." Retrieved 7/30/2012 from www.albany.edu/sourcebook/pdf/t2202007.pdf.

Sourcebook of Criminal Justice Statistics. 2011. "Respondents' Ratings of the Honesty and Ethical Standards of Police, Table 2.20." Retrieved 7/30/2012 from www.albany.edu/sourcebook/pdf/t2202011.pdf.

Souryal, S. 1992/2007. *Ethics in Criminal Justice: In Search of the Truth.* Cincinnati: Anderson.

Souryal, S. 1996. "Personal Loyalty to Superiors in Public Service." *Criminal Justice Ethics*, Summer/Fall: 44–62.

Souryal, S. 1999a. "Corruption of Prison Personnel." In *Prison and Jail Administration: Practice and Theory*, ed. P. Carlson and J. Garrett, 171–177. Gaithersburg, MD: Aspen.

Souryal, S. 1999b. "Personal Loyalty to Superiors in Criminal Justice Agencies." *Justice Quarterly* 16(4): 871–906.

Souryal, S. 2009. "Deterring Corruption by Prison Personnel: A Principle-Based Perspective." *Prison Journal* 89: 21–45.

South, N. 2001. "Police, Security and Information: The Use of Informants and Agents in a Liberal Democracy." In *Policing, Security and Democracy: Special Aspects of Democratic Policing*, ed. S. Einstein and M. Amir, 87–105. Huntsville, TX: Office of International Criminal Justice (OICJ), Sam Houston State University.

Spence, G. 1989. *With Justice for None.* New York: Penguin.

Spielman, F. 2013. "City Council OKs $10 Million Settlement in Burge Case." *Chicago Sun-Times*, July 24. Retrieved 8/3/2015 from http://articles.chicagotribune.com/2013-07-25/news/ct-met-chicago-police-brutality-burge-20130725_1_eric-caine-city-oks-police-misconduct.

Spielman, F. 2013. "$12.3 Million Settlement in Police Torture Case Spares Daley from Testifying." *Chicago Sun-Times.com*, September 5. Retrieved 8/3/2015 from www.suntimes.com/22374750-761/123-million-settlement-in-police-torture-case-spares-daley-from-testifying.html.

Starr, S. 2014. "Sentencing by the Numbers." *New York Times*, August 11: A17.

Stein, J. 2010. "Whitehurst's Legacy Still Haunts the FBI Lab." *Spytalk: A Washington Post Blog*, March 25. Retrieved 7/30/2012 from http://blog.washingtonpost.com/spy-talk/2010/03/whitehursts_legacy_still_haunt.html.

Stein, K. 2015. "8 Promises Alabama Just Made to Feds About Treatment of Female Inmates. *Al.com*, May 29. Retrieved 8/3/2015 from www.al.com/news/index.ssf/2015/05/8_promises_alabama_just_made_t.html#incart_river.

Stefanic, M. 1981. "Police Ethics in a Changing Society." *Police Chief*, May: 62–64.

Steffen, J. and C. Osher. 2015. "How Police Reliance on Confidential Informants in Colorado Carries Risk." *Denver Post*, April 17. Retrieved 8/3/2015 from www.denverpost.com/informants/ci_27937446/special-report-police-reliance-informants-colorado-brings-risks.

Stephens, D. 2011. *Police Discipline: A Case For Change.* (New Perspectives in Policing Series). Washington, DC: U.S. Department of Justice, National Institute of Justice.

Stern, R. 2013. "Andrew Thomas and Lisa Aubuchon Slapped by Ninth Circuit; No Immunity in Stapley Suit." *Phoenix New Times*, August 16. Retrieved 8/3/2015 from www.phoenixnewtimes.com/news/andrew-thomas-and-lisa-aubuchon-slapped-by-ninth-circuit-no-immunity-in-stapley-suit-6649229.

Sterngold, J. 2000. "Los Angeles Police Admit a Vast Management Lapse." *New York Times*, March 2: A14.

Stevens, D. 1999. "Corruption Among Narcotics Officers: A Study of Innocence and Integrity." *Journal of Police and Criminal Psychology* 14(2): 1–11.

Stewart, J. 2015. "When the Buck Doesn't Stop: Individual Accountability Is Elusive." *New York Times*, Feb.20: B1.

Stillman, S. 2013. "Taken." *The New Yorker*, August 12. Retrieved 8/3/2015 from www.newyorker.com/magazine/2013/08/12/taken.

Stinson, P., S. Brewer, and B. Mathna. 2015. "Police Sexual Misconduct: Arrested Officers and Their Victims." *Victims and Offenders* 10: 117–151.

Stinson, P., N. Todak, and M. Dodge. 2013. "An Exploration of Crime by Policewomen." *Police Practice and Research: an International Journal*, DOI: 10.1080/15614263.2013.846222.

Stohr, M., C. Hemmens, R. March, G. Barrier, and D. Palhegyl. 2000. "Can't Scale This? The Ethical Parameters of Correctional Work." *Prison Journal* 80(1): 56–79.

Stover, R. 1989. *Making It and Breaking It: The Fate of Public Interest Commitment During Law School*, ed. H. Erlanger. Urbana: University of Illinois Press.

Stroud, M. 2013. "Why Would A Prison Corporation Restructure as a Real Estate Company?" *Forbes*, January 31, 2013.

Sullivan, G. 2014. "Ex-Massey CEO Donald Blankenship Indicted for Coal Mine Disaster That Killed 29." *Washington Post*, November 14. Retrieved 8/3/2015 from www.washingtonpost.com/news/morning-mix/wp/2014/11/14/ex-massey-ceo-don-blankenship-indicted-for-coal-mine-disaster-than-killed-29.

Sulzberger, A. and J. Eligon. 2010. "2 Officers, 2 Courts, and Charges of Eliciting Sexual Favors." *New York Times*, May 18. Retrieved 7/30/2012 from www.nytimes.com/2010/05/19/nyregion/19cops.html.

Sunshine, J. and T.R. Tyler, 2003. "Moral Solidarity, Identification With The Community, and the Importance of Procedural Justice: The Police as Prototypical Representation of a Group's Moral Values." *Social Psychology Quarterly* 66: 153–165.

Sutherland, E. H. 1947. *Principles of Criminology*, 4th ed. Philadelphia, PA: J.B. Lippincott.

Swift, C. 2007. "The American Way of Justice." *Esquire*, June 26. Retrieved 7/30/2012 from www.esquire.com/print-this/features/ESQ0307swift.

Swisher, K. 2009. "The Judicial Ethics of Criminal Law Adjudication." *Arizona State Law Journal* 41: 755–828.

Sykes, G. 1980. "The Defects of Total Power." In *Keepers: Prison Guards and Contemporary Corrections*, ed. B. Crouch. Springfield, IL: Charles C. Thomas.

Sykes, G. 1989. "The Functional Nature of Police Reform: The Myth of Controlling the Police." In *Critical Issues in Policing*, ed. R. Dunham and G. Alpert, 292–304. Prospect Heights, IL: Waveland.

Sykes, G. M. and D. Matza. 1957. "Techniques of Neutralization: A Theory of Deviance." *American Sociological Review* 22(6): 664–670.

Tabish, S. and K. N. Jha. 2012. "The Impact of Anti-Corruption Strategies on Corruption Free Performance in Public Construction Projects." *Construction Management & Economics* 30(1): 21–35.

Tanay, E. 1982. "Psychiatry and the Prison System." *Journal of Forensic Sciences* 27(2): 385–392.

Tanner, R. 2002. "Central Park Case Puts Focus on Confessions." *Austin American-Statesman*, December 7: A9.

Tanner, R. 2006. "Bad Science May Taint Many Arson Convictions." *Austin American-Statesman*, May 3: A1, A5.

Tau, B. 2014. "Curbing Police Militarization Would be Uphill Battle." *Politico*, September 2014. Retrieved 8/3/2015 from www.politico.com/story/2014/09/police-militarization-110690_Page2.html#ixzz3ETGIi0nb.

Taylor, W. 1993. *Brokered Justice: Race Politics and Mississippi Prisons 1798–1992*. Columbus: Ohio State University Press.

Terrill, W. 2001. *Police Coercion: Application of the Force Continuum*. New York: LFB Scholarly Publishing.

Terrill, W. 2005. "Police Use of Force: A Transactional Approach." *Justice Quarterly* 22(1): 107–139.

Terrill, W. and S. Mastrofsky. 2002. "Situational and Officer-Based Determinants of Police Coercion." *Justice Quarterly* 19(2): 216–248.

Terrill, W. and E. Paoline. 2007. "Non-arrest Decision Making in Police-Citizen Encounters." *Police Quarterly* 10: 308–331.

Terrill, W. and E. Paoline. 2011. "Conducted Energy Devices (CEDs) and Citizen Injuries: The Shocking Empirical Reality." *Justice Quarterly* 29(2): 153–182.

Terrill, W., E. Paoline, and P. Manning. 2003. "Police Culture and Coercion." *Criminology* 41(4): 1003–1034.

Texas Bar Association. 2000. *Muting Gideon's Trumpet: The Crisis in Indigent Defense*. Report by the Committee on Legal Services to the Poor in Criminal Matters, Texas State Bar. Retrieved 7/30/2012 from www.uta.edu/pols/moore/indigent/last.pdf.

Texas Civil Rights Project. 2011. *Police Misconduct In San Antonio*. Austin, TX: Texas Civil Rights Project. Retrieved from www.texascivilrightsproject.org.

Texas District & County Attorneys Association (TDCAA). 2012. *Setting the Record Straight On Prosecutorial Misconduct*. Retrieved on March 23, 2014 from http://www.tdcaa.com/reports/setting-the-record-straight-on-prosecutorial-misconduct.

Thibaut, J. and L. Walker, L. 1975. *Procedural Justice*. Hillsdale, NJ: Erlbaum.

Thoma, S. 1986. "Estimating Gender Differences in the Comprehension and Preference of Moral Issues." *Developmental Review* 6: 165–180.

Thomas, E. 2001. "A Captain's Story." *Newsweek*. April 2. Retrieved 8/3/2015 from http://www.newsweek.com/captains-story-150105.

Thompson, C. 2015. "Dozens in D.C., Maryland Paid the Ultimate Price for Cooperating with Police." *Washington Post*, January 10. Retrieved 8/3/2015 from www.washingtonpost.com/local/dozens-in-dc-maryland-paid-the-ultimate-price-for-cooperating-with-police/2015/01/10/978b1a18-b5f6-11e3-b899-20667de76985_story.html.

Thompson, D. 1980. "Paternalism in Medicine, Law and Public Policy." In *Ethics Teaching in Higher Education*, ed. D. Callahan and S. Bok, 3–20. Hastings, NY: Hastings Center.

Thompson, D. 2004. "Prison System Blasted by Lawmakers, New Administration." *Sandiego.com*, January 20. Retrieved 7/30/2012 from http://signonsandiego.com/news/state/20040120-1658-ca-prisonhearings.html.

Thompson, D. 2013. "California Prison Abuse Detailed In New Report." *Huffington Post*, April 3. Retrieved 8/3/2015 from www.huffingtonpost.com/2013/04/03/california-prison-abuse-d_n_3009926.html.

Tobin, W. and C. Spiegleman. 2013. "Crime Labs Stained by 'Junk Science.'" *Austin American Statesman*, October 13, 2013, E1, E3.

Toch, H. 1977. *Living in Prison*. New York: Free Press.

Tonry, M. 2005. "The Functions of Sentencing and Sentencing Reform." *Stanford Law Review* 58: 37–67.

Toobin, J. 2014 "This is My Jail." *The New Yorker*, April 14, 2014.

Trager, R. 2014. "Hard Questions After Litany of Forensic Failures at US Labs. *Chemistryworld.com*, December 1. Retrieved 8/3/2015 from www.rsc.org/chemistryworld/2014/12/hard-questions-after-litany-forensic-failures-malpractice-labs-us.

Trainum, J. 2008. "The Case for Videotaping Interrogations." *Los Angeles Times*, October 24. Retrieved 7/30/2012 from www.latimes.com/news/opinion/commentary/la-oe-trainum24-2008oct24,0,7918545.story.

Transparency International. 2011. "Corruption Perceptions Index, 2011." Retrieved 7/30/2012 from http://cpi.transparency.org/cpi2011/results.

Transparency International. 2014. "Corruption Perceptions Index, 2013." Retrieved 7/4/2015 from https://www.transparency.org/cpi2013/results

Trautman, N. 2008. "The Ethics Continuum." Retrieved 7/30/2012 from www.ethicsinstitute.com/pdf/Corruption%20Continum.pdf.

Treatment Advocacy Center. 2014. *The Treatment of Persons with Mental Illness in Prisons and Jails: A State Survey*. Retrieved from www.tacreports.org/storage/documents/treatment-behind-bars/treatment-behind-bars.pdf.

Tuchman, G. and K. Wojleck. 2009. "Texas Police Shake Down Drivers, Lawsuit Claims." CNN.com, May 6. Retrieved 7/30/2012 from www.cnn.com/2009/CRIME/05/05/texas.police.seizures.

Tullio, E. 2009. "Comment: Chemical Castration for Child Predators: Practical, Effective and Constitutional." *Chapman Law Review* 13: 191–219.

Tullis, P. 2013. "Can Forgiveness Play a Role in Criminal Justice?" *New York Times*, January 4. Retrieved 8/3/2015 from www.nytimes.com/2013/01/06/magazine/can-forgiveness-play-a-role-in-criminal-justice.html?_r=0.

Turner, A. 2010. "Panel Cites 'Flawed Science' in Arson Case." *Houston Chronicle*, July 24. Retrieved 7/30/2012 from www.chron.com/disp/story.mpl/metropolitan/7122381.html.

Turner, C. 2007. "Ethical Issues in Criminal Justice Administration." *American Jails* (January/February): 49–53.

Tyler, T. 1990/2006. *Why People Obey the Law*. New Haven, CT: Yale University Press.

Tyler, T.R. 2003. "Procedural Justice, Legitimacy, and the Effective Rule of Law." In *Crime and Justice: A Review of Research*, Vol. 30, ed. M. Tonry. Chicago, IL: University of Chicago Press.

Tyler, T. 2010a. "Legitimacy in Corrections." *Criminology and Public Policy* 9: 127–134.

Tyler, T. R. 2010b. *Why People Cooperate: The Role of Social Motivations*. Princeton, NJ: Princeton University Press.

Tyler, T. R. 2011. *Why People Cooperate: The Role of Social Motivations*. Princeton, NJ: Princeton University Press.

Tyler, T. R. and J. Fagan 2008. "Legitimacy and Cooperation: Why Do People Help the Police Fight Crime in Their Communities? *Ohio State Journal of Criminal Law* 6: 231–75.

Tyler, T. and Y. Huo. 2002. *Trust in the Law: Encouraging Public Cooperation in the Police and Courts*. New York City: Russell Sage Foundation.

Tyler, T. and L. Wakslak. 2004. "Profiling and Police Legitimacy: Procedural Justice, Attributions of Motive, and Acceptance of Police Authority." *Criminology* 42(2): 253–281.

Umbreit, M. 1994. *Victim Meets Offender: The Impact of Restorative Justice and Mediation*. Monsey, NY: Criminal Justice Press.

Umbreit, M. and M. Carey. 1995. "Restorative Justice Implications for Organizational Change." *Federal Probation* 59(1): 47–54.

Umbreit, M., R. Coates, and B. Vos. 2002. "Peacemaking Circles in Minnesota: An Exploratory Study." *Crime Victims Report* 5(6): 81–82.

United States Attorney's Office. 2008a. "Boston Police Officer Pleads Guilty to all Charges." News Release: November 8. Boston, MA: U.S. Dept. of Justice, U.S. Attorney's Office, Michael J. Sullivan.

United States Attorney's Office. 2008b. "Correctional Officer Pleads Guilty to Bribery and Carnal Knowledge." News Release: June 23. Retrieved 7/30/2012 from www.justice.gov/oig/reports/press/2008/2008_06_23.pdf.

U.S. Attorney's Office. 2013. "25 Sentenced in Operation Prison Cell." U.S. Attorney's Office, Southern District, October 31, 2013. Retrieved 8/3/2015 from www.justice.gov/usao-sdtx/pr/25-sentenced-operation-prison-cell.

United States Department of Justice. 2012. *Report to Congress on the Activities and Operations of the Public Integrity Section For 2012*. Available via website: http://www.justice.gov/criminal/pin.

United States Department of Justice. 2014. *Justice Department Releases Findings Showing That the Alabama Department of Corrections Fails to Protect Prisoners from Sexual Abuse and Sexual Harassment at the Julia Tutwiler Prison for Women*, January 22, 2014. Retrieved from http://www.justice.gov/opa/pr/justice-department-releases-findings-showing-alabama-department-corrections-fails-protect.

United States Department of Justice. 2015. News Release. Retrieved 8/3/2015 from www.justice.gov/opa/pr/former-fbi-special-agent-sentenced-10-years-prison-bribery-and-obstruction-scheme.

Urza, G. 2014. "Indefensible: Why Khalid Sheikh Mohammed's Lawyer is Leaving the Defense Team – and the Army." *Slate*, August 26. Retrieved 8/3/2015 from http://www.slate.com/articles/news_and_politics/jurisprudence/2014/08/khalid_sheikh_mohammed_s_guantanamo_defense_lawyer_jason_wright_is_departing.html.

Valentine, D. 2009. "Police: Officers Under Investigation Removed from Patrols." *Gazette News*, July 20. Retrieved 7/30/2012 from www.gazette.net/stories/07202009/prinnew140235_32543.shtml.

Van Maanen, J. 1978. "The Asshole." In *Policing: A View from the Street*, ed. P. Manning and J. van Maanen, 221–240. Santa Monica, CA: Goodyear.

Van Ness, D. and K. Heetderks Strong. 1997. *Restoring Justice*. Cincinnati: Anderson.

Vaughn, M. and L. Smith. 1999. "Practicing Penal Harm Medicine in U.S. Prisons." *Justice Quarterly* 16(1): 175–231.

Vaznis, J. 2008 "Ex-Officer Gets 18 Years in Drug Plot." *Boston.com*. Retrieved 7/30/2012 from www.boston.com/news/local/articles/2008/03/11/ex_officer_gets_18_years_in_drug_plot.

Vedantam, S. 2007. "If It Feels Good To Be Good, It Might Be Only Natural." *WashingtonPost.com*. Retrieved 7/30/2012 from www.washingtonpost.com/wp-dyn/content/article/2007/05/27/AR2007052701056.html.

Verges, A. 2010. "Integrating Contextual Issues in Ethical Decisionmaking." *Ethics & Behavior* 20: 497–507.

Victor, B. and J. Cullen., 1987. "A Theory and Measure of Ethical Climate in Organizations." *Research in Corporate Social Performance and Policy* 9: 51–71.

Victor, B. and J. Cullen. 1988. "The Organizational Bases of Ethical Work Climates." *Administrative Science Quarterly* 33: 101–125.

Virtanen, M. 2014. "N.Y. Court: Some Lies to Suspects Are Unfair." *Associated Press*, February 21. Retrieved 8/3/2015 from http://www.nytimes.com/aponline/2014/02/20/us/ap-us-police-lies.html?_r=0.

Vitiello, M. 2008. "Punishing Sex Offenders: When Good Intentions Go Bad." *Arizona State Law Review* 40: 651–689.

Vodicka, D. 2009. *The Green Wall*. Bloomington, IN: iUniverse Inc.

Vogelstein, R. 2003. "Confidentiality vs. Care: Re-evaluating the Duty to Self, Client, and Others." *Georgetown Law Journal* 92: 153–171.

Von Hirsch, A. 1976. *Doing Justice*. New York: Hill and Wang.

Von Hirsch, A. 1985. *Past or Future Crimes*. New Brunswick, NJ: Rutgers University Press.

Walker, L. 1986. "Sex Difference in the Development of Moral Reasoning." *Child Development* 57: 522–526.

Walker, L. 2014. "Snowden Docs Lead to Discovery NSA Employees Spied on Spouses, Girlfriends." *Newsweek*, December 26. Retrieved 8/3/2015 from www.newsweek.com/snowden-docs-lead-discovery-nsa-employees-spied-spouses-girlfriends-294994.

Walker, S. 1985/2005. *Sense and Nonsense About Crime*. Monterey, CA: Brooks/Cole.

Walker, S. 2001. *Police Accountability: The Role of Citizen Oversight*. Belmont, CA: Wadsworth.

Walker, S. 2007. *Police Accountability: Current Issues and Research Needs*. Paper presented at National Institute of Justice, Policing Research Workshop: Planning for the Future, Washington, DC, November 28–29, 2006. (Available through National Institute of Justice, Washington, DC.)

Walker, S. and G. Alpert. 2002. "Early Warning Systems as Risk Management for Police." In *Policing and Misconduct*, ed. K. Lersch, 219–230. Upper Saddle River, NJ: Prentice Hall.

Walker, S., G. Alpert, and D. Kenney. 2000. "Early Warning Systems for Police: Concept, History, and Issues." *Police Quarterly* 3: 132–152.

Wallack, T., J. Ransom, and T. Anderson. 2015. "Boston Paid $36m to Settle Police Lawsuits." *Boston Globe*, May 15. Retrieved 8/3/2015 from www.bostonglobe.com/metro/2015/05/14/boston-spends-million-resolve-claims-against-police/KZ1NKhzahIDG51568m5FLK/story.html.

Walsh, A. 2000. "Evolutionary Psychology and the Origins of Justice." *Justice Quarterly* 17(4): 841–864.

Ward, M. 2004. "Echoes of Texas' Sordid Past in Iraq Prison Abuse." *Austin American-Statesman*, May 12: B4.

Ward, M. 2006. "Secrecy of Parole Files Opens Door for Abuses." *Austin American-Statesman*, March 18: A1, A11.

Ward, M. 2008. "Inquiry: New Trial Had Been Ordered by Federal Appeals Court Last August." *Austin American-Statesman*, April 23: A1, A9.

Ward, M. 2009. "Court Cases Forcing Change at Texas Parole Agency." *Austin American-Statesman*, August 31: A1, A9.

Ward, M. 2013. "Parole Officers, Youth-Prison Workers Busted in Separate Crackdowns." *American-Statesman*, July 1. Retrieved 8/3/2015 from www.statesman.com/news/news/parole-officers-youth-prison-workers-busted-in-sep/nYbXh/.

Ward, S. 2007. "Pulse of the Legal Profession." *ABA Journal* (October). Retrieved 7/30/2012 from www.abajournal.com/magazine/article/pulse_of_the_legal_profession.

Warren, J. 2004a. "Guards Tell of Retaliation for Informing." *Los Angeles Times*, January 21. Retrieved 7/30/2012 from http://articles.latimes.com/2004/jan/21/local/me-prison21.

Warren, J. 2004b. "State Penal System Is Hammered in Report." *Los Angeles Times*. Retrieved 7/30/2012 from http://articles.latimes.com/2004/jan/16/local/me-prisons16.

Warrick, J. and P. Finn. 2009. "Harsh Tactics Readied Before Their Approval." *Washington Post*, April 22. Retrieved 7/30/2012 from www.washingtonpost.com/wp-dyn/content/article/2009/04/21/AR2009042104055.html.

Wasikowska, M. 2013. "Spying on Law-Abiding Muslims." *New York Times* February 10, 2013: SR10.

Weber, D. 1987. "Still in Good Standing. The Crisis in Attorney Discipline." *American Bar Association Journal*, November: 58–63.

Weinstein, H. 2007. "ACLU: Company Aiding Torture." *Los Angeles Times*. Reprinted in *Austin American-Statesman*, May 31: A8.

Weisburd, D. and R. Greenspan. 2000. *Police Attitudes Toward Abuse of Authority: Findings from a National Study (Research In Brief)*. Washington, DC: U.S. Department of Justice.

Weiser, B. 2015. "Deal Is Near on Far-Reaching Reforms at Rikers, Including a Federal Monitor." *New York Times*, June 19: A1.

Weiser, B., M. Schwirtz, and M. Winerip. 2014. "U.S. Plans Suit Over Conditions at Rikers Island." *New York Times*, December 19: A1.

Weitzer, R. 1999. "Citizens' Perceptions of Police Misconduct: Race and Neighborhood Context." *Justice Quarterly* 16(4): 819–846.

Weitzer, R. and S. Tuch. 2002. "Perceptions of Racial Profiling: Race, Class, and Personal Experience." *Criminology* 40(2): 435–456.

Weitzer, R. and S. Tuch. 2004. "Race and Perceptions of Police Misconduct." *Social Problems* 51(3): 305–325.

Wells, W. and J. Schafer. 2006. "Officer Perceptions of Police Responses to Persons with a Mental Illness." *Policing: An International Journal of Police Strategies and Management* 29(4): 578–601.

Wendle, J. 2009. "New Rules for Russia's Cops: No Bribes or Wild Sex." *Time.com*, April 15. Retrieved 7/30/2012 from www.time.com/time/printout/0,8816,1891215,00.html.

Westmarland, L. 2005. "Police Ethics and Integrity: Breaking the Blue Code of Silence." *Policing and Society* 15(2): 145–165.

Wheeler, B. 2012. "The Rise of the Undercover Sting." *BBC News Magazine*, February 28. Retrieved 7/30/2012 from www.bbc.co.uk/news/magazine-17160690.

White, J. 2005. "Documents Tell of Brutal Improvisation by GIs." *Washington Post*, August 3: A1.

White, M. and J. Ready. 2009. "Examining Fatal and Nonfatal Incidents Involving the TASER." *Criminology and Public Policy* 8(4): 865–891.

White, R. 1999. "Are Women More Ethical? Recent Findings on the Effects of Gender on Moral Development." *Journal of Public Administration Research and Theory* 9: 459–472.

Whitehead, J. 1991. "Ethical Issues in Probation and Parole." In *Justice, Crime, and Ethics*, ed. M. Braswell, B. McCarthy, and B. McCarthy, 253–273. Cincinnati: Anderson.

Whitehead, S. 2015. "The Specter of Racism: Exploring White Racial Anxieties in the Context of Policing." *Contemporary Justice Review*. DOI: 10.1080/10282580.2015.1025622.

Whitlock, C. 2005. "CIA Role in Abductions Investigated." *Austin American-Statesman*, March 13: A5.

Whitman, J. 1998. "What Is Wrong with Inflicting Shame Sanctions?" *Yale Law Journal* 197(4): 1055–1092.

Wilder, F. 2013. "Give Us Your Tired, Your Poor, Your Huddled Masses—We Have Private Prisons to Fill." *Texas Observer*. May 1. Retrieved 8/3/2015 from www.texasobserver.org/give-us-your-tired-your-poor-your-huddled-masses-we-have-private-prisons-to-fill/.

Wilder, F. and P. Mosqueda, 2014. "Immigrants in Federal Prisons 'Subjected to Shocking Abuse and Mistreatment.'" ACLU/Texas, June 9, 2014. Available via website, www.prisonlegalnews.org/news/publications/aclu-warhoused-and-forgotten-immigrants-trapped-our-private-prison-system/.

Williams, B. 2009. "In Minneapolis, Costs of Police Misconduct Add Up." MPRNews, November 1. Retrieved 7/30/2012 from http://minnesota.publicradio.org/display/web/2009/11/02/police-misconduct.

Williams, C. 2008. "Prosecution of Youths at Guantanamo Spurs Outrage." *Los Angeles Times*, December 28: A1.

Williams, H. 2010. *Are the Recommendations of the Braidwood Commission on Conducted Energy Weapons Use Sound Public Policy?* Paper presented at the Academy of Criminal Justice Sciences Meeting, February, San Diego.

Williams, H. 2013. *Physiological Attributes of Arrest-Related Sudden Deaths Proximate to the Application of Taser Electronic Control Devices: An Evidence Based Study of the Theory of High Risk Groups.* Doctoral Dissertation. Texas State University.

Williams, M., J. Holcomb, T. Kovandzic, and S. Bullock. 2010. "Policing for Profit: The Abuse of Civil Asset Forfeiture." *Institute for Justice*, available via website, www.ij.org/images/pdf_folder/other_pubs/assetforfeituretoemail.pdf.

Williams, T. 2014. "Panel to Set Terms to End Abusive Reign at Jail System." *Los Angeles Times*, December 17: A18.

Williams, T. 2015a. "Inquiry to Examine the Extent of Racial Bias in the San Francisco Police." *New York Times*, May 8: A13

Williams, T. 2015b. "Jails Have Become Warehouses for the Poor, Ill and Addicted, a Report Says." *New York Times*, February 11: A19.

Wilson, J. Q. 1976. *Varieties of Police Behavior*. New York: Atheneum.

Wilson, J. Q. 1993. *The Moral Sense*. New York: Free Press.

Wilson, R. 2015. "Police Accountability Measures Flood State Legislatures After Ferguson, Staten Island." *Washington Post*, February 4. Retrieved 8/3/2015 from www.washingtonpost.com/blogs/govbeat/wp/2015/02/04/police-accountability-measures-flood-state-legislatures-after-ferguson-staten-island/.

Wiltrout, K. 2007. "Naval Officer Sentenced to Six Months in Prison, Discharge." McClatchy-Tribune Information Services, May 18. Retrieved 3/19/2008 from www.accessmylibrary.com/coms2/summary_0286-30808288_ITM.

Wimbush, J., J. Shepard, and S. Markham. "An Empirical Examination of the Relationship Between Ethical Climate and Ethical Behavior From Multiple Levels of Analysis." *Journal of Business Ethics* 16(16): 1705–1716.

Winerip, M. and M. Schwirtz. 2014a. "In Rare Rebuke for Rikers Officers, Judge Urges Firing of 6 Who Beat Inmate." *New York Times*, September 30: A18.

Winerip, M. and M. Schwirtz, M. 2014b. "Rikers: Where Mental Illness Meets Brutality in Jail." *New York Times*, July 14: A1.

Wines, M. 2014. "Are Police Bigoted?" *New York Times*, August 31: SR1.

Wines, M. and S. Cohen. 2015. "Police Killings Rise Slightly." *New York Times*, May 1: A1

Winston, A. 2013. "American Police Reform and Consent Decrees." *Truth-out.org*, August 31. Retrieved

8/3/2015 from www.truth-out.org/news/item/18455-american-police-reform-and-consent-decrees.

Wise, D. 2012. "Blumenfeld Finds D.A.'s Questioning of Suspects Violates Conduct Code." *New York Law Journal*, April 18. Retrieved 7/30/2012 from www.newyorklawjournal.com/PubArticleNY.jsp?id=1202549241241.

Witt, A. 2001. "Allegations of Abuses Mar Murder Cases." *Washington Post*, June 23: A01.

Wolfe, C. 1991. *Judicial Activism*. Pacific Grove, CA: Brooks/Cole Publishing.

Wolfe, S. and A. Piquero. 2011. "Organizational Justice and Police Misconduct." *Criminal Justice and Behavior* 38(4): 332–353.

Wood, D. 2015. "San Francisco Police Texting Scandal: How Can Police Root Out Racism?" *Christian Science Monitor*, March 19. Retrieved 8/3/2015 from www.csmonitor.com/USA/Justice/2015/0319/San-Francisco-police-texting-scandal-How-can-police-root-out-racism.

Wood, J. 1997. *Royal Commission into the New South Wales Police Service, Final Report*. Sydney, Australia: Government of the State of N.S.W. (cited in Prenzler and Ronken, 2001b).

Worden, R. and S. Catlin. 2002. "The Use and Abuse of Force by Police." In *Policing and Misconduct*, ed. K. Lersch, 85–120. Upper Saddle River, NJ: Prentice Hall.

Worley, R. and V. Worley. 2011. "Guards Gone Wild: A Self Report Study of Correctional Officer Misconduct and the Effect of Institutional Deviance on 'Care' Within the Texas Prison System." *Deviant Behavior* 32: 293–319.

Worrall, J. 2001. "Addicted to Drug War: The Role of Civil Asset Forfeiture as a Budgetary Necessity in Contemporary Law Enforcement." *Journal of Criminal Justice* 29(3): 171–187.

Worrall, J. 2002. "If You Build It They Will Come: Consequences of Improved Citizen Complaint Review Procedures." *Crime and Delinquency* 48(3): 355–379.

Worrall, J. and T. Kovandzi. 2008. "Is Policing for Profit? Answers from Asset Forfeiture." *Criminology and Public Policy* 7(2): 219–244.

Wren, T. 1985. "Whistle-Blowing and Loyalty to One's Friends." In *Police Ethics: Hard Choices in Law Enforcement*, ed. W. Heffernan and T. Stroup, 25–37. New York: John Jay Press.

Wright, K. 2001. "Management-Staff Relations: Issues in Leadership, Ethics, and Values." In *Discretion, Community and Correctional Ethics*, ed. J. Kleinig and M. Smith, 203–218. Oxford, England: Rowman and Littlefield.

Wyatt-Nichol, H. and G. Franks. 2010. "Ethics Training in Law Enforcement Agencies." *Public Integrity* 12(1): 39–50.

Yee, J. and A. Molloy. 2005. *For God and Country: Faith and Patriotism Under Fire*. New York: Public Affairs Press.

York, G. 2012. *Corruption Behind Bars: Stories of Crime and Corruption in Our American Prison System*. Available through Kindle Ebooks.

Yost, P. 2010. "FBI Looking Into Deadly Coal Mine Explosion." *Austin American-Statesman*, May 1: A9.

Yost, P. 2012a. "Concerns Raised About Investigation Tactic Before 'Fast and Furious.'" *Austin American-Statesman*, January 6: A13.

Yost, P. 2012b. "2,000 Exonerated in 23 Years." *Washington Times*, May 21. Retrieved 7/30/2012 from www.washingtontimes.com/news/2012/may/21/2000-exonerated-in-23-years/.

Zacharias, F. and B. Green. 2009. "The Duty to Avoid Wrongful Convictions: A Thought Experiment in the Regulation of Prosecutors." *Boston University Law Review* 89: 1–59.

Zak, P. 2012. *The Moral Molecule*. New York: Dutton.

Zalman, M., B. Smith, and A. Kiger. 2008. "Officials' Estimates of the Incidence of 'Actual Innocence' Convictions." *Justice Quarterly* 25(1): 72–100.

Zamora, J., H. Lee, and J. van Derbeke. 2003. "Ex-Cops Cleared of 8 Counts." *SFGate.com*, October 1. Retrieved 7/30/2012 from www.sfgate.com/bayarea/article/Ex-cops-cleared-of-8-counts-mistrial-on-27-2555011.php.

Zhao, J., N. He, and N. Lovrich. 1998. "Individual Value Preferences Among American Police Officers." *Policing: An International Journal of Police Strategies and Management* 21(1): 22–37.

Zimbardo, P. 1982. "The Prison Game." In *Legal Process and Corrections*, ed. N. Johnston and L. Savitz, 195–198. New York: Wiley.

Zimring, F., G. Hawkins, and S. Kamin. 2001. *Punishment and Democracy: Three Strikes and You're Out in California*. Oxford, England: Oxford University Press.

Zitrin, R. and C. Langford. 1999. *The Moral Compass of the American Lawyer*. New York: Ballantine Books.

Zohar, N. 2004. "Innocence and Complex Threats: Upholding the War Ethic and the Condemnation of Terrorism." *Ethics* 114: 734–751.

Author index

A

Abbey-Lambertz, J., 118
Acker, J., 71, 311
Adams, S., 58
Adams, V., 94
Adams, W., 430
Akers, R. L., 90
Albarazi, H., 132
Alderson, J., 458
Aleixo, P., 94
Alex, K., 94
Alexander, M., 132, 133, 334
Allen, H., 64
Allen, M., 319
Allen, R., 70, 101, 423
Allyn, B., 195
Alpert, B., 305
Alpert, G., 117, 119, 120, 148, 153, 158,
    161, 177, 194, 197, 217
Anderson, C., 169
Anderson, P., 276
Anderson, T., 198
Antes, A., 104
Apuzzo, M., 155, 165, 456
Arax, M., 405, 406
Archbold, C., 211
Ardichvili, A., 101
Ariens, M., 238, 240, 262
Aristotle, 9, 28–29, 31, 33, 44, 46,
    56–57, 63, 90, 137, 234
Armstrong, K., 296, 311
Aronson, R., 311
Arrigo, B., 209
Ashkanasy, N., 94
Ashkenas, J., 445
Atherley, L., 213
Attard, B., 216
Auerhahn, K., 337
Axtman, K., 175, 277

B

Baelz, P., 27, 42
Baker, A., 25, 26, 214, 216, 217
Baldwin, J., 140
Balko, R., 119, 167, 277, 316
Balko, S., 117–118
Balshaw-Biddle, K., 378
Bamford, J., 453, 454
Bandura, A., 90–91, 92, 96, 97, 98, 99
Banks, C., 121
Bannon, A., 245

Barber, B., 204
Barber, E., 315
Barker, K., 140, 210, 396, 397
Barker, T., 166, 170, 184, 191, 193
Barnes, R., 289
Barnhill, M., 378
Barrier, G., 346, 422
Barry, V., 10, 33, 38, 80
Barton, G., 147
Bateman, T. S., 101
Bayley, D., 184, 460
Bazelon, L., 68
Bazemore, G., 427
Bazerman, M., 90, 99, 100, 108
Bazley, T., 211
Beauchamp, T., 57
Beccaria, C., 67, 331
Beck, A., 376
Beckley, A., 459
Bedau, H., 70, 294, 342
Beecher-Monas, E., 281
Beehr, T. A., 70, 101
Bellamy, A., 436
Bells, J., 96
Bennett, S., 70
Bentham, J., 31, 38, 67, 331, 341
Berg, B., 358
Berman. M., 149
Bernard, T., 153, 154
Bernstein, N., 351
Berzofsky, M., 376
Billeaud, J., 153
Binelli, M., 346
Bjerregaard, B., 187
Blackwell, K., 288, 289
Blankstein, A., 214, 407
Blinder, A., 304
Blow, C., 352
Blumberg, A., 236
Blumenfeld, L., 449
Boccaccini, D., 278
Bomse, A., 404
Bonner, R., 358
Bono, C., 187, 188
Borchert, D., 33, 35, 341
Boss, J., 78
Bossard, A., 129
Bouie, J., 156
Bourge, C., 349
Bousquet, S., 412, 413
Bowes, M., 156
Bowie, N., 36

Bowker, L., 381
Boyce, W., 90, 92
Boyer, P., 46
Bradford, B., 423
Braithwaite, J., 76, 344, 428
Braswell, M. B., 8, 36, 38, 41, 75,
    385, 428
Brewer, S., 195, 212
Britt, C., 352, 353
Brockner, J., 102
Brown, B., 122
Brown, C., 461
Brown, J., 411, 412, 413, 414
Brown, M., 126
Brown, R., 104
Brown, S., 134, 205, 414
Brunson, R., 150
Bryson, D., 77
Buchholz, B., 371, 459
Buckle, S., 31, 32
Burgess, R. L., 90
Burrell, W., 425
Bursik, R., 89
Butterfield, F., 421

C

Cabana, D., 385
Caldero, M., 120, 130, 131, 133, 141, 197,
    206
Callahan, D., 80
Callanan, P., 385
Calnon, J., 153, 154
Caplan, D., 207
Carey, M., 428
Carr, R., 319, 463
Carroll. D., 257
Carroll, L., 381, 405
Carson, E. A., 349
Carter, D., 166, 170, 184, 191, 192,
    193, 208
Carter, J., 123
Casey, L., 245
Caspar, R., 376
Cassidy, R., 269
Cathcart, D., 313
Cathcart, R., 310, 313
Catlin, S., 160, 161
Cauvin, H., 379
Cergol, G., 191
Chang, C., 408, 409
Chappell, A., 203

Cheever, J., 132
Chen, K., 455
Chermak, S., 142
Chesney-Lind, M., 394
Christensen, D., 166
Christianson, S., 70
Clarridge, C., 127
Claussen, N., 209
Claussen-Rogers, N., 209
Claytor, S., 163
Clear, T., 333, 394
Clifford, S., 298
Close, D., 44
Coates, R., 428
Cochran, R., 238
Cohen, E., 238, 239
Cohen, H., 123, 124, 143, 186, 187
Cohen, L., 89
Cohen, M., 348, 350
Cohen, P., 59
Cohen, R., 255, 348, 350
Cohen, T., 256
Coherty, J., 377
Colarossi, A., 415
Cole, D., 155, 338, 453, 466
Cole, G., 269
Coleman, S., 187
Colloff, P., 224, 307
Conlon, E., 171
Connelly, S., 104
Conti, N., 139, 210
Contreras, R., 163
Cook, R., 162
Cooper, C., 134, 135
Cooper, J., 131
Copp, T., 355
Corey, G., 385
Corey, M., 385
Cormier, A., 25
Cotton, A., 384
Cox, D., 381
Coz, E., 409
Crank, J., 120, 130, 131, 133, 141, 152, 153, 197, 206, 437, 450, 457
Crouch, B., 358, 370, 380, 381
Cubellis, L. J., 117
Cullen, F., 333, 334
Cullen, J., 100
Cummings, L. P., 311, 312
Cunningham, L., 299
Curry, M., 169

D

Dalbert, C., 423
Dalbey, B., 152
Daly, K., 342
Dantzker, M., 209
Daratha, K., 156
Dardick, H., 198

Dart, B., 161
Davies, N., 294
Davis, J., 70
Davis, K., 127, 195
Davis, R., 142
De Angelis, J., 70, 101
Delattre, E., 6, 124, 137
Del Bosque, M., 96
de Oliveira-Souza, R., 88
Dershowitz, A., 237, 449
Deutsch, L., 218
Devenport, L., 104
Devine, T., 463
Dexheimer, E., 162
DeYong, K., 439
Dial, K., 378
Dilanian, K., 450
Dizikes, C., 416, 417
Dodge, M., 196, 202, 212
Dolnick, S., 395, 396, 418
Donner, F., 120
Dorschner, J., 196
Doyle, M., 155, 160
Draybill, D., 428
Drew, J., 299
Drizin, S., 176, 177
Ducrose, M., 160
Duncan, I., 172
Dunham, R., 120, 161
Dunningham, C., 170
Durkheim, E., 230, 336
Durose, M., 151
Dwyer, J., 171
Dzur, A., 76, 428, 429

E

Eads, D., 118, 119
Eban, K., 444, 445
Eckholm, E., 172, 274
Egelko, B., 196
Elder, L., 16
Eligon, J., 195, 444
Elinson, Z., 176
Elliott, A., 296
Ellis, L., 88
Emerson, T., 88
Emily, J., 418
Emling, S., 459
Engel, R., 151
Engel, R. S., 153, 154
Epp, C., 154
Eterno, J., 205
Ewin, R., 136

F

Fahrenthold, D., 344, 345
Fairfield, H., 445
Farmer, S. J., 70, 101
Farrar, T., 212

Faturechi, R., 407, 408
Fausset, R., 409
Faziollah, M., 205
Fecteau, L., 349
Feeney, J., 333
Feibleman, J., 56
Feinberg, J., 56
Feldberg, M., 123, 124, 143
Felkenes, G., 7
Felson, M., 89
Fender, J., 312
Fenton, J., 379
Ferdik, F., 217
Fessenden, F., 453
Feuer, A., 456
Filke, E., 423
Fink, P., 79
Finn, C., 302
Finn, M., 122
Finn, P., 444, 445, 446
Fischer, A., 94, 104
Fishbein, D., 87
Fisher, J., 278, 279, 280, 300, 301
Fitzgerald, D., 170
Fitzgerald, P., 246, 265
Flaherty, D., 141
Flanagan, D., 94
Fletcher, G., 136
Fogel, D., 332, 333
Fogelson, R., 120
Foot, P., 47
Ford, D., 225
Forrest, K., 176, 177
Fox, B., 442
Fox, L., 242
Frank, J., 151
Frankel, A., 302
Franks, G., 104
Freedman, M., 264
Friedman, B., 304
Friedrich, R., 160
Fritzsche, D., 91
Fuller, L., 67
Furst, R., 217
Fyfe, J., 184, 185, 186, 191, 193, 202, 209

G

Gallagher, M., 163
Galston, W., 57, 62
Garay, A., 294
Gardner, H., 101
Garland, D., 330, 333
Garner, J., 158, 160, 161
Garrett, B., 71, 280, 299, 300, 308, 316
Gass, H., 175
Gates, J., 409
Gau, J., 70
Gavaghan, M., 94
Geis, G., 349, 350

Gerber, J., 271
Gershman, B., 273, 300, 301, 310
Getlin, J., 176
Ghosh, B., 446
Giacomazzi, A., 141
Giannelli, P., 276, 277, 300, 301
Gibbs, J., 94
Gillers, S., 445
Gilligan, C., 41, 93, 94
Gilmartin, K., 206
Glaser, B., 389
Glaze, L., 333, 391
Glendon, M., 239, 246
Glenn, L., 380
Glover, S., 218
Golab, J., 45, 46, 218
Gold, J., 36, 41, 75, 428
Gold, S., 199
Golden, T., 447
Goldman, A., 456
Goldstein, J., 456
Golgowski, N., 114, 197
Gomme, I., 134, 160, 165
Gonnerman, J., 225
Goode, E., 199, 334
Goodman, J. D., 25, 26, 216
Goodsell, C., 283
Gordon, M., 74
Gormisky, L., 197
Gorta, A., 193
Gottschalk, P., 140
Gourevitch, P., 40
GrafmanMoll, J., 88
Graham, T., 197
Grasmick, H., 89
Gray, M., 379
Green, B., 298, 310, 313
Green, E., 152
Green, F., 278
Greenberg, J., 94
Greene, J., 203
Greenhouse, L., 320, 442
Greenhut, S., 216
Greenspan, R., 134, 161
Greenwald, S., 73, 275, 282, 296, 297,
    310, 314
Gregor, P., 437
Gregorian, D., 164
Griffin, M., 70, 101, 423
Grisso, T., 176, 177
Grissom, B., 267
Grometstein, R., 311
Gross, H., 56
Grossi, E., 358
Grotius, H., 436, 460
Grovum, J., 119
Gruenewald, J., 142
Guarnera, L., 278
Gudjonsson, G., 176, 177

Guerino, P., 376
Guilfoil, J., 190
Gundy, J., 160
Gurman, S., 384
Gutierrez, M., 166

H

Haag, A., 387
Haake, K., 268
Haberfeld, M., 190
Haederle, M., 88
Haider-Markel, D., 154
Haidt, J., 89
Hall, M., 73, 268, 278
Haney, C., 346, 347
Hansen, M., 263
Harmon, R., 198
Harris, J., 206
Harrison, P., 376
Hashimoto, E., 273
Hassell, K., 211
Hassine, V., 373, 376, 405
Hatamyar, P., 88
Hauser, C., 217
Hawkins, G., 338
Hays, K., 175
He, N., 130
Heath, B., 169, 302
Heffernan, W., 236
Heidensohn, F., 342
Heintze, I., 89
Hemmens, C., 346, 356, 422
Hennelly, R., 198
Hennessy, C., 104
Hennessy, J., 94
Henriques, Z., 376
Hensley, N., 458
Henych, M., 419, 422
Heraux, C., 161
Herbert, B., 299
Herbert, S., 130
Herman, H., 319
Hermann, P., 169, 170, 193
Hernandez, S., 273, 274, 311, 318
Hersh, F., 92
Hewer, A., 92
Hews, B., 408
Hickey, J., 343
Hickman, M., 158, 160, 203, 213
Hicks, J., 101
Hicks, W., 437
Hight, B., 19
Hinkel, D., 72
Hinman, L., 48
Hirschi, T., 89
Hobbes, T., 123, 226
Hofer, P., 288, 289
Hogan, N., 70, 101, 423
Holgersson, S., 140

Holley, P., 195
Holmes, M., 150
Hopfe, L., 34, 35
Hopkins, S., 101
Horn, D., 215
Horswell, C., 303
Horwitz, S., 168
Houston, J., 405
Hsu, S., 279
Hu, W., 192
Huberts, L., 206
Hume, D., 89
Huriash, L., 138
Huspek, M., 152
Hyde, J., 94
Hylton, W., 40

I

Iris, M., 214
Isikoff, M., 108
Israel, J., 176
Ivers, D., 217
Ivkovic, S., 190

J

Jablon, R., 218
Jackman, T., 308
Jackson, J., 423
Jackson, K., 94
Jacoby, J., 268
Jaffee, S., 94
James, L., 156
Jaycox, M., 457
Jeffrey, D., 275
Jensen, L., 90, 92
Jenson, E., 271
Jha, K.N., 89
Jiminez, L., 152
Johanek, M., 319
Johnson, C., 302, 334, 376
Johnson, K., 105, 159
Johnson, P., 150
Johnson, R., 358, 361, 370
Jondle, D., 101
Jones, D. A., 104
Jones, J., 142
Jones, N., 283

K

Kaeble, D., 333, 391
Kamin, S., 338
Kamisar, Y., 176
Kane, R., 184, 185, 186, 191, 193, 202,
    203, 209
Kania, R., 187, 354
Kant, I., 31, 35, 36, 37, 38, 341, 342
Kaplan, M., 61
Kaplan, T., 7, 43

Kappeler, V., 117, 119, 120, 148, 158, 194, 195, 196, 197
Kaptein, M., 206
Karp, D., 344, 428
Kassin, S., 176, 177
Kates, G., 347, 397
Katz, D., 101
Kauffman, B., 451
Kauffman, K., 358, 359, 361, 369, 374, 382
Keith, L., 460
Keller, J., 445
Kelly, J., 174
Kessler, G., 34, 35
Kiefer, M., 266
Kiger, A., 72
Kim, J., 218
Kim, V., 162, 168, 408, 409
Kindy, K., 159
King, R., 338
Kipnis, K., 390
Kirchmeier, J., 73, 275, 282, 296, 297, 310, 314
Klahm, C., 151
Klas, M., 414, 415
Klaver, J., 128
Kleinig, J., 236, 264, 341, 447, 448, 459
Klinger, D., 158
Klockars, C., 123, 131, 166, 190, 448
Knudten, M., 273
Kohlberg, L., 85, 91–95, 92, 103
Kohn, S., 174
Korecki, N., 99
Kottak, C., 47
Kovandzi, T., 167
Krajicek, D., 72
Kraska, P., 117, 194, 196
Kravets, D., 453
Krayewski, E., 138
Krebs, C., 376
Kreig, A., 319
Kreiger, M., 240
Kringen, A. L., 63
Kristian, B., 165
Krogstand, J., 44
Kroneberg, C., 89
Kronenwerter, M., 354
Krueger, F., 88
Kumar, A., 308
Kupchik, A., 70, 101

L

Lait, M., 218
Lamb, J., 132
Lambert, E. G., 70, 101, 423
Lamberth, J., 155
Land, K., 354
Lane, C., 304

Langan, P., 160
Langford, C., 263
Langton, L., 151
Larose, A., 141
Larrabee, M., 41
Lassek, H., 204
Lasthuizen., K., 206
Latessa, E., 334
Lavelle, J. J., 102
Law, V., 348
Lee, H., 200, 218
LeFave, W., 176
Lefstein, N., 236, 256
Leighton, P., 349, 350, 430
Leiser, B., 329
Leo, R., 176, 177
Leonard, J., 162, 166, 214, 338
Leonnig, C., 105
Lersch, K., 211
Levenson, M., 416
Levine, C., 92
Levine, J., 377
Lewis, M., 405
Lewis, N., 371
Lichtblau, E., 108, 445, 452
Lichtenberg, L., 387
Lighty, T., 416, 417
Lim, H., 218
Lindell, C., 224, 253, 281, 286, 287, 288
Lindquist, C., 278
Linzer, D., 440
Liptak, A., 71, 72, 256, 277, 355
Lisitsina, D., 419
Listwan, S., 334
Lithwick, D., 287, 300, 302
Loftus, B., 139, 141
Lombardo, L., 360, 374
Loo, R., 94
Lord, R., 170
Lord, V., 187
Love, K. G., 70, 101
Lovrich, N., 130
Luban, D., 464
Lucas, J., 55, 57
Lune, H., 387
Lush, T., 169
Lutwak, N., 94

M

Maas, P., 133, 415
MacDonald, J., 161
MacIntyre, A., 30, 31
Macintyre, S., 189
Mackie, J. L., 12, 225, 332, 342
Madden, M., 454
Mador, C., 114
Maestri, W., 31, 37
Magid, L., 177

Maguire, M., 196
Maher, T., 194, 196
Mahler, J., 247
Malloy, E., 207, 208
Maloney, D., 427
Manning, M., 70
Manning, P., 203
March, R., 422
Margasak, L., 446
Mariano, N., 256, 257, 273
Maril, R., 96
Marimow, A., 379
Markowitz, P., 257
Marks, F., 313
Marquart, J., 378, 380
Marsh, R., 346
Martin, D., 373, 375, 386
Martin, M., 346
Martin, N., 125
Martin, R., 171
Martinelli, T., 196, 210
Martinez, M., 297
Martinez, P., 256
Martinez, R., 152
Martyn, S., 242
Marx, G., 169, 171, 172, 210
Marzulli, J., 164, 298
Massimino, E., 443, 446
Mastrofski, S., 151
Mather, L., 239
Mathna, B., 195, 212
Mauer, M., 338, 394
Maxwell, C., 161
Mayer, J., 448, 449
Maynard-Moody, S., 154
Mazerolle, L., 70
McAnany, P., 127
McCabe, S., 185
McCaffrey, S., 267
McCarthy, B., 36, 38, 41, 360, 374, 403, 424
McCluskey, J., 151
McCollum, D., 235
McCoy, C., 304
McCoy, J. H., 209
McCready, D., 443, 449
McDonald, W., 131, 132
McGarrell, E., 142
McGinty, J., 214
McGurrin, D., 194, 195
McKelway, D., 273, 274
McKeown, M., 285
McKinley, J., 274
McKinney, J., 88
McKinney, M., 198
McKoski, R., 303
McMahon, P., 176
McManimon, P., 387
McMurtrie, J., 311

McNally, J., 147
McQuade, D., 304
McRoberts, F., 277, 279, 281, 301
Medina, J., 408, 409
Medwed, D., 297, 311
Meekins, T., 258
Mehlkop, G., 89
Meier, N., 44
Meincke, P., 197
Meisner, J., 99
Mejia, R., 279
Mellon, L., 268
Memmott, M., 108
Memory, J., 239
Mesloh, C., 419, 422
Metz, H., 106, 208
Meyer, J., 444
Meyer, R., 261
Micucci, A., 134, 160, 165
Mieczkowski, T., 171, 192, 193, 211
Milgram, S., 79
Miller, G., 439, 444
Miller, J., 142
Miller, J. M., 168
Miller, K., 353
Miller, L., 385
Mills, S., 99, 253, 277, 279, 280, 281, 301
Minugh, K., 166
Mitchell, A., 101
Mitchell, J., 138
Mobley, A., 349, 350
Moll, J., 88
Molloy, A., 371
Mondics, C., 271
Moore, D., 218
Moore, T., 123
Moran, J., 215
Moran, K., 201
Morgan, L., 411
Morganson, G., 59
Morris, E., 40
Morris, R., 429
Moskos, P., 131
Moskovitz, D., 191
Moss, M., 453
Muir, W., 126, 147
Mulgan, R., 100
Mulhausen, M., 240
Mumford, M., 104
Murphy, C., 165
Murphy, J., 66
Murphy, M., 277
Murphy, P., 201, 207
Murphy, S., 104
Murray, J., 122, 139, 197, 384
Murrie, D., 278
Murton, T., 361, 380
Muscat, B., 376, 377
Myers, S., 139

N

Nakamaura, D., 105
Nakashima, E., 454
Neufeld, P., 280, 299, 300
Neuschatz, J., 283
Newall, M., 205
Newport, F., 84
Neyfakh, L., 212, 213
Neyroud, P., 459
Noble, J., 177
Noddings, N., 39
Nolan, J., 210
Nolan, T., 196, 210
Norris, C., 94, 170

O

O'Brien, J., 162, 175
O'Brien, R., 285
O'Connell, P., 72
O'Harrow, R., 168
Olinger, D., 416
Olivo, A., 26
Ooi, Y., 94, 104
Organ, D. W., 101
Orlov, R., 26
Osher, C., 169, 416
Ostrow, R., 175
Owen, B., 376, 377

P

Packer, H., 116, 117
Packman, D., 195
Palhegyl, D., 422
Paoline, E., 129, 139
Papke, D., 234
Parascandola, R., 205
Parker, P., 199
Parks, R., 151
Parvini, S., 153
Paul, R., 16
Payne, D., 120
Pellicotti, J., 264, 265
Pender, G., 409
Peralta, E., 118, 119
Perez, N., 295
Perito, R., 184
Perksy, A., 302
Perry, J., 408
Perry, S., 270
Perry, T., 212
Peterson, R., 74
Pfaff, J., 334
Phillips, N., 139, 384
Phillips, S., 123
Piller, C., 279, 406
Pimental, D., 305
Pinker, S., 87
Pino, N. W., 121

Piquero, A., 70, 101, 158, 160, 202, 203, 207
Planas, R., 150
Plog, K., 377
Plohetski, T., 162
Pogarsky, G., 202, 203
Pollock, J., 88, 256, 334, 337, 340, 345, 348, 349, 370, 371, 374, 376, 377, 381, 423
Pont, J., 390
Pontius, A., 88
Possley, M., 277, 279, 281, 283, 296, 301, 311
Post, L., 279
Postema, G., 238
Poveda, T., 72
Powell, M., 169
Power, C., 92
Prendergast, A., 381, 403
Prenzler, T., 187, 189, 208, 210, 213, 216, 217
Price, M., 456, 457
Prior, W., 29
Purcell, D., 304
Putman, Y., 19
Putnam, C., 70, 294

Q

Quinlivan, D., 283
Quinn, M., 134
Quinney, R., 231

R

Rabin, J., 214
Radelet, M., 70, 294, 353
Raeder, M., 276, 282, 299, 300, 310, 314
Raftery, I., 360
Rahr, S., 117, 218
Raine, L., 454
Ramsey, R., 72
Ransom, J., 198
Raphael, D., 57
Raphael, S., 333, 334
Rashbaum, W., 7, 43
Ratcliffe, J., 122
Rawls, J., 31, 61, 65, 79, 342–343
Rayman, G., 205
Raymond, F., 313
Reagan, L., 245
Reasons, C., 231
Redlich, A., 71, 311
Reeves, B., 115
Reichel, P., 427
Reiman, J., 33, 63
Reimer, N., 175
Reisig, M., 151
Rejali, D., 449
Reuss-Ianni, E., 130, 131, 206, 209, 210
Reynolds, H., 73, 275, 282, 296, 297, 310, 314

Reynolds, K. M., 121
Reynolds, P., 70, 101, 102, 207
Rezendes, M., 169
Rice, S., 117, 218
Rich, S., 168
Richards, N., 136
Ridolfi, K., 296
Rimer, S., 255
Risen, J., 255
Ritter, N., 337
Robertson, C., 304, 308
Robertson, J., 44
Robles, F., 148, 298, 415
Rodin, D., 435
Roebuck, J., 373
Rogers, B., 416
Rojek, J., 217
Rokeach, M., 91
Romero, G., 216
Ronken, C., 210, 213, 216, 217
Rose, C., 239
Rosenbaum, D., 104
Ross, D., 199
Rossmo, K., 173
Roth, A., 234
Roth, J., 234
Rothlein, S., 196
Rothwell, G., 140
Rottman, D. J., 70, 423
Ruback, R. B., 288, 289
Rubin, J., 199
Rufino, K., 278
Ruggiero, V., 17, 41, 44
Ruiz, J., 187, 188
Rupp, D. E., 102

S

Saad, L., 229
Salins, L., 372
Saltzburg, S., 240
Saltzman, J., 190
Sanchez, Y., 266
Sandel, M., 54
Sanders, B., 209
Sanders, S., 163
Santo, A., 378, 379
Sapien, J., 273, 274, 311, 318
Sapp, A., 194
Sargeant, E., 70
Saul, J., 298
Savage, C., 17, 302, 437, 450, 453, 456, 457
Savage, D., 322, 442, 452
Schafer, J., 106, 127
Schaper, D., 4
Scharf, P., 343
Scheck, B., 71, 293, 314–315
Schehr, R., 71, 295, 308
Scheingold, S., 129, 130, 131, 169, 236

Schmadeke, S., 99
Schmidt, M., 158
Schoeman, F., 171, 261
Schuck, A., 104
Schwartz, J., 198
Schweigert, F., 76
Schwirtz, M., 360, 361, 382
Sears, J., 71, 295, 308
Seiler, S., 94, 104
Sekerka, L., 104
Selksky, A., 442
Selman, D., 349, 350
Semukhina, O., 121
Serrano, R., 175
Seville, L., 347, 397
Sewell, A., 408
Shaffer, T., 238
Shakespeare, W., 69
Shane, J. M., 70, 101
Shane, S., 444, 445, 455
Sharp, E., 150
Shaw, A., 99
Sheley, J., 231
Shelton, L., 99
Shepherd, J., 244, 245
Sherman, L., 10, 103, 130, 167, 201
Shermer, M., 14, 33, 87, 88
Shichor, D., 349, 350
Shiner, M., 423
Shukovsky, P., 247
Siegel, J., 317, 376
Siemaszko, C., 114
Silberman, M., 370
Silverman, E., 205
Simmons, A., 305
Simmons, K., 88
Simon, J., 372
Simonsen, C., 64
Simpson, S., 372
Skelton, A., 213
Skogan, W., 104, 121
Skolnick, J., 133, 164, 166, 176
Skutch, J., 190
Slackman, M., 441
Slobodzian, J., 205
Sluder, R., 117, 119, 120, 148, 158, 194, 197
Smilansky, S., 437
Smith, B., 72
Smith, E., 160
Smith, L., 389
Smith, M., 153
Smith, R., 440, 446, 447
Smith, S., 261
Smith, V., 138
Smith, W., 268
Sniffen, M., 175
Solomon, A., 349
Solomon, J., 174, 279

Sontag, D., 377, 380
Souryal, S., 105, 137, 391, 403, 404, 423, 425
South, N., 170
Spence, G., 246
Spiegleman, C., 277, 278, 279, 280
Spielman, F., 99
Stalans, L., 122
Starr, S., 337
Starr-Gimeno, D., 196
Steele, A., 205
Stefanic, M., 187
Steffan, J., 169
Stein, J., 174
Stein, K., 377
Stephens, D., 213, 214
Sterngold, J., 218
Stevens, D., 184
Stewart, D., 33, 35, 341
Stewart, J., 56
Stillman, S., 235
Stinson, P., 195, 202, 212
Stohr, M., 346, 422
Stoll, M., 333, 334
Stover, H., 390
Stover, R., 246
Strong, K. Heetderks, 75
Stroud, M., 349
Sullivan, G., 245
Sullivan, J., 127
Sulzberger, A., 195
Sunshine, J., 70
Sussman, J., 73, 275, 282, 296, 297, 310, 314
Sutherland, E. H., 90
Swift, C., 247, 447
Swisher, K., 305, 312
Sykes, G. M., 97, 128, 373

T

Tabish, S., 89
Tanay, E., 386
Tanner, R., 176, 279
Tau, B., 119
Taylor, D., 423
Taylor, W., 381
Tenbrunsel, M., 90, 99, 100, 108
Terrill, W., 126, 151, 152, 160, 161, 162
Teske, R., 354
Thibaut, J., 69
Thomas, P., 377
Thompson, C., 170
Thompson, D., 228, 405, 407
Tillyer, R., 151
Tobin, W., 277, 278, 279, 280
Toch, H., 64
Todak, N., 202, 212
Tonry, M., 289
Toobin, J., 378, 379

Toomey, P., 451
Torres, S., 376, 377
Trager, R., 277
Trainum, J., 177
Trautman, N., 105
Trevino, L., 94
Tuch, S., 151, 155
Tuchman, G., 235
Tullio, E., 340
Tullis, P., 66
Turner, A., 253
Turner, C., 383
Tyler, T. R., 70, 101, 142, 162, 207, 423

U

Umbreit, M., 427, 428
Urza, G., 442

V

Valentine, D., 197
Van Craen, M., 104
Vandecreek, L., 358
van Derbeke, J., 200
Van Maanen, J., 129, 130
Van Ness, D., 75
Vaughn, M., 389
Vaznis, J., 197
Vedantam, S., 89
Velasco, E., 245
Verges, A., 94
Verma, A., 205
Victor, B., 100
Vila, B., 156
Vitiello, M., 337
Vodicka, D., 406
Vogelstein, R., 239
Volpe, P., 445
Von Hirsch, A., 333
Vos, B., 428

W

Wagner, J., 379
Wagner, M., 114
Walker, L., 69, 94, 458
Walker, S., 134, 162, 206, 210, 211, 213, 216, 237, 354
Wallack, T., 198
Walsh, A., 55
Wanna, J., 100
Waples, E., 104
Ward, M., 410, 415, 416, 421, 423
Warren, J., 405
Warrick, J., 444, 445, 446
Wasikowska, M., 456
Wearne, P., 174
Weber, D., 302
Weinstein, H., 439
Weir, K., 285
Weisburd, D., 134, 161
Weiser, B., 296, 360
Weitzer, R., 151, 155
Wells, J., 376, 377
Wells, W., 127
Wendel, W., 242
Wendle, J., 121
Wertheimer, A., 76, 428, 429
Westmarland, L., 140
Wetmore, S., 283
Wheeler, B., 455
Whelan, A., 205
White, M., 202, 203
Wiatrowski,, M.D., 121
Wilkinson, M., 283
Williams, T., 196
Wilson, J. Q., 87, 124
Wilson, R., 216
Wiltrout, K., 463
Windsor, C., 94
Winerip, M., 360, 361, 382
Wines, S., 156

Winfree, L. T., 276
Winston, A., 199
Winton, R., 409
Wise, D., 274
Witt, A., 178
Wojleck, K., 235
Wolf, R., 419, 422
Wolfe, C., 321
Wolfe, S., 70, 101, 207
Wolff, H., 390
Wood, D., 148
Wood, J., 208
Woody, W., 176, 177
Worden, R., 139, 160, 161
Worley, R., 378
Worley, V., 378
Worrall, J., 167, 216
Wren, T., 136
Wright, K., 423, 424, 425
Wyatt-Nichol, H., 104
Wycoff, M., 121

Y

Yee, J., 371
York, G., 368
Yost, P., 16, 70, 245
Young, C., 285

Z

Zacharias, F., 298, 310, 313
Zahn, R., 88
Zak, P., 88
Zalman, M., 72
Zamora, J., 200
Zhao, J., 130
Zheng, H., 354
Zimbardo, P., 421
Zimring, F., 338
Zitrin, R., 263
Zohar, N., 437

Subject Index

Note: Page numbers followed by italic *f* or *b* refer to figures or boxes.

A

ABA Criminal Justice Standards, 255
ABA Standards for Prosecutors, 243
Abramoff, Jack, 4–5
absolutism, 46–49
absolutist system, 37
Abu Ghraib prison scandal, 422, 446, 462
abuse of authority, 184, 191
    on-duty drug use, 192–193
    professional courtesy, 191–192
    sexual misconduct, 193–196
    ticket fixing, 191–192
accepted lies, 166
act utilitarianism, 39
advantageous comparison, 97
ADX Florence, 346
affirmative action, 61, 62–63
African Americans
    discrimination against, 150–151
    police shootings of, 156–157
agape, 92
Alabama Bar Association Code of 1887, 239
al-Awlaki, Anwar, 437
Albuquerque, New Mexico, 163
alcohol, on-duty use, 193
Alito, Samuel, 322
allegiance effect, 278
altruistic acts, 89
American Bar Association (ABA), 234, 236, 239–240, 242, 256–257, 269
American Civil Liberties Union, 212
American Correctional Association's (ACA) Code of Ethics, 356, 357
American Correctional Health Services Association, 358
American Jail Association, 357
American Legal Institute (ALI), 242
Anderson, Ken, 224, 314
Anthony, Casey, 237
antipsychotic drugs, 386
applied ethics, 10
Aquinas, Thomas, 32, 35
arbitration, 213–215
Aristotle, 9, 28–30, 63
    on conception of justice, 56–57
Arizona Bar Association, 314
Arkansas Department of Correction, 361
Armani, Frank, 262, 263
Armstrong, David, 402

Arpaio, Joe, 153, 266
arson investigation, 279
Arthur Anderson scandal, 99–100
asset forfeiture, 167–168, 235, 270–271
attorney–client privilege, 261
Aubuchon, Lisa, 266
authority, 123

B

bad cops database, 212–213
Bagram prison, Afghanistan, 447
Baird, Charles, 254
baksheesh, 186
Balko, Radley, 117
ballistics testing, 279–280
Baltimore City Detention Center (BCDC), 379
Bandura, Albert, 90–91
    moral disengagement theory, 311
Batt, Keith, 200
"Beds for Kids Project," 115
behavior
    ethical beliefs and, 94–95
    informal code of, 131
behavior modification, 387
Belge, Francis, 263
Benjamin, Brent, 245
Bentham, Jeremy, 341
Beyler, Craig, 253
bias, 303–304
    confirmatory, 71, 309, 311
    racial, 308
Bill Clinton–Monica Lewinsky investigation, 233
bite mark comparison, 281
Bivens, Phillip, 308
Black Guerrilla Family (BGF), 379
Blacks. *see* African Americans
"blank slate," 87
blatant theft, 191
blind justice, 56
blue curtain of secrecy, 133–137, 139–140, 219
blue lies, 166
body cameras, 211–212
bounded ethicality, 99
Bradley, John, 224, 253
Brady list, 166
Brandley, Clarence, 293–294
Breivik, Anders Behring, 430

Browder, Kalief, 225
Brubaker (movie), 361
Buddhism, 34*b*
Buddy Boys, 197
budgetary abuse, 404
bureaucratic justice, 236
Burge, Jon, 98–99
Bush, George W., 247, 436, 452

C

CALEA. *see* Commission on Accreditation for Law Enforcement Agencies (CALEA)
California, corruption in prison/jail, 405–409
California District Attorneys Association (CDAA), 297
cameras, body, 211–212
Canons of Police Ethics, 128
capitalism, 42
capital punishment, 64, 352–355
Cardozo Law School, 257
care perspective, 93
caretaker style, policing, 126
caring, 30, 41
caseload supervision, 392–394
Casino Jack and the U.S. of Money (movie), 5
Catalog of Virtues, 29*b*
categorical imperative commands, 36
cavity search, 147
Ceballos, Richard, 317
CEDs. *see* conducted energy devices (CEDs)
Center for Public Integrity, 285
Central Park 5 case, 176
cheaters, 55
Chicago Police Committee, 184
Christopher Commission, 184
Church Committee, 120
Ciavarella, Mark, 302, 303
circle sentencing, 76
CIT. *see* Crisis Intervention Training (CIT)
Citizens for Responsibility and Ethics in Washington (CREW), 7
citizenship, 30
civil disobedience, 79, 79*b*, 80
Civilian Review Board, 216

civilian review/complaint model, 216–217
civil litigation, 138
civil service, 213–215
civil suits, 164
clean-beat officers, 126
Clemency Project 2014, 330
client–lawyer relationship, 240
Clinton, Bill, 10
A Clockwork Orange (movie), 387
Coalition for Public Safety, 328
code of ethics, 128
Code of Hammurabi, 225
Code of Judicial Conduct, 285
code of silence, 133, 134
codes of ethics, 356–358
codes of law, 225
Collins, James A. "Andy," 410
Colson, Charles "Chuck," 389
Colson Commission, 3
Commission on Accreditation for Law Enforcement Agencies (CALEA), 170
Commission on Safety and Abuse in America's Prisons, 422
community corrections, 390–392, 415–418
"community justice," 76
community policing movement, 121–122
community reparative boards, 76
Comprehensive Drug Abuse and Control Act of 1970, 270
Compstat, 205–206
Conahan, Michael, 302, 303
conducted energy devices (CEDs), 158
  Tasers, 161–163
"conduct unbecoming," 129
confidentiality, 261–264
confirmatory bias, 71, 257, 311
conflict paradigm, 231–232
conflicts of interest, 258–259, 270, 284–285
conflict theory, 232
Confucianism, 34–35*b*
connectedness, 41
Conner, Johnny, 288
consensus paradigm, 230–231
consent decrees, 2–3, 152, 198–199
continuum of compromise, 206
control, procedural justice, 69
conventional level, 92
conviction psychology, 311
cop code, 130–131
corporal punishment, 64
correctional officers
  discretion and, 369–372
  and morality in prison, 382
  relationship between inmates, 373–375
  and use of force, 380–382
correctional officer subculture, 358–362

correctional rehabilitation, 67
corrections
  ethical frameworks for, 340–343
  new era of, 372–373
  occupational subcultures in, 358–363
Corrections Corporation of America (CCA), 349
corrective justice, 57, 63–64
corruption, 96, 120, 403–418
  economic. *see* economic corruption
  investigative documentation of, 184
  noble-cause, 131–133
  responses to, 424–430
  scandals, 43
"Corruption Continuum," 105
"CREW's Most Corrupt" report, 7
crime control model, 116
crime fighter, 116
criminal cops, 196–197
criminal investigations, discretion and, 165–178
criminalistics, 278
criminalized poverty, 114
Criminal Justice Standards and Training Commission, 25
criminal law, 225
criminal siblings, 95
Crisis Intervention Training (CIT), 127
critical thinking skills, 16
Crosby, James, 411
cruel and unusual punishment, 343, 347
CSI and the courts, 276–282
cultural relativism, 47
culture, and ethics, 246
culture change, 217–218
culture of force, 164–165
Cummings, Jerry, 412–413
cynicism, 206, 362

D

Darby, Joseph (Joe), 39, 40
Daubert standard, 80, 276, 280
deception, 166
defense attorneys, ethical issues for, 15, 254–255
  confidentiality, 261–264
  conflicts of interest, 258–259
  duty regarding perjury, 264–265
  indigent defense, 256–257
  jury consultants, 260–261
  responsibility to client, 255
  specialty courts, 257–258
  zealous defense, 259–260
dehumanization, 97
Dekraai, Scott, 300
Denver jail, 384
deontological ethical system, 35–38
The Departed (movie), 169
Department of Homeland Security, 438
Department of Justice (DOJ), 155, 164, 268

Depo-Provera, 340
Dershowitz, Alan, 237
detainments, 438–439
deterrence, 67, 335
Development, Relief, and Education for Alien Minors Act (DREAM Act), 233
developmental theories, 91
deviance, explanations of, 200–208
  individual explanations, 201–204
  organizational explanations, 204–207
  societal explanations, 207–208
deviant lies, 166
"dialectic of the bargain," 120
diffusion of responsibility, 97
Dirty Harry problem, 131, 448
discipline matrixes, 215
discoverable evidence, 262
discretion
  correctional officers, 369–372
  and criminal investigations, 165–178
  in criminal justice system, 4–6
  defined, 4, 124
  and discrimination, 148–157
  and duty, 124–127
  judges use of, 285–286
  and law enforcement, 127
  power and, 123–124
  in probation, 391
  prosecutor's use of, 266–269
  right to use force, 157–165
discrimination, and discretion, 148–157
displacement of responsibility, 97
distortion of consequences, 97
distributive justice, 57–63
  perceptions, 101–102
Divine Comedy (Dante), 328
DNA evidence, 254, 280, 308, 315–316
Dodd-Frank law, 58
Dookhan, Annie, 277
Dorner, Christopher, 214
Dostoyevsky, Fyodor, 328
double effect principle, 437
double standards, 6
Dow, David, 287
Drug Enforcement Administration (DEA), 105
drug laws, 229
drug tests, during police hiring process, 193
drylabbing, 175, 277
due process, 6, 69, 102, 117, 319–320
  enhanced procedures, 316–318
Durk, David, 183
duty, 11
  and discretion, 124–127
  nonfeasance of, 125
  regarding perjury, 264–265
dynamic of desperation, 347

E

Eastern State Penitentiary, 345
ecology of cruelty, 347
economic corruption, 184, 186–191
    graft, 190–191
    gratuities, 187–189
economic goods, 57
Economic Policy Institute, 58–59
education, and training, 209–210
Edwards, John, 367–368
Egalitarian distribution systems, 59
Egalitarian theories, 57
egoism, 42–43
Eighth Amendment, 340, 343, 347
Ellington, Latandra, 411
emotion-based ethical systems, 89
emotions, and rationality, 89–90
enlightened egoism, 42
Enron's scandal, 99–100, 262
entitlement programs, 60
entrapment, 172
Epictetus, 9
Epps, Christopher, 409
equality, 55–56
Equitable Sharing program, 167, 168
ethical beliefs and behavior, 94–95
ethical climate of organization, 100–102
Ethical Climate Questionnaire (ECQ),
    100–101
ethical codes, 356–358
ethical decision making
    influences on, 85–86, 86f
    principles of, 44
ethical dilemmas, 3
    analysis of, 17–19
    resolution of, 44–45
ethical fading, 99, 100
ethical formalism, 35–38, 39, 55, 173,
    263–264
    criticisms of, 37
    decision making, 44
    deontological ethical system, 35–36
    punishment and, 341–342
    vs. rule utilitarianism, 39
ethical issues, 3, 25–26
    analysis of, 16–17
    with informants, 170
ethical leadership, 218
ethical misconduct, 294
    defense attorneys, 295
    judicial, 302–305
    prosecutorial, 296–302
ethical systems, 26, 28f
    based on care, 39–41
    characteristics of, 27
    defined, 27
    emotion-based, 89
    ethics of virtue, 28–30
    natural law, 30–32

ethics
    culture and, 246
    of defense attorneys, 15
    defined, 8, 10
    for legal professionals, 239–246
    of police, 15
    religious, 32–35
    situational, 48–49
    study of, 7–8
    timeline, 31b
    training, 103–104
ethics of care, 39–41, 48, 55
    punishment and, 342
ethics-of-care approach, 30
ethics of virtue, 28–30
ethnicity, 73–75
eudaimonia, 9, 28
euphemistic labeling, 97
excessive force, 158, 160
exchange system, prosecutors acting as,
    268–269
exclusionary rule, 286–287
ex parte communication, 303
expert witnesses, 275–276
    misconduct involving, 300–301
expiation, 332
Enron, 103, 107
eyewitness testimony, 307–308

F

factual judgments, 12
fairness, 30, 55, 61, 128
Fair Sentencing Act, 2010, 330
false confessions, 308
false convictions. see wrongful
    convictions
"Fast and Furious" operation, 16–17
Federal Probation and Pretrial Officers
    Association's ethical code, 357
federal sentencing guidelines, 288–289
feminine morality, 39–41
Ferguson, Missouri
    systemic racism in, 149
fingerprint analysis, 280
First Amendment, 317
FISA Amendments Reauthorization Act
    of 2012, 452–453
Fitzgerald, Patrick, 265
"Five Squad" scandal, 205
Florida, corruption in prison/jail,
    410–415
food stamps, 60
force, 123
    use of, discretion and, 157–165
Foreign Intelligence Surveillance Act
    (FISA), 108, 451
Foreign Intelligence Surveillance Court
    (FISC), 451
forensic evidence, 276, 281

forfeiture, principle of, 78
forgiveness, 66, 428
fortitude (virtue), 28
Fourth Amendment, 322
Freedom of Information Act, 452
free will, 14
"front page" test, 44
Fuller, Mark E., 304
fundamental liberties, 321

G

Gage, Phineas, 87
Gandhi, Mahatma, 78
"garbage calls" (social service), 130
Garrett, Brandon L., 56
Garrow, Robert, 262, 263–264
Gates, Darryl, 117
gender discrimination, 268
general deterrence, 335, 336
generalization principle, 44
genetics, personality and, 87
Geneva Conventions, 78, 247
GEO Group, 348, 349
Gilchrist, Joyce, 300
Giles, James Curtis, 294
Gilligan, Carol, 41, 93–94
godfather, 238
God's will, 33
Goethals, Thomas, 300
Golden Mean principle, 9, 29
Golden Rule, 33, 48, 49
Goldstein, Thomas Lee, 310
Gonzales, Alberto, 305, 319
Good Samaritan laws, 226
good will, 35
governmental "handouts," 60
governmental secrecy, 450–451
graft, 190–191
grass eaters, 186
gratuities, 187–189
"gray" area of crime, 229
Great Depression, 61
Gregory, Bernadette, 411
Grotius, Hugo, 436
"grudgers," 55
Guantanamo detainee abuses, 441–442
Gulf of Mexico oil spill, 232
gun trafficking operation. see "Fast and
    Furious" operation
guru, 238

H

"habitual-felon laws," 336
hair analysis, 278
halfway houses, 395–398
halo effect, 276
Hamdan, Salim Ahmed, 247
harm, prevention of, 227–230
harm principle, 227

Harris, Walter, 140–141
Hayes, Christopher, 195
hedonism, 43
hedonistic calculus, 67
Hidalgo County, corruption in, 96
Hinduism, 35*b*
Hippocratic Oath, 10, 128
hired gun, 238
Hispanics, discrimination against, 150, 152, 153
Hobbes, Thomas, 226
Holder, Eric, 256, 274
holy scriptures, 33
holy spirit, 35
homeless women, sexual extortion by police officers, 195
homicide, justifiable, 158
"honesty scores," 94
Hoover, J. Edgar, 120, 123
Hornung, Matt, 200
human rights–based policing, utilitarianism *vs.*, 458–461
Hurst, Gerald, 253
Hynes, Charles, 298
hypothetical imperatives, 36

I

IACP. *see* International Association of Chiefs of Police (IACP)
ideological toxicity, 347
Immigration Justice Clinic, 257
immorality, 8
immoral laws, 77–79
impartiality, 56
imperative principle, 44
imperfect duties, 11
incapacitation, 336–338
incriminating evidence, 262
indigent defense, 256–257
individual conscience, 33
individualism, subcultural norm, 362
ineffective counsel, 295
inequalities of society, 61
informal code of behavior, 131
informants, 168–170. *see also* jailhouse informants
Innocence Project, 3, 71, 224, 297, 314–315, 317
institutional corrections
    misconduct and corruption, 403–418
integrity testing, 210
intellectual virtues, 28
intelligence-led policing, 122–123
"Intelligence Squad," 171
internal affairs model, 213–215
International Association of Chiefs of Police (IACP), 128, 163, 209–210
interpretationists, 320
interrogation, 175–178

"investigatory stops," 154
Inwald Personality Inventory (IPI), 209
Irving, J. Lawrence, 289
Islam, 34*b*

J

jailhouse informants, 282–283, 298–300
jail officers, 382–383
Jessica's Law, 337
Jim Crow laws, 78
Jones, Julie, 414
Josephson Institute of Ethics, 6, 29
Judaism, 34*b*
judges, ethical guidelines for, 243–246
judges, ethical issues for, 284–289
    conflict of interest, 284–285
    use of discretion, 285–286
judicial activism, 320–322
judicial independence, 318–320
judicial misconduct, 302–305
judicial sanctions, 313–314
junk science, 277
jury consultants, 260–261
just deserts model, 333
justice, 28, 55, 61, 73–75
    corrective, 57, 63–64
    defined, 56
    distributive, 57–63
    organizational, 101
    origins of, 56–57
    procedural, 67–70
    remedial forms of, 64
    restorative, 75–77
    retributive, 64–67
    substantive, 64–67
    utilitarian, 67
Justice: What's the Right Thing to Do? (Sandel), 54
justice model, 332–333
justifiable homicide, 158

K

Kagan, Elena, 320
Kant, Immanuel, 36, 37, 48, 49
Kelly, Raymond, 214
"kids for cash" scandal, 302–303
King, Martin Luther, Jr., 78, 79–80, 120
Knapp Commission, 133, 183, 184, 186, 209, 210
Kohlberg's moral stages theory, 91–95, 93*f*
Kolts Commission, 184
Kraska, Peter, 117

L

LA County jail, 408
law
    as confidence game, 236

defined, 225
    justifications for, 226–230
    and legal professional, 234–237
    paradigms of. *see* paradigms, law
    role of, 225–226
law and rules, judges interpretation of, 286–288
law enforcement, 2, 117, 121
    codes of ethics for, 128
    discretion and, 127
    Equitable Sharing program and, 168
Law Enforcement Code of Ethics, 128–129, 246, 356
law scandals, 233
lawyers, public perceptions of, 233–234
leadership, 104–106
learning theory, criminality, 90–91
legal abuse, 191
legal agent, 238, 239
legal interests, 68
legalistic style of policing, 124
legal killings, 437
legal moralism, 228–230
legal paternalism, 227–228
legal professionals, ethics for, 239–246
legal rights, 68
Leonhart, Michele, 105
lethargy, subcultural norm, 362
lex salica, 64
lex talionis, 64
Libertarian theories, 57
Lichtblau, Eric, 108
"lifeboat" dilemma, 38–39
Lilly Ledbetter Equal Pay Act, 59
lobbying, 4–5
Los Angeles Police Department
    blue curtain of secrecy, 139–140
    culture of force, 164
    Ramparts Division scandal, 45–46
Louima, Abner, 163
Lowery, Eddie, 308
loyalty, in police work, 136–137
lying, 47

M

MacIntyre, Alasdair, 30
Madison, James, 124
Madoff, Bernard, 237
malfeasance, 404
malicious abuse, 404
Marie (Maas), 415
Marxist distribution systems, 59–60
Marxist theories, 57
Massey Coal Company, 245
mass imprisonment, 3
McCaffery, Seamus P., 304
McCarthy, Mary, 440
McCrory, Cecil, 409

meat eaters, 186
media relations, 274–275
Medill Innocence Project, 72
medroxyprogesterone acetate (MPA), 340
Megan's Law, 337
The Merchant of Venice (Shakespeare), 68
mercy, 65–66, 68–69
meta-ethics, 10
Miami Herald (investigative series), 411, 412
Miami River Rats, 196–197
Military Commissions Act, 441–442
Mill, John Stuart, 38, 227
mindfulness, 41
Minnesota Multiphasic Personality Inventory (MMPI), 209
Minority Report (movie), 336
Miranda warnings, 139, 176, 274, 442
misconduct, explanations for (court professionals)
    individual, 419–421
    judges, 312
    organizational, 421–423
    prosecutor, 309–312
    societal, 424
misconduct, responding to, 312
    conviction integrity units, 315
    DNA evidence, 315–316
    private crime labs, 316–318
    professional and judicial sanctions, 313–314
    rethinking prosecutorial immunity, 314
misconduct, types of, 186
misfeasance, 404
Mississippi, corruption in prison/jail, 409–410
mistaken eyewitness testimony, 307–308
Mitchell, Joyce, 328
Model Code of Judicial Conduct, 303
Model Code of Professional Responsibility, 234, 239, 246, 262
modeling, 90
Model Rules of Professional Conduct, 239, 240, 246, 262
Mohammed, Khalid Sheikh, 442
Mollen Commission, 133, 184, 186, 210
moral agency, 91
moral agent, 238
moral dilemma, 88–89
moral efficacy, 91
moral identity, 91
moral judgments, 12, 13–15, 27, 28f
moral justification, 97
"moral molecule," 88
"moral outrage," 55
moral pluralism, 48
moral principles, attorneys and, 238–239
moral rights, 68
moral rules, 27, 28f
morals/morality, 31, 36, 80, 92

defined, 8, 10
legal moralism, 228–230
in prison, 382
values and, 12–13
moral stage theory (Kohlberg), 91–95, 93f
moral theories/philosophies. *see* ethical systems
moral virtues, 28–29
Morton, Michael, 223–224
"motivated blindness," 99–100
Murton, Tom, 361
My Lai incident, 461–462

N

Nash, Craig, 195
National Academy of Sciences, 281
National Association of Small Businesses, 60
National bar association, 159
National Business Ethics Survey, 101
National Decertification Index, 212–213
National Forensic Science Commission, 282
National Law Journal, 234
National Police Misconduct Reporting Project, 195
National Police Misconduct Reports, 212
National Prison Project (ACLU), 407
National Prosecution Standards, 243
National Registry of Exonerations, 3
National Research Council, 279
National Security Agency, 107
national security letters, 452
natural law, 43, 46, 48, 56, 225, 436
natural rights, 321
negative retribution, 332
negligent abuse, 404
neutrality, as procedural justice element, 70, 73
"New Deal," 61
New Orleans Mayor's Advisory Committee, 184
New Orleans Police Department, 197
New York City
    civilian review board, 217
    integrity testing program in, 210
    prosecutor misconduct, 274
New York Legal Aid Society, 212
New York Police Department Internal Affairs Bureau, 214
New York Times, 43
Nietzsche, Friedrich, 368
Nifong, Mike, 275, 310, 314
9/11, response to, 438–458
    detainments, 438–439
    governmental secrecy, 450–451
    guantanamo and Military Commissions Act, 441–442
    privacy, threats to, 451–455

renditions and secret prisons, 439–441
    torture, 443–450
    undercover operations, 455–458
    wiretapping, 451–455
noble-cause corruption, 131–133, 317
"noble savage," 87
nonfeasance, 125, 404
Norfolk Four, 308
normative ethics, 10
"normative orders" of policing, 130

O

Oakland Police Department, 200
Oath of Honor, 128
Obama, Barack, 219, 442
"Obamacare," 60
Obergefell v. Hodges, 4
OCB. *see* organizational citizenship behaviors (OCB)
Occupy Protests, 121
Occupy Wall Street movement, 58
offensive behavior, prevention of, 217
old-style crime fighters, 126
on-duty drug use, 192–193
"One Squad" scandal, 205
open file policy, 3
Operation Greylord, 302
"Operation Prison Cell," 410
Operation Wide Receiver, 16
order maintenance, 122
organizational citizenship behaviors (OCB), 101
organizational culture, external influences and, 107
organizational incentives, 205–206
organizational justice, 101
Organized Crime Control Act of 1970, 270
overcriminalization, 2
oxytocin, 88

P

pantheistic religions, 32
paradigms, law, 230
    conflict paradigm, 231–232
    consensus paradigm, 230–231
    pluralist paradigm, 232–233
parole officers, 394
passive time server, 392
paternalistic laws, 227–228
Patient Protection and Affordable Care Act, 60
Patriot Act, 120, 438, 452
patrol officers, 126
peacemaking corrections, 428
peacemaking justice, 41, 75
Peasley, Kenneth, 314
penal harm, 333

perjury
  duty regarding, 264–265
  suborning, 298–300
permissive retribution, 332
Perry, Rick, 253, 254
personal conduct, police, 129
persuasion, 123
Philadelphia Police Study Task Force, 184
physical abuse, 191
physical evidence, 262
Piaget, Jean, 91–92
Pikett, Keith, 281
placebos, 166
Plato, 9, 28, 56
plea bargain, 258
plea bargaining, 272–274
pluralistic ignorance, 361
pluralist paradigm, 232–233
police
  ethics of, 15
  identity, after shooting, 25–26
  negative news about, 115
  as objective enforcers, 120
  public perception of, 150
  as public servants, 116–119
  subculture. *see* police subculture
  typologies of, 124, 126
police–citizen interactions, 160
police control, elements of, 123
police corruption
  costs of, 197–198
  organizational explanations, 204–207
  reducing, 208–219
  societal explanations, 207–208
police cynicism, 130
police misconduct, 2
police shootings, of Blacks, 156–157
police subculture, 129–142
  blue curtain of secrecy, 133–137
  cop code, 130–131
  current environment, 137–142
  noble-cause corruption, 131–133
  themes and value systems, 129–130
  weakening of, 137–138
police unions, 138
policing
  formal ethics for, 128–129
  future of, 122–123
  history of, 119–122
  "normative orders" of, 130
Ponzi scheme, 100
Poole, Russell, 45–46, 218
pornography, 173, 228
Porteous, Thomas, 305
Porter, Anthony, 72
positive retribution, 332
positivist law, 225, 436
post-conventional level, 92
power
  defined, 123

and discretion, 123–124
pre-conventional level, 92
predictive policing, 122
pretext stop, 152
prevention, 331, 335
Price, Dan, 59
principle of double effect, 437
principle of forfeiture, 47, 78
principle of need, 60
principle of the Golden Mean, 9, 29
Prison Fellowship Ministries, 389
Prison Litigation Reform Act of 1996
  (PLRA), 371
prison psychologists, 387
Prison Rape Elimination Act (PREA),
  375, 380
Prison Realty Trust (PRT), 349
privacy, threats to, 451–455
private crime labs, 316–318
private prisons, 348–352
proactive investigations, 166–170
probation/parole officer subculture,
  362–363
problem-solving policing, 122
procedural justice, 67–70, 423, 427–430
  elements of, 70
  perceptions, 101–102
professional courtesy, 191–192
professional ethics, 10, 30
professional-style officers, 126
The Project on Accountable Justice, 413
Propublica, 311
prosecutorial discretion, 269
prosecutorial immunity, 314
prosecutor misconduct, 274, 296–298,
  301
  explanations for, 309–312
prosecutors, ethical issues for, 265
  conflicts of interest, 270
  CSI and the courts, 276–282
  duty to disclose, 269
  expert witnesses, 275–276
  jailhouse informants, 282–283
  media relations, 274–275
  plea bargaining, 272–274
  use of discretion, 266–269
  zealous prosecution, 282
pro se defense, 255
prostitutes, sexual extortion by police
  officers, 195
prostitution, 173
Protect America Act, 452
protection of public morality, 4
psychological abuse, 191
psychological egoism, 42, 43
public action committees (PACs), 284
public defenders, 239, 256
public disclosure, 44
"public integrity" units, 268
public morality, protection of, 4

public perception, of police, 150
public safety, 4
public servants
  pensions of, 102
  police as, 116–119
punishment
  capital, 64, 352–355
  corporal, 64
  corrections and, rationale for,
    329–331
  cruel and unusual, 343, 347
  definition, elements essential to, 329
  for juvenile murder, 65
  Rawls defense of, 342–343
  retributive, 65
punitive law enforcer, 392
purposeful abuse, 404

R

races, 73–75, 149–152
racial bias, 288, 308
racial profiling, 152–154, 156
Rainey, Darren, 411
Rand, Ayn, 42
random integrity testing, 210
rape, 195
rape-shield laws, 260
rationality, emotions and, 89–90
rationalization, 47
Rawls, John, 342–343
reactive investigations, 173–175
Realignment Act, 372
Realty Trust (REIT), 349
reasonable force, 158
reciprocal altruism, 55
reciprocity, 373
recognition, 57
recognition tests, 94
Red Scare, 123
"Red Squads," 120
reinforcement, 90
reintegrative shaming, 344
relativism, 46–49
religious authorities, 33
religious ethics, 32–35, 46, 173, 263
rendition, 439–441
Rendition (movie), 441
respect, 30, 70, 73
responsibility, 30
Restatement of the Law Governing
  Lawyers, 242
restorative justice, 75–77, 427–430
restorative justice movement, 41
Rest's DIT (Defining Issues Test), 94, 103
retribution, 331, 332–335
retributive justice, 64–67
retributive punishment, 65
revenge killing, 159
rightful possession of goods, 57

Rikers, 360
Rimland, Jack, 72
The Rise of the Warrior Cop (Balko), 117
Robbins, Louise, 300
Roberts, John, 320, 322
"Robin Hood" laws, 61
Rokeach, Milton, 91
Roosevelt, Franklin Delano, 61
rotten-apple argument, 201
"rotten apple" responses
    bad cops database, 212–213
    body cameras, 211–212
    early warning/audit systems,
        210–211
    education and training, 209–210
    improved screening, 209
    integrity testing, 210
"rotten barrel" responses
    civilian review/complaint boards,
        216–217
    culture change, 217–218
    ethical leadership, 218
    internal affairs model/civil service/
        arbitration, 213–215
Rousseau, Jean-Jacques, 41
Royal Commission, 184
rule-based ethics, 41
rule-based utilitarianism, 49
rule utilitarianism, 39
    ethical formalism *vs.*, 39
Ryan, George, 3–4

S

same-sex marriage, 229
Sam Sheppard case, 275
San Antonio police department, 213
sanctions, 313–314
sanctuary, 65
Sandel, Michael
    What's the Right Thing to Do?, 54
Sarbanes-Oxley Act of 2002, 103, 107,
    233
Scalia, Antonin, 322
scent identification, 281
Sebesta, Charles, 314
secret prisons, 439–441
Secret Service agents scandals, 105
selective incapacitation, 337
self-defense, 47
self-efficacy, 91
self-preservation, 43
Seneca, 9
sentencing, 288–289, 332
September 11, policing approach
    following, 122
Serpico (Maas), 133
Serpico, Frank, 183–184
service, as law enforcement theme,
    128–129

service-style officers, 126
sex crimes investigator, 178
sex differences in ethical decision
    making, 88
sexual harassment, 196
sexual misconduct, 193–196
sexual relationships/abuse, in prison,
    375–380
shaming conditions, 344
"sheetrock" scandal, 169
Siapno, Jude, 200
Simon, Alstory, 72
Simpson, O. J., 237
Simpson case, 131
situational ethics, 48–49
Six Pillars of Character, 29–30
Sixth Amendment, 256
Skokomish Community Peacemaking
    Panel, 76
small work groups, 204–205
Smith, Adam, 42
smuggling, 379
sociability, 31
social contract, 123, 124
social contract theory, 226
social maturity, 91
societal responses, 218–219
Socrates, 9, 28, 78
"soft" stage of ethical awareness, 92
Sotomayor, Sonia, 320
special relationship, 238
"Special Responsibilities of a Prosecutor,"
    240
specialty courts, 257–258
Special Weapons and Tactics (SWAT)
    teams, 117–118
specific deterrence, 335, 336
St. Augustine, 32
St. Clair Commission, 184
Standing Committee on Ethics and
    Professional Responsibility (ABA),
    269
Starr, Kenneth, 233
Stevens, John Paul, 314
Stevens, Ted, 301–302
stigmatizing shaming, 344
Stinson, Philip, 212
Stoic philosophical school, 9
Stoics, 30–31
strict constructionists, 320
substantive justice, 64–67
success, in U.S., 13
Summa Theologiae (Thomas Aquinas), 32
supererogatories, 11
supermax prison, 345–348
SWAT teams, 117–118
Swift, Charles, 247
systemic abuse, 404
systemic racism, in Ferguson, Missouri,
    149

T

Tamm, Thomas, 107–108
TANF (Temporary Assistance for Needy
    Families), 60
Tarasoff rule, 388
targeted integrity testing, 210
Tasers, usage of, 161–163
Task Force on Policing in the 21st
    Century, 219
teleological ethical system, 38
temperance (virtue), 28, 56
Tenaha, Texas, 235
Ten Commandments, 32
terrorism, 435
testilying, 131, 132
Texas, corruption in prison/jail, 410
Texas Bar Association, 285
Texas Board of Pardons and Paroles, 253
Texas District & County Attorneys
    Association (TDCAA), 297
themes, of policing, 130
theory of justice (Rawls), 61, 65
    criticism of, 61–62
Thomas, Andrew, 266
Thomas, Clarence, 322
Thompson, John, 310
Thompson, Ken, 298
Thoreau, Henry David, 78
three-strikes laws, 338, 339
ticket fixing, 191–192
tolerated lies, 166
Too Big to Jail (Garrett), 56
*"Too Good to Be True: Private Prisons in
    America"* (Sentencing Project), 350
torture, 443–450
"traffic stops," 154
training, education and, 209–210
Training Day (movie), 200
"Transactions with Persons Other than
    Clients," 242
transgender inmates, prison rape and,
    377
treatment, 329, 339, 340–341
treatment ethic, 331, 385–390
treatment professionals, 415
treatment professionals subculture, 362
tribal justice, 76
tribal peacemakers, 76
Troubled Asset Relief Agency, 231
trustworthiness, 30, 70
Tucker telephone, 380
"tune-ups," 380
typologies, of police, 124, 126

U

undercover officers, 171–173
undercover operations, 455–458
"Unholy Alliance" (PICO National
    Network and Public Campaign), 350

United States Penitentiary (USP)
Florence, 403
universal healthcare, 60–61
universalism, 42–43, 46–49
unjust laws, 78, 79–80
utilitarianism, 43, 78, 172–173, 178
corrections and, 341
criticisms of, 38–39
defined, 38
rule-based, 49
vs. human rights–based policing,
458–461
utilitarian justice, 67
utilitarian principle, 44
Utilitarian systems of distribution, 60
Utilitarian theories, 57

V

values, 11–13, 12*b*
Vazquez, Frank (Choker), 200
veil of ignorance, 61
victim–offender mediation, 76
Violent Crime Control and Law
Enforcement Act of 1994, 152, 160,
198, 334

virtues, 56
defined, 28
intellectual *vs.* moral, 28–29
voice, procedural justice, 69

W

Waddle, Scott, 19
Walker, Samuel, 236
war, justifications for, 437
"war on terror," 435
Warren Court, 321
watchman style, policing, 126
Watkins, Craig, 315
wedding-cake illustration, 236, 237
Weiner, Anthony, 10
welfare/therapeutic worker, 392
West, Michael, 300
whistleblowers, 138, 462
Whitehurst, Frederic, 174
wholesight, 8
Willingham, Cameron Todd, 252–253,
279, 283
Wilson, Darren, 149
Wilson, Genarlow, 267
wiretapping, 451–455

wisdom (virtue), 28, 56
withholding evidence, 260
witness badgering, 260
workforce diversity, 137
workgroups, 96–106
WorldCom scandal, 262
wrongful convictions, 70–73
confirmatory bias and, 309
factors in, 306
false confessions and, 308
mistaken eyewitness testimony and,
307–308
racial bias and, 308
reasons for, 71

Y

Yee, James, 371
York, Gary, 368

Z

Zain, Fred, 301
zealous defense, 259–260
Zeno, 9

Table of Cases

A

Arizona v. United States, 567 U.S. __ , 132 S. Ct. 2492, 2012, 154
Atkins v. Virginia, 536 U.S. 304, 2002, 354

B

Batson v. Kentucky, 476 U.S. 79, 1986, 297
Baze v. Rees, 553 U.S. 35, 2008, 355
Berger v. United States, 295 U.S. 78, 88, 1935, 267
Bordenkircher v. Hayes, 434 U.S. 357, 1978, 272
Boumediene v. Bush, 553 U.S. 723, 2008, 247, 441
Bowers v. Hardwick, 478 U.S. 186, 1986, 228
Brady v. Maryland, 373 U.S. 83, 1963, 80, 166, 269, 273, 301
Brown v. Board of Education, 347 U.S. 483, 1954, 226
Brown v. Mississippi, 297 U.S. 278, 1936, 175
Brown v. Plata, 563 U.S. __, 131 S. Ct. 1910, 2011, 372, 389, 407
Bryan v. McPherson, 590 F.3d 767, 2009, 162
Bush v. Gore, 531 U.S. 98, 2000, 285

C

Callins v. Collins, 510 U.S. 1141, 1994, 355
Caperton v. Massey, 556 U.S. __, 129 S. Ct. 2252, 2009, 245
Citizens United v. FEC, 558 U.S. 310, 2010, 245
Clapper, Director of National Intelligence, et al. v. Amnesty International USA, et al., 568 U.S. ____ , 133 S. Ct. 1138, 2013, 453
Clark v. Martinez, 543 U.S. 371, 2005, 441
Cockrell v. Burdine, 262 F.3d 336, 2002, 295
Connick v. Thompson, 563 U.S. __, 131 S. Ct. 1350, 2011, 310
Copley Press, Inc. v. Superior Court of San Diego County (Cal., 2006), 215

D

Daubert v. Merrell Dow Pharmaceuticals Inc. 509 U.S. 579, 1993, 80, 276
District Attorney's Office for the Third Judicial District v. Osborne, 557 U.S. 52, 2009, 241

E

Ewing v. California, 538 U.S. 11, 2003, 338

F

Fisher v. University of Texas, 570 U.S. __, 133 S. Ct. 2411, 2013, 62

Florida v. Cayward, 522 So.2d. 971, 1989, 177
Ford v. Wainwright, 411 U.S. 399, 198, 354
Frazier v. Cupp, 394 U.S. 731, 1969, 176
Furman v. Georgia, 408 U.S. 238, 1972, 343

G

Gall v. United States, 552 U.S. 38, 2007, 289
Garcetti v. Ceballos, 547 U.S. 410, 2006, 317, 462
Giglio v. United States, 405 U.S. 150, 1972, 269, 299
Graham v. Connor, 490 U.S. 386, 1989, 157
Graham v. Florida, 560 U.S. 48. 2010, 65
Griffin v. Wisconsin, 483 U.S. 868, 1987, 417

H

Hall v. Florida, 572 U.S. __, 134 S. Ct. 1986, 2014, 354–355
Hamdan v. Rumsfeld, 548 U.S. 557 2006, 247, 304, 441, 442
Hamdi v. Rumsfeld, 542 U.S. 507, 2004, 441
Handschu v. Special Services Division, 349 F.Supp. 766, 1972, 456
Herrera v. Collins, 503 U.S. 902, 1993, 67
Holland v. Florida, 560 U.S. __, 130 S. Ct. 2549, 2010, 68, 288
Holt v. Sarver, 442 F.2d 304 (8th Cir. 1971), 361
Hudson v. McMillian, 503 U.S. 1, 1992, 381
Imbler v. Pachtman, 424 U.S. 409, 1976, 309

I

In re: National Security Letter v. Holder, (sealed), on appeal at the 9th Cir, 13-15957 & 13-16731, view at: www.ca9.uscourts.gov/content/view.php?pk_id=0000000715, 452
In re Troy Anthony Davis, 557 U. S. ____, 130 S.Ct. 1, 2009, 68

J

Jones 'El v. Berge, 374 F.3d 541 (Wisc. 2004), 347
Jones v. Town of E. Haven, 493 F.Supp.2d 302 (D. Conn. 2007), 133
Joslyn v. Armstrong, No. 3:01-cv-00198-CFD, slip op. at 1 (D. Conn., October 17, 2001), 347

K

Kansas v. Hendricks, 521 U.S. 346, 1997, 338
Katz v. United States, 389 U.S. 347, 1967, 451
Kennedy v. Louisiana, 554 U.S. 407, 2008, 355
Kimbrough v. United States, 552 U.S. 85, 2007, 289
Knecht v. Gillman, 488 F.2d 1136, 1973, 339
Korematsu v. U.S., 323 U.S. 214, 1944, 439
Kyllo v. United States, 533 U.S. 27, 2001, 451

L

Lane v. Franks, 571 U.S. __, 134 S. Ct. 2369, 2014, 463
Lawrence v. Texas, 539 U.S. 558, 2003, 228
Ledbetter v. Goodyear, 550 U.S. 618, 2007, 59
Lockyer v. Andrade, 538 U.S. 63, 2003, 338

M

Madrid v. Gomez, 889 F. Supp 1146 (N.D. Cal. 1995), 346, 347
Mapp v. Ohio, 367 U.S. 643, 1961, 286
McClesky v. Kemp, 481 U.S. 279, 1987, 354
McQuiggin v. Perkins, 569 U.S. __, 133 S. Ct. 1924, 2013, 241
Miller v. Pate, 386 U.S. 1, 1967, 301
Minnesota v. White, 536 U.S. 765, 2002, 244, 303
Missouri v. Frye, 566 U.S. __, 132 St. Ct. 1399, 2012, 272
Moran v. Burbine, 474 U.S. 412, 1986, 177

N

New York v. Quarles, 467 U.S. 649, 1984, 286
NFIB v. Sebelius, 567 U.S. __, 132 S.Ct 2566, 2012, 285
Nix v. Whiteside, 475 U.S. 157, 1986, 264
Nix v. Williams 467 U.S. 431, 1984, 286

P

Padilla v. Kentucky, 559 U.S. 356, 2010, 272
Papachristou v. Jacksonville, 405 U.S. 157, 1972, 227
Perry v. New Hampshire, 565 U.S. __, 132 S. Ct. 716, 2012, 307
Pottawattamie County v. McGhee, 556 U.S. 11981, 2009, 310
Purkett v. Elem, 514 U.S. 765, 1995, 297

R

Rasul v. Bush, 542 U.S. 466, 2004, 441, 463
Ricci v. DeStefano, 557 U.S. 557, 2009, 62
Riley v. California, __ U.S. __, 134 S.Ct. 999, 2014, 461
Roper v. Simmons, 543 U.S. 551, 2005, 65, 355
Rutherford v. Block, 2006 WL 3065781 (C.D. Cal. Oct 27, 2006), 407

S

Skilling v. U.S., 561 U.S. 358, 2010, 189

T

Taifa v. Bayhm, 846 F. Supp. 723 (Ind. 1994), 347
Tarasoff v. Regents of the University of California, 17 Cal. 3d 425, 1975, 388
Tennessee v. Garner, 471 U.S. 1105, 1985, 157
Thurman v. City of Torrington, 595 F. Supp. 1521 (D. Conn. 1984), 127

U

United States v. Agurs, 427 U.S. 97, 1976, 269
United States v. Bagley, 473 U.S. 667, 1985, 269
United States v. Booker, 543 U.S. 220, 2005, 289
United States v. Comstock, 560 U.S. 126, 2010, 338
United States v. Leon, 468 U.S. 897, 1984, 286
United States v. Martinez-Fuerte, 425 U.S. 931, 1976, 154
United States v. Russell, 411 U.S. 423, 1973, 172

V

Van De Kamp v. Goldstein, 555 U.S. 335, 2009, 310

W

Washington v. Harper, 494 U.S. 210, 1990, 339–340, 386
Whren v. U.S., 517 U.S. 806, 1996, 152
Wilkinson v. Austin, et al., 545 U.S. 209, 2005, 346, 347